WOMEN OF ASSUR AND KANESH

WRITINGS FROM THE ANCIENT WORLD

Theodore J. Lewis, General Editor

Editorial Board:
Edward M. Cook
Daniel Fleming
Theo P. J. van den Hout
Alice Mouton
Martti Nissinen
William M. Schniedewind
Emily Teeter
Steve Vinson

Number 42
Volume Editors
Jerrold S. Cooper, Benjamin R. Foster, and Klaas R. Veenhof

SBL PRESS

WOMEN OF ASSUR AND KANESH

Texts from the Archives of Assyrian Merchants

by

Cécile Michel

SBL PRESS

SBL PRESS

Atlanta

Library of Congress Cataloging-in-Publication Data

Names: Michel, Cécile, author, translator.
Title: Women of Assur and Kanesh : texts from the archives of Assyrian merchants / Cécile Michel.
Description: Atlanta : SBL Press, 2020. | Series: Writings from the ancient world ; 42 | Includes bibliographical references and index.
Identifiers: LCCN 2020012833 (print) | LCCN 2020012834 (ebook) | ISBN 9781628372823 (paperback) | ISBN 9780884144557 (hardback) | ISBN 9780884144564 (ebook)
Subjects: LCSH: Women—Iraq—Ashur (Extinct city) | Sex role—Iraq—Ashur (Extinct city) | Women—Turkey—Kanesh (Extinct city) | Sex role—Turkey—Kanesh (Extinct city) | Assyrian women—Iraq—Ashur (Extinct city) | Merchants—Turkey—Kanesh (Extinct city)—Archives. | Ashur (Extinct city)—History—Sources. | Kanesh (Extinct city)—History—Sources.
Classification: LCC HQ1137.A75 M53 2020 (print) | LCC HQ1137.A75 (ebook) | DDC 305.40935/4—dc23
LC record available at https://lccn.loc.gov/2020012833
LC ebook record available at https://lccn.loc.gov/2020012834

Contents

Series Editor's Foreword

Writings from the Ancient World is designed to provide up-to-date, readable English translations of writings recovered from the ancient Near East.

The series is intended to serve the interests of general readers, students, and educators who wish to explore the ancient Near Eastern roots of Western civilization or to compare these earliest written expressions of human thought and activity with writings from other parts of the world. It should also be useful to scholars in the humanities or social sciences who need clear, reliable translations of ancient Near Eastern materials for comparative purposes. Specialists in particular areas of the ancient Near East who need access to texts in the scripts and languages of other areas will also find these translations helpful. Given the wide range of materials translated in the series, different volumes will appeal to different interests. However, these translations make available to all readers of English the world's earliest traditions as well as valuable sources of information on daily life, history, religion, and the like in the preclassical world.

Covering the period from the invention of writing (by 3000 BCE) down to the conquests of Alexander the Great (ca. 330 BCE), the ancient Near East comprised northeast Africa and southwest Asia. The cultures represented within these limits include especially Egyptian, Sumerian, Babylonian, Assyrian, Hittite, Ugaritic, Aramean, Phoenician, and Israelite. It is hoped that Writings from the Ancient World will eventually produce translations of most of the many different genres attested in these cultures: letters (official and private), myths, diplomatic documents, hymns, law collections, monumental inscriptions, tales, and administrative records, to mention but a few.

The Society of Biblical Literature provided significant funding for the Writings from the Ancient World series. In addition, authors have benefited from working in research collections in their respective institutions and beyond. Were it not for such support, the arduous tasks of preparation, translation, editing, and publication could not have been accomplished or even undertaken. It is the hope of all who have worked on these texts or supported this work that Writings from the Ancient World will open up new horizons and deepen the humanity of all who read these volumes.

Theodore J. Lewis
The Johns Hopkins University

Acknowledgements

This research on women documented by the Old Assyrian cuneiform texts, while inspired by the unique content of these sources, has benefited from discussions with several colleagues in various projects and has received financial support from these projects. Within the joint research unit Archéologies et Sciences de l'Antiquité (ArScAn, dir. F. Villeneuve) and especially the team Histoire et Archéologie de l'Orient Cunéiforme (HAROC, dir. D. Agut and A. Tenu), Brigitte Lion and I have been working for many years together on women and gender studies, and our discussions have no doubt influenced my thoughts on certain aspects. Between 2012 and 2015, several members of the team HAROC participated in the bilateral French-Japanese project on the economic role of women in ancient Mesopotamia (ANR Chorus REFEMA, coordinated by Francis Joannès and Fumi Karahashi), a project in which I studied how Assyrian women earned money and managed their goods as businesswomen. The main results were published in 2016 in a collective volume dedicated to *The Role of Women in Work in Society in the Ancient Near East*, ed. Brigitte Lion and Cécile Michel, SANER 13 (Boston: de Gruyter, 2018).

Several of the Assyrian women settled in Anatolia as well as native women are well documented by the tablets unearthed at Kültepe. The Kültepe Archaeological Mission, with its director, Fikri Kulakoğlu, who invited me to join the archaeological team, has allowed me to immerse myself every summer in the site and to better understand the environment of the men and women living in the lower town of Kültepe. Within the framework of the Kültepe International Meetings (KIM) that we built up together in 2013, conferences every two years provide a multi- and interdisciplinary overview of the site and its surroundings. This approach was complemented by two projects that I have carried out in collaboration with Eva Andersson Strand, director of the Centre for Textile Research (Copenhagen, previously directed by Marie-Louise Nosch). The first one, within the framework of the International Research Network

Ancient Textiles from Orient to the Mediterranean (IRN ATOM), was dedicated to textile production in the Middle Bronze Age Near East and involved also Catherine Breniquet (Clermont-Ferrand). The study of Kültepe sealings with textile, thread, cords, and basket imprints, connected to textile tools (spindle whorl and loom weights, fig. 4.1) and data from the Old Assyrian texts, together with a sound knowledge of spinning and weaving techniques, made possible the estimation of the textile production of Assyrian women and the revenues they were earning (chapter 4). This research was further developed within the framework of another project, The Thread of Memory: Kültepe, a Pilot Laboratory for Interdisciplinary Research (Kül-TexT, LabEx Past in Present), which I am coordinating together with Vanessa Tubiana-Brun; this project will result in a documentary movie (*Thus Says Tarām-Kūbi*) and a book for the general public (*Daily Life at Kültepe-Kaneš*). Thanks to ATOM and Kül-TexT, but also to the Kültepe Archaeological Mission, our group could work every summer in the best possible conditions at Kültepe.

Since 2015, thanks to the kind invitation of its director, I have joined the Centre for the Study of Manuscript Cultures. There, I carried out research on Old Assyrian paleography together with my doctoral student Wiebke Beyer. This research is linked to the literacy of Old Assyrian individuals, including women (chapter 4), and I am most grateful to the DFG Sonderforschungsbereich 950 project, which supported our regular stays in Ankara to work on the cuneiform tablets at the Museum of Anatolian Civilisations. I wish to warmly thank Michael Friedrich and all the colleagues from Hamburg for lively and enlightening discussions.

I also give my warmest thanks to the Ankara museum staff and to the colleagues of the *tablet seksyonu*, who have always been very helpful, especially Şerife Yılmaz, Rukiye Akdoğan, and İsmet Aykut.

This book would not have been possible without a trio of dear friends who agreed, each in their own way, to review my work and contributed to improve it. The first to work over the text, Benjamin Foster, took on the heavy task of making my English readable, even going so far as to translate the introductions to chapters 2 to 5 from French. Not only did he work on the English text in depth, but he also made various suggestions on the translations of the texts themselves. The second, Klaas Veenhof, reread the texts' edition with the same patient attention as usual. It is not uncommon for the translation of Old Assyrian letters to give rise to different interpretations; it is therefore essential to compare your readings with those of another specialist in this corpus. The third and last, Jerry Cooper, is at the very origin of this book. It was he who suggested that I publish it in the Writings from the Ancient World series by the Society for Biblical Literature and kindly offered his help, in turn providing a review of the book and providing suggestions and discussions on the translation of certain terms. He also corrected the English of the introduction. I warmly thank Ted Lewis, the general editor in charge of SBL Press Writings from the Ancient World, for his infinite patience and regular reminders. I also address my thanks to the SBL editorial board for accepting this volume in their series and to Bob Buller, Director of SBL Press, for his careful work on the manuscript.

Last but not least, I wish to thank my family for their love, encouragement, and patience: Benoît, with whom I have shared everything for thirty-three years, and our three children, Coralie-Anne, Laureline, and Raphaël, who make us discover the diversity of biology. This book is dedicated to two great women who together total 183 years, Thérèse and Nelly, my mother and mother-in-law, both pioneers and active women, each in their own way, but also mothers, grandmothers, and great-grandmothers of twenty-five and nineteen descendants, respectively, who have thus given us a beautiful tribe that we enjoy bringing together.

Orsay, January 2019

Abbreviations and Conventions

Abbreviations and Conventions in Transliterations

le.e.	left edge
lo.e.	lower edge
obv.	obverse
r.e.	right edge
rev.	reverse
u.e.	upper edge
x$^{!}$(Y)	the correct reading is "x" but "Y" is written on the tablet/ envelope
*	collated sign / collated line
(°)	erased sign, erasure of several signs
(seal X)	seal imprint of X
[…]	broken signs
<x>	sign omitted
«x»	extra sign

Akkadian is in italics, while Sumerian logograms are written in roman. Assyrian and Anatolian proper names are capitalized; this concerns anthroponyms, toponyms, theonyms, months, and so on. But Sumerian logograms are never capitalized, even in proper names.

Numbers in **bold** refer to texts edited in this book.

Abbreviations and Conventions in Translations

Kaneš	Written most of the time *Kà-ni-iš* in the texts, is rendered as Kaneš in the translations and comments, following the recent choice of Old Assyrian specialists.
word	Tentative translation.

(word)	Word added in the translation to make the text intelligible in English.

Technical Abbreviations and Symbols

§	section
BCE	before the Common Era
bis	twice
ca.	circa
cf.	*confer*, compare
chap(s).	chapter(s)
cm	centimeter(s)
col(s).	column(s)
dir.	director, directed by
DN	divine name, name of deity
et al.	*et alii*, and others
etc.	*et cetera*, and so forth, and the rest
fem.	feminine
g	gram(s)
i.e.	*id est*, that is
kg	kilogram(s)
km	kilometer(s)
L	liter
m	meter(s)
masc.	masculine
n(n).	note(s)
no(s).	number(s)
n.p.	no place; no publisher; no page
n.s.	new series
pl.	plural; plate
PN	personal name
sg.	singular
sic	thus (indicating that the text is reproduced exactly as written)
sq.	square

Abbreviations for Journals and Series

AAA	*Annals of Archaeology and Anthropology* (Liverpool)

AfO	*Archiv für Orientforschung* (Vienna)
AfOB	Beihefte zum Archiv für Orientforschung (Vienna)
AHw	Soden, Wolfram von, ed. *Akkadisches Handwörterbuch*. 3 vols. Wiesbaden: Harrassowitz, 1965–1981.
AHDO	*Archives d'histoire du droit oriental* (Paris)
Akademi Günlüğü	*Akademi Günlüğü Toplumsal Araştırmalar Dergisi* (Ankara)
Akkadica	*Akkadica* (Brussels)
AMD	Ancient Magic and Divination (Leiden)
AMMY	*Anadolu Medeniyetleri Müzesi Yıllığı* (Ankara)
Anatolica	*Anatolica: Annuaire international pour les civilisations de l'Asie antérieure* (Istanbul)
AnOr	Analecta Orientalia (Rome)
AnSt	*Anatolian Studies: Journal of the British Institute of Archaeology at Ankara* (London)
AOAT	Alter Orient und Altes Testament (Münster)
AoF	*Altorientalische Forschungen* (Berlin)
ArAn	*Archivum Anatolicum* (Ankara)
Archibab	Archives babyloniennes (XXe–XXVIIe siècles av. J.-C.) (Paris)
ARMT	Archives royales de Mari, traduction (Paris)
ArOr	*Archív Orientální* (Prague)
AS	Assyriological Studies (Chicago)
ASJ	Acta Sumerologica (Hiroshima)
ATS	Ancient Textiles Series (Oxford)
AulaOr	*Aula Orientalis* (Barcelona)
BabBib	Babel und Bibel: Old Testament and Semitic Studies (Winona Lake, IN)
BBVO	Berliner Beiträge zum Vorderen Orient (Berlin)
BCAW	Blackwell Companions to the Ancient World (Oxford; Malden, MA)
Belleten	*Belleten*. Türk Tarih Kurumu (Ankara)
BiOr	*Bibliotheca Orientalis* (Leuven)
CAD	*The Assyrian Dictionary of the Oriental Institute of the University of Chicago*. Chicago: The Oriental Institute of the University of Chicago, 1956–2006.
CAHIJ	*Cappadocia Journal of History and Social Sciences*
CDLI	Cuneiform Digital Library Initiative. University of California, Los Angeles; University of Oxford; Max

	Planck Institute for the History of Science, Berlin. https://cdli.ucla.edu/ (Los Angeles; Oxford; Berlin)
CHANE	Culture and History of the Ancient Near East (Leiden)
CKLR	*Chicago-Kent Law Review* (Chicago)
ClioH	*Clio: Histoire, femmes et sociétés* (Toulouse)
CMRG	Colloques de la Maison René-Ginouvès (Paris)
CNIP	Carsten Niebuhr Institute Publications (Copenhagen)
CPOA	Civilisations du Proche-Orient. Série I: Archéologie et environnement (Neuchâtel; Paris)
CRRAI	Compte rendu de la Xe Rencontre Assyriologique Internationale (Leiden)
CSSH	*Comparative Studies in Society and History* (Cambridge)
Diogenes	*Diogenes* (London)
DTCFD	*Dil ve Tarih-Coğrafya Fakültesi Dergisi* (Ankara)
EO	*Estudios Orientais* (Lisbon)
FAOS	Freiburger Altorientalische Studien. Beihefte: Altassyrische Texte und Untersuchungen (Freiburg)
FM	Florilegium Marianum (Paris)
HANE	History of the Ancient Near East, Monographs (Padua)
HdO	Handbuch der Orientalistik (Leiden)
HSAO	Heidelberger Studien zum Alten Orient (Heidelberg)
HSS	Harvard Semitic Studies (Cambridge, MA)
HUCA	*Hebrew Union College Annual* (Cincinnati)
HUCASup	Supplements to Hebrew Union College Annual (Cincinnati)
Iraq	*Iraq* (London)
Isimu	*Isimu: Revista sobre Oriente Próximo y Egipto en la antiguedad* (Madrid)
JANEH	*Journal of Ancient Near Eastern History* (Boston)
JAOS	*Journal of the American Oriental Society* (Ann Arbor, MI)
JCS	*Journal of Cuneiform Studies* (New Haven; Boston)
JCSSup	Journal of Cuneiform Studies Supplemental Series (Boston; Atlanta)
JEOL	*Jaarbericht van het Vooraziatisch-Egyptisch Genootschap Ex oriente lux* (Leiden)

JESHO	*Journal of the Economic and Social History of the Orient* (Leiden)
JNES	*Journal of Near Eastern Studies* (Chicago)
JSOR	*Journal of the Society of Oriental Research* (Chicago, Toronto)
KASKAL	*Kaskal: Rivista di storia, ambiente e culture del Vicino Oriente antico* (Padua; Venice)
KIM	Kültepe International Meetings (Turnhout)
KMMCP	Kayseri Metropolitan Municipality Cultural Publication (Istanbul)
Ktèma	*Ktèma: Civilisations de l'Orient, de la Grèce et de Rome antiques* (Strasbourg)
LAPO	Littératures anciennes du Proche-Orient (Paris)
LO	Lettres Orientales (Leuven)
MAO	Monografie Archivu Orientálního (Prague)
Mari	*Mari: Annales de recherches interdisciplinaires* (Paris)
MC	Mesopotamian Civilizations (Winona Lake, IN)
Méditerranées	*Méditerranées: Revue du Centre d'Études Internationales sur la Romanité* (Paris)
Mesopotamia	Mesopotamia: Copenhagen Studies in Assyriology (Copenhagen)
MOS Studies	Middle Eastern Studies Programme (Leiden)
MVAG	*Mitteilungen der Vorderasiatischen Gesellschaft* (Berlin)
NABU	*Nouvelles Assyriologiques Brèves et Utilitaires* (Paris)
NdA	*Les Nouvelles de l'Archéologie* (Paris)
NIN	*NIN: Journal of Gender Studies in Antiquity* (Leiden)
OA	*Oriens Antiquus: Rivista del Centro per le Antichità e la Storia dell'Arte del vicino Oriente* (Rome)
OAA	Old Assyrian Archives (subseries of PIHANS, Leiden)
OAAS	Old Assyrian Archives Studies (subseries of PIHANS, Leiden)
OBO	Orbis Biblicus et Orientalis (Fribourg)
Or	*Orientalia* (Rome)
Orient	*Oriento: Bulletin of the Society of Near Eastern Studies in Japan / Nippon Oriento Gakkai* (Tokyo)
Paléorient	*Paléorient* (Paris)
PapVin	Papyrologica Vindobonensia (Vienna)
Philippika	Philippika (Wiesbaden)

PIHANS	Publications de l'Institut historique et archéologique néerlandais de Stamboul (Leiden)
RA	*Revue d'Assyriologie et d'archéologie orientale* (Paris)
REFEMA	Le rôle économique des femmes en Mésopotamie ancienne (Nanterre, France; Tokyo)
RGC	Recherche sur les grandes civilisations (Paris)
RHA	*Revue Hittite et Asianique* (Paris)
RHDE	*Revue historique de droit français et étranger* (Paris)
RIMA	Royal Inscriptions of Mesopotamia, Assyrian Periods (Toronto)
RlA	Ebeling, Erich, Michael P. Streck, Sabine Ecklin, Ernst Weidner, and Gabriella Frantz-Szabo, eds. *Reallexikon der Assyriologie und vorderasiatischen Archäologie*. Berlin: de Gruyter, 1932–.
RO	*Rocznik orientalistyczny* (Warsaw)
SANER	Studies in Ancient Near Eastern Records (Berlin)
SANTAG	SANTAG: Arbeiten und Untersuchungen zur Keilschriftkunde (Wiesbaden)
SAOC	Studies in Ancient Oriental Civilization (Chicago)
SDIO	Studia et documenta ad iura Orientis antiqui pertinentia (Leiden)
SMC	Studies in Manuscript Cultures (Berlin)
SSA	Saggi di Storia Antica (Rome)
SSN	Studia Semitica Neerlandica (Assen)
StCh	Studia Chaburensia (Wiesbaden)
Subartu	Subartu: European Centre for Upper Mesopotamian Studies (Turnhout)
Syria	*Syria: Revue d'art oriental et d'archéologie* (Paris)
T&C	*Techniques and Culture* (Marseille)
TMRG	Travaux de la Maison René-Ginouvès (Paris)
Topoi	*Topoi: Orient, Occident* (Lyon)
TopoiSup	Supplements to Topoi: Orient, Occident (Paris)
TTKY	Türk Tarih Kurumu Yayınları (Ankara)
TUAT	Texte aus der Umwelt des Alten Testaments (Gütersloh)
TÜBA-AR	*Türkiye Bilimler Akademisi Arkeoloji Dergisi* (Ankara)
UET	Ur Excavations Texts
VO	*Vicino Oriente* (Rome)
VS	Vorderasiatische Schriftdenkmäler der Museen zu Berlin (Berlin)

WAW	Writings from the Ancient World (Atlanta)
WO	*Die Welt des Orients* (Göttingen; Tübingen)
WSAWM	Why Sciences of the Ancient World Matter (Berlin)
WVDOG	Wissenschaftliche Veröffentlichungen der Deutschen Orient-Gesellschaft (Leipzig; Berlin)
WZKM	Wiener Zeitschrift für die Kunde des Morgenlandes (Vienna)
ZA	*Zeitschrift für Assyriologie und Vorderasiatische Archäologie* (Berlin; Munich)
ZAR	*Zeitschrift für altorientalische und biblische Rechtsgeschichte* (Wiesbaden)

Abbreviations for Old Assyrian Cuneiform Text Publications

AAA 1/3	Pinches, Theophilus G. 1908. "The Cappadocian Tablets Belonging to the Liverpool Institute of Archaeology." *AAA* 1:49–80.
Adana 237E	Matouš, Lubor. 1965. "Anatolische Feste nach kappadokischen Tafeln." Pages 175–82 in *Studies in Honor of Benno Landsberger on His Seventy-Fifth Birthday, April 21, 1965*. Edited by Hans Gustav Güterbock and Thorkild Jacobsen. AS 16. Chicago: University of Chicago Press.
AKT 1	Bilgiç, Emin, Hüseyin Sever, Cahit Günbattı, and Sabahattin Bayram. 1990. *Ankara Kültepe Tabletleri* 1. TTKY 6/33. Ankara: Türk Tarih Kurumu Basımevi.
AKT 2	Bilgiç, Emin, and Sabahattin Bayram. 1995. *Ankara Kültepe Tabletleri* 2. TTKY 6/33. Ankara: Türk Tarih Kurumu Basımevi.
AKT 3	Bilgiç, Emin, and Cahit Günbattı. 1995. *Ankaraner Kültepe-Texte* 3: *Texte der Grabungskampagne 1970*. FAOS 3. Stuttgart: Steiner.
AKT 4	Albayrak, İrfan. 2006. *(Ankara) Kültepe Tabletleri* 4: *(Kt o/k)*. TTKY 6/33b. Ankara: Türk Tarih Kurumu Basımevi.
AKT 5	Veenhof, Klaas R. 2010. *(Ankara) Kültepe Tabletleri* 5: *(Kt 92/k 188–263)*. TTKY 6/33c. Ankara: Türk Tarih Kurumu Basımevi.

AKT 6a	Larsen, Mogens Trolle. 2010. *The First Two Generations*. Vol. 1 of *(Ankara) Kültepe Tabletleri* 6a: *The Archive of the Šalim-Aššur Family*. TTKY 6/33d-a. Ankara: Türk Tarih Kurumu Basımevi.
AKT 6b	Larsen, Mogens Trolle. 2013. *Ennam-Aššur*. Vol. 2 of *(Ankara) Kültepe Tabletleri* 6b: *The Archive of the Šalim-Aššur Family*. TTKY 6/33d-b. Ankara: Türk Tarih Kurumu Basımevi.
AKT 6c	Larsen, Mogens Trolle. 2014. *Ali-ahum*. Vol. 3 of *(Ankara) Kültepe Tabletleri* 6c: *The Archive of the Šalim-Aššur Family*. TTKY 6/33d-c. Ankara: Türk Tarih Kurumu Basımevi.
AKT 6d	Larsen, Mogens Trolle. 2018. *Texts Concerning Non-Family Members*. Vol. 4 of *(Ankara) Kültepe Tabletleri* 6d: *The Archive of the Šalim-Aššur Family*. TTKY 6/33d-d. Ankara: Türk Tarih Kurumu Basımevi.
AKT 6e	Larsen, Mogens Trolle. Forthcoming. *Anonymous Texts and Fragments*. Vol. 5 of *(Ankara) Kültepe Tabletleri* 6e: *The Archive of the Šalim-Aššur Family*. TTKY 6/33d-e. Ankara: Türk Tarih Kurumu Basımevi.
AKT 7a	Bayram, Sebahattin, and Remzi Kuzuoğlu. 2014. *(Ankara) Kültepe Tabletleri* 7a: *Aššur-rē'ī Ailesinin Arşivi; Aššur-rē'ī'nin Kendi Metinleri*. TTKY 6/33e-a. Ankara: Türk Tarih Kurumu Basımevi.
AKT 8	Veenhof, Klaas R. 2017. *(Ankara) Kültepe Tabletleri* 8: *The Archive of Elamma, Son of Iddin-Suen, and His Family (Kt 91/k 285–568 and Kt 92/k 94–187)*. TTKY 6/33f. Ankara: Türk Tarih Kurumu Basımevi.
AKT 9a	Albayrak, İrfan, and Hakan Erol. 2016. *(Ankara) Kültepe Tabletleri* 9a: *Buzutaya ve Lipit-İštar Arşivleri 1950 Yılı Tabletlerinden (Kt c/k) Seçilmiş Metinler*. TTKY 6/33g-a. Ankara: Türk Tarih Kurumu Basımevi.
AKT 10	Günbattı, Cahit. 2016. *(Ankara) Kültepe Tabletleri* 10: *Anadolulu Tüccarlar Šarabunuwa ve Peruwa'nın Arşivleri*. TTKY 6/33h. Ankara: Türk Tarih Kurumu Basımevi.
AKT 11a	Erol, Hakan. 2018. *(Ankara) Kültepe Tabletleri* 11a: *Šu-İštar'a Ait Belgeler*. TTKY 6/33ı-a. Ankara: Türk Tarih Kurumu Basımevi.

Ankara 1938	Unpublished tablet from Ankara known by a transliteration of Benno Landsberger.
AoF 8	Jakob-Rost, Liane, and Hermann Freydank. 1981. "Eine altassyrische Votivinschrift." *AoF* 8:325–27.
ARMT 26	Charpin, Dominique. 1988. *Archives épistolaires de Mari*. 2 vols. Paris: Éditions Recherche sur les civilisations.
ArOr 47	Garelli, Paul. 1979. "Femmes d'affaires en Assyrie." *ArOr* 47:42–48..
Ass 13058h	Donbaz, Veysel. 1985. "More Old Assyrian Tablets from Aššur." *Akkadica* 42:1–23.
ATHE	Kienast, Burkhart. 1960. *Die altassyrischen Texte des orientalischen Seminars der Universität Heidelberg und der Sammlung Erlenmeyer*. Berlin: de Gruyter.
AulaOr 8	Farber, Walter. 1990. "Hanum kauft Gadagada: Eine altassyrische Selbstverfaufs-Urkunde." *AulaOr* 8:197–203.
BIN 4	Clay, Albert T. 1927. *Letters and Transactions from Cappadocia*. Babylonian Inscriptions in the Collection of James B. Nies 4. New Haven: Yale University Press.
BIN 6	Stephens, Ferris J. 1944. *Old Assyrian Letters and Business Documents*. Babylonian Inscriptions in the Collection of James B. Nies 6. New Haven: Yale University Press.
CCT 1	Smith, Sidney. 1921. *Cuneiform Texts from Cappadocian Tablets in the British Museum*. Part 1. London: British Museum.
CCT 2	Smith, Sidney. 1924. *Cuneiform Texts from Cappadocian Tablets in the British Museum*. Part 2. London: British Museum.
CCT 3	Smith, Sidney. 1925. *Cuneiform Texts from Cappadocian Tablets in the British Museum*. Part 3. London: British Museum.
CCT 4	Smith, Sidney. 1925. *Cuneiform Texts from Cappadocian Tablets in the British Museum*. Part 4. London: British Museum.
CCT 5	Smith, Sidney, and D. J. Wiseman. 1956. *Cuneiform Texts from Cappadocian Tablets in the British Museum*. Part 5. London: British Museum.

CCT 6	Garelli, Paul, and Dominique Collon. 1975. *Cuneiform Texts from Cappadocian Tablets in the British Museum*. Part 6. London: British Museum.
CTMMA 1	Larsen, Mogens Trolle. 1988. *Tablets, Cones and Bricks of the Third and Second Millennium B.C.* Edited by Ira Spar. Cuneiform Texts in the Metropolitan Museum of Art 1. New York: Metropolitan Museum of Art. Pages 92–143, 177–92, pls. 66–109, 129–56.
CUSAS 34	Hertel, Thomas K. 2017. "Old Assyrian Tablets." Pages 1–60 in *Assyrian Archival Texts in the Schøyen Collection and Other Documents from North Mesopotamia and Syria*. Edited by Andrew R. George, Thomas K. Hertel, Jaume Llop-Raduà, Karen Radner, and Wilfred Hugo van Soldt. Bethesda, MD: CDL.
HUCA 40	Lewy, Hildegard. 1969–1970. "Old Assyrian Texts in the University Museum." *HUCA* 40–41:46–85.
ICK 1	Hrozný, Bedrich. 1952. *Inscriptions cunéiformes du Kultépé*. Vol. 1. MAO 14. Prague: Státni Pedagogické Nakladatelstvi.
ICK 2	Matouš, Lubor. 1962. *Inscriptions cunéiformes du Kultépé*. Vol. 2. Prague: Státni Pedagogické Nakladatelstvi.
Ka 1044	Unpublished text known from a transliteration by Lubor Matouš.
Kalley C36	Unpublished text known by a transliteration by Benno Landsberger.
Kay 4369	Kienast, Burkhart. 1984. *Das altassyrische Kaufvertragsrecht*. FAOS 1. Stuttgart: Steiner.
KKS	Matouš, Lubor, and Marie Matoušová-Rajmová. 1984. *Kappadokische Keilschrifttafeln mit Siegeln aus der Sammlung der Karlsuniversität in Prag*. Prague: Karlsuniversität.
Kt ?/k	Tablet found during the 1948– Turkish excavations at Kültepe, in the lower town, and preserved in the Anadolu Medeniyetleri Müzesi (Ankara).
Kt ?/t	Tablet found during the 1948– Turkish excavations at Kültepe, on the tepe, and preserved in the Anadolu Medeniyetleri Müzesi (Ankara).
KTBl	Lewy, Julius. 1929. *Die Kültepetexte der Sammlung Rudolf Blanckertz*. Berlin: Heintze & Blanckertz.

KTH	Lewy, Julius. 1930. *Die Kültepetexte aus der Sammlung Frida Hahn, Berlin*. Leipzig: Hinrichs.
KTK	Jankovskaja, N. B. 1968. *Klinopisnye teksty iz Kjul'-tepe v sobranijah SSSR: Pis'ma i dokumenty torgovogo ob'edinenija v Maloj Azii XIX v. do n.e.* Moscow: Nauka.
KTP	Stephens, Ferris J. 1927. "The Cappadocian Tablets in the University of Pennsylvania Museum." *JSOR* 11:101–36.
KTS 1	Lewy, Julius. 1926. *Die altassyrischen Texte vom Kültepe bei Kaisarije*. Keilschrifttexte in den Antiken-Museen zu Stambul 1. Constantinople: Antiken-Museen.
KTS 2	Donbaz, Veysel. 1989. *Keilschrifttexte in den Antiken-Museen zu Stambul 2*. FAOS 2. Stuttgart: Steiner Verlag Wiesbaden.
KUG	Hecker, Karl. 1966. *Die Keilschrifttexte der Universitätsbibliotheke Giessen*. Giessen Universitätsbibliotheker 9. Giessen: Giessen Universitätsbibliothek.
LB 1201	Böhl, Franz M. Theodor. 1934. *Mededelingen uit de Leidsche Verzameling van Spijkerschriftinscripties*. Vol. 2. Amsterdam: Uitgave van de N. V. Noord-Hollandsche Uitgevers-Maatschappij.
LB 1209	Dercksen, Jan Gerrit. 2010b. "From the NINO Collections: An Unread Letter." Pages 22–25 in *Annual Report 2009: The Netherlands Institute for the Near East [and] the Netherlands Institute in Turkey*. Edited by J. Eidem and Carolien van Zoest. Leiden: Nederlands Instituut voor het Nabije Oosten.
LB 1217	Lewy, Hildegard. 1965. "Ištar-ṣâd and the Bow Star." Pages 273–81 in *Studies in Honor of Benno Landsberger on His Seventy-Fifth Birthday, April 21, 1965*. Edited by Hans Gustav Güterbock and Thorkild Jacobsen. AS 16. Chicago: University of Chicago Press.
Or 50	Moren, S. M. 1980. "Four Old Assyrian Tablets in a Private Collection." *Or* 50:98–105.
Or 52	Wilcke, Claus. 1983. "Drei altassyrische Kültepe-Texte aus München." *Or* 52:194–200.

POAT	Gwaltney, W. C. 1983. *The Pennsylvania Old Assyrian Texts*. HUCASup 3. Cincinnati: Hebrew Union College.
Prag I	Hecker, Karl, Guido Kryszat, and Lubor Matouš, eds. 1998. *Kappadokische Keilschrifttafeln aus den Sammlungen der Karlsuniversität Prag*. Prague: Universita Karlova Filozofická fakulta.
RA 51	Garelli, Paul. 1957. "Trois tablettes cappadociennes du musée de Rouen." *RA* 51:1–10.
RA 59	Garelli, Paul. 1965. "Tablettes cappadociennes de collections diverses." *RA* 59:19–48, 149–76.
RA 60	Garelli, Paul. 1966. "Tablettes cappadociennes de collections diverses." *RA 60*:93–152.
RA 76	Ichisar, Metin. 1982. "Un contrat de mariage et la question du lévirat à l'époque cappadocienne." *RA* 76:168–73.
RA 81	Michel, Cécile. 1987. Nouvelles tablettes cappadociennes du Louvre, *RA* 81.
RC 1749C	Larsen, Mogens Trolle. 2002. *The Aššur-nādā Archive*. OAA 1; PIHANS 96. Leiden: Nederlands Instituut voor het Nabije Oosten. No. 51.
RC 1749D	Larsen, Mogens Trolle. 2002. *The Aššur-nādā Archive*. OAA 1; PIHANS 96. Leiden: Nederlands Instituut voor het Nabije Oosten. No. 55.
Rendell	Unpublished text in the possession of K. Rendell; transliteration by Klaas R. Veenhof.
Sadberk	Donbaz, Veysel. 1999. *Sadberk Hanım Müzesi'nde bulunan çiviyazili belgeler / Cuneiform Texts in the Sadberk Hanım Museum*. Istanbul: Sadberk Hanım Müzesi.
Sch.	Tablet from the collection Schaeffer.
SUP	Sayce, A. H. 1912. "The Cappadocian Cuneiform Tablets of the University of Pennsylvania." *Babyloniaca* 6:182–92.
TC 1	Contenau, Georges. 1920. *Tablettes cappadociennes du Louvre*. Textes cunéiformes du Louvre 4. Paris: Geuthner.

TC 2	Thureau-Dangin, François. 1928. *Tablettes cappadociennes du Louvre*. Textes cunéiformes du Louvre 14. Paris: Geuthner.
TC 3	Lewy, Julius. 1935–1937. *Tablettes cappadociennes du Louvre*. 3 vols. Textes cunéiformes du Louvre 19–21. Paris: Geuthner.
TCL 1	Thureau-Dangin, François. 1910. *Lettres et contrats de l'époque de la première dynastie Babylonienne*. Textes cunéiformes du Louvre 1. Paris: Geuthner.
TPAK 1	Michel, Cécile, and Paul Garelli, eds. 1997. *Tablettes paléo-assyriennes de Kültepe* 1: *(Kt 90/k)*. Paris: de Boccard.
TTC	Contenau, Georges. 1919. *Trente tablette cappadociennes*. Paris: Geuthner. Collated by Michel, Cécile. 1986. "Réédition des trente tablettes 'cappadociennes' de G. Contenau." *RA* 80:105-40.
TuM 1	Lewy, Julius. 1932. *Die Keilschrifttexte aus Kleinasien: Autographiert und mit Inventarverzeichnis und Namenlisten versehen*. Hilprecht Collection 1/4. Leipzig: Hinrich.
VS 26	Veenhof, Klaas R., and Evelyn Klengel-Brandt. 1992. *Altassyrische Tontafeln aus Kültepe: Texte und Siegelabrollungen*. VS 26. Berlin: Mann.
WAG 48-1646	Lewy, Julius. 1937. "Old Assyrian Documents from Asia Minor I." *AHDO* 1:91–108.
Weir 1 Biggs	Biggs, Robert D. 1996. "A Woman's Plaint in an Old Assyrian Letter." Pages 47–52 in *Festschrift für Hans Hirsch zum 65. Geburtstag: Gewidmet von seinem Freunden, Kollegen und Schülern*. Edited by Arne A. Ambros, Markus Köhbach, and Claudia Römer. WZKM 86. Vienna: Institut für Orientalistik.

Translation Choices

ālum	This word means "city," and by default in Old Assyrian sources it represents "the city (of Aššur)."
amtum	This word has two different meanings in Old Assyrian sources: "second wife" and "female slave"; its translation in individual texts depends on context.

gubabtum — This word has been translated here as "consecrated woman," but in Assyriological literature it is often translated as "priestess." Since Old Assyrian sources do not document their cultic or religious activities, but only their economic activities, the chosen translation is in line with the data provided by the texts.

kārum, *bēt kārim* — The word *kārum* is often translated as "colony" or "trading colony" by scholars; however this term is not satisfactory since it often evokes some kind of domination of a state over a foreign territory (Michel 2014a). In the Old Assyrian texts, the *kārum* refers both to the part of the town where merchants were established and the institution represented by the assembly of the merchants who administered that center, and which had an office and officials. There is no word or expression in English that fits this definition, unlike the French expression *comptoir commercial*. Thus, the Akkadian word is kept in the texts' translations. In the commentary, the expression "commercial settlement" is used when referring to the area where merchants were established and carried out their activities.

bēt kārim — This is the office from which the center was administered; it is here translated as "trade bureau." Note that the building of the *bēt kārim* of Kaneš has not yet been identified.

mātum — "The country" refers to Central Anatolia.

ṣabātum — This verb is systematically translated by "to seize" in this volume, but it has a variety of meanings, including "to arrest," "to convene (witnesses)," "to depose," or "to question" to ascertain a legal fact.

ṣuhārtum — "(Young) girl," often a member of the family.

ṣuhārum — "Boy," "servant," "employee."

List of Figures

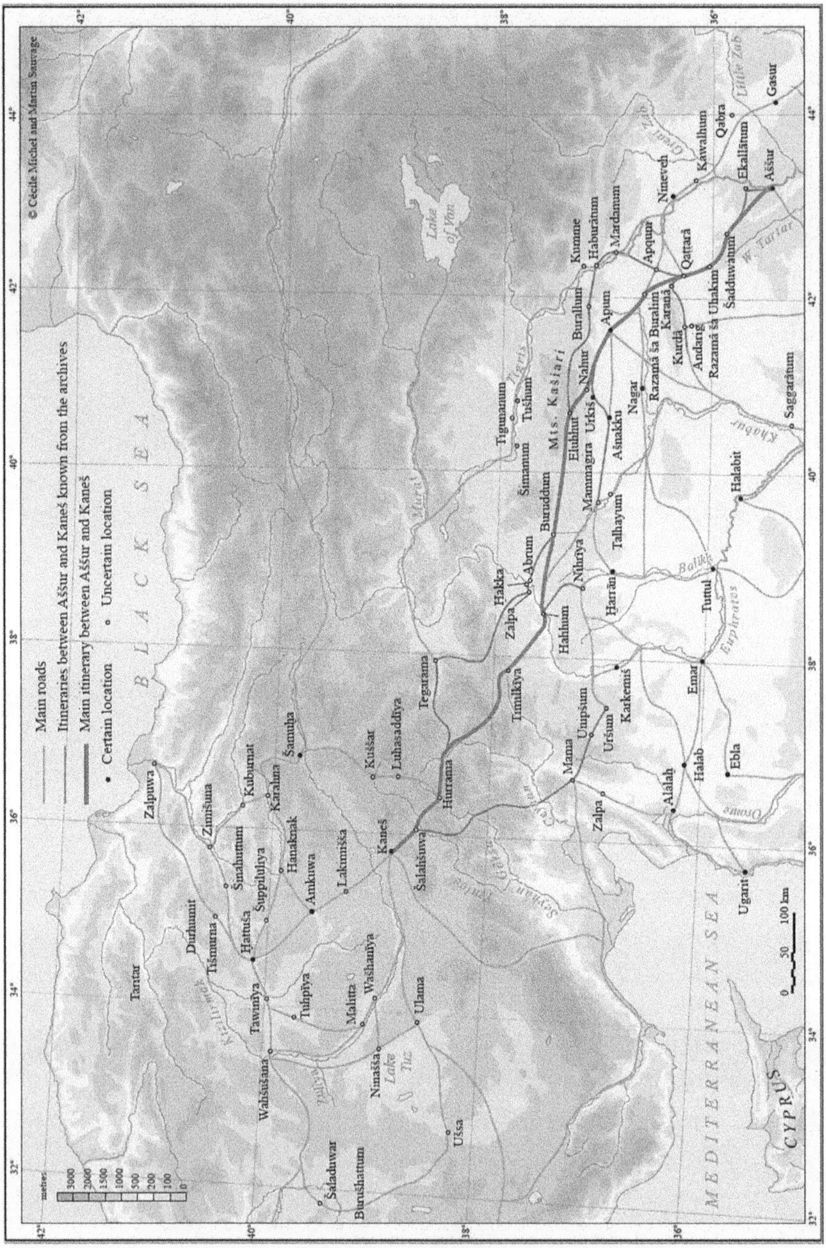

Map of the Old Assyrian Period

Introduction

"Why have you kept me confined inside the city (of Aššur) for ten months, as if I were a woman?"[1] This question, asked by a desperate man in Aššur in a letter sent to a colleague or family member in Kaneš, reveals both the condition of the Assyrian women, who remained alone in Aššur while their husbands traded in Anatolia, and the unenviable vision that men had of this life. It also illustrates the extraordinary richness, for the historian, of this correspondence, which unveils the daily life of women and men from Aššur (in the province of Mosul, northern Iraq), and more broadly of the many private archives found at the site of Kültepe, the former Kaneš, in Central Anatolia.

The Old Assyrian cuneiform tablets represent the very first corpus of archives found in private houses, providing substantial documentation of the female part of a society in a civilization where the male part regularly appears as dominant. Several specific studies have been dedicated to the women attested in these unique sources, but there has never been a comprehensive treatment.[2]

This volume is divided into six chapters, which cover as much as possible all aspects of the lives of Assyrian and Anatolian women from Aššur and Kaneš. The position and status of women in marriage are analyzed in the first chapter, which considers the different kinds of matrimonial relationships between men and women, but also the customs implemented

1. Letter to Aššur-idī from Aššur-malik, CCT 4, 45b:16–19: *mì-šu-um* : *ki-ma*, *sí-ni-iš-tim* : *iš-tù* iti-10-kam, *i-qé-ra-áb* : *A-lim*[ki], *ta-áp-ta-ah-a-ni-i*. We do not know what kind of relationships linked the two men. In his letter, Aššur-malik goes on complaining, with motifs that are recurrently found in letters sent by women: "Here winter has overcome me, there is not a single piece of bread."

2. Veenhof 1972, 103–23; Łyczkowska 1978; Garelli 1979; Günbattı 1992; Darga 1994; Kawasaki 1994; Sturm 1995; Kryszat 2007a; Kienast 2008; Thomason 2013, 2018; Veenhof 2015c; and the many articles by Michel since 1997.

in divorces and widowhood. Going further, the place of women in their family, especially in inheritance, is developed in chapter 2. The regulations concerning the responsibility of family members for debt are extended to debt slavery and female slaves. Chapter 3 considers mothers and their children, as well as all the activities of women in the domestic sphere, except spinning and weaving, which are part of chapter 4. Indeed, the textile production by women of Aššur exceeded family needs, and part of it was transported to and sold in Anatolia, thus providing the women with revenues. With the capital obtained for their work, Assyrian women acted as businesswomen, lending and investing gold and silver just as men.[3] Chapter 4 further deals with the existence of women's archives and the possibility that some of these active women were literate. The fifth chapter is dedicated to the precepts of life that women advocated and the moral values that they tried to transmit to their children and that they claimed from their male family members. It also examines their religious beliefs and practices and considers the consecration of some of them. The last and sixth chapter proposes portraits of nine women, five bearing Assyrian names and four Anatolian names, with various profiles. The analysis is illustrated by the complete edition of 334 Old Assyrian texts exemplifying the diversity of sources and unique data offered by these sources.[4]

At least in the first three chapters, women are considered in relation to men as daughters, sisters, mothers, and wives. A general study of Assyrian society, focusing on men, would not have the same structure; that is, it would not start with an analysis of their position as sons, brothers, fathers, and spouses. Examples where men are defined by the existence of a wife are rare, like in the following text:[5]

---

3. This has been regularly observed under the French expression *femmes d'affaires*; see, for example, Garelli 1979.

4. This book is intended both for Assyriologists, and thus includes the transliterations of the texts, and for a wider public curious to learn about the life and activities of Assyrian and Anatolian women, hence an accessible general introduction and elements on the chronology, calendar, and measures in use during the Old Assyrian period.

5. Kt n/k 1192:5–9, 38–42 letter from Laqēpum to a group of merchants and specifically to Aššur-taklāku: *mì-nam : ma-da-tim lu-lá-pí-ta-a-kum, a-hi a-ta be-lí* [*a-ta iš*]*-tù* mu-30-šè, *na-ru-qam a-dí-na-kum-ma : ta-ma-kár, bar-ki-tám-ma ù-lá té-er-ta-ka ú-lá, na-áš-pé-er-ta-ka* <*i-li-kam*>(…) *i-nu-mì na-ru-qám, a-dí-na-ku-ni : me-er-am am-tám* ìr$^{\textit{dam}}$, *ú* é$^{\textit{tám}}$ *ú-lá ti-šu* / *u*$_4$*-ma-am* kù-babbar$^{\textit{áp}}$, *na-ru-qí-a : a-na*

> Why should I write a lot to you? You are my brother and my master. Thirty years ago I gave you a joint-stock capital for you to conduct trade. Afterwards neither a letter of yours nor a message came to me.... When I gave you a joint-stock capital, you did not have a son, an *amtum*-wife, a slave, or a house. Today you have spent the silver from my joint-stock funds on your son and your wife!

In this case, it does not concern specifically the relation that this man had to a woman of the family, but it represents a stage in his life, the one of a married man with a family. Thus, the organization of these chapters is not only linked with a presumed preconception of the historian, but with a bias of the analyzed sources, in which women seem to be largely defined by their place in the family structure.

To better understand the data offered by the archives of Assyrian merchants, it is necessary to present the sources at our disposal and to analyze the part taken by women in these. We also need to consider more generally the historical context in which these women evolved, as well as the place given to women, compared to that given to men, in the society of Aššur and in that of Kaneš, where ethnic diversity was at work and mixed marriages a common phenomenon. Before undertaking such an analysis, I will briefly present the state of research on the history of women and gender in Assyriology.

The History of Women and Gender in Assyriology

It seems important to explain the approach implemented in this book and how it fits into the studies of women's history and gender history in Assyriology. The development of the feminist and postfeminist movement in humanities has been described as three overlapping waves.[6] During the 1960s and 1970s, scholars looked for women in primary sources in order to integrate them into history. In the 1980s, historians adopted the word *gender*, which represents the societal interpretation of sexual difference.[7] The third wave, developed since the early 1990s, questions the binary male/

ša me-er-i-kà, ù a-ší-tí-ka : ta-áš-ku-un-ma; text published by Sever and Çeçen 2000, 175–76.

6. Bahrani 2001, 14–25; see also van de Mieroop 1999, 138–60.

7. In 1989, the journals *Gender and History* (Wiley Online Library) and *Journal of Women's History* (Johns Hopkins University Press) both began publication.

female structure; what interests the historian is not so much the difference itself, but the way in which it has been culturally invested by societies. According to Joan Scott, gender remains "a useful category of analysis because it requires us to historicize the ways sex and sexual difference have been conceived."[8] Being man or woman, or considered as such, does not have the same meaning at all times and in all cultures.[9] Moreover, the way we write history is dependent on our own cultural and social context. This perspective was, for example, a concern of the French-Japanese program we conducted on the economic role of women in ancient Mesopotamia.[10]

The notion of gender was introduced in Assyriology in the early 1990s.[11] The idea was to distinguish gender, as a social and cultural construction, from sex, a biological identity, and to understand why women were less present in cuneiform texts and ancient Near Eastern iconography.[12] Studies focused first on elite women, queens and high priestesses, and the female workforce in large institutions.[13]

Archives found in private houses, quite sporadic in the third millennium, are extremely numerous at the beginning of the second millennium. This does not mean that they did not exist earlier; their scarcity may simply be linked to the hazards of discovery. David Owen published an Ur III letter sent by a woman that is very similar to some of the Old Assyrian women's letters:[14]

8. Scott 2010, 13.

9. Thébaud 1998, 114.

10. The REFEMA program was carried by Francis Joannès and Fumi Karahashi and involved several members of the team Histoire et Archéologie de l'Orient Cunéiforme (ArScAN laboratory, Nanterre) between 2012 and 2014. See Joannès and Karahashi 2014 and the proceedings of the final conference, Lion and Michel 2016.

11. Westenholz 1990. It really developed in the early 2000s with *NIN: Journal of Gender Studies in Antiquity* and the Forty-Seventh Rencontre Assyriologique Internationale, held in Helsinki in 2001 on "Sex and Gender in the Ancient Near East"; see Parpola and Whiting 2002. See also Asher-Greve 2000.

12. Asher-Greve 2002 published a bibliography of studies on women and gender in Near Eastern cultures up to 2001, which has been completed up to 2016 by Garcia-Ventura and Zisa 2017. Several recent books devote considerable space to the theoretical framework, as, for example, Svärd and Garcia-Ventura 2018.

13. For example, Maekawa 1980; Biga 1988, 2000, and 2016; Ziegler 1999; Gadaut 2009; Langlois 2017.

14. Owen 1980; translation after Michalowski 2011, 16–17. Its exact provenance is, unfortunately, unknown.

> Say to Kiaga: Why am I being maligned about the children, even though I bound up sixty half-loafs of bread and two ban of flour in leather sacks (for them)? There is grain in the household, but none was bound up for the woman. She would not allow me to enter into the storehouse without Atu's permission. Would I squander the property that belongs to him?
>
> The eleven beer-breads that were in his house have been taken out; they have been distributed as food for the household. The workers took away the seed grain, and (now) there is no grain whatsoever in the household....
>
> There is no grain in the household, and therefore he should dispatch grain to me. Please—let him come!

Many more such letters must have existed, and their reading could change our vision of Ur III society.

Publications linked to second-millennium private archives have focused on family contracts, legal documents, and law codes to assess the place of women in the family and society.[15] They also dealt with visible groups of women, like the *nadītum*-priestesses consecrated to the god Šamaš in Sippar and who remained single.[16]

The sources under study in this volume date back to the nineteenth and eighteenth centuries BCE and were found at Kültepe/Kaneš in the houses of Assyrian merchants temporarily settled in Central Anatolia. These texts have already been widely exploited for their rich data on trade and markets with important financial innovations, and the activities and lives of several important male merchants have been the subject of detailed studies.[17] However, some Assyrian women, residing in Aššur and known from the letters they sent to Kaneš, are particularly visible in these texts because, in the absence of the men away on business, they found themselves at the head of their households and were also active in inter-

---

15. For example, Westbrook 1988; Lafont 1999; for more references, see Michel 2015a. Stol 2016 proposes a comprehensive study of women over several millennia. See also the collective volume edited by Budin and MacIntosh Turfa 2016, which includes fourteen chapters on Mesopotamia and Anatolia showing various approaches to women and gender. Two collections of texts dedicated to women have been recently published: Chavalas 2014 and Halton and Svärd 2017.

16. Among others, Harris 1975; Lion 2009b, 2011; De Graef 2016; Nakata 2016.

17. For general studies on Old Assyrian trade, see, for example, Larsen 1967, 1976, 2015a; Veenhof 1972, 2008a; Dercksen 1996; Michel 2001a. For studies on specific merchants, see, for example, Ichisar 1981; Larsen 1982, 2002; Michel 1991; Stratford 2017, and volumes of publication of Old Assyrian tablets, starting with AKT 3.

national trade. The purpose of the present book is to make their voices heard, those of women.[18] But women do not exist without men, and vice versa; thus, this study about women is conducted from the perspective of gender: when applicable, I compare the place of women in the society and their activities with that of men, trying to emancipate myself from any preconceptions about gender division. For example, the following questions are raised: Who kept marriage contracts, husband or wife? Is there a great difference between men's and women's testaments, between men's and women's loans? What kind of mutual representations exist between men and women in business? And so on. This work thus inscribes itself in the first two feminist waves, and it provides unique textual material for more theoretical studies.[19]

Old Assyrian Archives and Women

The Old Assyrian corpus undoubtedly represents the oldest and largest group of private archives that gives a significant place to women. Of the 23,000 Old Assyrian cuneiform tablets, 99 percent were discovered at Kültepe, the ancient city of Kaneš, located in Central Anatolia, 22 km northeast of the modern city of Kayseri. The remaining tablets, some 180, come mainly from the sites of Boğazköy, ancient Hattuša; and Alişar, ancient Amkuwa, in Central Anatolia, two of the about forty other localities where Assyrian merchants settled.[20] A few remaining tablets were unearthed, discarded in Middle Assyrian levels at Aššur (on the Tigris river), at Gasur (east of the Tigris, later named Nuzi), and at Sippar (South Mesopotamia).[21]

---

18. This study is mainly based on a close reading of the texts. Garcia-Ventura and Svärd 2018, 8, note that "for Assyriologists, a close reading of the texts (based on the idea of the hermeneutic circle and source criticism) often works as a fruitful method."

19. I recognize, with Niek Veldhuis (2018, 453), that theoretical reflections on the researcher's historical and social location and global point of view are necessary. Such theoretical analyses need to rely on a real knowledge of the available documentation and must avoid mixing up corpuses from very different origins and written with different aims.

20. Barjamovic 2011.

21. For a detailed bibliography of Old Assyrian sources, see Michel 2003a, 2006c, 2011a, and 2015e.

Fig. 1. Kültepe: the circular mound and the lower town northeast of the mound. Source: © Google Earth, 2012.

Kaneš and Aššur

Kültepe was first excavated by illicit diggers and explored by scholars looking for written sources before being the object of regular excavations by Turkish archaeologists. These started in 1948 under the direction of Tahsin Özgüç, who worked there for fifty-seven years.[22] In 1955, Kutlu Emre joined the excavations and codirected them for fifty-nine years. Since 2006, Kültepe excavations have been directed by Fikri Kulakoğlu, who has invited colleagues from archaeobotany, zooarchaeology, and all subfields of archaeometry to investigate the site and its surroundings in order to know more about all aspects of daily life at Kültepe.[23]

22. Emre 2015.

23. T. Özgüç 2003; Kulakoğlu and Kangal 2010; the various contributions in Atici et al. 2014; Kulakoğlu and Michel 2015; and Kulakoğlu and Barjamovic 2017.

The site was occupied since the middle of the third millennium BCE. It is divided into two major sectors: the circular mound (tepe) and the lower town northeast of it. The mound was occupied from the Early Bronze Age to the Roman Empire, while the lower town was inhabited only from the last decades of the third millennium to the early sixteenth century BCE (Old Hittite period; fig. 1).[24] It shows four levels of occupation, but it seems that only level II (ca. 1945–1835 BCE) and Ib (ca. 1832–1700 BCE)—corresponding more or less to the Middle Bronze Age—yielded written documentation, some 22,200 and 560 tablets, respectively. Only forty scattered tablets were discovered on the mound where palaces and temples have been unearthed; thus, we do not have archives—if ever they have existed—of the local authorities.

During the nineteenth century BCE, Kaneš was a large site, measuring presumably between 170 and 230 hectares, and its population has been estimated between 25,000 and 30,000, including some 3,000 inhabitants in the 9 hectares of the lower town commercial district excavated up to now. Among these, there seem to have been a majority of Assyrians living there more or less temporarily, all of them involved in trade.[25]

The lower town was divided into districts separated by large streets and open spaces. The archives were discovered in the house storerooms, where merchandise was kept as well. They were classified and stored in sacks, baskets, boxes, or clay jars lying on the ground or on wooden shelves and identified by sealed clay labels.[26] Tahsin Özgüç described the discovery of the archives of Šalim-Aššur unearthed in 1994 as follows (fig. 3):[27]

---

24. The archaeologists refer to Kültepe's lower town by the Assyrian term *kārum*. This word means the merchant district and the organization of these merchants with its administrative building (see "Translation Choices," xxvii). Moreover, its stratigraphy is used as the chronological scale of reference for the whole Anatolian plateau between the end of the third millennium and the beginning of the seventeenth century BCE; see Michel 2011b. However, we do not know exactly what the word *kārum* referred to geographically, and since it is unlikely that it corresponded precisely to the lower town excavated up to now, the two entities, the lower town and the *kārum*, must be distinguished; see Michel 2014a.

25. Barjamovic 2014; Hertel 2014. Recent excavations focus on the mound; they have shown that Kültepe was a very prosperous regional center able to attract foreigners already during the Early Bronze Age; see Ezer 2014; Üstündağ 2014; Kulakoğlu 2015; Kulakoğlu and Öztürk 2015; Kulakoğlu 2017; Yazıcıoğlu-Santamaria 2017.

26. Michel 1998a, 2008e, 2018; Veenhof 2003e, 2013a; Larsen 2008.

27. T. Özgüç 2001, 370. See T. Özgüç 1994, 369, for the description of the discov-

Fig. 2. The house of Šalim-Aššur's family, excavated in 1994, in which letters sent or received by the woman Anna-anna were found (AKT 6). Photograph by Cécile Michel. © Archaeological Mission of Kültepe.

> An archive of 947 tablets and unopened envelopes and pottery were found in these two small rooms [5 and 6]. They were evidently kept on wooden shelves against the walls. The tablets that were found on the floor along the walls are those that fell off the shelves in the fire. The tablets that had been packed in bags, in straw wrappings, and sacks were discovered in piles at the middles of the rooms. A group of the tablets, as usual, were kept in pots.

The fire, which destroyed some houses at the end of level II, baked the tablets, helping to preserve them. Besides tablets, rich material lay in the houses and in the graves dug under the ground in some rooms: vessels and rhytons with original shapes, which presumably served cultic purposes, weapons, metal vases, statuettes, and jewelry items (see fig. 8).[28]

Kaneš was at the center of the Assyrians' commercial network in central Anatolia (which was designated by "the country"). These Assyrian merchants originated from Aššur—referred to as "the city" in the texts—a

ery of Elamma's archives excavated in 1991 and 1992: "The archive of the merchant was found along the base of the east wall of room 3 and in rooms 4–5, in groups once packed in boxes, bags, sacks and straw mats. On top of each group lay one or two bullae. Unopened envelopes were placed at the bottom, tablets on top. In contrast to other archives, here we did not find tablets stored in jars." See also T. Özgüç 2004 for level Ib archives.

28. See the objects presented in Kulakoğlu and Kangal 2010.

Fig. 3. Cuneiform tablets in situ from the archive of Šalim-Aššur, excavated in 1994. Source: Kültepe archives. © Archaeological Mission of Kültepe.

city built on a rocky headland on the western bank of the Tigris, in the north of Iraq. The first occupation of this site dates back to the beginning of the third millennium BCE. The town is mentioned in written documents from the mid-third millennium and was successively subject to the Akkad and Ur III dynasties. With the fall of Ur III at the very end of the third millennium BCE, Aššur became an independent city-state dominated by an oligarchy of merchants.[29] At the beginning of the second millennium, the town did not exceed fifty-five hectares and housed presumably between seven thousand and ten thousand inhabitants.[30] The archaeological discoveries for the Middle Bronze Age remain rare and scattered. Indeed, these levels have not been excavated since they are located under the first millennium ruins of the capital of the Assyrian Empire. The main constructions dated to the late third millennium and beginning of the second millennium are official and religious buildings. The Old Assyrian residen-

29. Veenhof 2008a, 28–32; 2017a; Larsen 2015a, 83–100.

30. Larsen 2000, 79.

tial district has not been identified, and the very rare tablets found for this period are, for the most part, school texts scattered in later levels.[31] Thus, all that we know about the Old Assyrian society of Aššur and its commercial activities is documented by the cuneiform tablets discovered at Kültepe, more than a thousand kilometers away.[32]

The Old Assyrian Archives of Kültepe/Kaneš

The tablets excavated at Kültepe represent, for the most part, the private archives of Assyrian merchants settled there during the nineteenth century BCE; very few of these archives belonged to native Anatolians who adopted the cuneiform script and the Old Assyrian dialect, mainly to record contracts.[33] Every year between 1948 and the end of the 1990s, the archaeologists excavated new houses in the lower town. Some of these contained archives made of a variable number of cuneiform clay tablets, from a few dozens to more than a thousand.[34]

These texts are written using the cuneiform script, with a repertoire limited mainly to simple syllabic signs and a few logograms, some of which appear very often.[35] Because of the reduced repertoire of signs, many have several alternative phonetic readings. In addition, orthographic conventions suggest an economy of writing—for example, the geminate consonants are rarely indicated—and errors of signs are not rare. Thus, some groups of signs can be interpreted in different ways.[36] Some writers use a word divider that is supposed to help the reader, but it appears very inconsistently. The script is often small and tight, with numerous wedges per sign; a great majority of tablets are covered with text all around, including the left edge. The simplicity of the syllabary suggests that, beside educated scribes, a large part of the Assyrian population was able to read and to write.[37] Paleographic analysis of Old Assyrian

---

31. Pedersen 1986, 26–27; Donbaz 1974, 1985.

32. Michel 2017.

33. Michel 2011c; Günbattı in AKT 10.

34. For the number of tablets excavated every year, see Michel 2003a, 2006c, 2011a, 2015e, and 2018.

35. A maximum of two hundred signs, including logograms, were in use during the Old Assyrian period; see Michel 2008b. See also Kryszat 2008a, with an estimation of one hundred twenty syllabic signs; and Barjamovic 2015.

36. Veenhof 2008a, 112; Kouwenberg 2017, 15–38.

37. Michel 2008b. See chapter 4, section "Women and Writing," in this volume.

tablets is in its infancy, and studies dedicated to Assyrian women's literacy and writing are still rare; up to now they have not found different writing habits between men and women.[38]

The Old Assyrian dialect belongs to the group of East Semitic languages and originates from Proto-Akkadian. It has some specificities, as vowel assimilation (*aššutum* versus *aššatum* in Old Babylonian) or the use of *-ni* as a marker of subordination, which indicate an independent development of the language; some of its innovations persisted in the state of the language spoken during the Middle Assyrian period, a few centuries later.[39]

The Old Assyrian archives, which predominantly date to the first half of the nineteenth century BCE, include different text genres, whose contents are usually trade oriented (fig. 6). Texts may be classified, according to modern categories, as letters, legal texts, personal memoranda, and noncommercial texts.

Between a third and two-fifths of an archive consists of private letters (*ṭuppum*, *našpertum*) received by the Assyrian population settled in Kaneš and were sent by their family members and colleagues living in Aššur or in other Assyrian settlements in Anatolia (fig. 4). There are also copies of letters sent to Aššur or to other Anatolian towns or originals sent from Kaneš and brought back to the town by their recipients. Such letters were protected during transport by clay envelopes, on which the writer usually unrolled his or her personal seal.[40] These letters provide precious data about the organization of long-distance trade, but also about domestic matters and daily life. The size of tablets bearing letters depended on the length of the message to be written. Letters usually contain twenty to forty lines, and their size does not exceed the palm of the hand. Even a letter of a small size could contain a lot of text: this is, for example, the case of text **264**, sent by Ummī-Išhara to her sister Šalimma, which measures 5 by 5.5 cm and includes forty-nine lines (fig. 15). Letters, and especially women's letters, were sometimes written in a language close to the vernacular, which makes them difficult to translate. Moreover, reading the correspondence of others is often challenging since we lack the context and thus do not always understand what is going on. Indeed, some letters are too elliptical and assume too much prior knowledge on the part of the recipient.

---

38. Michel 2015b; Stratford 2015b; Beyer 2019.

39. Kouwenberg 2017, 10–11.

40. Michel 2001a; 2008g; 2018, 52–53; Veenhof 2013a, 37.

Fig. 4. Letter 27, sent by a woman to her husband. Photograph by Cécile Michel. © Archaeological Mission of Kültepe.

Fig. 5. Marriage contract (facing page) and its envelope (above) (17). Photograph by Cécile Michel. © Archaeological Mission of Kültepe.

The Old Assyrian correspondence reflects, in general, an atypical situation. The letters come from a specific group, the merchants, a group that experienced very particular living conditions, where men and women were regularly separated. Merchants traveled frequently and were often far from home, hence the constant need to exchange information in writing. Such an abundance of private letters is not documented for other corpuses. Private archives from the early second millennium found at Larsa, or later ones from Nuzi, produced far fewer letters.

The second important group of tablets preserved by the Assyrian merchants in their Kaneš houses consists of legal texts, including contracts, whether family or commercial, and judicial records.[41] Marriage, divorce, and testaments (wills) represent the main types of records of family law (fig. 5); many of these are presented in chapters 1 and 2. There are a great variety of commercial contracts linked to international trade, among which one finds, for example, investments in joint-stock companies (*naruqqum*) and other types of partnerships, transport contracts, deeds of sale—several concerning the purchase of houses and slaves are presented in this book—transport contracts, and many types of debt notes. These consist of loan contracts from credit sales, straight loans

41. For these texts, see Hertel 2013, 133–83. A selection of legal texts is given in translation in Michel 2000a.

against interest, and loan contracts to the benefit of an anonymous creditor (*tamkārum*).

Many of these loans involving at least one woman, either as creditor or as debtor, are included in this study. Such loans are written on small tablets and were kept in the creditor's archive with their envelope, on which the text was copied and the witnesses and debtor(s) impressed their seal. The legal value of loan contracts lay in the presence of this sealed envelope (*ṭuppum harmum*). Loans agreements were usually written from the creditor's point of view: "PN_1 has loaned x silver to PN_2," hence their designation as debt claims.[42] Such a designation has to be understood in a broad sense and concerns every possible financial obligation, whatever its origin, and this obtains especially for Anatolian debts. The text never specifies the reason for the loan, and it is therefore difficult to distinguish between loans of necessity and commercial loans; the latter could involve large quantities of silver or copper, as well as small amounts—less than one mina of silver—corresponding to the sale on credit of textiles. Cereals, recorded in bags and jars, are also regularly lent, especially when Anatolians are involved. The duration of a loan, when specified, is generally indicated in *hamuštum*-weeks. Necessity loans were usually interest bearing from the beginning, while for loans that resulted from commercial credit, default interest could be charged for late repayment. A guarantor, sometimes a member of the family, could be named to secure the repayment of the debt. Contracts for loans of necessity also mention the provision of securities: a house, members of the debtor's family, and slaves often appear as collateral.[43] These could come into the creditor's possession until the repayment of the debt and work for the creditor in order to pay the interest on the loan; such a situation could be risky for the women of the family. Most of the occurrences of pledges concern loans granted to Anatolians, sometimes to a couple jointly responsible for the repayment, a liability that could also be extended to the children. Some loan contracts refer to a political measure of debt remission by Anatolian kings; they seek to protect their subjects who found themselves in a situation of debt slavery as a result of high interest rates applied by Assyrian creditors.[44]

When the debtor repaid his loan, the creditor gave him the document so that he could destroy it. In theory, therefore, loan contracts should

42. Veenhof 2012b, 155.
43. Veenhof 2001.
44. Balkan 1974.

not have survived the settlement of the debts they record. However, the large number of such texts indicates that the destruction of the tablet was far from systematic. A number of debts may not have been settled, and some were inherited by the descendants of the debtors, as evidenced by testaments. These loan contracts were often kept intact in their sealed envelopes. Some debtors, once their debt was settled, choose to break the envelope, removing any valid legal character from their contract, and to arrange the tablet in their archives in order to keep track of each of their transactions.[45] Finally, the repayment of a loan, in the absence of the original document, could generate the drafting of a receipt.

Besides contracts, judicial records included witnessed depositions, sometimes with sworn testimonies; records of private arbitration cases; verdicts, which could be transmitted to Kaneš by the king of Aššur; and so on.[46] Some of these legal texts, as private arbitrations, could be very long, presenting the arguments of both parties; for example, text **65** has ninety-two lines.

The merchants' archives also contain various private notices, lists, memoranda, and so on, which were usually anonymous. These texts are often short, but lists of expenses for a special occasion could reach more than sixty lines, as text **14**. Besides these three main groups of texts, a few incantations and historical, literary, and school texts were found scattered in some houses.

Clay labels (bullae) attached to tablet containers, jars closed with fabric secured by cord, tied up sacks, baskets, and bales of goods could bear a few lines of text specifying the content, and they were sealed by the owner of the goods. Such lumps of clay could as well be applied to a door to seal it and to prevent it from unexpected opening by an unauthorized person.[47] Thus goods and tablets could be kept in sealed containers, themselves preserved in a sealed room. Tablets were classified by dossiers or text genres, sealed envelopes being often kept together. Many letters allude to the opening of tablet containers, that is, breaking the seal on the container, to extract a tablet. Most of the seals applied on bullae or envelopes are uninscribed; thus it is not easy nowadays to identify their owner

45. Michel 2018, 54–56.

46. Hertel 2013, 137.

47. Michel 2016e; Andersson Strand, Breniquet, and Michel 2017. Due to an inventory of listed objects, not according to their precise provenance but according to their form or use, the link between the bullae and the tablets to which they refer is lost.

or user (figs. 13, 14, and 15). But in the past, people could easily recognize the seals of their relatives and colleagues, thanks to the miniature scenes represented.[48]

The archives excavated in the merchants' houses at the lower town of Kültepe are still in the phase of decipherment by a dozen Assyriologists from Turkey and elsewhere. For two decades, archives have been published as a group in volumes that allow a better understanding of family organization and the role and status of women.[49] For example, a dozen Assyrian archives, representing more than four thousand tablets, were unearthed between 1990 and 1994 (fig. 3); these include the following families, cited by the main male owner with his links to female members of the family, when known:[50]

- 1990a: Šumi-abiya, son of Puzur-Ištar, and Aššur-mūtappil (242 tablets published in TPAK 1)
- 1990b: Unknown owner (123 tablets currently studied by Salih Çeçen)
- 1991a + 1992a: Elamma, husband of Lamassatum, father of Ummī-Išhara and Šalimma, and father, with another wife, of Ištar-lamassī (282 tablets + 90 tablets from 1992 published in AKT 8)
- 1991b: Mixed archives (154 tablets)
- 1992b: Kuliya, husband of Ababaya (73 tablets + 3 tablets from 1989 published in AKT 5)
- 1992b: Šu-Ištar, son of Aššur-bāni (774 tablets partly published in AKT 11a)[51]
- 1993: Ali-ahum, son of Iddin-Suen, father of Tariša and Ištitiša, and his son Aššur-taklāku, husband of Lušitiya (915 tablets + 61 tablets from 1994 + 2 tablets from 1998)[52]
- 1994a: Irma-Aššur, husband of Suhkana (370 tablets)[53]

---

48. Larsen 1977; Teissier 1994; Lassen 2012; Ricetti 2017.

49. Volumes gathering archaeological excavated archives are the following: TPAK 1; AKT 3, 4, 5, 6a–e, 7a, 8, 9a, 10, and 11a.

50. Michel 2018, 61–62.

51. Erol 2015.

52. Michel 2008e (archive); Michel 2015b for the women of this family; the publication of this archive is currently being prepared; fig. 6 in this volume.

53. The publication of this archive is in the charge of Gojko Barjamovic.

Fig. 6. Groups of tablets excavated in 1993 in the house of Ali-ahum and his son Aššur-taklāku and daughter Tariša. Photograph by Cécile Michel. © Archaeological Mission of Kültepe.

- 1994b: Šalim-Aššur, son of Issu-arik, father-in-law of Anna-anna and Ištar-lamassī (1,101 tablets published in AKT 6a–e; figs. 2–3, 20 in this volume)

Other groups of archives are currently being prepared for publication, as, for example, the archive of Uṣur-ša-Ištar, brother of ᶠAkatiya and ᶠŠīmat-Suen (Çeçen et al.).[54] Most of these archives represent several hundreds of tablets, envelopes, and fragments testifying to the importance of written documents for Assyrian merchants and their families.

Texts Edited in This Volume

Most of the texts edited in this volume belong to the first two categories presented above, letters and legal texts. They document different groups of the population: the letters mainly refer to the activities and situations of their senders, who are living in Aššur or in Anatolian towns others than Kaneš; while the legal texts testify to agreements and cases that took place in Kaneš and concern either the Assyrians or native Anatolians. For example, the archives excavated in the houses of Kaneš's lower town contain both women's letters sent from Aššur illustrating the everyday life of Assyrian women in the mother city and family contracts documenting the marriage and divorce agreements of women living at Kaneš. We lack the archives kept by the Assyrian families in Aššur, including their family contracts. It is important to keep in mind this imbalance of sources when studying the place and role of women in families and in society, both in Aššur and in Kaneš.

This volume includes the edition of 334 Old Assyrian texts, nearly all discovered at Kültepe either before 1948 and scattered in different collections around the world (211 texts) or after 1948, during the regular Turkish excavations, and preserved in the Museum of Anatolian Civilizations at Ankara (121 texts). Most of these have been collated. Only two texts come from the Aššur excavations: one found in the Ištar temple (**122**) and the other one in a large house mixed in with a Middle Assyrian administrative archive (**242**). These 334 texts represent a sample of the Old Assyr-

54. See also the archives of Ali-ahum (Kt c/k), to be published by Jan Gerrit Dercksen, the volumes AKT 7a and AKT 9a, which represent the publication of parts of archives excavated respectively in 1988 (Aššur-rē'ī) and 1950 (Buzutaya and Lipit-Ištar).

ian sources documenting the status, role, and activities of women from Aššur and Kaneš.

More than half of the texts (176) are letters, and 54 percent of these (94) were sent by women.[55] Most of the time (78 letters), a woman was the only sender. However, some letters were sent by two women together, often sisters or a mother and daughter (**170, 211, 234, 237, 246, 249, 252, 254–256, 311**); others were sent by a couple (**50**), a woman and a man (**206, 287**), or a woman and several men (**59, 280**). Another important group of letters (72) were received by women. In contrast to the first group of letters, only a little more than half (41) of these were addressed to a woman alone. The others were mainly addressed to a woman and a man together (18 letters), to a woman and several men (6 letters), to two women and two men (**154**), or to two women, who might have family ties (6 letters: **126, 156, 221, 225, 290, 307**). Finally, ten more letters were included in this volume, even though exchanged only between men, because they document important aspects of women's life or status.

The headings of letters often provide evidence for the status of individual women. Letter headings traditionally followed a fixed formulation: "Say to PN_1: thus (says) PN_2." But, unlike Old Babylonian practice, in the Old Assyrian letters, the recipient is not systematically mentioned first; this position is usually reserved for the person with the highest social rank. Thus some letters start with a reverse heading: "Thus (says) PN_2: say to PN_1." The father places himself before his son, the elder before the younger, the boss before the employee, and the man usually before the woman. This tradition is complicated when several people send the same letter to different correspondents, and there is more than one sender and more than one recipient. In this relatively frequent situation, the individual who is the highest on the social scale is at the top of the letter-heading formula.

In twenty-two of the ninety-four letters sent by women, the letter heading starts with a female personal name; this woman is either the sender or recipient of the letter. We can observe that a wife usually places her husband first (Pūšu-kēn appears before Lamassī) and her sons after her (Ištar-baštī is mentioned before Puzur-Ištar). The status of some women seems to be so important that their names are placed before those of well-known merchants (Musa appears before Pūšu-kēn, but we do not know their rela-

55. See Michel 2010a.

tionship). However, this rule is not fixed and has exceptions: the order could be reversed, and this is especially interesting when it concerns siblings. Šīmat-Suen wrote twice to her brother, Uṣur-ša-Ištar, placing herself first (**272–273**), and a third time she appears after him (**274**). Her sister, Akatiya, systematically placed Uṣur-ša-Ištar first in her letters addressed to him (**265–269**), and the reciprocal is true (**240**). When the two sisters addressed a letter together to their brother, they mentioned him first, and Akatiya appears before Šīmat-Suen (**237**). This shows that the content of the letter could have an impact on the order of personal names in the letter formula; for example, if the sender had an important request to make, he or she could choose to honor the addressee by placing him or her at the top of the letter heading.

The information contained in the letters is quite variable, and some letters conveyed almost no particular message, just asking for news (**136**).[56] Even if the news was brief, it was essential to communicate, as the woman Narāmtum explained to her correspondents: "What is this that you do not even send me a tablet two fingers wide with good news from you?" (**235**).

Letters sent by women are of a particular interest since they deal not only with international trade—especially textile production and sale—and financial matters, but also yield unique insights into many everyday life aspects. These letters use a vernacular language, and some of them may even carry some personal feelings. Mogens Trolle Larsen noted:[57]

> It is deeply interesting to see that where men write about business and only rarely touch upon matters of family affairs or emotional problems, those topics are characteristic of women's letters. Not only are they often written in such agitation that the grammar suffers, they are full of words which belong to a very special sphere of life, one that is rarely attested in the entire cuneiform tradition, and they are therefore often very hard to understand.

Some lonely women at Aššur shared their feelings for their husbands: "When you hear (this) letter, come, look to Aššur, your god, and your home hearth, and let me see you in person while I am still alive!" (**129**). In

---

56. See Zaccagnini 2017 for a letter sent by a man to two women to reassure them and give them news.

57. Larsen 2015a, 5. See also Larsen 2001.

the letters they addressed to women, men usually conveyed instructions for tasks to be done, often linked to trade, and various recommendations.

Nearly all other texts edited in this book are legal texts, more specifically contracts (118 texts). These are represented by family contracts (42 texts); debt notes involving women either as creditor or as debtor (35 texts); deeds of sale concerning slaves and houses, in which women are either buyer or seller (28 texts); and transport or deposit contracts, where women appear often as owners of goods (13 texts).[58] The second group of legal texts are judicial records (27 texts). These consist of witnessed depositions (12 texts), verdicts (9 texts), records of private arbitration (4 texts), and two other documents.[59]

The last group of texts is more heterogeneous. Besides ten memoranda and inventories, often listing goods of women, there are two incantations related to women's health (**117–118**) and a votive inscription dedicated by a woman (**122**).[60]

The Role of Women in Society and Economy

The cuneiform archives excavated at the lower town of Kültepe document predominantly the intensive commercial exchanges developed by Aššur with Central Anatolia at the very beginning of the second millennium BCE. Political decisions were taken by kings of Aššur in order to set up free traffic of some goods traded by their subjects and to attract traders from southern Mesopotamia. Assyrian merchants settled in Anatolia, in foreign territory, more than a thousand kilometers away from their home city, to sell the tin and textiles brought from Aššur. Some of these textiles were produced by their female relatives back home. In return, they sent back gold and silver to Aššur. Their commercial activities, based on elaborate partnerships, were governed by trade agreements with the Anatolian

58. Marriage, divorce, and adoption contracts: **2, 5, 15, 17–26, 30–35, 37–47, 73, 120**; testaments and arrangements concerning successions: **54–62, 69**; debt notes involving women: **74–81, 83–91, 100–101, 177–189, 193–194, 261–262**; transport and deposit contracts: **121, 174, 196, 224, 285, 288, 292, 295–297, 320, 324, 334**; deeds of sale (slaves, houses): **52–53, 92–98, 102–109, 111, 138, 143–144, 148–153, 159**.

59. Witnessed depositions: **6–7, 10–11, 51, 64–65, 71, 82, 99, 112, 190**; records of private arbitration: **49, 115, 257, 258**; assertive oath: **72**; verdicts: **4, 8, 28, 36, 48, 191, 243–244, 276**; draft: **250**.

60. Private notices, memoranda, and inventories: **14, 110, 119, 131, 135, 251, 263, 275, 291, 321**.

princes in the various territories in which they had settled.[61] This long-distance trade with Anatolia lasted a little more than two centuries. At the end of the eighteenth century, the town passed under the authority of a local dynasty, then to the kings of the Mittani.

Being trade oriented, the Old Assyrian archives give the wrong impression that the great majority of the population in Aššur and Kaneš, both men and women, were involved in commercial exchanges. However, only part of the Assyrian society and a small proportion of the Kaneš native Anatolians are documented by the written sources. Because of their role in the society and in the economy, some women appear to us as visible, while others remain invisible. This study, necessarily, focuses on the status, social role, and economic activities of Assyrian and Anatolian women who appear with an active role in the texts.

Assyrian Society in Aššur and Kaneš

The Old Assyrian population was spread between Aššur and its surroundings, Kaneš, and the other trade settlements in Anatolia. The archives excavated in the houses of Kültepe's lower town belonged to Assyrian merchants settled there, and thus they provide data limited to the people first in Kaneš and secondarily in Aššur.[62] The written sources belong to two to three generations of Assyrian merchants; the bulk of the documentation is concentrated over a period covering the first half of the nineteenth century.[63] Texts give some hints on various aspects of the Assyrian society and the activities of its members.

The majority of the inhabitants of Aššur ("son/daughter of Aššur") mentioned in the sources were involved in the commercial exchanges with Anatolia, that is, the king and his family,[64] several eponyms and other high officials, priests and temple personnel, as well as men and women of wealthy families, presumably referred to as the "big men," as opposed to "small men."[65] In Kaneš, all the Assyrians who settled there, at least

61. Larsen 2015a.

62. Michel 2016a, 193.

63. Barjamovic, Hertel, and Larsen 2012. According to Stratford 2017, this period could even be narrowed down. Only a few texts belonged to native Anatolian merchants; Michel 2011c.

64. Larsen 1976, 129–246; Michel 2015c, 2017.

65. Hecker 2003; Veenhof 2014, 354–56.

during the first two generations, were involved in long-distance trade. There was a great variety of professions linked to international trade, from bankers and agents to donkey drivers and harnessers.[66] Some families built their fortunes on trade, owning large houses at Aššur, with many slaves.[67] Female slaves (*amtum*) helped women to manage the household and could contribute to the production of textiles, while some of the male slaves (*wardum*) could be employed as caravan personnel. Both men and women owned slaves, whom they inherited, bought, or received as pledges for unpaid debts.[68]

Besides people involved in trade, texts mention mainly male professions linked to the political, legal, or economic administration of Aššur or the Assyrian settlement at Kaneš, as, for example, scribes, officials, stewards, judges, interpreters, and so on. Priests were usually called after the deity whose temple they served ("priest of the god Aššur"; **174**:4′). Craftsmen appear sporadically, sometimes in the list of witnesses, as a carpenter, an innkeeper, or a textile cleaner; and one can imagine that leather workers were numerous, producing donkey harnesses and bags for transporting goods.[69]

In contrast, female professionals are scarce in the written sources. Their domains are often gender based, in food preparation or child care.[70] Flour grinders—who are often slaves—are mentioned, as well as an Amorite woman innkeeper; and we find the midwife (*šabsūtum*), nanny (*ēmiqtum*), or wet-nurse (*mušēniqtum*). A few female professionals in Aššur were linked to religious practices and were consulted only by women, as omen diviner (*bārītum*) and dream diviner or interpreter (*šā'iltum*); others were consecrated to a god (*gubabtum*, *qadištum*), and thus often remained single.[71]

The archives unearthed in Kaneš reflect the composition of families and the activities of their members, the family being the basic unit of Mesopotamian society, as evidenced, for example, in the extensive family law found in the Babylonian Code of Hammurabi, about a century later than

66. Michel 2015d.

67. Michel 2008a.

68. Larsen 2017; de Ridder 2017b.

69. Dercksen 2004a, 255–85; Michel 2015d.

70. Michel 2016a, 198.

71. Michel 2009b; note that *qadištum*-consecrated women could be married but were presumably not allowed to have children.

the texts in this volume.[72] Since no collection of laws has been found up to now for the Old Assyrian period, whether in Aššur or in Kaneš, our knowledge relies on family contracts, judicial texts, and letters.[73] These show that men and women enjoyed similar rights: both could ask for divorce and would then pay the same fines; both could inherit, lend silver, buy houses and slaves, or write their testaments. However, there were some differences, as, for example, in marriage contracts, where agency was on the part of the men who took a woman as a wife or gave her to the groom.[74] Women inherited their parents' possessions and, and unlike men, were not responsible for the debts of the deceased, even though they had an active role in the family business. Thus, following the definition proposed by Tonia M. Sharlach, Assyrian women may be considered as interdependent rather than independent.[75]

The terminology for family relationships was quite developed. A married man (*mutum*) could have two wives, the first to be married being called *aššutum* and the second usually *amtum*, a term whose use was ambiguous, as it also corresponded to a "female slave." They could be either Assyrian or Anatolian, but one was necessarily living in Aššur, while the other one was in Anatolia. "Father" (*abum*) and "mother" (*ummum*) had children, who were referred to with different words according to their age and gender: "baby" (*šerrum*) or the collective *ṣuhrum* to refer to small children; when mentioned individually, there were called "boy" (*ṣuhārum*) and "girl" (*ṣuhārtum*), and when grown up, "son" (*mērum*) and "daughter" (*mērtum*).[76] A man or a woman could mention his or her "brother" (*ahum*) or "sister" (*ahātum*); and, when referring to the in-laws, they used the word *emum* (and exceptionally *emātum*), which may be translated indistinctly as "father"/"son"/"brother-in-law."

These kinship terms have masculine and feminine forms, but the term *kallutum*, "fiancée"/"bride," has only a feminine form, indicating the specific status of a woman who was entering a new family structure through marriage. The family itself, sometimes over several generations, was referred to by the words *bēt abim*, "house of the father," an expression that could also refer to the "household" with its inhabitants, including the ancestors buried

72. Roth 1997.

73. Veenhof 2003a, 2012b.

74. See chapter 1.

75. Sharlach 2017, 54.

76. Veenhof 2014, 349.

under the ground of some rooms, and sometimes a chapel for the family god, or simply meant "the house" as a building.[77] The house itself had economic value, and could be transmitted, sold, or rented.[78] It was the women's domain par excellence: they lived, raised their children, and worked at home. All their possessions were preserved in their home; that is, bronze and copper vessels, wooden objects, textiles, and jewelry items. The house was also used as a warehouse, where merchants stored their goods and archives in sealed containers; thus, it needed to be guarded from robbers, and this task was the responsibility of women in the absence of their husbands.

Visible and Invisible Women

Such a picture of Old Assyrian society is made possible thanks to the archives discovered in the houses of the lower town at Kültepe. However, these written sources unevenly document men and women, and among the female Assyrian population, some women are more visible than others. The invisibility of many women is reflected by their scarcity in the family trees reconstructed by specialists in Old Assyrian sources. Unmarried young girls are rarely mentioned in the texts. After marriage, they left their family to enter their husband's family, where they could be very active and visible, but then texts no longer mention their patronyms, and historians often cannot reconstruct their filiation.[79]

Letters addressed or received by women represent approximately 20 percent of the letters excavated at Kültepe and available in transliterations up to now. Women's letters emanate mainly from those who remained alone at Aššur while their husbands were away, like Lamassī or Tarām-Kūbi, or because they were widows or consecrated to a deity and thus never married, like Ahaha. These women were at the head of their households and wrote to their husbands, brothers, or sons in Anatolia concerning both commercial and domestic matters.[80] They mostly belonged to the upper class of the society, earning money through their textile production and investing in trade. They often wrote alone, but could also send a letter together with other women of their family circle. Women who were living together with their husbands in Aššur had less need to write, and some remain unknown

77. Larsen 2007; Veenhof 2014, 350–53; Hertel 2015.
78. Michel 1997b; Veenhof 2011.
79. Michel 2015b; 2016a, 195.
80. Michel 2009c.

to us, like the wives of Aššur-idī or of Šū-Hubur. Letters written by a couple together are quite exceptional; this is, for example, the case of text **50**, addressed by Imdī-ilum and Ištar-bāštī to their daughter Zizizi.

Some letters of this female correspondence might mention the names of other women, occasionally daughters or sisters, who appear most of the time in a passive role. They also reveal the existence of anonymous female slaves bought or seized by authorities. As we lack Old Assyrian archives from Aššur, all other women living there remain invisible to us. Thus, the proposed analysis of status and activities of women of Aššur is necessarily incomplete, and oriented towards the wealthy segment of the population that used writing as a communication tool.

The situation is different for the Assyrian women living in Kaneš. The first Assyrians to settle at Kaneš were men; they left their wives and children at Aššur, and returned regularly to Aššur to deal with their family affairs. In a further stage, Assyrian women came with their husbands and brought up their children in Kaneš. Some of them, daughters or widows of Assyrians, married Anatolians. Women who received letters in the lower town from their fathers, their brothers, or their husbands, when these were traveling, appear regularly with other recipients. Many of these letters are motivated by commercial matters, informing the women of ongoing negotiations. Women are also involved in many of the contracts excavated in the Kaneš houses, both family and commercial. There, they often appear as active, buying slaves and real estate, lending or borrowing silver, and eventually being mentioned as witnesses. But they could also have a passive role, being sold as a slave or seized as a pledge. These women sometimes belonged to different segments of society, both rich and poor.

Among the archives excavated in the lower town, groups of tablets belonged to women, who sometimes wrote texts on their own initiative and kept them in their archives; these texts include family law documents, loan contracts, and transactions linked to the purchase of slaves and real estate. They kept these documents together with the letters they received in special containers, which they sealed with their seal (**223**) and deposited in a room of the house, alongside the archives of the other members of the family living there. These archives, presumably incomplete, belonged, for example, to the Assyrian women Lamassatum, wife of Elamma, and Ištar-lamassī, his daughter;[81] or Tariša, the daughter of Ali-ahum and sister of

81. Texts published by Klaas R. Veenhof in AKT 8.

Aššur-taklāku;[82] and exceptionally to some Anatolian women married to Assyrian merchants, such as Kunnaniya, wife of Aššur-mūtappil, or Hatala, wife of Laqēpum.[83]

Assyrians and Anatolians in the Lower Town

The Assyrians, because of their activities, were regularly in contact with foreigners. In Aššur or on the road to Anatolia, for example, they met the Elamites coming to sell their tin, the Babylonians with their Akkadian textiles, or the nomads with their sheep, which they plucked at the gate of the city. They identified them according to the language they spoke (Amorites, Subareans, Akkadians, etc.). Within Anatolia, whether in Kaneš or in the other Assyrian settlements, they were neighbors to locals.

Once across the Euphrates river, the Assyrians referred to the local population indistinctly as *nuā'um*, meaning "local," "native," a term that we translate simply as "(local) Anatolian," but which is very vague.[84] Indeed, the onomasticon of the local population in Kaneš suggests that there were various ethnic groups: Hattians, Luwians, Hittites, and Hurrians.[85] By contrast, Assyrians are referred to in the texts as *tamkārum*, "(Assyrian) merchant." Other visitors were traveling through Kaneš, originating from Upper Syria, such as Eblaites.[86] All these people interacted on a daily basis, without many communication problems, even though they had different mother tongues. Larsen has proposed this image of cosmopolitan life at Kaneš:[87]

> The lower town at Kanesh must have seemed like a veritable melting pot, where men and women of different ethnic backgrounds, many languages, distinctive clothes and different cultural and religious traditions were in constant interactions.... No one here could be unaffected by the fact that Kanesh was an international meeting-place, and the Assyrian presence in Anatolia must have had a powerful impact on life in the local states across the region.

82. Texts excavated in 1993 and prepared for publication by Cécile Michel.

83. For these two women, see, chapter 6, pp. 444–59 and 469–72.

84. Edzard 1989.

85. Goetze 1954; Garelli 1963, 127–68; Goedegebuure 2008; Wilhelm 2008; Michel 2014e.

86. Bilgiç 1992.

87. Larsen 2015a, 243.

The textual documentation, written in the Old Assyrian dialect with cuneiform script, offers an Assyrian-focused vision of what life was like in the lower town of Kaneš. There are only a few archives, small in size, which belonged to local Anatolians who adopted the language and script of the Assyrians for the occasion.[88] The material culture, on the other hand, shows more local characteristics since the Assyrians bought houses made according to local traditions, used Anatolian ceramics, and so on.

The Assyrians of the first generations, mainly men like Pūšu-kēn or Imdīlum who settled in Kaneš, were merchants, while professions held by local male Anatolians at Kaneš are more varied. Besides the fifty different officials working for the palace, there were specialized craftsmen, such as mason, potter, metalworker, confectioner, cook, gardener, shepherd, and so on. The relationships developed by the Assyrians with the local inhabitants were at first based on commercial interests. Anatolians acted as clients of the Assyrians, purchasing their merchandise and borrowing from them small amounts of silver, copper, or grain. Assyrians depended on the local markets for daily commodities, which they bought from Anatolians. These Assyrians regularly traveled back to Aššur to visit their families.

After one or two generations, the Assyrian merchants had developed links with the local society that went beyond strictly commercial transactions.[89] Some Assyrians, during their long stays in Anatolia, took a second wife in Kaneš, often from among local women, thus creating ties with some Anatolian families. They were no longer involved only in international trade; some of them engaged in local crafts like metallurgy.[90]

Some Anatolians involved in commercial exchanges with the Assyrians gradually became wealthier and integrated with Assyrian families through mixed marriages. Some of the houses excavated in the lower town, like those of Peruwa and Šuppiahšu, are very large, and reflect the wealth of the Anatolians who have left archives. Children of some of these

---

88. Michel 2011c. For studies focusing on the Anatolians, see, for example, Bilgiç 1954; Dercksen 2004b, 2016; Donbaz 1988, 1993, 2004, and 2008; Kryszat 2006b, 2008a; Matouš 1965, 1973; Michel 2011b, 2011c; Veenhof 1978, 1997b, and 2008a, 147–246. Dercksen 2007 lists the loanwords found in the cuneiform texts excavated at Kültepe, many of them borrowed from the different local dialects.

89. Barjamovic, Hertel, and Larsen 2012; Dercksen 2002, 2007; Kryszat 2008b, 2008c; Michel 2008c, 2014a, 2014e, 2017; Ulshöfer 2000; Veenhof 1982a.

90. Thomas Sturm studied the activities of the metallurgist Puzur-Anna, whose father was an Assyrian; see Sturm 2001.

mixed couples could bear either Assyrian or Anatolian names. For example, a daughter could have an Assyrian name, while her brother could have a name of native origin. This means that, at a certain point, the names of individuals do not allow us to distinguish between people of different ethnic origins. Thus, when speaking about Assyrian versus Anatolian women, the differentiation may sometimes be artificial.

The later phase, corresponding to the eighteenth century, is much less documented, with only a little more than a half-thousand tablets, many of them still unpublished.[91] The situation had changed considerably, and trade treaties distinguished the Assyrians still involved in the long-distance exchanges between Aššur and Kaneš, "the travelers on the road to the city (of Aššur)" (*ālikū ša harrān ālim*), and making profit out of the international trade, from those completely immersed in the Anatolian society, referred to as "the residents" (*wašbūtum*), whose activities were limited to intra-Anatolian trade; they had lost contact with the mother city.[92] This second group became impoverished, and some were indebted to Anatolians. Clauses in the treaties intended to protect them. When the first group stopped its activities in Anatolia, presumably because of political turmoil, the second group was not able to maintain Assyrian culture at Kaneš, and writing was abandoned, disappearing from Anatolia for about a century.[93]

The relationships developed between the Assyrians and the local people in the lower town of Kaneš and in several other settlements in Anatolia have prompted many studies concerning the various models that could be applied to such a situation. The term *colonies* to depict the Assyrian presence in Anatolia is regularly used, even if not adapted.[94] Stein has suggested that the expression *trade diaspora*, as trading groups settled in new areas with their own political organization and maintaining a separate cultural identity from their host community, would fit well the Assyrian presence in Kaneš.[95] Several aspects of the trade-diaspora model do fit the Old Assyrian settlements in Anatolia, as, for example, the indepen-

---

91. See Donbaz 1989, 1993, and 2004. Cahit Günbattı published treaties and a group of tablets excavated in 1989 and 2001; Günbattı 2004 and 2014.

92. Günbattı 2004; Veenhof 2008a, 147–82, and 2013b; Barjamovic, Hertel, and Larsen 2012, 78–80; Michel 2014a.

93. Michel 2014e.

94. Michel 2014a.

95. Stein 2008, 33–35.

dent political organization managed by the Assyrians in Kaneš. However, this model assumes a rather static situation, which was not the case as we observe important developments between the two groups of population over a few generations.[96]

Already in 2008, Lumsden suggested that the middle-ground model used by White to depict "the encounter between the French and the Algonquian Indians in North America during the 17th to the 19th centuries" would well fit the relationships between the Assyrians settled at Kaneš and the native Anatolians; his study took into account the material culture, in particular the seals, and the textual data.[97] In 2010, the notion of a hybrid community was introduced to depict the situation at Kaneš during the eighteenth century, as a result of an increase of mixed marriages during the previous century.[98] Both proposals, that is, the model of middle ground and the concept of hybridity, have been taken over by Larsen and Lassen in 2014, who proposed to use the first model to analyze the social and political relations between Assyrians and Anatolians, and applied the second concept to material culture, especially to seal styles, in order to highlight the cosmopolitan character of the family.[99]

The two new studies that appeared both in 2017 show that the debate is far from over. Highcock proposed to depict, with the help of textual sources, the relationships between Assyrians and Anatolians at Kaneš by borrowing elements from the trade diaspora model and to highlight the phenomenon of hybridization through seal styles.[100] Heffron, arguing "that hybridity is often the by-product of a wide range of cross-cultural encounters and not exclusive to the idiosyncratic circumstances of the middle ground," studied the various bigamous marriage agreements to detect elements of cross-cultural misunderstanding, as a key to the middle-ground model.[101] According to her study, the widespread practice of intermarriage would have allowed the Assyrians to integrate into the Anatolian society, thus facilitating trade transactions, while retaining their own identity.[102]

---

96. Gräff 2005; Michel 2014a.

97. Lumsden 2008, with the citation on p. 31.

98. Michel 2010f, 9. See also Michel 2014a, 79; 2014e, 124.

99. Larsen and Lassen 2014.

100. Highcock 2017.

101. See Heffron 2017, 79; she suggests that the notion of *bigamie autorisée* developed in Michel 2006a would fit perfectly the middle-ground model.

102. Heffron 2017, 80–81.

The ongoing theoretical discussion about which models may be used to depict the encounter between the Assyrians and the Anatolians in the lower town of Kaneš and in the other Old Assyrian settlements in Anatolia—for which we have much less data—is motivated by the originality of the Old Assyrian *kārum*s in Anatolia. These represent a unique system in the ancient Near East.

The Role of Women in Trade Networks

According to a shared consensus, mixed marriages between Assyrians and Anatolians have made possible the expansion of commercial networks. The role of women in these networks was variable and depended on their involvement in trade. In Kaneš, Anatolian women married to Assyrians could have agricultural activities providing the couple with daily products, while some Assyrian women married to Anatolians participated in long-distance trade.[103] Jewelry items and other valuable goods found in female graves at Kaneš suggest the wealth of some of these women.

Women in Aššur are documented through their correspondence with Assyrians settled in Kaneš. Among these letters, many involve couples, but also brothers and sisters. Indeed, family ties allowed a system based on trust, and some Assyrian merchants preferred to rely on their sisters rather than on their wives, like, for example, Imdī-ilum, who had close ties with his sisters, Tarām-Kūbi and Šīmat-Aššur (fig. 17).[104] The publication of Assyrian merchant family archives provides a better understanding of the internal organization of these family networks, which have often been presented as family firms, even though there is no real proof of common funds between members of a family.[105] In fact, the family structure often served as a basic framework for commercial relationships, which also grew outside of it.

---

103. According to Larsen and Lassen 2014, 186, Šāt-Anna, daughter of Šalim-Aššur and wife of the Anatolian Šuppinuman, son of Peruwa, invested in the Aššur caravan trade.

104. Larsen 2015a, 203–4.

105. See, for example, the reconstructions of the archives of Imdī-ilum (Ichisar 1981; Larsen 1982), Innaya, son of Elālī (Michel 1991), Aššur-nādā, son of Aššur-iddin (Larsen 2002), or the study of family archives discovered during regular excavations and published in TPAK 1 and several AKT volumes. See also Michel 2001a, 359–418; and, for the absence of common funds, see Larsen 2007.

The following reconstruction concerns only a few Assyrian families for which there is enough documentation linking those members living in Aššur and those settled in Anatolia.[106] The father or the eldest son, at the head of the family business, resided in Aššur. He raised important capital necessary for the purchase of tin, textiles, and donkeys, organized caravans, and managed the profits. His eldest son or a second brother, who usually lived in Kaneš, headed the Anatolian branch of the family business. He received the goods from Aššur, organized their sale on the spot at Kaneš, or entrusted the goods on credit to agents in charge of transporting them to other Assyrian settlements in Anatolia, where they were sold for cash, silver, or gold, or exchanged for copper and wool. When belonging to the first generation of Assyrians who came to Anatolia, this man might have left in Aššur his wife and young children for long periods. After a while, he could organize his life in Kaneš, where he established a new family with a native Anatolian woman.

The younger sons or brothers helped with the selling of goods in Anatolia, traveled between the various Assyrian settlements, or made round trips between Aššur and Kaneš. Some represented the family business in other Anatolian commercial centers, where they resided on a more or less temporary basis.

Over the years, members who had acquired some experience could redirect their activities and be promoted within the family structure. When the boss—the father, a brother, or an uncle—died, he could be replaced by a son, another brother, or a nephew, who then moved back to Aššur. A younger brother, who until then had been circulating inside Anatolia, replaced him in Kaneš to represent the Anatolian branch of the family business. This scheme, therefore, followed the evolution of the family.[107]

Furthermore, within the Assyrian commercial network, professional relations were modeled on family ties, and the specific vocabulary of the male family members took on a very particular technical meaning. For example, "father," *abum*, may be understood as the boss; "brother," *ahum*, represented a partner; and "boy" or "servant," *ṣuhārum*, referred to an employee. This vocabulary is used even though this reconstructed scheme

106. Michel 2001a, 359–418.

107. This is, for example, the case of Imdī-ilum, who stayed about twenty years in Kaneš before moving back to Aššur when one of his uncles died. His brother Ennam-Bēlum took over the family business in Kaneš (Larsen 2015a, 207–8).

does not work for all Assyrian families. Indeed, most of the time, the lack of documentation from Aššur hides existing contacts between family members; some families, like that of Šalim-Aššur, are only documented within Anatolia.[108] Also, a family member could decide to build up his own network apart from the rest of his family, and we have several cases of brothers who have few business contacts between them, as, for example, the sons of Iddin-Suen, Elamma and Ali-ahum.[109]

In various instances, we can observe the existence of other commercial networks that were not built on family ties but on commercial ventures based on the reputation of the involved individuals. This is, for example, the case of the joint-stock company (*naruqqum*) in which several persons invested funds entrusted to an agent to trade, with profits for an agreed number of years.[110] Each individual could belong both to the family business and to a trade network outside of the family through such types of partnerships; it is often difficult to trace a line between family links and trade network. As noted by Larsen, the firm or house to which a trader belonged should be seen "as a much wider circle of individuals reaching beyond the nuclear family," in which "marriage bonds and perhaps more distant blood relationships could play a vital role."[111] The economic reality of such a house was shared commercial interests, and the social position and reputation of an Assyrian was determined by the wealth of this house.

The place and role of the Assyrian women in these family and trade network systems was important. They contributed through their regular textile production to long-distance trade with Anatolia, and thus constituted an important link in the caravan trade. Their efforts to meet the demand are reflected in some of their letters. Tariša wrote to Bēlum-bāni that she even sent her own clothes:

108. See the reconstruction by Larsen in the introductions of the five volumes of AKT 6a–e.

109. Elamma's archives were excavated in 1991 and published in AKT 8; Ali-ahum's archives were excavated in 1993; see Michel 2008e. When in Kaneš, brothers were living across the street from one another (see the plan in Michel 2018, 62) and had then few opportunities to write to each other. But Ali-ahum had also a house in Aššur and another one in Durhumit, and might have kept in these houses some letters from his brother.

110. Larsen 1977, 1999, and 2007; Veenhof 1997a, 1999a; Dercksen 1999.

111. Larsen 2007, 103.

> The textile is with your textiles, and they are bringing (it) to you. I stripped my own garment (from my body), and I sent it to you! If you yourself do not intend to come, send the price of my garment with the first caravan. You, you know in your heart what you have left for me, and you know about my garment.[112]

So did Šāt-Tašmētum, writing to Puzur-Anna and Šu-Suen:

> You yourself know that I stripped the garment from my shoulder and gave it to you! Provide silver and let someone bring me it with the first caravan.[113]

Whether this is an image or a reality, there was a clear pressure on these women to provide high quality textiles for the Anatolian market.[114] For selling their textiles in Anatolia, they depended first on transporters, and second on the male members of their family who were aware of the demand and could negotiate the best prices. Their textile production, even if it did not fully meet demand, was at the heart of the international exchanges, and in turn it allowed them to earn revenues in silver with which to manage their households and invest in business operations. For their textile activities, they needed to buy wool on the market or at the gate of the city and went to shops and street stores to acquire food and daily needs.

Many of these women appear as creditors of loans within or outside their family; they could lend silver with interest to women and men, including their brothers and husbands. This suggests, as already noted by Larsen, that the capital was clearly individually owned, each individual enjoying rights and responsibility of personal property.[115] Several women invested

---

112. Prag I, 440:3–12: túg : *iš-tí* : túg$^{ba\text{-}tí}$-*kà-ma, na-áš-ú-ni-kum* : *ṣú-ba-at, ra-mì-ni-a-ma* : *ah-mu-uṣ-ma, ú-šé-bi$_4$-lá-kum* : *šu-ma, a-ta* : *lá ta-lá-kam, ší-im ṣú-ba-tí-a iš-tí, pá-ni-im-ma* : *šé-bi$_4$-lam, a-ta-ma* : *ša té-zi-ba-ni, i-na li-bi$_4$-kà-ma* : *tí-de$_8$-e, ú ṣú-ba-tí* : *a-ta-*[*m*]*a tí-de$_8$-e*. There are good chances that Tariša in this text is the daughter of Ali-ahum, whose archives were unearthed in 1993 in Kültepe's lower town.

113. AKT 8, 263:25–29: *a-ta-ma tí-de-e ṣú-ba-tam$_x$*(TUM), *bu-dé-a ah-mu-úṣ-ma, a-dí-na-kum* : *iš-tí, pá-ni-i*[*m*]*-ma a-li-ki-im*, kù-babbar *dí-in-ma lu-ub-lu-*[*nim*].

114. Even though they were spending most of their days producing textiles for international trade, they have never been referred to as professionals, and no profession connected with trade and business is expressed with a female gender; see Michel 2016a.

115. Larsen 2007; 2015a, 218–22; and chapter 4 in this volume.

in the caravan trade, owning tin and textiles transported to Anatolia for sale and holding capital in trade ventures. Capitalizing silver, they purchased slaves and real estate, showing off their high social status. Through their business activities, these women gained some economic and social independence, a phenomenon that has been well described by Laurence Fontaine. The market may be viewed as a place where women, thanks to their commercial presence, obtained rights and acquired more freedom within their families.[116] This power could even be reinforced by the fact that men had to depend on their female siblings for their business needs. As many of these women stayed in Aššur, at the head of the house during the long absence of their husbands or male relatives, they represented them locally, meeting colleagues and authorities to follow up on transactions, paying taxes or fines for them, delivering documents, and so on.

Already in 1979, Paul Garelli depicted the Assyrian women of Aššur as *femmes d'affaires*, that is, "businesswomen."[117] More recently, their activities have been characterized as those of female "entrepreneurs."[118] Such a word must be understood broadly and not restricted to the "owner or manager of a business enterprise," which is the basic definition given by most dictionaries. Those referred to as entrepreneurs set up businesses, taking on financial risks in order to make a profit. This word has been used by G. van Driel for agricultural managers of first-millennium Mesopotamia.[119] According to Laetitia Graslin-Thomé, who also focused on the Neo-Babylonian sources, long-distance trade remained a secondary activity for entrepreneurs who acted for palace and temples, mainly investing in local trade.[120] The few Assyrian women involved in financial operations do not appear as initiators of caravan contracts or trade ventures, but they occasionally took part in them. Even though they invested and took risks, it seems difficult to qualify them as female entrepreneurs.

116. Fontaine 2014.

117. Garelli 1979.

118. Thomason 2018, 414.

119. Van Driel 1999 defines the entrepreneur as "someone who does not belong to the (institutional) hierarchy and who (voluntarily) accepts the position of an agricultural manager without thereby becoming a member of the organisation within which he will act."

120. Graslin-Thomé 2016; see also Jursa 2010.

Chronology, Calendars, and Metrology

The Old Assyrian Eponym System

In Aššur, years were named after eponyms, *limum*, an individual of the Assyrian male elite who was chosen annually by lot. It was impossible to know in advance the name of the new eponym in Kaneš, since the information had to travel from Aššur to Anatolia. The Old Assyrian year started with the winter solstice (December 22).[1] During the first months of the year, dates in Kaneš referred to the name of the previous eponym: *limum ša qāti* PN, "the eponym following PN" (REL n + 1). The eponym played an important role in the city administration within the City Hall (*bēt ālim*); there he was involved in the administration of long-distance trade, collected taxes, and assessed fines.

Old Assyrian eponyms are known from date formulas, mainly in loan contracts, and by eponym lists unearthed in the houses of Kaneš's lower town. Over the last two decades, seven tablets containing lists of Aššur eponyms have been identified and published as "Kültepe Eponym List" (KEL); they cover the end of the twentieth, the nineteenth, and the eighteenth centuries BCE. The "Revised Eponym List" (REL) offers a continuous numbering of eponyms over more than two centuries.[2]

The letters and legal texts translated in this volume are primarily from the reigns of Šarru-kēn, Puzur-Aššur II, and Narām-Suen. For the two lower town levels at Kültepe, ancient Kaneš, see pages 8 and 40.

1. Dercksen 2011a.

2. Veenhof 2003d; Günbattı 2008; Barjamovic, Hertel, and Larsen 2012. The dates in the present book are given after Barjamovic, Hertel, and Larsen 2012.

Old Assyrian Kings

Kings of Aššur (years of reign)	Dates of reigns	REL numbers	Kültepe lower town levels
Erišum I (40)	1972–1933	1–40	Level II
Ikūnum (15)	1932–1918	41–55	
Šarru-kēn (40)	1917–1878	56–95	
Puzur-Aššur II (8)	1877–1870	96–103	
Narām-Suen (34)	1869–1836+	104–137+	
Narām-Suen / Erišum II	1835–1816	138–157	Level Ib
Erišum II (7)	+1815–1809	+158–164	
Šamšī-Adad I (33)	1808–1776	165–197	
Išme-Dagan	1775–1736(?)	198–237	
		238–255	

Old Assyrian Months, Half-Months, and Weeks

The Old Assyrian lunisolar calendar consisted of a solar year and twelve lunar months, iti (*warhum*), of twenty-nine or thirty days. The Old Assyrian months were named after cultic and seasonal events:

i.	*Bēlet-ekallim*	vii.	*Ṣip'um*
ii.	(*Narmak Aššur*) *ša Sarrātim*	viii.	*Qarrātum*
iii.	(*Narmak Aššur*) *ša Kēnātim*	ix.	*Kanwarta*
iv.	*Mahhur ilī*	x.	*Te'inātum**
v.	*Ab šarrāni*	xi.	*Kuzallu*
vi.	*Hubur*	xii.	*Allānātum*

*During level Ib, month ten is named after the moon god: *Suen* (36).

Intercalary months were added in some years to adjust the calendar to the agricultural cycle, but there was no fixed cycle of intercalation.

The Assyrians used a time unit, the *šapattum*, that in some texts corresponded to "the day of the full moon," that is, the middle of the month, and in other texts to the first half of the month ending with the *šapattum* day. There are also references to days corresponding to the moon's phases.

In loan contracts found at Kaneš, dates are often expressed in *hamuštum*-weeks, a time unit shorter than a month. These *hamuštum*, which correspond to a number of days, take the name of two, then one merchant (after REL 98).[3] The number of days forming a *hamuštum*-week is still debated. The most common proposals are seven days and ten days.[4] Another possibility would be that the *hamuštum*, as the *šapattum*, corresponded to phases of the moon, that is, quarters.[5]

The smallest unit of time used in the Old Assyrian corpus is *ūmum*, "day," which consisted of daytime and nighttime.[6] Note that the word "night," *mūšum* or *mušītum*, appears often in the texts. The word *bērum*, which usually corresponds to a time unit, a "double-hour," is always used in the Old Assyrian corpus as a length unit (see below).

The Anatolian Dating System

In Anatolia, loan contracts did not always use the Old Assyrian calendar but could be dated after important events linked to the local ruler or his family ("when PN became king"; "when the king died"; "when the queen gave birth": **119**), cultic activities of the king ("when the kind enters/comes out of the temple of DN": **91**), religious festivals, or agricultural activities.[7] The deadline of the loan is often fixed according to the festival in honor of an Anatolian god or goddess (Bēlum: **185**; Harihari: **189**) or seasonal agricultural activities. This dating system may be used alone or combined with the Assyrian dates.

Ten of the many Anatolian deities mentioned in the Old Assyrian texts appear in dates on the occasion of their main festival. In some cases, these festivals are combined with another type of dating, which makes possible the seasonal dating of these festivals within the year.[8]

3. Kryszat 2004, 157–98.

4. Seven days: Veenhof 1996, 2000; Kryszat 2004; Michel 2010e; Stratford 2015a. Ten days: Brinkman 1963; Dercksen 2011a.

5. Michel forthcoming b.

6. Michel 2010e.

7. Michel forthcoming b.

8. Kryszat 2006b; Veenhof 2008a, 238–45.

Festival	Season
ša Nipas (**85**)	beginning of spring
ša Parka (**75**)	summer (grain harvest)
ša Anna (**186**, main goddess of Kaneš)	late autumn*
ša Tuhutānim	autumn

Other festivals, which cannot be placed in the year, concern the following divinities: *Bēlim* ("Lord"), *Bēl qablim* ("Lord of the Battle"), *Harihari*, *Usumū*, and ^{d}UTU.

The loan contracts using the agricultural calendar predominantly deal with wheat, which was sown in autumn, and with barley, sown in the spring.[9] They follow the many agricultural events, from ploughing and seeding to the threshing floor, and cite seasons.

Seasons	Tasks	
autumn	*qitip kerānim*	picking of grapes (September)
	erāšum	ploughing (and seeding wheat, October–November)
	serdum	(time of) olives (October–December)
	eršum waṣā'um	coming up of the sown (late fall)
	buqlātum	sprouting (of barley seeds, late fall)
spring	*daš'ū*	spring (April–June, **314**)
	buqūnum	plucking (of wool, May–June)
summer	*harpū*	summer (July–September, **76**, **81**, **84**, **90**, **256**)
	kubur uṭṭitim	ripening of grain (July–October)
	ṣibit niggalim	seizing the sickle (July, 77, **100**)
	eṣādum	harvesting (July–August)
	ebūrum	harvest, crop (July–August)
	adrum	threshing floor (August–September)

9. Veenhof 2008a, 238–41; Dercksen 2008c; Michel forthcoming b.

Old Assyrian Weights and Measures

The Old Assyrian measures attested in this volume are units of weight, capacity, and length.[10]

Units of Weight

1 gú (talent) = 60 *mana* (mina)
1 *mana* (mina) = 60 gín (shekel)
1 gín (shekel) = 180 še (grain)
1 gú = ca. 30 kg; 1 *mana* = ca. 500 g; 1 gín = ca. 8.3 g; 1 še = ca. 0.05 g

When measuring copper or wool in Anatolia, the gú was not always used; instead, quantities could be given in thousands and hundreds of *mana*.

Units of Capacity

1 *naruqqum* (sack) = 4 dug = between 80 and 100 L
1 dug/*karpatum* (jar) = 2 *šaršarānum* = between 24 and 30 L
1 *šaršarānum* = 15 silà = between 12 and 15 L
1 silà (liter) = between 0.8 and 1 L

The Assyrians also use the baneš/*ṣimdum* measure, which equals 30 silà, thus corresponding more or less to the content of a *karpatum*-jar. There were also measuring vessels of standard capacity, such as *mašqaltum*-vessels of 1, 2, or 3 silà; or the *kirrum*, a pitcher of beer whose capacity is unknown.

Units of Length

The *bērum* is a length unit equal to the distance a walker may cover within a *bērum*, "double-hour," a little more than 10 km.

1 *ammatum* (cubit) = 2 *ūṭum* = between 50 and 52 cm
1 *ūṭum* (half-cubit) = 15 *ubānum* = 1/2 cubit = between 25 and 26 cm
1 *ubānum* (finger) = ca. 1.7 cm

---

10. For Old Assyrian measures, see Powell 1990; Michel 2006e; Dercksen 2016; Kulakoğlu 2017; Reculeau 2018; Michel forthcoming c.

1
Marriage and Divorce

The married couple and, by extension, the family formed the cornerstone of Mesopotamian society, as shown by the important place accorded to family law in the law collections issued by rulers in the ancient Near East. At the beginning of the second millennium BCE, the Assyrians refer to laws, at least for business matters, engraved on a stela, but no such stela has been found.[1] The historian, therefore, makes recourse to documents of the practice of law: contracts, lawsuits, and records of legal import, as well as a copious correspondence, to understand, among other things, Assyrian marriage customs. The archives of Kaneš include relatively few marriage contracts, or, more generally, contracts pertaining to family law, as the documentation is mostly concerned with business. Most of the marriages contracted between Assyrians must have taken place at Aššur, where one may suppose that the contracts, assuming there were any, were kept. Moreover, the examples discovered at Kaneš deal for the most part with specific situations. Certain marriage contracts, for instance, stipulate financial arrangements in case of divorce. Assuming that each standard marriage was accompanied by the drawing up of a contract, archaeologists should have discovered hundreds of examples of this type of document. Consequently, just as for the Old Babylonian period, marriage doubtless did not regularly entail drawing up a written document, but only agreements providing for specific terms were set down on tablets.[2]

The archives of Kaneš have yielded about forty marriage contracts or legal documents concerned with divorce, as well as about ten other legal records touching on these subjects. These documents concern Anatolians as well as Assyrians, and reflect different customs. The majority of the texts

1. Veenhof 2003a, 431.
2. For a study of Old Babylonian marriage contracts, see Westbrook 1988.

date to the principal occupation level of the lower town of Kaneš by the Assyrians (II), as well as a handful of later documents (Ib).[3]

Outside of legal documents strictly speaking, numerous letters refer to various matters related to the wedding ceremony and the status of the spouses; these communications are very valuable as well for prosopographical studies and allow a clearer understanding of the family situation, giving insight regarding the background of the partners, for example. The private archives of the merchants of Kaneš permit reconstruction of the different stages of marriage (betrothal, exchange of gifts, wedding), the circumstances of a second marriage, and breaking of betrothal and divorce.

Concubinage was practiced and seems to have been formally recognized in a division of inheritance where a son inherited a female slave living in concubinage with him, along with other female slaves with whom he had had sexual relations (**15**, **54**, **115**).

From Betrothal to Marriage

We do not know at what age young people could become betrothed to each other, nor at what age they could be when they married, but several years could go by between these two events (**1**, **6**). The oral or written agreement was made between the father or the parents of the young woman and the young man or sometimes the family of the latter. When the girl was an orphan, her brothers could arrange for her marriage using their shares of the paternal estate (**9**, **10**, **11**). According to the terminology, the girl was given (*tadānum*) in marriage by her family, or, in some cases, the man took her (*aḫāzum*) as wife.

The agreement must have dealt with the exchange of gifts, the indispensable condition for every matrimonial alliance (**2**). Unlike in Old Babylonian documents, the various wedding gifts are very seldom mentioned

---

3. Bibliography pertaining to marriage contracts: Lewy 1925; Eisser and Lewy 1930, nos. 1–6; Hirsch 1966; Matouš 1973; Ichisar 1982; Balkan 1986; Donbaz 1989; Sever 1992a, 1992b; Kawasaki 1994; Bayram and Çeçen 1995; Michel and Garelli 1996; Rems 1996; Jensen 1997; Veenhof 1997a; Łyczkowska 1998; Michel 2006a; Kienast 2008. This chapter was completed in 2012, and texts edited here are cited with their numbers in this volume in Justel 2014. Several texts have also been edited in Kienast 2015, with some different interpretations. This book was already finished when the article by Veenhof (2018a) appeared, which refers to the texts numbers as edited in this chapter.

in Old Assyrian marriage contracts.[4] However, allusions to these gifts in letters show that if the exchange of gifts had not taken place with a period specified in advance, the betrothal could be broken off (7).

Traditionally, the dowry, given to the girl when she went to live with her husband, remained her property and was passed on to her children. The bridegift paid by the groom to his in-laws was called in Old Assyrian *šīmum*, which could be translated as "price" and corresponds to a bride gift; it was paid over at the occasion of the wedding (**19**). Despite the ambiguity of the term, in no way did it correspond to a "purchase price" of a girl. Rather, it seems to have compensated her family for the loss of her labor capacity. The husband could also offer a gift to his wife (*iddinū*, **11**, **45**), and this could sometimes be substantial (one mina of silver, a house, and slaves); the future husband could receive various gifts, such as a belt (**7**, **14**).[5]

There must have been an exchange of goods before the marriage, because breaking off a betrothal incurred a penalty for the person breaking the contract, but the penalty could also result from breaking the solemn promise (**2**). Termination of the contract could be confirmed by a court decision freeing the young people.

At the time of the betrothal, both parties probably agreed on the date of the wedding. When the prospective husband, residing in a distant place for business reasons, failed to return to Aššur or Kaneš to marry his bride-to-be within the time specified, he would have to comply or release the girl from her engagement (**4**, **5**, **6**). In one case, the man tried to convince his bride-to-be to make the journey herself to him so they could marry, threatening, if she did not, that he would choose himself a wife locally (**3**).

The place chosen for the wedding was of some importance, as it necessitated not only the presence of the bride and groom, but also of the father of the bride, who, if he could not be there in person, had to be represented. Some documents emphasize the importance of a wedding at Aššur, requiring one or both of the couple to travel there (**12**, **13**). This choice could have been motivated by family custom, by legal considerations, such as making the union subject to Assyrian law, or by financial ones, but it could

4. Westbrook 1988.

5. On a husband's gift to his wife: Veenhof 2003a, 453. On silver, a house, and slaves as a gift: according to Kt 86/k 203:21; cited in Veenhof 2003a, 453.

also be the consequence of a tradition that permitted an Assyrian merchant to contract a second marriage elsewhere.[6]

We know little about the wedding ceremony itself. A feast was presumably put on, in the course of which could be heavy drinking. A long list of expenses paid by a merchant, probably on the occasion of his sister's marriage, itemizes various consumables served over several days to his in-laws. These included wine and numerous jars of beer; meat, such as cuts of beef and mutton; grain, including barley and wheat; fats, vegetable oil, and butter; onions, honey, nuts, and firewood for cooking (**14**). The text also mentions the guests who attended the marriage banquet and summarizes what happened on various occasions.

During the ceremony, guests used to give small amounts of silver, perhaps in the shape of jewelry items, to the bride.[7] The head of the girl was covered by her father or a male relative, apparently so that the groom could uncover her head. This short rite, consisting of "placing the scarf [*pusūnum*] over the girl's head," symbolized the woman's change of status; it need not imply that every married woman had to wear a scarf (**15, 16**).[8] According to section 40 of the *Middle Assyrian Laws*, married women wore scarfs, as well as unmarried women of good family; this was an external symbol for women marking their place in society.[9] According to these same laws, at the wedding ceremony, instead of a scarf, one could anoint the bride's head with oil (§42). But we do not know if these rules already applied in the Old Assyrian period.

After the ceremony, the bride joined her husband's household, if he had one of his own, or, if he did not have one, the household of her in-laws. Getting along with the husband's family was not always to be taken for granted (**146**).

---

6. Michel 2006a, and below, pp. 68–85.

7. The silver gifts amount regularly to 1½ shekels of silver; see Bayram and Kuzuoğlu 2015, and texts Kt 88/k 181, Kt 88/k 281, Kt 88/k 339, and Kt 88/k 340.

8. Dercksen 1991; Michel 1997d.

9. Roth 1997, 167–68.

1. Betrothal

Obv. [1]*um-ma Šu-Hu-bur-ma* [2]*a-na Pu-šu-ke-en*$_6$ [3]*qí-bi-ma* [...]
Rev. [17]*En-um-A-šùr* dumu [18]*Ša-lim-a-hi-im* [19]*iš-tí* ellat^{tim} *i-lá-ak* [20]*a-na-kam* : *i-na é*^{tim} [21]*ṣú-ha-ar-tám e-ha-az* [22]*a-ma-kam* : *ki-ma* : *i-a-tí* [23]*kà-bi-sú li-bu-šu* [24]*lá i-lá-mì*$^{!}$*-in* [25]*e-mì-i-ma* : *lá e-mu-kà* [26]*ar-hi-iš-ma* u.e. [27]*ṭur*$_4$*-da-šu-ma* le.e. [28]*ṣú-ha-ar-tám li-it-ru-ma* [29]*šu-ma a-hi a-ta* : *me-er-i-tí* [30]*lá me-er-at-kà* : *kà-bi-sú-ma* [31]*ṭur*$_4$*-da-šu*

[1-3]Thus (says) Šu-Hubur: say to Pūšu-kēn [...]

[17-19]Ennum-Aššur, son of Šalim-ahum, will travel with the caravan. [20-21]Here, at home (in Aššur), he will marry the young girl. [22-24]There (in Kaneš), honor him like myself so that he does not feel bad! [25]Is my son-in-law not your son-in-law? [26-27]Send him quickly [28]so that he can fetch the young girl. [29]If you are my brother, [29-30]is my daughter not your daughter? [30-31]Respect him and send him.

Bibliography: Text published in copy by Veenhof and Klengel-Brandt as VS 26, 64; see comments, p. 23.

Comments: The first part of this letter deals with commercial contacts between men. The girl, daughter of Šu-Hubur, who is supposed to marry Ennum-Aššur, son of Šalim-ahum, could be Nuhšatum, well known from the archives of Šalim-ahum's family, excavated in 1970 and published by Emin Bilgiç and Cahit Günbattı in *AKT* 3. See the review of that volume, Cécile Michel, *AfO* 44–45 (1997/1998):329–33; Michel 2001a, 508–11; and Veenhof 2015c.

2. Betrothal Confirmed by a Payment

Obv. [1]*[E-wa-ni-kà]* [2]*[ù] A-dí-ma-[tum]* [3]*[m]e-er*$^{!}$*-a-sí-[na]* [4]*[I]b-ni-sú-en*$_6$ dumu *E[n-nam-a]-/š[ur]* [5]*e-ha-az šu-ma a-na* [6]*ša*$^{!}$*-ni-im*$^{!}$ *me-er-a-sí-na* [7]*i-ta-ad-na* [8]2 *ma-na* kù-babbar *E-wa-ni-/kà* [9]*ù A-dí-ma-tum* [10]*a-na Ib-ni-sú-en*$_6$ [11]*[i-š]a*$^{!}$*-qá-lá* lo.e. [12]*[šu-ma] Ib-ni-sú-en*$_6$ rev. [13]*[a-n]a-kam* dumu-munus *A-šur* [14]*[ú-l]á* dumu-munus *nu-a-im* [15]*[e]-ta-ha-az-ma* [16]*me-er-a-sí-na* [17]*[lá] e-ta-ha-az* [18]*[2 ma]-na* kù-babbar *a-na E-wa-ni-/kà* [19]*[ù A-dí]-ma-tim Ib-ni-sú-e[n*$_6$*]* [20]*[i-ša-qá]l ṣú-ha-ar-tá[m]* [21]*[a-šar l]i-bi*$_4$*-šu i-d[a-an]* [22][...] x x [...] (end of the reverse destroyed)

$^{1-5}$Ibni-Suen, son of Ennum-Aššur, will marry the daughter of Ewanika and Adimātum. $^{5-7}$If they give their daughter to another (husband), $^{8-11}$Ewanika and Adimātum will pay 2 minas of silver to Ibni-Suen. $^{12-15}$If Ibni-Suen marries here a woman of Aššur or a woman from Anatolia and $^{16-17}$thus does not marry their daughter, $^{18-20}$Ibni-Suen will pay 2 minas of silver to Ewanika and Adimātum. $^{20-21}$He will (then) give the girl to (the husband) of his choice [...]

Bibliography: Text published in copy and edited by Donbaz as KTS 2, 55; edited by Kienast (2015, no. 1).

Comments: The girl, whose name is unknown, supposed to become the wife of Ibni-Suen, is designated as the daughter of two women, Ewanika and Adimātum: one might be her mother; the other a female member of the family. The betrothal seems to have been confirmed by a payment, because if the groom breaks off the agreement, he keeps control over the girl, whom he can give to the husband of his choice.

---

3. Threat of Breaking Off a Betrothal

Obv. ^{1}*um-ma Puzúr-A-šùr-*[*ma a-na*] ^{2}*Nu-ùh-ša-tim q*[*í-bi-ma*] ^{3}*a-bu-ki : a-šu-mì-ki* [*a-na*] ^{4}*ṣé-ri-a a-na a-ha-*[*zi-ki*] ^{5}*iš-pu-ra-am ù a-na-ku* ^{6}*ṣú-ha-ri-a ù na-áš-pè-er-tí* ^{7}*a-ṣé-er : a-bi-ki : a-šu-mì-ki* ^{8}*a-na šé-ṣú-i-ki* ^{9}*áš-ta-áp-ra-am a-pu-tum* lo.e. ^{10}*i-na* ^{d}utu^{ši} *ṭup-pí* ^{11}*ta-áš-me-i-ni : a-ma-k*[*am*] rev. ^{12}*a-na a-bi-ki : pu-nu-*[*i-ma*] ^{13}*iš-tí ṣú-h*[*a*]*-ri-a* ^{14}*tí-ib-e-ma a-tal-ki-im* ^{15}*we-da-ku : ma-ma-an : ša i-/na* ^{16}*re-šé-e-a : i-za-zu-ma* ^{17}*pá-šu-ra-am : i-ša-kà-na-/ni* ^{18}*lá-šu : šu-ma iš-tí* ^{19}*ṣú-ha-ri-a : lá ta-li-*[*ki-im*] ^{20}*i-na Wa-ah-šu-ša-na* u.e. ^{21}du[mu-munus] *Wa-ah-šu-ša-*[*na*] ^{22}*a-ha-az ih-*[*dí-ma a-tí*] le.e.^{23}*ù ṣú-ha-ru-a* ^{24}*lá ta-*[*sà-ha-r*]*a* ^{25}*a-tal-kà-*[*n*]*im*

$^{1-2}$Thus (says) Puzur-Aššur: say to Nuhšatum.

$^{3-5}$Your father wrote to me about you so that I marry you. $^{5-9}$And so I sent my servants and my letter concerning you to your father so that he lets you go. $^{9-11}$Urgent! The day you hear my tablet, there, ^{12}turn to your father (so that he agrees); $^{13-14}$set out and come here with my servants. ^{15}I am alone. $^{15-18}$There is none to serve me and set my table. $^{18-19}$If you will not come with my servants, $^{20-22}$then I shall marry in Wahšušana a woman from Wahšušana. $^{22-24}$See to it that you and my servants do not delay; ^{25}depart!

Bibliography: Text published in copy by Stephens as BIN 6, 104; edited by Lewy (1950, 374, n. 48); translated by Michel (2001a, no. 397; 2006a, 170, n. 55).

Comments: An agreement has been made between the father of the bride and the future husband, who are both Assyrians. The girl, who is living in Kaneš, is supposed to travel to Wahšušana, where the marriage must take place, some 200 km away. In his petition, Puzur-Aššur mentions the duties of the wife: serving the husband and cooking for him.

---

4. Deadline for the Marriage Promise

Obv. [1]*kà-ru-um dí-nam* [2]*i-dí-in-ma* [3]*iš-tù ha-muš-tim* [4]*ša A-šùr-ma-lik* [5]iti-kam *ša ke*[!]*-na-tim* [6]*li-mu-um* [7]*ša qá-tí* [8]*En-na-sú-en*$_6$ lo.e. [9]*šu-ma a-na* rev. [10]6 *ha-muš-tim* (*sic!*) [11]*A-šùr-ma-lik* [12]dumu *A-ni-nim* [13]*lá i-tal-kam* [14]*Iš*[?]*-tí-tí-ša* [15]dumu-munus[!] *A-lá-hi-im* [16]*a-na mu-ut* [17]*li-bi*$_4$*-šu* (*sic!*) u.e. [18]*ta-lá-ak*

[1–2]The *kārum* gave the following verdict: [3–9]if, reckoning from the week of Aššur-malik, month *ša Kēnatim* (iii), the eponym successor of Enna-Suen (REL 107 + 1), [9–13]within six weeks, Aššur-malik, son of Anīnum, has not come, [14–18]then, Ištitiša, the daughter of Ali-ahum, may go to the husband of her choice.

Bibliography: Text edited by Michel (2008e, 64–65, n. 54 [Kt 93/k 286]).

Comments: This tablet belongs to the archives of Ali-ahum and his son Aššur-taklāku, excavated in 1993. Ištitiša's marriage must have been arranged by her father, Ali-ahum, with Aššur-malik, son of Anīnum, but since the groom was away, the marriage could not take place. Ali-ahum died in REL 105 (ca. 1868), and his son Aššur-taklāku, brother of the bride, replaced him three years later (ca. 1865) and acted in his sister's interest. Lest she remain unmarried, a judgment was rendered by the *kārum* (authorities) to fix an ultimatum for the fiancée, who had to come and marry the girl within six weeks.

Line 17: One expects *libbiša* instead of *libbišu*.

5. Deadline for the Husband to Take Care of His Wife

Envelope

Obv. ^{1}kišib *E-na-na-tim* ^{2}(seal) ^{3}dumu *Tí-tí-na-tal* ^{4}kišib *Šu-Sú-en*$_{6}$ dumu *Il*$_{5}$*-mì-ti* ^{5}kišib ^{d}im-sig$_{5}$ dumu *Pì-lá-ah-Ištar* ^{6d}im-sig$_{5}$ *a-ša*$^{!}$(ŠU)*-tam* ^{7}*ṣú-ha-ar-tám* dumu-munus ^{8}*Ištar-na-da* : *e-hu-úz* ^{9}*a-ša-tám ša-ni-tám* lo.e. ^{10}*ú-lá e-ha-az* (seal) ^{11}*šu-ma a-ša*-tám* rev. ^{12}*ša-ni-tám e-ta-ha-az* ^{13}(seal) ^{14}1 *ma-na* kù-babbar *i-ša-qal* ^{15}*šu-ma a-na* iti 2-kam *lá i-tal-kam* ^{16}*ù da-tám ša a-ší-tí-šu* ^{17}*lá iš-ta-al* u.e. ^{18}*ṣú-ha-ar-tám* ^{19}(seal) le.e. ^{20}*a-na mu-tim ša-ni-im*$^{!}$ ^{21}*i-du-nu a-hi-sà*$^{!}$ (seal) ^{22}*lá ú-kà-sà* (seal)

$^{1-5}$Sealed by Ennanatum, son of Titinatal; sealed by Šu-Suen, son of Il(ī-i) mittī; sealed by Adad-damiq, son of Pilah-Ištar.

$^{6-8}$Adad-damiq married the girl, daughter of Ištar-nādā, as *aššutum*-wife. $^{9-10}$He shall not marry another *aššutum*-wife. $^{11-12}$If he marries another *aššutum*-wife, ^{14}he shall pay 1 mina of silver. $^{15-17}$If he does not come within 2 months and does not take care of his *aššutum*-wife, $^{18-21}$they shall give the girl to another husband. $^{21-22}$He (Adad-damiq) he shall not distrain the one who married her.

Tablet

Obv. ^{1} ^{d}*im-sig*$_{5}$ *a-ša*$^{!}$(ŠU)*-tam* ^{2} *ṣú-ha-ar-tám* ^{3}dumu-munus *Ištar-na-da** ^{4}*e-hu-úz a-ša-tám* ^{5}*ša-ni-tám* ^{6}*ú-lá e-ha-az* ^{7}*šu-ma a-ša-tám* ^{8}*ša-ni-tám* lo.e. ^{9}*e-ta-ha-az* rev. ^{10}1 *ma-na* kù-babbar ^{11}*i-ša-qal ù šu-ma* ^{12}*a-na* iti 2-kam ^{13}*lá i-tal-kam ù da-tám*$^{!}$ ^{14}*ša a-ší-tí-šu*$^{!}$ ^{15}*lá iš-ta-al* ^{16}*ṣú-ha-ar-tám*$^{!}$ *a-na* ^{17}*mu-tim ša-ni-im* ^{18}*i-«tí»-du-nu* u.e. ^{19}*a-hi*$^{!}$*-sà* le.e. ^{20}*ú-lá ú-ša-kà-ar*

$^{1-4}$Adad-damiq married the girl, daughter of Ištar-nādā, as *aššutum*-wife. $^{4-6}$He shall not marry another *aššutum*-wife. $^{7-9}$If he marries another *aššutum*-wife, $^{10-11}$he shall pay 1 mina of silver. $^{11-15}$If he does not come within 2 months and does not care about his *aššutum*-wife, $^{16-18}$they shall give the girl to another husband. $^{19-20}$He (Adad-damiq) will not take legal action against the one who married her.

Bibliography: Envelope published in copy by Contenau as TC 1, 67; edited by Eisser and Lewy (1930, no. 1); Michel 2006a, 162, n. 22; and edited by Kienast (2015, no. 3B). Tablet AO 7050, published by Ichisar as *RA* 76, 170.

Comments: The bride is given as wife to Adad-damiq by her mother, Ištar-nādā. The envelope, TC 1, 67, bears the seal imprints of the witnesses and the husband; thus the contract was kept in the bride's family archives. The marriage must be celebrated within two months, otherwise the betrothal will be canceled.

Line 22 of the envelope has _lā ukassa_, literally: "he shall not put under special strain" (_kassu'um_, "to bind"), and on the tablet, line 22: _ulaušakkar_, "he will not take legal action against."

---

6. A Long-Standing Betrothal

Obv. [1]_A-hu-wa-qar ù Zu-pá_* [2]_iṣ-bu-tù-ni-a-tí-ma_ [3]_um-ma A-hu-wa-qar-ma_ [4]_a-na Zu-pá-ma_ :* _a-ha-tí_ [5]_ir-tí-bi_$_4$: _ba-a-am_ [6]_a-ha-tí_ : _i-na Kà-ni-iš_ [7]_a-hu-úz um-ma Zu-pá-ma_ [8]_[l]u tù-ší-ib_ [9]_[u]m-ma A-hu-wa-qar-ma_ [10]_[i]-na Kà-ni-iš_ lo.e. [11]_[dí-i]n kà-ri-im_ :* _tí-šu_ rev. [12]_[š]é-ep-kà_ : _ru-qá-at_ [13]_a-dí ma-tí_ : _a-ha-tí_ [14]_lu tù-ší-ib_ [15]_um-ma Zu-pá-ma_ : _a-lik_ [16]_a-ha-at-kà a-šar_ [17]_li-bi_$_4$_-kà a-na mu-tim_ [18]_dí-in_ : _igi En-nam-A-šur_ [19]dumu _Bu-da-tim_ [20]_igi_ ^{d}_ab-ba-ni_ dumu _A-ba-ba_ [21]_a-na a-wa-tim a-ni-a-tim_ [22]_A-hu-wa-qar kà-ru-um_ u.e. [23]_Té-ga-ra-ma im-hu-ur-/ni-a-tí-ma_ (erased sign) [24]_kà-ru-um_ le.e. [25]_i-dí-in-ni-a-[tí-ma]_ [26]_ṭup-pá-am [ša] ší-[bu-t]í-[ni]_ [27]_i-ba-áb_ dingir _ni-dí-i[n]_

[1-2]Ahu-waqar and Zupa seized us (as arbitrators), and [3-4]Ahu-waqar (said) to Zupa as follows: "My sister has grown up! Come on and marry my sister in Kaneš." [7]Zupa (replied) as follows: [8]"Let her stay (at home)!" [9]Then Ahu-waqar (said): [10-11]"In Kaneš, you (already) had the verdict of the _kārum_. [12]You are far away! [13-14]How long should my sister stay?" [15-18]Then Zupa (said): "Go ahead and give your sister to a husband of your choice."

[18-20]In the presence of Ennum-Aššur, son of Budatum, and Enlil-bāni, son of Ababa. [21-25]For these proceedings, (concerning) Ahu-waqar, the _kārum_ of Tegarama approached us, and they appointed us (as arbitrators), and [26-27]we gave a tablet containing our testimony at the gate of the god.

Bibliography: Text published by Balkan (1986, 4–6 [Kt i/k 120]). Photo of the reverse of the tablet is published in Kulakoğlu and Kangal (2010, 337, no. 442); edited by Kienast (2015, no. 28). Collated May 2012.

Comments: This witness deposition between two Assyrians follows a verdict of the *kārum* that is lost. The formal declaration of Zupa, the engaged man, is enough to break off the betrothal.

Line 22: *kārum* is an error for *kāram*.

---

7. The Groom Who Did Not Receive a Gift Broke Off the Betrothal

Obv. ^{1}*Pí-lá-ah-Ištar a-na A-mur-Ištar* ^{2}*iṣ-ba-at-ni-a-tí-ma* ^{3}*um-ma Pí-lá-ah-Ištar-ma* ^{4}*a-na a-bi*$_4$*-a : pì-kà* ^{5}*ta-dí-in : ba-a-am* ^{6}*a-ša-at-kà a-hu-uz* ^{7}*um-ma A-mur-Ištar-ma* ^{8}*a-na a-bi-kà : pí-i* ^{9}*lu a-dí-in-ma* ^{10}*ki-ma : e-mì*$^{!}$*-a*$^{!}$ lo.e. ^{11}*[i]š-ra-am : a-na* rev. ^{12}*qá-áb-li-a* ^{13}*lá ta-dí-na-nim* ^{14}*ù a-he-a lá ta-sí-a* ^{15}*u*$_4$*-mu-ú : im-ṭù-ma* ^{16}*áš-tí-a-áb-ma ša-ni-tám* ^{17}dumu-munus *A-šùr a-ta-ha-az* ^{18}*a-ha-at-kà : ù-lá* ^{19}*a-ha-az a-na a-wa-tim* ^{20}*a-ni-a-tim kà-ru-um* ^{21}*Kà-ni-iš i-dí-ni-a-tí-/ma* u.e. ^{22}igi gír *ša A-šùr* ^{23}*ší-bu-tí-ni ni-dí-in* ^{24}igi *Ku-zi-zi-a* le.e. ^{25}dumu *Ì-lí-a-lim* igi *Ah-ša-/lim* ^{26}dumu *I-dí-Ištar* : igi *Bu-ur-/Sú-en*$_6$ ^{27}dumu *Da-da*

$^{1-2}$Pilah-Ištar seized us (as arbitrators) against Amur-Ištar, and ^{3}Pilah-Ištar (said) as follows: $^{4-5}$"You gave your word to my father. $^{5-6}$Come and marry your wife!" ^{7}Amur-Ištar (replied) as follows: $^{8-9}$"I indeed gave my word to your father, but $^{10-13}$as my in-laws, you (pl.) did not give me a belt for my waist, ^{14}nor did you invite my brothers. ^{15}Time passed, and ^{16}I have grown old, so $^{16-17}$I have married another woman of Aššur. $^{18-19}$Thus, I will not marry your sister."

$^{19-21}$For these proceedings, the *kārum* of Kaneš appointed us (as arbitrators), and $^{22-23}$we have given our testimony before Aššur's dagger.

$^{24-27}$In the presence of Kuziziya, son of Ilī-ālum; Ah-šalim, son of Iddin-Ištar; and Būr-Suen, son of Dada.

Bibliography: Text published by Sever (1992a, 670) and Çeçen (1995, 71, pl. 11 [Kt 88/k 625]); edited by Kienast (2015, no.27); translated by Hecker (2004b, 56). Lines 7–14 cited by Dercksen (2008a, 97, n. 22) and Michel (2006a, 160, n. 17). Collated May 2005.

Comments: The betrothal of two Assyrians should have been followed by an exchange of gifts. The engaged man, complaining that he had not received any gift from his future in-laws, broke off the betrothal. The argument of time passing and the man getting old is quite unusual.

Line 10: one must perhaps understand here, "as in-laws usually do ..."

Line 15: literally: "the time became little."

---

8. The Father May Marry His Daughter to Whom He Wishes

Obv. [1]*kà-ru-um Ha-hu-um* [2]*dì-nam* [3]*i-dí-in-ma* [4]ZU-*na-we-er* [5]*me-er-a-sú* [*a*]-*šar* [6]*li-bi-šu* [7]*i-da-an Da-dí-a* [8]*pá-šé-er a-wa-tim*

[1-3]The *kārum* of Hahhum gave the following verdict: [4-7]Suen-nawer may marry his daughter wherever he wishes. [7-8]Dadiya was the solver of the case.

Bibliography: Text published in copy by Stephens (1927); edited by Eisser and Lewy (1930, no. 275).

Comments: There must have been a betrothal, the obligations for which the groom did not fulfill; thus the agreement was canceled, and the father was free to marry his daughter to someone else.

---

9. Brothers Have to Arrange the Marriage of Their Sisters

[1]*a-na Ì-lí-a E-na-ah*-dingir [2]*ù En-um-A-šur* [3]*a-na E-na-ah*-dingir [4]*qí-bi*$_4$*-ma um-ma Ah-ša-lim-ma* [5]1 *a-ha-at-ni a-na qá-tí-kà* [6]*a-mu-tí-im ta-dí-in* [7]*ša-ni-tám Šu-Lá-ba-an i-dí-in* [8]*Ha-áš-ta-ah-šu-šar* [9]*Be-lá-num ù a-na-ku* [10]*a-na qá-tí-ni* [11]*ni-da-ší* [12]*ṣú-ha-ar-tám* [13]*a-na mu-tí-im* [14]*lá ta-da-an* [15]*ta-da-an-ma ga-am-ra-am* [16]*ša* 3 *ší-na-tí i-na* [17]*ra-mì-ni-kà tù-ma-lá* [18]2 *ma-na* 8½ gín kù-babbar [19]*qá-tí iš-tù li-mì-im* [20]*E-lá-li a-na ma-kà-ri-im* [21]*tal-qé*

[1-4]To Iliya, Ēnah-ilī, and Ennum-Aššur; say to Ēnah-ilī: thus (says) Ah-šalim.

[5-6]You have given one of our sisters to a husband on your share (of the inheritance). [7]Šu-Labān gave another one (on his share to a husband). [8-11]Bēlānum and myself, we will give Haštahšušar, (the third one), on our share (to a husband). [12-14]You shall not give the young one to a husband. [15-17]If you do give (her to a husband), you will then have to make good for the three other (sisters) from your own capital.

[18-21]You took 2 minas, 8½ shekels of silver, (corresponding to) my share, from the eponym Elālī (REL 92), to conduct trade.

Bibliography: Text published by Bayram and Çeçen (1995, 5–7 [Kt 84/k 281]); edited by Kienast (2015, no. 42). Collated May 2010.

Comments: After the death of their father, the four brothers, using their inheritance shares, have to arrange the marriages of their four sisters. One brother, who already took care of the marriage of one of his sisters, intends to marry off as well the youngest one, against the will of his brothers. The problem at issue is the amount to be spent from each brother's inheritance share, each share having perhaps been linked with a sister's marriage.

Eponym REL 92 corresponds to circa 1881 BCE.

---

10. Brothers Discuss How to Finance the Expenses of Their Sister's Marriage

Envelope

Obv. ^{1}(seal A) ^{2}[kišib] *A-bu-ša-lim* dumu *A-ta-a* ^{3}[kišib *A*]*-šùr-dan* dumu *I-ku-pí-*[*a*] ^{4}[kišib *A*]*-šùr-ma-lik* dumu *A-ni-n*[*im*] ^{5}[*a-n*]*a a-wa-tim* ^{6}[*a*]*-ni-a-tim* [*k*]*à-ru-um Kà-ni-i*[*š*] ^{7}*i-dí-ni-a-tí-ma* igi gír [*ša* ^{d}*A-šùr*] ^{8}(seal A) lo.e. ^{9}[…] rev. ^{10}(seal B) ^{11}(seal C) u.e. ^{12}(seal A) le.e. (seal C)

$^{1-4}$Sealed by Abu-šalim, son of Ataya; sealed by Aššur-dān, son of Ikuppiya; sealed by Aššur-malik, son of Anīnum.

$^{5-7}$For these proceedings, the *kārum* of Kaneš appointed us (as arbitrators) and, ^{7}before Aššur's dagger […]

Tablet

Obv. ^{1}*Pí-la-ah-Ištar a-na Ma-nu-um-ba-lu-/um-A-šùr* ^{2}*ù Šu-zu-zu iṣ-ba-at-ni-/a-tí-ma* ^{3}*um-ma Pí-la-ah-Ištar-ma* ^{4}*a-na Ma-nu-um-ba-lu-um-A-šùr* ^{5}*ù Šu-zu-zu-ma a-ha-at-ni* ^{6}*ir-tí-bi ba-a-nim* kù-babbar *ma-la* ^{7}*i-ga-mu-ru* 3 *né-nu a-na* ^{8}*ki-iš-da-tí-ni* : *lu ni-iš-ta-pá-ak-ma* ^{9}*ù-lá* é dam-gàr^{ri-im} kù-babbar *a-na* ^{10}*ṣí-ib-tim lu ni-il*$_{5}$*-qé-ma gam-ra-am* ^{11}*lu ni-*<*ig*>*-mu-ur-ma a-ha-at-ni* ^{12}*a-na mu-tim lu ni-dí-ší um-ma* ^{13}*Ma-nu-um-ba-lu-um-A-šùr ù* ^{14}*Šu-zu-zu-ma a-na Pì-la-ah-Ištar-ma* ^{15}kù-babbar *ú-lá ni-šu a-li-ik* ^{16}*i-na pí-ni* kù-babbar *ma-la* ^{17}*ta-ga-mu-ru* é dam-gàr^{ri-im} ^{18}*a-na ṣí-ib-tim le-qé-ma* lo.e. ^{19}*gam-ra-am gu*$_{5}$*-mu-ur-ma* ^{20}*a-ha-at-ni a-na mu-tim* rev. ^{21}*dí-ší-ma* kù-babbar *ù ṣí-ba-sú ša* ^{22}*i-na* é dam-gàr^{ri-im} ^{23}*ta-la-qé-ú-ma ta-ga-mu-ru* ^{24}*gu*$_{5}$*-mu-ur-ma* kù-babbar *ù ṣí-ba-sú* ^{25}*i-na* kù-babbar^{áp} *é a-bi-ni i-na* ^{26}*ma-aš-*<*qá*>*-al-tim pá-ni-tí-ma i-na* ^{27}*sú-hu-pí-im le-qé-ma a-na* ^{28}é dam-gàr^{ri-im} *a-šar ta-al-qé-ú* ^{29}*ta-er um-*

Fig. 7. Sworn testimony, text **10** (Kt 88/k 97b). Photograph by Cécile Michel. Anadolu Medeniyetleri Müzesi.

ma Pí-la-ah-Ištar-ma a-na ^{30}*Ma-nu-um-ba-lu-um-A-šùr ù Šu-zu-zu-ma* ^{31}*šu-ma*-BA kù-babbar *i-na* kù-babbar^{áp} é ^{32}*a-*bi_4*-ni la al-té-qé a-na* kù-babbar ^{33}*ù ṣí-ib-tí-šu ša é* dam-/gàr$^{ri\text{-}im}$ ^{34}*a-la-qé-ú-ma gam-ra-am* ^{35}*a-ga-mu-ru a-na ki-iš-da-tí-ku-nu* ^{36}*la ta-za-za-nim um-ma šu-nu-ma* ^{37}*ni-za-za-ku-um um-ma Ma-num-ba-lúm-A-/šùr-ma* ^{38}*ù Šu-zu-zu-ma a-na* ^{39}*Pí-la-ah-Ištar ki ma-ṣí-*BA kù-babbar ^{40}*ta*$^{!}$*-ga-ma-ar* (erased sign) *um-ma* u.e. ^{41}*Pí-la-ah-Ištar-ma* ^{42}*ú-*la_1 : 1⅔* *ma-na ú-la* ^{43}*e-li-iš ú-lá ša-áp-li-/iš* le.e. ^{44}*a-na a-wa-tim a-ni-a-tim kà-ru-um* ^{45}*Kà-ni-iš i-dí-ni-a-tí-ma* igi gír *ša* ^{46}^{d}*A-šùr ší-bu-tí-ni* : *ni-dí-in* ^{47}igi *A-bu-ša-lim* igi *A-šùr-dan* igi *A-šùr-/ma-lik*

$^{1-2}$Pilah-Ištar seized us (as arbitrators) against Mannum-balum-Aššur and $^{3-5}$Šuzuzu, and Pilah-Ištar (said) to Mannum-balum-Aššur and Šuzuzu as follows: $^{5-6}$"Our sister has grown up. $^{6-8}$Come, let the three of us put down, according to our shares, as much silver as is needed to pay the expenses, $^{9-10}$or let us borrow silver at interest from a money lender's house $^{10-11}$so that we may pay the expenses and $^{11-12}$give our sister to a husband."

$^{12-14}$Mannum-balum-Aššur and Šuzuzu (replied) to Pilah-Ištar as follows: ^{15}"We have no silver. Come! $^{16-17}$With our permission, as much silver as you will have to pay back, $^{17-18}$borrow silver at interest from a money lender's house and ^{19}pay the expenses, then $^{20-21}$give our sister to a husband. $^{21-23}$The silver and its interest that you will borrow from the house of the creditor and that you will have to pay back, $^{24-27}$pay it back, and take silver and its interest from the silver of our father's house that becomes available from the first installment, and $^{27-29}$give (it) back to the money lender's house where you borrowed (the silver)."

$^{29-30}$Then Pilah-Ištar (said) to Mannum-balum-Aššur and Šuzuzu as follows: $^{31-32}$"If, however, I have been unable to obtain the silver from the silver of our father's house, and $^{32-34}$I had to borrow silver and its interest from a creditor's house $^{34-35}$so that I may pay the expenses, $^{35-36}$will you then not stand by me with your assets?"

$^{36-37}$They (replied) as follows: "We will stand by you!"

$^{37-39}$Mannum-balum-Aššur and Šuzuzu (then said) to Pilah-Ištar as follows: $^{39-40}$"How much silver, then, are you going to spend?"

$^{40-41}$Pilah-Ištar (replied) thus: $^{42-43}$"1⅔ mina, more or less."

$^{44-46}$For these proceedings, the *kārum* of Kaneš appointed us (as arbitrators), and we gave our testimony before Aššur's dagger. ^{47}In the presence of Abu-šalim, Aššur-dān, and Aššur-malik.

Bibliography: Text published by Çeçen (1995, 56, 68 [Kt 88/k 97a–b]); translated by Hecker (2004b, 55); edited by Kienast (2015, no. 26AB). For the particle -BA, see Kouwenberg (2017, 475). Collated May 2007; see fig. 7.

Comments: Some time after the death of their father, three brothers discuss how to finance their sister's marriage. One of them is ready to borrow silver from a creditor, while the two others prefer to use silver from assets left by the father. The cost of the marriage amounts to one hundred shekels of silver. This text is the protocol of a testimony in court.

Line 26: the broken spelling is for *ina mašqaltim panītimma*.

---

11. Brothers Discuss Their Sister's Marriage Gift

Obv. ^{1}igi *A-šùr-i-m[i]-tí* ^{2}dumu *Ah-š[a-lim]* ^{3}igi *Im-li-ik-A-šùr* ^{4}dumu *Ku-ur-ku-ri-im* ^{5}*Ma-nu-um-ba-lu-um-A-šùr* ^{6}*ù Šu-zu-zu iṣ-ba-at-ma* ^{7}*um-ma a-na-ku-ma mì-nam* ^{8}*a-dí a-ha-tí-ni* ^{9}*ta-am-li-kà* (°erasure) lo.e. ^{10}*mì-nam i-dí-ni-ša* rev. ^{11}*ni-da-ší-im* (*) ^{12}*um-ma Ma-nu-um-ba-lu-um-/A-šùr* ^{13}*ù Šu-zu-zu-ma* ^{14}*a-na Pì-lá-ah-Ištar-ma* ^{15}*a-li kù-babbar i-na pì-ni* ^{16}1 *ma-na* kù-babbar *ša-wi-ri-/ša* (*) ^{17}*ù* 10 gín kù-babbar *a-na* (*) ^{18}*a-ni-qí-ša i-dí-ni-ša* ^{19}*qí-bi$_4$-ší-im um-*[*ma*] u.e. ^{20}*Pì-lá-ah-Ištar-*[*ma*] ^{21}*a-ma-lá pì-ku-*[*nu*] le.e. ^{22}*ta-dí-na-ni-ni i-dí-ni-/ša* ^{23}*lá a-qá-bi$_4$-ší-im um-ma* ^{24}*šu-nu-ma* [*ni-qá*]*-bi$_4$-ší-im*

$^{1-4}$In the presence of Aššur-im[i]ttī, son of Ah-š[alim], and Imlik-Aššur, son of Kurkurum.

$^{5-6}$He (Pilah-Ištar) seized Mannum-balum-Aššur and Šuzuzu, ^{7}(saying) as follows: $^{7-9}$"What did you decide concerning our sister? $^{10-11}$What gift will we give her?"

$^{12-14}$Mannum-balum-Aššur and Šuzuzu (replied) to Pilah-Ištar as follows: $^{15-18}$"Where is the silver? According to our agreement, (we need) 1 mina of silver (for) her bracelets, and 10 shekels of silver for her rings. $^{18-19}$Promise her (this as) her gift."

$^{19-20}$Pilah-Ištar (replied) as follows: $^{21-23}$"I will not promise her a gift according to your agreement that you have (just) given me." $^{23-24}$They (said) as follows: "We will promise her!"

Bibliography: Tablet published by Çeçen (1996a, 19–20 [Kt 88/k 651]). Collated May 2005.

Comments: After having discussed, in the previous text, how to finance their sister's marriage, the three brothers deliberate about the gift for their sister: bracelets and rings amounting to seventy shekels of silver. This leaves only thirty shekels for the other expenses. But this text could also be the start of the dispute, the refusal of Pilah-Ištar to pay being the reason for the proceedings recorded in the previous document.

---

12. Where Should the Marriage Take Place?

Obv. [1]*um-ma A-šur-i-mì-<tí>-ma* [2]*a-na Ú-ṣú-ur-š[a]-Ištar* [3]*qí-bi-ma : a-na šu-mì : a-ší-tí-kà* [4]*a-na A-šur-be-el-a-wa-tim* [5]*ù ku-a-tí : áš-pu-ra-ku-nu-tí* [6]*um-ma a-na-ku-ma : šu-ma* [7]*ta-ha-sí-ma iš-tí : a-bi-ša* [8]*ta-lá-kam : a-hu-sí : šu-ma* [9]*lá ta-lá-kam : lá ta-ha-sí* [10]*a-ni : šu-ma : Šu-Ku-bu-um* [11]*pá-ni : iš-tí-šu : lu ta-li-kam* [12]*šu-ma a-ta pá-ni-a-tí* lo.e. [13]*iš-tí-kà lu ta-li-kam* [14]*šu-ma a-ša-at-kà* rev. [15]*lá ta-ar-*de_8*-am* [16]*lá a-hi a-ta šu-ma a-hi* [17]*a-ta I-ku-pí-a ki-ma* [18]*ú-nu-tum : i-na* é-gal^{lim} [19]*ú-ṣa-ni :* u_4*-ma-kál :* [20]*lá i-bi-a-at* $ṭur_4$*-da-šu* [21]*a-na* túg *ku-ta-<né>-e-šu : iš-tí* [22]*a-hi-kà : ú e-eb-ri-kà* [23]*mì-iṭ-ra-tim e-r[i-š]u-[nu]* [24]*a-na-kam : a-dí ša-n[a]-at* [25]*ra-ku-sà-ku : i-na* [26]*a-lá-ki-kà* 2 gú urudu [27]sig_5 le.e. [28]*lu tal-qé-e : i-pá-ni-kà* [29]*ab-kà-am*

[1–3]Thus (says) Aššur-imittī: say to Uṣur-ša-Ištar.

[3–6]Concerning your *aššutum*-wife, I wrote to Aššur-bēl-awātim and to you as follows: [6–7]"If you want to marry her and [7–8]come here with her father, then marry her! [8–9]If you do not come here, you shall not marry her!" [10–11]Now, if Šu-Kūbum is the first (to travel), let her come here with him, but [12–13]if you are the first, let her come with you. [14–16]If you do not lead your wife here, you are no longer my brother!

[16–17]If you are my brother, [17–20]when the goods come out of the palace, Ikuppiya must not stay a single night; send him. [21–23]Ask *for help*? from your brother and your associate for his *kutānū*-textiles. [24–25]I am bound by contract for a whole year here. [25–29]At your arrival, you surely received 2 talents of good copper; bring it along personally.

Bibliography: Tablet published by Bayram and Çeçen (1995, 8 [Kt n/k 1138]); edited by Kienast (2015, no. 44). Lines 1–16 cited by Michel (2006a, n. 53; 2008d, 23, n. 14). The tablet is on display in the Museum of Anatolian Civilizations (Ankara) and could not be collated.

Comments: In order to conclude the marriage, both the future husband and wife must of course be present, but also the father of the bride. The town where the marriage ceremony should take place is presumably Aššur.

---

13. The Marriage Should Take Place in Aššur

Obv. ^{1}*um-ma I-ri-šum-ma* ^{2}*a-na Dan-A-šùr* ^{3}*ù I-dí-A-šùr* ^{4}*qí-bi*$_{4}$*-ma šu-ma* ^{5}dumu *Pá-na-kà* ^{6}*i-qá-bi*$_{4}$*-a-kum* ^{7}*um-ma šu-ut-ma* ^{8}*ṣú-ha-ar-tám* ^{9}*a-hu-uz* ^{10}*um-ma a-ta-ma* ^{11}*té-er-tí a-bi-a* ^{12}*a-na A-lim*^{ki} lo.e. ^{13}*a-lá-ak a-na* ^{14}*A-lim*^{ki} *šé-ri-ší-ma* rev. ^{15}*i-na A-lim*^{ki} ^{16}*a-ha-az a-pu-tum* ^{17}*a-ma-kam lá ta-ha-az* ^{18}4½ gín kù-babbar ^{19}*ša ha-mu-uš-tim* ^{20}6½ gín kù-babbar ^{21}*ša ni-is-ha-at kà-ší-im* ^{22}*ša i-na ba-áb A-šùr* ^{23}*ṭup-pì nu-lá-pì-tù* ^{24}dub-sar *ú-ša-bi*$_{4}$ ^{25}4 gín 15 še kù u.e. ^{26}*Ma-nu-ki-A-šùr na-ší* ^{27}*ší-na-tim ša-am-ma* le.e. ^{28}*a-na Na-áb-*dingir šé-*bi*$_{4}$*-il*$_{5}$ kù ^{29}*ša ba-ri-ni ša En-um-A-šùr* ^{30}*ha-bu-lu mu-nu-a-tí-a le-qé*

$^{1-4}$Thus (says) Irīšum: say to Dān-Aššur and Iddin-Aššur.

$^{4-7}$If the son of Panaka says to you as follows: $^{8-9}$"Marry the girl!" ^{10}then answer (him) as follows: $^{11-13}$"(According) to the instructions of my father, I will go to the city (of Aššur); $^{13-14}$bring her to the city (of Aššur), and $^{15-16}$I will marry her in the city (of Aššur)." ^{16}Urgent! ^{17}Do not marry her anywhere else!

$^{18-24}$I paid the scribe 4½ shekels of silver for the *hamuštum* and 6½ shekels of silver for the *nishātum*-tax of the *kaššum*, for which we drew up my debt note at the Gate of (divine) Aššur.

$^{25-26}$Mannum-kī-Aššur is bringing 4 shekels, 15 grains of silver. ^{27}Buy blades and ^{28}send (them) to Nab-ilī. $^{28-30}$Concerning the silver that it is ours in common that Ennum-Aššur owes, take my shares.

Bibliography: Tablet published by Bayram and Çeçen (1995, 6 [Kt 83/k 164]); edited by Kienast (2015, no. 43). Lines 18–24 cited by Çeçen (1998, 123); lines 1–17 cited by Michel (2006a, n. 54; 2008d, 23, n. 14); lines 18–24 by Dercksen (2004a, 101, n. 310). The tablet is on display at the Museum of Anatolian Civilizations (Ankara) and could not be collated.

Comments: The town where the marriage should take place seems to be significant; here again it is in Aššur.

The *hamuštum* corresponds usually to a calendar unit, a week; but in this context, it refers to the Assyrian official bearing this title. The *kaššum*-official might represent here the *kārum* (authorities).

---

14. Wedding Feast

[1]*i-nu-mì e-mu-ni nu-šé-ri-bu ki-ma* [2]*iš-ri-im* ⅔ gín 15 še *a-na mu-sà-ri-im* [3]*áš-qúl* ¼ gín *a-na ša-hi-re-en*$_6$ [4]⅔ gín 15 še *a-na* 3 *ki-ra-tim áš-qúl* [5]¼ gín *a-na ší-ri-im áš-qúl-ma* [6]*e-mu-ni ù e-ba-ru-tù-šu a-sí-i* [7]*e-mu-ni ù e-ba-ru-tù-šu a-sí-ma* [8]1½ gín kù-babbar *š*[*u*]* *ga-me-er i-nu-mì iš-tù* [9]*W*[*a-a*]*h-šu-ša-na i-li-kà-ni* ¼ gín *a-na* [10]*ša-hi-re-en*$_6$ ½ gín *a-na* 2 *ki-re-en*$_6$ *áš-qúl* [11]¼ gín *a-na ší-ri-im áš-qúl-ma e-mu-ni* [12]*ù e-ba-ru-tù-šu a-sí-i* 4½ gín *a-na* [13]2 *na-ru-uq ù* 1 dug *bu-uq-lim áš-qúl* [14]4 gín *a-na* 2 *na-ru-uq ba-pí-ri-im* [15]*áš-qúl* 7 gín lá 15 še *a-na* 6 *na-ru-uq* [16]še-*am áš-qúl* 6⅔ gín *a-na* 4 *na-ru-uq* [17]*ar-ša-tim áš-qúl* 2⅙ gín *a-na hi-im-tim* [18]*áš-qúl* 1⅓ gín *a-na dí-iš-pì-im áš-qúl* [19]2¼ gín *a-na pá-ni-re ša al-pì-im* [20]*ù e-me-re áš-qúl* 15 gín *a-na al-pì-/im* [21]*áš-qúl* ⅔ gín *a-na* udu *áš-qúl* ⅔ gín 15 /še [22]*a-na* udu-*ma áš-qúl* 1⅙ gín *a-na* udu [23][x] gín *a-na* udu *áš-qúl* 1 gín *a-na e-ri-qí-im /ša tí-ib-/nim* [24][x] lá ⅙ gín *a-ṣú-ri-im a-na* [25][*ú*]*-kul**-*tí*!* *al-pì-im ú e-me-re áš-qúl* lo.e. [26][x] gín *a-na* 2 *maš-ki ša-pá-tí-im* [27][*áš-q*]*úl* 3⅙ gín *a-na* 2 *e-ri-qé-*[*en*$_6$] [28][*ša e-ṣ*]*é áš-qúl* 1 gín lá 7½ še [x x] rev. [29][*a-na ki*]*-ra-ni áš-qúl* 2 gín [*a-na*] [30][*e*]*-ri-qí-im ša qá-nu-we* [31][*áš-qúl* x] gín *a-na a-lá-ni ù ki-ra-ni* [32][*áš-qúl* x +] 5 gín *a-na* 30 *ša-hi-ra-tim* [33][*áš-qúl* x +] 4 gín *a-na* ì-giš *áš-qúl* ⅙* [34][g]ín *a-na um-ṣí-im* ⅓ gín *a-na šu-um-ke* [35]*áš-qúl* ½ gín *a-na* 1 dug *ha-áš-lá-tim* [36]*áš-qúl* 1 lá ⅙ gín *a-na* <*na*>*-*ru-uq pá-e* [37]*áš-qúl* ⅙ gín *a-qá-nu-we ša ki-ra-tim* [38]1 gín *a-na zi-re ma-lá-he ú ha-ba-ša-tim* [39]¼ gín *a-na hi-im-tim bi*$_4$*-iš-tim áš-qúl* [40]½ gín lá 7½ še *a-na e-ṣé áš-qúl* 22½ še [41]«*a*» *a-qá-nu-we áš-qúl ša-ku-kam a-na** *a-*[*hi*]*-šu* [42]*a-dí-in* ¼ gín *a-na ak-le em-*[*ṣú*]*-tim* [43]15 še *a-ga/kà-ni* ⅔ gín 15 še *a-na ku-*[*a-t*]*im* [44]*áš-qúl* 15 še *a-na ki-ki-a-ni áš-qúl* [45]⅚ *ma-na a-na* 5 *ku-ta-ni áš-qúl* [46]4½ gín *a-na na-ah-lá-pá-tí-ša áš-qúl* [47]4 gín *a-na ší-it-ri-ša áš-qúl* [48]3 gín *a-na ší-it-re áš-qúl-ma a-ma-/tim* [49]*ar-ku-us*$_4$ ½ gín *a-na* 2 *ki-re-en*$_6$ [50]*áš-qúl* ⅓ gín *a-na ša-hi-re-en*$_6$ *áš**-*qúl** [51]*e-mu-ni ù e-ba-ru-*<*tù*>*-šu a-sí-i* [52]⅔ gín 15 še *a-na* 3 *ki-ra-tim* ⅙ gín [53]*a-na e-ṣé* ¼ gín *a-na ša-hi-re-en*$_6$ u.e. [54]⅔ gín 15 še *a-na šé-né-en*$_6$ *áš-qúl-/ma* [55]*i-ša-pá-*<*ar*> *be-el-ša* «x» *e-mu-ni ú* [56]*e-ba-ru-tù-*<*šu*> *a-sí-i e-mu-ni ù* le.e. [57]*e-ba-ru-tù-šu a-sí-ma* 2 gín kù-babbar *ga-me-er* 1½ gín *a-na* 5 [*ki-ra-tim*] [58]*áš-qúl* ⅓ gín *a-na e-ṣé* ⅙ gín *a-na a-lá-ni* 15 še *a-zu-*[x] [59]*áš-qúl e-mu-ni ù e-ba-ru-tù-šu i-ša-pá-ar a-sí-ma* [x gín] [60]7 *ki-ra-tim* 1¼ gín *a-na* udu ¼ gín *a-e-ṣé* 15 še *a-zu-*[x *áš-qúl*] [61]*a-ha-*<*at*>*-ni qá-qá-sà a-na Ištar ta-ag-lu-ub*

[1–3]When we introduced our father-in-law (into the house), I paid ⅔ shekel, 15 grains for a (metal) belt instead of a (woolen) belt; [3–4]I paid ¼ shekel for a pair of shoe straps (and) ⅔ shekel and 15 grains for 3 jars (of beer). [5]I paid ¼ shekel for meat and [6]invited our father-in-law and his friends. [7]As I invited our father-in-law and his friends (as well), [8]1½ shekel of this silver was spent.

[8–9]When he arrived from Wahšušana, [9–10]I paid ¼ shekel of silver for a pair of shoe straps (and) ½ shekel for 2 jars (of beer). [11–12]I paid ¼ shekel for meat and invited our father-in-law and his friends.

[12–13]I paid 4½ shekels for 2 sacks and 1 jar of malt. [14–15]I paid 4 shekels for 2 sacks of beer bread. [15–16]I paid 7 shekels minus 15 grains for 6 sacks of barley. [16–17]I paid 6⅔ shekels for 4 sacks of wheat. [17–18]I paid 2⅙ shekels for butter. [18]I paid 1⅓ shekels for honey. [19–20]I paid 2¼ shekels for the *pannurums* of oxen and sheep. [20–21]I paid 15 shekels for an ox. [21]I paid ⅔ shekel for a sheep. [21–22]I paid ⅔ shekel and 15 grains for another sheep. [22–23]I paid 1⅙ shekel for a sheep (and) [x] shekel for another sheep. [23–25]I paid 1 shekel for a wagonload of straw, [x shekels] minus ⅙ for a flint knife (to prepare) the food[?] of a calf and sheep. [26–27]I paid [x] shekels for 2 woolen fleeces. [27–28]I paid 3⅙ shekels for 2 wagonloads of firewood. [28–29]I paid 1 shekel minus 7½ grains [… for] wine. [29–31][I paid] 2 shekels for a wagonload of reeds; [31–32][I paid x] shekels for hazelnuts and wine. [32–33][I paid x +] 5 shekels for 30 shoe straps (and) [x +] 4 shekels for oil. [33–35]I paid ⅙ shekel for *umṣum* (and) ⅓ shekel for onions. [35–36]I paid ½ shekel for a jar of groats. [36–37]I paid 1 minus ⅙ shekel for sacks of chaff. [37–39]I paid ⅙ shekel for drinking straws for jars (of beer), 1 shekel for *zirums*, *malāhums*, and *habaštums*, (and) ¼ shekel for poor-quality[?] butter. [40]I paid ½ minus 7½ grains for firewood. [40–41]I paid 22½ grains for reed. [41–42]I gave a (metal) belt for his brother. [42–44]I paid ¼ shekel for sour bread, 15 grains for *g/kannum*, (and) ⅔ shekel, 15 grains for jugs. [44]I paid 15 grains for *kikkianum*. [45]I paid ⅚ mina for 5 *kutānum*-textiles. [46]I paid 4½ shekels for her tunics. [47]I paid 4 shekels for her shawl. [48–49]I paid 3 shekels for shawls and tied (them to) the female slaves. [49–50]I paid ½ shekel for 2 jars (of beer). [50]I paid ⅓ shekel for a pair of shoe straps.

[51]I invited our father-in-law and his friends. [52–54]I paid ⅔ shekel, 15 grains for 3 jars (of beer), ⅙ shekel for firewood, ¼ shekel for a pair of shoe straps, (and) ⅔ shekel, 15 grains for a pair of sandals; and [55–56]I invited her (future) husband (lit., "her master"), our father-in-law, and his friends at the *šaparrum*.

56–57I invited our father-in-law and his friends, and 2 shekels of silver were spent. 57–58I paid 1½ shekels for 5 [jars (of beer)]. 58–59I paid ⅓ shekel for firewood, ⅙ shekel for hazelnuts, 15 grains for *zu*[x x]. 59I invited our father-in-law and his friends at the *šaparrum*, and 59–60[I paid x shekels for] 7 jars (of beer), 1¼ shekel for a sheep, ¼ shekel for firewood, 15 grains for *zu*[x x].

61Our sister shaved her head for divine Ištar.

Bibliography: Text published by Albayrak (2002, 1–10 [Kt 88/k 71]); translated by Dercksen (2008a, 97–98, and n. 23). Collated May 2010.

Comments: This is a record of expenses incurred by a brother of the bride, who arranged the marriage of his sister and paid for the banquet, inviting the father-in-law and his friends. He probably expects to be partially reimbursed by the other brother(s). The Old Babylonian text UET 5, 636 is quite similar, listing expenses for visitors on several occasions.

The last line might be a reference to the consecration of the girl to the service of the goddess Ištar, meaning that she would have been married and consecrated at the same time. In Old Babylonian documents, the *nadītum* of Marduk, contrary to the *nadītum* of Šamaš, was allowed to get married but not to have children.[10] There could have been a similar distinction in Old Assyrian texts, where the consecrated *gubabtum*-women are not married, but the *qadištum* appears as a spouse in marriage contracts (**24**, **15**). The shaving of the woman's head during her consecration ceremony is known for the high priestess (nin-dingir) in Emar: she is compared to a bride, and her head is covered with a multicolored scarf.[11] In the Old Babylonian period, the *nadītum* seem in fact to have worn scarves.[12]

Line 1: the bride's brothers could call the groom's father "father-in-law."

Lines 2, 47–48: for *šitrum*, perhaps an "shawl," and *išrum*, a "belt" (or a "scarf"); see Michel and Veenhof 2010.

Line 19: the *pannurum* could be an animal brush made of date spadices, according to Sturm (1999), or it would denote a variety of dried meat; see Dercksen 2010a.

10. Barberon 2012.
11. Fleming 1992, 11.
12. Stol 1991; 2016, 22–28.

Line 34: the *umṣum*, according to Dercksen (2010a), could have been a raw dried piece of meat; it appears together with the *pannurum* in CCT 5 27c:1: 1 udu 1 *um-za-am* 1 *pannuram ina Tegarama ana bēt ubri addin* ("I gave one sheep, one *umzum*, (and) one *pannurum* to the caravanserai in Tegarama").

Line 38: the *zirum* usually denotes a kettle. Thus, both *malāhum* and *habaštum* may be kitchen ustensils (see BIN 4, 118; and **157**, where the last two words also appear together).

Line 43: according to Dercksen (2008a, 99), the *g*/*kannum* is a cut of mutton (*gannum*) or a jar (*kannum*); the *š*/*saparrum* would correspond to the place of the throw-net, symbol of an Assyrian deity in Kaneš.

Line 44: the word *kikkianum* is also attested in Kt 93/k 151:12–13 as an alternative for barley: *ù* ⅓ *ma-na lu še-am, lu ki-ki-a-ni*: "(Concerning the tin, 10 shekels) or ⅓ mina, (let them buy) either barley or *kikkianum*."

---

15. Head Uncovered but Bride Gift Not Paid

Envelope

Obv. [1][*kišib A-zu-a* dumu X-x]-*x-šar* [2][kišib *A-na-ah-a-š*]*ur* [3][kišib *Bu-ṣí* dumu X-x-*n*]*im* [4][*Šu-sú-en*$_6$ *E-ta-ri a-ha-sú ša E*]*n-nam-A-šur* [5][*e-hu-uz x x x š*]*a-sú* [6](seal A) [7][*qá-q*]*á-sà* : *pá-tí* : *ší-mu-ša* lo.e. [8](seal B) [9][*ú*]-*lá ša-aq-lu ša-wi-tám* rev. [10](seal C) [11]*i-na ša-ha-tí-ša ú-lá* [12]*ú-šé-ša-áb* : *qá-dí-iš-tám* [13]*i-na Kà-ni-iš ù Ni-ih-ri-a* [14]*ú-lá e-ha-az šu-ma a-na* [15]*a-ha-tí-šu-nu lu mu-sà lu nu-a-ú-um* [16]*lu* dumu *A-šur ma-ma-an* [17]*i-ṣa-ba-sí En-nam-A-šur* [18]*um-mu-šu ù Puzur*$_4$-sa-tu [19]*Š*[*u-s*]*ú-in* : *ú-bu-bu-ú* [20]*š*[*u-m*]*a e-zi-ib-ší* [21][2 *m*]*a-na* kù-babbar *i-ša-qal* [22][*šu-ma š*]*í-it* : *té-zi-ib-šu* [23][2 *ma-n*]*a* kù-babbar *šu-nu* u.e. [24][*i-ša-qú-lu*]

[1-3][Sealed by Azūa, son of X-x]-x-šar; [sealed by Ānah-A]ššur; [sealed by Buṣi, son of X-x-nu]m.

[4-6][Šu-Suen married Etari, the sister of E]nnam-Aššur [...]. [7-9]Her [hea]d is uncovered; her bride gift has not been paid. [9-12]He may not let a concubine? dwell next to her. [12-14]He shall not marry a *qadištum* in Kaneš or Nihriya. [14-17]If, for their sister, her husband, an Anatolian or an Assyrian creditor, or anyone else would seize her (for a debt), [17-19]Ennum-Aššur, his mother, and Puzur-šadūe will clear Š[u-S]uen. [20-21]If he divorces her, he will pay 2 minas of silver. [22-24][If s]he divorces him, [they will pay 2 min]as of silver.

Tablet

Obv. ^{1}*Šu-sú-en*$_6$: *E-ta-ri* ^{2}*a-ha-sú ša En-nam-A-šur* ^{3}*e-hu-uz qá-qá-sà* ^{4}*pá-tí* : *ša-wi-tám* ^{5}*i-na ša-ha-tí-ša* ^{6}*ú-lá ú-šé-ša-áb* ^{7}*qá-d[í-i]š-tám* : *i-na* ^{8}*Kà-ni-[iš] ù Ni-ih-ri-a* ^{9}*ú-lá [e]-ha-az* ^{10}*šu-ma a-na a-ha-tí-šu-nu* lo.e. ^{11}*lu mu-sà lu nu-a-ú-um* ^{12}*ù* dumu *A-šur* rev. ^{13}*a-na hu-bu-lim* ^{14}*ma-ma-an i-ṣa-ba-sí* ^{15}*En-nam-A-šur um-mu-šu* ^{16}*ù Puzur*$_4$-sa-tu ^{17}*Šu-sú-en*$_6$: *ú-bu-bu-ú* ^{18}*ší-mu-ša* : *ú-lá ša-aq-lu* ^{19}*šu-ma e-zi-ib-ší* ^{20}2 *ma-na* kù-babbar *i-ša-qal* ^{21}*šu-ma ší-it* : *té-zi-ib-šu* ^{22}2 *ma-na* kù-babbar *šu-nu* ^{23}*i-ša-qú-lu* igi *A-zu-a* u.e. ^{24}igi *A-na-ah-A-šur* ^{25}igi *Bu-ṣí*

$^{1-3}$Šu-Suen married Etari, the sister of Ennum-Aššur. $^{3-4}$Her head is uncovered. $^{4-6}$He may not let a concubine$^{?}$ dwell next to her. $^{7-9}$He shall not marry a *qadištum* in Kaneš or Nihriya. $^{10-14}$If, for their sister, her husband, an Anatolian or an Assyrian creditor, or anyone else would seize her for a debt, $^{15-17}$Ennum-Aššur, his mother, and Puzur-šadū'e will clear Šu-Suen. ^{18}Her bride gift has not been paid. ^{19}If he divorces her, ^{20}he will pay 2 minas of silver. ^{21}If she divorces him, $^{22-23}$they will pay 2 minas of silver.

$^{23-25}$In the presence of Azūa, Ānah-Aššur, and Buṣi.

Bibliography: Text published by Bilgiç, Sever, Günbattı, and Bayram as AKT 1, 77 (Kt a/k 55); edited by Kienast (2015, no. 9). Lines 1–18 cited by Rems (1996, 357–58, 362); lines 1–9 and 19–24 by Michel (2006a, respectively notes 33 and 19). See also Dercksen 1991. Collated May 2011.

Comments: The expression "her head is uncovered" perhaps means that since the bride gift has not been paid; the wedding has not yet been celebrated. The groom is not allowed to take as wife a *qadištum*, either at home (in Kaneš), or abroad, in Nihriya, an area where he might travel regularly for his business. He is not allowed also to install a concubine at her side; the word *šawītum* also appears in a testament (**54**) in the sentence, "The *šawītum* of Aššur-idī will stay with him." There we understand that Aššur-idī keeps as concubine a woman, perhaps a slave, with whom he had sexual relations.

Rems (1996) suggested that Etari might be herself a *qadištum*; this would explain the husband's prohibition from marrying another woman of the same status.

Line 5 of the envelope: should one perhaps read there [*a-š*]*a-sú*, "she is his wife"?

16. Covering the Bride's Head

Obv. ^{1}*um-ma En-um-A-šùr-ma a-na Lá-li-a* <*ú*> ^{2}*Nu-ùh-ša-tim* : *qí-bi-ma* ^{3}*mì-šu* : *ša ta-ki-li* ^{4}*ta-áš-ta-na-me-i-ni-ma* ^{5}*um-ma a-tí-ma* : *ṣú-ha-ra-am* ^{6}*ù ṣú-ha-ar-tám ú-lá-ma-nu* ^{7}*um-ma šu-nu-*<*ma*> *a-lá-nu-šu-nu* : *ma-nam tí-šu* ^{8}*ez-bi* : *ta-ki-li* : *lá ta-áš-ta-na-me-i* ^{9}*ù ší-it* : *lá ta-ša-me-ma* ^{10}*li-ba-ša* : *lá i-ma-ra-aṣ* ^{11}*iš-tù u*$_{4}$*-mì-im ša a-na A-lim*^{ki} ^{12}*e-ru-bu* kù-babbar 1 gú *ù* 2 gú ^{13}*ša-qú-ul* : *a-wa-tum ša ki-li-ma* ^{14}*gám-ra* : *ša* dumu-munus *a-hi-i-a* ^{15}*lá da-mì-iq-tim ša a-na-ku* ^{16}*áš-pu-ra-ma* : *ir-de*$_{8}$*-ú-ni-ší-ma* lo.e. ^{17}*ù* diri^{tám} *a-wa-sà-«ni»* ^{18}*ú-ṭá-ba-ma* : *ki-ma a-na* rev. ^{19}*wa-ar-ki-tí-a* : *ṣa-al-tum* ^{20}*mì-ma lá i-ba-ší-ú* : *e-pá-áš* ^{21}*Lá-li-a* : *ú-qá-a* : *Lá-li-a* ^{22}*i-na ma-qá-tim* : *pu-sú-nam* ^{23}*i-na qá-qá-ad ṣú-ha-ar-tim* ^{24}*a-ša-kán-ma* : *ha-ra-ni* ^{25}*e-pá-ša-am* : *lá ta-áš-ta-na-me-i* ^{26}*ki-ma* kù-babbar *ma-dam-ma* ^{27}*ag-d*[*a-a*]*m-ru* : *mì-šu-um a-wa-tim* ^{28}*li-*[*la-tim*] *ta-áš-ta-na-pì-ri-im* ^{29}*Lá-li-a* ^{30}*i-na ma-hu-ra-at* é^{tim} ^{31}*lu wa-ša-áb* : *e-er-šu-šu* ^{32}*áš-ra-kam* : *lu na-ad-a-at* ^{33}*ú-ku-ul-tù-šu* : *ga-ma-ar-šu* ^{34}*ša a-na-nim ù a-lá-nim ša-bu* u.e. ^{35}*ù ša a-dí a-ma-kam wa-áš-bu* ^{36}*lu a-li-ku* : *i-lu-ku* ^{37}*ša-bu-ma* : *pá-ší na-ki-pí* le.e. ^{38}*sí-pá-ra-tim sí-sí-ni mì-ma sà-he-er-tum* ^{39}*a-hu-ra-at-ni* : *ki-ta-am* : gal : *na-áb-ri-*[*a-tim*] ^{40}*ša i-lá-tim iš-ra-tim šé-na-tim šé-bi*$_{4}$*-lá* ^{41}*ta-as-kà-ri-nam a-na-kam im-ší-im*

$^{1-2}$Thus (says) Ennum-Aššur, say to Laliya <and> Nuhšatum.

$^{3-4}$Why do you keep listening to slander and ^{5}(saying) as follows: $^{5-6}$"They ill-treat the boy and the girl, saying, ^{7}'Besides them, whom else does she have?'" ^{8}Leave off and stop listening to slander. ^{9}She, too, she should not listen (to it) and ^{10}thus not become angry. $^{11-12}$Since I arrived in the city (of Aššur), $^{12-13}$silver has been spent, up to 1 or 2 talents; $^{13-14}$everyone's disputes are settled.

$^{14-16}$As to my bad niece, whom they brought here at my written request, $^{17-18}$I will also clear away her additional affair, $^{18-20}$and I will do my best so that there will be no disputes behind my back. ^{21}I am waiting for Laliya, $^{21-24}$and at the arrival of Laliya, I will place the scarf over the head of the girl, and (then) $^{24-25}$I will undertake my journey.

$^{25-27}$Do you not hear from various sides that I spent a lot of silver? $^{27-28}$Why do you keep writing me foolish words? $^{29-31}$Laliya must stay in the front part of the house; $^{31-32}$he must set up his bed at this place. $^{33-34}$His food and his expenses from there to here have been paid. $^{35-37}$Furthermore, all the travelers who came while he was staying over there have been paid. $^{37-40}$Finally, send axes, hammers, nails, date palm brooms, all the small wares that are delayed, a large linen textile, *nabrītums* for leather bags, (woolen) belts, and sandals. [41]Here, he *forgot* the boxwood.

Bibliography: Text published by Bilgiç and Günbattı as AKT 3, 80 (Kt v/k 95); translated by Michel (2001a, no. 399). See also Michel 1997d. Collated May 2011.

Comments: The bride is married off by her uncle, who will cover her head with a scarf during the marriage ceremony once he has settled his financial affairs.

Line 39: for a study of the word *nabrītum*, see Veenhof 2015a, 253–59.

Monogamy and Bigamy

The bulk of the documentation being concerned with business, the archives of the merchants of Kaneš contained only a limited number of contracts pertaining to family law. The marriage contracts involving Assyrians were kept at Aššur (**13**). Their discovery at Kaneš, involving marriages between Assyrians or between Assyrians and Anatolians, reflect generally atypical circumstances or contain special clauses. They provide for financial arrangements in case of divorce or stipulate steps to be taken in case of no offspring (**17**, **24**). The few marriage contracts involving only local people stipulate joint ownership of property or take up special situations such as adoption followed by marriage (**21**, **22**).

Marriage was normally monogamous in the ancient Near East, polygamy being the prerogative of kings; some contracts include a clause requiring monogamy. A man, upon marriage, could accept a marriage contract that forbade him to take another wife under a heavy penalty and breach of contract (**18**, **19**); as a prerogative, he had to take his wife with him on his business trips in Anatolia and had the obligation to bring her back to their home town (**23**). Thereby the penalty imposed on a man if he did marry another woman or if he divorced his wife could be the same and a strong deterrent, on occasion as much as 5 minas of silver, about 2.5 kg (**20**).

There were certain circumstances, however, in which a man could take a second wife.[13] The purpose of marriage was to provide offspring

13. Stol 2016, 165–92.

to inherit the family's assets, to support the aged parents, and to maintain the cult of dead ancestors. For couples that remained childless, only infertility in the woman was envisaged; thus, the Code of Hammurabi and Babylonian contracts dealt with the presumed infertility of a woman or the childlessness imposed upon certain priestesses who could nevertheless marry (Code of Hammurabi §§144–147). As in all other Mesopotamian documentation, infertility allowed the merchants to take a second woman in order to produce children. Two Old Assyrian marriage contracts, taking this possibility into consideration, specify the time after which, the wife having produced no child, the husband may have recourse to another woman; two or three years, as the case may be, relatively short compared to the seven years required of a man in a contract of the eighteenth century from Alalakh (**23**, **24**).[14] At Kaneš, the second woman, chosen solely to produce a child, was a slave; she did not gain the status of wife and could be sold after having given birth.

The special circumstances of the merchants who were absent from the conjugal abode for long periods, living in commercial settlements far from home in Asia Minor and in contact with peoples observing quite different legal practices, permitted them to take a second wife locally.[15] This custom, unique in the history of the ancient Near East, distinguished two types of wife: the principal wife (*aššutum*), who was often at Aššur, and the secondary wife, who most of the time lived in Asia Minor (**24**); after a few generations, the principal wife was often chosen in Kaneš. Thereby a man could have two wives but lived with only one of them at a time. Moreover, on the occasion of the second marriage, the contract stipulated that the secondary wife had to go with her husband on all his travels in Anatolia and that he was not allowed to take another wife in any locality in which there was a commercial settlement (**23**). This second marriage was possible only by observing two fundamental rules: an Assyrian merchant could not have two wives of the same status, and he could not have two in the same place. This restriction to two wives, one in the place of origin, the other in the place of secondary residence, was meant to protect their status; an Assyrian could not have a wife in each commercial settlement he visited!

---

14. Márquez Rowe 2003, 710; Justel 2008, 72. The unpublished text Kt 94/k 487 (courtesy Gojko Barjamovic) also mentions this possibility.

15. Michel 2006a; Heffron 2017.

Marriage contracts provide for the possibility of a husband marrying a second wife by using specific terms to refer to the status of the wives. The most common terms were *aššutum* and *amtum*. The former designates, in Akkadian, the wife vis-à-vis the husband (*mutum*). When a man had two wives, this word meant "principal wife." The latter term was used with different senses in Old Assyrian documents. According to context, it meant "female slave" or "secondary wife." The wives' statuses depended directly on the order in which the marriages were contracted: the first marriage or betrothal offered the woman the status of *aššutum*. A third term, *qadištum*, occurs only rarely (**15**, **24**; see chapter 5). In Old Babylonian documentation, the *qadištum* was a consecrated woman, sometimes of high rank, who could live in a family compound, inherit, and buy and sell real estate. According to Old Assyrian documentation, she could marry with the status of *amtum* (**24**). In marriage contracts, both Assyrian and Anatolian women could be *aššutum*, but it seems that only an Assyrian wife could be a *qadištum*.[16] The status of wives, although important, was not always specified, so in some cases the writers confuse them: a wife appears as an *aššutum* on a tablet of contract but as *amtum* on the corresponding envelope (**19**).[17] Letters seem to give the same rights to both wives, and each could inherit separately from their husband, but there is no testament in which both a primary and secondary wife are named. In the case of childlessness, the *aššutum* could herself purchase the female slave intended to provide her husband with heirs, then sell her again at will (**24**), whereas the *amtum* could have another female slave imposed upon her by her husband (**23**).[18] Finally, based on the study of several families, it seems that the children of the secondary wife had fewer inheritance rights than those of the principal wife.

An obligation imposed on the husband when he took a second wife involved where she could live. If he was already betrothed or married to an Assyrian woman in Aššur, his second marriage could take place only in Anatolia, and, vice versa, if he took a first wife in Anatolia, the second

16. The *qadištum*, presumably like the *nadītum* of Marduk in the Old Babylonian sources, was not allowed to have children; Barberon 2012. It is possible that text **14** concerns a double ceremony of marriage and consecration.

17. In AKT 3, 40, the wife of Erradi is referred to either as *amtum* (line 6) or *aššutum* (line 11). For the *amtum*, see Łyczkowska 1993.

18. This assertion is based on two texts and may be owing to the accident of discovery.

could only be in Aššur. There was no strict rule for where the first or second wife had to be; one or the other could live at Aššur or at Kaneš, but the two wives could not live together (**15**, **25**). In general, the documents distinguish between "the city," meaning Aššur, and "the countryside," which refers to central Anatolia, west of the Euphrates, where there were about thirty Assyrian commercial settlements (**24**, **15**). From the historical standpoint, the men of the first generation of Assyrians who ventured for business reasons into Asia Minor were probably already married in their native city; if a marriage contract had been drawn up, it was therefore kept at Aššur. Their Assyrian wives usually had the status of principal wife. Later, when they lived for increasingly prolonged periods in Anatolia, Assyrians contracted second marriages there, with local women. Various contracts drawn up in such instances have been found at Kaneš. One or two generations later, the situation had changed, in that some Assyrians had set up their primary households in Kaneš and only occasionally returned to Aššur, where, in due course, they might take a secondary wife (**29**).

Several contracts, taking into account the special circumstances of merchants who traveled a good deal, specified that the husband contracting the marriage at Kaneš was allowed to take his wife with him on all his trips into the Anatolian interior. For certain texts, it was sufficient to refer to Kaneš (**25**), the center for Assyrian administration in Anatolia, whereas others list different localities, thereby mapping out the marketing area of the Assyrian merchants: Kaneš, Burušhattum, Durhumit, Wahšušana, and Hattum, which corresponded to the area inside the Kızılırmak bend (**19**, **23**), representing the principal Assyrian commercial settlements of inner Anatolian trade, as well as the region between Nihriya and Kaneš (**15**), corresponding to the route the caravans took between Upper Mesopotamia and Anatolia, where the Euphrates flows through the Anti-Taurus range. In general, an Assyrian merchant who contracted a marriage in Asia Minor, especially with an Assyrian woman, had to be accompanied by his wife whom he had married at Kaneš; he was not supposed to leave her alone there when he traveled in Anatolia (**23**, **25**). This was a basic difference between the wife at Aššur and the one in Asia Minor: the former stayed at Aššur, awaiting her husband's return, while the latter went with him on his journeys in Anatolia, something not always to the wife's taste if she were left behind in a town and subsequently ignored (**27**). It follows that even if the Assyrian merchant was legally a bigamist, having contracted a second marriage in Anatolia when he was already married at Aššur, he was, for practical purposes, constrained to monogamy. By contrast, the few documents that attest to Anatolian practices of marriage and divorce suggest that marriage there was strictly monogamous.

These peculiar circumstances obliged married women to run their households alone during certain periods of their lives. The Assyrian wife often lived at Aššur and remained there, together with her younger children, during her husband's career in Anatolia, whereas the Anatolian wife lived with her husband, but found herself alone when he retired and moved back to Aššur.

The wife who went with her husband on his business trips insured that he remained faithful and that he provided her with food and lodging. When he married, a man committed to taking care of his wife, even in case of prolonged absence; if he did not maintain his wife, the contract could be annulled (**5**, **28**). This rule evidently applied as well to the wife at Aššur, so we may well suppose that only the more successful merchants allowed themselves two wives.

---

17. Clause Concerning a Possible Divorce

Envelope

Obv. [1](seal A) [2]kišib *Nu-ú-nu* dumu *E-ki-a* [3]kišib *[A-l]á-hi-im* kišib *A-ta* [4]ki[šib *T*]*ù-tù-pì-a-lá* kišib [5]*A-šùr*-gal dumu *A-ta-tí-a* [6]kišib *Ga-lu-a* dumu *A-kà-áb-ší* [7](seal B) [8](seal B) *Ga-lu-a* dumu *[A-k]à-[á]b-ší* lo.e. [9](seal B) [10]*Ta-am-na-ni-kà* dumu-munus rev. [11](seal C) [12]*Šu-be-lim e-hu-uz* : *šu-ma* [13]*Ga-lu-a* : *e-zi-ib-ší* [14]2 *ma-na* kù-babbar : *i-ša-qal* [15]*lam-nì-iš* : *ú-lá e-zi-ib-ší* [16]*ù šu-ma* : *Ta-am-na-ni-kà* [17]*te-zi-ib-šu*[!] (ŠÍ) [18](seal D) [19]2 *ma-na* kù-babbar u.e. [20](seal A) [21]*ta-ša-[qal]* le.e. [22](seal D) r.e. [23](seal C)

[1-7]Sealed by Nūnu, son of Ekiya; sealed by Ali-ahum; sealed by Ataya; sealed by Tutupiala; sealed by Aššur-rabi, son of Atatiya; sealed by Galua, son of Akabši.

[8-12]Galua, son of Akabši, married Tamnanika, daughter of Šu-Bēlum. [12-13]If Galua divorces her, [14]he shall pay 2 minas of silver—[15]he shall not leave her badly—[16-21]and if Tamnanika divorces him, she shall pay 2 minas of silver.

Tablet

Obv. [1]*Ga-lu-a* dumu *A-kà-áb-ší* [2]*Ta-am-na-ni-kà* dumu-munus [3]*Šu-be-lim* : *e-hu-uz* [4]*šu-ma* : *Ga-lu-a* : *e-zi-ib-/ší* [5]2 *ma-na* kù-babbar [6]*i-ša-qal* : *ù šu-ma* [7]*Ta-*

am-na-ni-kà [8]*te-zi-ib-šu*[!] (ŠÍ) [9]2 *ma-na* kù-babbar lo.e. [10]*ta-ša-qal* rev. [11]igi *Nu-ú-nu* : igi [12]*A-ta* : igi *A-šùr*-gal [13]igi *A-la-hi-im lam-ni-ìš* [14]*ú-lá e-pá*-ší**

[1–3]Galua, son of Akabši, married Tamnanika, daughter of Šu-Bēlum. [4]If Galua divorces her, [5–6]he shall pay 2 minas of silver; [6–10]and if Tamnanika divorces him, she shall pay 2 minas of silver.

[11–13]In the presence of Nūnu, Ataya, Aššur-rabi, and Ali-ahum.

[13–14]He shall not treat her badly.

Bibliography: Text published by Donbaz (2003 [Kt v/k 147]); text edited and photograph published in Michel 2010c; edited by Kienast (2015, no. 10). Collated May 2005; see fig. 5.

Comments: This contract mentions a reciprocal clause of divorce with the same penalty for both parties: two minas of silver (1 kg). But there is an additional clause intended to protect the wife: the husband must not leave her badly. The document is sealed by the groom and the witnesses and thus must have been preserved in the archives of the family of the bride. She could be a daughter from a mixed marriage, since the name of her father is Assyrian (Šu-Bēlum).

Line 15 of the envelope has *lamniš ezābum*, "to leave badly," while line 14 of the tablet has *lamniš epāšum*, "to treat badly."

18. Clauses Concerning Monogamy and Possible Divorce

Envelope

Obv. [1]kišib *A-gu$_5$-ú-a* dumu *Ba-zi-a* [2](seal A) [3]kišib *A-hu-wa-hi* dumu [d]mar-tu-*ba-ni* [4]kišib *A-ba-a-a* dumu du$_{10}$-*A-šùr* [5]kišib *Ku-ku-za-nim* dumu *A-ku-tim* [6][d]im-[d]utu[ši] [7]*A-ba-a-a* dumu du$_{10}$-*A-šùr* [8]*e-hu-sí šu-ma* [9]*e-zi-ib-ší* [10](seal A) [11] ⅓ *ma-na* kù-babbar [12](seal B) [13]*A-ba-a-a a-na* [d]im-[d]utu[ši] [14]*i-ša-qal a-ša-tám* [15]*ša-ni-tám lá e-ha-az* [16](seal C) [17]*šu-ma* [d]im-[d]utu[ši] [18](seal D) le.e. [19]*A-ba-a-a té-zi-ib* [20] ⅓ *ma-na* kù-babbar *a-na* [21]*A-ba-a-a ta-ša-qal* [22]*Ku-ku-za-num* dumu *A-ku-tim* [23]*ki-ma ší-a-tí i-zi-iz* r.e. [24](seal B)

[1–5]Sealed by Agūa, son of Baziya; sealed by Ahuwahi, son of Amurru-bāni; sealed by Abaya, son of Ṭāb-Aššur; sealed by Kukkuzānum, son of Akūtum.

[6–8]Adad-šamšī, Abaya, son of Ṭāb-Aššur, married her. [8–9]If he divorces her, [10–14]Abaya shall pay ⅓ mina of silver to Adad-šamšī. [14–15]He shall not marry another *aššutum*-wife. [16–19]If Adad-šamšī divorces Abaya, [20–21]she shall pay ⅓ mina of silver to Abaya. [22–23]Kukkuzānum, son of Akūtum, represented her.

Tablet

Obv. [1]^{d}im-^{d}utu^{ši} [2]*A-ba-a-a* dumu du$_{10}$-*A-šùr* [3]*e-hu-sí šu-ma* [4]*e-zi-ib-ší* [5]⅓ *ma-na* kù-babbar [6]*A-ba-a-a a-na* [7]^{d}im-^{d}utu^{ši} [8]*i-ša-qal* [9]*ša-ni-tám* [10]*a-ša-tám lá e-ha-az* [11]*šu-ma* ^{d}im-^{d}utu^{ši} [12]*A-ba-a-a té-zi-ib* [13]⅓ *ma-na a-na* [14]*A-ba-a-a ta-ša-qal* [15]*Ku-ku-za-num* dumu *A-ku*-tim [16]*ki-ma ší-a-tí i-zi-iz* [17]igi *A-gu*$_{5}$*-ú-a* le.e. [18]igi *A-hu-wa-hi*

[1–3]Adad-šamšī, Abaya, son of Ṭāb-Aššur, married her. [3–4]If he divorces her, [4–8]Abaya shall pay ⅓ mina of silver to Adad-šamšī. [9–10]He shall not marry another *aššutum*-wife. [11–12]If Adad-šamšī divorces Abaya, [13–14]she shall pay ⅓ mina of silver to Abaya. [15–16]Kukkuzānum, son of Akūtum, represented her.

[17–18]In the presence of Agūa and Ahuwahi.

Bibliography: Text published in copy by Smith and Wiseman as CCT 5, 16a; edited by Kienast (2015, no. 6); translated by Deller (1958, 62–63). The sealings of the envelope are published as CCT 6, nos. 36–39.

Comments: Husband and wife may both initiate a divorce, and the penalty is the same in both cases: ⅓ mina of silver. Adad-šamšī is mentioned first; she could be a widow who marries for the second time. The envelope bears the seals of the two witnesses, of the groom and of the man representing the wife.

---

19. Marriage Contract Mentioning the Bride Gift and Monogamy

Envelope

Obv. [1][kišib *Ta-ri-ku-d*]*a* dumu *Ki-ma-ar-ni-/ma-an* [2]kišib *A-š*[*ùr-na-da*] dumu *A-šùr*-du$_{10}$ [3]kišib *I-dí-*[*A-šùr*] dumu *E-lá-li-a* [4]kišib *Šu-pì-*[*el-kà*] 15 gín kù-babbar [5]*ší-mì ša* [munus] *Ha-ma-na-ni-kà* [6]*a-na um-m*[*ì-š*]*a* : *Šu-pì-el-kà* [7]*A-šùr-ma-lik iš-qú-ul* [8]*lu um-ma-ša* : *lu a-hu-ša* [9]*a-na A-šùr-ma-lik ma-ma-an* [10]*lá i-tù-ru-ú* lo.e. [11]*ù A-šùr-ma-lik* [12]*a-ša-tám* rev. [13]*l*[*u*] *i-na Bu-ru-uš-ha-tim* [14](seal) [15]*lu i-na Wa-ah-šu-ša-na* [16]*lu i-na Dur*$_{4}$*-hu-mì-it* [17]*lu i-na Kà-ni-iš* [18]*lá e-ha-az a-ša-sú* [19]*a-šar li-bi*$_{4}$*-šu* [20]*i-ra-dí* u.e. [21](seal A) le.e. [22](seal B) r.e. [23](seal C)

[1–4]Sealed by Tarikuda, son of Kimarniman; sealed by Aššur-nādā, son of Aššur-ṭāb; sealed by Iddin-Aššur, son of Elaliya; sealed by Šuppi-elka.

[4–7]Aššur-malik paid 15 shekels of silver, the bride gift of Hamananika, to her mother Šuppi-elka. [8–10]Nobody, either her brother or her mother, shall raise a claim against Aššur-malik. [11–18]And Aššur-malik shall not marry another *aššutum*-wife in Burušhattum, in Wahšušana, in Durhumit, or in Kaneš. [19–20]He shall take his *aššutum*-wife (*sic*!) along wherever he wishes.

Tablet

Obv. [1]15 gín kù-babbar *ší-im* [2]*Ha-ma-na-ni-kà* [3]*Šu-pì-el-kà* : *ta-al-qé* [4]*lu a-hu-ša* [5]*lu um-ma-ša* [6]*ma-ma-an* : *a-na* [7]*A-šùr-ma-lik* [8]*lá i-tù-ar* [9]*A-šùr-ma-lik a-ša-tám* [10]*lu i-na Kà-ni-iš* lo.e. [11]*lu i-na Bu-ru-uš-ha-tim* rev. [12]*lu i-na Dur*$_4$*-hu-mì-it* [13]*lu i-na* [14]*Wa-ah-šu-ša-na* [15]*lá e-ha-az* [16]*a-ma-sú* : *a-šar* [17]*li-bi*$_4$*-šu i-ra-de*$_8$ [18]igi *Ta-ri-ku-da* [19]igi *A-šùr-na-da* [20]igi *I-dí-A-šùr*

[1–3]Šuppi-elka received 15 shekels of silver, the bride gift of Hamananika. [4–8]Nobody, either her brother or her mother, shall raise a claim against Aššur-malik. [9–15]Aššur-malik shall not marry another *aššutum*-wife in Kaneš, in Burušhattum, in Durhumit, or in Wahšušana. [16–17]He shall take his *amtum*-wife along wherever he wishes.

[18–20]In the presence of Tarikuda, Aššur-nādā, and Iddin-Aššur.

Bibliography: Text published by Bayram and Çeçen (1995, 4–5), and Michel and Garelli (1996, 295–392, as Kt 90/k 108); edited by Kienast (2015, no. 12). Envelope opened in 1996.

Comments: The bride gift, called *šīmum* ("price"), is paid to the mother of the bride. The writer was mistaken about the status of the wife on the envelope: *aššutum* instead of *amtum* (on the envelope). The envelope bears the seals of the bride's mother and of the witnesses; thus, the contract was kept in the husband's archives as a proof of the payment of the bride gift.

According to this contract, a man who marries a girl in Kaneš is not allowed to marry a second wife in the whole Anatolian area where Assyrian merchants worked (Kaneš, Burušhattum, Durhumit, and Wahšušana).

20. Same Penalties in Case of a Second Marriage or a Divorce

Envelope

Obv. ^{1}(seal A) ^{2}kišib *Bu-ur-Sú-en* ^{3}dumu *I-ri-ší-im* ^{4}kišib du$_{10}$-*ṣí-la-A-šùr* ^{5}[dumu] *A-na-ah-*[*ì*]*-lí* ^{6}kišib *A-šùr-b*[*e*]*-li* ^{7}(seal A) ^{8}dumu *Ta-bi-na* lo.e. ^{9}(seal B) rev. ^{10}kišib *I-dí-*^{d}im dumu mi-[^{d}]im ^{11}(seal B) ^{12}*I-dí-*^{d}im *A-na-na* ^{13}*e-*[*h*]*u-úz i-na* gán^{lim} ^{14}*a-*[*š*]*a-tám* : *ša-ni-tám* ^{15}*ú-la e-ha-az šu-ma* ^{16}(seal C) ^{17}*e-ta-ha-az ú e-té-zi-ib-<ší>* u.e. ^{18}5 *ma-na* kù-babbar ^{19}(seal D) ^{20}*I-dí-*^{d}im *i-ša-qal*

$^{1-11}$Sealed by Būr-Suen, son of Irīšum; sealed by Ṭāb-ṣilli-Aššur, son of Ānah-ilī; sealed by Aššur-bēlī, son of Tabina; sealed by Iddin-Adad, son of Ṣilli-Adad.

$^{12-13}$Iddin-Adad married Anna-anna. $^{13-15}$He shall not marry another *aššutum*-wife in Anatolia. $^{15-17}$If he marries (another wife) and divorces her, $^{18-20}$Iddin-Adad shall pay 5 minas of silver.

Tablet

Obv. ^{1}*I-dí-*^{d}im ^{2}*A-na-na* : *e-hu-úz* ^{3}*i-na* gán^{lim} ^{4}*a-ša-tám* : *ša-ni-tám* ^{5}*ú-lá e-ha-az* ^{6}*šu-ma* : *e-ta-ha-az* ^{7}*ú e-té-zi-ib-ší* ^{8}5 *ma-na* kù-babbar ^{9}*i-ša-qal* lo.e. ^{10}igi *Bu-ur-sú-/en* rev. ^{11}igi du$_{10}$-*ṣí-la-A-šur* ^{12}dumu *A-na*$^{!}$*-ah-ì-lí* ^{13}igi *A-šur-be-li*

$^{1-2}$Iddin-Adad married Anna-anna. $^{3-5}$He shall not marry another *aššutum*-wife in Anatolia. ^{6}If he marries (another wife) ^{7}and divorces her, $^{8-9}$he shall pay 5 minas of silver.

$^{10-13}$In the presence of Būr-Suen, Ṭāb-ṣilli-Aššur, son of Ānah-ilī, and Aššur-bēlī.

Bibliography: Text published by Bilgiç, Sever, Günbattı, and Bayram as AKT 1, 76 (Kt a/k 894); edited by Kienast (2015, no. 5); cited by Rems (1996, 364). A photograph of the reverse of the envelope is published as Kulakoğlu and Kangal 2010, no. 439. This tablet could not be collated because it is in the restoration laboratory.

Comments: The envelope bears the seals of the groom and of the witnesses; thus, the contract was kept in the girl's family archives or with her own tablets. But Anna-anna appears alone, without filiation or family link.

21. Joint Property in a Marriage between Anatolians

Envelope

Obv. [1]kišib *Ha-nu* kišib *I-na-ar*-*/dingir [2](seal A) [3]kišib *A-šùr-ma-lik* [4]kišib *Za-ba-ra-áš-na* [5]kišib *Ku-ul-zi-a* [6]*Za-ba-ra-áš-na* [7]*Ku-ul-zi-a* : *e-hu-úz* lo.e. [8]é$^{be\text{-}tum}$ [9](seal A) [10]*ša ki-lá-le-šu-nu-ma* rev. [11]*i-lá-pì-nu*$^{!}$ *ù* [12](seal B) [13]*i-ša-ru-ú* : *a-na ba-ri-šu-nu-ma* [14]*šu-ma* : *Za-ba-ra-áš-na* [15]*Ku-ul-zi-a* : *e-té-zi-ib* [16]é$^{be\text{-}tám}$: *ki-lá-lá-šu-nu* [17]*i-zu-zu* : *i-nu-mì* [18]*i-mu-tù-ni* : *be-tám* [19]*Hi-iš-ta-ah-šu-šar* [20]*ù Pè-ru-wa* u.e. [21](seal A) [22]*i-lá-qé-ú* le.e. [23](seal B) [24](seal C) r.e. [25](seal B) [26](seal C)

[1–5]Sealed by Hanu; sealed by Inar-ilī; sealed by Aššur-malik; sealed by Zabarašna; sealed by Kulziya.

[6–7]Zabarašna married Kulziya. [8–10]The house is their joint property. [11–13]They will share poverty and wealth. [14–15]If Zabarašna divorces Kulziya, [16–17]they shall divide the house between them. [17–18]When they die, [18–22]Hištahšušar and Peruwa shall take the house.

Bibliography: Text published by Donbaz as KTS 2, 6; text published also by Bilgiç, Sever, Günbattı, and Bayram as AKT 1, 21; edited by Kienast (2015, no. 11).

Comments: The envelope of the contract is complete, with the tablet still preserved inside and thus not readable. Husband and wife act as two independent persons, by mutual agreement; they share everything, and if they divorce, they will each take half of the house. The two persons mentioned at the end could be children of a previous marriage or members of the family who will inherit if they have no children. Both the husband and the wife sealed the document, which was kept in the couple's archives.

22. Adoption and Marriage between Anatolians

Obv. [1]*Ta-ta-li-i ú T*[*í*-x]*-a-*/[*m*]*a* [2]*Šu-pì-a-ni-kà a-n*[*a*] [3]*me-er-ú-tim* : *i*[*l*$_5$*-qé-ú*] [4]*Ší-im-nu-ma-an* [5]dumu *Ta-ta-li-i* [6]*Šu-pì-a-ni-kà* : *e-h*[*u-uz*] [7]*bé*$^{!}$*-tám* : *iš-té-ni-*[*iš*] [8]*uš-bu-ú* : *šu-ma* lo.e. [9]*ṭá*$^{!}$*-bu-ú šu-ma* rev. [10]*lá i-ṭí-áb-šu-nu* [11]*Ší-im-nu-ma-an* [12]*ú Šu-pì-a-ni-kà lu* [13]*ú-šé-šu-bu-šu-nu* [14]igi *A-na-na* [15]igi *Ha-ma-na-ni* [16]igi *Ut-ni-ih-šu* [17]igi *Hi-iš-ta-ah-šu-šar*

[1-3]Tatalī and T[i-x]-ama ad[opted] Šuppianika a[s] daughter. [4-6]Šimnuman, son of Tatalī, marr[ied] Šuppianika. [7-9]They will (all) live togeth[er] in (one) house, if it pleases (them). [9-10]If it does not please them, [11-13]Šimnuman and Šuppianika will make them (the parents) live (separately).

[14-17]In the presence of Anna-anna, Hamanani, Urnihšu, and Hištahšušar.

Bibliography: Text published by Pinches (1908, 8); edited by Eisser and Lewy (1930, no. 7) and Veenhof (2017a, 5–8). Line 1 collated by Kawasaki (1998, 87). See also Donbaz 1993, 138, n. 37; 1997; Jensen (1997).

Comments: An Anatolian couple adopts a girl and gives her to their son as wife. The young couple joins their parents' household, but if the cohabitation does not go well, the parents will provide them with a separate dwelling.

---

23. Clause Concerning Infertility, Mention of Another Wife in Aššur

Obv. [1]*Ištar-lá-ma-sí* dumu-munus [2]*A-šùr-na-da Puzur*$_4$*-Ištar* [3]*a-na am-tù-tim* [4]*e-hu-uz-ma a-na* [5]*Bu-ru-uš-ha-tim* [6]*lu a-na Ha-tim a-šar* [7]*ha-ra-šu-ni iš-tí-šu* [8]*i-ra-de*$_8$*-ší ù qá-dí-šu-ma* [9]*a-na Kà-ni-iš* [10]*ú-ta-ra-ší šu-ma* [11]*e-zi-ib-ší* 5 *ma-na* [12]kù-babbar *i-ša-qal* lo.e. [13]*šu-ma ší-it-*[*ma*] rev. [14]*té-zi-ib-šu* 5 *ma-na* [15]kù-babbar *ta-ša-qal-šu-ma* [16]*a-lá-an a-ší-tí-šu* [17]*ša a-lim A-šur ša-ni-/tám* [18]*lá e-ha-az šu-ma* [19]*Ištar-lá-ma-sí a-dí* 3 *ša-/na-at* [20]*šé-ra-am lá e-mar* [21]gemé *i-ša-a-ma* [22]*e-ha-az A-šur-né-me-/dí* [23]*A-ni-na ù um-ma-ša* [24]*i-dí-nu-ší* [25][igi] *A-na-lí* le.e. [26]dumu *A-al-*du$_{10}$ [27]igi *Ma-nu-um-ba-lúm-/A-šur* [28]dumu *A-šur-ṣú-lu-lí*

[1-4]Puzur-Ištar married as an *amtum*-wife Ištar-lamassī, daughter of Aššur-nādā, and [4-8]he can take her along with him to Burušhattum or to Hattum, wherever his journeys will (lead) him, [8-10]but he must bring her back with him to Kaneš. [10-11]If he divorces her, [11-12]he shall pay 5 minas of silver. [13-14]If it is she who divorces him, [14-15]she shall pay him 5 minas of silver. [16-18]Also he shall not marry another (wife) apart from his *aššutum*-wife in the city of Aššur. [18-20]If, within 3 years, Ištar-lamassī does not see a baby, [21-22]he may buy a female slave and take her (for procreation).

[22-24]Aššur-nemēdi, Anīna, and her mother gave her (as wife).

$^{25-28}$In the presence of Annali, son of Āl-ṭāb, and Mannum-balum-Aššur, son of Aššur-ṣulūlī.

Bibliography: Text published by Hecker, Kryszat, and Matouš as Prag I 490; edited by Larsen (2002, no. 176); Kienast 2015, no. 37. See also Michel 2006a, 161–62, nn. 19 and 25.

Comments: This contract arranges the marriage of Puzur-Ištar to Ištar-lamassī, after the death of her father, Aššur-nādā (fig. 19). The girl, who bears an Assyrian name and is given as *amtum*-wife, is in fact given in marriage by her brother Aššur-nēmedī and her mother, Šišahšušar, the Anatolian wife of Aššur-nādā. Puzur-Ištar is already married in Aššur; he is the son of the well-known Imdī-ilum. The document stipulates that Puzur-Ištar shall not take another wife within Anatolia—Hattum corresponds to the territory within the Kızılırmak bend, and Burušhattum is the westernmost Assyrian settlement in Anatolia—and may take Ištar-lamassī along during his business trips, but must always take her back with him to Kaneš (see **27** for a wife left on a business trip). In case the couple does not have a child within three years, the husband is allowed to buy and "take" (*ahāzum*) a female slave; the verb *ahāzum* is understood here in its sexual meaning; see also **233**.

---

24. Clause Concerning Infertility: A Slave to Bear Children

Obv. ^{1}*Lá-qé-pu-um* : *Ha-ta-lá* ^{2}dumu-munus *E-ni-iš-ru* ^{3}*e-hu-úz* : *Lá-qé-pu-um* ^{4}*i-na ma-tim* dam$^{!}$ ^{5}*ša-ni-tám* : *lá e-ha-az* ^{6}*i-na A-lim*^{ki} : *qá-dí-iš-tám* ^{7}*e-ha-az* : *šu-ma* : *a-dí* ^{8}mu 2-šè *li-pè-e* ^{9}*lá ta-ar-tí-ší-šu-um* ^{10}gemé : *ší-it-ma* ^{11}*ta-ša-a-am-ma* ^{12}*ù wa-ar-kà-tám* ^{13}*iš-tù* : *ša-ra-am mì-/im* lo.e. ^{14}*ta-ra-ší-ú-ni* rev. ^{15}*ú a-šar li-bi*$_{4}$*-šu* ^{16}*a-na ší-mì-im i-da-/šu* (*sic!*) ^{17}*šu-ma* : *Lá-qé-pu-um* : ^{18}*e-té-zi-ib-šu* (*sic!*) ^{19}5 *ma-na* kù-babbar *i-ša-qal* ^{20}*ù šu-ma* : *Ha-ta-lá* ^{21}*e-té-zi-ib-šu* 5 *ma-na* ^{22}kù-babbar : *i-ša-qal* ^{23}igi *Ma-sà-a* ^{24}igi *A-šùr-iš-tí-kál* ^{25}igi *Ta-li-a* ^{26}igi *Šu-pì-a-ni-kà*

$^{1-3}$Laqēpum married Hatala, the daughter of Eniš(a)ru. $^{3-5}$Laqēpum shall not marry another *aššutum*-wife in Anatolia. $^{6-7}$In the city (of Aššur), he may marry a *qadištum*. $^{7-9}$If, within 2 years, she does not provide him with descendants, $^{10-11}$she herself shall buy a female slave, $^{12-14}$and later, after having a baby, $^{15-16}$she may sell her$^{!}$ where she$^{!}$ wishes. $^{17-18}$If Laqēpum divorces her[!], [19]he shall pay 5 minas of silver; [20-21]and if Hatala divorces[!] him, [21-22]she[!] shall pay 5 minas of silver.

[23-26]In the presence of Masaya, Aššuriš-tikal, Taliya, and Šuppianika.

Bibliography: Text published by Hrozný as ICK 1, 3; edited by Lewy (1956, 9–10); and Kienast (2015, no. 8). Lines 1–16 cited by Michel (2006a, 163, nn. 26–27) and lines 3–7 by Kienast (2008, 37).

Comments: In case Laqēpum and Hatala do not have a child within two years, a quite short period, the wife is allowed to buy a female slave for her husband. Once the female slave has had a child, the wife may sell the female slave.

Line 4: the reading "dam" is supported by the fact that the woman is designated in ICK 1, 67:2–3 as "dam *Laqēp*."

Lines 16 and 18: note the two masculine forms instead of feminine. As well, lines 21 and 22: the verbs show masculine forms with Hatala as subject. Such frequent gender errors could be marks of literate merchants writing their own tablets.

---

25. A Wife in Aššur, a Wife in Anatolia

Obv. [1]*A-šùr-ma-lik* [2]*Sú-ùh-kà-na* [3]dumu-munus *Ir-ma-A-šùr* [4]*e-hu-uz* [5]*a-šar A-šùr-ma-lik* [6]*i-lu-ku : iš-tí-šu* [7]*i-ra-dí-ší* [8]*ša-ni-tám* [9]*i-Kà-ni-iš* [10]*ú-lá e-[ha]-az-/ma* lo.e. [11]*i-na ša-ha-tí-ša* rev. [12]*ú-lá ú-šé-ša-áb* [13]*lu me-er-at* [14]*A-šùr : lu me-er-at* [15]*ma-tim : ú-lá e-ha-a[z]* [16]*šu-ma : e-ta-ha-az* [17]*5 ma-na* kù-babbar [18]*A-šùr-ma-lik* [19]*a-na Sú-ùh-kà-na* [20]*i-ša-qal* [21]*i-na a-lim*[ki] u.e. [22]*A-šùr :* dumu-munus *Da-da* [23]*e-ha-az* le.e. [24]igi *A-lá-hi-im* [25]igi *Ú-zu-a*

[1-4]Aššur-malik married Suhkana, daughter of Ir'am-Aššur. [5-6]Wherever Aššur-malik goes, [6-7]he shall take her with him. [8-10]He shall not marry another (woman) in Kaneš, [11-12]and shall not install (another one) at her side. [13-15]He shall not marry a woman from Aššur or a girl from Anatolia. [16]If he marries one, [17-20]then Aššur-malik shall pay 5 minas of silver to Suhkana. [21-23]In the city of Aššur, he shall marry the daughter of Dada.

[24]In the presence of Ali-ahum and Uzua.

Bibliography: Text published by Michel and Garelli (1996, 298–99 [Kt 94/k 149]); edited by Kienast (2015, no. 7.)

Comments: The marriage with Suhkana takes place in Anatolia, but the groom is already bound by a marriage promise to the daughter of Dada in Aššur. Ultimately, he will have two wives. He is forbidden to marry another woman in Anatolia, whether Assyrian or Anatolian. Ir'am-Aššur was married to Šalimma, a daughter of Elamma whose archives were excavated in 1991; see Veenhof 2007, 291, n. 22.

---

26. Wife Must Follow Her Husband

Obv. ^{1}*A-na-ah-ì-lí* ^{2}*me-er-a-sú* ^{3}*a-na am-tù-tim* ^{4}*a-na a-ha-zi-im* ^{5}[*a*]-*na* du$_{10}$-*ṣí-lá-A-šur* ^{6}[*i*]-*dí-in* lo.e. ^{7}*a-šar li-*[*bi-šu*] rev. ^{8}*ú-ru-ší* ^{9}(blank) ^{10}igi *Na-áb-Sú-en*$_{6}$ ^{11}igi *Dan-A-šur*

$^{1-6}$Ānah-ilī gave his daughter for marriage as *amtum*-wife to Ṭāb-ṣilli-Aššur. $^{7-8}$He may take her along wherever he wishes.

$^{10-11}$In the presence of Nab-Suen and Dān-Aššur.

Bibliography: Unpublished text, by courtesy of Dercksen (Kt a/k 616b); edited by Kienast (2015, no. 35).

---

27. Following the Husband's Travels across Anatolia

Obv. ^{1}*a-na I-na-sú-en*$_{6}$ ^{2}*qí-bi*$_{4}$*-ma um-ma Iš*$_{4}$*-tár-na-da-/ma* ^{3}*i-na Bu-ru-uš-ha-tim* ^{4}*té-zi-ba-ni-ma : i-na* ^{5}*qá-tí : mu-tim : ki-na-kam* ^{6}*ú-ṣí-ma : da-tí-ma* ^{7}*ú-lá ta-áš-a-al : a-li-kam-/ma* ^{8}*i-na Kà-ni-iš* ^{9}*ta-ad-ni-a-ni-ma* ^{10}1 *ša-na-at : a-na* ^{11}*er-ší-kà : la tù-šé-ra-ni* ^{12}*iš-tù Tí-mì-il*$_{5}$*-ki-a* ^{13}*ta-áš-pu-ra-ma : um-ma* ^{14}*a-ta-ma šu-ma lá ta-li-ki-/im* ^{15}*ú-lá am-tí : a-tí-i* ^{16}*ù a-ṣé-er* ^{17}*ša Bu-ru-uš-ha-tim* ^{18}*ú-ša-áb-ra-a-ki-im* ^{19}*iš-tù Tí-mì-il*$_{5}$*-ki-a* ^{20}*a-na Kà-ni-iš* ^{21}*ta-ta-lá-ak-ma* ^{22}*um-ma a-ta-ma : a-na* ^{23}15 *u*$_{4}$*-me-e : a-ta-lá-kam* ^{24}*a-pu-ùh* 15 *u*$_{4}$*-me-e* ^{25}1 *ša-na-at : ta-ta-ša-áb* ^{26}*iš-tù Kà-ni-iš* ^{27}*ta-áš-pu-ra-ma : um-ma* ^{28}*a-ta-ma : a-na Ha-hi-im* ^{29}*e-li-i : u*$_{4}$*-ma-am* ^{30}*i-na Ha-hi-im : iš-/tù* ^{31}1 *ša-na-at : wa-áš-ba-ku-ma* ^{32}*i-na šé-bu-ul-tim* ^{33}*šu-mì-ma : lá ta-za-kàr* ^{34}*ša ki-ma : a-ma-kam* ^{35}*i-na ša-ha-tí-kà : wa-áš-bu-ni* ^{36}*u*$_{4}$*-mì : e-mu-ru : um-ma šu-nu°-ma* ^{37}*né-nu : ni-iq-bi*$_{4}$*-ší-im : um-ma* ^{38}*ni-nu-ma a-na ṣé-er*

$^{1-2}$Say to Enna-Suen: thus (says) Ištar-nādā.

[3–4]You left me in Burušhattum, [4–6]and there I have escaped from the hand of death, [6–7]but you do not take care of me! [7–9]I came here, and in Kaneš you humiliated me, and [10–11]for one (full) year you did not let me come to your bed. [12–13]You wrote to me from Timilkiya [13–14]as follows: "If you do not come here, [15]you are no longer my *amtum*-wife! [16–18]I will make it last for you even longer than in Burušhattum." [19–21]From Timilkiya, you went to Kaneš, [22](saying) as follows: [22–23]"I will leave within fifteen days (to come to you)." [24–25](But) instead of 15 days, you stayed there one year! [26–27]From Kaneš you wrote to me [27–28]as follows: [28–29]"Come up to Hahhum!" [29–31]Today, I have been living in Hahhum for one year, and [32–33]you have not even sent me an attention! [34–36]All those who live there at your side have seen my (long lonely) days; they (say) as follows: [37–38]"We, we told her as follows: [38]'[Go] to [...]'"

Bibliography: Tablet published by Sever (1995, 14 [Kt h/k 73]); translated by Michel (2014b, 210); edited by Kienast (2015, no. 46). Collated May 2005, and is complete; see fig. 4. Therefore, the end of the text must have been written on a second or supplementary tablet, as it sometimes happens.

Comments: It appears that Enna-Suen is often on the road for his trade activities, and his wife, Ištar-nādā, has to travel alone to join him (see the map at the beginning of this volume), but she did not succeed.

Line 5–6: the translation of *kinnikīam* and of these lines is proposed by Kouwenberg (2017, 400, n. 26).

Line 18: the verb could be *šutabrûm*, "to make last"; literally: "I will make it last for you." See Veenhof 2015a, 259, no. 20.

---

28. Obligation for a Husband to Support His Wife

Obv. [1]kišib *kà-ri-im Wa-ah-šu-ša-/na* [2]*ṣa-he-er* gal *kà-ru-um* [3]*ṣa-he-er* gal *dí-nam i-dí-ma* [4]*Ta-ta-na me-er-a-at A-gi-a* [5]*a-ša-at Pí-lá-ah-Ištar a-na-kam* [6]*kà-al-a-at* gán^{lam} *ú-lá* [7]*tù-ṣí a-dí Pí-lá-ah-Ištar a-na* [8]*Kà-ni-iš i-li-ku-ma* é *a-bi-/šu* [9]*ú-ṭù-up-tù-šu ù* [10]*ṭup-pí-šu e-šu-ru* lo.e. [11]8 *ma-na*-ta urudu *ší-kam* rev. [12]*a-na ú-kúl-tí-ša* ì-giš [13]*ù e-ṣí-ša i-na* iti-kam$^{/im}$ [14]*Pí-lá-ah-Ištar a-na* [15]*Ta-ta-na a-ší-tí-šu* [16]*i-da-ší-im ù i-na* [17]*ša-tim* túg *i-da-ší-im* [18]*ta-ah-sí-is-tum a-ni-tum* [19]*me-eh-ra-at ṭup-pí-im* [20]*ha-ar-mì-im ša dí-in* [21]*kà-ri-im me-he-er-ša* u.e. [22]*iš-tí ṭup-pí-im ha-ar-/mì-im* le.e. [23]*i-na Wa-ah-šu-ša-na* [24]*e-zi-ib*

[1-2]Seal of the *kārum* of Wahšušana, (the whole assembly) small and big. [2-3]The *kārum*, (the whole assembly) small and big, gave a verdict. [4-6]Tatana, daughter of Agiya (and) wife of Pilah-Ištar, is detained here; [6-7]she cannot depart overland. [7-8]Until Pilah-Ištar has gone to Kaneš and [8-10]has taken control of the house of his father, his furniture, and his tablets, [11-16]Pilah-Ištar shall give each month 8 minas of *šikkum*-copper to his wife Tatana for her food, oil, and firewood; [16-17]he will also give her one textile per year. [18-21]This memorandum is a copy of the certified tablet containing the verdict of the *kārum*. [21-24]A copy of it was left together with the certified tablet in Wahšušana.

Bibliography: Text published by Bayram and Çeçen (1995, 11), Çeçen (1995, 57–58; copy, 70 [Kt 88/k 269]), and Bayram (2018, 33); edited by Kienast (2015, no. 34); translated by Hecker (2004b, 56). Lines 11–17 cited by Dercksen (1996, 42, n. 142). Collated May 2005.

Comments: This tablet, which begins with the mention of the seals (*kišib*) of the witnesses and parties, has a copy of the original verdict before it was enclosed in its sealed envelope, and which was left in Wahšušana, together with another copy.

---

29. Do the Two Wives Know Each Other?

Envelope
[1]kišib *A-šùr-ták-lá-ku* dumu *A-šùr-i-dí* [2]*a-na Ištar-um-mì am-tí-šu* [3]*ù Ša-A-šùr-ma-da* [4]*a-pu-tum a-pu-tum lá ta-sá-hi-i*

[1]Sealed by Aššur-taklāku, son of Aššur-idī.

[2-4](Letter) to Ištar-ummī, his *amtum*-wife, and Ša-Aššur-mā'da. Urgent, urgent! Do not make trouble!

Tablet
Obv. [1]*um-ma A-šur-ták-lá-ku-ma a-na* [2]*Ištar-um-mì ù Ša-A-šur-ma-da* [3]*a-na Ištar-um-mì qí-bi-ma* [4]*mì-nam hi-im-ṭá-tim* [5]*ša ta-áš-ta-na-pí-ri-ni* [6]*m*[*a-na*]*m* : *e-lá-nu-ki i-šu-ma* [7]*a-*[*ma-lá*] *i-li-bi-ki* 1 *ma-na ša* gú [8][*ú ša*] 2 gú *al-qé-ú* : *ú* u_4*-me-e-a* [9]*m*[*a-d*]*u-ti*[*m*] *uq-ta-ri-ba-ni* [10]*mì-nam i-li-bi-ki ša ta-áš-ta-/na-ki-ni-/ni* [11]*a-šu-mì-i* : *i-ṣé-ri-a* [12]*a-wa-tum ša ma-al-a* [13]*ša-me-e na-ad-a-ni* lo.e. [14]*ú a-tí hi-im-ṭá-tim* rev. [15]*ta-áš-ta-na-pí-ri-im* [16]10 gín kù-babbar *ú* ⅓ *ma-na* [17]*uš-té-bi-lá-ki-im ki ma-ṣí-i* [18]*lu* kù-babbar^{pí}*-ma ù a-a-am* [19]*ṣú-*

ba-tám ša a-bu-ki i-a-tí [20]*i-dí-na-ni a-pu-tum a-pu-tum* [21]*iš-tí a-li-ki-im pá-nim-ma* [22]*lu iš-tí A-šur-ták-lá-ku ú Ša-a-A-šur-/ma-da* [23]*tí-ib-e-ma : a-tal-ki-im* [24]*ṣú-ha-ra-am lá té-zi-bi-im* [25]*ú šu-ma* kù-babbar *mì-ma ta-ha-ší-hi* [26]*iš-tí A-šur-ták-lá-ku* 1 gín kù-babbar [27]*ú-ul* 2 gín *ir-ší-ma* u.e. [28]*li-dí-na-ki-im i-na* [29]*ṣí-ib-tim*[!] *lá al-té-e* [30]*ú šu-ma ki-na-tim* le.e. [31]*ta-ra-i-mì-ni tí-ib-e-ma a-tal-ki-/im* [32]dam[!] *a-ni-tum ša a-hu-zu tù-ṣa-ma-ra-/ki-im* [33]*mì-ma i-li-bi-ki* [34]*lá ta-[ra-ší-i*[?]] u_4*-ma-am* [35]*a-na-ku [qá-t]í-x*[?] *úṣ-lá-at* [36]*šé-e-ni-in iš-tí-ni-a-tim* [37]*dam-qá-tim bi-li-ší-im ar-hi-iš e lá tù-ṣí-ma* [38]*e*[!]*-lim mì-ma e tù-ha*[!]*-li-qí-ni* [39]*i-pá-nim-ma ṭé-eb-e-ma* [40]*a-tal-ki-im*

[1–3]Thus (says) Aššur-taklāku: to Ištar-ummī and Ša-Aššur-mā'da; say to Ištar-ummī.

[4–5]Why do you keep writing me heated (words)? [6]Whom do I have except you, [7–8]even though I have received from you 1 mina per talent or even per 2 talents, [8–9]and now *he has shortened* my numerous repayment periods!

[10]Why do you always put me down in your heart? [11–13]Not only are troubles big enough to fill the heavens loaded upon me, [14–15]but you keep writing me heated (words)!

[16–17]I sent you 10 or 20 shekels of silver; how much (more do you want)? [18]It is surely my silver! [18–20]And what kind of a textile was it that your father gave to me? Urgent, urgent! [21–23]Get started and come here with the next traveler or with Aššur-taklāku and Ša-Aššur-ma'dā. [24]Do not leave the boy behind! [25]And if you need any silver, [26–28]ask Aššur-taklāku to give you 1 or 2 shekels of silver. [28–29]I can manage no more because of the interest. [30–31]So, if you truly love me, then get started and come here.

[32]This wife (*aššutum*) I have married desires to see you, [33–34]do not worry! [34–35]Today, *my hand is impeded* (?). [36–37]Bring along for her one pair of sandals of good quality.

[37–38]Do not fail to leave and come up here quickly! Do not ruin me! [39–40]Get up and come as soon as possible!

Bibliography: Text published by Garelli as *RA* 51, 6; translated by Michel (2001a, no. 396) and Larsen (2002, no. 134); edited by Kienast (2015, no. 45). Lines 7–10 are cited by Hirsch (2007).

Comments: Contrary to the common situation, Ištar-ummī was Aššur-taklāku's *amtum*-wife in Aššur (fig. 19); his *aššutum*-wife, whose name is unknown, was living with her husband in Anatolia. It seems that the husband would like to have both wives with him in Kaneš, which we suppose was against the tradition. It seems clear that the family in Aššur knew the existence of the second wife in Kaneš; see also letter **172**, in which the presumed daughter of Aššur-nādā writes to her father: "I shall love your *amtum*-wife who is with you in Kaneš."

Aššur-taklāku, mentioned on line 22, is a homonym of this letter sender.

Divorce

Separation of spouses was sometimes envisaged in Old Assyrian marriage contracts, and some contracts and court decisions dealing with divorce have been discovered at Kaneš. Conditions for divorce seem to have been far less severe than in contemporaneous Old Babylonian northern documentation, in which the penalty for the husband was high, and in which sometimes even death was imposed on a woman who wanted to separate herself from her husband. In most of the divorces recorded in Old Assyrian documents, all of which were consensual, the man and the woman seem to enjoy the same status; either one could initiate divorce, and the fine for breach of contract was the same for both parties and often served as a deterrent. A contractually arranged "divorce compensation" or "divorce money" (*ēzibtum*) was regularly paid by the husband to the wife.

The issues of the documents focused on could be different, depending on whether they dealt with Assyrians, Anatolians, or mixed couples. In the case of divorce between Assyrians, the compensation to be paid by the instigator of the divorce, either husband or wife, could amount to twenty shekels of silver (**18**), two minas (**17**, **15**) and, more often, five minas (2.5 kg) of silver (**20**, **23**, **25**). Such a sum could allow a divorced wife to maintain herself; her husband could not leave her destitute (**17**). The reasons for divorce varied depending on who initiated it and hence bore the onus, man or woman. Thus, if the husband took another wife although it was forbidden, he divorced his wife and had to pay her a compensation: divorce was thus similar to marrying a second wife (**20**, **25**).[19] One document appears to prohibit divorce, at the same time setting the compensation to be paid by the husband if he mistreated his wife (**30**); this was an exceptional case in that the husband stood guarantor for his father-in-law (**72**).

19. Veenhof 2003a, 453–54. For divorces in Old Assyrian sources, see also Stol 2016, 217–19.

The great majority of divorces were between mixed couples.[20] This situation arose from the possibility, for Assyrian merchants, of taking a second wife in Anatolia. Some Assyrians, after a business career in Anatolia, during which they set up a second household locally, decided to return to Aššur for their declining years. This was the case with Imdī-ilum, who spent twenty-years at Kaneš;[21] of Ali-ahum, who stayed some twenty years at various places in Anatolia;[22] and of Enlil-bāni, who resided at Kaneš for fifteen years.[23] Their departure from Anatolia therefore obliged them to divorce their Anatolian wives. Some of these divorces contain the regular clauses of divorce contracts, such as financial compensation by the instigator of the divorce; in these instances, the husband (**24**, **32**, **31**, **35**). Possible misconduct by the wife is also taken into account, the consequence of which is not her paying compensation, for she doubtless lacked the means, but rather leaving the household empty-handed, after having symbolically removed her garment pin fixing her clothing (**31**, **32**).[24] However, in **30**, note that her misconduct does indeed result in her having to pay compensation. When the man had moved in with his in-laws at marriage, he might have to pay them compensation as well (**33**, **47**).

The majority of the documents are intended to provide resources for the Anatolian wife after divorce and to determine the future of children from the marriage. Young children were entrusted to either of the parents, depending on the circumstances. In some cases, the father, departing for Aššur, took charge of his children. Pilah-Ištar was allowed to take his daughter Lamassī with him, after having paid to his wife and her family the costs of the girl's prior education and sustenance (**35**). Another document, dating to Level Ib, allows the father to leave with his three sons after having paid the divorce compensation to his wife (**36**). The father did not, however, always receive custody of all his children; in one case, the mother, Talhama, kept her daughter with her and could marry as she chose, while

20. Michel 2008c, 222–25. See also, as an example the divorce between Ir'am-Aššur and his Anatolian wife, Kt 94/k 154 and 158.

21. Ichisar 1981; Larsen 1982.

22. Michel 2008e.

23. Veenhof 1998. Others stayed their whole life in Anatolia, as Aššur-nādā; see Larsen 2002.

24. Similar clauses may be found, for example, at Nuzi; when a widow, deemed a "mother," after having inherited from her husband, wanted to remarry; she had to leave the house "naked," thus giving up everything (see Lacheman 1962, no. 19); see Michel forthcoming c.

the father, Atata, could take the little boy once he had reached a certain age and after the father had paid compensation to his ex-wife (**37**).

Divorces between Anatolians and Assyrians were not always consensual and sometimes ended up with an appeal to the authorities and administration of an oath before Assyrian (Aššur) and Anatolian (Anna) gods, as well as by the local authorities: the king and sometimes the *rabi sikkitim* (**34**, **35**). The marriage contracts and divorce documents suggest that the Anatolian women never contemplated following their husbands to Aššur, no doubt constrained by the presence of another wife in that city.

When marriage contracts were drawn up between Anatolians, one sees joint ownership of property by the spouses, which, in case of divorce, resulted in even division (**21**). In one instance, the husband, initiating the divorce, cedes to his wife all the household goods and real estate, but also his debts (**39**). Once the divorce had been finalized, contestation incurred the penalty of a heavy fine that probably served as a deterrent (one mina: **39**; two minas: **40**; and five minas: **41**), or even death.

The majority of the divorce documents involving Anatolian couples found at Kaneš date to level Ib; these were regularly overseen by the king of Kaneš and a government authority.[25] According to these documents, the woman left with the divorce compensation, the furniture, and the servants, and she was not bound to any service obligation connected with the ownership of real estate (**42**, **43**, **44**). Contesting a divorce that had been executed was punishable by a heavy fine or death (**45**, **46**).

---

30. Divorce Prohibited

Obv. [1]kišib *Ib-ni-li* dumu *A-al*-du$_{10}$ [2](seal A) [3]kišib *A-šùr-i-mì-tí* dumu *I-dí-We-er* [4]kišib *Du-du* dumu *A-šùr*-du$_{10}$ [5]kišib *En-um-A-šùr* dumu *Na-ra-am-*ZU [6]kišib *Puzur$_{4}$-A-šùr* dumu *A-šùr-i-dí* [7]kišib dingir-*ba-ni* dumu *A-šùr-i-mì-tí* [8](seal B) [9]kišib *Ta-ta-a* dumu-munus *Ša-lim-Ištar* lo.e. [10](seal C upside down) rev. [11]dingir-*ba-ni a-ša-sú* [12](seal D) [13]*Ta-ta-a šu-ma ú-lá-ma-an-/ší* [14]*ú-lá e-zi-ib-ší* [15]½ *ma-na* kù-babbar dingir-*ba-ni* [16]*a-na Ta-ta-a i-ša-qal* [17]*šu-ma ší-it ší-lá-tám* [18](seal E) [19]*ta-ar-tí-ší ma-a* [20]*e-ta-mar-ší* [21](seal) [22]*ú-lá* «*té*» *té-zi-ib-šu* [23]½ *ma-na* kù-babbar le.e. [24]*Ta-ta-a a-na* dingir-*ba-ni* [25]*ta-ša-qal Šál-lim-Ištar* [26]*ki-ma Ta-ta-a i-zi-iz*

---

25. Veenhof 2003a, 454; Dercksen 2004b, 140–45, 168, 172–73.

[1-10]Sealed by Ibni-ilī, son of Āl-ṭāb; sealed by Aššur-imittī, son of Iddin-Wēr; sealed by Dudu, son of Aššur-ṭāb; sealed by Ennum-Aššur, son of Narām-Suen; sealed by Puzur-Aššur, son of Aššur-idī; sealed by Ilī-bāni, son of Aššur-imittī; sealed by Tataya, daughter of Šalim-Ištar.

[11-13]Ilī-bāni, whose *aššutum*-wife is Tataya, if he maltreats her, [14]he shall not divorce her, [15-16](but) Ilī-bāni shall pay ½ mina of silver to Tataya. [17-20]If she commits a misdeed and he moreover sees her (doing it), [22]she shall not divorce him, [23-25](but) Tataya shall pay ½ mina of silver to Ilī-bāni. [25-26]Šalim-Ištar represents Tataya.

Bibliography: Text published by Veenhof (1997a, 358–60 [Kt 91/k 132]); edited by Kienast (2015, no. 4). Collated May 2012.

Comments: The envelope is perfectly preserved, with its tablet inside. It bears the sealings of the witnesses and of the husband and wife. The following inscription can be read on seal A: kišib dingir-*ba-ni*. Tataya was not there when the document was written since her father represented her; he would have used her personal seal to sign the contract.

Divorce is prohibited; even in the case of bad conduct (by the wife) or maltreatment (by the husband), there will be a financial compensation. This exceptional arrangement is due to the fact that we know, from another text (72), that the husband is at the same time the guarantor of a loan for his father-in-law, so that the family relationship must remain intact. In that text, Tataya is protected against her father's creditors.

---

31. Marriage Contract Giving Grounds for Divorce

Obv. [1]*Lu-ší-tí-a : a-na* [2]*A-šùr-ma-lik me-er-i-/ša* [3]*Šu-pì-a-šu* dumu-munus *Ha-pu-a-/šu* [4]*ù Ú-ni-ú-ni* [5]*a-na am-tù-tim* [6]*tal-qé : šu-ma* [7]*sà-ra-at ù-ul mì-ma* [8]*ta-ša-lá-al* [9]*ṣú-ba-sà ù na-ah-lá-áp-/ta-ša* lo.e. [10]*i-ha-ma-ṣí-ma* [11]*e-za-za-am-ri-ša* rev. [12]*i-ṭá-ra-sí a*$^{?}$*-ma-s*[*ú*] [13]*a-šar : li-bi-šu* [14]*i-ta-ru-ší : šu-ma* [15]*šu-ut : i-ze-ar-ší-ma* [16]*i-ṭá-ra-sí* ½ *ma-na* [17]kù-babbar *e-zi-ib-ta-ša* [18]*i-da-an* igi *A-mur-A-šur* [19]dumu *A-lá-hi-im* [20]igi ^{d}nin-šubur-*ba-ni* [21]dumu *Ah-ša-lim* u.e. [22]igi *Ha-šu-i* [23]dumu *Pá-lu-i*

[1-6]Lušitiya took as an *amtum*-wife for her son Aššur-malik, Šuppiašu, daughter of Happuašu and Uniuni. [6-8]If she is deceitful or misbehaves in any way, [9-10]he shall strip (her) of her cloth and her tunic [11-12]and drive her

away *naked.* $^{12-14}$He shall take along his *amtum*-wife wherever he wishes. $^{14-15}$If he comes to despise her, and ^{16}drives her away, $^{16-18}$he shall give (her) ½ mina of silver as her divorce money.

$^{18-23}$In the presence of Amur-Aššur, son of Ali-ahum; Ilabrat-bāni, son of Ah-šalim; and Hašui, son of Palui.

Bibliography: Unpublished text quoted by Michel (2008c, 223, n. 77 [Kt 94/k 141]) and deciphered in September 1995 with the kind permission of T. Özgüç.

Comments: Lušitiya, presumably the wife of Aššur-taklāku, son of Ali-ahum, whose archives were excavated in 1993, organizes the marriage of her son. The husband is allowed to divorce his wife if she misbehaves or if he comes to despise her, but the wife does not seem to be allowed to initiate a divorce. The verb "to hate" is a technical term in divorce, meaning that the husband "wants to get rid of" his wife. The *ṣubātum*-cloth and *nahlaptum*-tunic seem to correspond to a normal set of clothing of a woman.

---

32. Different Penalties for Man and Woman

Envelope

Obv. ^{1}[kišib *A-šù*]*r-ma-lik* dumu *A-mu-ur-lu-ṣú* ^{2}[kišib *Pè-r*]*u-a* dumu *Šu-pì-e-eb-ra* ^{3}(seal A) ^{4}kišib *Sá-ak-*[*lá-nim*] dumu [...]*-lim* ^{5}kišib *Puzu*[r_4]-^{d}utu dumu *Da-*[...] ^{6}(seal A) ^{7}*Puzur*$_4$-^{d}utu *Ha-šu-ša-ar-/ni-kà* lo.e. ^{8}(seal B) ^{9}[*a*]-*na am-tù-tim* rev. ^{10}*e-hu-uz šu-ma Puzur*$_4$-^{d}utu ^{11}(seal C) ^{12}*i-ša-mu-ùh-ma* ^{13}*e-zi-ib-ší*$^{!}$(BU) 1 *ma-na* kù-babbar ^{14}*i-ša-qal šu-ma Ha-šu-ša-ar-ni-/kà* ^{15}*ší-lá-ta-am i-ra-ší* ^{16}*i-ší-hi-iṭ tù-dí-tim* ^{17}(seal D) u.e. ^{18}(seal A) le.e. ^{19}[*tù*]-*ṣ*[*í*]-*i* r.e. ^{19}(seal D)

$^{1-6}$[Sealed by Aššu]r-malik, son of Amur-luṣi; sealed by Per]ua, son of Šuppibra; sealed by Sak[lānum,] son of [X-x-]lum; sealed by Puzur-Šamaš, son of Da[x-x].

$^{7-10}$Puzur-Šamaš married Hašušarnika as *amtum*-wife. $^{10-13}$If Puzur-Šamaš breaks the contract and divorces her, $^{13-14}$he shall pay 1 mina of silver. $^{14-15}$If Hašušarnika commits a misdeed, $^{16-19}$she shall leave (the house), drawing out the garment pin (of her cloth).

Tablet

Obv. ^{1}*Puzur*$_{4}$-^{d}utu ^{2}*Ha-šu-ša-ar*$^{!}$(RI)*-ni-kà* ^{3}*a-na am-tù-tim* ^{4}*e-hu-uz šu-ma* ^{5}*Puzur*$_{4}$-^{d}utu ^{6}*i-ša-mu-ùh-ma* ^{7}*e-zi-ib-ší* ^{8}1 *ma-na* kù-babbar lo.e. ^{9}*i-ša-qal* rev. ^{10}*šu-ma Ha-šu-ša-ar-ni-kà* ^{11}*ší-lá-ta-am* ^{12}*ta-ar-ší* ^{13}*i-na ší-hi-iṭ* ^{14}*tù-dí-tim* ^{15}*tù-ṣí* ^{16}igi *A-šùr-ma-lik* ^{17}igi *Sá-ak-lá-nim* u.e. ^{18}igi *Pè-ru-a*

$^{1-4}$Puzur-Šamaš married Hašušārnika as *amtum*-wife. $^{4-7}$If Puzur-Šamaš breaks the contract and divorces her, $^{8-9}$he shall pay 1 mina of silver. $^{10-12}$If Hašušarnika commits a misdeed, $^{13-15}$she shall leave (the house), drawing out the garment pin (of her cloth).

$^{16-18}$In the presence of Aššur-malik, Saklānum, and Perua.

Bibliography: Tablet edited by Michel (2008c, 223, n. 76 [Kt d/k 29]), Kienast (2008, 46–47; 2015, no. 36B), and published after collations by Günbattı as AKT 10, 41A–B.

Comments: The envelope is sealed by the witnesses and the husband.

The divorce clauses of this contract are asymmetrical. If the husband decides to divorce, he has to pay divorce money to his wife, but if the wife commits a serious offense, she shall leave the house almost naked, after the garment pin holding her cloth has been striped off; this means that she will leave everything to her husband (see **31**).

---

33. Divorce of an Assyrian from His Anatolian Wife

Envelope (ICK 2, 221 + 237[?])

Obv. ^{1}[x x x] *ú I-a-[ta-al-kà]* ^{2}[x x x] *Lá-li-[a]* ^{3}[x x *I-a-t]a-al-kà* ^{4}(seal) (lacuna)

Lo.e. $^{1'}$*e-hu-uz* : *Al-ga-ri-[a ú]* rev. $^{2'}$(seal A) $^{3'}$*[I-a]-ta-al-kà* : *a-ša-sú* $^{4'}$*[Lá-li-a] e-zi-bu-ma* : *a-wa-tí-šu-nu* $^{5'}$*[ú-ga-me-ru]-ma* 10½ [g]ín kù-babbar $^{6'}$*[Lá-li-a a]-na Al-[ga-ri-a]* $^{7'}$*[iš]-qú-ul*

$^{1-4}$… and Ia[talka] … Lali[a … Iat]alka (lacuna)

$^{1'}$… married … $^{1'-4'}$[Laliya] left Algariy[a and Ia]talka, his *aššutum*-wife, $^{4'-5'}$and [they settled their matter], $^{5'-7'}$thus [Laliya] paid 10½ [sh]ekels of silver [t]o Al[garia].

Tablet (Prag I, 513)

Obv. [1]*Lá-li-a* dumu *A-šur-i-<dí>* [2]*me-er-a-at* : *Al-ga-ri-a* [3]*Kà-áp-sí-a-áš-we* : *e-hu-uz* [4]*Lá-li-a* : *Al-ga-ri-a* [5]*ú I-a-<ta>-al-kà* : *e-zi-bu-ma* [6]*a-wa-tí-šu-nu ú-ga-<me>-ru-ma* [7]10½ gín kù-babbar *Lá-li-a* [8]*a-na Al-ga-ri-a* [9]*ú I-a-ta-al-kà* [10]*iš-qú-ul Al-ga-/ri-a* lo.e. [11]*I-a-ta-al-kà* rev. [12]*a-ša*[!]*-sú* : *ú Kà-áp-sí-a-áš-/we* [13]*me-er-a-sà* : *a-na* [14]*La-li-«li»-a lá i-tù-/ru* [15]*šu-ma* : *i-tù-ru* 1 *ma-na* [16]kù-babbar *a-na La-li-a* [17]*i-ša-qú-lu* : igi *Pè-ru-a* [18]igi *Lá-ba-ar-ša* [19]igi *Tù-ma-na*

[1–3]Laliya, son of Aššur-idī, married the daughter of Algariya, Kapsiašwe. [4–5]Laliya and Algariya and Iatalka divorced, and [6]they settled their affairs; [7–10]thus Laliya paid 10½ shekels of silver to Algariya and Iatalka. [10–14]Algariya, Iatalka, his wife, and Kapsiašwe, his daughter, shall not raise claim against Laliya. [15–17]If they do raise a claim, they shall pay 1 mina of silver to Laliya.

[17–19]In the presence of Perua, Labarša, and Tumana.

Bibliography: Tablet published by Matouš (1973, 309–18), as Prag I, 513. The join with the envelope, ICK 2, 221 + 237[?] was made by Kryszat (2001, 271); and the text edited by Michel (2008c, 221, n. 65) and Kienast (2015, no. 14A).

Comments: Laliya married Kapsiašwe, daughter of Algariya and Iatalka, and moved into the house of his in-laws. The divorce is here consensual with a financial settlement; the husband leaves both his wife and his parents-in-law.

---

34. Divorce Settlement under Oath

Obv. [1']*[Pu-šu-ke]-en*$_6$ *[ù]* [2'][X-*ma-z*]*i ni-i*[*š*] [3'][*A-lim*] *it-mu-*[*ú*] [4'][x *m*]*a-na* (erasure) [5'][kù-babbar] *e-zi-ib-ta-ša* [6'][X-*m*]*a-zi ta-al-q*[*é*] [7'][*a-n*]*a Pu-šu-ke-en*$_6$ [8'][*me-e*]*r-<i>-šu me-er-ú-a-t*[*í*]*-/šu* [9'][*ù*] *kà-ṣa-ri-šu* [10'][X]-*ma-zi ù* lo.e. [11'][gem]é[?]-*sà lá i-tù-*[*ra*] [12'][*n*]*i-iš A-šùr* rev. [13'][*n*]*i-iš A-na ni-iš* [14']*ru-ba-e ù ni-iš* [15']*ra-bi*$_4$ *sí-ki-tim* [16'][*i*]*t-mu-ú-ma* [17'][*a*]-*mì-ma šu-um-šu* [18'][*a-h*]*u-um a-na a-*[*hi-im*] [19'][*lá*] *i-tù-a-a*[*r*] [20'][x x x]-*bi* igi *A-lu-*[x x] [21'][x x x] x igi *Ha-nu-*[x] u.e. [22'][x x x] *li* [x x] [23'][igi *A*]*-šùr-*[x x]

[1'–3'][Pūšu-k]ēn [and X-maz]i swore the oa[th by the city]. [4'–6'][X-m]azi received [x m]inas of [silver] as her divorce money. [7'–11'][X-]mazi and her [female serv]ant shall not raise a [claim agai]nst Pūšu-kēn, his [sons], his daught[ers, or] his harnessors. $^{12'-16'}$[Th]ey swore the [oa]th by Aššur, Anna, the king, and the *rabi sikkitim*, and $^{17'-19'}$[o]ne shall [not] raise a claim against the o[ther] regarding anything whatsoever.

$^{20'-23'}$[In the presence of NP], Alu-[x-x x x] x, Hanu-[x, Aš]šur-[x-x].

Bibliography: Tablet published by Kryszat, Hecker, and Matouš as Prag I, 651; edited by Kienast (2015, no. 30).

Comments: This divorce, drawn up in Anatolia, between Pūšu-kēn and his wife, [X]-mazi (the X stands for the beginning of her name, which is broken on the tablet), does not involve the famous Pūšu-kēn and his wife Lamassī, since she never traveled to Anatolia and died while she was still married to Pūšu-kēn (TC 1, 30). It could deal with the second wife of Pūšu-kēn, an Anatolian lady who is still unknown. But the Pūšu-kēn involved in this divorce could also be the son of Buzāzu and grandson of the famous Pūšu-kēn.

The wife receives her divorce money and shall not ask for more. The oath is taken by Assyrian and Anatolian deities, and Anatolian dignitaries.

---

35. Divorce and Clauses about the Children

Obv. ^{1}*Pí-lá-a[h-Ištar Wa-l]á-wa-/lá* ^{2}*a-ma-sú* [*e-zi-ib*]-*ma* ^{3}*e-zi-ib-ta-š*[*a* x *ma-na*] kù-babbar ^{4}*ša-bu-a-at a-*[*na*] ^{5}*a-wa-tim a-ni-a-*[*tim*] ^{6}*Pí-lá-ah-Ištar W*[*a-lá-wa*]-*lá* ^{7}*Ša-at-Ištar um-ma-*[*ša*] ^{8}*Nu-nu ú A-mur-A-šùr* ^{9}*a-hu-ša* : *i-ša-ha-tí-ša* ^{10}*i-zi-zu-ma ni-iš* ^{11}*A-šùr ni-iš A-na* ^{12}*ni-iš ru-ba-im* ^{13}*it-mu-ú-ma* lo.e. ^{14}*a-na Pí-lá-ah-Ištar* ^{15}*me-er-e-šu* ^{16}*ú a-na mì-ma šu-mì-*[*šu*] rev. ^{17}*ú-lá i-tù-ru-šu-um* ^{18}*šu-ma i-tù-ru-šu-um* ^{19}10 *ma-na* kù-babbar *i-ša-*[*qú-lu*] ^{20}*Lá-ma-sí me-er-a-sú* ^{21}*Pí-lá-ah-Ištar i-nu-mì* ^{22}*a-na A-lim*^{ki} ^{23}*i-lu-ku i-ra-dí-ší*$^{!}$ ^{24}*ta-ar-bi-tám* ^{25}*ú-ku-ul-ta-ša* ^{26}*ša-bu-ú mì-ma* ^{27}*ú-lá e-ru-šu-šu* ^{28}igi *En-nam-A-šùr* ^{29}igi *E*[*n-na-sú*]-*in* ^{30}igi [PN]^{31}igi *Da-lá-áš* ^{32}igi *A-da-da*

$^{1-2}$Pila[h-Ištar divorced] his *amtum*-wife, [Wal]awala, and $^{3-4}$she is satisfied with h[er] divorce money: [x minas] of silver. $^{4-10}$F[or] the[se] proceedings, Pilah-Ištar (and) W[alawa]la—with [her] mother, Šāt-Ištar, (and) her brothers Nūnu and Amur-Aššur assisting her—$^{10-13}$swore the oath by Aššur, Anna, and the king $^{14-17}$that they will not raise a claim, whatever the iss[ue], against Pilah-Ištar and his sons. ^{18}If they raise a claim, ^{19}they shall [pay] 10 minas of silver. $^{20-23}$As to his daughter Lamassī, Pilah-Ištar may take her along when he goes to the city (of Aššur). $^{24-26}$They have received satisfaction for her upbringing and her food; [26–27]they shall not ask anything further from him.

[28–32]In the presence of Ennum-Aššur, E[nna-Sî]n, [PN], Dalaš, and Adada.

Bibliography: Text published in copy by Hrozný as ICK 1, 32; edited by Lewy (1956, 3, n. 7; 4–5, nn. 21–22); Kienast 2015, no. 38.

Comments: This verdict concerns the divorce of an Assyrian merchant who intended to go back to Aššur from his wife, who has an Anatolian name (contrary to her mother and brothers). They had to swear by the main divinities of Aššur and Kaneš, Aššur and Anna, and the ruler (of Kaneš). The father is allowed to take his daughter with him to Aššur.

---

36. The Husband May Take His Children with Him (Ib)

Obv. [1]*kà-ru-um Kà-ni-iš* [2]*dí-nam i-dí-in-ma* [3]*A-šùr-a-ma-ru-um* [4]dumu *E-nam-A-šùr* [5]*Zi-be-zi-be* [6]dumu-munus *A-šùr-be-li* [7]*a-ša-sú-ú* [8]*e-zi-ib-ší-ma* lo.e. [9]1 *ma-na* kù-babbar [10]*e-zi-ib-ta-ša* [11]*A-šùr-a-ma-ru* rev. [12]*a-na Zi-be-zi-be* [13]*a-ší-tí-šu i-dí-in-ma* [14]3 *me-er-e-šu A-šùr-a-ma-ru* [15]*i-ta-ru Zi-be-z*[*i-be*] [16]*a-na A-šùr-a-ma-r*[*u*] [17]*ù* 3 *me-er-e-šu* [18]*ú-lá i-tù-a-ar* [19]iti-kam *Sú-en*$_6$ [20]*li-mu-um* u.e. [21]*A-wi-li-a*

[1–2]The *kārum* of Kaneš gave a verdict as follows: [3–8]Aššur-amārum, son of Ennum-Aššur, divorced Zibezibe, daughter of Aššur-bēlī, his *aššutum*-wife, and [9–13]Aššur-amārum paid 1 mina of silver, her divorce money, to Zibezibe, his wife; [14–15]thus Aššur-amārum is allowed to take (with him) his three sons. [15–18]Zibezibe shall not raise a claim against Aššur-amārum and his three sons.

[19–21]Month Suen, eponym Awiliya (REL 194).

Bibliography: Text published in copy by Lewy as TuM 1, 21d; edited by Eisser and Lewy (1930, no. 276), Larsen (1976, 327–28), Kienast (2015, no. 33), and Bayram (2018, 35).

Comments: This text is dated to level Ib, month x of the eponym Awiliya, REL 194, which corresponds to circa 1779. The divorced husband is allowed to take with him his three sons after having paid one mina of silver as divorce money to his wife.

37. The Husband Keeps the Son; the Wife the Daughter

Obv. ^{1}*Tal-ha-ma* : *ù A-ta-ta* ^{2}*ki-ma* : *Ì-lí-áš-ra-ni* ^{3}*ni-iš A-lim*^{ki} : *it-mu-ú-/ma* ^{4}*a-hu-um* : *a-na a-hi-im* ^{5}*a-na mì-ma* : *šu-um-šu* ^{6}*lá i-tù-wa-ar* ^{7}*ṣú-ha-ar-tám* : *Tal-ha-ma* ^{8}*a-šar* : *li-bi-ša a-na mu-tim* ^{9}*tá-dá-an i-nu-mì* : *A-ta-ta* ^{10}11½ gín kù-babbar *i-ša-qú-lu* ^{11}*ù ṣú-ha-ra-am* ^{12}*i-ta-ru* igi *En-na-nim* ^{13}dumu *A-lá-bi-im* rev. ^{14}igi *En-na-Sú-en*$_{6}$ ^{15}dumu *A-mur-*^{d}utu^{ši} ^{16}igi *Ma-num-ba-lúm-A-šur* ^{17}dumu *Ep-qí-im* ^{18}igi *E-lá-li-iš-kà* ^{19}*ša qá-nu-e* ^{20}igi *Pé-ru-a ša qá-nu-e*$^{!}$(A) ^{21}*i-nu-mì ṣú-ùh-ru-um* ^{22}*i-pá-ni* : gu$_{4}$ *i-pá-ri-du* ^{23}*ù* kù-babbar *i-dá-an*

$^{1-3}$Talhama and Atata, in place of Ilī-ašranni swore the oath by the city that $^{4-6}$one will not raise a claim against the other with respect to anything. $^{7-9}$Talhama may give her daughter to the husband of her choice. $^{9-10}$When Atata pays the 11½ shekels of silver, $^{11-12}$he may take away the boy.

$^{12-17}$In the presence of Ennānum, son of Ali-abum; Enna-Suen, son of Amur-Šamaš; Mannum-balum-Aššur, son of Epqum; $^{18-20}$Elališka of the reeds; and Perua of the reeds.

$^{21-23}$When the little boy will become frightened in front of an ox, he (the father) will give the silver.

Bibliography: Text published in copy by Thureau-Dangin as TC 2, 76; edited by Eisser and Lewy (1930, no. 6), and Kienast (2015, no. 31).

Comments: Even if there is a reference to an oath sworn by the city (*Alim*^{ki}), which normally refers to Aššur, this contract was sworn in Anatolia, with Anatolians among the witnesses.

Atata is acting here as a representative of Ilī-ašranni; this could suggest that Ilī-ašranni was the husband of Talhama. It is curious that only the name of the father's representative, Atata, is mentioned in what follows concerning the little boy.

In their commentary, Eisser and Lewy (1930, 7, n. b), consider that the word "gu$_{4}$" should be here a divine name, even if the sign "dingir" is missing; they translate the sentence as follows: "An dem Tage, da die Kleinen vor dem Stier sich trennen warden, wird er auch das Silber geben"; this translation is repeated in *CAD* Ṣ, 236b, as follows: "When the children separate (?) (at the ceremony) before the (sacred ox), he shall hand over the silver," which is grammatically impossible. Hans Hirsch (1961, 70–71) also translates "gu$_{4}$" by "Stier(gottes)" and suggests that this religious rite could be linked to puberty. The translation proposed here considers that fear is not innate but appears between two or three years old, an age that coincides with weaning (see Michel 2008c, 224, n. 81). Thus, the father would be allowed to take with him his young boy after payment of an amount of silver, and once the boy was old enough to be separated from his mother.

---

38. The Wife Keeps the Bride Gift

Obv. [1]*Ša-ak-ri-uš-we a-ša-at* [2]*A-šùr-ták-lá-ku* : *mu-tum* [3]*ù a-ša-tum i-né-zi-bu* [4]*a-hu-um a-na a-hi-im a-na* [5]*mì-ma šu-mì-šu lá i-tù-wa-ar* [6]*lu a-na ší-mì-ša* : *lá i-tù-ru* [7]*Ša-ak-ri-uš-we lu a-na* [8]*nu-a-im* : *lu a-na* dam-gàr [9]*a-šar li-bi-ša ta-lá-ak* [10]*ù A-šùr-ták-lá-ku* [11]*a-ša-at li-bi-šu* [12]*e-ha-az* lo.e. [13]*a-hu-um a-na* rev. [14]*a-hi-im a-na* [15]*mì-ma šu-mì-šu* [16]*lá i-tù-wa-ar* [17]igi *A-lu-lu* dumu *Wa-al-ha-aš-na* [18]igi *Ša-da-ah-šu* : dumu *Da-lá-áš* [19]igi *A-ni-na* igi *I-dí-A-šur* [20]igi *Uš-ma-na-ah-šu*

[1–3]Šakriušwe (was) the wife of Aššur-taklāku; husband and wife divorced. [4–5]One shall not raise a claim against the other with respect to anything. [6]They shall not raise a claim with respect to her bride gift. [7–9]Šakriušwe may go to (the husband) of her choice, either an Anatolian, or an (Assyrian) merchant, and [10–12]Aššur-taklāku may marry the wife of his choice. [13–16]One will not raise a claim against the other with respect to anything.

[17–20]In the presence of Alulu, son of Walhašna, Šadahšu, son of Dalaš, Anīna, Iddin-Aššur, and Ušmanahšu.

Bibliography: Text published by Sever (1992a, 668 [Kt n/k 1414]); edited by Kienast (2015, no. 19). The tablet is on display in the Museum of Anatolian Civilizations (Ankara) and could not be collated.

Comments: The bride gift (lit., "[bride-]price": *šīmum*) was given at the moment of the marriage to the family of the girl; after the divorce, Aššur-taklāku cannot get back the bride-price. Remarriage is allowed for both the man and the woman, but it is expressed differently. While Aššur-taklāku is allowed to marry any woman he wishes, Šakriušwe is allowed to marry again either a *nuā'um* (Anatolian) or a *tamkārum* (Assyrian, lit. "merchant").

39. Divorce of Anatolians; the Wife Keeps Everything

Obv. ^{1}*A-ra-wu-ur-h[i-na]* ^{2}*a-ša-sú e-zi-i[b]* ^{3}*ṣú-ha-ri-šu ú-nu-tám* ^{4}*ša be-tí-šu mì-ma a-al*-šu** ^{5}*lá il$_5$-qé hu$^{!}$-bu-lu-šu* ^{6}*e-zi-ib ú ú-ṭù-up-/tù-šu$^{!}$* ^{7}*e-zi-ib ú-ṭù-up-tám* ^{8}*ṣú-ha-ri-šu ú-nu-tám* ^{9}*ša be-tí-šu ú hu-bu-/lam* ^{10}*a-ša-sú* ^{11}*Ma-lá-wa-áš*-hi-na* lo.e. ^{12}*tal-qé a-na* ^{13}*A-ra-wa-ar-hi-/na** rev. ^{14}*lá i-tù-wa-ar* ^{15}*šu-ma i-tù-wa-ar* ^{16}1 *ma-na* kù-babbar *ta-ša-/qal* ^{17}*ú i-du-ku-ší šu-ma* ^{18}*A-ra-wa-ar-hi-na* ^{19}*i-tù-wa-ar-ší-im* ^{20}1 *ma-na* kù-babbar *i-ša-qal* ^{21}*ú i-du-ku-šu* ^{22}igi *Tí-ri-ku-da* ^{23}igi *Du-hu-ší-li* ^{24}igi *Ki*-ni-a-ah-šu* ^{25}igi *Da-ra-ak-šu*

$^{1-2}$Arawurhina has divorced his *aššutum*-wife. $^{3-5}$He did not take his servants, the goods of his house, or anything of his estate; $^{5-6}$(but) he left his debts, $^{6-7}$and he left his furniture. $^{7-12}$Malawašhina, his wife, took the furniture, his servants, the goods of his house, and the debt. $^{12-14}$She$^{!}$ shall not raise a claim against Arawarhina. ^{15}If she$^{!}$ raises a claim against him, ^{16}she shall pay 1 mina of silver, ^{17}or they will put her to death. $^{17-19}$If Arawarhina raises a claim against her, $^{20-21}$he shall pay 1 mina of silver, or they will put him to death.

$^{22-25}$In the presence of Tirikuda, Duhušili, Kiniahšu, and Darakšu.

Bibliography: Text published in copy by Contenau as TC 1, 100; edited by Eisser and Lewy (1930, no. 4), Joachim Hengstl (1992, 213), and Kienast (2015, no. 18).

Comments: The divorce is initiated by the husband, who leaves assets and debts to his wife. This contract forbids any claim.

Lines 14 and 15: the verbal form is masculine, even if the subject is feminine.

40. Divorce of Anatolians

Obv. ^{1}kišib *Da-ku-na* kišib ^{2}*Ša-hi-iš-kà-an* ^{3}(seal) ^{4}kišib *Zu-zu* : kišib *Da-ar-ha-ší-/at* ^{5}kišib *Na-ki-le-e-ed* ^{6}gal *ša-ri-qé* ^{7}kišib *Šu-hu-ur-pí-a* ^{8}*Ta-li-a* : *a-ša-sú* ^{9}*Ha-šu-ša-ar-na* lo.e. ^{10}dumu-munus *Ud-ga-ri-a* ^{11}(seal) ^{12}*e-zi-ib* : *šu-ma* ^{13}*Ta-li-a* rev. ^{14}*a-na Ha-šu-šar-na* ^{15}*a-ší-tí-šu i-tù-wa-/ar* ^{16}2 *ma-na* kù-babbar ^{17}*i-ša-qal ú i-na* ^{18}*i-dí-nim* ^{19}(seal) ^{20}*i-du-ku-šu* ^{21}*šu-ma* : *Ud-ga-ri-/a* ^{22}*ú Ha-šu-šar-na* ^{23}*a-na Ta-li-a* ^{24}*i-tù-ru* u.e. ^{25}2 *ma-na* ^{26}kù-babbar le.e. ^{27}*i-ša-qú-lu* ^{28}*ú i-na i-dí-/nim* ^{29}*i-du-ku-šu-nu*

[1-7]Sealed by Dakuna; sealed by Šahiškan; sealed by Zuzu; sealed by Darhašiat; sealed by Nakile'ed, chief of oblates; sealed by Šuhurpiya.

[8-12]Taliya divorced his wife Hašušarna, daughter of Udgariya. [12-15]If Taliya raises a claim against Hašušarna, his wife, [16-17]he shall pay 2 minas of silver, [17-20]or they will put him to death in the countryside. [21-24]If Udgariya and Hašušarna raise a claim against Taliya, [25-27]they shall pay 2 minas of silver, [28-29]or they will put them to death in the *steppe*.

Bibliography: Text published in copy by Thureau-Dangin as TCL 1, 242; edited by Eisser and Lewy (1930, no. 5), and Kienast (2015, no.15). Unopened envelope; the tablet is preserved inside.

Comments: The divorce is decreed, and in case of a claim there is a fine of two minas of silver or the death penalty. The contract is made with the wife and her father, which could suggest that the wife was still young and would return to her father's house.

---

41. The Divorce is Decreed; No Possibility of Claim

Envelope

Obv. [1](seal A) [2]kišib *Dí-ik-šar* dumu *Sà-sú-um* [3]kišib *Ku-lá-ku-lá* [dumu *Ša-r*]*u-a* [4]kišib *Pè-ru-wa* dumu [5]*Kà-ru-<nu>-wa* kišib *Ha-nu* [6]dumu [d]im-*ba-ni* [7](seal B) [8]*Ha-ar-na-šar-na* lo.e. [9](seal A) [10]dumu *Sà-sú-um* rev. [11](seal C) [12]*ù Ha-na-ha-na* [13]*mu-tum ú a-ša-tum* [14]*i-té-zi-bu-ú a-hu-um* [15]*a-na a-hi-im* [16]*lá i-tù-wa-ar* [17]*ša i-tù-ru-ú* [18]5 *ma-na* kù-babbar [19]*i-ša-qal* [20]*ú i-na i-dí-nim* [21]*i-du-ku-šu* u.e. [22](seal D) le.e. [23](seal D) r.e. [24](seal B)

[1-7]Sealed by Dikšar, son of Sāsum; sealed by Kulakula, [son of Šar]ua; sealed by Peruwa, son of Karu<nu>wa; sealed by Hanu, son of Adad-bāni.

[8-14]Harnašarna, son of Sāsum, and Hanahana, husband and wife, divorced. [14-16]One shall not raise a claim against the other. [17-19]The one who raises a claim shall pay 5 minas of silver [20-21]or they will put that one to death in the *steppe*.

Tablet

Obv. [1]*Ha-ar-na-šar-na* [2]*ù Ha-na-ha-na a-ša-tum* [3]*ú mu-tum i-té-zi-bu-ú* [4]*a-hu-um a-na* [5]*a-hi-im* [6]*lá i-tù-ar* [7]*ša i-tù-ru* [8]5 *ma-na* kù-babbar lo.e. [9]*i-ša-qal* rev. [10]*ù i-na i-dí-nim* [11]*i-du-ku-šu* [12]igi *Dí-ik-šar* dumu *Sà-sà-ma* [13]igi *Ku-*

lá-ku-lá dumu *Ša-ru-a* ^{14}igi *Pè-ru-wa* dumu *Kà-ru-nu-wa* ^{15}igi *Ha-nu* dumu ^{d}im-*ba-ni*

$^{1-3}$Harnašarna and Hanahana, wife and husband, divorced. $^{4-6}$One shall not raise a claim against the other. $^{7-9}$The one who raises a claim shall pay 5 minas of silver, $^{10-11}$or they will put that one to death in the *steppe*.

$^{12-15}$In the presence of Dikšar, son of Sasaku; Kulakula, son of Šarua; Peruwa, son of Karunuwa; and Hanu, son of Adad-bāni.

Bibliography: Text published by Matouš (1973), and again by Matouš as KKS, 36.

Comments: The divorce is settled. This contract forbids any claim; the one who raises a claim shall pay a fine of five minas of silver or shall be put to death.

---

42. The Wife Keeps the Furniture and Slaves (Ib: Harpatiwa)

Obv. ^{1}*be-tám* i*$^{!}$*-ga-ra-tim* ^{2}*ra-bi-<a>-tim a-lam* ^{3}*ú tù-zi-nam* ^{4}*[H]u-ta-lá a-Ta-ha* ^{5}*té-zi-ib am-tám* ^{6}*mì-ma : i-be-tim* ^{7}*ib*-ší-ú Hu-ta-lá* ^{8}*tù-šé-ṣí : a-tù-zi*-/nim* ^{9}*lá ṭá-hu-at* ^{10}*šu-ma a-ma-tí-ma* lo.e. ^{11}*Ta-ha* dumu-*ú-šu* rev. ^{12}*lu tù-zi-num* ^{13}*a-Hu-ta-lá ú* dumu-*e-ša* ^{14}*i-tù-ar* «1 *ma-na*»* ^{15}1 *ma-na* kù-babbar *i-da-an ú i-/du-ku*-<šu>* ^{16}*šu-ma Hu-ta-lá* ^{17}[dumu]-*ú-ša a-Ta-ha* ^{18}[*ú*] dumu-*e-šu* «*a-Hu-ta-lá*» ^{19}*i-tù-ar* 1 *ma-na* kù-babbar ^{20}*i-da-an ú i*$^{!}$*-du-ku-/šu* ^{21}*i-qá-tí Ha-ar-pá-tí-wa* u.e. ^{22}igi *Ha-li-kà* ^{23}igi *Šu-pu-nu-ma-/an* le.e. ^{24}igi *Pè-*[x-x igi] *I-na-ar-me-/I*

$^{1-5}$Hutala left to Taha the house (with) the large walls, the village, and the *tuzinnum*-obligation. $^{5-8}$Hutala brought out (of the house) female slave(s) (and) whatever (other goods) there were in the house. $^{8-9}$She is not liable for the *tuzinnum*-obligation.

$^{10-14}$If in future Taha (or) his sons or the *tuzinnum* raise a claim against Hutala and her sons, ^{15}he shall give 1 mina of silver, or they will put him to death. $^{16-19}$If Hutala (or) her sons raises a claim against Taha or his sons, $^{19-20}$she$^{!}$ shall pay 1 mina of silver, or they will put her$^{!}$ to death.

^{21}Under the jurisdiction of Harpatiwa.

$^{22-24}$In the presence of Hali(t)ka, Šuppunuman, Pe[…], and Inar-mei.

Bibliography: Text published by Donbaz (1989, 80–81, 95 [Kt r/k 19]); edited by Dercksen (2004b, 168) and Kienast (2015, no. 16A). Collated May 2010 (no museum inventory number).

Comments: The wife took everything out of the house, including the slaves, gave up her rights to the real estate, and is free from the linked service obligation (*tuzinnum*).

---

43. The Wife Keeps a Slave and Is Exempt from the Service Obligation (Ib: Waršama)

Obv. ^{1}*Hu-ma-da-šu* ^{2}*ú Ha-ha-lu-wa-an* ^{3}*mu-tum ú a-šu-tum* ^{4}*i-tap*-ru-sú ur-dam*$^{!}$ *A-li-li* ^{5}*e*-zi-ib-ta-ša* ^{6} *[i-dí]-ší-ma Ha-ha-lu-an* ^{7} *[a-na a]r-ha-lim** ^{8}*[e-lá-at ...]* (lacuna)
Rev. $^{1'}$*[H]u-ma-da-šu* $^{2'}$*i-tù-ar a-hu-um* $^{3'}$*a-na a*$^{!}$*-hi-im* $^{4'}$*lá i-tù-ar* $^{5'}$*ša i-tù-ru-ni* $^{6'}$5 *ma-na* kù-babbar $^{7'}$*i-da-an [ú] i-du-ku-šu* $^{8'}$*i-qá-tí Wa-ar-šu*$^{!}$*-ma* u.e. $^{9'}$*ru-ba-im [H]al-ki*$_5$*-a-šu* $^{10'}$gal *sí-mì-il*$_5$*-tim* le.e. $^{11'}$igi *I-na-ar* $^{12'}$igi *Šu-hu-ur-[pì-a]* $^{13'}$igi *Pè-ru-[wa]*

$^{1-4}$Humadašu and Hahaluwan, husband and wife, have separated. $^{4-6}$[He gave] her the slave Alili as her divorce compensation, $^{6-8}$and Hahaluwan [is exempt from the *a*]*rhālum*. (lacuna)

$^{1'-2'}$[If in the future the one who] raises a claim against [H]umadašu—$^{2'-4'}$one will not raise a claim against the other— $^{5'-7'}$he who raises a claim shall pay 5 minas of silver, [or] they will put that one to death.

$^{8'-10'}$Under the jurisdiction of King Waršuma (and of) Halkiašu, the chief of the staircase.

$^{11'-13'}$In the presence of Inar, Šuhurpiya, and Peruwa.

Bibliography: Text published in copy by Contenau as TC 1, 122; edited by Eisser and Lewy (1930, no. 3), Balkan (1957, 45–47), Garelli (1963, 68–69, n. 2), Dercksen (2004b, 172–73), and Kienast (2015, no. 25).

Comments: The wife receives a slave as divorce compensation, and she is exempt from the *arhālum* service that was linked to a house or real estate.

44. The Wife Is Exempt from the Service Obligation (Ib: Pithana)

Envelope

Obv. ^{1}kišib *Pè-ru-wa* gudu$_{4}$ *ša* ^{d}i[m] ^{2}*ša qá-qí-dim* kišib *E-lá-ni* [...] ^{3}gal$^{!}$ *na-gi-ri* ^{4}kišib *Šu-*(seal A)**-hu-ur-pì-a* ^{5}gudu$_{4}$ *ša* ^{d}im ^{6}kišib *Ha-du-wa-an ša ṭab*$^{!}$*-tim* ^{7}kišib *Ši-*(seal B)*-li-a-ra* ^{8}[*Ni-ki*]*-li-it* ^{9}[*ú Ša-ša*]*-li-kà* ^{10}[*mu-tu*]*m ú a-šu-tum* ^{11}[*i-tap-ru*]*-sú Ša-*[*ša*]*-li-kà* (end destroyed)

$^{1-2}$Sealed by Peruwa, priest of the Storm-God-of-the-Face, $^{2-3}$sealed by Elani [...], chief of the heralds, $^{4-5}$sealed by Šuhurpiya, priest of the Storm-God, ^{6}sealed by Haduwan, of the salt, ^{7}sealed by Šiliara.

$^{8-11}$Nikilit and Šašalika, husband and wife, have separated. Šašalika (end destroyed)

Tablet

Obv. ^{1}*Ni-ki*$^{!}$*-li-it* ^{2}*ú Ša-ša-li-kà* ^{3}*mu-tum ú a-šu-tum* ^{4}*i-tap-ru-sú* ^{5}*Ša-ša-li-kà* ^{6}*a-na ar-ha-lam* ^{7}*e-lá-at a-šar* ^{8}*li-bi*$_{4}$*-šu i-lá-ak* ^{9}*šu-ma a-ma-tí-ma* ^{10}*lu ú-ba*$^{!}$*-dí-num* x x lo.e. ^{11}*lu ma-ma-an* rev. ^{12}*lu ú-ba-dí-nu* ^{13}*lu* dam-gàr-*šu* ^{14}*ša a-na Ša-ša-li-kà* ^{15}*i-tù-wa-ar* ^{16}5 *ma-na* kù-babbar ^{17}*i-da-an* ^{18}*ú i-du-ku-šu* ^{19}*i-qá-té Pì-it-ha-na* ^{20}*ru-ba-im* lo.e. ^{21}*A-ni-ta* ^{22}gal *sí-mì-il*$_{5}$*-tí* le.e. ^{23}*ar-nu ša : Ni-ki-li-/it*

$^{1-4}$Nikilit and Šašalika, husband and wife, have separated. $^{5-7}$Šašalika is exempt from the *arhālum* service. $^{7-8}$She$^{!}$ may go wherever she$^{!}$ wishes. $^{9-15}$If, in the future, either the *ubadinnum* [...] or anyone else, either the *ubadinnum* or his creditor, raises a claim against Šašalika, $^{16-18}$he shall pay 5 minas of silver, or they will put that one to death.

$^{19-22}$Under the jurisdiction of King Pithana (and of) Anitta, the chief of the staircase. ^{23}The culpability is Nikilit's.

Bibliography: Text published in copy by Lewy as TC 3, 214; edited by Lewy (1938, 123); Garelli (1963, 68–69, n. 2), Dercksen (2004b, 173–74), and Kienast (2015, no. 24).

Comments: This text and the following concern mutual divorce among Anatolians. Here, the wife, Šašalika, is exempt from the *arhālum* service linked to the house, but we do not know who kept the house, husband or wife. This verdict is phrased to concern the husband, Nikilit. The text is badly written.

Line 10: Balkan (1957, 46, n. 72) suggested that the word *ubadinnum* is an error for *tuzinnum*.

Šuhurpiya, priest of the Storm-God, is also attested in Kt 89/k 376:2 (courtesy Kawasaki).

---

45. The Wife Receives Her Divorce Compensation and a Gift (Ib: Zuzu)

Obv. [1]kišib *Pè-ru-wa* dumu *Ku-ur-ku-ri* [2]kišib *Tù-ut-ha-li-a* [3]gal *ša-qí-e* [4]kišib (stamp seal) *Pì-it-ha-na* [5][gal$^{?}$] *qá-qí-dí* [6][kišib] *Kán$^{?}$-ma-li-a* [7][gudu$_4$] (stamp seal) ša ^{d}im [8][kišib] *Ar-šu-lá* [9][kišib *K*]*u-be-a-tal*[10][X-x]-*wa* : *A-wi-a-lá* [11][*mu*]-*tum ú a-šu-tum* [12][*i-tap-r*]*u-sú* [13][*ù*] 6½ gín kù-babbar lo.e. [14][*e*]-*zi-ib-ta-ša* rev. [15][*i*]-*dí-ni$^{!}$-ša* [16][*i*]-*dí-ší-ma* [17][*a*]-*hu-um* [18][*a*]-*na* (stamp seal) *a-hi-im* [19][*l*]*á i-tù-wa-ar* [20]*ša i-tù-ru-ni* [21]10 ma-na (stamp seal) kù-babbar [22]*i-da-an* [23]*ú* i-du-ku-šu* [24][*i*]-*qá-tí Zu-zu* [25]*ru-ba-im* gal [26][*Ištar*]-*ib-ra* [27]gal *sí-mì-il$_5$-tí*

[1]Sealed by Peruwa, son of Kurkuri; [2–3]sealed by Tudhaliya, the chief cupbearer; [4–5]sealed by Pithana, [chief] of …; [6–7][sealed] by Kanmalia, [priest] of the Storm-God; [8–9][sealed] by Aršula; [sealed by K]ūbe-atal.

[10–12][X-x]wa (and) Awiala, [hu]sband and wife, [have] separated, [13–16][and] he gave her 6½ shekels of silver as divorce compensation and her gift. [17–19]One shall not raise a claim against the other. [20–22]The one who raises a claim shall pay 10 minas of silver, [23]or they will put that one to death.

[24–27]Under the jurisdiction of Zuzu, great king, (and of) [Ištar]-ibra, the chief of the staircase.

Bibliography: Text published by Donbaz (1989, 84, 97 [Kt j/k 625]); edited by Kienast (2015, no. 22). Collated May 2010.

Comments: The divorce is decreed, and the wife receives divorce money, and the gift she had been given at her marriage is returned to her. Raising a claim is then prohibited.

---

46. The Wife Receives Her Divorce Compensation

Obv. [1]kišib *Ha-pu-a-*[x-(x)] [2]kišib *Pè-er-wa-áš-x-*[(x)] [3]gudu$_4$ *ša Ku-ba-ba-at* [4]kišib *Tár-hu-šé-et* [5]gudu$_4$ (seal A) *ša I-lá-li-an-ta* [6]ir^{ad}-*Ku-be Mu-a-tí* [7]*mu-*

(seal B)-*tum* [8]*ú a-ša-tum* [9]*i-tap-ru-šu* [10]15 gín kù-babbar rev. [11]*e-zi-ib-ta-ša* [12]*i-dí-ší-ma* [13]*i-tap-ru-šu a-hu-um* [14]*a-na a-hi-im* [15]*lá i-tù-ar* [16]*ša i-tù-ru-ni* [17]5 *ma-na* kù-babbar [18]*i*-(seal C)-*da-an* [19]*ú i-du-ku-šu* [20]*i-qá-tí ru-ba-im* [21]*Zu-zu Ištar-ib-ra* u.e. [22]gal _sí-mì-il$_5$-ti_ [23]_ar-nu ša Dí-iš-tí*-x*_

[1]Sealed by Happua[x-x]; [2–3]sealed by Perwaš-[x-(x)], priest of Kubabat; [4–5]sealed by Tarhušet, priest of Ilalianta.

[6–9]Warad-Kūbi (and) Muati, husband and wife, have separated. [10–12]He paid her 15 shekels of silver as divorce compensation, and [13]they have separated. [13–15]One will not raise claim against the other. [16–18]The one who raises a claim shall pay 5 minas of silver, [19]or they will put that one to death.

[20–22]Under the jurisdiction of King Zuzu (and of) Ištar-ibra, the chief of the staircase.

[23]The culpability is Dišti-[x]'s.

Bibliography: Text published by Donbaz (1989, 83, 97 [Kt k/k 1]); tablet with stamp seals on its surface; edited by Kienast (2015, no. 23). Collated May 2011; the lower edge is not inscribed.

Comments: After the wife has received her divorce compensation, they are officially divorced. Raising a claim is forbidden. It is strange that the verdict names someone other than the husband.

Widowhood and Remarriage

Once divorced, the woman could remarry as she liked; the same applied to her former husband. Several verdicts may be understood this way (**47**, **48**). One even specifies that the divorced woman, Šakriušwe, is free to marry an Assyrian or an Anatolian as she likes (**38**).

The widow's future was generally guaranteed by a testament left by her husband.[26] The eldest son often received a larger inheritance than the other sons, including the main house where his mother lived; in return for that, he had to support her and to pay for the funeral (**49**). Otherwise, the merchant provided for his wife by will: besides a sum of money that she could use as she wished, the widow sometimes inherited the house where

26. Testaments involving women are included in chapter 2, pp. 113–45.

she lived (**54**, **56**). Thus provided with shelter and resources, she was free from want.

A widow, like a divorced woman, could remarry but without disinheriting the children by her first marriage; she nonetheless kept her dowry.[27] Letters and testaments of women give several instances of widows who remarried, some of them Assyrian widows who remarried with Anatolians. For example, the daughter of Imdī-ilum and Ištar-baštī, Zizizi, widow of an Assyrian merchant, Āl-ṭāb, who died in an epidemic, married for the second time an Anatolian from Kaneš. Her father complained in a letter to her of the combined costs of these two marriages, for which he paid the exorbitant sum of ten minas of silver (**50**, **230**). These Assyrian women may well have been attracted by the apparent equality of husband and wife in Anatolian marriages. Anatolian queens reigned together with their husbands, and ordinary women had equal rights with their husbands.

If an Assyrian married to an Anatolian woman died intestate, her situation could be delicate. Normally, when an Assyrian merchant died in Anatolia, his goods and debts were sent back to Aššur, where his heirs paid his debts and then divided his effects.[28] The Anatolian wife in these circumstances had considerable difficulty asserting her rights and those of her children against the estate of her husband, to whom she was only the secondary wife. This befell Kunnaniya, widow of Aššur-mūtappil, son of Pūšu-kēn, who became embroiled in a dispute with her husband's family. Her subsequent efforts, including making the journey to Aššur to defend her interests and those of her daughter, went unrewarded.[29] In the best of circumstances, these women might keep the use of their house, the disposition of which was not always decided at Aššur, and in which the Anatolian wife probably had the right to reside. Several contracts for the sale of real estate at Kaneš refer to the presence of a woman, generally a widow, allowed to reside there for life (**51**, **52**). Kunnaniya had a house at her disposal, which she leased out; but, after her husband's death, she lost that income because the rent devolved to a nephew of her husband (**310**). She further lost ownership of the house she lived in and for which her in-laws demanded that she pay rent (**312**).

27. Stol 2016, 288–90.

28. Michel 1994, 2008c; Veenhof 1997b.

29. Michel 1997e; 2001a, 493–99. See also chapter 6, texts **299–312**.

47. Compromise after a Divorce: Husband and Wife Are Free to Remarry

Envelope

Obv. $^{1'}$(seal) $^{2'}$[*ú*] *Hu-na* : *a-na mu-tí* : *li*-[*bi*$_{4}$-*ša*] $^{3'}$*ta-lá-ak* : *mì-ma* : *tù-šé-r*[*i-bu*] $^{4'}$*tù-šé-ṣí lu ú-nu-tám lu* 16½ gín [kù-babbar] $^{5'}$*ša a-na nu-a-im* : *iš-qú-lu* $^{6'}$2 gín kù-babbar : [*ú-r*]*a-dí-ší-ma* [*lu* dub] $^{7'}$*ša hu-bu-ul a-bi-ša* : *ta*-[*al-qé*] $^{8'}$*lu mì-ma a-bu-ša* : *šál-ṭám h*[*a-bu-lu*] $^{9'}$*kà**-*bu**-*ús**-*ma** *mì**-*ma** *a**-*nim** [*a-na*]* $^{10'}$*e-zi-ib-tí*-[*š*]*a* : *a-na H*[*u-na*] $^{11'}$*ú um-mì-ša* [*Puzur*$_{4}$]-*Ištar* [*i-dí-in*] $^{12'}$*a-na* [...]

$^{1'-3'}$[... and] Huna will go to the husband of [her choi]ce. $^{3'-4'}$Whatever she brou[ght] into (the house), she has taken out: $^{4'-5'}$both the goods, and the 16½ shekels of [silver] that he had paid to the Anatolian creditor. $^{6'}$[He ad]ded for her 2 shekels of silver, and $^{6'-9'}$ she [took] her father's debt [note] and, as well, whatever cash he owed (to her husband) was forgiven; $^{9'-11'}$all this [Puzur-Ištar gave] to H[una] and her mother [as he]r divorce compensation. $^{12'}$For [...]

Tablet

Obv. ^{1}*Puzur*$_{4}$-*Ištar ú Hu-na* ^{2}*a-ša-sú* dumu-munus *Pí-la-ah**-*a-a** ^{3}*ú A-la-a-a-ga-a* : *um-ma-áš-nu* ^{4}*iṣ-bu-tù-ni-a-tí-ma* : *ni-iš* ^{5}*A-lim*^{ki} *ú ru-ba-im* : *it-mu-ú-/ma* ^{6}*Puzur*$_{4}$-*Ištar a-ša-at* ^{7}*li-bi*$_{4}$-*šu* : *e-ha-az* ^{8}*ú Hu-na* : *a-na mu-tí* ^{9}*li-bi*$_{4}$-*ša* : *ta-lá-ak* ^{10}*mì-ma tù-šé-ri-bu* ^{11}*tù-šé-ṣí* : *lu ú-nu-tám* ^{12}*lu* 16½ gín kù-babbar ^{13}*ša a-na nu-a-im iš-qú-lu* lo.e. ^{14}2 gín kù-babbar : *ú-ra-dí-ší-ma* rev. ^{15}*lu ṭup-pá-am ša hu-bu-ul* ^{16}*a-bi-ša*$^{!}$*(ŠU) : *ta-al-qé* ^{17}*lu mì-ma a-bu-ša* : *šál-ṭám* ^{18}*ha-bu-lu* : *kà-bu-ús-ma* ^{19}*mì-ma a-ni-im* : *a-na e-zi-ib-tí-/ša* ^{20}*Puzur*$_{4}$-*Ištar a-na Hu-na* ^{21}*ú um-mì-ša* : *i-dí-in* ^{22}*a-na mì-ma šu-um-šu* : *a-na* ^{23}*Puzur*$_{4}$-*Ištar lá i-tù-ru* ^{24}*ú Puzur*$_{4}$-*Ištar* <*šu-nu-tí*> ^{25}*a-na mì-ma šu-um-šu ú-lá* ^{26}*i-tù-ar-šu-nu-tí* ^{27}igi *A-šùr-i-mì-tí* ^{28}igi *Ma-nu-ki-A-šùr* u.e. ^{29}igi *En-um-A-šùr* le.e. ^{30}igi *Šu-be-lim* igi *Tù-ta-a*

$^{1-4}$Puzur-Ištar and Huna, his wife, daughter of Pilahaya, and Alayaga, their mother, seized us (as arbitrators), and $^{4-5}$they swore the oath by the city (of Aššur) and the king concerning the fact that $^{6-7}$Puzur-Ištar will marry the wife of his choice, $^{8-9}$and Huna will go to the husband of her choice. $^{10-11}$Whatever she brought into (the house), she has taken out: $^{11-13}$both the goods and the 16½ shekels of silver that he had paid to the Anatolian creditor. ^{14}He added for her 2 shekels of silver, and $^{15-18}$she took her father's debt note, and as well, whatever cash he owed (to her husband) was forgiven; [19–21]all this Puzur-Ištar gave to Huna and her mother as divorce compensation. [22–23]They shall not raise a claim against Puzur-Ištar for anything whatsoever, [24–26]and neither shall Puzur-Ištar raise a claim against them for anything whatsoever.

[27–30]In the presence of Aššur-imittī, Mannum-kī-Aššur, Ennum-Aššur, Šu-Bēlum, and Tutaya.

Bibliography: Text published by Veenhof (1997a, 373 [tablet: Kt 91/k 158; envelope: Kt 91/k 240]); edited by Kienast (2015, no. 29A). Collated May 2012; line 9′ of the envelope was omitted by the editor.

Comments: This text is an arrangement worked out by the persons seized as mediators by the parties to settle the financial consequences of divorce between an Assyrian man and his Anatolian wife living with the woman's mother. Huna is allowed to leave with all the assets and goods she brought, and her deceased father's debts are canceled. Both husband and wife may remarry as they wish.

---

48. Possibility of Remarriage after a Divorce

Obv. [1]*kà-ru-um Kà-ni-iš* [2]tur gal *dí-nam* [3]*i-dí-in-ma* [4]*Hu-na-na-a* [5]*A-li-na* [6]*me-er-a-sà-*[*a*] [7]dam *A-šur-ma-lik* [8]*u*$_4$*-ma-ma* lo.e. [9]*a-na mu-ut* rev. [10]*li-bi*$_4$*-ša* [11]*ta-da-an* (the rest of the tablet is not inscribed)

[1–3]The *kārum* of Kaneš, (the whole assembly) small and big, gave a verdict according to which [4–11]from this day, Hunanaya may give Alina, her daughter, (ex)-wife of Aššur-malik, to the husband of her choice.

Bibliography: Tablet published by Bayram and Çeçen (1995, 12); edited by Kienast (2015, no. 32). The excavation inventory number of the text given there, Kt 78/k 176, in the Museum of Anatolian Civilizations (Ankara), is assigned to a transport contract.

Comments: From this verdict, we guess that, the promise of marriage being not honored, the bride's mother is free to marry her daughter according to her wish. It is also possible that this legal document refers to a divorce.

49. Sons to Take Care of Their Mother

Obv. ^{1}kišib *Ni-mar-Ištar* dumu *Ba-la*$_{1}$ ^{2}(seal A) ^{3}kišib *En-um-A-šur* dumu ^{4}*I-dí-Sú-en*$_{6}$ kišib *En-um-A-šur* ^{5}dumu *E-lá-ma* ^{6}(seal B) ^{7}[*I-dí-Išta*]*r ù* ^{d}nin-šubur-*ba-ni* lo.e. ^{8}[*i-mì*]-*ig-ru-ma* ^{9}(seal B) rev. ^{10}(seal C) ^{11}é^{tù} *ša Kà-ni-iš* ^{12}*ù ú-ṭù-up-tum ša I-dí-Ištar* ^{13d}nin-šubur-*ba-ni lá ṭá-hu a-na* ^{14}*hu-bu-ul a-bi-šu-nu ki-la-la-šu-nu-ma* ^{15}*i-za-zu a-na qú-bu-ur Pu-zu-ur* ^{16}*um-mì-šu-nu* ^{17}(seal D) ^{18}*a-na gam-ri-im ù hu-bu-ul* ^{19}*Pu-zu-ur um-mì-šu-nu* u.e. ^{20}(seal A) ^{21}*I-dí-Ištar-ma i-za-az* le.e. ^{22}*i-nu-mì ša i-na A-l*[*im*^{ki}] ^{23}*i-za-ku-ú-ni* é^{tù} ^{24}*ša Kà-ni-iš lá i-ša-ku-nu*

$^{1-6}$Sealed by Nimar-Ištar, son of Bala; sealed by Ennum-Aššur, son of Iddin-Suen; sealed by Ennum-Aššur, son of Elamma.

$^{7-8}$[Iddin-Išta]r and Ilabrat-bāni reached (the following) agreement:

$^{10-12}$The house in Kaneš and the furniture belong to Iddin-Ištar. ^{13}Ilabrat-bāni shall not approach (them). $^{13-15}$Both are mutually responsible for their father's debt. $^{15-21}$For the burial of Puzur, their mother, for expenses, and for the debt of their mother, Puzur, Iddin-Ištar alone is responsible. $^{22-24}$When the property in the c[ity (of Aššur)] is cleared (for distribution), they shall not include the house in Kaneš.

Bibliography: Unopened case edited first by Veenhof (1997a, 141–42), then as AKT 8, 297 (Kt 91/k 389). Collated May 2012.

Comments: After the father's death, the two sons inherit. The eldest son inherits the house in Kaneš together with its belongings, and he must take care of his mother as long as she lives, assume responsibility for her expenses and debts, and pay for her burial. The definitive division must take place in Aššur.

50. The Cost of a Remarriage

Obv. ^{1}[*um-ma Im-dí*]-*lúm-ma* ^{2}[*ù Ištar-ba*]-*áš-tí-ma* ^{3}[*a-na Zi-z*]*i-zi qí-bi-ma* ^{4}*u*[*m-mì-ki*] *ù a-bu-ki* ^{5}*ú-*[*lá*] : [*t*]*í-de*$_{8}$*-i* : *i-nu-mì* ^{6}*a-na mu-tim* : *A-al-*du$_{10}$ ^{7}*a-dí-nu-ki-ni* : 5 *ma-na* kù-babbar ^{8}*ag-mur* : *ù iš-tù A-al-*du$_{10}$ ^{9}*mu-ut-ki* : *i-mu-tù-ú-/ni* ^{10}[*n*]*u-a-um* : *e-hu-uz-ki-ma* ^{11}[5] *ma-na-ma* kù-babbar : *a-na* ^{12}[*šu-mì a-ha-z*]*i-ki* ^{13}[*ag-mu-ur-ma* x x *á*]*š*$^{?}$*-a-am* ^{14}[…-*u*]*m* (lacuna)

Rev. $^{1'}$[…] x […] $^{2'}$[…] *lá-a a-*[*ma* : *a-na-ku*] $^{3'}$[*ù*] *me-er-ú-a* : *i-na* $^{4'}$*e-né-ki* : *ú-lá kà-ab-tá-/ni* $^{5'}$*šu-ma-me-en* : *a-na-ku* $^{6'}$*ù me-er-ú-a* : *i-na* $^{7'}$*e-né-ki*$^{!}$(KÀ) :

kà-ab-tá-ni 8′*ù a-na-ku : ki-ma* 9′*me-er-ú-a-tim ú-kà-bi-/it-ki-me-en* 10′*iš-tù* 11′*a-na A-lim*^{ki} *a-li-kà-ni* 12′*i-bi-sà-i : a-mur-ma* 13′*šu-mì : ú-lá ta-az-ku-ri* 14′[d]am : *E-na-ma-nim : i-na* 15′[é^{t}]^{i}*-a : mì-nam tal-qí-ma* 16′[*ki-iš-d*]*a-tù-ša ù mu-t*[*ù*-x] 17′[x x x *w*]*e-du-um ú-q*[*á*] 18′[x x x x x x]-*iš-té-nu-ma* le.e. 19′[x x *a*]-*wi-lim tal-*[*x x a-na lá*] 20′[*a-wi-li*]-*im-ma Ištar-ba-*[*áš-tí* x x *a-lá*] 21′[*a-wi-lim*] *i-na* igi : *ì-lí a-bi*$_4$*-ku*$^!$*-n*[*u*] 22′[*lá*] *ta-ša-ki-ni-ni : ta-t*[*a-lá-ak*]

1–3 [Thus (say) Imdī-i]lum [and Ištar-b]āštī: say [to Ziz]izi.

4–5 [Don't you] know [your] m[other] and your father?

5–7 When I gave you as spouse to Āl-ṭāb, 7–8 I spent 5 minas of silver. 8–9 And after Āl-ṭāb, your husband, died, 10 an Anatolian married you, and 11–13 [I spent 5] more minas of silver for your [marriage, and …] I bought […] (lacuna)

2′–4′ [I and] my sons, we are not important in your eyes. 5′–7′ If I and my sons had been important in your eyes, 8′–9′ then I myself would have honored you like a daughter.

10′–11′ Since I left for the city (of Aššur), 12′ I have suffered losses, 13′ but you did not invoke my name anymore. 14′–15′ What did the [w]ife of Ennam-Anum take from my [house]? And 16′–17′ her [acqui]sitions and […] I am waiting [a]lone […] 18′–21′ man [… not (acting) as a gentlem]an, and Ištar-bā]štī […] 21′–22′ Before god, you do [not] treat me, yo[ur] father, (like) [a gentleman]! You have l[eft] (the family)!

Bibliography: Text published in copy by Veenhof as VS 26, 33; edited by Michel (2001a, no. 355), Kryszat (2007a, 213–15), and Kienast (2015, no. 48).

Comments: Zizizi is the daughter of Imdī-ilum and Ištar-baštī. An epidemic killed first her sister, Šiduna, then her husband, Āl-ṭāb (**230**). The cost of each of her marriages amounted to five minas, not including her dowry, which a widow could keep with her.

---

51. A Widow Is Allowed to Remain in a House Now Belonging to Someone Else

Obv. 1 *Mu-sà* dumu-munus dingir-*ìš-tí-kál* 2 *a-ša-at I-lá-áb-ra-at-ba-/ni* 3 *i-na* é$^{be-ti}$ *ša A-šur-ma-/lik* 4 dumu *Puzur*$_2$*-Ištar a-dí* 5 *ba-al-ṭá-at-ni* 6 *tù-ša-áb i-na* é^{tim} 7 *ša A-šur-ma-lik-ma* 8 *ta-ša-bi*$_4$*-ir A-šur-ma-lik* 9 *ù me-er-ú-šu lá i-ṭá-ru-/du-ší* 10 é^{tám} 6 *gu*$_5$*-šu-ri* 11 *da-lá-tim ù-ṭù-up-/tám* 12 *lá ta-da-an* 13 *ú-lá tù-ra-áb* lo.e. ^{14}igi (blank) rev. ^{15}igi *A-ta-a* ^{16}igi *I-dí-A-šur* ^{17}igi *A-mur-A-šur* ^{18}igi *Ma-ṣí-ì-lí*

$^{1-6}$Musa, daughter of Iliš-tikal, wife of Ilabrat-bāni, may live in the house belonging to Aššur-malik, son of Puzur-Ištar, as long as she lives. $^{6-8}$(If,) in the house belonging to Aššur-malik, she becomes disabled, $^{8-9}$Aššur-malik and his sons shall not expel her. $^{10-13}$She shall neither sell nor pledge the house, six beams, doors, and the furniture.

$^{14-18}$In the presence of (blank), Ataya, Iddin-Aššur, Amur-Aššur, and Maṣi-ilī.

Bibliography: Text published by Donbaz as Sadberk 28; cited by Veenhof (1997b, 143–44; 2017b).

Comments: The house in which Musa, widow of Ilabrat-bāni, is living, has changed ownership. This contract guarantees her right to live in this house during the rest of her life.

---

52. A Woman Has the Right to Live in Someone's House or to Be Compensated

Envelope

Obv. ^{1}(seal A) ^{2}[kišib *A*]*-ba-ba* dumu dingir*-[…] ^{3}kišib *A-šùr-ma-lik* [dumu…] ^{4}kišib *I-ku-*[*pí-A-šùr* dumu…] ^{5}*a-na* 2 [*ma-na* kù-babbar] ^{6}é *A-ba-ba* [*I-ku-pí-a*] ^{7}(seal B) ^{8}*iš-a-am lu* [*ú-ṭù-up-tù-um*] lo.e. ^{9}*lu ku-s*[*í-u*]*m* rev. ^{10}*lu pá-šu-ru-u*[*m mì-ma*] ^{11}[*šu-um-šu*] *ú-*[*la ú-šé-ṣa*] u.e. ^{12}[*Ga-mu-*x-(x) *ma*]*-ma*$^{?}$*-a*[*n*] ^{13}[*la i-ṭá*]*-ra-sí* [kù-babbar 1 *ma-na*] le.e. ^{14}*i-ša-qal-ší-im-ma*

$^{1-4}$Sealed by Ababa, son of […]; sealed by Aššur-malik, [son of …]; sealed by Ikuppī-[Aššur, son of …].

$^{5-8}$[Ikuppiya] has bought the house of Ababa for 2 [minas of silver]. $^{8-11}$Neither [the furniture], nor a ch[ai]r, nor a tabl[e, (nor) anything else shall be *taken out*.… $^{12-14}$[Nob]ody shall [ex]pel [Gamu-x-(x)], (or) he shall pay her [1 mina of silver,] and [*she shall then leave the house*].

Tablet

Obv. ^{1}*a-na* 2 *ma-na* kù-babbar ^{2}é : *A-ba-ba* ^{3}*I-ku-pí-a* ^{4}*iš-a-am* : *lu ú-ṭù-*[*up-tù-um*] ^{5}*lu ku-sí-um* ^{6}*lu pá-šu-ru-um* ^{7}*mì-ma šu-um-šu* ^{8}*ú-la ú-*[*šé-ṣa*] ^{9}é$^{\textit{bé-tù}}$ ^{10}é *I-ku-*[*pí-a*] lo.e. ^{11}*a-dí ba-al-*[*ṭá-at-ni*] rev. ^{12}*Ga-mu-*[…] ^{13}*tù-ša-ab* ^{14}*ma-*

ma-an ^{15}*la i-ṭá-ra-sí* ^{16}*a-dí ba-*[*al*]*-ṭá-at-/*[*ni*] ^{17}[é^{tù}] é$^{bé-}$[*sà*$^{!}$] ^{18}*šu-*[*ma iš-t*]*ù-mu-ùh-ma* ^{19}[*i-ṭ*]*á-ra-sí* kù-babbar ^{20}1 *ma-na* : *i-ša-qal-ší-im-ma* ^{21}*tù-ṣí* ^{22}igi *A-šùr-ma-lik* ^{23}igi *I-ku-pí-A-šùr*

$^{1-4}$Ikuppiya has bought the house of Ababa for 2 minas of silver. $^{4-8}$Neither furniture, nor a chair, nor a table, (nor) anything else shall be [*taken out*]. $^{9-10}$The house is Iku[ppiya]'s house. $^{11-13}$As long as [she] li[ves], Gamu-[x-x] shall inhabit (it); $^{14-15}$nobody shall expel her. $^{16-17}$As long as she lives, [the house] is [he]rs. $^{18-19}$I[f he b]reaks the agreement and [e]xpels her, $^{19-20}$he shall pay her 1 mina of silver, and ^{21}she shall leave (the house).

$^{22-23}$In the presence of Aššur-malik and Ikuppī-Aššur.

Bibliography: Text edited by Bayram and Veenhof (1992, 98 [Kt a/k 1255]). Collated May 2010.

Comments: Gamu-[x-x] is not explicitly said to be a widow, but she is probably an elderly woman. She must have lived in the house, with permission of Ababa—probably a relative—and when the latter sold it, he stipulated that Gamu[x-x] was entitled to live in the furnished house.

---

53. Sons to Take Care of Their Widowed Parents in an Anatolian Family (Ib)

^{1}kišib *Wa-*[x-x-x-x] ^{2}*ša* mun$^{?}$ [kišib x x x] ^{3}dumu *Ba-a*[*r-*x x x] ^{4}dumu *Wa-ší-nu-m*[*a-an*] ^{5}*Tù-ut-ha-li-*[*a*] ^{6}*ú A-*(seal A)*-na-na* (seal A) *a-bu-*[*um*] ^{7}*um-mu-um Zu-ru* ^{8}*A-ta-ta ú I-na-ar* ^{9}3 *at-hu-ú be-tám* ^{10}*pu-hu-ur uš-bu* ^{11}*a-be-tim iš-té-en*$_{6}$ ^{12}*ú-kà-šu-ú ú šu-ma ma-ma-an* ^{13}*i-ba-ri-*[*šu-nu*] *i-ṣé-er* lo.e. ^{14}*a-bi*$_{4}$*-im um-mì-im* ^{15}*i-ša-lá mì-ma* rev. ^{16}*ú-pá-za-ar* 10 *ma-na* kù-babbar ^{17}*i-ša-qal-ma šu-ma A-na-na* ^{18}*um-*(seal B)*-ma-šu-nu i-mu-a-at* ^{19}*ú* 3 *at-hu-*(seal B)*-ú* ^{20}*Tù-ut-ha-li-a* <*a*>*-bu-šu-nu* ^{21}*i-na-ṣú-ru-ú šu-ma* ^{22}*Tù-ut-ha-li-a i-mu-at* ^{23}3 *at-hu-ú A-na-na um-ma-šu-nu* ^{24}*i-na-ṣú-ru i-nu-mì* ^{25}*a-bu-um um-mu-um* ^{26}*i-mu-tù-ni* 3 *at-hu-*[*ú*] ^{27}*i-zu-uz-zu* [x x x] ^{28}*ša ur-d*[*im* x x x] ^{29}*be-tám* [x x x x] u.e. ^{30}*zi-tám* [x x x x] ^{31}*a-bi-šu-*[*nu* x x x] ^{32}*i-da-*[*gal* x x] le.e. ^{33}*ar-ha-lam ša na-ṣir* ^{34}*a-lim ú-kà-lu i-qá-at Zu-zu* ^{35}*ru-ba-im Ištar-ib-ra* gal *sí-mì-il*$_{5}$*-tí*

$^{1-4}$Sealed by Wa-[x x x x], of the salt (?); [sealed by X x x], son of Ba[r x x x], son of Wašinuman.

[5–7]Tudhaliya and Anna-anna are father (and) mother; [8–9]Zuru, Atata, and Inar are three brothers. [9–10]They shall live together in one single house. [11–12]They will profit from this one house. [12–15]If anyone among them does harm to (his) father (and) mother, [15–16]conceals anything, [16–17]he shall pay 10 minas of silver. [17–18]If Anna-anna, their mother, dies, [19–21]the three brothers shall take care of their father, Tudhaliya. [21–24]And if Tudhaliya dies, the three brothers shall take care of their mother, Anna-anna. [24–26]When father (and) mother (both) have died, [26–27]the three brothers will divide (the inheritance). [27–32]… the house … the share … their father … he will own. [33–34]The … the *arhālum* of the protector of the city they will hold (together). [34–35]Authorized by King Zuzu and by Ištar-ibra, chief of the stairway.

Bibliography: Text published by Donbaz (1993, 140–41; 153, pl. 28, 2a–b [Kt 89/k 370]); translated by Veenhof (1997b, 146–47), Dercksen (2004b, 170). Hecker 2004b, 57. Sealings studied by Nimet Özgüç (1996, 272).

Comments: An Anatolian couple is dwelling together with their three sons in a house. When both parents die, the sons will divide the property and share the services due to the Anatolian authorities.

2
Women and Family

A woman's status within her family was long seen as secondary, but this has changed markedly in recent years. Understanding family in the ancient Near East requires setting aside presuppositions about patriarchal societies, according to which women were always dominated by men. Although the husband's family was the locus of identity and oversaw the inheritance of real property and maintenance of the family ancestor cult, the woman's influence at home was by no means inconsiderable, in the first instance through the bearing of children. True, if the father's name was often carried on by one of his grandsons, typically the eldest, nothing similar was done for the mother's name. Yet every woman who became a mother was honored because producing a child, especially a son, assured the couple of an heir to the family patrimony, support when they were elderly, and even an existence beyond death through the ancestor cult.[1] Depending on the period and circumstances, certain women seem to have enjoyed considerable independence in family life, and this is indeed the case with the wives and daughters of the Assyrian merchants at Aššur and Kaneš.[2] This chapter takes up more specifically the place of women in their families from a legal standpoint, through inheritance, and in loans. It considers as well the status of the female slave.

The internal structures of the great Assyrian merchant families cannot be reconstructed in detail because their archives were kept at Aššur in the paternal homestead (*bēt abim*) and have not been discovered.[3] The Kaneš

1. For references to ancestor worship in the Old Assyrian Sources, see Michel 2008f; Veenhof 1982b; 1997b, 141–45 (Kt 91/k 389); 2014.

2. For the Late Bronze Age, see, for example, Justel 2008, 2014, and 2018.

3. We do not know much about the *bēt abim*, "the house of the father," where ancestors were buried; see Larsen 2007 and Veenhof 2014. Hertel 2015 interpretated the expression *bēt abim* as the paternal estate. In this volume, *bēt abim* is translated

documentation includes letters from the members of the family living at Aššur, especially the wives and female relatives of merchants who had gone off to live in Anatolia. This is especially true of the first two generations of Assyrians residing at Kaneš. After that, entire Assyrian families either moved to or were created in Anatolia, at Kaneš, where their archives were found, or in other Assyrian commercial settlements. In these, therefore, are found, among other documents, various types of family records, such as marriage and divorce contracts and wills. These families still had some relatives at Aššur, perhaps parents, grandparents, or relatives, or an eldest daughter consecrated to the city god.

The conventional, recognized status of the adult woman was as a wife. She was in all respects the legal equal of her husband in marriage (see chapter 1). Daughters received a dowry when they married, made up of a sum of money and household goods. They left home when they married.[4] If the father had died before being able to marry off his daughter, his sons were supposed to arrange for and finance their sister's marriage from their shares of the inheritance (**9**, **10**). Sometimes daughters of merchants inherited equally with their brothers, especially eldest daughters who had been consecrated to a deity and remained unmarried. They could inherit a sum of money, sometimes in the form of loan documents, and could also receive an annuity and even the paternal cylinder seal, a privilege normally reserved for sons.[5]

Assyrian women enjoyed some particularly favorable legal protections. Unlike sons, daughters inherited only assets, such as obligations due the family, and were not held responsible for debts left by their deceased fathers.[6] Among Anatolians, by contrast, collective family responsibility often forced wives and daughters of merchants into debt slavery to the creditors of their husbands and fathers. Assyrian and Anatolian women could sometimes borrow small amounts of money or grain to pay house-

---

literally as the "father's house." In fact, it can refer to various realities, from the building itself to the "family" over three generations.

4. The daughters of Aššur-nādā decided to leave their grandfather, who was in charge of their education. In a letter sent to his son, Aššur-idī complained: "I have also raised your daughters, but they said: 'You are not our father.' Three days later, they got up and left to go to you" (CCT 3, 6b:27–32, translated by Michel 2001a, no. 254, and Larsen 2002, no. 22).

5. Michel 2009c.

6. Michel 2003b.

hold expenses, though if they lacked the means to repay, they, too, could go into their creditors' service in debt bondage.

Slavery at Aššur and Kaneš has been recently analyzed, but studies focused on the male terms.[7] Assyrian society distinguished a citizen with full legal rights (*awīlum*, dumu *Aššur*) from a slave. The term for male slave, *wardum*, poses no problem, but the word *amtum* for female slave is sometime ambiguous because it can also be translated "secondary wife."[8] In Anatolia, there was a third social class in that dependents of the palace and important officials were distinguished from the rest of the population, made up mostly of farmers with small holdings (*hupšum*). A substantial number of Anatolian slaves in Kaneš were no doubt men and women who had become slaves through debt. The sale of slaves was overseen by the local ruler or his representative.[9]

Most Assyrian households in Aššur and Kaneš had slaves. These could be acquired by inheritance, unpaid debts, or purchase. Slaves had various duties. Women kept house, made meals, minded children, and most likely wove textiles for export, whereas men could work in a business capacity like transporting goods or accompanying caravans.[10] Not uncommonly, young merchants had their sexual initiation with household slave women.

Women and Inheritance

According to Mesopotamian law, when one parent died, his sons inherited his or her property, including real estate, cash assets, slaves, and belongings.[11] If the mother died first, they divided her dowry; if the father, they inherited his estate but with the obligation to support their mother. Beyond

7. Larsen 2017; de Ridder 2017b.

8. Slaves could also appear under the general designation *subrum* (Larsen 2017, 291; de Ridder 2017b, 52–54). There is one mention of a palace slave named Asqudum, *Ás-qú-dim* ìr *ša* é-gal^{lim} (KTS 1, 55b:2–3), see Michel 2012. The words *ṣuhārum* and *ṣuhārtum* could also be used as male and female slave but not exclusively. They also referred to a young employee or to a young woman; see Larsen 2017, 295–98, and de Ridder 2017b, 54–55. On the "secondary wife," see chapter 1, pp. 68–85.

9. For Anatolian society, see Dercksen 2004b and Michel 2011c. Note the existence of a chief slave, *rabi urdē*, named Hudarlani in KKS 57:1 and Kuwatar in the Level Ib text Kt n/k 32:5.

10. Then, their owner would receive the *tadmiqum*-trust as wages; for example, ICK 1, 10:11–15.

11. For an inventory of goods left by a merchant to his heirs, see, for example,

these general rules of inheritance, Assyrian merchants drew up wills that could demonstrate their concern for protecting the financial interests of all the women in their families.[12] Most Assyrian merchants may have written wills, as the lack of one could leave the heirs in an awkward situation: "Alas! Elālī has died without drawing up his will!"[13] Many of these wills were likely at Aššur in the primary residences of Assyrian families, but some, and perhaps also duplicates, have been found at Kaneš. The goods left by merchants consisted of one or more pieces of real estate, notes of debts due to them, cash assets in silver or gold, utensils and objects of bronze, male and female slaves, and their personal cylinder seal. Assyrian merchants did not own arable land or vineyards, so such properties are not mentioned in the wills found at Kaneš.

According to Assyrian wills (*šīmtum*), divisions of the paternal estate in the presence of executors of the will (*bēl šīmātim*), and court verdicts pertaining to a disputed inheritance, the widow's support was provided for, either by a share in the estate or by the children. Even if there was no hard and fast rule, custom could bestow a larger share of the inheritance on the eldest son, who often got the family home where his mother lived but had to support her. Wills give the impression that their main intent was to provide for the support of women after the testator's demise, be it a wife (**54**, **55**, **56**), sister (**57**), or a consecrated daughter who had remained in the family unmarried (**56**). The will drawn up by Agūa shows this intent clearly: he provided in the first instance for his wife, who received his assets and the use of the house she was living in at Aššur; next his daughter, who inherited gold, silver, and a servant (**54**). By constituting his wife "father and mother" (*abat u ummat*) over the silver that she received, Agūa granted her full ownership. She could use her silver as she wished, on the condition that it remained in the family so that, at her death, the eldest son would inherit it, along with the family home in Aššur (**55**).

Prag I, 705: a house located in Kaneš, slaves, and household goods, including containers, tables, forks, knives, bowls, and hides.

12. Von Soden 1976; Wilcke 1976; Veenhof 1997b, 2012a; Michel 1997g, 2000b; Albayrak 2000, 2010; Hecker 2004a; Veenhof 2008b; de Ridder 2017a.

13. BIN 6:2: [3]*E-lá-lí me-et* [4]*ší-im-tù-šu ú-lá* [5]*i-ší-im*. See also the letter AKT 6d, 765, sent by a woman announcing the death of the father's sister of her correspondent and warning him that the brothers intend to take away the house—presumably the family house—since there is no heir.

The peculiar status of "father and mother" anticipates expressions used in certain legal documents from Emar and Nuzi, dating to the fourteenth century BCE, in which wives and daughters were given, in a written document, masculine gender, according them rights normally reserved to men. Thus legal gender trumped biological sex.[14] The progressiveness of family law in Aššur is in striking contrast to the conservatism of contemporaneous Babylonia, where wills are practically unknown. Numerous Old Babylonian divisions of inheritances according to different regional traditions would seem to suggest that dispositions by will were made only in exceptional cases.[15] By contrast, the numerous wills found at Nuzi and especially Emar would seem to indicate the absence of specific rules of inheritance; the same is true of the Assyrian archives at Kaneš. Drawing up of wills with a view to providing for inheritance by women shows clearly that women enjoyed important socioeconomic status, and the numerous letters found at Kaneš sent to and by women serve to reinforce this impression.

A father's provision for his succession was not always carried out. One set of documents reveals a dispute between two brothers after their father's death (**64**, **65**). Amur-Šamaš took care of his father during the last months of his life in Asia Minor. According to his brother, Ikūnum, who refused to hand over to him money to pay for their father's funeral, Amur-Šamaš kept for himself the entire estate, as well as their father's cylinder seal, wronging his siblings, including their consecrated sister.[16] Amur-Šamaš conceded only that he had received from their father, before he died, a lapis-lazuli seal intended for their sister. Three years later, the dispute was still not settled.

When their mother died, the children naturally inherited her goods. Certain widows deemed it worthwhile to draw up their own wills to distribute their belongings as they wanted, but that portion of their goods which properly belonged to them and that which was inherited from their husbands was not always specified.[17] Lamassatum, widow of Elamma, whose archives were found in 1991, made a list of her goods which, after

14. Michel 2000b; Justel 2008, 156–67; Lion 2009a; Veenhof 2012a, 185 n. 35; Justel 2018, with previous literature.

15. Westbrook 2001, 395–99, with previous literature.

16. Hecker 2004a.

17. The Elamma archives, discovered in 1991, included two texts related to wills of widows: **61** and AKT 8, 179; for the second text, see also Veenhof 1997b, 137. For

her death, were to be taken to Aššur and divided among her consecrated daughter and her sons (**61**). This inventory includes valuable dishes, jewelry, money from votive offerings, debt notes in her favor, merchandise, and slaves. A group of a dozen texts found in the same house is concerned with the funeral and legacies of Ištar-lamassī, widow in the first instance of the Assyrian Kūn-ilum, with whom she had three children, and in the second of the Anatolian Lulu.[18] One document specifies the share she intended to go to her two sons and to her consecrated daughter, Šīmat-Ištar, who was supposed to receive gold, silver, and a cylinder seal.[19] But part of the legacy ended up being used to pay off debts of the deceased husband and to pay the funeral expenses for her mother and her two sons, both of whom died not long after her. Thus Šīmat-Ištar was left as the sole residuary legatee. While the primary purpose of men's wills is to protect women's rights, starting with their wives, the situation is not symmetrical. The only two wills of women known to date are from widows, so husbands are not present.[20]

The status of daughters mentioned in Old Assyrian wills and who inherited portions of their fathers' estates was not always specified. They seem as a rule to have been unmarried, and it is most likely that in every case they were consecrated daughters, even if not all documents state that (**54**). When they themselves had no heirs, the paternal family apparently received their goods when they died.

Most of the wills found at Kaneš belonged to Assyrian families. According to a marriage contract between Anatolians, man and wife were

---

Emar, see, for example, the following texts: Arnaud 1986, nos. 30, 32, and 69; and for Nuzi: HSS 5, 74.

18. This dossier is studied by Veenhof 2008b, where texts are classified in the following order: AKT 8, 179 (Kt 91/k 453): will of Ištar-lamassī; **59**: letter from Lamassatum to family members among Šīmat-Ištar, who lives in Aššur; AKT 8, 181 (Kt 91/k 425): draft of a letter sent to Šīmat-Ištar; AKT 8, 182 (Kt 91/k 438): contract dealing with gold and silver left by Ištar-lamassī to Lamassatum and entrusted to Ennma-Aššur and Šumi-abiya; AKT 8, 183 (Kt 91/k 413): contract explaining that gold and silver were entrusted to Ennum-ilī in order to be sent to Šīmat-Ištar; **60**: memorandum indicating that all what is left from the silver given by Ištar-lamassī to her sons will go to Šīmat-Ištar at Aššur.

19. AKT 8, 179:4–12: "Iliya will take 37 shekels of the 1 mina minus 3 shekels of [silver] that are available. Ilī-bāni will take ⅓ mina. They will send 2¼ shekels of gold and 7½ shekels of silver, plus the seal, to my daughter, the consecrated woman."

20. Lion 2018, 238.

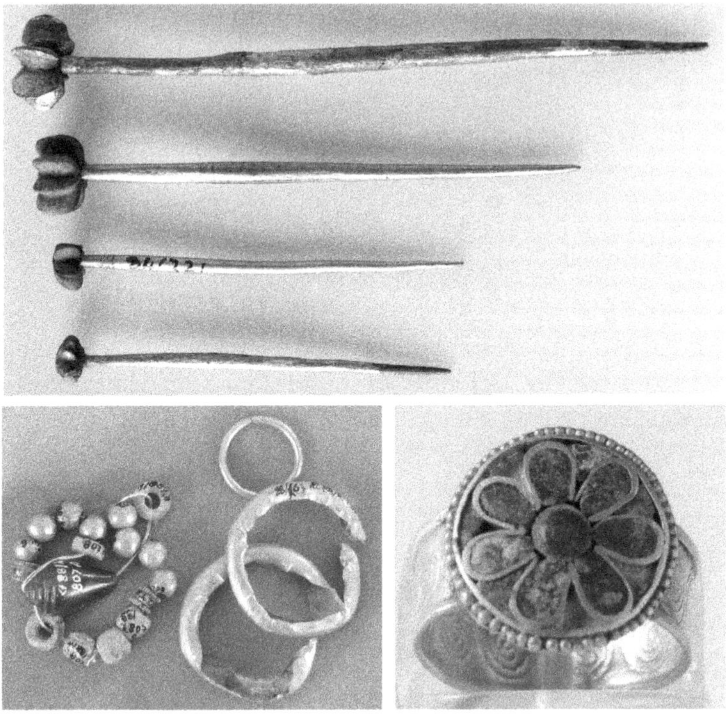

Fig. 8. Jewelry items of women found at Kültepe: (top) garment pins; (left) Kayseri Museum; (right) lapis lazuli ring (Ankara Museum). © Kültepe Archaeological Mission.

joint owners of their house, and their children inherited it when both parents had died (**21**). Some estate documents belonging to Anatolian families show that after the father's death, the sons inherited his goods in undivided shares (*ahhūtum*) and had to take care of their mother. Daughters are not mentioned, which leads one to suppose that they had already left the family by marrying (**53**).[21] In one instance, when the eldest brother decided to withdraw from the undivided partnership, a woman with the Assyrian name of Lamassī was mentioned along with the two male heirs; there is no way of knowing whether she was the widow or the daughter of the decedent (**69**).

21. Veenhof 1997b, 146–50; Albayrak 2010.

54. Wife and Daughter Inherit First

Envelope

Obv. ^{1}(seal A) ^{2}kišib *I-dí-Sú-en*$_6$ ^{3}dumu *Puzur*$_4$*-Ištar* ^{4}kišib *A-šùr-na-da* ^{5}dumu *Pu*<*zur*$_4$>*-A-na* ^{6}(seal B) ^{7}kišib *A-pí-il*$_5$*-ke-en*$_6$ ^{8}[dumu *Ì*]*-lí-dan* ^{9}[kišib *I-ku-pì-a* dumu PN] ^{10}(seal B) lo.e. ^{11}kišib *Sà-li-a* dumu *Ú-ṣú-ur-*[x-x] rev. ^{12}(seal C) ^{13}(seal D) ^{14}*ša ší-ma-at A-gu-a* ^{15}dumu *Šu-A-nim* ^{16}(seal D) ^{17}(seal E) u.e. ^{18}(seal F) le.e. ^{19}(seal F) r.e. ^{20}(seal E)

$^{1-13}$Sealed by Iddin-Suen, son of Puzur-Ištar; sealed by Aššur-nādā, son of Puzur-Anna; sealed by Apil-kēn, [son of I]lī-dān; [sealed by Ikuppiya, son of PN]; sealed by Salliya, son of Uṣur-[x-x].

$^{14-15}$(Text) concerning the will of Agūa, son of Šu-Anum.

Seal C Inscription

^{1}*I-d*[*í*?]*-sú-en*$_6$ ^{2}dumu *Puzur*$_4$-[*Ištar*]

Seal D Inscription

^{1}*A-pí-il*$_5$*-ke-en* ^{2}dumu *Ì-lí-dan*

Seal E Inscription

^{1}*A-šùr-na-da* ^{2}dumu *Puzur*$_4$*-A-na*

Tablet

Obv. ^{1}*A-gu-a* : *ší-im-tù-šu* ^{2}*i-ší-ma* : *bé-tum ša A-lim*^{ki} ^{3}*ša a-ší-ti-a* : *i-na* kù-babbar ^{4}*qá-dì* : *me-er-e-a-ma* ^{5}*ta-zu-az i-na* kù-babbar ^{6}*zi-ti-ša* : *a-ba-at ù um-ma-/at* ^{7}*bé-tù-um ù* kù-babbar *wa-/ar-kà-/sà* ^{8}*ù mì-ma ti-šu-ú* ^{9}*ša Šu-Be-lim bé-tù-um* ^{10}*ša Kà-ni-iš* : *ša Šu-Be-lim* ^{11}*um-me-a-ni* : *me-er-ú-a* ^{12}*e-pu-lu-ma i-na* kù-babbar ^{13}*ša i-a-ti* : *i-šé-ta-ni* ^{14}⅓ *ma-na* kù-gi 1 *ma-na* ^{15}kù-babbar *ù am-tám Áb-ša-lim* ^{16}*tù-ša-ra-ma* : *ta-lá-qé* ^{17}*ù i-na ší-ta-tim* ^{18}*me-er-ú-a* lo.e. ^{19}*ša bé-ta-tim* ^{20}*lá il*$_5$*-qé-ú-ni* 4 gú-ta rev. ^{21}urudu *ki-ma bé-ta-tí-šu-/nu* ^{22}*i-lá-qé-ú* : *i-na* ^{23}*ší-tí* kù-babbar *am-tim wa-ar-dim* ^{24}*a-ší-tí Šu-Be-lim ù me-er-ú-a* ^{25}*mu-ta mu-ta-ma* ^{26}*i-zu-zu* : *ša-wi-sú ša A-šùr-/i-dí* ^{27}*wa-šu-ra-sú-um šu-ma* kù-babbar ^{28}*i-a-ti* : *mì-ma ú-la iš-té-/tám* ^{29}4!(2*) gú-ta urudu ^{30}*ša bé-ta-ti-šu-nu* ^{31}*me-er-ú-a* : *ú-lá i-lá-qé-/ú* ^{32}2 *ma-na* kù-babbar ^{33}*Puzur*$_4$*-Ištar ú-wa-da*! ^{34}2 *ma-na* kù-babbar *Ú-ṣú-ur-/ša-A-šùr* ^{35}*ú-ta-ar* ^{36}*e-li-a-tù-šu-nu** ^{37}*a-pu-a-ti-šu-nu-ma* u.e. ^{38}*i-ta-pu-lu* ^{39}*A-bi-ì-lí šu-ma* 10 *ma-na* ^{40}kù-babbar *i-ša-qal* le.e. ^{41}*qá-dì* : *a-hi-šu-ma* : *i-zu-az šu-ma* 10 *ma-na* ^{42}kù-babbar *lá iš-qúl* : *na-sí-ih ù* 10 *ma-na*-ta

[43]kù-babbar *a-na a-he-šu* : *i-na-pá-al* igi *I-dí-Sú-en*$_6$ [44]igi *A-šùr-na-da* igi *A-pí-il*$_5$*-ke-<en>* igi *I-ku-pì-a* [45]igi *Sà-li-a*

[1-2]Agūa drew up his will as follows. [2-3]The house in Aššur is the property of my wife. [3-5]She shall share the silver with my children. [5-6]She is father and mother over the silver (that is) her inheritance share. [7-9]After her (death), the house and silver and everything that she owns is the property of Šu-Bēlum. [9-10]The house in Kaneš is the property of Šu-Bēlum. [11-12]My sons shall pay back my investors, and [12-16]of my remaining silver, Ab-šalim shall be the first to take ⅓ mina of gold, 1 mina of silver, as well as a female slave. [17-22]Then, from what remains, my sons who did not receive houses shall each take 4 talents of copper instead of their (share of) real estate. [22-26]Of the remaining silver and male and female slaves, my wife, Šu-Bēlum, and my sons shall share in equal parts. [26-27]The *šawītum*-concubine of Aššur-idī is ceded to him. [27-28]In the case there is no more silver of mine, and [29-31]my sons will not be able to each take the 4 talents of copper instead of their (share) of real estate, [32-33]Puzur-Ištar shall designate 2 minas of silver, [34-35]Uṣur-ša-Aššur shall give back 2 minas of silver. [36-38]They shall mutually balance their *elītum*-share at their discretion. [39-41]If Abi-ilī pays 10 minas of silver, he shall take a share together with his brothers, [41-42](but) if he does not pay 10 minas of silver, then he shall be disinherited and [42-43]shall have to compensate 10 minas of silver to each of his brothers.

[43-45]In the presence of Iddin-Suen, Aššur-nādā, Apil-kēn, Ikuppiya, and Salliya.

Bibliography: Text published by Albayrak (2000 [Kt o/k 196a envelope; Kt o/k 196c tablet]); edited by Hecker (2001, 28); studied within its context by Michel (2000b); translated by Albayrak (2010, 144); commented on by Veenhof (2012a, 183–84) and de Ridder (2017a, 63). Photos of the reverse of the envelope and tablet published by Kulakoğlu & Kangal (2010, 338–39, nos. 443–44). The tablet is on display in the Museum of Anatolian Civilizations (Ankara) and could not be collated; collations indicated for the reverse of the tablet were made from the photograph.

Comments: Agūa wrote a will in order to leave assets first to his wife and to his daughter Ab-šalim, who is single, then to his five sons. The wife receives a house in usufruct and has full authority over the silver corresponding to her share, since she is said to be "father and mother." But after her death, the eldest son will inherit from her. The daughter receives gold, silver, and a female slave. The eldest son, Šu-Bēlum, receives a house, while the other sons get copper. The ten minas of silver that Abi-ilī must give to receive a legacy are presumably commercial inheritance rights computed separately. This tablet, discovered in 1963, was kept in a container together with other documents dealing with the succession of Agūa, as we can guess from an inscribed bulla (Kt o/k 203): "tablets of the will of Agūa"; see Michel 2000b.

Line 25: for the expression *muttā muttāma*, see Hertel 2010; but correct "the wife of Šu-Bēlum" to "my wife, Šu-Bēlum." Since there are more than two persons concerned, the translation cannot be "half and half each" as suggested by Hertel but might be a standardized expression meaning "in equal parts."

Line 36: the word *elītum* should be the object; see Veenhof 2012a, 183–84: "What remained of the assets, after the itemized assignments had been realized, would be shared equally between them." According to him, there are two types of assets to share in an inheritance. The word *elītum* would correspond to "commercial 'assets,' such as investments and claims on agents and debtors, merchandise in transit, etc., frequently represented by relevant records," while the *zittum* might deal with "private, 'domestic' assets, such as the house, furniture, slaves, bronze objects, stocks, and cash silver."

---

55. A Woman Inherits All Her Husband's Assets in Kaneš

Obv. [1]*A-mur-Ištar ší-im-tí* [2]é^{tí}*-šu ša Kà-ni-iš* [3]*i-ší-im-ma* : é [x x (x)] [4](line erased) [5]*ú a-ma-tim ú šé-r*[*a*]*-áš-/*[*n*]*a* [6]*ma-lá i-šu-ú* [7]*Ú-ší-nu-ma-an ú-ra*$^{!}$*-sú* [8]*ša Lá-ma-sí a-š*[*í-tí-šu*] [9]*qá-dí-iš-ti*[*m* x x x] [10]kù-babbar *ša* [x x x] [11]*ú ṣí-*[x x x x] (lacuna)

Rev. [1']*x* [x x x x x x] [2']*ša Lá-*[*ma-sí* x x x] [3']*ša* é^{tí} [x x x x x] [4']*i-na me-er-i-*[*šu*$^{?}$] [5']*i-na* é^{tim} [6'][x]*-ta-ra-ma* [7']igi *Ú-ra-a* [8']igi ^{d}mar-tu-*ba-ni* [9']igi *E-lá-ma* [10']igi *A-gu*$_{5}$*-a i-na* [11']*wa-ar-kà-at* le.e. [12']*Lá-ma-s*[*í q*]*á-du-u*[*m*] [13']x [x x x] x *a* : *ša* x [(x x)] [14'][x x x x]*-im i-*[x] [15'][x x x x x] x [x x]

[1–3]Amur-Ištar drew up a will concerning his household in Kaneš. [3–9]The house [x x x], the female slaves and their toddlers, all that he owns, Ušinuman, his slave, (shall) belong to Lamassī, [his] wi[fe], the (consecrated) *qadištum* [x x x]. [10–11]The silver that [x x x] and [...]

[…] [2'-6']belongs to La[massī x x x] from the house […] among [*his*] sons, in the house, [x] shall return.

[7'-10']In the presence of Uraya, Amurru-bāni, Elamma, and Agūa.

[11'-12']Of what Lamassī will leave behind, including […]

Bibliography: Text published in copy by Stephens as BIN 6, 222; edited by von Soden (1976, 216–17). Restorations of lines 5 and 7 proposed by Veenhof (2012a, 176). According to Wilcke (1976, 197), the piece BIN 6, 224, would belong to the same tablet. But in a review, Foster (1981, 621 n. 8) wrote that it cannot be part of this tablet, "for the ductus is quite different."

Comments: Amur-Ištar gives all his belongings (house in Kaneš, female slaves, children, and slave) to his wife Lamassī, who is a (consecrated) *qadištum* (for this word, see pp. 377–78 in this volume). Because of her status, he had presumably no children with her. The sons mentioned line 4' could be the children he had with his first wife, possibly in Aššur. After the death of his wife (*warkat* Lamassī), all the assets that she received might go to Amur-Ištar's relatives.

56. The Wife Receives the Kaneš House; the Daughter, a Full Share

Envelope

Obv. [1'](seal A) [2']kišib *Il*$_5$*-ba-ni* dumu *I-a-a* [3']kišib *I-ku-pì-a* dumu *A-šur-ba-ni* [4'](seal A) [5']kišib *Ku-ṣí-a* [dumu] *Bu-zi-zi* [6']kišib *A-šur-m*[*a-lik* dumu *Puz*]*ur*$_4$*-A-šur* /x[x] [7'](seal A, lacuna)

Seal A Inscription

[1]kišib *Ku-mi-im* [2]dumu *E-pí-iš-qá-bi*

Seal of Kumum, son of Epiš-qabi.

[1'-6']Seal of Il(ī)-bāni, son of Iaya; seal of Ikuppiya, son of Aššur-bāni; seal of Kuziya, [son of] Buzizi; seal of Aššur-m[alik, son of Puz]ur-Aššur (lacuna)

Tablet

Obv. [1]*Il*$_5$*-ba-ni ší-im-tí bé-tí-/šu* [2]*i-ší-ma* : *ṭup-pu-um* <*ša*> [3]1 gú 12 *ma-na* an-na *ša Šu-Ištar* [4]dumu *Me-na-nim* : *ṭup-pu-um ša* 1½ /gú [5]urudu *ša* dingir-sipa dumu *Sá-li-ma-nim* ^{6}*ṭup-pu-um ša* 1½ *ma-na* kù-babbar ^{7}*ša Ib-ni-lí ù En-um-A-šur* ^{8}*me-er-i-šu ṭup-pu-ú a-ni-ú-tum*$_8$ ^{9}*ša A-ha-tim me-er-i-tí-a* ^{10}*gu*$_5$*-ba-áb-tim : ší-tí : ṭup-pè-a* ^{11}*lu ša A-lim*^{ki} *lu ša eq-lim* ^{12}[*ša*] *me-er-e-a ki-li-šu-nu-ma* ^{13}[*ú me-e*]*r-í-tí-a gu*$_5$*-ba-áb-tim* ^{14}[*qá-tum*] *iš-té-tù-ma* ^{15}[*be-tum š*]*a Kà-ni-iš* ^{16}[*ša Lá-ma*]*-sí a-ší-tí-a* lo.e. ^{17}[*i-na me-er*]*-e-<a> a-na* ^{18}[*Lá-ma-sí ma*]*-ma-an : ú-lá* ^{19}[*i-tù-a-a*]*r-ší-im* rev. ^{20}[*i-na ṭu*]*p-pè-a ša Kà-/ni-/iš* ^{21}[*iš-té-e*]*n-ma : ša* 1½ *ma-na* ^{22}[kù]-babbar *ṭup-pè-e : na-bu-tim :* ^{23}*a-na Lá-ma-sí : i-da-an* ^{24}*I-a-a : ù I-ku-pí-a* 6 *ma-na*-ta ^{25}urudu *i-na ša-tim a-na A-ha-tim* ^{26}*me-er-i-tí-a i-du-nu : kà-lu* ^{27}*me-er-e-a : a-na hu-bu-li-a* ^{28}*i-za-zu : a-hu-um ba-lu-um* ^{29}*a-hi-im lu i-na A-lim*^{ki} ^{30}*lu i-na eq-lim ṭup-pè-a* ^{31}*lá i-pá-té : i-na ni-qé-e-/šu-nu* ^{32}*i-ra-tim a-na A-ha-tim* ^{33}*i-du-nu : ku-nu-ki : I-a-a* ^{34}*i-lá-qé : ša be-el ší-ma-tí-/a* ^{35}*a-na ma-mì-tim : i-ra-de*$_8$*-ú* ^{36}*na-sí-ih*$^{!}$(HI) *ù hu-bu-lam* u.e. ^{37}*šu-ut-ma : i-ša-qal* 1 *ma-na* ^{38}kù-babbar *ša ik-ri-bi*$_4$*-a ša I-ku-pì-a* ^{39}*ú-kà-lu : I-a-a : ú I-ku-pì-a* le.e. ^{40}*i-ma-ku-ru-ma : ik-ri-bi*$_4$*-a* [*ša* DN *A-ha-tám*] ^{41}*me-er-i-tí : šu-nu-ma : e-ki-mu* [igi *I-ku-pì-a*] ^{42}dumu *A-šur-ba-ni* igi *Bu-zi-zi* ig[i …] ^{43}(erasure) dumu *A-šur-d*[*an*$^{?}$]

$^{1-2}$Ilī-bāni drew up a will concerning his household.

$^{2-4}$One tablet (of debt) for 1 talent, 12 minas of tin amount from Šu-Ištar, son of Menānum, $^{4-5}$1 tablet (of debt) for 1½ talent of copper amount from Ilī-rē'ī, son of Salimanum, $^{6-8}$1 tablet (of debt) for 1½ minas of silver amount from Ibni-ilī and Ennum-Aššur, his son; $^{8-10}$these tablets (of credit) belong to Ahattum, my daughter, the consecrated woman. $^{10-14}$My remaining tablets (of debts owed me), in both Aššur and Anatolia, go to all my sons and to my daughter, the consecrated woman, as one [share. $^{15-16}$The house i]n Kaneš [is the property of Lama]ssī, my wife. $^{17-19}$None of my [children shall rais]e a claim against [Lamassī. $^{20-22}$Among] my [ta]blets at Kaneš, [there is one] concerning 1½ minas of [si]lver. $^{22-23}$He shall give the mentioned tablets to Lamassī. $^{24-26}$Iaya and Ikuppiya shall give 6 minas of copper a year to Ahattum, my daughter. $^{26-28}$All my sons are responsible for my debt. $^{28-31}$None (of them), without the others, shall open any of my tablets (of debt owed me), either in Aššur or in Anatolia. $^{31-33}$From their (meat) offerings, they shall give breast cuts to Ahattum. $^{33-34}$Iaya shall take my seal. $^{34-36}$Whoever shall require my executors to accompany (him) to swear an oath shall be disinherited; $^{36-37}$moreover, he shall be the one to pay (my) debts. $^{37-39}$With the mina of silver from my votive offerings, which Ikuppiya is holding, $^{39-40}$Iaya and Ikuppiya shall do business, $^{40-41}$and they shall take away from my daughter [Ahattum] the votive offerings [of DN].

$^{41-43}$[In the presence of Ikuppiya], son of Aššur-bāni, Buzizi, and [PN], son of Aššur-d[ān$^{?}$].

Bibliography: Text published in copy by Hrozný as ICK 1, 12; edited by von Soden (1976, 212–16) and Wilcke (1976, 202–3); translated by Michel (1998a, 432); cited by Dercksen (1997, 91 n. 60) and Veenhof (2012a, 36 n. 29; 178).

Comments: Ilī-bāni divides his assets among his wife, Lamassī, his two sons, Iaya and Ikuppiya, and his daughter, Ahattum, who was single because she was a (consecrated) *gubabtum* (Michel 2001a, 504–5). The wife receives the house in Kaneš in which she lives as well as a tablet of credit. The daughter inherits several credit tablets in copper, tin, and silver, plus one share equal to her brothers. But, contrary to them, she is not responsible for her father's debt. Moreover, they have to give her an annual allowance of six minas of copper and cuts of meat from their offerings.

The reference to votive offerings that the brothers of Ahattum should take away from her is not clear: maybe it means they have to take on her obligation for the offerings (Dercksen 1997, 90–91).

---

57. A Sister Inherits from Her Brother Who Has No Heirs

Obv. ^{1}^{d}im-*b[a-ni ší-im-tí* é-*šu]* ^{2}*i-ší-ma* é[^{tum} *ša Kà-ni-iš]* ^{3}*ša a-bi-i* [x x x] ^{4}*ša Ša-at-*^{d}i[m *a-ha-/tí-a]* ^{5}*a-hu-ša* : *i-š[a*$^{?}$ x x] ^{6}*šu-ma mì-ma tù-*[x x x] ^{7}*ta-lá-ak iš-t[é-ni-iš]* ^{8}*ú-ša-ba* 9 *ma-n[a* kù-babbar] ^{9}*ša Da-da-a* dumu [PN] ^{10}*ha-bu-lá-ni lu ṭup-p[u-um]* ^{11}*lu* kù-babbar *lu sí-pá-ru lu ú-ṭù-up-/tum* ^{12}*lu ṣú-ub-ru-um qá-tí* ^{13}[*š*]*a wa-ar-kà-at um-mì-ni* ^{14}*ik-šu-dí-ni lu sí-pa-ri pá-ni-ú-/tim* ^{15}*ša a-na-ku* : *e-zi-bu* ^{16}*lu sí-pá-ri* : *ša iš-tí A-ni-na* ^{17}*áš-ú-mu-ma* : *a-na a-ha-tí-a* ^{18}*e-zi-bu* : *lu kur-sí-na-ti*[*m*] ^{19}*qá-tí ša a-ha-tí tal-ta-q[é-ú]* ^{20}*lu ṣú-ub-ra-am pá-ni-tám* lo.e. ^{21}*lu i-na* kù-babbar *ša Da-da-a* ^{22}*lu i-na ša um-mì-ni* ^{23}*lu i-na kur-sí-na-t*[*i*]*m* rev. ^{24}*qá-tí i-mì-ma a-nim* ^{25}*i-sú-hu-pí-im a-hu-ša* ^{26}*e-ki-mu-ší-ma i-ší-tim* ^{27}5 *ma-na* kù-babbar *a-ṣí-ib-tim* ^{28}*i-na-dí-ú-ma ṣí-ba-sú ší-it*$^{!}$(DA) ^{29}*ù um-ma-ša e-kà-lá* ^{30}*i-mì-m*[*a*] *a-*[*n*]*i*[*m š*]*a e-zi-bu* ^{31}2 *qá-té-en*$_{6}$ *a-wi-lá-tum* ^{32}*i-lá-qé-a*$^{!}$ *iš-té-et qá-tám* ^{33}*Šu-A-nim i-lá-qé iš-té-et* ^{34}*qá-tám En-um-A-šur i-lá-qé* ^{35}*i-na* 5 *ma-na* kù-babbar *ša a-ṣí-ib-/tim* ^{36}*i-na-dí-ú* 3 *ma-na* kù-babbar ^{37}*Šu-A-nim i-lá-qé* 2 *ma-na* kù-babbar ^{38}*En-um-A-šur i-lá-qé wa-ar-kà-/at* ^{39}*a-wi-lá-tim* é^{tum} *lu* kù-babbar ^{40}*lu sí-pá-ru lu ú-ṭù-up-tum* ^{41}*lu ṣú-ub-ru-um ša Šu-A-núm-m*[a] ^{42}*ša ma-hu-ur-tí* é$^{be\text{-}tí\text{-}i}$[^{m} *a-na*$^{?}$] ^{43}*qá-tí-šu En-um-A-šu*[*r i-lá-qé* /*a-na*] ^{44}*a-hu-a-tí-šu-nu* x [x x x] ^{45}*i-du-nu* [x x x x] u.e. ^{46}kù$^{!}$-babbar *i*-[x x x x] ^{47}*ma-du* [x x x x] ^{48}*ta* x [x x x] le.e. ^{49}*i-du-nu-ší-im* gémé *ša Kà-ni-iš ša Ša-at-*^{d}/im ^{50}*a-hu-bu-lim ša Sú-e*[*n*] *a-na ṭup-pì-a ša* gán^{lim} ^{51}*ki-lá-lá-šu-nu-ma i-za-*[*z*]*u e-li-a-tù-šu-nu ša-lu-ṭá*$^{!}$ ^{52}*A-lá-bu-um* dumu *Il*$_5$*-ba-ni I-k*[*u*]*-pì-a* dub-sar *ù Lá-qé-ep b*[*e-e*]*l* ^{53}[*š*]*í-ma-tí-a*

$^{1-2}$Adad-b[āni] drew up [a will concerning his household]. $^{2-4}$The house [in Kaneš] that my father [*bought*] is the property of Šāt-Ad[ad, my sister]. $^{5-7}$Her brothers […] if she […] anything, she may go. $^{7-8}$They may (continue to) live tog[ether].

$^{8-10}$As to the 9 min[as of silver …] that Dadaya, son of [PN], owes me, $^{10-14}$or the tabl[e]t, the silver, the bronze, the furniture, or the slaves which are mine, from what was left by our mother that accrued to me, $^{14-18}$or the previous bronzes that I leave, the bronzes that I bought from Anīna and that I left to my sister, $^{18-19}$the *kursinnātum*-bags, my share that my sister repeatedly took, $^{20-23}$the previous slaves, or the silver of Dadaya, or that of my mother, or what (is) in the *kursinnātum*-bags, $^{24-26}$(and) my share of whatever there is of the stock, her brothers shall take away from her. $^{26-28}$Of the remainder, they shall deposit 5 minas of silver at interest, $^{28-29}$and she (Adad-bāni's sister) and her mother shall benefit from the interest. $^{30-32}$Of all that I leave, the women shall take 2 shares, $^{32-33}$Šu-Anum shall take one share, $^{33-34}$Ennum-Aššur shall take one share. $^{35-36}$Of the 5 minas of silver that they shall deposit at interest, $^{36-37}$Šu-Anum shall take three minas of silver, $^{37-38}$Ennum-Aššur shall take 2 minas of silver. $^{38-41}$Whatever shall be left (after their deaths) by the women (Šāt-Adad and her mother), be it silver, bronze, furniture, or slaves, (it shall) go to Šu-Anum.

$^{42-43}$As to the […] which is facing the house, Ennum-Aššu[r shall take it for] his share. $^{44-45}$They will give to their sisters […] $^{46-49}$silver […] they will give her […]. ^{49}The female slave from Kaneš is for Šāt-Adad. $^{50-51}$For the debt owed (the god) Suen, and my debt tablets in Anatolia, they both shall be responsible. ^{51}Their *elīatum*-shares will be at their full disposal.

$^{52-53}$Ali-abum, son of Ilī-bāni; Ikuppiya, the scribe; and Laqēp are the executors of my will.

Bibliography: Text published by Garelli in *RA* 60 (1966): 133, as "Tablette de la collection Thierry"; edited by Wilcke (1976, 204–8) and de Ridder

(2017a, 81–82). Restoration of line 51 proposed by Veenhof (2012a, 183). The tablet was bought in Kayseri.

Comments: According to the reconstruction of Wilcke (1976), the testator's father had married twice, and Šāt-Adad is his half-sister from a different mother. Adad-bāni, the testator, is single and has no heirs, but he has brothers and sisters. He leaves to his half-sister his house in Kaneš, which he inherited from his father, but she will have to share it with his other brothers and sisters. Šāt-Adad and her mother receive each one share from the assets left by Adad-bāni; two other shares are left to his brothers, who are also responsible for his debts. After the death of Šāt-Adad and her mother, their belongings shall go to one of Adad-bāni's brothers. Šāt-Adad is not married and was presumably consecrated to a god. According to de Ridder (2017a, 81), Šāt-Adad would be the wife of the testator. In his reconstruction, it is not clear why the goods left by the testator's mother are involved.

Lines 18, 23: the *kursinnum*-bag contained assets (like the *narruqum*-bag); it was used for particular goods and could be associated with specific people.

Line 51: for the *elītum*-share, see the comments to **54**; they concerned only male heirs because they had to be balanced with the commercial debts, which were the responsibility of the sons.

---

58. A Consecrated Woman and Her Brother Inherit a House Plot

Obv. ^{1}*iš-tí Um-mì-Iš-ha-ra* ^{2}*ù En-um-A-šùr Pí-lá-ah-Ištar* ^{3}*ù Šu-Be-lúm i-mì-ig-ru-ma* ^{4}kù-babbar 6⅔ *ma-na ša* é ^{5}*Hi-na-a* 4 *ma-na* kù-babbar ^{6}*ša Kur-ub-Ištar* dumu *A-lá-hi-im* ^{7}*ù i-na ku-ur-sí-nim* ^{8}*ša Ištar-pì-lá-ah* 1⅓ *ma-na* kù-babbar ^{9}*na-dí-šu-nu-tí* : kù-babbar *a-nàm* ^{10}*Pì-lá-ah-Ištar ù Šu-Be-lúm a-na* ^{11}*Um-mì-Iš-ha-ra ù En-um-A-šùr* ^{12}*qá-sú-nu* : *ik-bu-sú-ma ša-lá-áš* ^{13}*šu-ba-tim* : *qá-qí-ri ša* 5-*tum* ^{14}*i-dí-nu-šu-nu-tí-ni* : *iš-tí um-mì-a-an* ^{15}*E-lá-ma* : *a-bi-šu-nu Um-mì-Iš-ha-ra* ^{16}*ù En-um-A-šùr ú-bu-bu* ^{17}*qá-qí-ri-šu-nu* : *i-lá-qé-ú* lo.e. ^{18}iti-kam : *Té-i-na-ti*[*m l*]*i-mu-um* ^{19}*En-na-Sú-en*$_6$ dumu *Šu-A-šùr* rev. ^{20}*a-na* 3 *ša-na-tim* ^{21}*qá-qí-ri-šu-nu ú-bu-bu-šu-nu-tí* ^{22}*šu-ma* : *lá ú-bi-bu-ú* ^{23}3 *ma-na* kù-babbar *i-na* ^{24}*ša Kur-ub-Ištar i-lá-qé-ú-/ma* ^{25}*ší-im qá-qí-ri-šu-nu* ^{26}*uš-ta-bu-ú-ma a-na qá-qí-ri-/ šu-nu* ^{27}*ù-lá i-tù-ru* : *i-na* ^{28}3 *ma-na* kù-babbar *ša Kur-ub-Ištar* ^{29}*qá-tí Pì-lá-ah-Ištar ù* ^{30}*Šu-Be-lim* : *ša-ak-na-at* ^{31}*šu-ma té-bi-ib-tum i-tab-ší* ^{32}*qá-dí*

: *a-hi-šu-nu-ma* : *e-bi-bu* ^{33}*ki-ma Um-mì-Iš-ha-ra Ir-ma-/A-šur* ^{34}*i-zi-iz* : *šu-ma* : *a-na* ^{35}3 *ma-na* kù-babbar *ša Kur-ub-Ištar* ^{36}*ša qá-tí Pì-lá-ah-Ištar ù* ^{37}*Šu-Be-lim ša-ak-na-at-ni* ^{38}*ma-ma-an i-na me-er-e* u.e. ^{39}*E-lá-ma* : *i-tù-ar* ^{40}*En-um-A-šùr ù Um-mì-Iš-ha-/ra* ^{41}*ù-bu-bu-šu-nu* igi *I-dí-*^{d}im le.e. ^{42}dumu *Šu-Ištar* igi *En-um-A-šùr* dumu *Ṣí-li-Ištar* ^{43}igi *En-na-nim* dumu *A-bu-sà* igi *Šu-A-nim* ^{44}dumu *Lá-qé-ep a-na ma-lá ší-ma-tí-šu-nu*

$^{1-3}$With Ummī-Išhara and Ennum-Aššur, Pilah-Ištar and Šu-Bēlum reached the following agreement:

$^{4-9}$Silver (in the amount of) 6⅔ minas of the house of Hinnaya, 4 minas of silver of Kurub-Ištar, son of Ali-ahum, and from the *kursinnum*-bag of Ištar-pilah, 1⅓ minas of silver have been deposited for them. $^{9-12}$Concerning this silver, Pilah-Ištar and Šu-Bēlum have dropped their claim in favor of Ummī-Išhara $^{12-14}$and Ennum-Aššur, and a house plot of 108 square meters that the committee-of-five had given them. $^{14-16}$When Ummī-Išhara and Ennum-Aššur shall clear it of claims from the investors of Elamma, their father, ^{17}they shall take it as their house plot. $^{18-21}$(Beginning with) the month Te'inātum (x), eponym Enna-Suen, son of Šu-Aššur (REL 107, ca. 1866), they shall clear their house plot of claims against them within three years. $^{22-24}$If they do not clear it of claims, they shall take 3 minas of silver from that of Kurub-Ištar and $^{25-26}$so then shall be satisfied with the price of their house plot, $^{26-27}$and they shall not raise a claim against their house plot. $^{27-30}$Of the 3 minas of silver of Kurub-Ištar, on which Pilah-Ištar and Šu-Bēlum have a claim, $^{31-32}$it has been cleared; they shall be clear of claims, along with their brothers. $^{33-34}$Ir'am-Aššur represented Ummī-Išhara. $^{34-39}$If anyone among the sons of Elamma shall raise a claim on the 3 minas of silver belonging to Kurub-Ištar, on which Pilah-Ištar and Šu-Bēlum (now) have a claim, $^{39-41}$Ennum-Aššur and Ummī-Išhara shall clear them (Pilah-Ištar and Šu-Bēlum).

$^{41-44}$In the presence of Iddin-Adad, son of Šu-Ištar; Ennum-Aššur, son of Ṣilli-Ištar; Ennānum, son of Abusa; and Šu-Anum, son of Laqēp. ^{44}In accordance with the testamentary dispositions applying to them.

Bibliography: Text edited by Veenhof (2012a, 187–93) as Kt 91/k 420, then as AKT 8, 175; collated May 2012.

Comments: This text refers to the division of some assets left by Elamma among his three sons and his consecrated daughter, Ummī-Išhara. His other daughter, Šalimma, is not mentioned here because she was married in Aššur to Ir'am-Aššur (**264**). Elamma left a will (Veenhof 2012a, 194), but Elamma's children decided to make an exchange. Ummī-Išhara, living in Aššur, is represented by her brother-in-law, Ir'am-Aššur. Together with her brother Ennum-Aššur, Ummī-Išhara negotiates for a house plot in Aššur. Note the rare mention of a house plot in an Old Assyrian inheritance; last wills usually refer to built houses, see also no. **62**.

Line 19: this agreement was reached during the eponym Enna-Suen, son of Šu-Aššur, REL 107 (ca. 1866), and not his homonym, son of Šu-Ištar, as indicated by Veenhof (AKT 8, 244).

---

59. A Consecrated Woman Inherits from Her Mother

Obv. [1]*um-ma Lá-ma-sà-tum Puzur*$_2$*-A-šùr* [2]*ù En-um-A-šur-ma a-na A-ta-a-/a* [3]*Ir-ma-A-šur Um-mì-Iš-ha-/ra* [4]*ù Ší-ma-at-Ištar qí-bi*$_4$*-ma* [5*]*a-na Ší-ma-at-Ištar qí-bi*$_4$*-ma* [6]*lá li-bi i-lim-ma : um-mì-ki* [7]*ù ki-lá-lá-ma : a-hu-ki : me-tù* [8]*i-na ba-áb : mu-wa-tim* [9]*ša um-mì-ki* 3 *me-er-e* [10]*um-mì-a-ni ni-iṣ-ba-at-ma* [11]*a-na ṣé-er : um-mì-ki* [12]*né-ru-ub-ma* : igi 3 *me-er-e* [13]*um-mì-a-ni : ta-ma-lá-ki-ša** [14]*Ištar-lá-ma-sí um-mì-ki* [15]*i-na bu-ul-ṭí-ša-ma* [16]*ta-ap-ṭù-ur-ma* kù-babbar [17]1 gín *i-šu : qá-tí-ša* lo.e. [18]*ša ib-ší-ú e-mu-ru-ma* [19]2¼ gín kù-gi *ù* [20]8 gín babbar *a-na ku-a-tí* rev. [21]*ta-dí-in* ½ *ma-na* 7 gín [22]kù-babbar *a-na Ì-lí-a : a-he-ki** [23]*ta-dí-in* ⅓ *ma-na* kù-babbar [24]*a-na* ^{d}nin-šubur-*ba-ni* [25]*ta-dí-in : i-na bu-lu-uṭ* [26]*um-mì-ki-ma : lá-ma a-na sí-kà-/tim* [27]*nu-úṣ-ú Ì-lí-a : i-na* [28]*ki-ša-ar-ší-im : i-ni-dí* [29]*iš-tù i-šu : qá-tí-šu : ig-mu-ru* [30]*ù nu-a-um ša um-mì-ki e-hu-zu* [31]*Ì-lí-a : me-er-a-sú : a-hi-iz* [32]*nu-a-um gám-ra-am a-na* [33]*ki-ša-ar-ší-im ig-mu-ur-ma* [34]*iš-tù nu-a-um : ga-ma-ar-šu* [35]*il*$_5$*-qé-ú : lu a-na bi-ki-tim* [36]*ša um-mì-ki ù a-he-ki* (°kù-babbar° erased) [37]⅓ *ma-na* 7 gín kù-babbar *ga-me-er* [38]*a-na-kam : ša ki-ma* dumu *Hi-na-a* [39][d]am-gàr^{ru-um} *ša a-he-ki* [40]*a-na ṣa-ba-at* kù-babbar le.e. [41][*i-z*]*i-iz-ma En-um-A-šùr ù* [42][*Šu-mì-a-b*]*i-a ša ki-ma : ku-a-tí* [43][x x x]*-ma um-ma né-nu-ma* kù-babbar [44][*lá i*]*-ṣa-ba-at* : kù-babbar *ma-nu-šu*

[1-5]Thus (say) Lamassatum, Puzur-Aššur, and Ennum-Aššur: say to Ataya, Ir'am-Aššur, Ummī-Išhara, and Šīmat-Ištar. Say to Šīmat-Ištar.

[6-7]Alas, your mother and both your brothers are dead. [8-10]Just before the death of your mother, we took 3 recognized traders, [11-12]went to your mother's place, [12-16]and in front of the three recognized traders, your mother, Ištar-lamassī, as she was still alive, opened her *tamalakkum-*

chests, [16–18]and they saw every shekel of silver, her cash assets, that was there. And [19–21]she gave 2¼ shekels of gold and 8 shekels of silver to you; [21–23]she gave ½ mina and 7 shekels of silver to Iliya, your brother; [23–25]she gave ⅓ mina of silver to Ilabrat-bāni. [25–27]While your mother was still alive and before we had left for the *sikkātum*-expedition, [27–28]Iliya was thrown into jail. [29]After he had spent (all) he had available, [30]the Anatolian who married your mother, [31]and whose daughter Iliya married, [32–33]that Anatolian has paid for the jail expenses. [34–35]After the Anatolian has recovered what he had spent, [36–37]both for the mourning of your mother and your brothers, ⅓ mina and 7 shekels of silver were spent. [38–41]Here, the representative of Hinnaya's son, the creditor of your brothers, intended to seize silver [41–43]and [*we went to*] Ennum-Aššur and [Šumi-ab]ia, your representatives, and [43–44]said as follows: "He shall not seize silver! Who is he (that …) the silver."

Bibliography: Text edited by Veenhof (2008b, 107–9) as text B (Kt 91/k 423), then as AKT 8, 180; collated May 2012. Line 5 was omitted by the editor.

Comments: Fifteen tablets, unearthed in 1991 and studied by Veenhof (2008b; 2012a; AKT 8, 266–69), document the burial and legacy of Ištar-lamassī, widow first of the Assyrian Kūn-ilum, with whom she had three children, and second of the Anatolian Lulu. In her will (AKT 8, 179), Ištar-lamassī mentions the shares she leaves to each of her children: Iliya, Ilabrat-bāni, and their consecrated sister, respectively 37 shekels and 20 shekels of silver for her sons; and 2¼ shekels of gold, 7½ shekels of silver, and a seal for her daughter. But, according to this letter, addressed to Šīmat-Ištar, daughter of Ištar-lamassī and Kūn-ilum, a consecrated woman living in Aššur, the situation changed. Part of the inheritance was used to pay the debts of the deceased husband as well as the burials of the mother and the two sons who died a short time after her.

The mentioned "Anatolian" is Lulu, the second husband of Ištar-lamassī. Since the tablet does not seem to be broken, there could have been a small second page containing the end of the text.

Other texts belong to this dossier besides the following (**60**), include the continuation of a letter addressed to Šīmat-Ištar (AKT 8, 181), a record mentioning gold and silver left by Ištar-lamassī (AKT 8, 182) and entrusted to Ennum-ilī for shipment to Šīmat-Ištar (AKT 8, 183), various memoranda (AKT 8, 184–85, 188), and legal texts (AKT 8, 186–87).

Lines 7 and 22: read respectively "*a-hu-ki*" and "*a-he-ki*," the personal pronoun *-ki* referring to Šīmat-Ištar.

---

60. A Consecrated Woman, Sole Remaining Heiress of Her Mother

Obv. [1]*i-na* kù-babbar^{dáp} *Ištar-lá-ma-/sí* [2]*ša* : *a*-dumu-*e-ša* [3]*ta-dí-nu-ma* kù-babbar *i-na*$^{!}$(ŠU) [4]é$^{!}$ *E-lá-ma a-na-áb-šé-em* [5]*ib-ší-ú* šà-ba 7 gín [6]kù-babbar *Ì-lí-a i-bu-ul-ṭí-šu* [7]*i-qá-tí-šu il*$_5$*-qé iš-tù* [8]dumu-*ú Ku-ni-lim me-tù* lo.e. [9]*lu a-na bi-ki-tí-šu-nu* rev. [10] *lu a-ku-sí-im ša* rev. [11]*um-mì-šu-nu ṭá-bu-im* [12]*a-hu-ni e-ru-bu-ni-ma* [13]⅓ *ma-na* lá ½ gín kù-babbar [14]*lu a-bi*$_4$*-ki-tí-šu-nu lu a-na* [15]*ku-sí-im ša um-mì-šu-nu* [16]*lu a-na nu-a-im a-šu-mì Ì-lí-a* [17]7½ gín kù-/babbar [18]*a-hu-bu-*<*li*>*-šu i-ší-qí-il*$_5$ u.e. [19]*ší-tí* kù-babbar *a-ṣé-er* [20]*a-ha-tí-šu-nu* dumu-munus *Ku-ni-lim* le.e. [21]*a-na A-lim*^{ki} dumu *A-šur-dan* [22]*ù Šu-mì-a-bi-a ša ki-ma* [23]dumu-*e Ku-ni-lim ú-šé-bi*$_4$*-lu*

[1–3]From the silver of Ištar-lamassī that she gave to her sons [3–5]and which was a safe deposit in Elamma's house, [5–7]from it, Iliya, while he was still alive, took 7 shekels of silver as his share. [7–8]After the sons of Kūn-ilum died, [9–12]our brothers came for bewailing them, for removing the chair of their mother, and [13–18]19½ shekels of silver were paid for bewailing them and for the chair of their mother, and 7½ shekels of silver to the Anatolian, because of Iliya, for his debt. [19–23]The remainder of the silver was sent to the address of their sister, daughter of Kūn-ilum, to the city (of Aššur), by the son of Aššur-dān and Šumi-abiya, the representatives of Kūn-ilum's sons.

Bibliography: Text edited by Veenhof (2008b, 113) as text F (Kt 91/k 441), then as AKT 8, 184. Lines 6–18 cited by Michel (2008f, 186 n. 25); collated May 2012.

Comments: This memorandum records the expenses for the burial of the mother and the two sons, during which their "chairs" were removed. All that remains of the silver left by Ištar-lamassī goes to her daughter. Šīmat-Ištar, a (consecrated) *gubabtum*, was the sole heiress, and she sent representatives from Aššur to settle the estate so as not to be used by others.

The chair (*kussium*) of the deceased mother, mentioned several times here, is intended to replace her soul between the time of her death and her burial.[22] A ceremony was performed in which the ghost of the dead mother participated through her chair. "Removing the chair" of the deceased woman would then symbolize her departure.

---

61. Assets of a Woman to Be Divided according to Her Will

Obv. [1]3 *kà-sá-tum ù tù-dí-na-/tum* [2]*šu-qú-ul-ta-áš-na* [3]1 *ma-na* kù-babbar *ku-nu-ku-a* [4]*a-ha-ma* ⅓ *ma-na* 6* gín kù-babbar [5]*ku-nu-ku-a-ma ik-ri-bu* [6]*ša E-lá-ma* 2 *ṭup-pu-ú* [7]*ša* 2 *ma-na* 15 gín kù-babbar [8]*ša hu-bu-ul nu-a-im* 1 *ṭup-pu-/um* [9]*ša* 1½ *ma-na* kù-babbar *ša hu-bu-/ul* [10]*Na-ni-a* 1 *ṭup-pu-um* [11]*ša* 1 *ma-na* 6 gín kù-babbar [12]*ša hu-bu-ul Bur-Sú-en*$_6$ [13]1 *ṭup-pu-um ša* ⅓ *ma-na* 4 gín [14]kù-babbar *ša hu-bu-ul Il*$_5$*-tap-pá* [15]1 *ma-na* kù-babbar *a-na Ir-ma-A-/šùr* lo.e. [16]*a-na ší-a-ma-tim* [17]*a-dí-in* 1 *ma-na* kù-babbar rev. [18]*a-na Ah-ša-lim a-na* [19]*ší-a-ma-tim a-dí-in* [20]9 túg *pí-ri-kà-ni ù* 1 túg : /*A-bar-ni-am* [21]*a-na Pí-lá-ah-Ištar* [22]*a-na ší-a-ma-tim a-dí*-in** [23]5 ìr^{du} *ù* 5 *a-ma-tum* [24]šà-ba 1 *am-tum* : *I-a-an-tal-/kà* [25]*ša Ì-lí-na* dumu-munus *A-šur*-du$_{10}$ [26]*mì-ma a-nim Lá-ma-sà-tum* [27]dam *E-lá-ma* [28]*té-zi-ib* : *Ištar-pá-li-il*$_5$ [29]*En-na-Sú-en*$_6$ *ù Ma-ṣí-ì-lí* [30]*ša ki-ma Lá-ma-sà-tim a-na* [31]dumu *um-mì-a-nim ù ma-ri-/ša* [32]*i-pá-qí-du-ma a-na* [33]*A-lim*^{ki} *ú-bu-lu-ú-ma* [34]*a-ma-lá* [35]*ší-ma-tí-šu-nu me-er-i-tí* : nin-dingir [36]*ù ma-ru-ú-a e-pu-š*[*u*]

[1–3]Three cups and garment pins, their weight: 1 mina of silver, under my seal; [4–6]separately ⅓ mina, 6 shekels of silver under my seal, votive offerings of Elamma; [6–8]2 tablets for 2 minas, 15 shekels of silver regarding the debt owed by an Anatolian; [8–10]1 tablet for 1½ minas of silver regarding the debt owed by Naniya; [10–12]1 tablet for 1 mina, 6 shekels of silver regarding the debt owed by Būr-Suen; [13–14]1 tablet for ⅓ mina, 4 shekels of silver regarding the debt owed by Il(ī)-tappa; [15–17]I gave 1 mina of silver to Ir'am-Aššur for making purchases; [17–19]I gave 1 mina of silver to Ah-šalim for making purchases; [20–22]I gave 9 *pirikannum*-textiles and 1 Abarnian-textile to Pilah-Ištar for making purchases; [23–25]5 slaves and 5 female slaves, of which 1 female slave, named Iantalka, belongs to Ilina, daughter of Aššur-ṭāb. [26–28]All this, Lamassatum, wife of Elamma, left (at her death). [28–32]Ištar-pālil, Enna-Suen, and Maṣi-ilī, representatives of Lamassatum, shall entrust it to a recognized trader and to her sons; [32–33]they shall bring it to the city (of Aššur), and [34–36]my daughter, the (consecrated) *gubabtum*,

22. Scurlock 2002.

and my sons shall act in accordance with the testamentary dispositions applying to them.

Bibliography: Text edited by Veenhof (2012a, 196–97) as Kt 91/k 421, then as AKT 8, 164; collated May 2012.

Comments: Lamassatum makes a list of her belongings that, after her death, should be brought to Aššur and divided among her (consecrated) *gubabtum* daughter and her two sons. This inventory includes valuable cups, jewelry items, votive offerings, loan contracts, and slaves.

---

62. A Consecrated Woman and Her Brothers Share a House Plot with Their Uncle

Envelope

Obv. $^{1'}$[*A-šùr*-du$_{10}$] *me-er-ú A-*[*gu$_5$-za ù*] $^{2'}$[*a-ha-sú-nu*] *gu$_5$-ba-áb-tum* [*ni-iš*] $^{3'}$[*A-lim*^{ki}] *it-mu-ú a-n*[*a* é$^{be\text{-}tim}$] $^{4'}$[*ša Kà-n-iš*] *ša A-šùr*-gal *w*[*a-aš-bu*] (lacuna)
u.e. $^{?\,1''}$[x x x x *a*]*-na ba-ri-šu-nu* [*i-za-zu*] (lacuna)

$^{1'-3'}$[(Šu-Ištar and) Aššur-ṭāb], the sons of A[guza, and their sister,] the consecrated woman, swore [the oath of the city (of Aššur). $^{3'-4'}$On the house in Kaneš] in which Aššur-rabi i[s living *they will not raise a claim*] (lacuna) [x x x] $^{1''}$[it belongs t]o them jointly (lacuna)

Tablet

Obv. ^{1}*A-mur*-^{d}utu *a-hu-ú A-gu$_5$-za* ^{2}*A-šùr*-gal dumu *A-gu$_5$-za* ^{3}*Šu-Ištar A-šùr*-du$_{10}$ *me-er-ú* ^{4}*A-gu$_5$-za ù a-ha-sú-nu* ^{5}*gu$_5$-ba-áb-tum ni-iš A-lim*^{ki} ^{6}*it-mu-ú a-na bé-tí-im* ^{7}*ša Kà-ni-iš ša A-šùr*-gal ^{8}*wa-áš-bu ù ší-ma-at* ^{9}*a-bi-šu-nu ù a-na mì-ma* ^{10}*šu-um-šu A-mur*-^{d}utu lo.e. ^{11}*a-na A-šùr*-gal ^{12}*ù a-hi-šu me-er-e* rev. ^{13}*A-gu$_5$-za ú-lá i-tù-ar* ^{14}*ù me-er-ú A-gu$_5$-za a-na* ^{15}*A-mur*-^{d}utu *ù me-er-e-šu* ^{16}*a-na mì-ma šu-um-šu ú-lá i-tù-ru* ^{17}*qá-qú-ru ša ṭé-hi-i* ^{18}é *I-dí-A-šùr* dumu *Ku-bi$_4$-dí* ^{19}*a-na ba-ri-šu-nu i-za-zu* ^{20}igi *Ku-ku-wa* igi *Il$_5$-ba-ni* ^{21}igi (erasure) ^{22}igi *A-šùr-lá-ma-sí*

$^{1-6}$Amur-Šamaš, brother of Aguza, Aššur-rabi, son of Aguza, Šu-Ištar, Aššur-ṭāb, the sons of Aguza, and their sister, the consecrated woman, swore the oath of the city (of Aššur). $^{6-8}$On the house in Kaneš, in which

Aššur-rabi is living, [8–10]and the will of their father and anything else, [10–13]Amur-Šamaš shall not raise a claim against Aššur-rabi and his (other) brothers (and sister), the children of Aguza. [14–16]And the children of Aguza shall not raise a claim about anything against Amur-Šamaš and his sons. [17–19]The house plot next to the house of Iddin-Aššur, son of Kūbi-(i)dī, belongs to them jointly.

[20–22]In the presence of Kukuwa, Ilī-bāni, and Aššur-lamassī.

Bibliography: Tablet published by Jankovskaja as KTK 103; envelope published in copy by Contenau as TC 1, 93; both edited by Eisser and Lewy (1930, no. 9).

Comments: Aššur-rabi, as the oldest son of the deceased Aguza, lives in the house in Kaneš. Šu-Ištar and Aššur-ṭāb are his two younger brothers, and he also has a sister who has been consecrated to the god and may live in Aššur. After the death of Aguza, there was a dispute among his children and his brother's family; this witnessed agreement is intended to put an end to the dispute. The consecrated woman has a share in the inheritance along with her brothers. Note the very rare mention of land in an Old Assyrian inheritance; see also text **58**.

---

63. A Woman Wants to Open Her Father's Will before Her Brothers' Arrival

Obv. [1]*a-na Dan-A-šur E*[*n-am-A-šur*] [2]*ù Puzur*$_4$*-A-šur qí-*[*bi*$_4$*-ma*] [3]*um-ma A-zi-a-ma a-na* [*Dan-A-šur*] [4]*ù En-nam-A-šur qí-bi*$_4$*-ma* [5]*a-hu-ú-a a-tù-nu be-lu-ú-*[*a*] [6]*a-tù-nu a-na-kam a-dí* 5$^{\text{ší-[šu]}}$ [7]*a-ha-at-ni A-lam ta-ak-šu-ud* [8]*um-ma ší-it-ma ší-ma-at* [9]*a-bi*$_4$*-ni lá-áš-me a-na-ku** [10]*ak-ta-na-lá-ší um-ma a-na-ku-/ma* [11]*a-hu-ni ra-bi*$_4$*-ú-tum* [12]*li-li-ku-ni-ma ù* kù-babbar [13]1 gín *ša* gán^{lim} *li-ip-hu-ra-/ma* [14]*ù ší-ma-at a-bi*$_4$*-ni* [15]*ku-lu-ni-ma lu ni-iš-me* [16]*i-na wa-ar-ki-tim* lo.e. [17]*a-na A-lim ta-li-kà-ma* [18]*um-ma ší-it-ma ší-ma-tim* rev. [19]*lá-áš-me a-na-ku a-na A-lim*^{ki} [20]*ki-ma ku-nu-tí ú-ta-er-ma* [21]*um-ma a-na-ku-ma a-hu-ni* [22]*ra-bi*$_4$*-ú-tum i-na* gán^{lim} [23]é *ku-nu-ki ù ší-ma-tim lá ni-pá-té* [24]*a-lu-um dí-nam i-dí-ma a-dí* [25]*ta-lá-kà-ni-ni* é *ku-nu-ki* [26]*ù ší-ma-tum lá i-«i»-pá-té-a* [27]*ù* kù-babbar *i-ba-ab-tim la*$_1$ *ni-*[*lá-qé*] [28]*ša i-lá-qé-ú i-ša-ri-iq-šu-um* [29]*a-hu-a a-tù-nu be-lu-a a-tù-nu* [30]*a-na-kam lá wa-áš-ba-ku-ma* [31]*a-ha-at-ni lá tú-sà-ha-ha-ni* [32]*i-*kù-babbar *ša a-bi*$_4$*-ni ša a-m*[*a-kam*] [33]*i-ba-ší-ú* 10 *ma-na-*ta [34]kù-babbar *šé-*

bi$_4$-lá-nim-ma ší-m[a-am] ^{35}*lá-áš-a-ma a-mì-ša-am* u.e. ^{36}*lu-ṣa-ma i-na re-ší-ku-[nu]* ^{37}*lá-zi-iz lu wa-á[š-ba-ku]* ^{38}*a-na-ku [a-n]a-[kam]* le.e. ^{39}*lá a-sà-hu-ur be-lu-a a-tù-nu* ^{40}*ki-ma a-bi$_4$-a ku-nu-tí ta-ak-lá-ku* ^{41}*ep-ša-at a-ha-tí-ni tí-de$_8$-a* é ^{42}*a-bi$_4$-ni lá tù-ha-lá-aq ší-ma-tim* ^{43}*lá t[a-š]a-me-«ma»*

$^{1-3}$Say to Dān-Aššur, E[nnum-Aššur,] and Puzur-Aššur: thus (says) Aziya. $^{3-4}$Say to [Dān-Aššur] and Ennum-Aššur.

$^{5-6}$You are my brothers; you are [my] masters. $^{6-7}$Here, our sister approached the city (authorities) up to five times, $^{8-9}$(saying) as follows: "I want to hear the will of our father!" $^{9-10}$For my part, I keep trying to prevent her, $^{10-12}$(saying) as follows: "Let our older brothers come, $^{12-13}$let it come to gather each shekel of silver abroad, $^{14-15}$and then, let us all together hear the will of our father!"

$^{16-17}$Later on, she went to the city (authorities) and $^{18-19}$(said) as follows: "I want to hear the will!" $^{19-20}$For my part, as your representative, I responded to the city (authorities) $^{21-22}$as follows: "Our older brothers are abroad. ^{23}We must not open the strong room or the will!"

^{24}The city (authorities) gave a verdict: $^{24-25}$until your arrival, $^{25-26}$the strong room and the will shall not be opened, ^{27}and we shall not collect any silver from outstanding claims (owed to our dead father); ^{28}whoever takes any, shall be considered as having stolen (it). ^{29}You are my brothers; you are my masters. ^{30}I don't want to stay here, and ^{31}our sister should not persecute me! $^{32-33}$From the silver of our father that is available ov[er there], $^{33-35}$each of you must send me ten minas of silver, so that I can make purcha[ses], then $^{35-37}$I will leave for over there to be at your disposal and to st[ay (with you)]. $^{38-39}$For my part, I do not want to remain here! ^{39}You are my masters; ^{40}I trust you as (if you were) my father. ^{41}You know the acts of our sister! $^{41-42}$She shall not ruin the house of our father! $^{42-43}$[She sh]all not hear the will!

Bibliography: Text published by Bilgiç and Günbattı as AKT 3, 94 (Kt v/k 77); translated by Michel (2001a, no. 289). Lines 6–26 cited by Albayrak (2000, 19); collated May 2012.

Comments: Šāt-Aššur, daughter of Šalim-ahum and sister of Dān-Aššur, Ennum-Aššur, and the youngest, Aziya, is living in Aššur; she might be single and consecrated to a deity. She is impatient to open the will of her father but is prevented from doing so before the arrival of her brothers by a verdict of the city authorities. The opening of a will had to be done in the presence of all the heirs.

---

64. Quarrel among Brothers; Their Consecrated Sister Shall Inherit

Obv. ^{1}*I-ku-num : A-mur-*^{d}utu *iš-a-a[l-ma]* ^{2}*um-ma I-ku-nu-um-ma a-na-ku* ^{3}*a-na mì-ma ša a-bu-ni : e-zi-[bu-ma]* ^{4}*a-ta tù-kà-lu-ni : a-li-k[à-kum]* ^{5}*a-ta : a-ha-at-ni : gu*$_{5}$*-ba-áb-tá[m]* ^{6}*a-he-e-ni : ù tám-kà-ar : a-b[i*$_{4}$*-ni]* ^{7}*t[ù-r]a*-pì-id-ma : iš-tù :* kù-[babbar] ^{8}*[ta-a]t*-bu-lu : ù um-ma a-ta-ma* ^{9}*[2 ma-na]* kù-babbar : é$^{be\text{-}et}$ *: nu-a-im a-[al-qé-ma]* ^{10}*[a-qú-b]u-ú-ur : a-bi*$_{4}$*-ni : ag-mu-u[r]* ^{11}*[ša i-n]a mu-a-at : a-bi*$_{4}$*-ni : a-t[a]* ^{12}*[ù a-na-k]u : ki-lá-lá-ni : wa-áš-ba-ni-[ni-ma]* ^{13}*[a-n]a qú-b[u]-ú-ur* : a-bi*$_{4}$*-ni : i-na* kù-babbar^{á}[^{p}] ^{14}*[a]-bi*$_{4}$*-ni-ma ½ ma-na* 4 gín kù-babbar ^{15}*ni-ig-mu-ru-ma : wa-ar-ki-a-ma* ^{16}*a-na kà-ri-im : ta-li-ku-ma* ^{17}*½ ma-na* kù-babbar : *kà-ru-um : i-dí-na-ku-ni* ^{18}*a-na a-ha-ti*-ni* a-he-e-ni : ú tám-kà-ar* ^{19}*a-bi*$_{4}$*-ni ra-pu-dim : ta-tí-zi-iz* ^{20}5⅓ *ma-na* kù-babbar 3 gín : *ú-qú-ur-tám* ^{21}*ša* kù-gi *ik-ri-be* ^{22}*ša Ta-áš-me-tim* 2⅔ gín ^{23}2 *uq-ru-a-tim ša* kù-gi-*ma* ^{24}3 lá ¼ gín kù-gi-*ma* ⅓ gín *i-lu-ú* ^{25}*ša a-bi*$_{4}$*-ni* 2 *ma-na sú-a-an ša* zabar ^{26}2 *ha-ṣí-nu : ú sà-sú-šu-nu : kà-sà-tum* ^{27}*ša* <2> *qá-áb-li-a-tim :* 2 *sú-pá-nu* ^{28}*ša* 2 *ma-na-*ta : *ša* zabar ^{29}2 *qá-áb-li-a-tim ša ½ ma-na-*ta ^{30}*a-hu-za-tim* 2 *qá-áb-li-a-tim* ^{31}*ša* 1 *ma-na-*ta 1 *a-hu-za-at* ^{32}1 lá *a*-hu-za-at* 1 *ma-na pá-šu-um* ^{33}*ar-za-lu-um : šu-ga-ri-a-an* ^{34}3 *ú-ru-za-na-tim :* 2 gú 10 *ma-na* ^{35}*lu-lá-a-am* 1 *ṭup-pá-am* ^{36}*ha-ar-ma-am ša ší-im* lo.e. ^{37}*A-ra-lá* 1 *ṭup-pá-am ha-ar-ma-am* ^{38}*ša ší-im : Ha-pu-a-ah-šu-šar* ^{39}1 *ṭup-pu-um : ša ší-im* rev. ^{40}*Hi-iš-ta-ah-šu-šar* 1 *ṭup-pu-u[m]* ^{41}*ša hu-bu-ul : nu-a-im* ^{42}*ku-nu-kam : ša a-bi*$_{4}$*-ni : ú me-he-er* ^{43}*ta-ah-sí-is-tim : ša* é$^{be\text{-}et}$ ^{44}*kà-ri-im : mì-ma a-nim* ^{45}*ša a-bu-ni : e-zi-bu-ni : tal-qé-e* ^{46}*lá tal-qé :* igi *a-né-e-em-ma* ^{47}*i-ki-ir : ú-ul : kà-i-in*$_{4}$ ^{48}*ú mì-ma : ša a-na-ku : i-na ša a-bi*$_{4}$*-ni* ^{49}*al-qé-ú-ni : qí-ib-a-am* ^{50}*A-mur-*^{d}utu *: I-ku-nàm : e-pu-ul* ^{51}*um-ma A-mur-*^{d}utu*-ma : tí-ma-li-ma* ^{52}*ta-áš-a-lá-ni-ma : a-pu-ul-kà* ^{53}*i-na mu-a-at a-bi*$_{4}$*-ni : ki-lá-lá-ni-ma* ^{54}*wa-áš-ba-ni : iš-tù* mu 3-šè : *a-bu-ni* ^{55}*me-et :* 1 gín kù-babbar : *a-bu-ni : lá e-zi-ib* ^{56}*iš-tù : a-bu-ni : a-na Kà-ni-iš :* ^{57}*e-ru-ba-ni : a-ta : i-na re-ší-šu* ^{58}*ta-za-az : a-na-ku* é *a-hi-tám wa-áš-ba-ku* ^{59}*ša a-bu-ni : mì-ma : lá e-zi-bu* ^{60}*ù i-na ša a-bi*$_{4}$*-a : mì-ma lá : al-qé-ú* ^{61}*ú ṭup-pì : a-ta : ù a-bi*$_{4}$ *: lá tù-kà-lá-ni* ^{62}*[a-w]a-tim ma-da-tim* ^{63}*[t]ù-ul-[t]a-pì-tám : lu ṭup-pì* ^{64}*[ha-a]r-ma-am : tù-kà-al : lu ší-be-e* ^{65}*tí-[šu]-am : ša i-na ša a-bi*$_{4}$*-a [al-qé]-ú* ^{66}*a-na a-né-e-em-ma : ru-a-am-ma* ^{67}*mì-nam : a-qá-bi : ku-nu-ku-um : ú [ší-im-tum]* ^{68}*ša a-bi*$_{4}$*-a : i-na A-lim*^{ki} *: ba-a-a[m]* ^{69}*a-ma-lá : ší-ma-at a-bi*$_{4}$*-ni* *i-na* [*A-lim*^{ki}] ^{70}*lu né-ta-ú* : *ma-ah-ri-kà* ^{71}*ù* igi 3 du[mu] *um-mì-a-nim* 2 *m*[*a*-x (x)] ^{72}é [x x x (x)] *al-qé-ma* ^{73}*a*-na*-k*[*u** x x x x-*t*]*im* : *ag*-[x x] u.e. ^{74}*a-na* [*a-wa-tim a-ni-a-tim*] ^{75}*kà-ru-u*[*m Kà-ni-iš* tur gal] ^{76}*i-dí-n*[*i-a-tí-ma* igi gír *ša A-šùr*] ^{77}*ší-bu-tí-ni ni-dí-in* le.e. ^{78}igi *A-šùr-*^{d}utu^{š}[^{i} dumu x-x]-x$^{!}$-[x] igi *Da-dí-a* dumu *Šu-mì-a-bi*$_4$*-a*

^{1}Ikūnum question[ed] Amur-Šamaš, and Ikūnum $^{2-4}$(saying) as follows: "I came [to you] personally concerning all that our father le[ft behind and] that you kept with you. $^{5-7}$You, you bothered our sister the consecrated woman, our brothers, and the creditor of [our] father, $^{7-8}$and after [you had] taken away sil[ver], $^{8-9}$then you (said) as follows: '[I borrowed 2 minas] of silver at the house of the Anatolian creditor, [and] ^{10}I spent (them) [for the gr]ave of our father.' $^{11-12}$[While, a]t the death of our father, both yo[u and I] were present, $^{13-15}$we spent [fo]r the grave of our father ½ mina, 4 shekels of silver from our [f]ather's silver; $^{15-17}$and later on, you went to the *kārum*, and the *kārum* gave you ½ mina of silver. $^{18-19}$(But even then,) you started to bother our sister, our brothers, and the creditor of our father! $^{20-22}$5⅓ minas of silver, a precious golden object (weighing) 3 shekels, a votive offering for (the goddess) Tašmētum, $^{22-24}$2 gold precious objects as well, (one weighing) 2⅔ shekels, (the other) 2¾ shekels of gold, $^{24-25}$⅓ shekel (weight of) the gods (figurines) of our father, 2 minas (weight of) 2 bronze discs-*su'ums*, $^{26-28}$2 axes and their *sāsum* (stone?), cups from <2> *qablītum*-containers, 2 bronze *supānum*-bowls of 2 minas each, 2 plated *qablītum*-containers of ½ mina each, $^{29-32}$2 *qablītum*-containers of 1 mina each, 1 plated (and) 1 not plated, $^{32-33}$1 hatchet (weighing) 1 mina, an *arzallum*-implement, 2 small knives, $^{34-35}$3 *uruzzannum*-tables, 2 talents, 10 minas of antimony, $^{35-37}$1 certified tablet concerning the sale of Arala, $^{37-38}$1 certified tablet concerning the sale of Happuahšušar, $^{39-40}$1 tablet concerning the sale of Hištahšušar, $^{40-44}$1 tablet concerning the debt of an Anatolian, the seal of our father, and the copy of the memorandum of the trade bureau; $^{44-46}$did you or did not take all this that our father left behind? $^{46-49}$Confirm or deny (it) before these two (present), and tell me anything I myself took from what belonged to our father!"

$^{50-51}$Amur-Šamaš replied to Ikūnum; thus Amur-Šamaš (said) as follows: $^{51-52}$"Yesterday, you (already) asked me, and I answered you. $^{53-54}$At the death of our father, both of us were present. $^{54-55}$Our father died 3 years ago! He did not leave even a shekel of silver! $^{56-58}$Since our father came to Kaneš, you were close to him; but as for me, I lived in a house separately. $^{59-61}$Despite the fact that our father left nothing behind, that I did not take anything from our father's belongings, and that yourself and my father hold no (debt) tablet from me, [62–63]you write to me many words! [63–65]If you hold a certified tablet concerning me, or if you have witnesses (able to prove) that [I too]k something from my father, [66]then bring them (the witnesses) here for this. [67–68]What (else) can I say? The seal and the [will] of my father are in the city (of Aššur). [68–70]Com[e], let us discuss according to the will of our father in [the city (of Aššur)]. [70–72]In your presence and in presence of 3 recognized traders, I did borrowed 2 mi[nas of silver from] the house [of the Anatolian (creditor)], and [73]I, for my part (lacuna)

[74–76]For [these proceedings], the *kārum* of [Kaneš], [(the whole assembly) small and big,] appointed [us] (as arbitrators), and [76–77]we have given our testimony [before Aššur's dagger]. [78]In the presence of Aššur-šamšī, [son of PN], and Dadiya, son of Šumi-abiya.

Bibliography: Text translated by Hecker (2004b, 54 [Kt m/k 1]). Lines 8–18, 42–44, 50–52, and 67–68 cited by Hecker (2004a, 291, nn. 35–36, 38–39). Lines 20–41 are quasi duplicates of **65**:15–30; collated May 2010.

Comments: According to Kt m/k 2 (envelope Kt m/k 65), the father of Amur-Šamaš and Ikūnum, perhaps Puzur-ilī (Hecker 2004b, 283), died during month twelve of REL 128 (ca. 1845). He left several sons and a consecrated daughter whose name is unknown. According to this private summons and the next one, the father is supposed to have left many objects made of gold and silver, as well as several tablets dealing with slave property. The sister was supposed to get a share from her father's inheritance together with her brothers.

It is noteworthy that the assets left by this man—precious objects made of gold and silver, votive offerings, some tools and weapons, bronze vessels, containers, tables, antimony, deeds of slave purchases, and loan contracts—are quite similar to those left by a woman (**61**), except that the tools and weapons are the equivalent of jewelry in the woman's properties (figs. 2.1, 3.2).

65. Same Quarrel among Brothers; Their Consecrated Sister Inherits a Seal

Envelope

This fragment of envelope is not inscribed. There are three sealings on one side, one on the other side, and one on each of the lower, left, and right edges.

Tablet

Obv. [1]*I-ku-num : a-na A-mur-*^{d}utu : *iṣ-ba-at-ni-a-tí-ma* [2]*um-ma I-ku-nu-um-ma : i-na mu-a-at* [3]*a-bi*$_4$*-ni : ba-lúm* : kù-babbar 1 gín [4]*a-na ki-dim : ta-aṭ-ru-da-ni-ma* [5]*iš-tí* : dumu *um-mì-a-nim : be-ú-lá-tim* [6]*al-qé-ma : a-na A-lim*^{ki} : *a-lá-ak* [7]*a-ta : ta-aṣ-ba-ta-ni-ma a-dí : mu-a-tim* [8]*ta-du-kà-ni-ma : hu-ur-ší-a-ni* [9]*qá-du-um : be-ú-lá-tim : ta-aṣ-ba-at-ma* [10]*um-ma a-ta-ma* : kù-babbar : *i-a-tí : ú a-na a-ší-tí-a* [11]*ha-bu-lá-tí : e-né-a : tù-ki-il-ma* [12]*i-na* kù-babbar^{áp} : *a-bi*$_4$*-a-ma : ša* 10 gín kù-babbar : *ṭup-pì* [13]*ta-ah-tí-ri-im : u*$_4$*-ma-am : lá tù-na-ha-ni* [14]*ú a-na* é *hu-bu-lim : lá ta-ša-pá-ra-ni* [15]5⅓ *ma-na* kù-babbar : 3 gín *ú-qú-ur-tum ša* kù-ki [16]*ik-ri-bu : ša Ta-áš-me-tim* : 2⅔ gín [17]2 *uq-ru-a-tum : ša* kù-ki : 3 lá ¼ gín kù-ki-*ma* [18]⅓ gín *i-lu : ša a-bi*$_4$*-ni* : 2 *ma-na sú-a-an* [19]*ša* zabar : 2 *ha-ṣí-nu : ú sà-sú-šu-nu* [20]*kà-sà-tum : ša* 2 *qá-áb-li-a-tim : mì-ma a-nim* [21]*ša i-na ta-ma-lá-ki : ku-nu-ku : ša a-bi*$_4$*-ni : ib-ší-ú* [22]2 *sú-pá-nu : ša* 2 *ma-na*-ta : *ša* zabar [23]1 *ma-na pá-šu-um : ar-za-lúm : šu-ga-ri-a-an* [24]2 *qá-áb-li-a-tum : ša* ½ *ma-na*-ta : *a-hu-za-tum* [25]2 *qá-áb-li-a-tum* <*ša* 1 *ma-na*-ta> : 1 *a-hu-za-at* : 1 lá *a-hu-za-at* [26]3 *ú-ru-za-na-tum : ša ta-as-kà-ri-nim* [27]2 gú 10 *ma-na lu-lá-am* : 1 *ṭup-pá-am : ha-ar-ma-am* [28]*ša ší-im : A-ra-lá* : 1 *ṭup-pá-am : ša ší-im : Ha-pu-ah-šu-šar* [29]1 *ṭup-pá-am : ša ší-im : Hi-iš-ta-ah-šu-šar* [30]<1 *ṭup-pá-am*> *ša hu-bu-ul : nu-a-im : mì-ma : a-nim : ša a-bu-ni* [31]*e-zi-bu-ma : a-ta : tù-kà-lu-ni : bi*$_4$*-lá-ma* [32]*a-na A-lim*^{ki} : *a-ṣé-er : a-ha-tí-ni : gu*$_5$*-ba-áb-tim* [33]*ù a-he-ni : lu nu-bi*$_4$*-il*$_5$*-ma : tám-kà-ar a-bi*$_4$*-ni* [34]*lu nu-ša-bi*$_4$*-ma : ší-tám : a-ma-lá : ší-ma-at : a-bi*$_4$*-ni* [35]*lu né-pu-uš : ú a-na a-i-tim : ta-tí-ki-il*$_5$*-ma* [36]*ba-lu-um : a-ha-tí-ni : gu*$_5$*-ba-áb-tim : a-he-ni* [37]*ú ší-ma-at : a-bi*$_4$*-ni : ša-ma-e-em : ku-nu-kam : ša a-bi*$_4$*-ni* [38]*tal-qé : A-mur-*^{d}utu : *I-ku-na-am : e-pu-ul* [39]*um-ma A-mur-*^{d}utu : *a-na I-ku-nim-ma* lo.e. [40]*i-na mu-a-at : a-bi*$_4$*-ni : a-na-ku ú a-ta* [41]*uš-ba-ni : a-bu-ni* : 1 gín kù-babbar : *lá e-zi-ib* [42]*a-na* é *nu-a-im : a-na-ku : e-ru-ub-ma* [43]2 *ma-na* kù-babbar : é *nu-a-im : al-qé-ma* [44]*a-na qú-bu-ur* : [*a*]*-bi*$_4$*-ni : ag-mu-ur* rev. [45]*iš-tù* : 3 *ša-na-tim : a-bu-ni* [46]*me-et : ša mì-ma : ša a-bi*$_4$*-a : lá al-qé-ú* [47]*ú mì-ma : a-na a-bi*$_4$*-a : ú* *ku-a-tí : lá ha-bu-lá-ku-ni* ^{48}*ú ṭup-pì : a-bi : ú a-ta : lá tù-kà-lá-ni* ^{49}*ú a-ta : i-ṣé-ri-a : mì-ma* ^{50}*lá tí-šu-ú : i-na dí-tim : tù-ša-a-lá-ni* ^{51}*ša ṭup-pá-am : ha-ar-ma-am : a-bi*$_4$ *ú a-ta* ^{52}*lá tù-kà-lá-ni : ta-ar-ta-ag-ma-am* ^{53}*lu ṭup-pì-i : ha-ar-ma-am : tù-kà-lá : lu ší-be-e* ^{54}*tí-šu-a-nim : a-na a-num-ma : ru-a-nim-ma* ^{55}*mì-nam : a-qa-bi*$_4$: iti-3-kam : *a-bi*$_4$: *e-er-šu-um* ^{56}*ú-kà-il*$_5$*-šu : ki-ma :* kù-babbar : *i-šu-ú : ú-lá i-šu-ú* ^{57}*mì-ma : lá iq-bi*$_4$ *: ú a-ta : i-na re-eš*$_{15}$ *: a-bi*$_4$*-ni* ^{58}*ta-za-az : ki-ma* kù-babbar : *a-bu-ni* ^{59}*lá e-zi-bu : a-[t]a-ma : tí-de*$_8$*-e : ú a-na a-wa-tim* ^{60}*a-ra-tim : ki-a-ma : i-na dí-tí-im* ^{61}*tù-ša-a-lá-ni : [u*$_4$*]-ma-am : i-na ṭup-pì-im* ^{62}*a-wa-tim : ma-[da]-tim : tù-ul-ta-pì-tám* ^{63}*ṭup-pì-ni : lu nu-ha-ri-im-ma : ší-ma-at* ^{64}*a-bi*$_4$*-ni : lu ni-iš-me-ma : a-ma-lá : ší-ma-at* ^{65}*a-bi*$_4$*-ni : i-na A-lim*^{ki} *: lu né-tù-wu-ú* ^{66}*ú iš-tù : a-bu-ni : me-tù-ú* ^{67}(erasure) *a-ma-at-kà : ú-ša-kà-al : ú ú-lá-ba-áš* ^{68}*i-na sú-ku-ur-tim : a-na ni-ší-a : ba-lu-ṭim* ^{69}1½ *ma-na* kù-babbar : é *nu-a-e : a-sí-ma : qá-qí-dí* ^{70}*ú ni-ší-a : ú-ba-li-iṭ-ma : u*$_4$*-ma-am* ^{71}*nu-a-um : i-šé-a-ni : i-a-tí : a-na me-tim* ^{72}*ta-áš-ku-ni-ma : ša a-na-ku : mì-ma : i-na* ^{73}*ba-áb-tim ša a-bi*$_4$*-ni lá al-qé-ú : a-ta* ^{74}*ta-lik-ma : i-na Lu-hu-sà-dí-a : iš-tí : Ha-nu-nu* ^{75}*ú A-ni-na :* ½ *ma-na* kù-babbar : *tal-qé-e* ^{76}*ba-a-am : i-na A-lim*^{ki} *: a-ha-at-ni : gu*$_5$*-ba-áb-tum* ^{77}*ú a-hu-ú-ni : i-na A-lim*^{ki} *: A-šùr : uš-bu* ^{78}*a-ma-lá : ší-ma-at : a-bi*$_4$*-ni : lu né-pu-uš* ^{79}*ší-ma-at : a-bi*$_4$*-ni : i-na A-lim*^{ki} *: a-ta* ^{80}*ki-ma : li-bi*$_4$*-im : ta-da-nim ú* kù-babbar ^{81}10 gín-ta : *ta-da-nim-ma : ni-ší-a : ba-lu-ṭim* ^{82}*e-ša-ni-ma : a-na gám-ri-im : ú hu-bu-lim* ^{83}*ta-áš-ta-áp-ra-ni : iš-tù* u.e. ^{84}*[a-b]u-ni : me-tù* : 10 gín-ta kù-babbar ^{85}*a-na ni-ší-a : a-na A-lim*^{ki} *: uš-té-bi*$_4$*-i[l*$_5$*]* ^{86}*iš-tù : a-bi*$_4$ *: a-Kà-ni-iš : i-li-kà-ni* ^{87}*a-na-ku : a-hi-tám : wa*$^{!}$*-áš-ba-ku : a-ta : i-na* ^{88}*re-ší-šu : ta-zi-iz : e-mu-uq : a-bi*$_4$*-a* ^{89}(erased line) le.e. ^{90}*lá-mì-dí* : (erasure) *a-na a-wa-tim : a-ni-a-tim : kà-ru-um Kà-ni-iš : ṣa-he-er* : gal ^{91}*i-dí-ni-a-tí-ma* : ká dingir^{lim} : igi gír *ša A-šùr ší-bu-tí-ni : ni-dí-in* ^{92}igi *I-ší-im-Sú-en*$_6$: dumu *Šál-ma-A-šùr* : igi *Dan-A-šùr* dumu *A-šùr-iš-tí-kál*

^{1}Ikūnum seized us (as arbitrators) against Amur-Šamaš, and $^{2–3}$Ikūnum (said) as follows: "At the death of our father, $^{3–4}$you sent me off without a single shekel of silver, and $^{5–6}$I took a working capital from a recognized trader, then I intended to go to Aššur. $^{7–8}$You, you seized me and almost had me executed. $^{8–9}$Also, you seized (the contents of) my storehouse together with the working capital, and $^{10–11}$(said) as follows: 'You owe silver to me and to my wife.' $^{11–13}$You made my eyes bloodshot, (because) from the silver of our own father, you certified my tablet for an amount of (only) 10 shekels of silver. ^{13}Now, you must not make trouble for me, ^{14}and you must not send me to (work off) my debt (in a creditor's) house!

[15–17]5⅓ minas of silver, a precious golden object (weighing) 3 shekels, a votive offering of Tašmētum, 2 precious golden objects, (one weighing) 2⅔ shekels, (the other) 2¾ shekels of gold, [18–20]⅓ shekel (weight of) the gods (figurines) of our father, 2 minas (weight of) 2 bronze discs-*su'ums*, 2 axes and their *sāsum* (stone?), cups from 2 *qablītum*-containers; [20–21]all this is kept in chests under the seal of our father. [22–23]2 bronze *supānum*-bowls of 2 minas each, 1 hatchet (weighing) 1 mina, an *arzallum*-implement, 2 small knives, [24–25]2 plated *qablītum*-containers of ½ mina each, 2 *qablītum*-containers <of 1 mina each>, 1 plated (and) 1 not plated, [26–27]3 *uruzzannum*-tables made of boxwood, 2 talents, 10 minas of antimony, [27–28]1 certified tablet concerning the sale of Arala, 1 tablet concerning the sale of Happuahšušar, [29–30]1 tablet concerning the sale of Hištahšušar, <1 tablet> concerning the debt owed by an Anatolian. [30–31]All this that our father left and that you hold back, bring (it) here [32–33]so that we can bring it to Aššur to our sister, the consecrated woman, and to our brothers, [33–35]pay the creditors of our father and act for the rest according to the will of our father. [35–38]Why are you so sure that without our sister, the consecrated woman, our brothers, and without hearing the will of our father, you could take our father's seal?"

[38–39]Amur-Šamaš replied to Ikūnum; Amur-Šamaš (said) to Ikūnum as follows: [40–41]"At the death of our father, you and I were (both) present. [41]Our father did not leave even 1 shekel of silver! [42]I entered the house of an Anatolian (creditor) and [43]borrowed 2 minas of silver from the house of the Anatolian (creditor) and [44]spent (it) for our [fa]ther's grave. [45–46]Our father died 3 years ago! Even though I did not take anything from our father's belongings, [47]I do not owe anything to our father or to you, [48]neither you nor my father hold a (debt) tablet from me, (and) [49–50]you yourself have no claim on me, you interrogate me in court! [51–52]Even though my father and you held no certified tablet, you have raised a claim against me! [53–54]If you (pl.) hold a certified tablet of me, or witnesses against me, then bring them here for this. [55–56]What (else) can I say? For 3 months, my father remained confined to bed. [56–57]He did not tell me whether he had silver or not. [57–59]Since you were the one close to him, you must know that our father left no silver! [59–61]Even so, you interrogate me thus in court for false purposes. [61–62]Now, you write me ma[n]y words on a tablet! [63–65]Let us seal our tablet, hear the will of our father, and discuss in accordance with the will of our father in Aššur! [66–67]Moreover, since our father died, I feed and cloth your female slave. [68–69]During the suspension (of commerce), for the well-being of my people, I asked for 1½ minas of silver from the house of an Anatolian (creditor) and [69–70]thus kept alive myself and my people, but today [71]the Anatolian (creditor) sues me! [71–73]You have turned me into a dead (man), and although I myself took nothing from the outstanding claims owed by our father, [73–75] you yourself went and took ½ mina of silver from Hanunu and Anīna in Luhusaddiya. [76–77]Come to the city (of Aššur), our sister the consecrated woman and our brothers are in the city (of Aššur). [78]Let us act according to the will of our father. [79–82]The will of our father (is) in the city (of Aššur). You, instead of encouraging me by giving me some silver, 10 shekels for each, and thus (helping) to keep my people in good health, [82–83]you repeatedly write me for expenses and debts! [83–85]Since our [fa]ther died, I have sent 10 shekels of silver for each of my people in the city (of Aššur). [86–87]After my father went to Kaneš, I was the one who lived in a house separately. [87–90]You, you were the one close to him! Inform me about my father's assets!

[90–91]For these proceedings, the *kārum* of Kaneš, (the whole assembly) small and big, appointed us (as arbitrators), and [91]we have given our testimony before Aššur's dagger at the Gate of the God. [92]In the presence of Išim-Suen, son of Šalim-Aššur, and Dān-Aššur, son of Aššuriš-tikal.

Bibliography: Text published by Hecker 2004a, 286–91 (Kt m/k 69); duplicate of Kt m/k 70. Lines 15–30 are quasi duplicates of **64**:20–41. The tablet is on display in the Museum of Anatolian Civilizations (Ankara) and could not be collated. A photo of the obverse of the tablet in its envelope has been sold for more than twenty years as a museum postcard.

Comments: Ikūnum accuses his brother Amur-Šamaš of having taken for himself their father's seal. But, according to the unpublished text Kt m/k 2:32–38 (envelope Kt m/k 65), the father bequeathed his personal seal to his (consecrated) *gubabtum* daughter, who was living in Aššur:[23] "Our father died during the eponym Isaya (REL 128, ca. 1845). While he was still alive, in the presence of Inah-ilī and Ikūnum, our father gave me a seal of lapis lazuli saying as follows: 'The seal is for your sister. Go and give it to your sister in the city (of Aššur).' Our father did not put under

23. Kt m/k 2:32-38: [30]*a-bu-ni* : *i-na* [31]*li-mì-im I-sá-a* : *lu me-et* [32]*a-bu-ni* : *i-na bu-ul-ṭí-šu-ma* : *ma-ah-ri-kà* [33]igi *I-na-ah-*dingir *ú I-ku-nim* : *ku-nu-kam* [34]*ša* $^{na}{}_{4}$za-gìn : *a-bu-ni* : *i-dí-nam* [35]*um-ma šu-ut-ma* : *ku-nu-ku ša a-ha-tí-kà* [36]*a-lik-ma* : *i-na A-lim*^{ki} : *a-na a-ha-tí-kà* [37]*dí-šu* : *a-bu-ni* : *ku-nu-kam* : *šu-a-ti* [38]*lá ik-nu-uk*. Lines cited by Hecker 2004a, 292 n. 42.

seal this (cylinder)-seal." We do not know what else the daughter was supposed to inherit from her father.

---

66. Dispute among Heirs; the Sister Is Asked to Send a Copy of the Father's Will

Obv. ^{1}*a-na A-šur-ma-sú-wi ú Lá-ma-sí qí-bi$_4$-/ma* ^{2}*um-ma En-um-A-šùr-ma a-šu-mì* ^{3}*ší-ma-tim ša a-bi-ni* ^{4}*té-er-tí a-dí 5$^{ší-šu}$ áš-pu-ra-ki-ma* ^{5}*ma-tí-ma té-er-tí ú-lá e-zi-ba-am-/ma* ^{6}*úz-ni lá ta-p[á-t]í-i* ^{7}*ù li-ba-am ú-[lá] ta-dí-ni-im* ^{8}*a-na-ku a-lá-nu-tí* (*sic!*) *[a]-ha-tám* ^{9}*ú bé-el-tám ša-ni-tám ma-nam* ^{10}*i-šu-ú* : *iš-tù u$_4$-mì-im* ^{11}*ša a-bi-i i-mu-tù a-šu-mì* ^{12}*mu-ší ú ú-ri lá a-ša-ga-šu-/ni* lo.e. ^{13}*A-šur ú i-lá-bi-ni* ^{14}*li-ṭù-lá um-ma a-na-ku-ma* ^{15}*ma*-dí-iš a-h[a]-tí ú-za-kà ú* ^{16}*bé-tí-ša ú-ba-áb-ší-ma* ^{17}*pá-ni-ša ṣa-al-mu-tim* ^{18}*ú-ša-an-wa-ar a-tí ma-tí-ma* ^{19}*té-er-tí-ki lá i-li-kam-ma li-ba-am* ^{20}*ú-lá ta-dí-ni-im i-na u$_4$-mì-im* ^{21}*ša ṭup-pí ta-ša-me-a-ni* ^{22}*A-šur-ma-sú-i ù a-tí me-eh-ra-at* ^{23}*ší-ma-tim šu-ba-al-ki-tù-ma* ^{24}*iš-tí A-lu-wa šé-bi$_4$-lá-nim* ^{25}½ *ma-na* kù-babbar *Ku-da-tum ub-lá-ki-/im* ^{26}½ *ma-na* kù-babbar *a-ha-ma* 2 gín ^{27}*a-me-er-i-tí-ki* : *A-lu-wa* ^{28}*na-áš-a-ki-im* : *bé-el-tí a-tí* ^{29}*mu-ší ú ú-ri ša-zu-za-tí-a* ^{30}*ša-am-ṭí-i-ma a-ma-lá* ^{31}*áš-pu-ra-ku-nu-tí-ni* 2 *ṭup-pé-e* ^{32}*ša dí-in A-lim^{ki} le-qé-a-ma* le.e. ^{33}*Áš-du ú A-lu-wa ṭù-ur-/da-nim* ^{34}*ú mì-ma ša la$_1$** é *a-bi$_4$-<ni>* ^{35}*a-hu-ur-tám šu-up-ra-nim-ma* ^{36}*uz-ni pé-té-a um-mì-a-nu a-bi$_4$-ni* ^{37}*be-tám ik-ta-an-ku*

$^{1-2}$Say to Aššur-massu'ī and Lamassī: thus (says) Ennum-Aššur.

$^{2-4}$Concerning our father's will, I wrote to you (fem.) up to five times, $^{5-7}$but no news ever came to me, nor have you informed me or encouraged me. $^{8-10}$As for me, apart from you, what [si]ster and lady do I have? $^{10-11}$From the day our father died—$^{13-14}$may Aššur and our father's god be my witnesses—$^{11-12}$did I not try to do my utmost, night and day? $^{14-15}$I (said) to myself as follows: "I will fully clear my sister, ^{16}free her house of claims, $^{17-18}$and light up her frowning face!" $^{18-20}$But as for you, no news from you ever came to me, and you did not encourage me! $^{20-21}$The very day you hear my tablet, $^{22-24}$you and Aššur-massu'ī should have a copy made of the will and send it to me with Aluwa.

^{25}Kudātum brought you (fem.) ½ mina of silver. $^{26-28}$Aluwa is bringing you ½ mina of silver and another 2 shekels for your daughter. $^{28-30}$You are my lady. Pester my representatives night and day, and $^{30-32}$according to what I wrote, get 2 tablets with verdicts of the city (assembly of Aššur),

^{33}send (pl.) Ašdu and Aluwa, and $^{34-35}$write me concerning all the remainder that is not of our father's house, and $^{36-37}$thus inform me! Our father's investors have just sealed the house.

Bibliography: Text published by Larsen as AKT 6a, 233 (Kt 94/k 739); collated May 2012.

Comments: Šalim-Aššur had two sons, Ennum-Aššur, married to Anna-anna, and Ali-ahum, married to Ištar-lamassī; and two daughters, Lamassī, a consecrated woman living in Aššur, and Šāt-Anna, married to Šuppinuman, son of Peruwa (fig. 20; Larsen, AKT 6a, 7). When he died in Durhumit, in circa 1756 or 1755 (REL 103 or 104), there was a dispute among his children concerning the inheritance, which is documented by no fewer than eighty-eight texts. In one of those, Ennum-Aššur accuses his brother of having influenced their father to make an additional oral codicil to his will before his death. He asks his sister for a copy of the father's will and a tablet of the city. The official tablet was sent with an attorney (**67**) but not the copy of the will. One or two years later, Ennum-Aššur was killed in the country of Tawiniya (ca. 1754 or 1753, REL 105 or 106).

Line 13: note the writing *i-lá-bi-ni* for *ilu abini.*

67. The Sister Sends an Attorney but Not the Copy of the Will

Obv. ^{1}*um-ma La*$_1$*-ma-sí-ma* ^{2}*a-na En-nam-A-šùr ù* ^{3}*A-la*$_1$*-hi-im qí-bi-ma* ^{4}*ta-áš-pu-ra-nim um-ma a-tù-nu-/ma* ^{5}*ra-bi-ṣa-am : ah-za-nim* ^{6}*ù ṭup-pá-am ša A-lim*^{ki} ^{7}*le-qé-a-nim ra-bi*$_4$*-ṣa-am* ^{8}*ni-hu-za-ku-nu-tí ù ṭup-pá-am ša A-lim*^{ki} ^{9}*ni-il*$_5$*-<qé> a-ma-kam ki-ma ša bu-lu-uṭ* ^{10}*a-bi-ku-nu la*$_1$ *tù-úš-té-ṣa-a-/ma* ^{11}*ša-li-um i-ṣé-er* ^{12}é *a-bi*$_4$*-ku-nu lá i-ša-lá* ^{13}*lu ší-ta-am a-tù-nu-ma* ^{14}kù-babbar^{áp} *a-bi-ni ma-lá* ^{15}*a-wi-lu-tí-ku-nu pá-hi-ra-/ma* rev. ^{16}*ù pu-ut a-bi-ni ù* é$^{/et}$ ^{17}*a-bi*$_4$*-ni e-bi-ba-ma* ^{18}*ša-li-um i-ṣé-er* é^{et} ^{19}*a-bi*$_4$*-ni lá i-ša-lá : lá tù-uš-té-/ṣa-a* ^{20}*a-pu-tum šu-ma a-hu-a a-tù-nu* ^{21}*ra-bi*$_4$*-ṣú-um e-ku-ša-ku-nu-tí* ^{22}kù-babbar 10 *ma-na ma-lá a-wi-lu-tí-ku-nu* ^{23}*lu da-pu-ur-tí* é *a-bi*$_4$*-ni* ^{24}*ù* é *a-bi-ni e-bu-bi-im* ^{25}*ep-ša-ma ù ra-ma-ku-nu* ^{26}*za-ki-a-nim tí-ib-a-nim-ma* ^{27}*a-tal-kà-nim-ma ú iš-tí* dam-gàr ^{28}*ù um-mì-a-ni a-bi*$_4$*-ku-nu* u.e. ^{29}*zu-ku-a [a-p]u-tum šu-ma a-ma-kam* ^{30}*a-tù-nu ša-tám iš-té-et* ^{31}*sà-ah-ra-tù-nu za-lu-ar-[t]ám* le.e. ^{32}*a-šar 1 ma-na ù 2 ma-na-e* kù-babbar ^{33}*a-bu-ni ha-bu-lu šé-bi*$_4$*-lá-nim-ma* ^{34}*lu ni-iš-qú-ul i-na da-ma-am-tum*$^{?}$ ^{35}*a-na ma*$^{!}$*-e : lá tù-ṣí-i*

[1-3]Thus (says) Lamassī: say to Ennum-Aššur and Ali-ahum.

[4]You wrote me as follows: [5]"Contract an attorney for me [6-7]and get hold of a tablet from the city (of Aššur)." [7-8]We have gotten an attorney for you, and [8-9]we got hold of a tablet from the city (of Aššur). [9-10]Just as during the life of your father, do not quarrel there, [11-12]so that no troublemaker does any harm to your father's house. [13-15]As for the remainder, it is you who must collect the silver of our father, inasmuch as you (are responsible) gentlemen, and [16-19]clear (from claims) our father and our father's house so that no troublemaker does any harm to your father's house, and you must not quarrel. [20-21]Urgent! If you really are my brothers, when the attorney comes to you, [22-25]move to realize at least 10 minas of silver—inasmuch as you (are responsible) gentlemen—by clearing both the *satisfaction*? of our father's house and our father's house itself, and [25-26]then clear yourselves. [26-27]Set out, come here [27-29]and clear (things) with the creditors and your father's investors. [29-31][Ur]gent! If you are delayed for one entire year, [31-33]send a … wherever our father owes 1 or 2 minas of silver, and [34]let us pay it. [34-35]When *mourning*?, don't go out for water!

Bibliography: Text published by Larsen as AKT 6a, 236 (Kt 94/k 772); collated May 2012.

Comments: Lamassī blames her brothers for their attitude and asks them, instead of starting quarrels, to clear their father's debts.

Line 23: the meaning of the word *dappurtum* is unknown. Veenhof in VS 26, 70:5, translated it as "quickly," or "in time"; this translation does not fit here. Larsen, in AKT 6a, 384, supposes that it is built on the D-stem of *dapārum*, with the meaning "to satisfy"; but it does not really make sense in this text.

Line 32: the word *za-lu-ar-tám* is unknown; since the sign "*lu*" seems to be clear, one could also read *za-lu-ùh*!*-tám*.

Line 34: the word *da-ma-am-tum*? is also unkown; it could be linked to mourning activities. The meaning of the last sentence, a proverbial expression, is unknown. Wells were located outside of the house, at several points of the town, and it might not have been appropriate to quit the house, even to fetch water, when performing morturary rites.

68. Brother and Sister Dispute over a Female Slave Left by Their Father

Obv. [1]*um-ma La*$_1$*-ma-sí-ma a-na* [2]*A-la*$_1$*-hi-im qí-bi*$_4$*-ma* [3]*mì-šu ša ta-áš-pu-ra-ni* [4]*um-ma a-ta-ma a-*[*m*]*a-kam* [5]*a-na* kù-babbar 1 gín *e-né-ki* [6]*a-he-e-eš*$_{15}$ *ra-k*[*i-i*]*s* [7]*Ší**-[*ma*$^?$*-at*$^?$] *-Ištar e úṣ-ri-/ma* [8]*e tù-úṣ-a-am* [9]*ke-e a-bi*$_4$*-i* : *i-na* lo.e. [10]*re-ší-a i-zi-zi-im* [11]*ù qá-qí-dí-a* : *na-ṣa-ri-im* [12]*e-zi-ba-ši a-na-ku* <*a-na*>[13]kù-babbar 1 gín *e-né-a* [14]*a-na-ší-ma ù ú-ša-ra-ší* [15][x x *k*]*à-tù-kà lá ta-ša-/kán* [16]*lá ú-ša-ra-ší mì-*[*š*]*u-/um* [17]*a-ma-kam um-ma Kà-lá-ta***-šar-*<*ma*> [18]*a-hu-kà* é *a-bi*$_4$*-ni* [19]*a-na ha-lu-qí-im* [20]*i-tí-zi-iz a-pu-tum* [21]*i-hi-id i-*[*ša*]*-ha-at* [22]*ra-bi*$_4$*-ṣí-im ša ki-ma* [23]*E-dí-*[x]*-a-ša i-zi-za-ma* le.e. [24][kù]-babbar *ša l*[*i-bi-šu*]*-nu* [25][x]*-lá***-tí-*[x x x] *šu-uq***-/lá***-ma* [26][é$^{be-et}$] *a-bi*$_4$*-ni e x-šu***-ma* [27]*x a-ta ú* x [x x]

[1–2]Thus (says) Lamassī: say to Ali-ahum.

[3–4]Why have you written me as follows: [4–6]"There, your eyes are fixed on every single shekel of silver. [7–8]Should you not watch Šīmat$^?$-Ištar lest she cannot leave to come here"? [9–12]For certain, my father left her to be at my disposal and to take care of me. [12–14]Would I lift my eyes <for> just one shekel of silver and so release her? [15]You shall not place your [...] [16]and I shall not release her. [16–17]Why does Kalatašar (say) there as follows: [18–20]"Your brother was ready to destroy the house of our father!"

[20–23]Urgent! Be careful to assist the attorney, representative of Edi[x]aša, and [24–25]pay them the silver that [...] [26]so that our father's [house ...] [27]you [...]

Bibliography: Text published by Larsen as AKT 6a, 247 (Kt 94/k 719); collated May 2012.

Comments: In an earlier message, Ali-ahum has warned his sister against wasting money on the release of a female slave left by their father. The brother ready to destroy the family house might be Ennum-Aššur.

69. Division between Anatolians Involving a Woman

Envelope (TC 3, 215):
Obv. [1](seal A) [2]kišib *Šu-p*[*u-na-ah* x x x x] [3]kišib *Pé-ru-*[*wa* kišib *Šé-pá-na*] [4]*Lá-bar-ša Š*[*u-pí-ša-am-nu-ma-an*] [5]*ù Lá-ma-*[*sí i-zu-zu-ma ù*] [6]*Lá-bar-ša i*[*š-tí bé-tim*] [7](seal A) (lacuna)

U.e. [1'](seal B)
[2]Sealed by Šupp[unah …]; [3]sealed by Peru[wa; sealed by Šepana].
[4–5]Labarša, Šuppišamnuman, and Lama[ssī made the division (of property), and] [6]Labarša [*left* the house].

Tablet
Obv. [1]*Lá-bar-ša Lá-ma-sí* [2]*ù Šu-pí-ša-am-nu-ma-an* [3]*i-zu-zu-ma ù* [4]*Lá-bar-ša iš-tí bé-tim* [5]*i-tí-ṣí a-hu-um* [6]*a-na a-he-e* [7]*lá i-tù-wa-ar* [8]*ša i-tù-ru* rev. [9]5 *ma-na* kù-babbar [10]*i-ša-qal ù i-na* [11]*i-dí-nim i-du-ku-uš* [12]igi *Šu-pu-na-ah* [13]igi *Pè-ru-wa* [14]igi *Šé-pá-na*

[1–3]Labarša, Lamassī, and Šuppišamnuman made the division (of property), and [4–5]Labarša left the house. [5–7]One shall not raise a claim against the other; [8–10]the one who does raise a claim shall pay five minas of silver, [10–11]or they will put that one to death in *the steppe*.
[12–14]In the presence of Šuppunah, Peruwa, and Šepana.

Bibliography: Tablet published in copy by Thureau-Dagin as TC 2, 73; envelope published in copy by Lewy as TC 3, 215; text edited by Eisser and Lewy (1930, no. 10). Lines 3–7 of the envelope restored by Donbaz (1989, 89).

Comments: Labarša and Šuppišamnuman, presumably two brothers bearing Anatolian names, divided an inheritance, probably a paternal estate. According to Veenhof 1997b, 159, Labarša, mentioned first, possibly the eldest brother, decided to leave the common household. The woman, Lamassī, bears an Assyrian name; she could be either the wife of the deceased man or his daughter.

Women Protected against Their Father's or Husband's Creditors

Several Assyrian wills, according to which daughters (generally consecrated) received shares of inheritances, show that they did not thereby incur their fathers' liabilities.[24] Parental debts, presumably commercial in nature, had to be paid by the male heirs before any division of the estate. Next the women of the family, mothers and daughters, received their shares; they were, moreover, often the first to do so (**54**, **57**). This rule, which seems to have been the norm, is invoked by Ili-bāni in his will, "All my sons are responsible for my debts" (**56**).[25] In fact, responsibility for a father's debts regularly fell upon the male heirs, as shown in a letter sent by Ali-ahum, who, after his father's death, made the inventory of his house, in which several women of the family were still living (**70**). The storerooms and strong room turned out to be bare to the walls, so Ali-ahum suspected that the women had helped themselves, "You are women, but he (is) a man, and they will bring action against him for his father's debts." Clearly one fundamental difference between men and women in a family was that the daughters of Assyrian merchants were not responsible for any commercial debts contracted by their deceased fathers. Certain merchants had the foresight to make provisions during their lifetimes lest their wife and children find themselves deep in debt after their demise (**71**).

In like manner, some parents, when marrying off their daughters, tried to protect them from liability for their husbands' future debts by adding a clause specifying this in the marriage contract. The groom had to promise not to allow creditors to distrain his future wife, not to sell her (**73**), and to undertake to find a third party who would stand guarantor for his debt (**72**).

The letters sent by wives in Aššur to their husbands in Asia Minor gives ample testimony, however, for debts their husbands had incurred to associates or to the city authorities. Indeed, women in Aššur were regularly dunned by creditors to pay off their husbands' debts, especially for sums owed to the authorities for taxes or fines.[26] The eponym-official could seize

24. Michel 2003b.

25. In the inheritance agreement AKT 8, 297, the two sons are also responsible for their father's debts, but the eldest son alone, who inherited the house, is responsible for the care, the debts, and the burial of his mother.

26. See chapter 4, pp. 301–14.

wives' property, such as slaves or bronze objects, for collateral, and even close and seal their houses to force them to pay.[27]

---

70. Sons Inherit Assets and Liabilities; Daughters Receive Only the Assets

Obv. ^{1}*a-na I-na-a qí-bi$_4$-ma* ^{2}*um-ma ra-bi$_4$- ṣú-ma* ^{3}*ù A-lá-hu-um : a-na-kam* ^{4}*a-na ša ki-ma a-bi$_4$-a áp-nu-ma* ^{5}*um-ma a-na-ku-ma er-ba-ma* ^{6}*ší-tí* é *a-[b]i$_4$-a kà-li-ma-/ni* ^{7}*e-ru-bu-ma um-ma šu-nu-/ma* ^{8}*a-lá-an* 70 túg *pì-ri-kà-/ni* ^{9}*mì-ma ú-lá ni-il$_5$-qé* ^{10}*ù ma-ṣa-ar-tám* ^{11}*ni-ip-té-m[a] mì-ma* ^{12}*i-ma-ṣa-ar-tim lá-šu* ^{13}*ù a-wi-lá-tim* ^{14}*aṣ-ba-at-ma um-ma* ^{15}*né-nu-ma : ú-zu-um* ^{16}kù-babbar^{áp} *a-bi$_4$-a : i-ha-li-/iq* ^{17}*um-ma ší-na-ma* ^{18}*a-na kà-ri-im lá ta-ra-/de$_8$-ni-a-tí* ^{19}5 *ma-na* kù-babbar ^{20}*iq-bi$_4$-a-nim wa-<ar>-ki-tá-ma* ^{21}*Puzur$_4$-Sú-en$_6$ ù* lugal-*Sú-/en$_6$* ^{22}*ù a-hu-šu* dumu$^{er-ú}$ *Ma-ni-/a* ^{23}*a-na a-wi-lá-tim im-li-ku-ma* ^{24}*um-ma šu-nu-ma* kù-babbar ^{25}*ta-be-a-lá sí-ni-ša-tí-ni* ^{26}*šu-ut za-kà-ar a-hu-bu-ul* ^{27}*a-bi$_4$-šu i-ṣa-bu-tù-šu* ^{28}*a-na-kam a-bu-tám i-za-zu* ^{29}*a-na-ku ù ra-bi$_4$-ṣú-um* le.e. ^{30}*tí-iq-[ni] ù* kù-babbar^{áp}*-kà* ^{31}*ú e-ri-ku a-bi$_4$ a-ta be-lí a-ta* ^{32}*a-ma-kam ṭup-pá-am ša kà-ri-im*

$^{1-3}$Say to Innaya: thus (say) the attorney and Ali-ahum.

$^{3-4}$Here, I have turned to the representatives of my father, and ^{5}I (said) as follows: "Enter and ^{6}show me what remains of my father's household!" ^{7}They entered and (said) as follows: $^{8-9}$"Apart from the 70 *pirikannum*-textiles, we took nothing! $^{10-11}$We also opened the strong room, $^{11-12}$and there was nothing in the strong room!"

$^{13-15}$(Then) I seized the women, and we (said) as follows: $^{15-16}$"Alas! Will my father's silver get lost?" ^{17}They (replied) as follows: ^{18}"You must not take us to the *kārum*!" $^{19-20}$And they promised us 5 minas of silver.

$^{20-23}$Later on, Puzur-Suen, as well as Šarra-Suen and his brother, the sons of Manniya, gave advice to the women, $^{24-25}$(saying) as follows: "You can keep the silver; $^{25-27}$you are women, but he (is) a man, and they will seize him for his father's debts." ^{28}Here, they will give fatherly protection. $^{29-31}$The attorney and myself ... ornaments and your silver.... You are my father and master. ^{32}There, ... a tablet of the *kārum*.

---

27. See Dercksen 2004a, 40–51.

Bibliography: Text published in copy by Smith as CCT 5, 8b; edited by Michel (1991, no. 54).

Comments: Ali-ahum's father died, leaving some debts to his son. His house is inhabited by some ladies who had family links with the dead merchant (wife, daughters, or sisters). They have taken goods left by the deceased needed to pay his debts.

Line 31: the first word, not understood, should be a verb.

Line 32: the last sentence of this letter is incomplete, lacking a verb. There might have been a small second page, lost today.

---

71. Debt of the Husband and Father Paid by Representatives

Envelope

Obv. ^{1}(seal A) ^{2}[kišib] *Lá-ba-na-da* ^{3}dumu *I-dí-Sú-en*$_{6}$ ^{4}kišib *I-ku-pí-A-šur* ^{5}(seal B) ^{6}dumu *P*[*í-lá*]*-ah-A-šur* lo.e. ^{7}(seal B) rev. ^{8}(seal A) ^{9}*a-na a-wa-tim* ^{10}*a-ni-a-tim kà-ru-um* ^{11}*Dur-hu-mì-it i-dí-ni-a-tí-ma* ^{12}igi gír *ša A-šur* ^{13}(seal B) ^{14}*ší-bu-tí-ni* : *ni-dí-in* u.e. ^{15}*I-dí-Da-gán* ^{16}(seal A) le.e. ^{17}[dumu *Sà-a*]*r-ni-ki-im* ^{18}(seal A) ^{19}*ù Ša-lim-a-hu-um* ^{20}dumu du$_{10}$*-ì-lí tap-pá-ú-ni* r.e. ^{21}(seal B)

$^{2-3}$[Sealed by] Labā(n)-nādā, son of Iddin-Suen; $^{4-6}$sealed by Ikuppī-Aššur, son of P[ila]h-Aššur.

$^{9-11}$For these proceedings, the *kārum* of Durhumit appointed us (as arbitrators), and $^{12-14}$we gave our testimony before Aššur's dagger. $^{15-17}$Iddin-Dagan, [son of Sa]rnikum, $^{19-20}$and Šalim-ahum, son of Ṭāb-ilī, were our partners.

Tablet

Obv. ^{1}*En-na-Sú-en*$_{6}$ dumu *I-ku-a* ^{2}*ù Puzur*$_{4}$*-Ištar* dumu *A-lá-bi-lim* ^{3}*i-na ša-ha-at* ^{4}dam *I-ku-pí-a me-er-a-at* ^{5}*I-ku-pí-a ù me-er-e* ^{6}*I-ku-pí-a ki-ma šu-nu-tí* ^{7}*i-zi-zu-ma* 40 *ma-na* kù-babbar ^{8}*hu-bu-ul I-ku-pí-a* ^{9}*a-na A-šur-mu-ta-pí-il*$_{5}$ ^{10}dumu *Pu-šu-ke-en*$_{6}$ ^{11}*ù Bé-lá-nim ra-bi*$_{4}$*-ṣí-lim* lo.e. ^{12}*ša Pu-šu-ke-en*$_{6}$ rev. ^{13}*iš-qú-lu a-na* ^{14}*a-wa-tim a-ni-a-tim* ^{15}*kà-ru-um Dur-hu-mì-it* ^{16}*i-dí-in-ni-a-tí-ma* ^{17}igi gír *ša A-šur ší-bu-tí-ni* ^{18}*ni-dí-in* igi *Lá-ba-na-da* ^{19}dumu *I-dí-Sú-en*$_{6}$ ^{20}igi *I-ku-pí-A-šur* dumu *Pí-lá-lah-A-šur* ^{21}*I-dí-Da-gán* ^{22}dumu *Sà-ar-ni-ki-im* ^{23}*ù Ša-lim-a-hu-um* u.e. ^{24}dumu du$_{10}$*-ì-lí* le.e. ^{25}*tap-pá-ú-ni*

[1-2]Enna-Suen, son of Ikua, and Puzur-Ištar, son of Ali-abum, [3-7]assisted Ikuppiya's wife, Ikuppiya's daughters, and Ikuppiya's sons as their representatives [7-13]and paid to Aššur-mūtappil, son of Pūšu-kēn, and Bēlānum, the attorney of Pūšu-kēn, forty minas of silver, (corresponding to) the debt of Ikuppiya.

[13-16]For these proceedings, the *kārum* of Durhumit appointed us (as arbitrators), and [17-18]we gave our testimony before Aššur's dagger.

[18-19]In the presence of Labā(n)-nādā, son of Iddin-Suen, [20]and Ikuppī-Aššur, son of P[ila]h-Aššur. [21-25]Iddin-Dagan, son of Sarnikum, and Šalim-ahum, son of Ṭāb-ilī, were our partners.

Bibliography: Text edited by Kienast as ATHE, 22.

Comments: The enormous amount of Ikuppiya's debts, forty minas of silver, is paid by representatives in Durhumit, not by his wife and children.

Line 16: the writing *i-dí-in-ni-a-tí-ma* with a double "n" is exceptional.

---

72. A Married Woman Protected from Her Father's Debts

Obv. [1]⅓ *ma-na* 5 gín kù-babbar [2]*hu-bu-lam ša nu-a-e* [3]*ša Ša-lim-Ištar* [4*]gír *ša A-šur* dingir-*ba-ni* [5]*ú-ta-mì-ú-ma* [6]*iš-tù li-mì-im* [7]*Ma-ṣí-ì-lí* [8]*a-na hu-bu*[!](IM)*-li-im* [9]*šu-a-tí* : dingir-*ba-ni* [10]*i-za-az šu-ma* lo.e. [11]*nu-a-ú Ta-ta-a* rev. [12]*a-ša-sú i-ṣa-áb-/tù* [13]dingir-*ba-ni* [14]*ú-ba-áb-ší* [15]*Ib-ni-lí* dumu *A-al*-du$_{10}$ [16]*A-šur-i-mì-tí* dumu *I-dí-we-/er* [17]*Du-du-ú* dumu *A-šur*-du$_{10}$ [18]*En-nam-A-šur* dumu *Na-ra-am-/*ZU [19]*Puzur*$_4$*-A-šur* dumu *A-šùr-i-/dí* [20]*ma-ah-ri-šu-nu* [21]*ni-iš A-lim*[ki] [22]*it-mu-ú* [23]*a-wa-tù-šu gám-ra* u.e. [24]*Ša-lim*[!](WA)*-Ištar ki-ma* le.e. [25]*me-er-i-tí-šu* dingir-*ba-ni* [26]*ki-ma ra-mì-ni-šu*

[1-2]⅓ mina, 5 shekels of silver, debt of the native Anatolians, [3-5]about which Šalim-Ištar made Ilī-bāni swear the following oath by the dagger of Aššur: [6-10]"From the year-eponymy of Maṣi-ilī (REL 109, ca. 1864), Ilī-bāni will be responsible for that debt. [10-12]Should the native Anatolians seize his wife Tataya, [13-14]Ilī-bāni shall clear her." [15-19]Ibni-ilī, son of Āl-ṭāb, Aššur-imittī, son of Iddin-Wēr, Dudu, son of Aššur-ṭāb, Ennum-Aššur, son of Narām-Suen, Puzur-Aššur, son of Aššur-idī, [20-22]in their presence they swore the oath by the city (of Aššur). [23]His case is settled, [24-26]Šalim-Ištar representing his daughter, Ilī-bāni acting for himself.

Bibliography: Text published by Veenhof (1997a, 360–62 [Kt 91/k 200]); collated May 2012.

Comments: Ilī-bāni, as he married Tataya and moved into the house of her father, undertook the responsibility for a debt of his father-in-law (see text **30**) and promises that he will not give his wife as a pledge for this debt.

Line 18: Ennum-Aššur is a variant for Ennum-Aššur: the son of Narām-Suen is written Ennum-Aššur in text no. **30**:5.

---

73. A Woman Protected from Her Husband's Debts

[1]*Ki-tí-tí-a** : *ša Ša-lim-/be-lí* [2]*e-hu-zu-ni* [3]*Ša-lim-be-lí a-na* [4]é$^{\textit{bé-et}}$ *A-mur-A-šùr* [5]*ú-lá ú-šé-ra-áb-ší* [6]*a-šar* : *li-bi*$_4$*-šu* [7]*i-ra-de*$_8$*-šu* : *a-na* [8]*ší-mì-im lu A-mur-A-šùr* [9]*lu* dumu$^{\textit{me-er-ú}}$-*šu* rev. [10]*ù Ša-lim-be-lí* [11]*ú-lá i-du-nu-šu* [12]*ú-lá ú-ru-bu-šu* [13]*šu-ma* : *ma-ma-an* [14]*i-tí-dí-šu* : 1 *ma-na* kù-/babbar [15]*Ša-lim-be-lí* [16]*a-na Ša-at-ì-lí* [17]*i-ša-qal* : igi *A-šùr-/*du$_{10}$ [18]igi du$_{10}$-*a-he-e* [19]igi *I-ku-nim*

[1–2]Kititiya, whom Šalim-bēlī married, [3–5]Šalim-bēlī shall not make her enter the house of Amur-Aššur. [6–7]He shall take her along wherever he wishes. [7–11]Neither Amur-Aššur, his sons, nor Šalim-bēlī shall sell [12]or pledge her$^{!}$. [13–14]If anyone does sell her, [14–17]then Šalim-bēlī shall pay one mina of silver to Šāt-ilī.

[17–19]In the presence of Aššur-ṭāb, Ṭāb-ahhē, and Ikūnum.

Bibliography: Text published in copy by Lewy as KTS 1 47a; edited by Eisser and Lewy (1930, no. 2). Line 1 collated by Donbaz (2015, 67 [Ka. 146]).

Comments: In this contract, a specific clause protects the wife and forbids her husband or a family member, who might be the creditor of her mother, Šāt-ilī, to give her as a pledge.

Women in Debt

It was not unusual for an Assyrian or Anatolian woman to borrow money herself, with or without interest, from a man or another woman; numerous instances of this have turned up among the hundreds of loan contracts found in the houses of the lower town at Kaneš. Such texts almost never state the reason for the loan, so it is very difficult to distinguish loans driven by need from business loans. Business loans can often involve substantial amounts of silver or copper, but smaller sums as well, less than a mina of silver, the equivalent of a sale or credit for two bolts of cloth. The Old Assyrian loan contract was drawn up from the point of view of the creditor, so it is often referred to as a "debt (owed to)" or, for business loans, a "promissory note." Loans taken out by women were often for small sums of silver (**74**) or sacks of grain (**81**), so seem in general to have been for their own subsistence and that of their family in time of shortage, as shown by the repayment dates linked to the harvest (**79**, **76**, **77**).

Like any other debtor, women were of course held responsible for repaying their loans. Some creditors required of them some sort of guarantee, which could take different forms: pledge of an object or a person or designation of a guarantor, man or woman.[28] The guarantor had a subsidiary hability for the case in which the debtor defaulted, by paying the debt himself, in exchange for which he took possession of the debt note and assumed the creditor's rights over the debtor and her property. Among the property put up as pledges by women could be houses, implying that they were the owners of them (**78**). The creditor could decide to move into the debtor's house until the debt was paid off (**79**). In some cases, one or more slaves could be pledged, as well as a house (**75**); in others, holding a person as pledge was enough, either a slave or a member of the family (**80**).

Women's debts seem to have been incurred on their own, independently of their husbands, and any line between individual and common property, if ever a common fund existed, does not seem to have been clearly drawn.[29] A complaint filed by a merchant illustrates this: he demanded the return of objects that his wife gave to another woman for safekeeping, but that woman explained that the objects were in fact pledges for the loan of a small amount of money (**82**).

---

28. On guarantees for creditors, see Veenhof 2001; Michel 2003b. There are several examples of a woman designated as guarantor (**193**, **194**).

29. See Larsen 2007 and chapter 4 of this volume, pp. 271–82.

Whatever the amount borrowed, the examples given below show that more guarantees were required of Anatolian women who took out loans than of Assyrian women; the same was true for loans made to men.

---

74. An Assyrian Woman Owes Twelve Shekels of Silver

Envelope

Obv. [1](seal A) [2][kišib du$_{10}$-*ṣí-lá-A-š*]*ùr* dumu *Da-ki-i*-[(x)] [3][kišib *I-ku-pí-a* dumu] *A-gi$_5$-a-a* [4][kišib *Ša-té-a me-er-a*]*t Sú-e-ta-ta* [5]12 [gín kù-babbar] *i-ṣé-er* [6]*Ša-té-a* [*Pu-š*]*u-ke-en$_6$* [7](seal A) [8]*i-šu* [*i*]*š-tù* [9][*ha*]*-muš-ti*[*m*] [10][*ša A-šur-ták-lá-ku*] rev. [11]*a*-[*na*] [12]5 [*ha-am-ša-tim ta-ša-qal*] [13]*šu-ma* [*lá ta-áš-qúl*] [14]1½ [gín-ta *a-na* 1 *ma-na-im i-na*] [15]iti-kam [*ṣí-ib-tám tù-ṣa-áb*] le.e. [16](seal B) r.e. [17](seal C)

[2][Sealed by Ṭāb-ṣilli-Aš]šur, son of Daki-[x-x]; [3][sealed by Ikuppiya, son of] Agiya; [4][sealed by Šāt-Ea, daugh]ter of Su'etata.

[5–8][Pūš]u-kēn has loaned 12 [shekels of silver] to Šāt-Ea. [9–12][F]rom the [w]eek [of Aššur-taklāku], [she shall pay] i[n] 5 [weeks]. [13]If [she has not paid, [14–15]she shall add 1½ [shekels per mina] per month [as interest].

Tablet

Obv. [1]12 gín kù-babbar *i-ṣé-er* [2]*Ša-té-a Pu-šu-ke-en$_6$* [3]*i-šu iš-tù ha-muš-tim* [4]*ša A-šur-ták-lá-ku* [5]*a-na* 5 *ha-muš-tim* (*sic*!) [6]*ta-ša-qal šu-ma* [7]*lá ta-áš-qúl* [8][1½] gín-ta *ṣí-ib-tám* [9][*i*]-iti-kam *a-na* rev. [10]1 *ma-na-im tù-ṣa-/áb* [11]iti-kam [12]*A-lá-na-tim* [13]*li-mu-um* [14]*Ì-lí-dan* [15]igi du$_{10}$-*ṣí-lá-A-šùr* [16]igi *I-ku-pí-*[*a*]

[1–3]Pūšu-kēn has loaned 12 shekels of silver to Šāt-Ea. [3–6]From the week of Aššur-taklāku, she shall pay in 5 weeks. [6–7]If she has not paid, [8–10]she shall add 1½ shekels per mina per month as interest.

[11–14]Month Allānātum (xii), eponym Ilī-dān (REL 98/123, ca. 1875/1850).

[15–16]In the presence of Ṭāb-ṣilli-Aššur and Ikuppi[a].

Bibliography: Text published in copy by Smith as CCT 1, 8c; edited by Eisser and Lewy (1930, no. 60). Envelope published in copy by Garelli as CCT 6, 1b.

Comments: This loan contract is quite similar to those concerning men; an Assyrian lady borrowed a small amount of silver from the well-known Assyrian merchant Pūšu-kēn. The default interest corresponds to 30 percent per year and is the one in use among Assyrians.

---

75. An Assyrian Woman Promises to Sell a House and Slave in Case of Default

Envelope

Obv. ^{1}[kišib *Šu-ma-bi$_4$-a* ki]šib *E-lá-lí* ^{2}(seal A) ^{3}kišib *Ištar-lá-ma-sí* ^{4}[*ša* ½ *ma-na* <lá ¼ gín> kù-babbar *i-ṣé-er* ^{5}*Ištar-lá-ma-sí Na-na-a* ^{6}*tí*$^{!}$(I)-*šu i-*[*na*] *ša Pá-ar-kà* ^{7}(seal A) ^{8}*ta-ša-qal šu-ma* lo.e. (seal) rev. ^{9}*lá ta-áš-qú-ul* ^{10}(seal B) ^{11}géme *ú* é^{tám} ^{12}*ta-dá-ma* kù-babbar^{áp}*-ša* ^{13}*ta-lá-qé* ^{14}(seal C) u.e. ^{15}(seal C) le.e. ^{16}(seal A) r.e. ^{17}(seal A)

$^{1-3}$[Sealed by Šumi-abiya; sea]led by Elālī; sealed by Ištar-lamassī.

$^{4-6}$[Concerning] the ½ mina minus ¼ shekel of silver (that) Nanaya has loaned to Ištar-lamassī, $^{6-8}$she shall pay during the Parka festival. $^{8-9}$If she has not paid, $^{11-12}$she (Ištar-lamassī) shall sell the female slave and the house, $^{12-13}$and she (Nanaya) shall take her silver.

Tablet

Obv. ^{1}½ *ma-na* lá ¼ gín kù-babbar ^{2}*i-ṣé-er Ištar-lá-ma-sí* ^{3}*Na-na-a tí-šu* ^{4}*i-na ša Pá-ar-kà* ^{5}*ta-ša-qal šu-ma* ^{6}*i-na u$_4$-me-ša* ^{7}*lá ta-áš-qú-ul* ^{8}géme é^{tám} lo.e. ^{9}*ta-dá-ma* rev. ^{10}kù-babbar^{áp}*-ša* ^{11}*ta-lá-qé* ^{12}igi *Šu-ma-bi$_4$-a* ^{13}igi *E-lá-lí*

$^{1-3}$Nanaya has loaned ½ mina minus ¼ shekel of silver to Ištar-lamassī. $^{4-5}$She shall pay during the Parka festival. $^{6-7}$If she has not paid by the end of her term, $^{8-9}$she (Ištar-lamassī) shall sell the female slave and the house, and $^{10-11}$she (Nanaya) shall take her silver.

$^{12-13}$In the presence of Šumi-abiya and Elālī.

Bibliography: Text published by Matouš (1965, 178) as Adana 237E.

Comments: The Assyrian woman owes half a mina of silver. She pledged her house to her creditor, another woman, in case of default payment, for her to sell, in order to recover her silver.

76. Debt of an Anatolian Woman, with Interest in Case of Default

Envelope

Obv. [1][kišib *Ma-ṣ*]*í-lí* [2](seal) [3]kišib *Šar-ma-ma* [4]kišib *Ha*!*-li-it-*[*kà*] [5]kišib *Ku-šu*!*-ma-an* [6]kišib *Ma-wa-áš-hi* [7](seal) [8]*ša* 1 *ma-na* 7!½ gín [9](seal) [10]kù-babbar *i-ṣé-er* [11]*Ma-wa-áš-hi* rev. [12](seal) [13]*A-šur-na*!*-da*! *i-šu* [14]*iš-tù ha-mu-uš-tim* [15]*ša Na-ra*!*-am-*ZU [16]*a-na ha-ar-pè* [17](seal) [18]*ta-ša-qal šu-ma* u.e. [19](seal) le.e. [20][*lá t*]*a-áš-qú-ul* [21](seal) [22]3 gín-ta *i-na* iti-1-kam! [*a-n*]*a*! [23]1 *ma-na-em tù-ṣa-áb*

[1–6][Sealed by Maṣi-]ilī; sealed by Šarmama; sealed by Halit[ka]; sealed by Kušuman; sealed by Mawašhi.

[8–13]Concerning 1 mina, 7½ shekels of silver, (which) Aššur-nādā has loaned to Mawašhi, [14–18]from the week of Narām-Suen; she shall pay by the summer. [18–20]If [she] has [not] paid, [22–23]she shall add 3 shekels [pe]r mina per month.

Tablet

Obv. [1]1 *ma-na* 7½ gín [2]kù-babbar *i-ṣé-er* [3]*Ma-wa-áš-hi* [4]*A-šur-na-da* [5]*i-šu* : *iš-tù* [6]*ha-mu-uš-tim* [7]*ša Na-ra-am-*ZU [8]*a-na ha-ar-pè* rev. [9]*ta-ša-qal* [10]*šu-ma lá ta-áš-qú-/ul* [11]3 gín-ta [12]*i-na* iti-1-kam [13]*a-na* 1 *ma-na-em* [14]*tù-ṣa-áb* [15]igi *Me-ṣí-li* [16]igi *Šar*!*-ma-ma* [17]igi *Ha-li-it-kà* [18]igi *Ku*!*-šu-ma-an*

[1–5]Aššur-nādā has loaned 1 mina, 7½ shekels of silver to Mawašhi. [5–9]From the week of Narām-Suen, she shall pay by the summer. [10]If she has not paid, [11–14]she shall add 3 shekels per mina per month.

[15–18]In the presence of Maṣi-ilī, Šarmama, Halitka, and Kušuman.

Bibliography: Text published in copy by Smith and Wiseman as CCT 5, 48b–c; obverse and reverse must be inverted on the copy of the envelope; text edited by Rosen (1977, 119–20) and Larsen (2002, no. 148).

Comments: The default interest imposed on this Anatolian woman, who owes more than a mina of silver, is the equivalent of 60 percent per year.

77. Debt of an Anatolian Woman, with Interest in Case of Default

Obv. [1]8½ gín kù-babbar [2]*i-ṣé-er* : *Šu-pì-ma-ni* [3]*Pu-šu-ke-en*$_6$ [4]*i-šu* : *iš-tù ha-muš-/tim* [5]*ša Im-dí-lim* [6]*ù Pì-lá-ah-Ištar* [7]*a-na ṣí-bi*$_4$*-it* lo.e. [8]*ni-ga-li* rev. [9]*ta-ša-qal* : *šu-ma* [10]*lá ta-áš-qú-ul* [11]*ki-ma* : *a-wa-at* [12]*kà-ri-im* : *i*-iti-kam^{im} [13]*tù-ṣa-áb* : iti-kam [14]*Ṣí-ip-e-em* : *li-/mu-/um* [15]*A-šur-i-dí* igi u.e. [16]*A-šur*-du$_{10}$ igi [17]*A-lá-hi-im*

[1–4]Pūšu-kēn has loaned 8½ shekels of silver to Šuppimani. [4–9]From the week of Imdī-ilum and Pilah-Ištar, she shall pay at the taking up of the sickle. [9–10]If she has not paid, [11–13]she shall add monthly interest according to the rate of the *kārum*.

[13–15]Month Ṣip'um (vii), eponym Aššur-idī (REL 95, ca. 1878).

[15–17]In the presence of Aššur-ṭāb and Ali-ahum.

Bibliography: Text published by Lewy as KTH, 20; studied by Eisser and Lewy (1930, no. 81); edited by Ichisar (1981, 123).

Comments: An Anatolian woman owes a small amount of silver to the well-known Assyrian merchant Pūšu-kēn; the default interest will be computed according to the official rate of Kaneš.

78. Debt of an Anatolian Woman, Who Pledges Her House(s)

Obv. [1]⅓ *ma-na* kù-babbar [2]*i-ṣé-er* : *Zi-a* [3]*I-dí-Ištar i-šu* [4]2 gín-ta : *ṣí-ba-sú* [5]*iš-tù ha-mu-uš-tim* [6]*ša A-mu-a* [7]*i-na* iti-1-kam lo.e. [8]*ta-ša-qal* [9]*bé-tù e-ru-ba-tù*$^!$*-a* rev. [10]igi *I-ri-šum* [11]igi *Ma-nu-um-ki-ì-lí-a* [12]igi *A-šùr-iš-tí-kál*

[1–3]Iddin-Ištar has loaned ⅓ mina of silver to Ziya. [4–8]She shall pay 2 shekels as its interest per month from the week of Amua. [9]The houses are my pledges.

[10–12]In the presence of Irīšum, Mannum-kī-iliya, and Aššuriš-tikal.

Bibliography: Text published in copy by Lewy as TC 3, 222.

Comments: Line 19: the plural of the word *bētum* might refer to a multiroom house; see Michel 1997b and Veenhof 2011.

79. Debt of Two Anatolian Women Who Pledge Their House

Envelope

Obv. ^{1}kišib *Ku-lu-na-*[*ah-šu*] ^{2}(seal) ^{3}kišib *Za-ba-ra-*[*áš-na*] ^{4}kišib *Šar-n*[*i-kà-an*] ^{5}kišib *Pì-tí-*[*a-na-al-kà*] ^{6}(seal) ^{7}18 gín kù-babbar ^{8}(seal) ^{9}*i-ṣé-er Ha-na* rev.^{10}(seal) ^{11}*ù Pì-tí-a-na-al-kà* ^{12}*Hu-ma-da-šu ù I-lá-li-i*[*š-kà-an*] ^{13}*i-šu-ú* kù-babbar *i-na i-tí* ^{14}[*e-r*]*a-ší-im i-ša-qá-lá* ^{15}[é]$^{be\text{-}tám}$ *a-na ša-pár-tim* ^{16}*ú-kà-lu* kù-babbar *i-ša-qá-la*$_5$*-ma* ^{17}*ù i-na* é$^{be\text{-}tim}$ ^{18}*ú-ṣí-ú*

$^{1-5}$Sealed by Kuluna[hšu]; sealed by Zabara[šna]; sealed by Šarn[ikan]; sealed by Piti[an-elka].

$^{7-13}$Humadašu and Ilali[škan] have loaned 18 shekels of silver to Hana and Pitian-elka; $^{13-14}$they (fem.) shall pay the silver at the time of [cul]tivation. $^{15-16}$They (masc.) hold the [house] as pledge. ^{16}They (fem.) shall pay the silver ^{17}and they (masc.) shall go out from the house.

Tablet

Obv. ^{1}18 gín kù-babbar ^{2}*i-ṣé-er* : *Ha-na* ^{3}<*ù*> *Pì-tí-a-na-al-kà* ^{4}*Hu-ma-da-šu ù I-lá-li-/iš-kán* ^{5}*i-šu-ú* kù-babbar ^{6}*i-na* : *i-tí* ^{7}*a-ra-ší-im* lo.e. ^{8}*ta-ša-qal* rev. ^{9}é^{be}*-sà* : *a-na ša-pár-tim* ^{10}*ú-kà-lu* kù-babbar ^{11}*ta-ša-qal-ma ù i-na* ^{12}é$^{be\text{-}tim}$ *ú-ṣí-ú* ^{13}igi *Ku-lu-na-ah-šu* ^{14}igi *Za-ba-ra-áš-na* ^{15}igi *Šar-ni-kà-an*

$^{1-5}$Humadašu and Ilališkan have loaned 18 shekels of silver to Hana <and> Pitian-elka; $^{5-8}$she (*sic*) shall pay the silver at the time of cultivation. $^{9-10}$They (masc.) hold her house as pledge. $^{10-11}$She shall pay the silver, $^{11-12}$and they (masc.) shall go out from the house.

$^{13-15}$In the presence of Kulunahšu, Zabarašna, and Šarnikan.

Bibliography: Tablet published in copy by Lewy as TC 3, 240; envelope published in copy by Thurean-Dangin as TC 2, 66; text edited by Eisser and Lewy (1930, no. 99).

Comments: Two women are indebted, but, on the tablet, the subject of the verb "to pay" is singular; since the envelope bears only the seal of Pitian-elka, she might be the principal debtor.

80. An Indebted Woman Pledges a Boy

Envelope

Rev. $^{1'}$(seal A) $^{2'}$[*i-ṣé-er Ha-tí-tim* dumu]-munus *Zu-pá Ku-tal-ba* $^{3'}$[*tí*]-*šu-ú* kù-babbar $^{4'}$*i-na ga-ma-ar* $^{5'}$*er-ší-im ta-*[*ša-qal*] $^{6'}$*a-*[*na* k]ù-babbar (lacuna)

$^{2'-3'}$Kutalba has loaned [(9 shekels of silver) to Hattītum, dau]ghter of Zupa; $^{3'-5'}$she shall [pay] the silver when the cultivation is finished. $^{6'}$F[or the s]ilver [...]

Tablet

Obv. ^{1}9 gín kù-babbar ^{2}*i-ṣé-er Ha-tí-tim* ^{3}*Ku-tal-ba tí-šu* ^{4}kù-babbar *i-na ga-ma-/ar* ^{5}*er-ší-im* : ^{6}*ta-ša-qal* ^{7}*a-na* kù-babbar ^{8}dingir$^{\textit{lúm}}$-*i-mì-tí* lo.e. ^{9}*ta-dá-gal* rev. ^{10}igi *Lá-ma-sí* ^{11}dumu-munus *Ma-sà-a* ^{12}igi *A-šur-dan* ^{13}dumu *En-um-A-šur*

$^{1-3}$Kutalba has loaned 9 shekels of silver to Hattītum; $^{4-6}$she shall pay the silver when the cultivation is finished. $^{7-9}$For the silver, she has claim on Ilum-imittī.

$^{10-13}$In the presence of Lamassī, daughter of Masaya, and Aššur-dān, son of Ennum-Aššur.

Bibliography: Text published by Bilgiç, Sever, Günbattı, and Bayram as AKT 1, 45 (Kt a/k 889a); collated May 2011.

Comments: Hattītum has borrowed silver, for which she has a claim on a third party.

81. Debt of a Woman in Grain

Obv. ^{1}kišib *A-ta-ta* kišib *Me-ṣí-*[*lí*] ^{2}(seal A) ^{3}kišib *Šar-ma-ma* kišib *Ni-ni* ^{4}*ša* 21 *na-ru-uq* gig ^{5}20 še *i-ṣé-er* ^{6}(seal B) ^{7}[*Ni*]-*ni A-šùr-na-da* lo.e. ^{8}[*i-šu*] : *i-na kà-ar-pì-tí-a* ^{9}(seal C) ^{10}*ta-ma-dá-dam* (°erasure) rev. ^{11}*šu-ma i-na ha-ar-pè* ^{12}(seal C) ^{13}*lá ta-am-du-dam* ^{14}*ki-ma a-wa-at Kà-ni-iš* ^{15}*ṣí-ib-tám tù-ṣa-áb* ^{16}(seal D) u.e. ^{17}(seal D) le.e. ^{18}(seal A) r.e. ^{19}(seal B)

$^{1-3}$Sealed by Atata; sealed by Meṣi-i[lī]; sealed by Šarmama; sealed by Nini.

[4–8]Concerning the twenty-one sacks of wheat (and the) twenty sacks of barley (that) Aššur-nādā [has] loaned to [Ni]ni, [8–10]she shall measure (them) out to me according to my *karpatum*-measuring jar. [11–13]If she has not measured (them) out to me by the summer, [14–15]she shall add interest according to the rate of Kaneš.

Seal C Inscribed (Teissier 1994, no. 47b)
A-mu-ur-A-šur
dumu *Ì-lí-kur-ub*

Bibliography: Text published in copy by Lewy as TC 3, 239. Lines 3–7 cited by Balkan (1974, 39). Collated March 2018.

Comments: The woman has borrowed both wheat and barley, which she has to repay after the harvest. Note that the name inscribed on seal C does not correspond to any of the names written on the envelope.

---

82. Dispute between Two Women Concerning Pledged Objects

Obv. [1]*A-šùr-na-da ù Zu-uš-kà-na* [2]*a-na Zu-uš-kà* : dam *Ú-zu-a* [3]dumu *Li-pá-a* : *iṣ-bu-tù-ni-a-tí-ma* [4]*Ú-zu-a w*[*a*]*-ša-áb um-ma* [5][*A*]*-šùr-na-da-ma ú-nu-tí* [6]*ša a-na na-áb-šé-em a-ší-tí* [7]*a-mu-tí-ki ša-zu-úz-tí-a* [8]*ù ku-a-*[*t*]*í* : *ta-dí-nu* : *dí-nim* [9]*um-ma Zu-uš-kà-ma ke-na* [10]*ú-nu-ut-kà* : *ma-lá a-ša-at-kà* [11]*ta-dí-na-ni* : *i-ba-ší* (erasure) lo.e. [12]*šu-ma* : *i-na ú-nu-tim* [13]*ša ta-dí-na-ni* : *mì-ma* rev. [14]*lá-šu* 12-ta-a : *lá-dí-na-kum* [15]*a-ša-at-kà* 1½ gín kù-/babbar [16]*a-ṣí-ib-tim* : *iš-tí-a* [17]*tal-qé-ma* : *ú-nu-ut-kà* [18]*aṣ-ba-at a-ha-ma* 1½ gín [19]kù-babbar *ša-ni-a-am a-dí-ší-ma*[!] [*ú*[?]] [20]*kà-ta-pá-am a-ša*[!]*-pár-ti*[*m*]*-ma* [21]*ta-dí-a-am* kù-babbar *lu ta-dí-nam* [22]*ù ú-nu-ut-kà le-qé* : *um-ma* [23]*Zu-uš-kà-na-ma* : *ke-na* [24]1½ gín kù-babbar *ta-dí-nim-ma* [25]*kà-ta-pá-am* : *a-ša-pár-tim* u.e. [26]*a-dí-a-ki-im* : 1½ gín kù-babbar [27]*mì-ma ša-ni-a-am lá ha-*<*bu*>*-lá-ki-im* [28]*ù ú-nu-tám mì-ma* le.e. [29]*a-ša-pár-tim lá a-dí-a-ki-im* [30]igi *Zu-zu-a* dumu *Ì-lí-dan* [31]igi *Sú-en*$_6$-sipa dumu *A-mur-Ištar* [32]*Ú-zu-a mu-sà wa-ša-áb*

[1–3]Aššur-nādā and Zuškana seized us (as arbitrators) against Zuška, wife of Uzua, son of Lipaya, [4]and while Uzua was present, [4–5][A]ššur-nādā (said) as follows: [5–8]"Give (fem.) me my goods, which my wife gave to your husband, to my representative and to you for deposit!" [9]Zuška (replied) as follows: "True, 10–11all your goods that your wife gave me are here. 12–14If any of the goods she gave me is missing, I will repay you twelvefold. 15–18Your wife took from me 1½ shekels of silver at interest, and I took your goods. 18–19Moreover, I gave her another 1½ shekels of silver, and 20–21she made available to me a *katappum*-container as a pledge. 21–22Let her pay me the silver, and then take your utensils." 22–24Zuškana (then said) as follows: "True, you gave me 1½ shekels of silver, and 25–26I gave you as a pledge a *katappum*-container. 26–27I do not owe you anything more than 1½ shekels of silver, 28–29and I did not make available to you any goods as pledge."

30–31In the presence of Zuzua, son of Ilī-dān, and Suen-rē'ī, son of Amur-Ištar. 32Uzua, her husband, was present.

Bibliography: Text published in copy by Lewy as TC 3, 266; edited by Eisser and Lewy (1935, no. 292, where it is quoted as L 20).

Comments: The plaintiff asks for the return of objects that his wife gave to another couple for safekeeping, according to his wife, or as pledge for a debt, according to the lady who retains these objects.

Women and Family Responsibility for Debt

Women, Assyrian or Anatolian, appear regularly in loan contracts, taken out in time of need, along with their husbands. Loans to multiple debtors are very numerous, and most contain a clause of mutual responsibility on the part of the borrowers.[30] Old Assyrian documents show every imaginable instance: an Anatolian couple may borrow from an Anatolian man or woman; an Assyrian may loan to several Anatolian couples or an Assyrian to an Assyrian and an Anatolian woman (**87**, **84**) or an Assyrian man and woman may borrow from an Assyrian.[31] In any case, the great majority of couples in debt for sums of money or sacks of grain are Anatolians; this is clear from the formulary of the documents, even if the name of the wife is not always given (**83**). The joint responsibility clause often includes, besides

30. Rosen 1977, 93–159, lists more than thirty loans to multiple debtors. See also Veenhof 2001 and Michel 2003b.

31. Anatolian couple borrows from Anatolian: ICK 1, 16, or ICK 1, 130. Assyrian loans to Anatolian couples: ICK 1, 115. Assyrian man and woman borrow from an Assyrian: in the loan contract ICK 1, 104, the debtors, Šāt-Ea and Atata, are not necessarily husband and wife, but could be mother and son, or have no family relationship.

the borrowers, their children, their house, and their possessions (**84, 85**).[32] The frequent mention of joint obligation of Anatolian couples for debt would be a consequence of Anatolian family law, which seems to have provided for some sort of joint ownership of property by married couples (**21**).

When Assyrians made loans to Anatolians, they not uncommonly required extra guarantees beyond the joint responsibility clause. Real estate and family members were thus often put up as pledges, including the wife, daughters, or female slaves of the borrower (**90, 89, 91**). The borrower could offer himself as pledge for his own debt. The lender took possession of the pledges until the debt was paid off (**88**). Instances of female family members ceded to the creditor for debt mostly involve Anatolian families.[33] Among the rare cases involving an Assyrian family, a merchant in debt for two minas of silver found himself obliged to offer as pledge his wife, female slave, and house (**86**). This practice is also attested for mixed couples, where an Assyrian man has married an Anatolian woman (**87**). The Assyrian authorities in Asia Minor sometimes used merchants' wives as pledges in order to receive from a husband payment for his debts. For example, Tatana, the Anatolian wife of Pilah-Ištar, had to be detained in Wahšušana on account of his debts; the verdict required the debtor to pay his wife a monthly allowance in copper so that she could sustain herself with food, cooking oil, and firewood, as well as an annual allowance of cloth. These payments, in some cases, calculated annually, show how slowly debt could be paid off (**28**).

In normal circumstances, the person put up as pledge could not be sold by the creditor, save in certain cases whereby the loan contract specified a period after which he could dispose of the person as he wished (**97**).[34] The entry of a pledged woman into a household nevertheless caused a problem: to what extent was she, wife or daughter of another man, under the control of the head of the household?[35] In order to avoid putting female members of their families into an embarrassing situation

---

32. See also TC 3, 218; TC 3, 237. In such cases, the wife is not necessarily mentioned as codebtor, as, for example, in ICK 1, 41.

33. See Veenhof 2001, 148–52.

34. See below, pp. 169–93, concerning slaves. According to the Hammurabi Code §117, if the debtor was not able to repay, pledged members of his family were released after three years.

35. Concerning this question, see Westbrook 1995, 1669; according to him, only the Bible was concerned by this problem in Lev 19:20–22.

of this type, some borrowers thought up new solutions; for example, by finding a third party who would agree to endorse the loan (**72**). Anatolian families in pressing need sometimes sold family members to the creditor or became his slaves (see below).

Joint responsibility of family members for debt mostly fell upon the wife and children of the debtor; they could be taken as pledges or become the creditor's slaves. This was especially true of Anatolian families, whereas Assyrian merchants often took measures intended to protect the status of the women in their families.

---

83. Indebted Anatolian Couple; The Wife's Name Is Not Given

Envelope

Obv. ^{1}(seal A) ^{2}kišib *Ku-ku-a* ^{3}kišib *Kà-lu-lu* ^{4}kišib *Ki-kà-ar-ša* ^{5}*ù a-ší-tí-šu* ^{6}(seal A) ^{7}[½] *ma-na* 5 gín kù-babbar lo.e. ^{8}[(seal)] ^{9}[*li-tí* s]ig$_{5}$ rev. ^{10}(seal B) ^{11}*i-ṣé-er K*[*i-k*]*à-ar-*[*ša*]* ^{12}*ú a-š*[*í-t*]*í-šu* ^{13}*P*[*uzu*]*r*$_{4}$*-A-šùr i-šu* ^{14}[*i*]*š-tù ha-muš-tim* ^{15}*ša I-na-a* ^{16}*ú A-šùr-i-mì-tí* ^{17}*a-na* 5 *ha-am-ša-tim* ^{18}17½ gín *i-ša-qal* ^{19}*ú* 5 *ha-am-ša-tum* u.e. ^{20}*i-lá-kà-ma* ^{21}(seal B) ^{22}17½ gín *i-ša-/qal* le.e. ^{23}*šu-ma i-na u*$_{4}$*-mì-šu* ^{24}*ma-al-ú-tim lá iš-qúl* ^{25}3 gín-ta *i-na* iti-kam ^{26}*ṣí-ib-tám ú-ṣa-áb* r.e. ^{27}(seal A)

$^{2-3}$Sealed by Kukua; sealed by Kalulu; $^{4-5}$sealed by Kikarša and his wife.

$^{7-13}$P[uzu]r-Aššur has loaned [½] mina, 5 shekels of [good] quality [*litum*] silver to K[ik]ar[ša] and his w[if]e. $^{14-18}$[F]rom the week of Innaya and Aššur-imittī, he shall pay 17½ shekels of silver in 5 weeks; $^{19-22}$(after) another 5 weeks goes by, he shall pay (the remaining) 17½ shekels. $^{23-24}$If he has not paid by the end of his term, $^{25-26}$he shall add 3 shekels monthly as interest.

Tablet

Obv. ^{1}½ *ma-na* 5 gín ^{2}kù-babbar *li-tí* ^{3}*i-ṣé-er* ^{4}*Ki-kà-ar-ša* ^{5}*ú a-ší-tí-šu* ^{6}*Puzur*$_{4}$*-A-šùr i-/šu* lo.e. ^{7}*iš-tù ha-muš-tim* ^{8}*ša I-na-a* rev. ^{9}*ú A-šùr**-i-mì-tí* ^{10}*a-na* 5 *ha-am-ša-tim* ^{11}17½ gín *i-ša-qal* ^{12}*ú* 5 *ha-am-ša-tum** ^{13}*i-lá-kà-ma* u.e. ^{14}17½ gín-«ta» ^{15}*i-ša-qal* le.e. ^{16}igi *Kà-lu-lu* ^{17}igi *Ku-ku-a*

$^{1-6}$Puzur-Aššur has loaned ½ mina, 5 shekels of *litum* silver to Kikarša and his wife. $^{7-11}$From the week of Innaya and Aššur-imittī, he shall pay 17½ shekels in 5 weeks; $^{12-15}$(after) another 5 weeks go by, he shall pay (the remaining) 17½ shekels.

16–17In the presence of Kalulu and Kukua.

Bibliography: Text published by Bilgiç, Sever, Günbattı, and Bayram as AKT 1, 57 (Kt a/k 501); collated May 2011.

Comments: The text on the envelope is more complete than the one on the tablet; it bears a default interest. Both husband and wife are debtors, but the name of the wife is not given, and the subject of all the verbs appears to be in the masculine singular.

Line 1: according to Dercksen (2005b), the *litum* might denotes a specific object made of silver. It usually occurs in loan contracts to Anatolians, and this type of silver is never sent to Aššur.

---

84. Joint Responsibility of an Assyrian Merchant and His Anatolian Wife

Obv. 12 *ma-na* 12 gín kù-babbar 2*i-ṣé-er A-mur-A-šur* dumu *A-lu* 3*Za-az-hu-na a-ší-tí-šu* 4*ša-ri-šu ú be-tí-šu* 5*E-ni-iš-ru ú Ta-mu-ur-a* 6*i-šu-ú a-na* 4 *ša-na-tim* 7*i-na ša-tim i-na ha-ar-/pè* 8½ *ma-na* 3 gín kù-babbar 9*i-ša-qú-lu ú kà-ar-pá-at* 10*šu-um-ki i-du-nu* lo.e. 11*šu-ma lá iš-qú-lu* rev. 123 gín-ta kù-babbar 13*ṣí-ib-tam i-na* 14iti-kam *ú-ṣú-bu-ú* 15kù-babbar *i-na qá-qá-ad* 16*šál-mì-šu-nu ra-ki-is* 17igi *Ša-ra-bu-nu-wa* 18dumu *Ší-pá-na* 19igi *A-šur-mu-ta-pì-il*$_5$ 20dumu *En-um-A-šur* 21igi *Šu-pì-a-ah-šu*

1–6Eniš(a)ru and Tamura have loaned 2 minas, 12 shekels of silver to Amur-Aššur, son of Alu, Zazhuna, his wife, his children, and his house. 6–9For 4 years, each year in the summer, they shall pay ½ mina, 3 shekels of silver, 9–10and give a pot of onions. 11If they have not paid, 12–14they shall add 3 shekels of silver as interest per month. 15–16The silver is charged to them as a joint responsibility.

17–21In the presence of Šarabunuwa, son of Šipana; Aššur-mūtappil, son of Ennum-Aššur; and Šuppiahšu.

Bibliography: Text published in copy by Lewy as TC 3, 237.

Comments: The debt lies on the husband, his wife, his children, and his house as a joint responsibility.

85. Anatolian Wives and Children Included in the Joint Responsibility Clause

Envelope

Obv. [1]ki[šib x x x x (x)] [2](seal destroyed) [3]kišib *A-ma-Š[í-wa-á]š-[mì]-iš* [4]kišib *Ha-pu-a-šu* [5]kišib *Hu-pì-iš-nu-ma-an* [6]kišib *Ší-li-ú-ma-an* [7][kiši]b x][x] [x x (x)] [8](traces of a seal) [9]*ša* 2 [*ma-na* kù-babba]r lo.e. [10](seal B) [11]*ṣa-ru-pá-am i-ṣé-er* rev. [12](seal B) [13]*Hu-pì-iš-nu-ma-an* [14]*ù Ší-li-ú-ma-an* [15]*Me-ra-lí <i-šu-ú> i-na ša* [16]*Ni-pá-as i-ša-qú-lu* [17]*šu-ma lá iš-qú-lu* [18]*a-na* 1 *ma-na-em* [19]3 gín-ta [20](seal C) *i-na* (seal C) [21]iti-kam [22]*ú-ṣú-bu* kù-babbar *i-na* u.e. [23][*q*]*á-qá-a*[*d šál-mì-š*]*u-nu* [24](traces of a seal) [25]*ke-*[*ni-šu-nu*] le.e. [26]*šé-ri-šu-nu ù a-ša-ti**-*šu-nu* [27](seal E?) [28]kù-babbar[pì] *ra-ki-is* r.e. [29](seal B)

[1-7]Se[aled by …]; sealed by Ama-Š[iwa]š[mi]š; sealed by Happuašu; sealed by Hupišnuman; sealed by Šiliuman; [seal]ed by […].

[9-15]Concerning the 2 [minas of] refined [silver] (that) Merali has loaned to Hupišnuman and Šiliuman, [15-16]they shall pay (it) at the Nipas festival. [17]If they have not paid (it), [18-22]they shall add 3 shekels per mina per month. [22-28]The silver is charged to them, as well as to their children and wives, [as a join]t responsibility.

Tablet

Obv. [1]2 *ma-na* kù-babbar *ṣa-ru-p*[*á-a*]*m* [2]*i-ṣé-er Hu-pí-iš-nu-*[*m*]*a-an* [3]*ù Ší-li-ú-ma-*[*a*]*n* [4][*M*]*e-*[*r*]*a-lí i-šu-ú* [5]*i-na ša Ni-pá-a*[*s*] [6]*i-ša-qú-lu* [7]*šu-ma lá iš-qú-lu* lo.e. [8]*a-na* 1 [*m*]*a-na-em* [9]3 gí[n]-t[a] rev. [10]*i-na* iti-kam *ú-ṣú-bu* [11]kù-babbar[pí] *i-na* (erasure) [12]*qá-qá-ad ke-n*[*i*]*-š*[*u-n*]*u* [13]*šál-mì-šu-nu a-ša-t*[*í-š*]*u-n*[*u*] [14]*ù šé-ri-šu-nu* [15]*ra-ki-is* [16]igi *A-ma-*(erasure)*-šu-*[*i*]*š-mì-*[*i*]*š* [17]igi [*H*]*a-*[*p*]*u-a-šu* u.e. [18]igi *Ší-*[*l*]*i-ú-m*[*a*]*-an* [19]igi [*H*]*u-*[*p*]*í-i*[*š-n*]*u-*[*m*]*a-an*

[1-4][M]e[r]ali has loaned 2 minas of refi[ne]d silver to Hupišnu[m]an and Šilium[a]n. [5-6]They shall pay (it) at Nipas festival. [7]If they have not paid (it), [8-10]they shall add 3 she[ke]ls per [m]ina (and) per month. [11-15]The silver is charged to [th]em, as well as to the[ir] children and wives, [as a join]t responsibility.

[16-19]In the presence of Ama-Šu[i]šmiš, [H]a[p]uašu, Ši[l]iuman, and [H]u[p]i[šn]u[m]an.

Bibliography: Text published by Balkan (1992, 35–36, no. 4 [Kt b/k 260]), photos, 41–44; collated May 2011. The tablet has been damaged since its publication.

Comments: The names of the two Anatolian debtors' wives are not mentioned. The default interest amounts to 60 percent per year. The joint responsibility clause first mentions the children, then the wives.

---

86. Debtor's Wife and Female Slave Given as Pledges (Assyrians)

Obv. ^{1}2 *ma-na* kù-babbar ^{2}*i-ṣé-er* ^{3}*Puzur*$_4$*-A-na* ^{4}*Puzur*$_4$*-Ištar i-šu* ^{5}*iš-tù ha-mu-uš*$_{10}$*-/tim* ^{6}*ša A-la*$_1$*-hu-um* ^{7}*a-na* 13 ^{8}*ha-am-ša-tim* ^{9}kù-babbar *i-ša-qal* ^{10}*a-ša-sú : a-ma-sù* lo.e. ^{11}*bé-sú e-ru-ba-/tum* rev. ^{12}igi *Da-da-nu-um* ^{13}igi *Sú-kà-li-a* ^{14}dumu *A-mur-A-šur* ^{15}*šu-ma i-na ú-me-šu* ^{16} kù-babbar *la*$_1$ *iš-qú-ul* ^{17}*e-ra-áb-ma* ^{18}*i-na* é dam-gàr ^{19} kù-babbar *a-na* ^{20}*ṣí-ib-tim* ^{21}*a-lá-qé-ma ṣí-ib-/tam*$_x$ u.e. ^{22}*ù-ma-lá*

$^{1-4}$Puzur-Ištar has loaned 2 minas of silver to Puzur-Anna. $^{5-9}$From the week of Ali-ahum, he shall pay the silver within 13 weeks. $^{10-11}$His wife, his female slave, (and) his house are pledges.

$^{12-14}$In the presence of Dadānum and Sukkalliya, son of Amur-Aššur.

$^{15-16}$If he has not paid the silver by the end of his term, $^{17-21}$I shall proceed to a merchant's house and borrow the silver at interest, $^{21-22}$(then) he shall compensate the interest.

Bibliography: Text published by Hecker, Kryszat, and Matouš as Prag I, 475.

Comments: For an amount of two minas of silver to be paid within three months, the debtor's wife, female slave, and house are pledged. An additional clause concerns default payment and allows the creditor to borrow the two minas and impose on the debtor the interest of this new loan.

---

87. Indebted Mixed Couple; the Wife Serves as Pledge

Obv. $^{!1}$(seal B) ^{2}kišib dingir-*ma-lá-ak* dumu$^{!}$(I) *Sú-en*$_6$-sipa ^{3}kišib *Bé-lá-nim* dumu *Šu-Ku-bi-im* ^{4}kišib *E-ni-ba-áš* dumu *A-šùr*-du$_{10}$ ^{5}(seal C) ^{6}[kišib *W*]*a-*<*lá*>*-wa*$^{!}$*-lá* lo.e. ^{7}(seal C) rev. $^{!8}$(seal: two circle impressions) ^{9}[⅓ *ma*]-

na kù-babbar *ṣa-ru-pá-am* 10[*i-ṣé-e*]*r* dingir-*ma-lá-ak* 11[dumu *Sú-en*$_6$]-sipa *ù Wa-*<*lá*>*wa-lá* 12[*am*]*-tí-šu* dEn-líl-*ba-ni i-šu* 13[*i*]*š-tù ha-muš-tim ša kà-ší-im* 14(seal A) 15*ša qá-tí E-na-nim* <iti>-kam 16*A-lá-na-tim li-mu-um* u.e. 17(seal B) 18*A-ku-tum* ½ gín-ta *i*-iti-kam 19*ṣí-ib-tám ú-ṣú-bu* kù-babbar 20*i-qá-qá-ad šal-mì-šu-nu ra-ki-is* le.e. 21*qá-tí* dEn-líl-*ba-*[*ni i-ṣé-er*] 22(seal B) 23*Wa-*<*lá*>*wa-lá* [*ša-ak-na-at*] r.e. 24(seal A)

2–6Sealed by Ilī-malak, son of Suen-rē'ī; sealed by Bēlānum, son of Šu-Kūbum; sealed by Ē-nibâš, son of Aššur-ṭāb; [sealed by W]a<la>wala.

9–12Enlil-bāni has loaned [⅓ mi]na of refined silver [to] Ilī-malak, [son of Suen]-rē'ī, and Wa<la>wala his [*am*]*tum*-wife. 13–19[F]rom the week of the *kaššum*-official that followed the one of Ennānum, month Allānātum (xii), éponym Akūtum (REL 108), they shall add ½ shekel per month as interest. 19–20The silver is charged to them as a joint responsibility. 21–23Enlil-bā[ni]'s hand [has been laid on] Wa<la>wala, (who is the pledge).

Bibliography: Text published in copy by Smith as CCT 1, 11b; edited by Eisser and Lewy (1930, no. 24). Lines 15–16 cited by Larsen (1967, 31). Obverse and reverse are inverted on the copy.

Comments: The joint responsibility clause includes both the Assyrian merchant and his Anatolian wife, and, moreover, the wife serves as pledge. The text OIP 27, 59, which is recapitulative of loans, includes on lines 22–30 the one written on this tablet; it gives the complete name of Ilī-malak's wife: Walawala.

---

88. Debtor's Wife and Daughter Are Pledged (Mixed Couple?)

Envelope

Obv. 1(seal A) 2kišib *En-*[*um-a-a* k]išib *A-šùr-ma-lik* 3(seal B) 4[*ša hu-b*]*u-ul Šu-Be-lim ša* ⅓ *ma-na* k[ù-babbar] lo.e. 5(seal B) rev. 6*iš-tù ha-mu-uš-tim* 7*ša A-gu*$_5$*-a ù Iš-me-*dim 8½ gín *i-na* iti-kam *ú-ṣa-áb* 9*Ha-ti* ù me-er-a-sà e-ru-ba-tù-a* 10*a-dì** kù-babbar *ú-ša-ba-a-ni-ni* 11*ma-ma-an ú-lá i-ṭá-hi-ší-na-tí* 12(seal A) 13(seal A) 14(seal B)

2Sealed by Ennum-Aya; sealed by Aššur-malik.

4[Concerning the de]bt of Šu-Bēlum amounting to ⅓ mina of s[ilver], 5–8from the week of Agūa and Išme-Adad, he shall add ½ shekel monthly (as interest). [9]Hatti and her daughter are my pledges; [10–11]until they satisfy me with the silver, nobody shall approach them.

Tablet

[1]⅓ *<ma>*-na* kù-babbar *i-na* [2]*ṣé-er Šu-Be-lim* [3]*A-šùr-i-dì** *i-šu* [4]*iš-tù ha-mu-uš-tim* [5]*ša A-gu*$_5$*-a* ½ gín-ta [6]*i-na* iti-kam *ú-ṣa-áb* [7]*Ha-ti** *ù me-er-a-sà* [8]*e-ru-ba-tù-a* [9]*a-dì** kù-babbar *ú-ša-ba-a-ni-ni* [10]*ma-ma-an ú-lá* [11]*i-ṭá-hi-ší-na-tí* [12]igi *En-um-a-a* [13]igi *A-šùr-ma-lik*

[1–3]Aššur-idī has loaned ⅓ <mi>na of silver to Šu-Bēlum. [4–6]From the week of Agūa, he shall add ½ shekel monthly (as interest). [7–8]Hatti and her daughter are my pledges; [9]until they satisfy me with the silver, [10–11]nobody shall approach them.

[12–13]In the presence of Ennum-Aya and Aššur-malik.

Bibliography: Text published by Bilgiç, Sever, Günbattı, and Bayram as AKT 1, 44 (Kt a/k 454); collated May 2011.

Comments: The Anatolian wife and daughter of the Assyrian debtor are pledges, and seem to be in the possession of the creditor, perhaps working for him, since nobody shall approach them. This verb could have a legal or a sexual meaning: "nobody should have sexual relationships with them." This concerns anybody else, and could be meant to protect the pledges. The name of the creditor is missing on the envelope, and the name of the *hamuštum*-week is incomplete on the tablet.

---

89. House, Wife, and Children of an Indebted Anatolian Given as Pledges

Obv. [1]1 *ma-na* kù-babbar *li-tí* [2]sig$_5$ *ša Kà-ni-iš* [3]*i-ṣé-er Ta-ar-hu-nu* [4]*A-na-ah-ì-lí i-šu* [5]*iš-tú ha-muš-tim* [6]*ša A-šùr-ma-lik* [7]dumu *Sú-kà-li-a* [8]iti-kam *Áb-ša-ra-ni* [9]*a-na* iti-10-kam [10]*i-ša-qal* [11]igi *Tù-ma-na* lo.e. [12]*kà-ší-im* rev. [13]igi *Tù-ub-tù-ku* [14]igi *Me-me-ib-ri* [15]*é-sú ú a-ša-sú* [16]*ú šé-ru-šu a-da-gal*

[1–4]Ānah-ilī has loaned one mina of *litum* silver of good quality from Kaneš to Tarhunu. [5–10]From the week of Aššur-malik, son of Sukkalliya, month Ab-šarrāni (v), he shall pay within ten months. [11–14]In the presence of Tumana, the *kaššum*-official, Tubtuku, and Memē-ibri. 15–16I have a claim on his house, as well as on his wife and his child.

Bibliography: Text published by Jankowskaja as KTK, 96; edited by Eisser and Lewy (1930, no. 14).

Comments: Though the name of the wife is not mentioned, she may be Anatolian.

---

90. Indebted Anatolian Couple Pledges Their Daughter

Obv. 1kišib *A-lu-wa-zi* 2kišib *Šu-pu-na-ah-šu* 3kišib *Ha-pí-a* kišib *Wa-ak-le* 4kišib *Kà-áp-sí-a a-ší-tí-šu* 5(seal A) 615 gín kù-babbar *ù* 3 *na-/ru-uq* 7*še-a-am i-ṣé-er* 8*Wa-ak-le-e* 9*ù Kà-áp-sí-a* 10*a-ší-tí-šu* 11(seal B) 12*E-na-áš-ru-ú* 13*i-šu* rev. 14kù-babbar *ú še-a-am* 15*a-na ha-ar-pé* 16*i-du-nu-ú* 17*Ku-uk-ra-an* 18(seal B) 19*me-ra-sú-ú* 20*a-na ša-pá-ar-tim* 21*ú-kà-al* kù-babbar 22*i-na qá-qá-ad* 23*šál-mì-šu-nu ú ke-ni-šu-nu* 24*ra-ki-is* u.e. 25(seal B) le.e. 26(seal A) r.e. 27(seal)

1–4Sealed by Aluwazi; sealed by Šuppunahšu; sealed by Happiya; sealed by Wakle; sealed by Kapsiya, his wife.

6–13Eniš(a)ru has loaned 15 shekels of silver and 3 sacks of barley to Wakle and Kapsiya, his wife. 14–16They shall give (back) the silver and the barley in the summer. 17–21I hold Kukran, their! daughter, as pledge. 21–24The silver is charged to them as a joint responsibility.

Bibliography: Text published in copy by Smith as CCT 1, 10b–11a; edited by Eisser and Lewy (1930, no. 15). Enišaru has been the subject of a study by Veenhof (1978).

Comments: An Anatolian couple have borrowed a small amount of silver and barley and pledged their daughter.

91. An Anatolian, His Sister, His Slaves, and His House Given as Pledges

Envelope

Obv. [1]kišib *Bu-li-na* kišib *Wa-lá-wa-lá* [2](seal A)* [3]*a-ší-tí-šu* kišib *Kà-lu-lu* [4]kišib *Zu-lá* kišib *I-dí-Ištar* [5]kišib *Ha-nu* kišib *Ku-lá-na-lá* [6]⅔ *ma-na* 5 gín kù-babbar *i-ṣé-er* [7]*Bu-li-na ù Wa-lá-wa-lá* [8]*Bu-za-zu-um ù Ma-nu-ki-A-šùr** [9]*i-šu-ú* [10](seal B)* [11]*iš-tù ha-mu-uš-tim* [12]*ša A-šur-i-dí ù Šu-Ištar* [13](seal C)* [14][iti]-kam *Ma-hu-ri-li* [15][*l*]*i-mu-um Ì-lí-*[*dan*] [16]*a-na ša-na-at* (end of line erased)* [17]*i-nu-mì ru-ba-um i-na* é [18]*Ni-pá-as ú-ṣí-a-ni* [19]kù-babbar *i-ša-qú-lu šu-ma lá iš-qú-lu* [20]*ki-ma a-wa-at Kà-ni-iš* [21]*ṣí-ib-tám ú-ṣú-bu* [22]*Mu-sà* :* *a-ma-sú Zi-it-wa-an* [23]ìr-*sú Ga-na-na a-ha-sú* [24]*Zi-a ù* é-*sú e-ru-ba-tù-/šu-nu* [25](seal D)* u.e. [26](seal E)* le.e. [27](seal F)* r.e. [28](seal E)*

[1–5]Sealed by Bulina; sealed by Walawala, his wife; sealed by Kalulu; sealed by Zula; sealed by Iddin-Ištar; sealed by Hanu; sealed by Kulanala.

[6–9]Buzāzum and Mannum-kī-Aššur have loaned ⅔ mina, 5 shekels of silver to Bulina and Walawala. [11–15]From the week of Aššur-idī and Šu-Ištar, month Mahhur-ilī (iv), eponym Ilī-dān (REL 98/123, ca. 1875/1850), [16–19]within one year, when the king comes out of the temple of Nipas, they shall pay the silver. If they have not paid, [20–21]they shall add interest according to the rate of Kaneš (authorities). [22–24]Musa, his female slave; Zitwan, his slave; Ganana, his sister; Ziya; and his house are their pledges.

Seal A Inscription* **(CS 359)**
A-šùr-^{d}utu^{ši}
dumu *Šu-A-n*[*im*]

Aššur-šamšī, son of Šu-A[num]

Tablet

Obv. [1]⅔ *ma-na* 5 gín kù-babbar [2]*i-ṣé-er Bu-li-na* [3]*ù Wa-lá-wa-lá a-ší-tí-šu* [4]*Bu-zu-zu ù Ma-nu-ki-A-šùr* [5]*i-šu-ú iš-tù ha-mu-*<*uš*>*-tim* [6]*ša A-šùr-i-dí ù Šu-Ištar* iti-kam [7]*Ma-hu-ri-li li-mu-um* [8]*Ì-lí-dan a-na ša-na-at* [9]*i-nu-mì ru-ba-um i-na* [10]é *Ni-pá-as* [11]*ú-ṣí-a-ni i-ša-qú-lu šu-ma* [12]*lá iš-qú-lu ki-ma* [13]*a-wa-at Kà-ni-iš* [14]*ṣí-ib-tám ú-ṣú-bu* [15]*Mu-sà a-ma-sú* [16]*Zi-it-wa-an* ìr-*sú* [17]*Ga-na-na Zi-a ù* [18]é-*sú e-ru-ba-tum* [19]igi *I-dí-Ištar* [20]igi *Kà-lu-lu* [21]igi *Ku-za-za a-ší-tí-šu* [22]igi *Zu-lá* igi *Ha-nu* [23]igi *Ku-lá-na-lá*

1–5Buzāzum and Mannum-kī-Aššur have loaned ⅔ mina, 5 shekels of silver to Bulina and Walawala, his wife. 6–8From the week of Aššur-idī and Šu-Ištar, month Mahhur-ilī (iv), eponym Ilī-dān (98/123, ca. 1875/1850), 8–11in one year, when the king comes out of the temple of Nipas, they shall pay (the silver). 11–14If they have not paid, they shall add interest according to the rate of Kaneš (authorities). 15–18Musa, his female slave; Zitwan, his slave; Ganana, his sister; Ziya; and his house are his pledges.

19–23In the presence of Iddin-Ištar, Kalulu, Kuzaza, his wife, Zula, Hanu, and Kulanala.

Bibliography: Tablet and envelope published by Bayram (1990, 461 [Kt n/k 1716]); tablet edited by Çeçen (1998, 120) and translated by Kuzuoğlu (2005, 82); collated May 2012.

Comments: The debtors, an Anatolian couple, give their slaves and house as pledges to their Assyrian creditors. We do not know the link between the debtors and Musa. Among the witnesses, the woman Kuzaza, wife of Kalulu, has not imprinted her seal on the envelope.

Female Slaves

A fair number of people, generally Anatolians, and more often women and children than men, became slaves for debt, sold by a parent or self-sold (**92**, **93**, **94**, **95**, **96**).[36] They could be redeemed within a fixed period upon payment of a higher price than that for which they were originally sold. For example, a woman named Huzura was sold for debt by three Anatolians to a compatriot; they were authorized to redeem her within a month. Once the month had passed, the purchaser was free to sell her where he wished, even in the town of Talhad (**97**).[37] Several texts thus document the sale of women in Talhad.[38] The Assyrian purchaser of a girl, in order to recover the

36. See also Kt 88/k 1003, in which a child was sold for 33 shekels of silver by his mother and another woman; redemption was permitted for an amount of 45 shekels of silver; Kt v/k 65, in which a boy has been sold for 37½ shekels of silver by his mother and his eldest brother. More examples may be found in Kienast 1984; Bayram and Çeçen 1996. For female debt slaves, see also Stol 2016, 314–15.

37. Talhad was probably located to the south of Viranşehir, possibly at Tell Chuera; see Veenhof 2008c, 18–21, and Michel 2012.

38. This dossier was published by Hecker 1997. See also Dercksen 2008b, 19–21.

silver owed by the parents of the girl, could not sell her in Kaneš; instead, according to the contract, he was allowed to sell her to people from Talhad (**98**).[39] Since the Euphrates seems to have served as a boundary for "the land [*mātum*]" (Anatolia), and since Talhad—like the town of Nihriya mentioned in a marriage contract (**15**)—was located on the other side of the Euphrates, and so in foreign territory, these contracts appear to prohibit resale of slaves in their country of origin, perhaps to avoid complications with members of their families or with people who might have the right to redeem them (**99**; see the map in the front matter). It seems evident that the resale of slaves at Talhad, in foreign territory, ruled out any possibility of redemption and protected the purchaser from any edict canceling debts.

In fact, the excessive indebtedness of some Anatolian families, forced to offer various of their relatives as pledges to Assyrians who charged very high rates of interest, caused local rulers to issue edicts canceling debts (**100**).[40] This changed over the course of time. In the eighteenth century (level Ib), although residents of Aššur involved in the caravan trade between Aššur and Kaneš still profited from it, some Anatolians had moved up in the social scale, while some Assyrians at Kaneš lost contact with their compatriots at Aššur and had become impoverished. Specific clauses included in commercial treaties dating to this second phase (Ib) tended to protect the last mentioned, though they were by then submerged in a hybrid Assyro-Anatolian community.[41] Thus the treaty drawn up between the Assyrians and the ruler of Kaneš contained clauses protecting Assyrian property from appropriation by Anatolians or other inhabitants of Kaneš. This clause applied particularly to widows and Assyrian children born and living in the city of Kaneš, as well as to male and female slaves belonging to Assyrians.[42]

39. Veenhof 2008c, 18–19, gives more examples of the sale of female slaves to people from Talhad and to the prohibition to bring the female slave back to the vicinity of Kaneš. The three related texts (correct 91/k to 92/k) Kt 92/k 120, Kt 92/k 139, and Kt 92/k 181 deal with a female slave who has behaved badly.

40. "To wash the debt," *hubullam masāʾum*; see Balkan 1974. It is also mentioned in the treaty between the Assyrians and the ruler of Kaneš: "When you [bring about] in your city … the liberation [*andurārum*] of female and male slaves …" (Kt 00/k 6:81–83: *i-nu-mì* : *i-na a-l*[*i*]-*kà*, [*ša*]-*dí-tim* : [*a*]-*du-ra-ar am-ti*[*m*], [*ú ur-dim* x x] *ta-ša*-[*ku-nu-šu*]-*ni*; Günbattı 2004, 252; restorations according to Veenhof 2008a, 193).

41. For the treaties of level Ib, see Veenhof 2008a, 188–218; Michel 2011b, 2014a, 2014e; Barjamovic, Hertel, and Larsen 2012, 73–80.

42. Kt 00/k 6:61–63; Günbattı 2004; Veenhof 2008a, 192–93; 2013b.

The basis for the sale of a person cannot usually be deduced from the documents; it is often impossible to distinguish debt slaves from slaves by birth. Just as with debt slaves, redemption was possible for slaves by birth who had been given by their owners in pledge or for payment of a debt (**101**, **102**, **103**). The redemption price to be paid by the former owner was often substantially higher than the purchase price or the amount of the debt (**104**). The sale price of a female slave was about two thirds or a half that of a male slave, on the average twenty shekels of silver, but that could vary according to the age or skills of slaves, and could be higher (**105**, **106**, **107**, **108**, **138**). A female slave could be sold with her child, boy or girl; the price for a mother and child might then be forty-five shekels of silver (**104**, **109**).[43] The price of slaves could also be paid in kind: four women and nine children were sold for stones, wool, various kinds of cloth, and sheep (**110**).

Slaves could also be acquired for unpaid or inherited debts due a deceased parent; they could then be resold or given various domestic tasks (**57**, **61**, **68**, **139**). In a time of famine, a slave couple was turned over to a new owner, who undertook to provide for the man and woman (**111**). A symbolic gesture, doubtless cutting off a piece of the slave's garment fringe, marked his change of ownership (**112**).

Outside of sale contracts, the name of slaves was seldom mentioned, so it is difficult to reconstruct their lives. Only rarely do letters give the identity of a female slave (**113**, **114**). There are likewise few indications of the duties slaves were obliged to perform. The correspondence of wives at Aššur suggests that their slaves helped them in their everyday activities, such as preparing meals, taking care of children, and housework.[44] Some female slaves could have more specific tasks, for example, as grinding grain to make flour (TC 3, 88).

Most families at Aššur or Kaneš had a few slaves, male and female, who were an integral part of the household. Some documents show that merchants' sons had their sexual initiation with young slaves of their parents, who thus became their concubines, but were still slaves. They could inherit their concubines after their fathers' death, along with any children

---

43. Prices for a man varied between thirty shekels and one mina of silver. See Garelli 1963, 315–16; Hecker 1980; Kienast 1984, excurses 2 and 3; Bayram and Çeçen 1996, 606; Sever 1998; Veenhof 2003b.

44. See chapter 3, "Housewives."

they had had with them (**54**, **115**), or they could simply take them without the consent of their brothers (**233**).[45]

---

92. An Anatolian Is Sold by His Parents and His Brother

Obv.[1] ½ *ma-na* kù-babbar *ší-mì-šu* [2]*ša Ti*$_1$*-kà-nu-ú* [3]*En-na-Sú-en*$_6$ *a-na* [4]*Ša-ra-bu-nu-a a-bi-šu* [5]*Pé-ru-a ù A-šu-a-al-kà* [6]*um-mì-šu iš-qú-ul* [7]*šu-ma ma-ma-an* [8]*a-na Ti*$_1$*-kà-nu-ú* [9]*i-tù-a-ar* [10]3 *ma-na* kù-babbar lo.e. [11]*Ša-ra-bu-nu-a a-b*[*u-šu*] [12]*Pé-ru-a a-hu-šu* rev. [13]*ù A-šu-a-al-kà u*[*m-mu-šu*] [14]*a-na En-na-Sú-en*$_6$ [15]*i-ša-qú-lu* igi *Ha-nu-nu* [16]igi *Kà-ba-nu-ú* [17][igi (*A*)]*-li-le-e* [18][igi *A*]*-šùr-i-mì-tí*

[1–6]Enna-Suen paid ½ mina of silver, price of Tikanu, to Šarabunua, his father, Peru(w)a, (his brother), and Ašua-elka, his mother. [7–9]If anyone raises a claim against Tikanu, [10–15]Šarabunua, [his] father, Peru(w)a, his brother, and Ašua-elka, [his] m[other], he shall pay 3 minas of silver to Enna-Suen.

[15–18]In the presence of Hanunu, Kabanu, [A]lilē, [and A]ššur-imittī.

Bibliography: Text published by Yılmaz (1998, 109 [Kt 92/k 1033]); collated May 2011.

Comments: An Anatolian is sold, certainly for a debt, by his father, his brother, and his mother, who is mentioned last.

---

93. An Anatolian Female Slave Is Sold by Her Sister

Envelope (unpublished fragment)

Obv. [1][kišib PN] [2](seal A) [3]dumu *I-tur*$_4$-[dingir] [4]*šu-ma Bé-dí-*[*bé-dí*] [5]dumu-munus X-[x-x *a-na*] [6]*H*[*a*]*-nu ta-*[*tù-wa-ar*] [7]½ *ma-na* [kù-babbar] [8]*ta-ša-*[*qá-al ù šu-ma*] [9]*a-hi-u*[*m i-tù-ar-šum*] [10]*Bé-dí-be-*[*dí*] [11]*tù-ša-h*[*a-sú*] lo.e. [12](seal B) (lacuna)

[1–3][Sealed by PN], son of Itūr-[ilī].

[4–6]If Bedi[bedi], daughter of [PN, raise]s a claim [against] H[a]nu,

---

45. The concubine would be referred to by the word *šawītum*, or by the abstract noun *ištariuttum*. The verb *ahāzum*, usually translated, in marriage contracts, by "to take (as a wife)," would mean in these texts "to take sexually."

$^{7-8}$she shall [pay] ½ mina [of silver; $^{8-9}$and if] a strang[er raises a claim against him], $^{10-11}$Bedibe[di] shall clear [him] of claims. (lacuna)

Obv. ^{1}*Tí-ta-wa-áš-hi* : *am-tám* ^{2}*Bé-dí-bé-dí* : *a-ha-sà* ^{3}*a-na ší-mì-im* : *ta-d[í-in]* ^{4}*Ha-nu* dumu *I-tur*$_4$-dingir ^{5}*iš-a-am-[š]í šu-ma B[e]*-dí-[b]é*-dí* ^{6}*a-na Ha-nu* : dumu *I-tur*$_4$-dingir ^{7}*ta-tù-wa-ar* ^{8}½ *ma-na* kù-babbar : *ta-ša-/qal* ^{9}*ù šu-ma* : *ma-ma-an* lo.e. ^{10}*a-hi-um i-tù-ar-šu[m]** rev. ^{11}*Be-dí-be-dí* : *tù-ša-ha-sú* ^{12}*šu-[ma] Tí-ta-wa-áš-hi* ^{13}*tù-uš-té-ṣa* : *a-na [m]a*-hi-re-/e* ^{14}*ú-šé-lu-ú-ší-ma a-na* ^{15}*ší-mì-[i]m* : *i-du-nu-uš* ^{16}igi *Ku-lá-a* ^{17}igi *A-šùr-i-mì-tí* ^{18}igi *Šu-pì-áš-we* ^{19}*kà-li-tí-kà*

$^{1-3}$Bedibedi, her sister, sold the female slave Titawašhi; $^{4-5}$Hanu, son of Itūr-ilī, bought [he]r. $^{5-7}$If B[e]di[b]edi raises a claim against Hanu, son of Itūr-ilī, $^{7-8}$she shall pay ½ mina of silver; $^{9-10}$and if any stranger raises a claim against him, ^{11}Bedibedi shall clear him of claims. $^{12-15}$If Titawašhi is quarrelsome, they shall bring her up to the market and sell her.

$^{16-19}$In the presence of Kulā, Aššur-imittī, and Šuppiašwe, your daughter-in-law.

Bibliography: Text published by Yılmaz (1998, 108 [Kt j/k 288]). Lines 13–14 corrected by Veenhof (2003b, 697); collated May 2011.

Comments: An Anatolian woman sells her sister, already referred to as a female slave. Perhaps she was already pledged for a debt, and Bedibedi was not able to redeem her? She is then considered a chattel slave, to be sold on the market if misbehaving.

---

94. A Mother Sells Her Daughter

Envelope

Obv. ^{1}dumu-munus *Ha-na A-ha-at-tum*$_8$ ^{2} (seal A) ^{3}*ta-ša-am* ½ *ma-na* 1½ gín ^{4}kù-babbar *ta-áš-qú-ul* ^{5}*šu-ma Ha-na me-er-e-sà* ^{6}*ta-ṣa-ba-at* 1 *ma-na* kù-babbar ^{7}(seal A) ^{8}*[Ha-n]a a-na A-ha-at*$^{!}$(TÍ)-*tim* lo.e. ^{9}*[ta]-ša-qal me-er-e-sà* ^{10}(seal B, four times) ^{11}*ta-ta-ar*$^{!}$(RI)-*ru*$^{!}$(UR) rev. ^{12}*šu-ma ar-na-am* ^{13} (seal C) ^{14}*ù ší-lá-tám té-pá-ší*$^{!}$(ŠA) ^{15}*A-ha-at*$^{!}$(TÍ)-*tum*$_8$ *a-šar li-bi-ša* ^{16}*a-na ší-mì-im ta-da-/ša* ^{17}*šu-ma ma-ma-an* ^{18}*i-ṣa-ba-at-sí* ^{19} (seal C) ^{20}*Ha-na A-ha- at*$^{!}$(TÍ)-*tum*$_8$ u.e. ^{21}*ta-ṣa-ba-at* ^{22} (seal B, four times) ^{23}kišib *Ha-na* le.e. ^{24}kišib *Da-lá-ša* ^{25}kišib *Pé-ri-wa*

Inscription on Seal A
^{1}*Pè-ru-a* ^{2}dumu *Ha-mu-ri-a*

$^{1-3}$Ahattum bought the daughter of Hana. $^{3-4}$She paid ½ mina, 1½ shekels of silver. $^{5-6}$If Hana wants to take her daughter (back), $^{6-9}$Hana shall pay to Ahattum 1 mina of silver, (then) $^{9-11}$she shall take her daughter along. $^{12-14}$If she commits an offense or a misdeed against her, $^{15-16}$Ahattum may sell her wherever she wishes. $^{17-18}$If anyone seizes her, $^{20-21}$Ahattum shall take Hana.

$^{23-25}$Sealed by Hana; sealed by Dalaša; sealed by Periwa.

Tablet
Obv. ^{1}dumu-munus *Ha-na A-ha-at*$^{!}$(TÍ)-/*tum*$_{8}$ ^{2}*ta-ša-am* ½ *ma-na* /1½ gín ^{3}kù-babbar *ta-ša-qú-ul* ^{4}*šu-ma Ha-na me-er-e-sà* ^{5}*ta-ṣa-ba-at* 1 *ma-na* /kù-babbar ^{6}*Ha-na ta-ša-qal* ^{7}*me-er-e-sà ta-ta-ru*$^{!}$(UR) ^{8}*šu-ma ma-ma-an* lo.e. ^{9}*i-ṣa-ba-at-sí* rev. ^{10}*Ha-na A-ha-at*$^{!}$(TÍ)-/*tum*$_{8}$ ^{11}*i-ṣa-ba-at* ^{12}*šu-ma mì-ma ar-na-/am* ^{13}*ù ší-lá-tám té-pá-ša* ^{14}*A-ha-at*$^{!}$(TÍ)-*tum*$_{8}$ *a-šar li-bi-/ša*$^{!}$(ŠÍ) ^{15}*a-na ší-mì-im*$^{!}$ ^{16}*ta-da-ša* ^{17}igi *Da-lá-ša* ^{18}igi *Pé-ri-wa*

$^{1-2}$Ahattum bought the daughter of Hana. $^{2-3}$She paid ½ mina, 1½ shekels of silver. $^{4-5}$If Hana takes her daughter (back), $^{5-6}$Hana shall pay 1 mina of silver, (then) ^{7}she shall take her daughter along. $^{8-9}$If anyone seizes her, $^{10-11}$Ahattum shall take Hana. $^{12-13}$If she commits an offense or misdeed against her, $^{14-16}$Ahattum may sell her wherever she wishes.

$^{17-18}$In the presence of Dalaša and Periwa.

Bibliography: Text published in copy by Hrozný as ICK 1, 27; edited by Kienast (1984, no. 10).

Comments: A woman sold her own pledged daughter; she is allowed to redeem her for double the price paid. This text is carelessly written, with many mistakes.

---

95. A Mother Sells Her Son

Envelope
Obv. ^{1}kišib [*Ú-šu-na*]-*ma-an* ^{2}(seal A) ^{3}dumu *Zi*-[x-x kišib *Ha*]-*ma-ar-a* ^{4}[dumu PN$_{1}$ kišib] *A-bi-a-at* ^{5}[dumu PN$_{2}$ kišib *Ta-at*]-*ki-pu-uš* ^{6}[dumu

PN$_3$] kišib *Šu-pì-a-ni-kà* ^{7}(seal A) ^{8}*Zu-li-i um-mu-šu-ú* lo.e. ^{9}*Šu-pì-a-ni-kà a-na* ^{10}(seal B, five times) ^{11}*ší-mì-im i-dí-šu-ú* rev. ^{12}(seal C) ^{13}*Ša-lu-a-ta-a i-iš-a-am-šu* ^{14}*ša i-tù-ru-šu-ni* ^{15}½ *ma-na* kù-babbar *i-ša-qal* ^{16}(seal D)

$^{1-6}$Sealed by [Ušuna]man, son of Zi-[x-x; sealed by Ha]marā, [son of PN$_1$; sealed by] Abiat, [son of PN$_2$; sealed by Tat]kipuš, [son of PN$_3$]; sealed by Šuppianika.

$^{8-11}$His mother Šuppianika sold Zulī; ^{13}Šaluata bought him. ^{14}Anyone who raises a claim for him ^{15}shall pay ½ mina of silver.

Tablet

^{1}*Ša-lu-a-ta* ^{2}*Zu-li-i* ^{3}*i-ša-a-am-šu* ^{4}*um*$^{!}$*-mu*$^{!}$*-šu-ú* (°erasure) ^{5}*Šu-pì-a-ni-kà a-na* ^{6}*ší-mì-im i-dí-šu-ú* ^{7}*ša i-tù-ru-ú-šu-/ni* ^{8}½ *ma-na* kù-babbar ^{9}*i-ša-qal* lo.e. ^{10}igi *Ú-šu-na-ma-<an>* rev. ^{11}igi *Ha-ma-ra-a* ^{12}igi *A-ba-lá-lá-a* ^{13}igi *Ta-at-kà-pu-/ú*

$^{1-3}$Šaluata bought Zulī; $^{4-6}$his mother Šuppianika sold him. ^{7}Anyone who raises a claim for him $^{8-9}$shall pay ½ mina of silver.

$^{10-13}$In the presence of Ušunaman, Hamaraya, Abalalaya, and Tatkapū.

Bibliography: Text published in copy by Hrozný as ICK 1, 35; edited by Kienast (1984, no. 17).

Comments: Šuppianika sold her own son; she could be the same woman as the daughter of Kurukuru mentioned in text **97**. The names of two Anatolian witnesses are different on the tablet and on the envelope: Tatkipuš is written Tatkapū on the tablet; Abiat (envelope) might be a different person than Abalalaya (tablet).

---

96. An Anatolian Woman Sells Herself

Obv. ^{1}kišib *Wa-li-iš-ra* ^{2}(stamp seal A) kišib *Ší-wa-áš-me-i* (stamp seal A) ^{3}*ú-tù-ú ša a-bu-ul* ^{4}*a-da-ah-ší* kišib *Ha-pu-a-šu* ^{5}dumu *Kà-zu-ba* ^{6}kišib *Na-ki-le-e-ed* ^{7}dumu *Šu-pí-ú-ma-an* ^{8}kišib *Ga-da-ga-da* ^{9}*Ga-da-ga-da* ^{10}(stamp seal A) *ší-it-ma* ^{11}*«a»-ra-ma-šu* (stamp seal A) ^{12}*a-na ší-mì-im* lo.e. ^{13}(double stamp seal B) rev. ^{14}(stamp seal D) *ta-dí-in* (stamp seal D) ^{15}*Ha-nu-um iš-a-am-ší*$^{!}$ ^{16}*šu-ma tù-zi-nu-um ú-ul* ^{17}*be-el hu-bu-li*$^{!}$ ^{18}*ú-ul mu-sú a-šu-mì* ^{19}*Ga-da-ga-da a-na* ^{20}*Ha-nu-um i-tù-wa-ar* ^{21}½ *ma-na* kù-babbar *a-na* [22]*Ha-nu-um i-ša-qal* [23](imprint of textile) [24]*ú Ga-da-ga-da* u.e. [25](seal C) le.e. [26](twofold stamp seal B) *i-ta-ru*

[1-8]Sealed by Wališra; sealed by Šiwašme'i, keeper of the *addahšu* gate; sealed by Happuašu, son of Kazuba; sealed by Nakile'ed, son of Šuppiuman; sealed by Gadagada.

[9-14]Gadagada sold herself personally; Hanum bought her. [16-20]If the *tuzinnum* or the creditor of the debt, or her[!] husband raises a claim against Hanum concerning Gadagada, [21-22]he shall pay ½ mina of silver to Hanum, [24-26]and he shall take along Gadagada.

Bibliography: Text published by Farber (1990).

Comments: The married woman Gadagada sells herself, certainly to pay a debt; her husband may buy her back for ½ mina of silver. This text, as **94** and **95**, shows a gender error typical of tablets belonging to and written by Anatolians; see Michel 2011c, 108.

Lines 3–4: for *andahšum*, see Veenhof 1991, 293.

---

97. Possible Redemption of a Female Slave

Obv. [1](seal A and imprint of textile) [2]kišib *A-pì-zi-a-šu* dumu *Ha-al-ki-/a-šu* [3]kišib *Ta-ar-hu-a-lá* dumu *Tal-wa-na* [4]kišib *Šu-pì-a-ni-kà* dumu-munus *Ku-ru-ku-/ru* [5]kišib *Ni-wa-ah-šu-šar* [6]kišib *Ha-pì-a* kišib *Pè-ru-wa* [7]*Ni-wa-ah-šu-šar Ha-pì-a* [8]*ù Pè-ru-wa : ki-ma* [9]*⅔ ma-na* 5 gín kù-babbar [10](seal B) lo.e. [11]*Hu-zu-ra : a-na* [12]*E-ni-iš-ru i-dí-nu-ší-ma* [13](seal C) [14]*a-ma-sú šu-ma a-šu-mì* rev. [15]*Hu-zu-ra*[!] *ma-ma-an* [16]*lu tù-zi-nu-um* [17](seal D) [18]*lu be-el hu-bu-lim i-tù-ar-šu-um* [19]*Ni-wa-ah-šu-šar ù Pè-ru-wa* [20]*Ha-pì-a a-na E-ni-iš-ru* [21]*ú-ta-ru-šu-ma ú ú-ra-sú* [22]*šu-ma Hu-zu-ra ta-ba-at* [23]*Ha-pì-a : a-na* é[ti]*-šu* [24]*i-ta-ru-šu-ma ù ú-ra*[!]*-sú* [25]*šu-ma i-na ga-ma-ar* [26]iti-kam *a-nim <½ ma-na>* 15 gín kù-babbar u.e. [27]*ší-mì-ša i-tab-lu-nim* [28]*ú i-ta-ru-ú-ší* [29]*šu-ma lá ub-lu-nim* (seal A) [30]*a-ma-sú a-na Tal-ha-dí-e* [31]*ú-ul a-šar* le.e. [32]*li-bi*$_4$*-šu i-da-ší* [33](seal E) r.e. [34](seal D)

[1-6]Sealed by Apiziašu, son of Halkiašu; sealed by Tarhuala, son of Talwana; sealed by Šuppianika, daughter of Kurukuru; sealed by Niwahšušar; sealed by Happiya; sealed by Peruwa.

[7–14]Niwahšušar, Happiya, and Peruwa sold Huzura to Eniš(a)ru instead of ⅔ mina, 5 shekels of silver, and she (is) his female slave. [14–18]If, concerning Huzura, someone, either the *tuzinnum* or a creditor of the debt, raises a claim against him, [19–21]Niwahšušar and Peruwa shall turn over Happiya to Eniš(a)ru, and he shall be his slave. [22]If Huzura runs away, [23–24]they shall take Happiya to his house, and he shall be his slave. [25–28]If, by the end of this month, they bring <½ mina and> 15 shekels of silver, her price, they shall take her along. [29–32]If they do not bring (it), she (becomes) his female slave; he can sell her to an inhabitant of Talhad or wherever he wishes.

Bibliography: Text published in copy by Lewy as TC 3, 252; edited by Kienast (1984, no. 32).

Comments: An Anatolian girl, daughter or sister of the debtor, is sold and can be redeemed within one month, after which the creditor, Enišaru, is free to sell her wherever he wishes, even abroad, at Talhad, where no redemption is then possible.

---

98. Sale of a Female Slave; Sale Abroad Permitted

Obv. [1](seal A, inscribed) [2]kišib *I-ku-nim* dumu ^{d}utu-*ba-ni* [3]kišib *A-šur*-gal dumu *Lá-qé-ep* [4]kišib *Lu-lu-ú* dumu *Du-du* [5]kišib *Hi-iš-ta-ah-šu* kišib *A-du-ma-an* [6]*ša qá-nu-e* : kišib *Ší-ša-wa-da* [7][dumu]-munus *Ma-li-ah-šu* [8][⅓ *m*]*a-na* 2½ gín kù-babbar [9][*Wa-lá*]-*wa-lá* dumu-m[unus x x] [10][*a-na ší*]-*mì-im* [x x (x)] [11](seal B) [12][x x x] *x ma x* [x x x] lo.e. [13](seal C) [14]*A-lá-hu-um a-na Ší-ša-wa-da* [15]dumu-munus *Ma-li-ah-šu iš-qúl* rev. [16](seal D) [17]*za-ku-tám lá ha-bu-ul-tám iš-a-am* [18]*šu-ma* : *ma-ma-an* : *a-na Wa-lá-wa-lá* [19]*ú A-lá-hi-im i-*<*tù*>*-wa-a-ar* [20]2 *ma-na* kù-babbar *a-na A-lá-hi-im* [21]*i-ša-qú-ul*!(LU) *a-šar li-*bi_4*-šu i-ra-*de_8*-ší* [22]*šu-ma li-bu-šu a-ta-al-ha-dí-e* [23]*i-da-ší a-na hu-bu-ul* [24]*um-mì-ša a-*bi_4*-ša ú a-ha-tí-ša* [25](seal E) [26]«*a-na*» *Wa-lá-wa-lá ú-lá i-da-ší* [27]4 gín kù-babbar *ša Ha-nu-nu a-šu-*[*mì*] u.e. [28]*A-lá-hi-im* [29]*Ší-ša-*[*wa*]*-da e-pu-lu* kù-babbar [30]*Ší-ša-*[*wa*]*-da* : *ša-bu-a-at* [31]*a-na Ha-nu-nu* (erasure) le.e. [32]*ú-lá i-tù-ru Ší-ša-*[*wa-da*] [33]*ú a-ha-sà a-na A-lá-*[*hi-im*] [34](seal E) [35]*me-er-i-šu ú Wa-lá-wa-lá* [*a*]*m-tí-šu* [36]*ú-lá i-tù-ru* r.e. [37](seal C?)

Seals

Seal A: *I-ku-num*, dumu ^{d}utu-*ba-ni*

Ikūnum, son of Šamaš-bāni.

[1-7]Sealed by Ikūnum, son of Šamaš-bāni; sealed by Aššur-rabi, son of Laqēp; sealed by Lulu, son of Dudu; sealed by Hištahšu; sealed by Aduman of the reeds; sealed by Šišawada, [dau]ghter of Maliahšu.

[8-12][⅓ m]ina, 2½ shekels of silver, [Wala]wala, daug[hter of PN for the pr]ice [...] [14-15]Ali-ahum paid to Šišawada, daughter of Maliahšu. [17]He bought (her) cleared and without debt. [18-19]If anyone raises a claim against Walawala and Ali-ahum, [20-21]he shall pay 2 minas of silver to Ali-ahum. [21]He may take her along wherever he wishes. [22-23]He may sell her, if he wishes, to Talhadites. [23-26]For debts of her mother, her father, or her sisters, he shall not sell Walawala.

[27-29]Concerning the 4 shekels of silver that Hanunu paid back to Šiša[wa]da in the name of Ali-ahum, [29-30]Šiša[wa]da has been satisfied with the silver; [31-32]she shall not raise a claim against Hanunu. [32-36]Šiša[wada] and her sister shall not raise a claim against Ali-a[hum], his sons, or Walawala, his female slave.

Bibliography: Text edited by Hecker (1997, 162–64, as no. 4 [Kt 87/k 99]); collated May 2012.

Comments: An Assyrian merchant bought a female slave from an Anatolian woman and is allowed to sell her abroad, where redemption will no longer be possible. This is clearly stated in the unpublished text AKT 8, 217:6–19: "Deprive her of her garment and head scarf; do not sell her to an Assyrian or Kanešite; sell her to an inhabitant of Talhad, and where you sell (her), you must say: 'Do not bring the woman (back) to the land of Kaneš.'"

The letter sent to Hanunu by Walawala may concern the same people (Pinches 1908, 13; translated by Michel [2001a, no. 387]).

---

99. Selling a Female Slave in the Land of Kaneš Prohibited

Obv. [1]kišib *A-šùr-ma-lik* dumu *E-lá-lí* [2](seal A) [3]*Puzur$_4$-A-šùr ù Ma-num-ki-*^{d}im [4]*a-na Pá-pá-an-ta-ah-e* [5]*iṣ-bu-tù-ni-ma* [6]*um-ma*$^{!}$ *Puzur$_4$-A-šùr* [7]*ù Ma-num-ki-*^{d}im-*ma* [8]*a-ma* : *am-tám* : *ša* ⅓ *ma-na* kù-babbar [9](seal B) [10]*tù-bu-lu a-na hu-lu-uq* lo.e. [11]*a-na du-ba-bi* lo.e. [12](seal A) [13]*ni-dí-na-kum** rev. [14]*šu-ma a-na Ha-tim* [15](seal A) [16]*lu a-na ma-tim* : *am-tám* [17]*ri-de$_8$-e* :

i-na Kà-ni-iš [18]*ù ma-at* : *Kà-ni-iš* [19]*lá ta-da-an-ší* [20]*um-ma Pá-pá-an-tá-ah-e-ma* [21]*Pu-ra-tám ú-šé-ba-ar-ší* [22]*a-na a-wa-tim* [23](seal B) [24]*a-ni-a-tim kà-ru-um* u.e. [25](seal B) [26]*Kà-ni-iš* tur gal le.e. [27]*i-dí-na-ni-ma* igi *šu-ga-ri-a-en* [28](seal A) [29]*ša A-šùr* ší-bu-tí a-dí-in* r.e. [30](seal A)

[1]Sealed by Aššur-malik, son of Elālī.

[3-5]Puzur-Aššur and Mannum-kī-Adad seized me (as arbitrator) against Papantah'e, and [6-7]Puzur-Aššur and Mannum-kī-Adad said as follows: [8-13]"Look, we gave you the female slave, who cost ⅓ mina of silver, (with guaranty) against loss or contestation. [14-17]Take the female slave along either to Hattum or to the country; (you may sell her there), [17-19]but you shall not sell her in Kaneš or in the land of Kaneš." [20]Papantah'e (replied) as follows: [21]"I will take her across the Euphrates."

[22-27]For these proceedings, the *kārum* of Kaneš, (the whole assembly) small and big, appointed me (as arbitrator), [27-29]and I gave my testimony before Aššur's pair of swords.

Bibliography: Text edited by Hecker (1997, 165–67, as no. 6 [Kt 87/k 275]); collated May 2011.

Comments: According to Hecker (1997, 166 n. 14), the expression "(be it at a) loss (or with) dissatisfaction (later)," which is a *hapax*, would refer to purchase at the buyer's risk; no claim seems possible. The female slave, whose name is not given, might have been a native of the land of Kaneš; she shall not be sold there to avoid either the right of redemption or royal remission of debts.

---

100. Anatolian Couple Indebted; Debt Not to Be Canceled by the Ruler

Obv. [1]13 [gín kù-babbar]* [2]*i-ṣé-er Hi-iš-ta-/ah-šu* [3]*ù I-lá-li-/iš-kà-an* [4]*a-ší-tí-šu* [5]*A-du-ma-an** [6]*i-šu* kù-babbar [7]*a-na ṣí-bi-it*!(IŠ) [8]*ni-ga-lim* lo.e. [9]*i-ša-qú-lu* rev. [10]kù-babbar *i-qá-qá-/ad* [11]*šál-mì-šu-nu* [12]*ù ki-ni-šu-nu* [13]*ra-ki-is* [14]igi *T[a-m]u-ri-a* [15]igi *Pí-[it-ha-n]a* [16]*šu-ma [ru-ba-um]** [17]*hu-b[u-lam]* lo.e. [18]*i-ma-[sí* x x] [19]*ša* [x x x] le.e. [20]*a-nim hu-bu-lá-šu-nu* [21]*lá i-ma-sí*

[1-6]Aduman has loaned 13 [shekels of silver] to Hištahšu and Ilališkan, his wife. [6-9]They shall pay the silver at the taking up of the sickle. [10-13]The

silver is charged to them as a joint responsibility. $^{14-15}$In the presence of T[am]urya and Pi[than]a. $^{16-21}$If the [king] (decides to) ca[ncel] de[bts ...] he will not cancel their debt.

Bibliography: Text published by Balkan (1974, 36 [Kt e/k 164]); collated May 2011.

Comments: The end of the contract makes an allusion to a possible remission of debts by the Anatolian ruler; this is also attested in the Old Babylonian southern Mesopotamia (Charpin 2000). By such measures, the Anatolian rulers tried to protect the property of their subjects who were deeply in debt because of high interest imposed by Assyrian creditors.

---

101. Young Girl and Female Slave Taken as Collateral

Obv. ^{1}1½ *ma-na* kù-babbar ^{2}*i-ṣé-er* ^{3}*Pá-la-a-na-áš-wa* ^{4}*Ta-mu-ri-a i-šu* ^{5}*a-na* kù-babbar *a-ni-im* ^{6}é$^{\textit{be-tám}}$ *Ku-lu-ma-a* ^{7}*ṣú-ha-ar-tám* ^{8}*ù* géme *i-da-gal* ^{9}*ša* kù-babbar *a-na* ^{10}*Ta-mu-ri-a* lo.e. ^{11}*i-ša-qú-lu* ^{12}é$^{\textit{be-tám}}$ rev. ^{13}*i-lá-qé* ^{14}igi *Pè-er-wa-ah-šu* ^{15}dumu *Ma-lá-áš* ^{16}igi *Na-ki-le-ed* ^{17}dumu *Šu-pì-a-ah-šu*

$^{1-4}$Tamuriya has loaned 1½ minas of silver to Palanašwa. $^{5-8}$For this silver, (Tamuriya) has a claim on the house, Kulumaya the young girl, and the female slave. $^{9-11}$Whoever pays the silver to Tamuriya $^{12-13}$may take the house.

$^{14-17}$In the presence of Perwahšu, son of Malaš, and Nakile'ed, son of Šuppiahšu.

Bibliography: Text published in copy by Clay as BIN 4, 190; edited by Eisser and Lewy (1930, no. 92).

Comments: A female slave is given as collateral together with a servant and a house.

Line 12: the mention of the sole house may suggest that it concerns the house with the slaves in it.

102. Possible Redemption of a Female Slave

Obv. [1]*Tí-ri-ku-da ú* [2]*Ha-áš-<ta>-ah-šu-šar* dam-/*sú* [3]géme *A-*bi_4*-du-ri* [4]dumu-munus *Ša-li-ni* [5]*a-na ší-mì-im i-dí-nu-/ma* [6]*Tù-hu-ší-ip-ha* [7]*iš-a-am* : *šu-ma* [8]*ma-ma-an a-na* lo.e. [9]*Tù-hu-ší-ip-ha* rev. [10]*i-tù-ar* [11]*Tí-ri-ku-da ú* dam-*sú* [12]*ú-ša-hu-tù-šu šu-ma* [13]*ma-ma-an i-pá-ṭá-ar-/ší* [14]1 *ma-na* kù-babbar [15]*i-ša-qal* : igi *Ša-zu-/a* [16]igi *A-nu-lá* [17]igi *Ša-at-A-na*

[1–5]Tirikuda and Haštahšušar, his wife, sold the female slave Abī-dūrī, daughter of Šalini, and [6–7]Tuhušipha bought (her). [7–10]If anyone raises a claim against Tuhušipha, [11–12]Tirikuda and his wife shall clear him. [12–13]If anyone wants to redeem her, [14–15]he shall pay 1 mina of silver.

[15–17]In the presence of Šazua, Anula, and Šāt-Anna.

Bibliography: Text published in copy by Stephens as BIN 6, 225; edited by Kienast (1984, no. 21). Lines 7–15 cited by Hecker (1980, 73).

Comments: An Anatolian couple sells a female slave bearing an Assyrian name to an Anatolian. Note that Kienast (1984, no. 21) reads the female slave's name as Appituri, making her an Anatolian woman, which is also possible. The contract stipulates a possible redemption for one mina of silver.

Lines 3–4: the unsual mention of the slave mother's name suggest that Abī-dūrī is a debt slave.

103. Redemption of a Female Slave Possible for the Double of Her Price

Envelope

Obv. [1]kišib *A-bi-b*[*a-áš-tí*] [2]kišib *Šé-zi-z*[*i*] [3][kiš]ib *Ku-ur-ma-*[*lá*] [4][kiši]b *Zu-mu* kišib [*Ma-hi-/ra*] [5][kišib *H*]*a-lu-pá* ki[šib *Du-du* …] (the remainder of the envelope is broken)

[1]Sealed by Abi-b[aštī]; [2]sealed by Šeziz[i]; [3][seal]ed by Kurma[la]; [4][seale]d by Zumu; sealed by [Mahira]; [5][sealed by H]alupa; se[aled by Dudu…]

Tablet

Obv. [1]½ *ma-na* 5 gín [2]kù-babbar *ṣa-ru-pá-am* [3]*ší-im I-*[*x-x*]*-kà* [4]*a-na Du-du* [5]*ù Ku-zi-zi* [6]*Ištar-ba-áš-tí* [7]*ta-áš-qú-ul* [8][géme] : *a-ma-sà* [9][*a-n*]*a ší-mì*$^{!}$*-im* lo.e. [10][*lá t*]*a-da-ší* [11][*lá*] *tù-ha-lá-aq*$^{!}$(AH)*-ší* rev. [12][*š*]*u-ma Du-du* [13]*ù Ku-zi-zi* [14]*i-pá-ṭù-ru-ší* [15]1 *ma-na* kù-babbar [16]*a-na Ištar-ba-áš-tí* [17]*i-ša-qú-lu-ma* [18]*i-ta-ru-ší-im-ša* [19]*ha-lu-qá-*[*at*] igi *A-bi*$_4$*-ba-áš-tí* u.e. [20]*il*$_5$*-*[*qé* igi] *Šé-zi-zi* u.e. [21]igi [*K*]*u-ur-ma-lá* [22]igi *Ma-hi-ra* le.e. [23][igi *Ha*$^{?}$*-l*]*u-pá* [24][igi *Zu*]*-mu*

[1–7]Ištar-baštī paid to Dudu and Kuzizi ½ mina, 5 shekels of refined silver, price of I-[x-x]-ka. [8–10]The [female slave] (is) her female slave, (but) she shall [not] sell her (and) [11]shall not make her perish. [12–14]If Dudu and Kuzizi decide to release her, [15–17]they shall pay 1 mina of silver to Ištar-baštī, and [18]they shall take her back to her. [19–20]She will be lost (for them). He to[ok (her) in the presence] of Abi-baštī. [20–24][In the presence of] Šezizi, [K]urmala, Mahira, [Hal]upa, [and Zu]mu.

Bibliography: Text published as two fragments in copy by Matouš as ICK 2, 68, and ICK 2, 116; ICK 2, 69, is a fragment of its envelope. Fragment ICK 2, 116, edited by Kienast (1984, no. 27). Lines 1–8 and 12–18 cited by Hecker (1980, 68 n. 23).

Comments: The buyer of the slave shall not sell her. Redemption is possible at twice the original sale price.

---

104. A Female Slave Sold with Her Son

Obv. [1]*Nu-hu-ša-tù a-ma-sú* [2]*Ku-ru-ba-na-a i-dí-nu-šu* [3]*ša Nu-hu-ša-tí-im* [4]*Nu-hu-ša-tù a-na* [5]*ší-mì-im i-dí-in* [6]*ú A-áb-ša-lim* (°*lim*° erased) [7]⅔ *ma-na* 5 gín kù-babbar [8]*ta-áš-qú-ul* : *ú am-tám* lo.e. [9]*Ku-ru-ba-na ú* [10]*ma-ra Áb-ša-lim* [11]*ta-áš-a-am šu-ma* [12]*ma-ma-na-a a-na* [13]*am-tim*$_x$ (DAM) *ú ma-ri-šu i-tù-/wa-/ar* [14]⅔ *ma-na* 5 gín kù-babbar [15]*a-na Áb-ša-lim* [16]*i-ša-qal* igi *E-na-A-šùr* [17]dumu *Ib-ni-lí* igi *Me-ra-lí* [18]<dumu> *En-um-A-šur*

[1–3]Nuhušatum, Kurubanaya, his female slave—she is the gift of Nuhušatum—[4–5]Nuhušatum sold (her). [6–8]And Ab-šalim paid ⅔ mina, 5 shekels of silver, [8–11]and so Ab-šalim bought the female slave Kurubanaya and (her) son. [11–13]If anyone raises a claim for the female slave and her son, [14–16]he shall pay ⅔ mina, 5 shekels of silver to Ab-šalim.

[16–18]In the presence of Enna-Aššur, son of Ibni-ilī, and Merali, <son> of Ennum-Aššur.

Bibliography: Text published by Michel and Garelli as TPAK 1, 159 (Kt 90/k 120); Bayram and Çeçen 1996, no. 1, 613–14.

Comments: Nuhušatum sold her female slave and her son to Ab-šalim for forty-five shekels of silver. In this text, Nuhušatum is a man; the female name is usually written Nuhšatum; see Michel 2001a, 507–11, and Veenhof 2015c.

Line 13: the writer made a mistake using the masculine pronoun instead of its feminine form; it should be *ma-ri-ša*.

---

105. Sale of a Female Slave for Twenty Shekels of Silver

Obv. [1]kišib *Bu-kà-nim* dumu *Šu-Sú-en*$_6$ [2](seal A) [3]*ša* ⅓ *ma-na* kù-babbar [4]*ṣa-ru-pá-am ší-im* géme^{tim} [5]*ša* é *Na-áp-li-is* [6]*ki-ma* [7](seal A) [8]dumu-munus *Na-áp-li-is gu*$_5$*-ba-áb-tim* lo.e. [9]*I-dí-A-šùr* dumu *Pá-pá-lim* [10](seal A) [11]*i-na Kà-ni-ìš** kù-babbar rev. [12]*il*$_5$*-qé-ú* [13](seal A) [14]dumu-munus *Na-áp-li-is* [15]*a-na Ku-ra ú-lá* [16]*ta-tù-ar* [17](seal A) le.e. [18](seal A)* r.e. [19](seal A)*

[1]Sealed by Bukānum, son of Šu-Suen.

[3–5]Concerning ⅓ mina of refined silver, price of the female slave from the house of Naplis [6–12]that Iddin-Aššur, son of Pappalum, received in Kaneš in place of the consecrated daughter of Naplis. [14–16]The daughter of Naplis shall not raise a claim against Kura.

Bibliography: Text published by Bayram and Çeçen (1996, no. 3, 615–16 [Kt n/k 1772]); collated May 2011.

Comments: The female slave was sold for twenty shekels of silver by a consecrated woman who was represented by a man during the transaction.

106. Female Slave Sold on the Market for Twenty Shekels of Silver

Obv. [1]kišib *A-šùr-ba-ni* [2](seal A, inscribed) [3]dumu *Ì-lí-e-mu-qí* [4]kišib *Sú-en$_{6}$-na-da* [5]dumu *En-nam-A-šùr* [6]kišib *E*-num*-Ištar ša-wi-it* [7]*Lá-qé-pì-im ša* ⅓ *ma-na* [8]kù-babbar *ṣa-ru-pá-am* [9](seal B) [10]*ší-im* : *Ku-ur-ma-lá* lo.e. [11](seal C, inscribed) [12]*E-num-Ištar tal-qé-ú* rev. [13](seal C) [14]*i-na ma-hi-ri-im* [15]*A-mur*-dingir : *ú-ṭá-bi$_{4}$-ší* [16]*am-tum a-ma-sú a-šar* [17]*li-bi$_{4}$-šu i-ta-<na>-dí-ší* [18]*ma-ma-an a-na A-mur*-dingir [19]*ú-lá i-tù-wa-ar* [20](seal B) [21]*šu-ma* [x x] [22][x x x x] *a-na A-mur*-dingir u.e. [23](seal A) le.e. [24]*i-tù-wa-ar E-num-Ištar* [25](seal A) [26][*tù-š*]*a-ha-sú* r.e. [27](seal B)

Seals

Seal A: [d]*A-šur-ba-ni*, dumu *Ì-lí-e-mu-qí*

Aššur-bāni, son of Ilī-emūqi.

Seal C: *E-num-Ištar*, *ša-wi-i*[*t*], *Lá-qé-ep*

Ennum-Ištar, concubine of Laqēp.

[1–7]Sealed by Aššur-bāni, son of Ilī-emūqi; sealed by Suen-nādā, son of Ennum-Aššur; sealed by Ennum-Ištar, the *šawītum*-concubine of Laqēpum.

[7–12]Concerning the ⅓ mina of refined silver, price of Kurmala, Ennum-Ištar received. [14–15]Amur-ilī removed her from the market; [16]the female slave is his female slave; [16–17]he is free to sell her wherever he wishes. [18–19]No one shall raise a claim against Amur-ilī. [21–24]If [...] raises a claim against Amur-ilī, [24–26]Ennum-Ištar shall clear him of obligations.

Bibliography: Text edited by Hecker (1997, 160–61, as no. 2 [Kt 87/k 287]); collated May 2011.

Comments: The seller, Ennum-Ištar, is referred to as a concubine of an Assyrian merchant, as her seal inscription states. She sold her female slave on the market for twenty shekels of silver.

107. Possibility to Redeem a Woman Sold by Her Family

Obv. [1]⅓ *ma-na* 2½ gín [2]kù-babbar *ší-im* [3]*Ša-am-na-ni-kà* [4]*A-ha-tum a-na* [5]*Ku-na-ni-a ù* [6]*Na-ki-iš-du-ar* [7]*ta-áš-qú-ul* [8]⅔[!] (3) *ma-na* 5 gín lo.e. [9]kù-babbar *ší-im* rev. [10]*Ša-[a]m-na-ni-kà* [11]*ša i-ša-qú-lu-ú* [12]*ù ší-a-tí i-ta-ru-ší* [13]igi *Li-ih-šu-ma-an* [14]igi *Hu-za-a*

[1-7]Ahattum paid ⅓ mina, 2½ shekels of silver to Kunnaniya and Nakišduar, as price for Šamnanika. [8-12]Who pays ⅔[!] mina and 5 shekels of silver as purchase price for Šamnanika can take her along.

[13-14]In the presence of Lihšuman and Huzaya.

Bibliography: Text published in copy by Clay as BIN 4, 183; edited by Eisser and Lewy (1930, no. 214) and Kienast (1984, no. 26); lines 1–12 are cited by Balkan (1974, 31 n. 14).

Comments: The amount of silver needed to redeem the female slave equals the double of her purchase price.

108. A Girl Sold by Her Mother May Be Redeemed

Envelope

Obv. [1]kišib *Ša-na-bu-ú* [2](seal A, stamp seal, 5 times) [3]kišib *Ba-dí-da-a* [4]kišib *Hi-iš-ta-ah-šu-ša-/a[r]* [5]*Za-za-tí-i ṣú-ha-ar-t[ám]* [6]*ta-áš-a-am-ší* «*šu-m[a]*» [7]*Ni-wa-[ah-š]u-ša-[ar]* [8]*[lá ta-tù-a-ar-ší-im]* lo.e. [9][(seal[?])] rev. [10][(seal[?])] [11]*[šu-ma ta-tù-a-a]r-[ší-im]** [12]15 gín kù-babbar [13]*ta-ša-qá-al-ma* [14]*[m]e-er-a-sà ta-ta-ru-/ú** u.e. [15](seal A, stamp seal, 5 times) le.e. [16](seal B)* r.e. [17](seal B)*

[1-4]Sealed by Šanabū; sealed by Badidaya; sealed by Hištahšušar.

[5-6]Zazatī bought a girl. [7-8]Niwahšušar shall not raise a claim against her. [11]If she raises a claim against her, [12-13]she shall pay 15 shekels of silver and [14]take her daughter along.

Tablet

Obv. [1]*Za-za-a ṣú-ha-ar-tám* [2]*ta-áš-a-am-ší*[!](ŠU)*-ma* [3]*Ni-wa-ah-šu-ša-ar* [4]*lá ta-tù-a-ar-ší-im* [5]*šu-ma : ta-tù-ar-ší-/im** [6]15 gín kù-babbar [7]*ta-ša-qá-*

al-ší-ma [8]*me-er-a-sà* lo.e. [9]*ta-ta-ru-ú* le.e. [10]igi *Ša-na-bu-ú* [11]igi *Ba-dí-da** [12]igi *Hi-iš-ta-ah-šu-ša-/ar**

[1–2]Zazaya bought a girl, and [3–4]Niwahšušar shall not raise a claim against her. [5]If she raises a claim against her, [6–7]she shall pay her fifteen shekels of silver and [8–9]take her daughter along.

[10–12]In the presence of Šanabū, Badidaya, and Hištahšušar.

Bibliography: Text edited by Balkan (1974, 31 [Kt a/k 554a/b]), and by Kienast (1984, no. 4); collated May 2012.

Comments: The price the mother sold her daughter is not known, but the amount for redemption is quite low: fifteen shekels of silver.

---

109. A Woman and Her Daughter Are Sold as Slaves

Obv. [1]*Lá-ba-ar-ša a-na* [2]*A-šur-be-el-a-wa-tim* [3]*a-na ší-mì-im* [4]*Šu-pì-a-ni-kà* [5]dam *Ha-pí-a* [6]*ù Ša-ri-ša* [7]*me-ra-ša i-dí-nu-šu* [8]*šu-ma Š[u-p]ì-a-ni-kà* lo.e. [9]dam *Ha-pí-a* rev. [10]*ù Ša-ri-kà* [11]*me-ra-ša a-na Lá-bar-ša* [12]*i-tù-ru* 1 *ma-na* [13]kù-babbar *a-na Lá-bar-ša* [14]*i-ša-qú-lu* [15]igi *Puzúr-A-na* dumu dingir-*na-da* [16]igi *Ba-ru-uš-ga* [17]dumu *Ha-al-ki-a-šu* u.e. [18]igi *Ha-zi-me-el* le.e. [19]dumu *Ha-lu-pá*

[1–7]Labarša sold Šuppianika, wife of Happiya, and Šariša, her daughter, to Aššur-bēl-awātim. [8–12]If Šuppianika, wife of Happiya, and Šarika, her daughter, raise a claim against Labarša, [12–14]they shall pay one mina of silver to Labarša.

[15–19]In the presence of Puzur-Anna, son of Ilī-nādā; Barušga, son of Halkiašu; and Hazimel, son of Halupa.

Bibliography: Text published by Sever (1998, 493–94, copy, pl. 150 [Kt v/k 125]) and again by Bilgiç and Günbattı as AKT 3, 42; collated May 2011.

Comments: An Anatolian sold a woman, wife of another Anatolian, with her daughter to an Assyrian. The name of the daughter is either Šariša (line 6) or Šarika (line 10).

110. Price in Kind of Female Slaves and Their Children

Obv. [1]65 *áb-ni* [2]*ša-áp-tum* 31 túg [3]80 *e-me-ru* [4]*ší-im* 4 *a-ma-tim* [5]*ú* 9 *ṣú-uh*[!]*-ri-im* [6]*qá-dum* [7]*ṣú-ha-ri-im*

[1-2]Sixty-five stones of wool, thirty-one textiles, [3]eighty sheep; (all this is) [4-7]the price of four female slaves and nine children, including the boy.

Bibliography: Text published in copy by Lewy as TC 3, 183. Lines 4–7 collated by Garelli (1966, 137).

Comments: The "stones of wool" refer to weights used specifically for wool; see Dercksen 2016, 18.

111. A Slave Couple Moves to a New Owner Because of Famine

[1]kišib *Ma-ra ša Kam-ma-li-a* [2]kišib *Šu-li-a Sá-sú-e-im* [3]kišib *Kam-ma-li-a-ta-ra-wa* [4]kišib *Du-wa-zi* [5](seal A) [6]kišib *Ša-ar-ba* : *A-lu-lu-wa* [7]*ú a-ša-sú* : *Bu-na-mu-wa-/dí* [8]*i-na da-na-tim* [9]*a-na Wa-al-ku-a* [10]*i-dí-šu-nu* lo.e. [11]*i-na* (stamp seal B) *dá-na-tí* rev. [12]*ú-ba-li-sú-nu* [13]*A-lu-lu-wa* [14](2 stamp seal B) [15]*ur-a-sú* : *a-ša-sú* [16]*am-a-sú* : *šu-ma* [17]*a-*(stamp seal C)*-ma-tí-ma* [18]*ma-ma-an* [19]*ib-ta-qar-šu-nu* le.e. [20]2 *ma-na* kù-babbar *a-na* [21]*Wa-al-*(stamp seal D)*-ku-wa i-ša-qal* [22]*ú-šé-ṣa*

[1-6]Sealed by Mara, from Kammaliya; sealed by Šuliya, the Sasuean; sealed by Kammaliya-ammatarawa; sealed by Duwazi; sealed by Šarba.

[6-10](As to) Aluluwa and his wife, Bunamuwadi gave them during a famine to Walkua; [11-12]during a famine he kept them alive. [13-16]Aluluwa (is now) his slave; his wife (is now) his female slave. [16-19]If, at any time in the future, someone claims them, [20-22]he shall pay 2 minas of silver to Walkuwa, and he will (then) take (them) out.

Bibliography: Text published by Lewy (1937, 106–8 [WAG 48-1464]); photo of the sealed envelope online on the CDLI as P272900.

Comments: Because of famine, Bunumuwadi sells a couple of slaves to another man so that they can survive. Husband and wife are given together, and it is together that they can be released if someone pays two minas of silver.

112. A Symbolic Act for the Transfer of a Female Slave

Obv. ^{1}*am-tám* : *Ku-uk-ra* ^{2}*ša* ^{d}utu-*a-bi* dumu *Zu-za-nim* ^{3}*iš-tí ṣu-ha-ri-im* ^{4}*ša Ha-da-i-kur* ^{5}*a-lá-hi-nim* ^{6}*Ša-lim-A-šur* ^{7}dumu *Ip-hu-ri-im* ^{8}*iš-a-am ha-ma-am* ^{9}*ma-ah-ri-ni* ^{10}*ib-tù-uq* (lacuna of about six lines)
Rev. $^{1'}$[*a-na a*]*-wa-*[*tim*] $^{2'}$[*a-ni*]*-a-tim* $^{3'}$*kà-ru-um Dur-hu-m*[*ì-it*] $^{4'}$*i-dí-ni-a-tí-ma* $^{5'}$igi gír *ša A-šur* $^{6'}$«*ša A-šur*» *ší-bu-tí-ni* $^{7'}$*ni-dí-in* $^{8'}$igi *Lá-ba-na-da* $^{9'}$dumu *I-dí-Sú-en*$_{6}$ $^{10'}$igi *Na-áb-Sú-en*$_{6}$ $^{11'}$dumu *Šu-Be-lim* u.e. $^{12'}$igi *I-dí-Ištar* $^{13'}$dumu *I-dí-A-bi*$_{4}$*-im* le.e. $^{14'}$igi *Puzur*$_{4}$*-Ištar* $^{15'}$dumu *Dan-A-šur*

$^{1-8}$Šalim-Aššur, son of Iphurum, bought the female slave Kukra of Šamaš-abī, son of Zuzānum, from the employee of Hadaikur, the *alahhinnum*-official. $^{8-10}$He cut off the *hāmum* in our presence, and (lacuna).

$^{1'-4'}$[For the]se [pr]ocee[dings], the *kārum* of Durhumit appointed us (as arbitrators), and $^{5'-7'}$we gave our testimony before Aššur's dagger.

$^{8'-14'}$In the presence of Labān-nādā, son of Iddin-Suen; Nab-Suen, son of Šu-Bēlum; Iddin-Ištar, son of Iddin-abum; and Puzur-Ištar, son of Dān-Aššur.

Bibliography: Text published by Veenhof (2003b, 699–705, as no. 3 [Kt 91/k 410]), then as AKT 8, 156; collated May 2012.

Comments: This document belongs to a small dossier published in AKT 8; according to AKT 8, 154, Kukra has been previously bought by Šamaš-abī from Lamassatum and still owes her some copper.

Line 8: as the female slaves leaves her previous master, Šalim-Aššur cuts off the *hāmum*. According to Veenhof, it means literally: "to cut (off) the (upper) stalk (of grain)," and would symbolize the link between slave and owner.

113. The Female Slave Is Named Utruwaššu

Obv. ^{1}*um-ma* ^{d}*En-líl-ba-ni-*<*ma a-na*> ^{2}*Áb-ša-lim* : *qí-bi-ma* ^{3}*ha-ra-ni* : *wa-ar-kà-/at* ^{4}*Puzúr-A-šùr* : *a-dí* 10 *u*$_{4}$*-me-e* ^{5}*A-šùr-lá-ma-sí* : *ma-ha-i* ^{6}[*a*]*-mì-ša-am* : *a-ṭá-ra-/dam* ^{7}[*a*]*-pu-tum* : *iš-tí-šu* ^{8}*ṣú-ha-ar-tám* ^{9}*lu-šé-ṣí-am*

3 gín kù-babbar [10]*ku-nu-ki-a ù* 1 túg lo.e. [11]*kam-sú-um : ša ṣú-ùh-ri-/im* rev. [12]*a-na ṣú-ha-ar-tim* [13]*Puzúr-A-šur : na-áš-a-ki-im* [14]*a-šu-mì : am-tim* [15]*Ut-ru-wa-šu : šu-ma a-ma-kam* [16]*iš-tí-ki : wa-áš-ba-at* [17]*ù-lá-ma : a-a-kam-ma* [18]*wa-áš-ba-at : té-er-tí-ki* [19]*li-li-kam : a-šu-mì* [20]*ha-muš-tim : ša a-bi-ni* [21]*ša-áš-hu-tim : a-ša ki-ma* [22]*i-a-tí : ù um-mì-ni* u.e. [23]*áš-ta-pár ù a-ma-kam* [24]*šu-ma : ha-muš-ti* le.e.[25]*a*$^{!}$-[*bi-ni* ...] [26][...]

[1-2]Thus (says) Enlil-bāni: say <to> Ab-šalim.

[3]I (am leaving) on my journey. [4-6]After (the departure of) Puzur-Aššur, within ten days I will send Aššur-lamassī, my uncle, over there. [7-9]Urgent! Make him take the young girl out with him. [9-13]Puzur-Aššur is bringing you three shekels of silver under my seal and one child(-size) *kamsum*-textile (cloth) for the young girl. [14-19]As for the female slave Utruwaššu, let your report come to me as to whether she is staying there with you, or whether she is staying somewhere else.

[19-23]As for letting our father's one-fifth share be cleared, I have written to my representatives and to our mother, [23-25]and there, if [our father's] fifth share [...]

Bibliography: Text published in copy by Clay as BIN 4, 68; translated by Michel (2001a, no. 340). Lines 19–25 cited by Larsen (1976, 384).

Comments: Ab-šalim married a member of Enlil-bāni's family, possibly him or his brother Aššur-lamassī; she is living in Kaneš. Enlil-bāni writes to her concerning two servants who are supposed to be in Ab-šalim's house.

---

114. The Female Slaves Are Named Utruwaššu and Gadada

Obv. [1]*um-ma* ^{d}*En-líl-ba-ni-ma* [2]*a-na Áb-ša-lim* [3]*qí-bi-ma* : 7 gín kù-babbar [4]*tù-dí-tam*$_4$ *ku-nu-ki-a* [5]*a-na ṣú-ha-ar-tim* [6]*En-na-Sú-en*$_6$ *na-ší* [7]*a-ma-kam* 2 *a-ma-tim*

[8]*Ut-ru-a-šu : ù Ga-da-da* [9]*a-na é*$^{\text{bé-tí}}$*-ki* lo.e. [10]*šé-ri-bi-ší-na* [11]*ù ṣú-ha-ra-am* rev. [12]*ša a-*[*šar*] : *Áb-ša-lim* [13]*ù-ra-bu-ú-ni* [14]*a-na é*$^{\text{bé-tí}}$*-ki* [15]*ta-ru-e-šu* 2$^{?}$ sìla *sà-ar-dam* [16]*le-qí-ma* [17]*ṭá-i-bi-šu : a-na* [18]*ha-ra-ni-a* : 5 gín kù-babbar [19]*En-na-Sú-en*$_6$ *ir-ší-ma* [20]*ta-ar-bi-it* [21]*ṣú-ha-ri-im dí-ni*

[1-3]Thus (says) Enlil-bāni: say to Ab-šalim.

[3–6]Enna-Suen is bringing you a garment pin of 7 shekels of silver under my seal for the young girl. [7–10]There, bring into your (fem.) house the two female slaves Utru(wa)ššu and Gadada, [11–15]and take to your (fem.) house the boy, where one raised him with Ab-šalim (*sic*!). [15–17]Take 2 liters of *sardum*-oil$^?$ and refine it. [17–19]Enna-Suen had five shekels of silver for my travel, [20–21]so give (them) as payment for raising the boy.

Bibliography: Text published in copy by Lewy (1969–1970, 59–60 [L 29-590]); edited by Gwaltney as POAT 31; translated by Michel (2001a, no. 341).

Comments: Ab-šalim is living on her own, and Enlil-bāni mentions two female slaves by their names (see **113**) that she is supposed to take to her home, as well as a boy who might have been the son of Utruwaššu or Gadada. In fact, he made a mistake by writing the name of "Ab-šalim" on line 12, since the letter is addressed to her.

---

115. Female Slaves Inherited as Concubines

Obv. [1]*A-zu : A-gi-a ù A-lá-hu-u*[*m*] [2]*i-mì-ig-ra-tí-šu-nu* [3]*ú-šé-ri-bu-ni-a-tí-m*[*a*] [4]*ni-iš A-lim*^{ki} *it-mu-*[*ú-ma a-ma-lá*] [5]*ší-ma-at* : *a-bi*$_4$*-šu-nu né-*[*pu-uš*] [6]*lu i-ba-áb-tim ša Puzur*$_4$*-*[*A-šur*] [7]*lu i-ba-áb-tim ša A-mur-A-šur* [8]*A-zu* kù-babbar *ma-lá il*$_5$*-ta-qé-ú* [9]*i*[*š-t*]*a-kà-ma ù šu-ut* kù-babbar [10]*ma-l*[*á a*]*-na hu-bu-ul* [11]*Puzur*$_4$*-A-šur* [*ù h*]*u-bu-ul* [12]*A-mur-A-šur ú-ša-qí-lu ṭup-pì* [13]*ha-ru-mu-tim iš-ku-un-ma* [14]*nu-ṣa-he-er-ma* : *iš-tù hu-bu-lam*$_5$ [15]*ša A-lim*^{ki} *ša um-me-a-ni* [16]*uš-ta-bu-ú* 10 *ma-na* 12 gín [17]*ú-ša-ra-ma A-zu* lo.e. [18]*i-lá-qé ù ší-tám lu ú-ṭá-tám* rev. [19]*lu am-tám lu* [ì]r [20]*lu zi-*[*tám*] *a-ma-lá* [21]*ší-ma-at a-bi*$_4$*-šu-nu* [22]*i-zu-zu* : *i-wa-ar-kà-at* [23]*Ša-Ša-ma-áš ù Ta-ri-iš-ma-tàm* [24]*ú-ša-ra-ma* (erasure) [25]*A-gi-a* : *lu a-na-kam lu i-na* [26]*A-lim*^{ki} *am-tám a-na iš-ta-ri-ú-tí-šu-nu* [27]*i-lá-qé za-ak* : *A-zu* [28]*Puzur*$_4$-sa-tu *ù A-lá-hu-um* [29]*i-na a-ma-tim ša lá-am-du* [30]1$^{iš\text{-}té\text{-}na}$ *i-ṣa-bu-tù-ni-ma* [31]*i-qá-tí-šu-nu i-ṣa-he-er* [32]*li-li-sí-na šu-nu-um-m*[*a*] [33]igi *Ku-lá* : igi *A-mur-A-šur* [34]igi *Puzur*$_4$*-Tí-am-ti*[*m*] [35]igi *Puzur*$_4$-sa-tu [36]igi *Il*$_5$*-ba-ni* igi *Šu-A-*[*šur*] u.e. [37]igi *A-šur*-utu^{ši} : igi *A-šur-ni-*[*šu*] [38]igi *Šu-Be-lim* igi *En-um-ì-lí* le.e. [39]igi *En-um-A-šur* igi *Dan-A-šur* igi *Šu-A-nim* [40]é^{tum} *ša A-lim*^{ki} *zi-tum ša Šu-mì-a-bi*$_4$*-a* [41]*a-ma-lá ší-ma-at a-bi-šu-nu ku-lu-šu-nu-ma i-zu-zu*

[1–3]Azu, Agiya, and Ali-ahu[m], upon their mutual agreement, brought us inside and [4–5]swore by the city (of Aššur) that we will act [according] to the will of their father.

[6–9]Azu has put down all the silver that he has collected on the outstanding claims of Puzur-[Aššur] or of Amur-Aššur, [9–13]and, himself, he has presented certified tablets concerning the silver he paid on the debts of Puzur-Aššur and Amur-Aššur; [14–16]we will deduct (it) and after he has satisfied his debt to his investors in the city (of Aššur); [16–18]he will be the first to take 10 minas, 12 shekels (of silver), and Azu will take (it). [18–22]Concerning the rest (of the inheritance), either grain or female or male slave, or (any other) share, they will divide according to the will of their father. [22–27]From what is left behind by Ša-Šamaš and Tarīš-mātum, Agiya will be the first to take, either here (in Anatolia) or in the city (of Aššur), a female slave as his concubine; he is quit. [28–30]Azu, Puzur-šadū'e, and Ali-ahum, each will (then) take one of the female slaves with whom they had intercourse, and [31](they) will be deducted from their shares; [32]their offspring too belong to them.

[33–39]In the presence of Kulā, Amur-Aššur, Puzur-Tiamtum, Puzur-šadū'e, Ilī-bāni, Šu-A[ššur], Aššur-šamšī, Aššur-nī[šu], Šu-Bēlum, Ennum-ilī, Ennum-Aššur, Dān-Aššur, and Šu-Anum.

[40]The house in the city (of Aššur) belongs to the share of Šumi-abiya. [41]They will divide everything according to the will of their father.

Bibliography: Text published in copy by Lewy as TuM 1, 22a; edited by Eisser and Lewy (1930, no. 287). Lines 25–35 cited by Veenhof (2014, 348).

Comments: Three brothers share the assets left by their parents. Among the goods they receive are the female slaves of the household family. We learn from this agreement that the sons had already sexual relations with the female slaves, and thus they are allowed to take each their concubine. The last words of the agreement imply that households could also comprise children born from sons' concubines. The two women, Ša-Šamaš and Tarīš-mātum, were perhaps the widow living in Kaneš and a sister of the testator, who could have been a consecrated woman in Aššur.

116. A Woman Asks Her Son-In-Law to Buy a Slave for Her Daughter

Obv. [1]*um-ma A-na-ah-Ištar-ma* [2]*a-na Áb-ša-lim qí-bi*$_4$*-ma* [3]*ší-it-ra-am ša tù-šé-bi*$_4$*-li-/ni* [4]*A-šur-*^{d}utu^{ši} *ší-im-šu* kù-babbar [5]*ú-šé-bi*$_4$*-lá-ki-im : am-tám* [6]*a-ma-kam ša-li-ší : a-wi-lam* [7]*ší-it tí-de*$_8$*-e : ša* kù-babbar [8]*ub-lá-ni : a-na-ku a-na-kam* [9]*a-wi-lam aṣ-ba-at-ma* [10]*um-ma a-na-ku-ma am-tám* [11]*a-na me-er-*<*i*>*-tí-a* lo.e. [12]*ša-am um-ma šu-ut-ma* [13]*i-Kà-ni-iš a-ša-am* rev. [14]*šu-ma lá iš-a-ma-ki-im*$^{!}$(AM) [15]*té-er-tí-ki li-li-kam* [16]3 gín kù-babbar *a-na mu-tí-ki* [17]*a-dí-in i-dí-na-ki-im* [18]*lá i-dí-na-ki-im um-ma Ha-tí-tum-ma* [19]*a-na Áb-ša-lim qí-bi*$_4$*-ma ší-it-ra-/am* [20]*ša Ì-lí-uṣ-ra-ni tù-šé-bi*$_4$*-lá-/ni* [21]3 gín kù-babbar *ší-im-šu* [22]*I-dí-*^{d}utu *na-áš-a-ki-im* [23]*um-ma A-na-ah-Ištar-ma* [24]*a-na Áb-ša-lim qí-bi*$_4$*-ma* u.e. [25]1 gín kù-babbar *I-dí-*^{d}utu [26]*na-áš-a-ki-im* le.e. [27]*šál-ma-ni ṭup-pá-am* [28]*ša tù-šé-bi*$_4$*-li-ni* [29]*ú-lá za-ku mì-ma* [30]*ú-lá ni-iš-me*

[1-2]Thus (says) Ānah-Ištar: say to Ab-šalim.

[3]Concerning the shawl that you sent, [4-5]Aššur-šamšī sent you its price in silver. [5-7]There, ask the female slave whether she knows the man who brought the silver. [8-9]Here, I personally seized the man [10-12](saying) as follows: "Buy a female slave for my daughter." He (answered) as follows: [13]"I will buy (one) in Kaneš." [14-15]Let your report come to me if he has not bought (a female slave) for you.[16-17]I gave three shekels of silver to your husband. [17-18]Did he or did he not give it to you?

[18-19]Thus (says) Hattītum: say to Ab-šalim.

[19-20]Concerning the shawl that you sent with Ilī-uṣrannī, [21-22]Iddin-Šamaš is bringing you 3 shekels of silver, (corresponding to) its price.

[23-24]Thus (says) Ānah-Ištar: say to Ab-šalim.

[25-26]Iddin-Šamaš is bringing you 1 shekel of silver. [27]We are well. [27-29]The tablet you sent was not explicit. We understood nothing.

Bibliography: Text published by Larsen as AKT 6d, 732 (Kt 94/k 1248).

Comments: From this letter, Ānah-Ištar appears to be Ab-šalim's mother, and Hattītum could be her sister, still living with their mother. Ab-šalim's husband, during his travels has been in contact with his mother-in-law, and she asked him to buy a female slave for her daughter. Perhaps Ab-šalim complained to her mother that she had too much work to do and had not enough domestics. She sent a letter to her mother that was not understandable.

Lines 29–30: literally, "We have heard nothing."

3
Housewives

What the Assyrian male wanted in his marriage was primarily a helpmeet who would give him children, keep house, and cook for him (**3**). But the women who sent the letters found at Kaneš did not accompany their husbands to Anatolia; they remained at Aššur in charge of their households. The solitude of these women, left alone for many months by their husbands, was notorious, as shown by the remark of a merchant who reproaches his correspondent for having forgotten him entirely:[1] "Why have you kept me confined inside the city (of Aššur) for ten months, as if I were a woman?" At Aššur, besides representing their husbands in business transactions and producing textiles for export to Anatolia, these women were active in various capacities that reflect the daily life of women at home as well as their roles as heads of families.[2] At Kaneš, merchants' wives had to contend with their husbands' frequent absences. They received letters full of instructions about business matters in progress, in which they were expected to take part, as well as about proper upkeep of the household.

Both Assyrian and Anatolian women spent much of their time looking after and educating their children, though how many is seldom known. Prosopographical studies can give some indication of the number of children women had to raise, and the reconstructed family trees of several large Assyrian merchant families show at least how many sons reached adulthood. The wife of Aššur-idī had at least three sons active in business.[3] One of them, Aššur-nādā, married an Assyrian woman, perhaps named Parrurtum, who presented him with a son and several daughters, although she could not bring them up, perhaps because she died in child-

1. See introduction, note 1.
2. See chapter 4.
3. Larsen 2002, xix.

birth or from the complications of a difficult delivery.[4] The second wife of Aššur-nādā, an Anatolian woman, produced at least one daughter and a son who reached adulthood.[5] Tarām-Kūbi, wife of Innaya, had five sons, all of whom joined the family business (fig. 19);[6] likewise, Lamassī, wife of the well-known Pūšu-kēn, raised his five sons and at least one daughter, if not two (fig. 16).[7] Nuhšatum, wife of Ennum-Aššur, gave birth to at least two sons and a daughter.[8] Lamassatum, wife of Elamma, bore four or five sons and two daughters who reached adulthood.[9] Daughters were not generally mentioned, and they remain rare in the reconstructed family trees. Also infant mortality was probably high. For the three to six children of a woman who reached adulthood, there were perhaps two or three additional ones who, if not stillborn, did not survive childhood diseases. Finally, wills and texts referring to division among heirs after the death of the head of a family give an indication of the number of children surviving their father, although such documents do not mention married daughters, who would already have received their portion as their dowry.[10] More prosperous families, it seems, tended to have more children than less advantaged ones, because they could provide for them and leave an estate sufficiently large to be distributed among a fair number of people.

For household help, a woman could have a few or many slaves, depending on her standard of living. Estimating the number of persons per household in Aššur or Kaneš is difficult because two, even three, generations might live in the same house. Besides family members and domestics, traveling business associates were regularly accommodated, to the extent that some left their archives along with those of the head of the household in Kaneš.[11] In her husband's absence—the length of which is difficult to evaluate—the housewife had to keep up the family home and manage any other family real estate, as well as keep track of everything in the home: furnishings and utensils, documents, and merchandise.

4. Michel 2001a, 363–70.

5. Larsen 2002, xxv–xxix.

6. Michel 1991, 76–88, 126–40.

7. Michel 2001a, 426.

8. Michel 2001a, 507–11; according to Veenhof (2015c, 279), she was the mother of the girl Šazua.

9. Veenhof 2007.

10. See chapter 2 and Michel 2015b.

11. Michel and Garelli, TPAK 1, 27–34.

Motherhood

How old men or women tended to be at marriage or procreation is practically unknown for ancient Mesopotamia.[12] Although there are images of mothers or wet nurses, of indefinable age, nursing babies and children are rarely depicted, in contrast to ancient Egypt.[13] Maternity is referred to in medical, divination, and magical texts, including conception, pregnancy, childbirth, and problems with nursing.[14] Law codes are concerned with miscarriages and abortions, wet nursing, and adoptions.

Old Assyrian documentation is no exception to this: aside from the mention of a midwife (*šabsūtum*), mother of a merchant, maternity occurs only in magical texts, which are rare in the Kaneš archives.[15] Three incantations of the ten now known are concerned with the pregnant woman and the infant. One of them is intended to ease the labor of a woman in childbirth, comparing her to the cow impregnated by the moon god Suen, as well as to the outlet of a watercourse (**117**). In fact, the child's watery surroundings were seen as something he had to be freed from. Because the moment of birth was particularly dangerous for both mother and child, incantations were recited that were supposed to help the mother give birth. This was done crouched over, with the knees braced on bricks.[16]

The other two incantations deal rather with childhood diseases: one is concerned with the jaundice that often affects newborns; the other is directed at the demon Lamaštum, who attacked mothers with puerperal fever, as well as babies (**117**, **118**). Infants were particularly subject to

12. Roth (1987, 747) analyzed two population groups of the Neo-Babylonian period and proposed that "there is more than a decade age difference between spouses.… A bride will be in her middle or late teens, with a father in his fifties and a mother in her early to mid-forties. The bride's husband would be about thirty and her mother-in-law about fifty, almost the age of her own father."

13. Parayre 1997. Ancient Near Eastern iconography shows mainly queens, elite women, and high priestesses; see, for example, for the third millennium BCE, Asher-Greve 2006; Suter 2008.

14. Farber 1989; Stol 2000a; Lion, Michel, and Villard 1997. The more recent study by Couto-Ferreira 2016 on mothers does not take into account the Old Assyrian sources.

15. TC 3, 219a:8–9: *Šu-Ištar*, dumu *ša-ab-sú-tim*; and TC 3, 219b:11–13: *Šu-Ištar* (seal C), dumu *ša-áb-sú-tim*.

16. Stol 2000a.

digestive troubles or to fretfulness, as shown by crying and agitation.[17] The demon Lamaštu was deemed responsible for most childhood illnesses, the crying of babies, and the death of newborns. Passing herself off as a midwife, she might strangle the baby or poison him with her milk. She was warded off by exorcistic rituals and the recitation of incantations, so it is no surprise that an incantation of this type was found in an Assyrian merchant's house in Kaneš.

Among the rare references to birth is that of a child of a king used to date a loan between Anatolians (**119**). Lack of children is more frequently referred to. Thus, certain marriage contracts provide for the case that the couple has not succeeded in having a child (**23**, **24**). According to the world order established in the myth of Atra-hasīs, there were in fact women who gave birth and women who did not, the latter including both barren and consecrated women, who were forbidden to bear children.[18] Adoption of either babies or adults could remedy childlessness. A childless couple could adopt a man to maintain them in their old age and inherit their property at their death. The adopted child enjoyed the same rights as the biological one. The Kaneš archives have yielded several adoption contracts among Anatolians (**22**, **120**), but only one among Assyrians has been discovered so far, clearly later than most of the documentation found at Kaneš and perhaps from Aššur.[19] One may suppose that adoption contracts, like marriage contracts, were kept at Aššur.

In well-to-do families, the newborn could be turned over to a wet nurse. This practice is well attested among elites, for example at Ebla and Mari,[20] but must have been current among ordinary people as well, as shown by the Code of Hammurabi, where section 194 punishes a nurse who had several contracts at the same time with different families, to the detriment of the children in her care.[21] Some Old Babylonian contracts do

17. Farber 1989; Cadelli 1997.

18. See chapter 5, pp. 376–93.

19. This text, preserved in Amsterdam and published by Veenhof (1982b), shows both Babylonian and Assyrian characteristics. The proper names it quotes are not attested in the Old Assyrian documentation but are well known from the Middle Assyrian onomastic. It is dated to the eponym Išme-Dagan, son of Šamšī-Adad, who is not known as such in the Kültepe Eponym List.

20. See Biga 1997 and 2000; Ziegler 1997. At Urkeš, storeroom doors were sealed by Zamena, nurse of a royal child and employed by Uqnītum, queen of Urkeš; see Buccellati and Kelly-Buccellati 2002, 132, fig. 9.

21. Roth 1997, 120.

show that children could be nursed two or three years. Only one text from Kaneš mentions a wet nurse, who received a small sum of money (**121**).

---

117. Incantation to Help a Woman in Labor; Incantation against Jaundice

Obv. [1]*ar-hu-um a-ra-ah* [2]*a-ra-ah-tum ar-ha-at* [3]*ar-hi-iš : ta-ri-i : ar-hi-iš* [4]*tù-lá-ad ar-hi-iš : i-lu-ku* [5]*ma-ú i-pí-ša : i-na* [6]*a-pí-ša : qá-qá-ra-am : té-sú-uq* [7]*i-zi-bi-tí-ša : ta-ša-bi-iṭ* [8]*bé-tám ma-na-me : lá-áš-pur* [9]*ú lu-wa-e-er a-me-er*[!]*-ú-at ša-sú-ra-tim* [10]*7 ù 7-ma : ma-ri-ki-/na* [11]*ù ta-áp-šu-kà-tí-ki-na* [12]*le-qé-a-nim-ma : ba-áb* [13]*a-ra-ah-tim ha-ba-tum* lo.e. [14]*hu-ub-ta : šu-ma : za-kàr* [15]*e-tù-da-ni šu-ma* rev. [16]*sí-ni-ša-at ša-pá-ra-ni* [17]*šu-ma : sà-ak-pu-um : sà-ki-ip* [18]*i-li-šu : li-ší-lá-ma : k[i]-i* [19]*ṣa-ru-ú : ki-ra-nim : li-i[m-q]ú-tám* [20]*qá-qá-ar-šu : ší-ip-tu[m]* [21]*lá i-a-tum ší-pá-at Ni-ki-l[i-il*$_5$*]* [22]*be-el ší-pá-tim ù be-el tí-i-i[m]* [23]*be-lá-at ša-sú-ra-tim l[i-dí]* [24]*e-er-qú-um e-ri-iq* [25]*e-ri-iq-tum e-er-qá-at* [26]*i-ṣí-li : mì-iṭ-ra-tim* [27]*e-ri-iq-tim e-zu-um* [28]*ba-ru-ma-tum ta-ar-té-/e* u.e. [29]*a-dí-ší-im kà-kà-a-am* [30]*lá a-ba-ra-ší : a-dí-ší-im* [31]*ší-bi*$_4$*-r[a-a]m* le.e. [32]*lá a-ṣa-áb-ta-ší : a-[d]í-ší-im ba-pì-ra-/am* [33]*ha-šu-a-am ù [ṭá]-áb-tám i-na* [34]*[š]u-ur-ší-ša šu-ba-al-ku-tu[m]* [35]*uš-ba-al-k[i-s]í*

[1]A cow, O cow!

[2]The Arahtum-canal is rapid.

[3]Rapidly she becomes pregnant,

[3–4]Rapidly she gives birth,

[4–5]Rapidly water flows out of her "mouth,"

[5–6]She scrapes the ground with her nose,

[6–8]She brushes the house with her tail.

[8–10]Whom shall I send with orders to the twice seven daughters of the birth goddesses, (saying): [10–12]"Take your spades and your baskets and [12–14]clear quickly out the mouth of the Arahtum-canal"?

[14–15]If it is a male, like a wild ram,

[15–16]If it is a female, like a wild cow,

[17–18]If it is a stillborn child, one rejected by his god,

[18–20]May (the baby) be brought forth, and may he drop towards to the ground like a snake (from) a vineyard.

[20–22]The spell is not mine. It is a spell of Ninkilil, master of spells and lord of incantation. [23]May the Mistress of the birth goddesses cast it!

24–25 Yellow one, O yellow one!
The yellow one is yellow!
26 In the shade of the green orchard,
27–28 The spotted goat has come to graze.
29–30 I cast a weapon at it (but) did not bag it,
30–32 I cast a shepherd's crook at it (but) did not catch it,
32–33 I cast beer bread, thyme, and salt at it:
34–35 Then did I surely make it move from where it stood.

Bibliography: Text published by Michel (2004 [Kt 90/k 178]); translated by Hecker (2008, 65–66). There are two fragmentary duplicates for the first incantation, see Kouwenberg and Fincke (2013 [CCT 5, 50e]) and Barjamovic (2015, 75 [Kt 94/k 429]).

Comments: This tablet contains two incantations, both starting with a pseudo-abracadabra formula using wordplays. The link between these two incantations is obvious since the first one is intended to help a woman in labor, while the second one is for a newborn baby suffering from jaundice.

The first two lines of the first incantation may be also translated: "The rapid male is (quite) rapid / The rapid female is (quite) rapid!" meaning that the baby can be of either sex and should come quickly. The two first lines of the second incantation refer first to the boy baby, then to the girl baby with the same construction: "The yellow male is (quite) yellow, the yellow female is (quite) yellow."

Line 1: the word for "speedy male" (*arhum*) is a homonym of the word for "cow," and this animal reminds of the moon god both because of its bull-like horns and of the word play with *warhum*, "month." Moreover, the word for "speedy female" (*arhatum*) is also the name of the canal, which is a metaphor for the vagina of the woman giving birth; for a detailed analysis of these figures, see Michel 2004.

The badly preserved copy CCT 5, 50e, duplicates lines 5–12 with few variants (Kouwenberg and Fincke 2013); the most noticeable one is lines 3′-5′: *i-na dí-im-a-té-š*[*a*], *ta-sà-ra-aq*, é^{tám}, "with her tears she sprinkles the house." The last lines of the duplicate Kt 94/k 429 also differ; lines 21–24: *i-na ṣé-er, ki-ra-nim* : *ki-i* še-gig, *a-ša-ar-šu*, *li-iṣ-ba-at*, "May it take place like barley on top of the vineyard" (Barjamovic 2015).

Line 26: note that "yellow" and "green" are the same word in Akkadian.

118. Incantation against Lamaštum

Obv. [1]*e-za-at pu-ul-ha-at* [2]*i-lá-at na-ma-ra-at* [3]*ba-ar-ba-ra-tum* [4]*ma-ra-at A-ni-im* [5]*i-na sà-sí-im* [6]*mu-ša-*(erasure)*-bu-ša* [7]*i-na el-pé-tim* [8]*ru-úṣ*!*-pá*!*-sà* [9]*eṭ-lá-am lá-sí-ma-am* l.o. [10]*ta-kà-lá* [11]*ma*!*-ra-am ar-ha-am* rev. [12]*ta-na-sà-ha-am* [13]*zi-ba-sú ṣa-hu-ru-tim* [14]*na-pu-ṣú-um tù-na-pì-is* [15]*ší-bu-tum ta-ša-qí* «*a-me*» [16]*me-e bi-iš-ri-im* [17]*ší-ip-tum lá i-a-tum* [18]*ši-pá-at Ni-ki-li-il*$_5$ [19]*be-el ší-pá-tim* [20]*Ni-kà-ra-ak* [21]*ta-dí-ší-ma* le.e. [22]*a-na-ku al-qé-ší*

[1]She is furious, she is terrifying,
[2]She is evil, she has an awful glamour,
[3–4](She is) a she-wolf, the daughter of Anum.
[5–8]Her dwelling is in grass, her lair is in weeds.
[9–10]She holds back the youthful runner,
[11–13]She pulls out by his tail the rapid child.
[13–14]She brains little babies,
[15–16]She makes the old ones swallow the birth fluids.
[17–19]The spell is not mine; it is a spell of Ninkilil, master of spells.
[20–22]Ninkarrak casts it, so I took it up.

Bibliography: Text published by Michel (1997c [Kt 94/k 821]); translated by Foster (2005, 77) and Hecker (2008, 64). Lines 1–2 cited by Barjamovic and Larsen (2008, 147).

Comments: This incantation is written on a tablet with a clay handle by which to hang it in the house, perhaps near the baby's bed. The object was thus used both as an amulet and as an incantation to be recited by the exorcist.

Lamaštum weakens the young one and attacks both babies and the elderly, making them drink the amniotic fluids. The "rapid" child seems to be premature.

119. A Birth Used to Date a Document

Obv. ^{1}⅚ *ma-na* ½ gín ^{2}kù-babbar *ší-im* kù-gi ^{3}*ù* 15 gín kù-babbar ^{4}*ša i-ší-im* kù-gi ^{5}*pá-*[*ni*]*-im i*-ší-ta-ni* ^{6}*iš-tí Ta-ta-áš-mì-šu* lo.e. ^{7}3 gín kù-gi rev. ^{8}*i-nu-mì be-lá-at* ^{9}é$^{be\text{-}tim}$ *tù-ul-du** ^{10}*iš-tí Me-i-iš-mì-iš* ^{11}*ù Ta-ta-áš-mì-iš* ^{12}⅓ *ma-na* 1 gín kù-babbar ^{13}*ší-im-šu*

$^{1-2}$⅚ mina, ½ shekel of silver, price of the gold, $^{3-5}$and 15 shekels of silver, which remained as due to me from the price of the previous gold, ^{6}are on the account of Tattašmiš. $^{7-9}$3 shekels of gold (borrowed) when the Lady-of-the-House gave birth $^{10-11}$are on the the account of Meišmiš and Tattašmiš; $^{12-13}$its price is ⅓ mina, 1 shekel of silver.

Bibliography: Text published by Balkan (1992, 20; photo, 39 [Kt a/k 851]); collated May 2012.

Comments: The Lady-of-the-House seems to be the queen of Kaneš, the "house" being interpreted here as the Anatolian palace.

120. Adoption among Anatolians

Obv. ^{1}*Ha-ba-ta-li ki-ma*$^{!}$(LÁ) *Na-ah-šu-/ša-r*[*a*] ^{2}*Šé-li-a-ra me-ra-šu* ^{3}*šu-ma Šé-li-a-ra* ^{4}*ṣú*$^{!}$(KI)*-ha*$^{!}$(IL$_5$)*-ra*$^{!}$(BA)*-am mì-ma* <*a*>*-a-kam-ma* ^{5}*i-kà-ša-du-ni a-na* é$^{be\text{-}/et!}$ ^{6}*Ha-ba-ta-li ú-ba-al* ^{7}*šu-ma iš-tù Ha-ba-ta-li* ^{8}*mì-ma ú-pá-za-ar* 2 *ma-na* kù-babbar ^{9}*i-ša-qal šu-a-tí i-du-/ku-šu* lo.e. ^{10}*e-sú-nu* rev. ^{11}*ma-sú-nu ša* 3 *šu-nu-tí* ^{12}*šu-ma ša Ha-ba-ta-li* ^{13}*ṣú-ha-ar-šu ú-lá-ad* ^{14}6 gín kù-babbar *a-na e-le-e* ^{15}*i-za-zu du-nam ša Ha-ba-ta-li* ^{16}*Šé-li-a-ra il*$_5$*-qé šu-ma ki-ša*$^{!}$*-sú* ^{17}*a-na ba-tim i-pá-nu* 2 *ma-na* kù-babbar ^{18}*i-ša-qal ú šu-a-tí i-du-ku-šu šu-ma* ^{19}*Ha-ba-ta-li i-lá-pì-in Šé-li-a-/ra*$^{!}$(ŠA) ^{20}*a-na ší-mì-im i-dí-šu šu-ma* ^{21}*Ha-ba-ta-li Ni-wa-ah-šu-ša-ar* ^{22}*i-mu-tù Šé-li-a-ra* ^{23}*i-lá-qé šu-ma ṣú-ha-ra-am ú-lá-ad* ^{24}*mì-ma* é$^{be\text{-}tim}$ *i-*[*lá-qé*] le.e. ^{25}igi *Tù*$^{!}$(MA)*-hu-ší* igi *Wa-za-wa* ^{26}igi *Ša-áb-ta*

$^{1-2}$Habatali represents Nahšušara; Šeliara (is) his son. $^{3-5}$If Šeliara acquires any male slave anywhere, $^{5-6}$he shall bring him to the house of Habatali. $^{7-8}$If he conceals anything (he has acquired) from Habatali, $^{8-9}$he shall pay 2 minas of silver, or they will put him to death. $^{10-11}$All their income belongs to the 3 of them. $^{12-13}$Should the (wife) of Habatali give birth to a boy,

[14–15]there will be 6 shekels of silver on top of it. [15–16]Šeliara took the fortified house of Habatali. [16–18]If he (the adoptive son) has gone elsewhere, he shall pay 2 minas of silver, or they will put him to death. [18–20]If Habatali becomes poor, he may sell Šeliara. [20–23]When Habatali (and) Niwahšušar die, Šeliara shall take (everything). [23–24]Even if she (the wife of Habatali) gives birth to a boy, he [shall take] all the household property.

[25–26]In the presence of Tuhuši, Wazawa, and Šabta.

Bibliography: Text published in copy by Thureau-Dangin as TCL 1, 240; edited by Eisser and Lewy (1930, no. 8); Veenhof 2017a, 8–11.

Comments: Habatali and Nahšušara are husband and wife; they have no children and adopt Šeliara. Clauses refer to the status of the adoptive son in his new family and his rights of inheritance. He has to work for his parents' household and to share everything with them. He has already acquired part of the house and ultimately will obtain all their belongings, even if they have their own child. There are unclear penalties: the meaning of *e-le-e* is unknown.

If he becomes poor, the Anatolian father may sell his adopted son; this clause could have been inspired by Assyrian practice.

The literal translation of lines 16–17 is: "He has turned his neck to elsewhere."

Line 20: the writing *i-dí-šu* is a mistake for *i-da-šu*.

---

121. Payment for a Wet Nurse

Obv. [1]1 *ma-na* 6½ gín kù-gi [2]*pá-ša-lúm* 5 *ma-na* kù-babbar [3]*ša ik-ri-bi-a* 2½ *ma-/na* [4]*ša ni-qí-im a-na um-mì-a-/ni-a* [5]2 *ma-na* kù *ša Šu-Be-/lim* [6]*ù i-a-tí ša ba-ri-ni* [7]4 *ma-na* kù *ša* é *Ì-lí-/dan* [8]⅓ *ma-na ša ik-ri-bi*$_4$*-šu-/nu* [9]*i-pá-ni né-pí-ší-im* [10]*na-dí* 1 *ma-na ša-wi-ru* [11]*ša ṣú-ha-ar-tim* [12]*mì-ma a-nim ni-is-ha-sú* lo.e. [13]diri *ša-du-a-sú* [14]*ša-bu* ½ *ma-na* lá 1½ /gín rev. [15]*ta-ad-mì-iq-tum* [16]*ša I-li-a* 10 gín [17]*šé-bu-ul-tum ša Ištar-um-/mì* [18]2 gín *A-gi*$_5$*-a-a* 2 gín *Me-me* [19]2 gín *I-li-a* 2 gín [20]é *Ì-lí-dan* 2 gín [21]*Ší-ma-at-Ištar* ½ gín [22]*La-qé-ep* 1½ gín [d]im-sig$_5$ [23]1½ gín *Ší-la-ma-sí* [24]1½ gín *mu-šé-ni-iq-tum* [25]3 gín *ša La-ma-sí* [26]*a-na La-ma-sà-tim* [27]10 gín kù *ik-ri-bu* u.e. [28]*ša Be-lim a-na Bu-ṣí-/a* [29]*a-dí* 10 gín *ik-ri-bu* [30]*ša Be-lim* 5 gín kù [31]*ik-ri-bu ša* [d]utu *a-na A-šùr-dan* [32]*a-dí mì-ma a-nim a-na A-šùr-dan áp-qí-id* [33]igi *A-šùr-ba-ni* igi *Šu-lí* dumu *Me-ra-lí*

[1–3]1 mina, 6½ shekels of *pašallum*-gold, 5 minas of silver from my votive offerings, [3–6]2½ from the sacrifices for my investor, 2 minas of silver belonging to Šu-Bēlum and myself, it is ours in common; [7–10]4 minas of silver from the house of Ilī-dān, ⅓ mina from their votive offerings, (which) is placed uppermost in the pack; [10–11]1 mina of bracelets belonging to the young girl: [12–14]all this—its import tax added, its transport fee paid for. [14–16]One-half mina minus 1½ shekels from the *tadmiqum*-trust of Iliya; [16–17]10 shekels, consignment for Ištar-ummī; [18–20]2 shekels: Agiya; 2 shekels: Memē; 2 shekels: Iliya; 2 shekels: the house of Ilī-dān; [20–23]2 shekels: Šīmat-Ištar; ½ shekel: Laqēp; 1½ shekels: Adad-damiq; 1½ shekels: Šī-lamassī; [24–26]1½ shekels: the wet nurse; 3 shekels from Lamassī to Lamassatum. [27–29]I deposited 10 shekels of silver, votive offerings of Bēlum, for Buṣia. [29–32]I deposited 10 shekels, votive offerings of Bēlum; 5 shekels of silver, votive offerings of Šamaš for Aššur-dān.

[32]All this, I entrusted to Aššur-dān.

[33]In the presence of Aššur-bāni, and Šu-(i)lī, son of Merali.

Bibliography: Text published in copy by Lewy as TC 3, 207. Lines 1–10 and 14–33 cited by Hirsch (1961, 36–37 n. 191).

Comments: This text lists several amounts of gold and silver as expenses. Among these, a wet nurse receives 1½ shekels of silver. Other women are also recipients of small quantities of silver: Šīmat-Ištar, Šī-Lamassī, and Lamassatum.

Line 15: the word *tadmiqtum* refers to merchandise entrusted in good faith to a relative to sell it for as favorable terms as possible, with the obligation to give the yield to the owner, and without guaranteed commission or profit (Veenhof 2008a, 131 n. 595).

Line 17: the *šēbultum* corresponds to small amounts of silver or gold meant for women, usually as payment for textiles they had sent to Kaneš for sale.

Raising Children

There is very little iconography of women as mothers, although excavations at Kültepe have yielded depictions of Anatolian divine couples. A steatite mold dating to the eighteenth century BCE shows a couple with their two children: one standing, dressed like his parents, whereas the other,

Fig. 9. Mold for lead figurine showing an Anatolian divine couple with two children. Source: Kulakoğlu and Kangal 2010, 272, no. 240. © Archaeological Mission of Kültepe.

in his mother's arms, is entirely swaddled. The two children are shown as being approximately the same size (fig. 9).[22]

The father, as legal guardian of his children, decided his daughters' futures; it was he who arranged for their marriages.[23] Nevertheless, at Aššur, in the absence of their husbands, women raised their youngest children, who grew up in an environment dominated by women. Some women made recourse to acts of piety to assure the well-being and prosperity of their families, especially their children; for example, by commissioning a votive inscription (**122**).

Besides the moral and intellectual upbringing of their children, women also had to see to their nurture (**126**). In letters exchanged with the male members of their family living in Anatolia, they commonly give

22. Emre 1971; T. Özgüç 2003, 274, no. 305.
23. Michel 1997g and chapter 1 in this book.

news of their offspring only in a brief formula: "Your household and (all) the children are fine."[24]

Lack of news of their wives and children could be worrisome to merchants, who could ask their associates and representatives to protect and advise their wives and to take care of them: "Look after the young woman and the children. Instruct the woman to make (others) pay the expenses."[25] This implied making certain that women and children were not in need, to the extent of advancing money needed for their support (**123**).

A good part of women's correspondence is taken up by material concerns about the rearing of the child: they had to be fed and clothed (**142**, **166**). Children could go through a considerable amount of food, as Aššur-idī observed, when, in the absence of their father, he brought up his grandchildren and kept an account of what they consumed: "I spent one mina of silver to buy two oxen and grain to feed (your) sons."[26]

A husband had to provide for his wife and children, as some merchants were reminded by their representatives or by their wives: "Send to your kitchen enough food for your children and your wife so that we can give them their rations!"[27] One woman compared her food allowance to that for servants and considered herself particularly badly treated; indeed, servants received additional rations for their children (**124**). Lack of food was a major source of anxiety for mothers, and, in order to arouse the compassion of their correspondents for the fate awaiting their little ones as a consequence of paternal neglect, they could invoke their children's death from malnourishment and even their own (**125**, **127**).[28]

---

24. **133**, **206**, **308**. This expression can also be found in letters sent by representatives in Aššur in contact with the merchants' wives; see, for example, VS 26, 9:23–25 (Michel 2001a, no. 199); CCT 2, 38:32–33; CCT 4, 28b:27.

25. TPAK 1, 22:23–28: *i-ṣé-er* : [*a*]*m-tim*, *ù ṣú-ùh-ri-im*, *e-k*[*u-n*]*u li-li-kam*, dam *na-hi-da-ma*, *a-na gam-ri-im*, *lu tù-uš-ta-dí-in*. See also: "You are our brother. Look after our *amtum*-wives and your children"; ICK 1, 65:15–18, *a-hu-ni a-ta*, *a-ṣé-er* : *a-ma-tí-ni* :, *ú ṣú-ùh-ri-kà*, *e-kà* : *li-li-ik*. Even if the two authors of this letter are in debt to their correspondent, they ask him to look after their wives, which could also mean to pay their expenses.

26. KUG 27:50–53: 1 *ma-na* kù-babbar [*a*]*-ší-im* 2 $gu_4^{hi\text{-}a}$, *ù ú-ṭí-tim*, *a-na me-er-e ša-ku-li-im*, *ag-mu-ur*. See Michel 1997g, 98–101.

27. KTH 9:33–36: *a-na hu-ur-ší-kà šé-*bi_4*-lam-/ma*, *ma-lá a-kà-al šé-ri-kà*, *ù a-ší-tí-kà né-nu*, *ip-ri-šu-nu lu-ni-/dí-*in_4. Note that the word *tarbitum* corresponds to the payment for raising children (by others).

28. Men, too, could worry about not having the means to feed their children,

Besides food and shelter, women had to provide their children with a wardrobe, generally one or two garments of the right size. As children grew, their wardrobe had to be replaced regularly (**166**). Intensive production of cloth intended for export to Anatolia took its toll on weaving of textiles for home use.[29] Among the different types of cloth mentioned is "cloth for a child," no doubt a piece of a size to make a child's garment (**173**; **158**; KTS 2, 31).[30] To judge from the steatite mold mentioned above (fig. 9), children of the Anatolian residents of Kaneš were dressed in the same style as their parents. Some children could receive finery such as golden earrings or copper crescents: "I will send gold for the girls' ears. Urgent! Wait for me to send the gold and look after the children."[31]

Besides material maintenance, the young were supposed to be provided with professional or academic training, a system of moral values, and the basis for a future.[32] At Aššur, girls from a young age no doubt worked in the weaving establishment of their home, there learning the rudiments of the craft.[33] Training of boys is almost never mentioned in texts. The only known reference comes from the eldest son of Pūšu-kēn. While he was with his mother in Aššur, he learned writing and arithmetic with a teacher.[34] Several school texts used for scribal education have been discovered at Aššur and Kaneš.[35] These young boys presumably learned their future profession as merchants after they joined their fathers in Anatolia.

---

as in BIN 6, 183:10–13, 14–17, presumably sent to Puzur-Anna by Ir'am-Aššur (see BIN 6, 73): "What shall I give to the children? What shall I say to our mother about food?… My eyes have become bloodshot (trying to find) food for myself and the children!"; *a-na ṣú-ùh-ri-/im, mì-nam lá-dí-in a-na um-mì-/ni, a-na ú-ku-ul-tí-a mì-nam, lá-aq-bi … a-na-kam-ma, a-na ú-ku-ul-tí-a ù ú-ku-ul-ti, ṣú-ùh-ri-im e-na-a, i-ta-na-ki-lá.*

29. Veenhof 1972, 103–23; Michel 1997g, 101–2; 2006b; in this book chapter 4, pp. 256–70.

30. Michel and Veenhof 2010, 36–37. See, for example, Kt 75/k 78:3–4: "I (gave) his daughter a garment for a child to wear"; 1 túg *ša ṣú-ùh-ri-im me-ra-sú, ú-lá-bi₄-iš.*

31. KTS 2, 23:13–18: kù-gi *a-na ú-za-an, ṣa-ha-ra-tim ú-šé-*[*ba-lam*?], *a-pu-tum i-hi-id-*[*ma*], kù-gi *šé-bi₄-la*[*m*], *ù šé-ri-kà, a-šu-ur*. See also BIN 6, 175:16–18.

32. See chapter 5.

33. Michel 2006b and, in this book, chapter 4.

34. "As you know, we are learning the scribal art. Send me an *ēpattum*-garment for my teacher!"; CCT 4, 6e:4–8: dub-sar-*tám wa-dí, lá-am-da-ni, e-pá-tá-am, a-na um-me-a-ni-a, šu-bi-lam*. See Larsen 1976, 305 n. 47.

35. Michel 2008b and 2010b for an overview.

122. Votive Inscription of a Woman to Protect Her Family

Col. I. ^{1}*i-nu-ma* ^{2d}lugal-gin ^{3}ensí *A-šùr* ^{4}*a-na* ^{d}inanna ^{5}*A-šu-ri-tim* ^{6}nin-a-ni ^{7}*Ha-ti-tum* ^{8}dam *En-na-da-[gan]* ^{9}*ta-ak-ru-ub* ^{10}*a-na ba-lá-aṭ* ^{11}*mu-ti-ša* ^{12}*ba-lá-ṭì-ša* col. II. ^{1}*ù* ^{2}*ba-lá-aṭ* ^{3}*šé-ri-ša* ^{4}téš ^{5}*tù-šé-ri-ib*

$^{i1-3}$When Sargon (was) the vice regent of Aššur, $^{i4-6}$to Ištar Aššurītum, her mistress, $^{i7-9}$Hattītum, wife of Enna-Dagan, made an offering (and) $^{i10-ii5}$dedicated (this bronze) vulva for the life of her husband, her own life, and the life of her children.

Bibliography: Votive inscription written on a bronze plaque in the shape of a female sex organ, found during the excavations of the Ištar temple at Aššur, and published by Jakob-Rost and Freydank (1981 [VA Ass 4286]), and Grayson (1987, 46, no. 2001).

Comments: Written in the third-person, this votive inscription was commissioned by Hattītum, wife of Enna-Dagan, to protect her family. The text is dated to the reign of Sargon I (ca. 1917–1878), who belonged to the so-called Puzur-Aššur dynasty. As shown by his title, he was considered as governor appointed by the god of Aššur, the true king of the city of the same name.

Line 10: the various Assyrian votive inscriptions of the type *ana balāṭ*, "for the life of," do rarely mention the children. Here, the word *šerrum* refers to all Hattītum's children, boys and girls, which she already has or will give birth to in the future; thus it could also be translated "descendants."[36]

123. A Merchant's Anxiety about His Wife and Daughter

^{1}*a-na Ni-mar-Ištar Šu*$^{!}$*-ma-bi*$_{4}$*-a* ^{2}*I-dí-Sú-en*$_{6}$ *Ha-nu qí-bi*$_{4}$*-ma* ^{3}*a-hu-ú-a be-lu-ú-a a-tù-nu* ^{4}*a-na šu-mì : ni-šé-e-a : a-na* ^{5}*me-er-e I-dí-a-bi*$_{4}$*-im a-tí-ki-il*$_{5}$*-ma* ^{6}*ma-tí-ma : lá áš-pu-ra-ku-nu-tí* ^{7}*ma-ma-an : i-na ba-ri-ku-nu* ^{8}*[p]á-ni-ú-ni : ni-šé-e :* ^{9}*li-ir-de*$_{8}$*-a-ma : ga-mar-šu* ^{10}*a-na-kam : a-da-šu-um* ^{11}*a-na-kam : I-dí-Sú-en*$_{6}$ ^{12}*a-wa-tim :* sig$_{5}$$^{qá\text{-}tim}$ ^{13}*a-šu-mì ni-šé-e-a : e-ta-wa-am* ^{14}*šu-ma : a-na Kà-ni-iš* lo.e. ^{15}*lá e-ru-ba-am* rev. ^{16}*a-hu-ú-a be-lu-ú-a* ^{17}*a-tù-nu : ki-ma ṣú-ha-ar-tum* ^{18}é *Šu-ma-bi*$_{4}$*-a : wa-áš-ba-at-ni*

36. For another votive inscription written by a woman, see below, 377 n. 50.

[19]*I-tur*$_4$-dingir *iq-bi*$_4$*-a-am* [20]*a-na Šu-ma-bi*$_4$*-a qí-bi*$_4$*-ma* [21]*iš-tí-kà : Mu-na-iš-kà-an* [22]*lá té-zi-ba-am : am-tí : ù ṣú-ha-ar-tum* [23]*sà-he-er-tum : mì-ta : ú ba-al-ṭá* [24]*ú-lá i-de*$_8$ *: a-hu-ú-a* [25]*a-tù-nu : šu-ma : ba-al-ṭá* [26]*ú ší-na-tí : ta-ru-a-am* [27]*ga-mar-ší-na : ta-da-na-am* [28]*a-le-e : a-hu-ú-a be-lu-a* [29]*a-tù-nu za-ku-sà : šu-up-ra-nim* u.e. [30]*šu-ma ba-al-ṭá* le.e. [31]kù-babbar 1 gín *a-na a-kà-li-ší-na* [32]*dí-na-ma : šu-up-ra-nim*

[1–2]Say to Nimar-Ištar, Šumi-abiya, Iddin-Suen, (and) Hanu.

[3]You are my brothers and masters. [4–5]I relied on the sons of Iddin-abum in the matter of my people, and [6]I never wrote to you (about it). [7–9]Whoever among you is first (to depart), let him take along my people, [9–10]and here I will pay for his expenses. Here, Iddin-Suen spoke to me friendly about my people. [14–17]If I am not back in Kaneš—you are my brothers and masters—[17–19]you (must know that) Itūr-ilī told me that the girl is living in the house of Šumi-abiya.

[20]Say to Šumi-abiya.

[21–22]You should not leave behind Muna'iškan in your place. [22–24]I do not even know whether my *amtum*-wife and the little girl are dead or alive! [24–25]You are my brothers. If they (fem.) are alive, [26–28]then, take them along to me, I am able to pay for their expenses! [28–29]You are my brothers and masters. Send me exact information [30–32]whether they are alive. Give silver for their food, every shekel (you can), and send (them) to me!

Bibliography: Text published by Michel and Garelli as TPAK 1, 34.

Comments: The author of this letter is unknown. He has been away for a long time, either in Aššur or in another Anatolian town, without news from his wife and daughter left in Kaneš. During his absence, representatives had to take care both of his affairs and his family.

---

124. Complaints about Food Rations

Obv. [1]*um-ma Ša-at-A-šur-ma* [2]*a-na Pu-šu-ke-en*$_6$ [3]*qí-bí-ma a-šu-mì* [4]*mì-ih-ṣí-im ku-lu* é^{tim} [5]*ma-sú-uh šu-ma pá-nu-kà* [6]*a-na A-lim*$^{\text{ki!(LIM)}}$ *ša-ak-nu* [7]*a-na i-li ša-qí-i* [8]*ú*$^!$ *a-bu ú-lá e-ta-áš*$^!$*-ru-ni* [9]*ú a-ta : a-ma-«nu»-kam*$^!$(HI) [10]*lá ta-ša-ra-ni* [11]*a*$^!$(Ú)*-lá-ku-a-ti ma-ma-an*$^!$ [12]*ša-ni-a-am lá i-šu* [13]*a-šu-mì iš-tù Be-el*$^!$*-/té-é-*<gal^{lim}> [14]*a-dì kán-bar-ta* lo.e. [15]*qú-ta-a-«da»-/tù-ni* [16][x]*-ma* : rev. [17]*a-ni ur-ta-i-bu* [18]20 silà *ma-da-dam* [19]*iš-tí a-ma-tí-kà-ma*

[20]*lu*!(Ú)-*uš-ta-am-he-ru-ni* [21]gemé 20 silà *e-kà-lá* [22]*ú a-na-ku* 20 silà *a-kál* [23]*a-ni šu-mì ṣú-uh-ri-im* [24]*lá i-za-ku-ru a-na-nu-um* [25]*a-ta : lá ta-za-kár-šu-nu* [26]*a-li-ku i-li-ku*!*-nim-ma* [27]*šu-mì lá ta-az-ku-ur* [28]*ma-nu-*BA : *šu-mì* (erasure) [29]*li-iz-ku-ur* [30]*a-lá-ku-a-tí ma-ma-an* u.e. [31]*ša-ni-a-am* [32]*lá i-šu* le.e. [33]*ma*?*-lá iš-*(erasure)*-tù i-Na-ar-ma-ak-/A-šur* [34]*ni-qí-a-am i-dí-nu-nim* [35]an?-na *ší-*[x]*-tù-um* x x

[1–3]Thus (says) Šāt-Aššur: say to Pūšu-kēn.

[3–5]As for illness, the entire house is affected! [5–6]If you intend to go to the city (of Aššur), [7]have an offering made to the gods. [8–9]The fathers have not taken care of me; neither do you, over there, [10–12]take care of me, although I have no one but you!

[13–15]Because you kept waiting from month Bēlet-ekallim (i) until month Kanwarta (ix) […] [17]they now have made me tremble!

[18–20]They have made me equal to your female slaves by measuring out (to me) a ration of only 20 silas. [21–22]If female slaves get (a monthly ration of) 20 silas, should I too get 20 silas only?

[23–24]Now, they do not even mention the names of the children; [24–25]should you, over there, then not mention them? [26–27]Travelers came, but you did not mention my name! [28–29]Who else is there to mention my name? [30–32]I have no one but you!

[33–35]All (I obtained) since (the month) Narmak-Aššur (ii or iii), (is) a sacrifice (that) they gave me! […]

Bibliography: Text published in copy by Clay as BIN 4, 22; translated by Michel (2001a, no. 375).

Comments: Šāt-Aššur is the daughter of Šalim-ahum, a close colleague of Pūšu-kēn. She married Aššur-malik, son of Innaya, who travels to Anatolia. She is complaining that her food rations are no bigger than those of the female servants. According to her, the children of the female servant should not be taken into account in the rations.

Šāt-Aššur feels isolated and lonely; she is asking Pūšu-kēn to get news of him and her distant family members.

125. Children Dying of Hunger

Obv.$^{1'}$[x x x x x x] *i-d*[*í* x x] $^{2'}$[*a-na* X-x]*-hu za ar* [x] $^{3'}$[*ù* X x] *qí-bi*$_4$*-ma um-ma* $^{4'}$[x x] *ma Ba-zi-tim-ma* $^{5'}$[*i-na*] kù-babbar^{pì}*-a ša qá-bi*$_4$*-a-ni* $^{6'}$[kù]-bab-bar *uš-ta-qí-*[*il*$_5$] ^{d}im-dùl $^{7'}$[*ša-zu-uz*]*-tám i-zi-iz-ma ša* é $^{8'}$[*Pì-l*]*á-ah-Ištar* kù-babbar *ša i-a-tí* $^{9'}$*i-lá-kà-ni* : *a-na* é *Pì-lá-ah-Išt*[*ar*] $^{10'}$*iš-ta-aq-lu-šu* : *ú qá-t*[*ám*] $^{11'}$*ša A-šùr-na-da* : *a-na* é $^{12'}$*A-lim*^{ki} *a-na hu-bu-li-šu* $^{13'}$*iš-ta-aq-lu-šu a-na-kam* : kù-babbar $^{14'}$1 gín *a-na ba-lá-ṭí-ni* : *lá-šu-m*[*a*] $^{15'}$*ṣú-ùh-ru-um i-na bu-bu-tim* $^{16'}$*i-mu-a-at-ma lá ta-ša-ra* $^{17'}$*a-dí* : *a-i-im* : *ú-mì-im* : *a-ba-*[*ri*] $^{18'}$*lá t*[*ù*]*-ha-da-ar-ni-*[*a-tí*]
(the rest of the tablet is destroyed)

$^{1'-4'}$[…]: thus (say) […] Bazītum.

$^{5'-6'}$[From] my silver that has been promised to me, I paid the [sil-]ver. $^{6'-7'}$Adad-ṣululī acted as the [represent]tative, and concerning [Pil]ah-Ištar's house, $^{7'-10'}$the silver that should come to me, they paid it to Pilah-Išt[ar]'s house; $^{10'-13'}$but (as for) Aššur-nādā's share, they paid it to the City Hall for his debts.

$^{14'}$Here there is not even a single shekel of silver for us to live from, and $^{15'-16'}$the children are dying of hunger, and you are not taking care (of them). $^{17'}$How long must I starve?

$^{18'}$You should not make us miserable!

Bibliography: Text published in copy by Stephens as BIN 6, 197.

Comments: The names of the correspondents of this letter are broken; the only name left among the senders belongs to a woman, Bazītum. She complains that she has no silver to buy food for the children.

126. A Man Urges a Woman Not to Let the Child Starve

Obv. ^{1}*u*[*m-m*]*a* [*Šu*]*-Ištar-ma a-na* ^{2}*Zi-z*[*i*]*-zi-i* : *ù* ^{3}*Ištar-lá-ma-sí qí-bi*$_4$*-ma* ^{4}1[0$^?$ gí]n an-na *A-nu-pí-a* ^{5}*na-*[*áš*]*-a-ku-nu-tí um-mì a-tí* ^{6}*e-lá-nu-ki ma-ma-an* ^{7}*lá i-šu ṣú-ùh-ra-am* ^{8}*l*[*á t*]*ù-me-ṣí* : *a-ṣé-er* ^{9}[X-x-x] *ú A-nu-pì-a* ^{10}[x x] *kà* [x-*z*]*i-ik* lo.e. ^{11}[x dug *a*]*r-ša-tim* rev. ^{12}[*l*]*i-dí-na-ki-na*$^!$(UN)-*ti* ^{13}*ú-dí a-na-ma a-na-kam* ^{14}*ú-ša-hi-*[*sú*] *ú a-ti* ^{14}*a-wa-tim* : *ša nu-a-im* 3 gín ^{15}kù-babbar *ša e-zi-bu* kù-babbar ^{16}*lu a-na-ku á*[*š*]*-qúl lu A-bu-ša-/lim* ^{17}*iš-qúl té-er-ta-ku-nu* ^{18}*li-li-kam*

$^{1-3}$T[hu]s (say) [Šu]-Ištar: say to Ziz[i]zi and Ištar-lamassī.

$^{4-5}$Anupiya is bringing you t[en shek]els of tin. You are my mother; $^{6-7}$I have no one but you! $^{7-8}$D[o n]ot let the child starve. $^{8-10}$To [X-x-x] and Anupiya [...]

$^{11-13}$I instructed (him) that he should give you (fem. pl.) [x jars of] wheat. $^{13-14}$And as for the matter of the Anatolian, $^{17-18}$let your message come here, $^{14-15}$about the 3 shekels of silver that I left, $^{15-17}$whether I myself paid the silver or whether Abu-šalim paid it.

Bibliography: Tablet published by Larsen as AKT 6c, 646 (kt 94 k 1405).

Comments: Zizizi was the nickname of the daughter of Imdī-ilum and his wife Ištar-baštī (see fig. 17 for her family tree); she was first married to Āl-ṭāb, and then to Annuwa. Ištar-lamassī was the wife of Ali-ahum, son of Šalim-Aššur, whose archives were excavated in 1994 (figs. 2–3). The letter is addressed to both women on lines 4–5, using the masculine *-kunūti* instead of the feminine *-kināti* (on line 17, there is *-kunu* instead of *-kina*), then presumably only to Zizizi on lines 5–8, then again to both women on the following lines.

---

127. Lack of Food for the Children

Obv. ^{1}*a-n*[*a* X-x-x-x] ^{2}*qí-bi-*[*ma um-ma*] ^{3}*Ší-ma-S*[*ú-en*$_{6}$*-ma*] ^{4}*a-šu-mì še-i*[*m* x x (x)]*-a-ni* ^{5}*um-ma a-ta-*[*m*]*a a-*[*na*] *E-na-A-šur* ^{6}*a-qá-bi*$_{4}$*-*[*m*]*a* 10 dug *še-im* ^{7}*i-da*$^{!}$*-na-ki-im mì-ma* ^{8}*ù-lá i-*[*d*]*í-nam* lo.e. ^{9}*bé-lí a-ta* ^{d}utu^{ši} ^{10}*a-ta qá-qú-ru-um* rev. ^{11}dan^{an} *ṣú-ha-ar-kà* ^{12}*i-bu-bu-tim* ^{13}*lá i-mu-a-at šu-ma* ^{14}*a-ta* : *sà-ah-ra-at a-na* ^{15}*ú-ku-ul-tí ṣú-ùh-ri-kà* ^{16}*šé-bi*$_{4}$*-lam* : *a-ma-/kam* ^{17}*Hu-du-ur-lá* ^{18}*ṣa-*[*ba-at-ma*] 12 gín u.e.^{19}k[ù-babbar x-*n*]*i*$^{?}$*-li*

$^{1-3}$Say to [X-x-x-x: thus (says)] Šīmat-S[uen].

$^{4-6}$Concerning barley [...] you (said) as follows: "I will speak t[o] Enna(m)-Aššur, [an]d $^{6-7}$he will give you ten jars of barley." $^{7-8}$He did not give me anything. $^{9-11}$You are my lord; you are my sun. The situation is difficult. $^{11-13}$Your children should not die of hunger! $^{13-16}$If you are delayed, send me (silver) for your children's meals. $^{16-19}$There, s[eize] Hudurla [and ...] twelve shekels of s[ilver].

Bibliography: Text published in copy by Stephens as BIN 6, 124.

Comments: Šīmat-Suen informs her correspondent—my lord, my son—that she never received the promised jars of barley, and she asks him for food for their children's meals.

Provisioning and Food

Women had to care for the members of the older generations living in their house, as well as their domestic staff. Lack of means to buy grain, the basic food item, was one of their principal worries. At Aššur, they could buy grain after the harvest with money sent by their husbands or with the proceeds from their sale of textiles. They had to estimate the quantities needed to feed all the members of their household and sometimes found themselves coming up short (**127**, **128**, **129**, **130**).

Grain, ground into flour, was used to make various kinds of bread (**131**; CCT 3, 7b–8a; **201**).[37] It was also the principal ingredient of beer: "Give it (the silver) to Tarīš-mātum, and according to my instructions, let her buy barley and make malt and 'beer bread.'"[38] This alcoholic beverage was made by the lady of the house using malt (*buqlum*) and beer bread (*bappirum*) as needed (**129**, **166**).[39]

Like the women at Aššur, Anatolian merchants' wives had the daily chore of preparing the beer for household consumption (**132**, **319**). They got from their husbands the money and various commodities for cooking, such as lard, oil, nuts, and assorted condiments and spices (**319**, **202**, **303**). Women's diet included meat as well: mutton, beef, and pork were sold and dried, smoked, stewed, or conserved for long-term storage (**133**, **307**).[40]

For food preparation, the inhabitants of Kaneš had an impressive array of utensils. The merchants' houses in Kaneš have yielded a considerable assemblage of clay pots in many shapes.[41] Some inventories as well give an idea of the equipment women used to store and prepare food. Since

---

37. Michel 1997f.

38. AKT 2, 26:14–18: *a-na, Ta-ri-iš-ma-tim dí-na-šu-ma, a-na ma-lá té-er-tí-a še-am, lu ta-áš-a-ma bu-uq-lam, ù ba-pì-ra-am lu*[!] *té-pu-uš.*

39. For the preparation of beer, see Michel 2009d. See also AKT 2, 26, in which Tarīš-mātum is supposed to buy barley with the proceeds of copper, and then to prepare the ingredients for brewing beer.

40. Michel 1997f; Dercksen 2008a.

41. See, for example, T. Özgüç 2003, 142–229, for the pottery, and 242–44 for some metal vessel.

Fig. 10. Bronze vessels excavated in 2003 in a Ib grave; from Kutlu Emre (2008): (left) bronze ladle with sieve; (top right) fruit stand; (bottom right) frying pan. © Archaeological Mission of Kültepe.

only metal objects were normally inventoried in texts, wooden objects are rarely and ceramics are almost never mentioned (**135**).[42] Some cooking pots could be specially made according to very precise directions (**134**).

Even if these furnishings are Anatolian, one can suppose that women at Aššur used the same types of household utensils. In fact, an unpublished document shows that the wife of Hunniya, who lived at Aššur, owned at least forty minas worth of bronze objects, dishes, and pots and pans (fig. 10).[43] Also, merchants sent from Anatolia to their wives at Aššur all sorts of copper or bronze objects, including cups and bowls (**134**, **166**, **210**).

42. See also Kt c/k 1517, edited by Dercksen 1996, 76–77, which mention 1 talent, 17 minas of bronze objects belonging to Aššur-emūqī.

43. Kt n/k 212:11–14, cited by Dercksen 1996, 78 n. 261: "I (Hunia's sister) handed over to her (Hunia's wife), before your representatives, her belongings and bronze objects, weighing 40 minas, from your kitchen, and she took them out (of the house)."

128. Famine in Aššur and No Barley at Home

Obv. [1]*a-na I-na-a qí-bi-m*[*a*] [2]*um-ma Ta-ra-am-Ku-bi-ma* [3]*ta-áš-pu-ra-am um-ma a-ta-ma* [4]*ša-wi-ru-ú : ù a-nu-qú-ú* [5]*ša i-ba-ší-ú-ni : ša-ṣí-ri* [6]*a-na a-kà-li-ki : li-ib-ší-ú* [7]*ke-na*$^{!}$*-tim-ma* : ½ *ma-na* kù-gi [8]dingir-*ba-ni* : *tù-šé-bi-lam* [9]*a-i-ú-tim* [*š*]*a-wi-ri* [10]*ša té-zi-ba-ni i-nu-mì* [11]*tù-úṣ-ú* kù-babbar 1 gín [12]*ú-lá té-zi-ba-am* : é^{tam} [13]*tù-lá-qí-it-*[*ma*] : *tù-šé-ṣí* [14]*iš-t*[*ù*] *t*[*ù*]*-úṣ-ú-ni* [15]*da-nu-tum* [*bu-bu*]*-tum* [16]*i-n*[*a*] *A-lim*^{ki} : *ù-lá še-am* [17]1 silà : *té-zi-ba-am* : *še-am* [18]*a-n*[*a*] *ú-kúl-tí-ni* : *áš-ta-na-am* [19]*ù tap-hi*$^{!}$*-ra-am ša šu-ri-nim*$_{x}$ [20]*i-na it-*[x x x x] [21]*a-dí-in-ma* [*i-šu*]*-ú* [22]*qá-tí-a* : *ag-da-ma-ar* rev. [23]*ù a-na* é *A-lim*^{ki} : *a-na* [*ša*] [24]é *A-da-da i-šu-ú*$^{!}$*-ma áš-t*[*a*]*-/qá-al* [25]*mì-num* : *ri-ip-šu* [26]*ša ta-áš-ta-na-pá-ra-ni* [27]*a-na a-kà-li-ni-i* [28]*lá-šu* : *né-nu* : *ri-ib-ší* [29]*né-ta-na-pá-áš ša i-qá-tí-a* [30]*ib-ší-ú* : *ú-lá-qí-it-ma* [31]*uš-té-bi*$_{4}$*-lá-kum* : *u*$_{4}$*-ma-am* [32]*i-bé-tim* : *e-ri-im* : *wa-áš-ba-ku* [33]*ša-tum* : *ša-na-at* [34]*i-hi-id-ma* : *me-eh-ra-at* [35] [túg] *ṣú-ba-tí-a* : kù-babbar : *i-na* [36][*ša*] *i-qá-tí-kà-ma* : *i-ba-ší-ú* [37]*šé-bi*$_{4}$*-lam-ma* : *še-am* 10 baneš [38]*lá-áš-am* : *a-šu-mì* : *ṭup-pí-im* [39]*ša A-šùr-i-mì-tí* dumu *Ku-ra* [40]*ša ší-bi*$_{4}$: *ša il*$_{5}$*-qé-ú* [41]é^{tám} : *ú-ša-ah-dí-ir-ma* [42]*a-ma-tim* : *ú-kà-tí-ma* [43]*ša-zu-úz-ta-kà* : *a-wa-tám* [44]*ig-mu-ru-ma* le.e. [45]⅔ *ma-na* kù-babbar *áš-ta-qal* : *a-dí ta-lá-kà-/ni* [46]*lá*$^{!}$ *i-ra-ga-am* : *i-na a-lá-ki-kà* [47]*ta-ta-ú-wu* : *mì-šu-um* : *ta-ki-li* [48]*ta-áš*$^{!}$*-ta-na*$^{!}$*-me-ma hi-im-ṭá-tim* /*t*[*a-á*]*š-*[*ta-na-pá-ra-am*]

[1–2]Say to Innaya: thus (says) Tarām-Kūbi.

[3]You wrote me as follows: [4–6]"Watch over the bracelets and rings that are there, so that they can serve to provide you with food." [7–8]Certainly, you had Ilī-bāni bringing me ½ mina of gold, [9–10]but what bracelets did you leave me? [10–13]When you left, you did not leave me silver, not even a single shekel! You emptied the house and took (everything) out! [14–17]After you had gone, there was a severe famine in the city (of Aššur) while you had not left me barley, not even a single liter! [17–18]I must try to buy barley for our sustenance. [19–22]And, as to the treasure for the temple collection, I gave an emblem in/among […], and I spent what is at hand. [23–24]Moreover, I just paid to the City Hall for [what] the house of Adada owed. [25–26]What protests do you have to keep writing me about? [27–29]There is nothing for our sustenance, so we are the ones to keep making complaints! [29–31]I scraped together what I had at my disposal and sent it to you. [31–32]Now, I am living in an empty house. [33–37]The (harvest) season is now! Be sure to

send me the silver for my textiles from what you have as your share $^{37–38}$so that I can buy barley, about ten *ṣimdu* measures (ca. 300 liters).

$^{38–41}$Concerning the tablet giving (the list) of witnesses which Aššur-imittī, son of Kura, took, he caused the house much trouble, ^{42}took maids as collateral, then $^{43–44}$your representatives settled the matter. ^{45}But I finally had to pay ⅔ mina of silver. $^{45–46}$He must not contest before you arrive. At your arrival, $^{47–48}$you will discuss it. Why do you keep listening to slander and sending me heated (letters)?

Bibliography: Text published in copy by Smith as CCT 3, 24; edited by Michel (1991, no. 3); translated by Michel (2001a, no. 348; 2014b, 206–7); lines 1–38 cited by Dercksen (2004a, 23–24).

Comments: Tarām-Kūbi writes to her husband, Innaya, stressing her critical financial situation (fig. 17). She accuses him of leaving nothing in the house and complains that she has no more money to buy barley. This letter belongs to a group of a dozen letters sent by this woman. Most of these are very emotional and give the image of a strong-minded person.

---

129. Management of Food Products

Obv. ^{1}*a-na I-na-a qí-bi-ma um-ma Ta-ra-<am>-Ku-<bi>-ma* ^{2}*a-wa-tám* : *ša* é *Ku-ra ša ta-wa-tù-ú* ^{3}*ṭá-bu-a-at* : kù-babbar *iš-tí pá-nim-ma* ^{4}*šé-bi-lá-ma* : *ṭup-pu-šu a-na* é^{tí}*-kà* ^{5}*li-ip-hu-ru*$^{!}$ *ú* : *ṭup-pu-um ša* é ^{6}*En-na-Sú-en*$_6$: é *Šu-Be-lim pá-qí-id* ^{7}*ù ṭup-pu-um ša* é *Ku-ra* : *Puzúr-A-šùr* ^{8}*ù-kà-al* : kù-babbar *i-na pá-ni-kà* ^{9}*šé-bi-lá-ma* : *i-na* é *ku-nu-ki-kà* ^{10}*li-ni-dí* kù-babbar *a-na šé-bu-li-im* ^{11}*mì-ma* : *lá ta-pá-lá-ah* : kù-babbar : *a-na* ^{12}é$^{\text{bé-tí}}$*-kà-ma* : *e-ra-ab* : *ša-tum* ^{13}*ša-na-at* kù-babbar *šé-bi-lá-ma* ^{14}*ú-ṭá-tám a-pá-ni-kà li-iš-pu-/ku-ni-kum* ^{15}*ba-pí-ra-am ša e-pu-ša-ku-ni* ^{16}*il*$_5$*-té-bi*$_4$*-ir* : *a-šu-mì ša* é *Ku-ra* ^{17}*Puzúr-A-šùr a-šu-mì-kà* : *ip-lá-ah-ma* ^{18}*um-ma né-nu-ma mì-ma lá ta-pá-lá-ah* ^{19}*a-wa-tám* : *ku-bu-ús-ma ú a-wi-lúm* rev. ^{20}*šé-ep-šu* : *a-na A-lim*^{ki} *li-iq-ru-ba-/am* ^{21}*ú-sá-li-šu-ma* : *a-wa-tám* ^{22}*ig-mu-ur a-pu-tum ki-ma* ^{23}*ṭup-pá-am ta-áš-me-ú* : *al-kam-ma* ^{24}*e-en*$_6$: *A-šùr* : dingir-*kà ù li-bi*$_4$*-/tí-ka* ^{25}*a-mu-ur* : *ú a-dí* : *ba-al-ṭá*$^{!}$*-ku-ni* ^{26}*e-né-kà lá-mu-ur* : *du-lu-um*$^{!}$(ZU) *a-na li-bi*$_4$*-/ni* ^{27}*e-ta-ra-ab* : *ki-ta-am* : *ú iš-ra-am*$^{!}$ ^{28}*a-na* ^{d}mar-tu-*im ša* dumu *Šu-Ku-bi-im* ^{29}*ub-lá-ni* : *i-na* é$^{\text{bé-tí}}$*-šu-ma* : *i-ba-ší* ^{30}*ṭup-pá-am* : *šé-bi-lá-šu-ma* : *ki*$^{!}$*-ta-a-am* ^{31}*ù iš-ra-am* : *li-dí-in-ma* : *i-na* ^{32}*bé-tí-kà* : *li-bi-ší* : *a-šu-mì* : *am-tim* ^{33}*A-šùr-ták-lá-ku iš-pu-ra-ma i-na ṭup-pì-šu*

[34]⅓ *ma-na* kù-babbar *a-na E-lá-lí* dumu *Šu-Ku-bi*$_4$*-im* [35]*a-dí-in : am-tám : šu-ub-ri-tám li-iš-/a-ma*$^!$*-ki-im* [36]dumu *Šu-Ku-bi*$_4$*-im* : *áš-al-ma* [37]*um-ma šu-ut-ma* kù-babbar *A-šùr-ták-lá-ku lá i-dí-/nam* [38]*ṭup-pá-am šé-bi*$_4$*-lá-šu-ma* : *am-tám* [39]*li-iš-a-am-ni-a-tí* le.e. [40]*bé-tám ša ṭé-hi* é^{tí}*-ni* : *qá-ra-be-e Puzúr-A-šùr* [42]*iš-a-ma-kum ša* é *na-ga-ri-im kà*$^!$(IK)*-lá-šu* [43]*i-lá-qé*$^!$*-ma* : *iš-tí pá-nim-ma* : *ú-šé-ba*$^!$*-lá-kum*

[1]Say to Innaya: thus (says) Tarām-Kūbi.

[2–3]The matter concerning Kura's household, about which you spoke, is resolved. [3–5]Send silver with the next (caravan) and let them bring together his tablets in your house. [5–6]The tablet from the house of Enna-Suen has been entrusted (to) the house of Šu-Bēlum. [7–8]As to the tablet of the house of Kura, Puzur-Aššur holds (it). [8–10]Send me silver before your arrival, and let it be deposited in your sealed storehouse. [10–12]Concerning all the silver to be sent, do not be afraid; the silver will indeed come to your house. [12–14]Now is the (harvest) season! Send silver so they can store barley for you before your arrival. [15–16]The beer bread I made for you has become too old.

[16–17]Concerning the house of Kura, Puzur-Aššur became afraid of you, so [18–20]we (said to him) as follows: "Do not be afraid, drop the case and let the man come to the city (of Aššur)." [21–22]I asked him and he settled the case.

[22–23]Urgent! When you hear (this) letter, come, [24–27]look to Aššur, your god, and your home hearth, and let me see you in person while I am still alive! Misery has entered our minds.

[27–29]Concerning the linen and the belt for the god Amurrum that the son of Šu-Kūbum brought here, they are in his house. [30–32]Send him a tablet so he gives the linen and the belt: they must be in your house.

[32–33]Aššur-taklāku wrote to me about the servant, and in his tablet (he said as follows): [34–35]"I gave ⅓ mina of silver to Elālī, son of Šu-Kūbum. He should buy you a Subarean female slave." [36–37](So) I asked the son of Šu-Kūbum, and he (told me) as follows: "Aššur-taklāku did not give me silver!" [38–39]Send him a tablet so he buys the female slave for us.

[40–42]Puzur-Aššur bought for you the house near to ours [...] [42–43]As to the carpenter's house, he will take the whole complex and will send you by the next (caravan a tablet about it).

Bibliography: Text published in copy by Smith as CCT 3, 25; edited by Michel (1991, no. 3); translated by Michel (2001a, no. 345).

Comments: As in the previous letter, Tarām-Kūbi deals with various topics, acting as a representative of her husband in Aššur. She feels lonely and asks him to come back to Aššur. The beer bread she prepared to make beer for her husband got too old since Innaya did not come back to Aššur for a long time.

Line 2: the form *ta-wa-tù-ú* is an error for *ta-ta-wu-ú* (*tatawwû*).

---

130. Seasonal Purchase of Grain

Obv. ^{1}[*a-na* PN$_1$] *qí-bi*$_4$*-ma* ^{2}[*um-ma* PN$_2$]*-ma* ^{3}2 [x x x x] x ^{4}*a-h*[*a-ma*$^?$ x x x] dam-gàr ^{5}1 *ma-na* kù-babbar *ú* ^{6}6 gín kù-ki *mì-ma* ^{7}*a-nim ša ta-áp-qí-/da-ni* ^{8}*a-na-kam A-ha-/ha* lo.e. ^{9}*ta-ṣa-ba-at-ma* ^{10}*um-ma ší-it-ma* rev. ^{11}*a-na-kam ša-tum* ^{12}*ša-na-at ú-ṭá-tám* ^{13}*a-ša-pá-ak* ^{14}*a-dí ma-lá ú šé-ni-šu* : <igi> 4 ^{15}*um-mì-a-ni aṣ-ba-sí-ma* ^{16}*ú-šu-ra-am lá ta-mu-a* ^{17}*Pì-lá-ha-a-a ú* du$_{10}$*-A-šur* ^{18}*i-ma-li-ku-ši-im* ^{19}*um-ma šu-nu-ma ṣa-áb-tí* u.e. ^{20}*a-bi*$_4$ *a-ta be-lí a-/ta* ^{21}[*a-ta a-ma*]*-kam* le.e. ^{22}*ma-lá-kà*

$^{1-2}$Say [to PN$_1$]: [thus (says) PN$_2$].

$^{3-6}$[…] bes[ide…] the creditor, 1 mina of silver and 6 shekels of gold; $^{6-9}$all this that you have entrusted to me, Ahaha took it here, $^{10-13}$saying as follows: "Now is the (harvest) season. I will stock up on grain." $^{14-16}$I took her to task several times in the presence of four investors, but she refused to release (it). $^{17-18}$Pilahaya and Ṭāb-Aššur gave advice to her, ^{19}saying as follows: "Take (it)."

$^{20-22}$You are my father and my master. [The]re, it is up [to you]!

Bibliography: Text published in copy by Stephens as BIN 6, 118.

Comments: Ahaha, daughter of Pušū-kēn, lived with her mother in Aššur. She became a consecrated woman, wrote letters to her brothers, and managed her own affairs. According to this letter, she took some gold and silver in order to buy grain and refused to give it back. It is not impossible that one of her brothers is the author of this letter.

131. Flour for a Woman

Obv. [1]1 dug *qé-ma-am* [2]*ù* 1 gín kù-babbar [3]*a-na am-tí-šu* [4]*ša Be-lá-nim* [5]*a-dí-in*
(the remainder of the tablet is not inscribed)

[5]I gave [1–2]1 jar of flour and 1 shekel of silver [3–4]to the *amtum*-wife of Bēlānum.

Bibliography: Text published in copy by Lewy as TC 3, 172.

132. Preparing Beer with Malt and Beer Bread

Obv. [1]*um-ma A-šùr-na-da-ma* [2]*a-na A-šùr-ta-ak-/lá-ku* [3]*ù Ší-ša-ah-šu-šar* [4]*qí-bi-ma* [5]*mì-šu ša um-ma a-tí-ma* [6]*e-lá* 20 *na-ru-uq* [7]gig *ù* 15 *na-ru-uq* [8]*še-im ša Ku-du-bi*$_4$*-iš* [9]*i-dí-na-ni mì-ma* [10]*ša-ni-um lá-šu* [11]*a-li* 40 *ma-na* lo.e. [12]*ni-ga-lu* 2½ *ma-/na* rev. [13]an-na *ša a-na* [14]*Ša-na-a* [15]*Ì-lí-šar ù Hu-lu-/ba* [16]*ub-lu-ni a-pu-tum* [17]kù-babbar *ša Ha-lu-le* [18]*A-zu ù Du-du-li* [19]*ù Kà-ú-ba* [20]*ša*[!]*-ah-dí-ra-ma* [21]10 *na-ru-/uq* [22]*bu-uq-lúm* 10 *na-ru-/uq* [23]*ba-pì-ra-am* u.e. [24]*ṣí-pì-ma ep-ší* [25]*šu-ma ú-ṭá-tám* [26]*ta-ha-ší-hi* le.e. [27]*ša-mì šu-ma a-ba-a-ba-/tim* [28]*lá na-ah-du té-er-tí-ki* [29]*li-li-kam* ì-giš *šé-bi*$_4$*-lim*

[1–4]Thus (says) Aššur-nādā: say to Aššur-taklāku and Šišahšušar.

[5]Why did you (say) as follows: [6–10]"Apart from 20 sacks of wheat and 15 sacks of barley that Kudubiš gave me, there is nothing else!" [11–16]Where are the 40 minas in sickles and the 2½ minas of tin that Ilī-išar and Huluba brought to Šanā?

[16–20]Urgent! Put pressure on Azu and Duduli, as well as Ka'uba, concerning the silver of Halule, and [21–24]soak 10 sacks of malt and 10 sacks of beer bread to prepare (beer). [25–27]If you want any grain, then buy it. [27–28]If they are not careful with the outstanding claims, [28–29]let your report come to me. Send me some oil.

Bibliography: Text published as copy by Veenhof as VS 26, no. 19; edited by Larsen (2002, no. 54); translated by Michel (2001a, no. 359).

Comments: Šišahšušar is the Anatolian wife of Aššur-nādā living in Kaneš. This letter concerns domestic affairs, among which is the preparation of beer. In Aššur, malt was prepared from barley, but in Kaneš it could also be made from germinated wheat, dried and crushed. To prepare beer, malt was then thrown into hot water, and beer bread, made of barley, was added before fermentation with yeast; then it was brewed (see Michel 2009d).

---

133. Slaughtering an Ox for Meat

Obv. [1]*a-na Ku-li-a* : *qí-bi$_4$-ma* [2]*um-ma A-ba-ba-a-ma* [3]*šál-ma-ni ṣu-hu-ur-kà* [4]*ša-lim ni-šu-kà šál-*[*m*]*u* [5]*ki-ma ku-a-tí i-*[x] x [6]*a-bi$_4$-kà a-*[x x x] [7]*a-wa-tí-kà* [x x x x] [8]*i-ṣé-r*[*i-a* x x x x] [9]*ma-num* : [x x x x x] [10]*li-dí-n*[*am* x x x x] [11]*ša ta-*x-[x x x x] [12]*té-tap-ša-n*[*i* x x x] [13]*n*[*a-*x x x x x x] [14]*lá i-*x [x x x x x] lo.e. [15]*e tù-kà-*x [x] *t*[*a*]* *ú** [x] rev. [16]*iš-tù na-áš-pè-er-t*[*a-/k*]*à* [17]*lá ta-lá-kà-ni* [18]*mì-nam ša ta-áš-ta-n*[*a*]*-/pá-r*[*a-n*]*i* [19]*um-ma a-ta-ma ṣú-ba-tí* [20]*ha-am-ša-at šé-bi$_4$-li-/i*[*m*] [21]*mì-nam ṣú-ha-ar-kà* [22]*li-ku-ul* : *mì-nam* [23]*a-ṣí-tí-kà lá-áš-qú-ul* [24]*šu-ma a-na a-bi$_4$-kà* [25]*lá uš-té-ri-id um-ma šu-u*[*t*]*-/ma* [26]*ú-ha-lá-qú-nu* GA *ša-ni-a-tù* [27]*i-pì-šu ša-ak-na* [28]*me-er-a-at-*[*kà*] *iš-tí-a* [29]*ta-al-ta-*[x x *-u*]*m* u.e. [30]*wa-áš-ba-at* [x x x (x)] [31]*ša* é *a-bi$_4$-ni tim* [x x x] [32]*áb e ta-hi-ri-/*x le.e. [33]*ta-áp-hi-ra-am a-dí-in-ma* gu$_4$ *aṭ-bu-ùh* [34]*ší-ru-um ša i-ri-hu ša-áp-lá-nu-um i-tab-ku* [35]4 gú urudu *ag-mur a*[!]**-na**-kam ṣú-ùh-*[*ur-kà*] [36]*lá i-mu-tù*

[1-2]Say to Kuliya: thus (says) Ababaya.

[3-4]We are well, your children are well, and your people are well.

[5-8]Like/instead of you [...] of your father [...] your words [...] on me (?)[...]

[9-12]Who could give me [...] that you [...] you have treated me [...]

[13-17][...] Do not [...] since no letter of yours arrives here.

[18-19]What is the purpose of constantly writing me as follows: [19-20]"Send me five textiles!" [21-25]What would your children eat, what would I (use to) pay your expenses if I had not *humbled myself* to your father?

He said: [26-27]"He is destroying you [...]; he has evil intentions!"

[28-31]Your daughter is/keeps [...] with me [...] she lives [...] of our paternal house [...] [32-33]I have spent the savings and slaughtered the ox. [34]The meat that remained they have *stored* below. [35-36]I have spent four talents of copper [...] (lest) your children die!

Bibliography: Text published by Veenhof as AKT 5, 9 (Kt 92/k 211). For philological comments, see AKT 5, 96–98; collated May 2012.

Comments: Ababaya is the Assyrian wife of Kuliya, messenger of the *kārum* Kaneš, whose archives were unearthed in 1992 and published by Veenhof in AKT 5. She was living in Aššur, together with her daughter and perhaps a younger son. In this letter, she gives good news of her children and household staff but, at the same time, asks urgently for money to buy food. Her situation is not so desperate, since she mentions that she has slaughtered an ox and stored—certainly dried or cooked—meat; for the consumption of meat, see Michel 1997f; Dercksen 2008a, 2010a.

Line 20: the number five is written in Akkadian.

---

134. Making a Kettle for the Kitchen

[1]*um-ma Bu-za-zu-ma* [2]*a-na Lá-ma-ša qí-bi-ma* [3]10 *ma-na* urudu sig$_5$ [4]*a-na ša-ni-im* [5]*e-pá-ší-im Kà-as-ha-nu-el* [6]*na-áš-a-ki-im* : urudu [7]*a-dí a-lá-kà-ni* lo.e. [8]*li-bi-ší i-na* rev. [9]*a-lá-ki-a* : *mu-lá-e-šu* [10]*ú-ba-lam-ma* : *ša-nam* [11]*ú-šé-pá-áš* : 1 *ma-na* urudu [12]*A-ni-na li-dí-in-ma* [13]*i-ša-ad* : *ša-nim* [14]*ša* 20 *ma-na* : *ta-ba-kà-tám* [15]*li-dí-ú-ma* : *a-dí* [16]*a-lá-ki-a* : *kà-i-lá-ší* [17]4 *ma-na* urudu *a-na lu-bu-uš* u.e. [18]*Ša-ak-ri-ú-ma-an* [19]*Kà-as-ha-nu-el* le.e. [20]*na-ší na-hi-dí-šu-ma* [21]*qá-nu-e lu-pá-he-er* [22]*ù e-ṣí*

[1-2]Thus (says) Buzāzu: say to Lamaša.

[3-6]Kashunuel is bringing you 10 minas of fine copper to make a kettle. [6-8]The copper should be stored until I arrive. [8-11]When I arrive, I will bring (with me) what is missing for it, and I will have a kettle made. [11-12]Let Anīna give 1 mina of copper, and [13-16]let them deposit bit by bit 20 minas worth for a stand for the kettle, and keep it until I arrive.

[17-20]Kashanuel is (also) bringing four minas of copper (to buy clothes) for Šakriuman. [20-22]Instruct him to collect reeds, also wood.

Bibliography: Text published as copy by Lewy as TC 3, 97; translated by Michel (2001a, no. 366). Lines 3–16 cited by Dercksen (1996, 74 n. 254).

Comments: Buzāzu sent to his wife, Lamaša, the metal necessary to make a kettle but instructs her to wait for his return so he can supervise the work.

Line 14: the word *tabākattam* would derive from the verb *tabākum*.

135. Inventory of Bronze Vessels in a Woman's House

Obv. [1]10 *ša-áp-lá-tum ša tí-ra-ni* [2]1 *ša-pí-il*$_5$*-tum ša šu-ru-um* [3]2 *ús-hi-ú* : *ša bi-ṣí-ni* [4]1 *ša-pì-il*$_5$*-tum ša sà-pé-e* [5]2 *ṣú-ur-ṣú-pá-tum* [6]3 *zu-pá-nu* : *ša Kà-ni-iš*^{ki*} [7]*maš-qal-tum ša* 2 sìla [8]*maš-qal-tum ša* 1 sìla [9]9 *ha-bu-ra-a-tum* [10]šà-ba *sà-pu-um ša na-aṣ-bi*$_4$*-tim* [11]18 *ša-ha-tum* [12]4 *hu-ub-lu*-ú ra-bi*$_4$*-ú-tum* [13]4 *hu-ub-lu*-ú ṣa-hu-ru-tum* [14]6 *sà-pu-ú ša mu-sà-ri* lo.e. [15]5 *ku-na-ki-ú* rev. [16]2 *zu-ur-ša-tum* [17]5 *hu-tù-lá-tum* [18]2 *áš-hu-lu* 2 *mu-ša*-lá-/tum* (*sic*) [19]3 *sà-pu-ú* [20]*ša-ah-tù-tum* [21]1 *a-ga-nu-um* 1* *ša-kà-nim** [22]1 *it-qú-ru-um ša qá-tim* [23]šunigin 1 gú 40 *ma-na* zabar [24]14 gú urudu *ša ṣí-ib-tim* [25]14 *pá-šu-ru* 7 *ú-ru-za-na-tum* [26]6 *qá-áb-li-a-tum* : 3 *zi-ra-tum* [27]*ša* 30 *ma-na*-ta *mì-ší-it* [28]*zi-ri-im ša hu-ur-ší-a* [29]1 *lu-ru-um* 2 *qá-áb-li-a-/tum* [30]*ša* 15 *ma-na*-ta u.e. [31]3 *pá-šu-ru* 2 *pì-it-nu* le.e. [32]*iš-tù A-a me-ta-at-ni tal*-qé** [33]*mì-ma a-nim iš-tí Ša-at-A-šur*$^!$

[1–4]10 grooved stands, 1 stand for a sieve, 2 duck-shaped figures with lamp wicks, 1 stand for *sappum*-bowls, [5–6]2 *ṣurṣuppum*-containers, 3 *supānum*-bowls of Kaneš-type, [7–10]a measuring cup of 2 sila, a measuring cup of 1 sila, 9 *haburrum*-vessels, one among them is a *sappum*-bowl with a handle, [11–13]18 *šāhum*-pitchers, 4 large and 4 small *hublum*-vessels$^?$, [14–15]6 *sappum*-bowls with metal bands, 5 *kunakkium*, [16–18]2 *zuršum*-cups, 5 *hutūlum*-vessels, 2 *ašhalum*-vessels, 2 mirrors$^?$, [19–22]3 stripped *sappum*-bowls, 1 *agannum*-large bowl, 1 *šakanum*, 1 spoon; [23]in total 1 talent, 40 minas of bronze (objects).

[24–25]14 talents of copper bearing interest, 14 tables, 7 *urunsannum*-tables, [26–28]6 *qablītum*-containers, 3 cauldrons of 30 minas each (from) the stock of cauldrons in my kitchen. [29–31]1 *lurum*, 2 *qablītum*-containers of 15 minas each, 3 tables, 2 chests, [32–33]she received since Aya died.

All this is with Šāt-Aššur.

Bibliography: Unpublished text known as Kt h/k 87. Lines 1–28 and 30–33 cited by Dercksen (1996, 77); lines 1–2, 4–5, 7–11, 15–16, 18–19, 21–24 cited by Balkan (1965, 160); lines 6–14, 16, 19–20, 26–30 cited by Gökçek (2003, 74–75, 81, 84–86); collated May 2011.

Comments: This inventory lists predominantly the bronze and copper items in a woman's house in Kaneš (fig. 10). A few items, presumably made of wood, are mentioned at the end of the text: tables, chests, and unknown objects. Most of these objects are still not identified. Among archaeological artifacts—predominantly consisting of pottery—metal objects are quite rare; they were often reused. On the contrary, vessels made of clay are usually not mentioned in the texts because they were less valuable.

Lines 4 and following: for the different uses of the *sappum*-bowl in the Mari texts, see Michaël Guichard (2005, 292–95).

Line 5: the *ṣurṣuppum* could be a container provided with teat-shaped protuberances.

Line 11: the *šāhum* is a drinking vessel in Mari; see Guichard 2005, 301–2.

Line 18: the word *mušālum* is a mirror or a cosmetic vase according to Guichard (2005, 243–44), but it is a masculine word in Mari, while here we have a feminine plural form.

Line 21: the proposed reading of Dercksen (1996, 77): "one *agannum ša qātim*," which he translates by "one a.-hand bowl," needs correction.

The left edge is written upside down.

Heads of the Household

In the absence of their husbands, merchants' wives found themselves alone, at the head of their households, called simply "the house" (*bētum*; **136**, **137**). Besides children, this could sometimes include the young wife of a married son without his own house. Sharing of quarters by mothers- and daughters-in-law was not always harmonious, and Tarīš-mātum complained bitterly about the conduct of her son's wife, who regularly took refuge with her own father at nightfall, behaved badly, and refused to obey her mother-in-law (**146**). Although we have no direct evidence, it is very probable that the women of Aššur also took care of aged family members.[44] These could, for their part, look after the children, and the Kaneš documentation shows that several generations could live together under one roof. At Kaneš too, and in the other Assyrian commercial settlements in Anatolia, the wives of the Assyrian merchants had to accommodate, for more or less extended stays, other members of the family and associates traveling from Aššur who had no other place to stay. Thus, certain households could provide shelter to more than a dozen people.

44. For the elderly, see Veenhof 1997b.

To help out with domestic tasks, especially meal preparation, a woman could have domestics, especially female slaves, who could be of different ethnic backgrounds: one letter mentions a Hurrian woman (**129**).[45] Such slaves were part of the household, so women had to see to their maintenance, both clothing and food, in the form of a ration entitlement (**124**). Some women complained in their letters of the high cost of keeping domestic help. However, these female slaves could be given important responsibilities; one took care of the children when her mistress was absent (**303**).

Even if they were sometimes purchased with money sent by their husbands (**129**), these slaves were the property of their mistress, whether they were Anatolian or Assyrian. Sometimes they were part of a wife's dowry or were inherited from deceased merchants or from daughters who were consecrated (**139**, **54**); they could even be purchased by a wife from her own husband (**138**).[46] Their mistresses disposed of them as they wished, and could decide to sell certain of their domestics if they were no longer useful and keep the proceeds for themselves (**140**).

Several Assyrian wives defend, in their letters, their ownership of these slaves. It could happen that, when their husbands had neglected to pay certain taxes, the city authorities could put pressure on their wives by impounding their slaves. These women would then put pressure on their husbands to pay the amount due so they could get their slaves back (**141**, **142**).

Assyrian merchants' wives, whether they were Assyrian or Anatolian, bought or sold slaves as they liked, as shown by numerous sale contracts for them found in their houses in Kaneš (**144**, **143**). The purchase could also be made by their relatives, with property belonging to the women:

---

45. Food preparation: female slaves had, for example, to grind grain, see CCT 3, 7b + 8a:29–32: "Give instructions to the female slave, she should grind me the old barley for food"; *am-tám ša-hi-za-ma*, gig *la-bi*$_4$*-ra-tim*, *a-na ku-ru-ma-tim*, *li-ṭé-na*. This was a hard job, and it was sometimes difficult to get slaves to do their work: "Forgive me, but you left a real female slave behind to work for me. The female slave quarrels with me. When I tell her, 'Grind 5 liters,' she refuses. Even as little as 2 liters she refuses to grind. Over there, you have 10 female slaves at your disposal. Here, I appeal to the whole city for a (single) female grinder!"; Kt c/k 266:25–34: *ki-ša-ma gemé ša ke-na-tim*, *i-na ma-ah-ri-a té-zi-ib*, gemé *iš-tí-a tù-uš-té-ṣa i-nu-mì*, *a-qá-bi-ú-ší-ni um-ma a-na-ku-ma*, 5 silà *ṭé-ni lá ta-mu-a*, *ù* 2 silà *e-ṣa-am ṭé-a-na-am lá ta-mu-a*, *a-tù-nu a-ma-kam* 10 *a-ma-tum*, *ma-ah-ri-ku-nu uš-ba a-na-ku a-na-kam*, *a-na ṭé-i-tim A-lim*^{ki}, *ki-li-šu ú-sà-la*; unpublished text cited by Dercksen (2014, 105 n. 135).

46. See also text **61**.

funds received from the sale of rings and garment pins of Kunnaniya were used to buy two female slaves, who then belonged to her (**307**).

It is difficult to estimate the number of slaves, men or women, per household at Aššur and Kaneš, but it is certain that well-to-do families could acquire and maintain a whole staff of them. Slaves were a public sign of wealth.[47]

---

136. News from the Household

Obv. [1]*a-na Ša-at-A-/šùr* [2]*qí-bi-ma* [3]*um-ma A-šùr-ma-lik* [4]*šál-ma-ku : mì-ma* [5]*li-bi-ki* [6]*lá i-pá-ri-id* [7]2 *pá-ni-ri* [8]*ša al-pè-e* [9]*Ì-lí-ma-lik* [10]*na-áš-a-ki-im* [11]*a-pu-tum i-na* [12]^{d}utu$^{\textit{ši}}$: *na-áš-pár-tí* [13]*ta-ša-me-i-ni* [14]*šu-lu-um-ki* [15]*ú šu-lu-um* [16]*é*$^{\textit{be-tim}}$ [17]*šé-bi*$_4$*-lìm*

[1–3]Say to Šāt-Aššur: thus (says) Aššur-malik.

[4–6]I am well; do not worry. [7–10]Ilī-malik is bringing you 2 *pannurum* for/of oxen.

[11–13]Urgent! The day you hear my letter, [14–17]send me news about your well-being and about that of the household.

Bibliography: Text published in copy by Smith as CCT 4, 15b; translated by Michel (2001a, no. 373).

Comments: Some lines duplicate text **137**.

There are several women called Šāt-Aššur. In this text and the following, she is the daughter of Šalim-ahum and wife of Aššur-malik, son of Innaya.

Line 7: the word *pannurum* has been interpreted by Bilgiç (1954, 73) as a utensil for oxen and by the dictionaries as a "brush" or a "curry comb?"[48] Thomas Sturm (1999) proposed to translate it as a "Bürsten aus Dattelrispen" because it occurs very often with *sissinnum* "Dattelrispe(nbesen)." Dercksen (2010a) studied this word together with *umṣum*, which, according to him, would correspond to "raw dried meat"; he then translates *pannurum* by "a piece of dried sheep or ox meat." If this translation fits well in

47. Michel 2008a.

48. *AHw* 2:818b and *CAD* 15:326. In *CAD* 12:83 it has been interpreted as "a textile?"

the examples chosen by Dercksen, where other foodstuffs are mentioned, it does not in other texts where *pannurum* occurs with various utensils; for example, with wool, textiles, and brooms made of date spadices, such as **158**.

---

137. News from the Household

Obv. [1]*a-na Ša-at-A-šùr* [2]*qí-bi-ma um-ma A-šur-ma-lik-ma* [3]*šál-ma-ku* : *li-bi-ki* [4]*lá i-pá-ri-id* [5]*a-pu-tum i-na* [6]^{d}utu$^{\check{s}i}$ *na-áš-pè-er-tí* [7]*ta-ša-me-i-ni* [8]*šu-lu-um-ki* lo.e. [9]*ù*$^{!}$ *šu-lu-um* rev. [10]*é*$^{bé\text{-}tim}$ [11]*še-bi*$_4$*-lìm-ma* [12]*ù li-bi-i* [13]*lá pá-ri-id* [14]1 *ší-it-ra-am ku-nu-ki-a* [15]*I-dí-Sú-en*$_6$ *na-áš-a-/ki-im* [16]2 *pá-na-re-e* : [17]*ša* gu$_4$ u.e. [18]*Ì-lí*$^{!}$*-ma-lik* le.e. [19]*ṣú-ha-ru-um ša I-ku-pì-/a* [20]*na-áš-a-ki-im*

[1–2]Say to Šāt-Aššur: thus (says) Aššur-malik.

[3–4]I am well; do not worry. [5–7]Urgent! The day you hear my letter, [8–10]send me news about your well-being and about that of the household, [12–13]so that I do not worry.

[14–15]Iddin-Suen is bringing you one shawl under my seal. [16–20]Ilī-malik, the servant of Ikuppiya, is bringing you 2 *pannurum* for/of oxen.

Bibliography: Text published in copy by Clay as BIN 4, 75; translated by Michel (2001a, no. 374).

Comments: Lines 1–11 and 16–20 duplicate **136**, see Michel 2001a n. 373; both texts use the sign *lam* with the rare value *lìm*. For *pannurum*, see comments on text **136**.

---

138. A Woman Buys a Female Slave from Her Husband

Envelope

Obv. [1]kišib *Ma-ṣí-ì-lí* dumu *Bu-zu-zi-im* [2](seal A) [3]kišib *Bu-ta* dumu *I-dí-A-šùr* [4]kišib *Ta-mu-ri-a* dumu *Ha-pu-a-šu* [5]kišib *Ša-ak-ri-ú-ma-an* dumu *A-lá-ri-/a* [6]kišib *Tal-ha-ma* kišib *Hi-iš-ta-ah-šu* [7]*me-er-i-ša* kišib *Ha-pu-a-lá* [8]*ša* ⅓ *ma-na* ¼ gín kù-babbar *li-/tí* [9](seal B) [10]*ší-im Šu-pí-a-ni-kà Wa-la-wa-/la* [11]*a-na Ha-pu-a-la mu-tí-ša* [12]*ta-áš-qú-lu-ni-ma* [13](seal B) [14]*am-tum a-ma-sà-ni a-na am-tim* lo.e. [15](seal C) rev. [16]*ma-ma-an ú-lá i-tù-a-ar-ší-im* [17]*a-na am-tim Tal-ha-ma ù Hi-iš-ta-/ah-šu* [18]*me-ra-ša qá-ta-tum šu-ma a-šu-mì* [19]*am-tim a-na Wa-la-wa-la ma-ma-an* [20]*i-tù-a-ar-ší-im Tal-*

ha-ma ^{21}*ù Hi-iš-ta-ah-šu me-ra-ša am-tám* ^{22}*a-na Wa-la-wa-la ú-bu-bu-/ší-im* ^{23}*šu-ma* (seal D) *am-tám* (seal D) ^{24}*la ú-ta-bi-bu-ší-im* 1 *ma-na* u.e. ^{25}kù-babbar *li-tí Tal-ha-ma* ^{26}(seal E) le.e. ^{27}*ù Hi-iš-ta-ah-šu me-ra-ša a-na* ^{28}*Wa-la-wa-la* ^{29}(seal F) ^{30}*i-ša-qú-lu-ší-ma ù am-tám* ^{31}*i-ta*$^{!}$*-ru-ú*

Inscription on Seal E
^{1}dingir-*ba-ni* ^{2}dumu *Ištar-b*[*a-ni*]

Ilī-bāni, son of Ištar-bāni.

$^{1-7}$Seal of Maṣi-ilī, son of Buzuzim; seal of Butaya, son of Iddin-Aššur; seal of Tamuriya, son of Happuašu; seal of Šakriuman, son of Alaria; seal of Talhama, seal of Hištahšu, her sons; seal of Happuala.

$^{8-10}$(Contract) concerning ⅓ mina, ¼ shekel of silver of *litum*-quality, price of Šuppianika, $^{10-12}$that Walawala paid to Happuala, her husband, and ^{14}the female slave is her female slave. $^{14-16}$No one shall raise a claim against her concerning the female slave. $^{16-18}$For the female slave, Talhama and Hištahšu, her sons, are guarantors. $^{18-20}$If anyone raises a claim against Walawala concerning the female slave, $^{20-22}$Talhama and Hištahšu, her sons, shall clear the female slave (from claims) for Walawala. $^{23-24}$If they do not clear the female slave (from claims), $^{24-30}$Talhama and Hištahšu, her sons, shall pay one mina of silver to Walawala, $^{30-31}$and (they) shall take along the female slave.

Tablet
Obv. ^{1}⅓ *ma-na* ¼ gín kù-babbar ^{2}*li-tí ší-im Šu-pí-a-ni-kà* ^{3}*Wa-la-wa-la a-na* ^{4}*Ha-pu-a-la* : *mu-tí-ša* ^{5}*ta-áš-qúl am-tum* ^{6}*a-ma-sà a-na am-tim* ^{7}*ma-ma-an lá i-tù-a-ar-ší-/im* ^{8}*a-na am-tim Tal-ha-ma* ^{9}*ù Hi-iš-ta-ah-šu* ^{10}*qá-ta-tum šu-ma a-šu-mì* ^{11}*am-tim a-na Wa-lá-wa-/lá* lo.e. ^{12}*ma-ma-an i-tù-a-ar* rev. ^{13}*Tal-ha-ma ù Hi-iš-ta-/ah-šu* ^{14}*am-tám a-na* ^{15}*Wa-lá-wa-lá* ^{16}*ú-bu-bu-ší-im šu-ma* (erasure) ^{17}*am-tám lá ú-ta-bi-bu-/ší-im* ^{18}1 *ma-na* kù-babbar ^{19}*li-tí Tal-ha-ma ù Hi-iš-ta-/ah-šu* ^{20}*a-na Wa-lá-wa-lá* ^{21}*i-ša-qú-lu-ší-ma am-tám i-ta-ru-ú* u.e. ^{22}igi *Ma-ṣí-ì-lí* dumu *Bu-zu-zi-/im* ^{23}igi *Bu-ta-a* dumu (erasure) ^{24}*I-dí-A-šùr* igi *Ta-mu-ri-a* le.e. ^{25}dumu *Ha-pu-a-šu* igi *Ša-ak-/ri-ú-ma-/an* ^{26}dumu *A-lá-ri-a*

$^{1-5}$Walawala paid to Happuala, her husband, ⅓ mina, ¼ shekel of silver of *litum*-quality, (corresponding to) the price of Šuppianika. $^{5-7}$The female slave is her female slave. No one shall raise a claim against her concerning the female slave. [8–10]For the female slave, Talhama and Hištahšu are guarantors. [10–12]If anyone raises a claim against Walawala concerning the female slave, [13–16]Talhama and Hištahšu shall clear the female slave (from claims) for Walawala. [16–17]If they do not clear the female slave (from claims), [18–21]Talhama and Hištahšu shall pay one mina of silver to Walawala, and (the claimants) shall take away the female slave.

[22–26]In the presence of Maṣi-ilī, son of Buzuzim; Buta, son of Iddin-Aššur; Tamuriya, son of Happuašu; and Šakriuman, son of Alaria.

Bibliography: Text published by Hrozný as ICK 1, 19a + b; edited by Kienast (1984, no. 28).

Comments: The price of the female slave is 20¼ shekels of silver. One wonders why Walawala's husband sold his female slave to his wife, and why the sons are guarantors. There are several women called Walawala (see Michel 2001a, 499–500), and thus it is difficult to identify the one of our text. Since Talhama and Hištahšu are said to be the sons of Walawala and not of Happuala, we may imagine that she was married twice.

---

139. Getting Back Slaves from the Husband's Household in Kaneš

Obv. [1]*a-na Pu-šu-ke-en*$_{6}$ [2]*Zu-pá Puzur*$_{4}$*-A-šur* [3]*A-šur-tù-ku-*<*ul*>*-tí* [4]*ù A-šur-ša-du-ni* [5]*qí-bi-ma um-ma La-ma-/sà-tum-ma* [6]*šu-ma a-ba-ú-a* [7]*a-tù-nu a-na ma-lá* [8]*ṭup-pí-im ša A-lim*^{ki} [9]é$^{bé\text{-}tám}$ *ša Kà-ni-iš*$^{/ki}$ [10]<*ú*>*-ṭù-up-ta-am : lu a-ma-tim* [11]*lu ṭup-pé-e : lu a-li* [12]kù-babbar 1 gín *i-ba-ší-*<*ú*> [13]*ih-da-ma : ku-un-kà-ma* [14]*šé-bi-lá-nim : a-pu-tum* rev. [15]^{d}im-*ba-ni* [16]*ù* túg^{tù} : *a-na* [17]*ší-mì-im : lá ta-da-/na* [18]*a-na ma-lá ṭup-pí-im* [19]*ša A-lim*^{ki} *i-na ša-ha-/at* [20]*ra-bi-ṣí-im* [21]*i-zi-za-ma ṭup-pá-am* [22]*ša kà-ri-im Kà-ni-iš* [23]*a-na ṣé-er ṭup-pí-im* [24]*ša A-lim*^{ki} *le-qé-a-ma* [25]*a-na Wa-ah-*<*šu*>*-ša-na* [26]*a-na ṣé-er : Am-ri-a* [27]*ṭur*$_{4}$*-da-šu : lá i-sà-hu-ur*

[1–5]Say to Pūšu-kēn, Zupa, Puzur-Aššur, Aššur-tukultī, and Aššur-šaduni: thus (says) Lamassatum.

[6–7]If you are my fathers, [7–8]in accordance with the tablet of the city (of Aššur) [9–13]concerning the house in Kaneš, take care to put under seal (all that it contains): furniture, female slaves, tablets, or wherever there is, (as little as) 1 shekel of silver, and [14]send (it) to me. Urgent! [15–17]Do not sell Adad-bāni and the textiles!

[18-21]In accordance with the tablet of the city (of Aššur), assist the attorney and [21-24]take a tablet from the *kārum* of Kaneš in addition to the tablet from the city (of Aššur), and [25-27]send him to Wahšušana at Āmria's place. He should not tarry.

Bibliography: Text published in copy by Smith as CCT 4, 40b + 41a; translated by Michel (2001a, no. 392). Lines 6–14 cited by Kienast (1984, 96).

Comments: Lamassatum is living in Aššur, but she was married to a merchant who had a house in Kaneš. The mention of an attorney might indicate that he died in Anatolia and that his goods had to be brought back to Aššur for the settlement of his affairs. The slave Adad-bāni is also mentioned in the letter **239**:4–5, sent by Lamassatum to Pūšu-kēn.

---

140. Selling an Unsatisfactory Female Slave

Obv. [1]*um-ma Lá-qé-pu-ma* [2]*a-na Hu-ta-lá qí-*bi_4*-/ma* [3]*a-na-kam* 9 gín kù-/babbar [4]*ša a-ša-at : A-bu-qár* [5]*ha-bu-lá-at-ni : ša-dí-ni-/ší-ma* [6]*nu-a-am : ša-*bi_4*-i* [7]*šál-ma-ku*$^{!}$(IB) *šu-ma* [8]*am-tum : i-ṣé-ri-/ki*$^{!}$ [9]*lá ṭá-ba-at* lo.e. [10]*a-na ší-mì-im* rev. [11]*dí-ni-ší-ma* [12]*ší-im-ša*$^{!}$ *: le-qé* [13]*a-ma-kam : A-šùr-ma-lik* [14]dumu *A-šùr-*^{d}utu^{ši} *ṭup-pá-/am* [15]*ša* ^{d}im-gal : *lu*$^{!}$*-šé-lí-/ma* [16]kù-babbar ^{d}im-gal *ša /ṭup-pè-šu*$^{?}$ [17]*li-iš-qú-ul-ma* [18]kù-babbar *a-tí : le-qí* [19]*a-pu-tum* kù-babbar *ú ṣí-ba-/«ba»-sú* u.e. [20]*li-iš-qú-ul* le.e. [21]*a-pu-tum be-tám* [22]*ša-ṣí-ri*

[1-2]Thus (says) Laqēpum: say to Hutala.

[3-5]Here, (concerning) the 9 shekels of silver that Abu-(wa)qar's wife owes, [5-6]make her pay (it back) and thus satisfy (the demands of the) Anatolian (creditor). [7]I am well. [7-9]If the female slave is unsatisfactory to you (fem.), [10-11]sell her and [12]keep the price you receive for her.

[13-15]There, let Aššur-malik, son of Aššur-šamšī, produce the tablet of Adad-rabi, and [16-17]let Adad-rabi pay the silver of his tablet; then [18]you take the silver. [19-20]Urgent! Make him pay the silver and its interest.

[21-22]Urgent! Watch the house!

Bibliography: Text published by Hrozný as ICK 1, 69; translated by Michel (2001a, no. 389).

Comments: Hutala, written elsewhere Hatala, daughter of Enišru, married Laqēpum according to **24**. She is living in Kaneš, where she manages her household while her husband is traveling. She is free to sell her female slave, and must watch carefully the house and its contents, among which is her husband's merchandise.

---

141. Female Slaves Taken as Collateral by Aššur Authorities

Obv. [1]*a-na A-šùr-mu-ta-pì-il*$_5$ [2]*Bu-za-zu ú I-ku-pá-ša* [3]*qí-bi-ma um-ma A-ha-ha-ma* [4]*a-na-kam* é *Šu-*^{d}*En-líl* [5]*a-na* kù-babbar *is-ni-qú-ni-a-tí-ma* [6]*a-na ṣí-ib-tim ni-il*$_5$*-qé-/ma* [7]*nu-ša-bi-šu-nu* : *li-mu-/um* [8]*ù-ša-ah-da-ra-ni* [9]*ù* géme$^{hi\text{-}tí\text{-}}$*a* [10]*ik-ta-na-ta* [11]kù-babbar 10 *ma-na* rev. [12]*šé-bi-lá-nim-ma* [13]*ša-zu-za-tù-ku-nu* [14]*lu-kà-i-lá-šu-ma* [15]*a-ša i-ta-ṣí-a-ni* [16]*li-iš-qú-lu* : *a-ma-kam* [17]*a-tù-nu tí-dá ki-ma* [18]*a-na-kam pu-ru* [19]*é a-bi-ni ša-ki-in* [20]*a-hu-ú-a a-tù-nu* [21]*a-na a-wa-tim* [22]*a-ni-tim ih-da* [23]*a-na-ku ša-zu-za-tí-ku-nu* le.e. [24]*lá a-sà-hu-ur*

[1–3]Say to Aššur-mūtappil, Buzāzu, and Ikuppaša: thus (says) Ahaha.

[4–5]Here, Šu-Enlil's house put pressure on us for the silver, [6–7]so we borrowed (some) at interest and satisfied them. [7–8]The eponym is intimidating me, and [9–10]he keeps seizing my female slaves as collateral. [11–12]Send me silver, about 10 minas, and [13–14]let your representatives offer (it) to him and [15–16]pay the amount that has been declared against me.

[16–19]You know over there that here the house of our father is getting unfair treatment. [20–22]Pay attention to this case, as to me; [23–24]let me not have to wait for your representatives.

Bibliography: Text published in copy by Thureau-Dangin as TC 2, 46; translated by Michel (2001a, no. 315). Lines 7–19 cited by Larsen (1976, 202 n. 4).

Comments: Ahaha, from Aššur, writes to her brothers about debts of the family to the City Hall of Aššur—also called the House of the Eponym—perhaps after the death of their father. These debts might result from a delay in the payment of the export tax (use of the verb *waṣûm*, line 15). The authorities put pressure on the family members still in Aššur, in this case Ahaha, a consecrated woman, by taking their slaves as collateral.

142. Bronze and Female Slaves Taken as Collateral by Aššur Authorities

Obv. ^{1}*a-na* ^{d}*A-šùr-ta-ak-lá-ku* ^{2}*qí-bí-ma um-ma Ší-ma-Sú-/en*$_{6}$*-ma* ^{3}*še-am* : *a-wi-lu-ú* ^{4}*la i-du-nu* : *a-šu-mì* ^{5}*ṭup-pá*$^{!}$*-am* : *ša ta-áš-pu-ru-/šu-nu-tí-/ni* ^{6}*um-ma a-ta-ma* : *mì-šu-um* ^{7}*ha-ri-tí* : *ta-áp-ta-na-té-e* ^{8}*ú še-um* : *ta-da-na-šu-nu-tí* ^{9}*i-na e-ne-a* (erasure) ^{10}*tù-*°x-x°*-ku-ma* : *um-ma a-ta-ma* ^{11}*hu-bu-la-am* : *lu t*[*a*-x-x]*-/ki-n*[*i*] lo.e. ^{12}[*ṣ*]*ú-ùh-ri* ^{13}*lu tù-ša-ki-il*$_{5}$ *lá šé-bu-ul-tum*$_{x}$ rev. ^{14}*lá ta-ak-ší-tum* ^{15}*i-na A-lim*^{ki} : *a-ta a-ni-a-tím* ^{16}*ta-ša-pá-ra-am* (erasure) ^{17}*sí-pá-ru ú* géme^{hi}*-kà* ^{18}*li-mu-um* : *ik-ta-ma* ^{19}*a-ni* : *li-mu-um ú-ṣí-ma* ^{20}*a-ší-im ú-ká-lu-ú* ^{21}*kà-sí-lu-ta-am* : *e-ri-iš-/ma* ^{22}é$^{bé-tám}$: *ip-té-ú-ma* ^{23}*i-dí-nu-nim* : *ú-ri-qá-e* ^{24}*a-mu-ur-ma* : *ša-bu-lu ú* ^{25}*sú-qú-um i-na ṣé-ri-a*$^{!}$(E) u.e. ^{26}*i-za-az šu-ma* le.e. ^{27}*li-bi-kà* : *šé-bi-lá-ma* ì-gi[š] ^{28}*li-iš-pu-ku lá i-kà-le-ma* (erasure)

$^{1-2}$Say to Aššur-taklāku: thus (says) Šīma(t)-Suen.

$^{3-4}$The men did not give the barley. $^{4-6}$Concerning the tablet about which you wrote them as follows: $^{6-8}$"Why do you time and again open my *harītum*-containers and give them barley?" $^{9-10}$In my eyes, you [...] and (said) as follows: ^{11}"Certainly, you should [...] me (with) a debt." $^{12-14}$Indeed, you gave food to my children. (However,) there is neither a consignment nor a share of the profit in the city (of Aššur). $^{15-16}$You, you write this to me! $^{17-18}$The eponym has taken the bronze objects and your female slaves as collateral, and $^{19-21}$now the eponym has gone out, and has made senseless (?) demands for the purchase goods I hold, and $^{22-23}$they opened the house and sold (them).

$^{23-24}$I saw my *vegetables*; $^{24-26}$they are dry and hunger is upon me! $^{26-27}$If you agree, send me (silver), and $^{27-28}$let them store oil. He should not detain me!

Bibliography: Text published in copy by Clay as BIN 4, 67. Lines 17–23 cited by Hecker (1968, 144) and Larsen (1976, 203 n. 42).

Comments: Šīmat-Suen's husband has large debts with the Aššur authorities, who put pressure on his wife to recover them. They took female slaves and bronze as collateral and sold some goods that were kept inside the house. She needs silver both to buy food and to pay his debts. She is afraid that she herself could be detained for the debt of her husband.

Line 7: *ha-ri-tí* could be the Assyrian form *harītum* of the word *harûm*, whose plural is *hariātum*.

Line 10: the two middle signs of the verbal form are written over erasure. The word *uriq(q)û* could refer to vegetables (*urqû*).

Line 25: *sú-qú-um* would stand for *sunqum*.

---

143. An Anatolian Woman Buys a Female Slave from an Assyrian Merchant

Envelope

Obv. 1(seal A) [2]kišib *A-bu-ša-lim* dumu *A-šur-du*$_{10}$ [3]kišib [d]*En-líl-ba-ni* dumu *Ì-lí-*[*a-lim*] [4]kišib *Lá-qé-pí-im* dumu *A-šùr-*[gal] [5](seal B) [6][*A-ra-lá*] [7][dumu-munus] *Šál-ma-A-šur* [8][dumu *A-šur-ma-lik*] [9][a-na 14 gín kù-babbar] [10][*Lá-qé-ep* dumu *A-šur*-gal rev. [11][a-na š]í-m[ì-im a-na] [12][*Wa-lí-wa-lí*] dam *Lá-q*[*é*]*-ep* [13][dumu *A-šu*]*r-ma-lik* [14](seal C) [15][*i-dí-in-ší*] le.e. [16][*šu-ma*] *a-na Wa-lí-wa-lí* [17](seal C) [18][*ma-ma-an a*]*-šu-mì A-ra-lá* [19][(x-x)] *i-tù-wa-ar* [20][*L*]*á-qé-pu-um* [21][*ú-ba-áb-ší*]

Inscription on Seal A

[1][*Za-at-ip-ra*] [2]gal *ha-ṭí-im*

Zatipra *rabi haṭṭim.*

[1–4]Seal of Abu-šalim, son of Aššur-ṭāb; seal of Enlil-bāni, son of Ilī-[ālum]; seal of Laqēpum, son of Aššur-[rabi].

[6–15]Laqēp, son of Aššur-[rabi, sold to Waliwali], wife of Laqēp, [son of Aššu]r-malik, [Arala, daughter of] Šalim-Aššur, [son of Aššur-malik], [for 14 shekels of silver]. [16–19][If anyone] raises a claim against Waliwali concerning Arala, [20–21][L]aqēpum shall clear her (from claims).

Tablet

Obv. [1]*A-ra-lá* dumu-mu[nus] [2]*Šál-ma-A-šur* [3]dumu *A-šur-ma-lik* [4]*a-na* 14 gín kù-bab[bar] [5]*Lá-qé-ep* dumu *A-šur*-gal [6]*a-na ší-mì-im a-n*[*a*] [7]*Wa-lí-wa-lí* [8]dam *Lá-qé-ep* [9]dumu *A-šur-ma-lik* [10]*i-dí-in-ší* [11]*šu-ma* : *ma-ma-an* lo.e. [12][*a*]*-na Wa-lí-wa-/lí* rev. [13][*a-šu-mì A-ra-lá*] [14][*i-tù-wa-ar*] [15][*Lá-qé-pu-um*] [16][*ú-ba-áb-ší*] [17][igi *A-bu-ša-lim*] [18][igi [d]*En-líl-ba-ni*]

$^{1-10}$Laqēp, son of Aššur-rabi, sold to Waliwali, wife of Laqēp, son of Aššur-malik, Arala, daug[hter of] Šalim-Aššur, son of Aššur-malik, for 14 shekels of sil[ver]. $^{11-14}$If anyone [raises a claim a]gainst Waliwali [concerning Arala], $^{15-16}$[Laqēpum shall clear her (from claims)].

$^{17-18}$[In the presence of Abu-šalim and Enlil-bāni.]

Bibliography: Text of the tablet published in copy by Matouš as ICK 2, 76; text of the envelope in several pieces, published in copy by Hrozný as ICK 1, 46a, and by Matouš as ICK 2, 77, and KKS 45b; edited by Kienast (1984, no. 2); translated by Hecker (1980, 66). The seal of the official chief scepter bearer is Teissier 1994, no. 221.

Comments: The Anatolian woman, Waliwali, purchaser of the female slave, is married to an Assyrian merchant called Laqēp. The female slave, Arala, is a daughter and granddaughter of Assyrian merchants.

---

144. An Anatolian Woman Buys a Female Slave from Another Anatolian Woman

Envelope

Obv. $^{1'}$ki[šib …] $^{2'}$[(seal)] $^{3'}$[ki]šib *A-*[*zu* 15 gín kù-babbar] $^{4'}$*ší-i*[*m am-tí-šu Ni-wa-al-ki*] $^{5'}$*ta-a*[*l-qé* …] $^{6'}$*Na-ki-*[*il*$_5$*-wi-iš-we* dam] $^{7'}$(seal A) $^{8'}$[*A-šùr-mu-ta-pì-il*$_5$ *i-ša-am šu-ma*] $^{9'}$(seal A) lo.e. $^{10'}$(seal B upside down) rev. $^{11'}$*ma-ma-an* : *i-pá-ṭá-ar-*[*ší*] $^{12'}$(seal B upside down) $^{13'}$1 *ma-na* kù-[babb]ar [*a-n*]*a* [d]am$^!$ $^{14'}$*A-šùr-mu-t*[*a-pì-il*$_5$] $^{15'}$*Na-ki-il*$_5^!$*-w*[*i-iš-we i-š*]*a-*[*qal*] $^{16'}$*šu-ma ša ú*$^!$(W[A)*-ba-dí-ni ma-ma-an*] $^{17'}$(seal C) $^{18'}$[*i-t*]*ù-r*[*a*$^!$*-am* …] (lacuna) le.e. (seal B)

$^{1'-3'}$S[eal of … se]al of A[zu. $^{3'-5'}$Niwalka] rece[ived 15 shekels of silver], pri[ce of his female slave]. $^{6'-8'}$Naki[lwišwe, wife of Aššur-mūtappil, bought (her). $^{8'-11'}$If] anyone redeems her, $^{13'-15'}$he s[hall pay] one mina of si[lver [to the wi]fe of Aššur-mūt[appil], Nakilwišwe. $^{16'-18'}$If [anyone r]ais[es a claim] from the *u*[*badinnum*, …]

Tablet

Obv. ^{1}15* gín kù-babbar ^{2}*ší-im am-tí-šu** ^{3}*Ni-wa-al-ki* ^{4}*ta-al-qé* ^{5}*Na-ki-il*$_5$*-wi-iš-/we* ^{6}dam : *A-šùr-mu-ta-pì-/il*$_5$ ^{7}*i-ša-am* : *ša* ^{8}*i-tù-ru-šu-ni* lo.e. ^{9}[1 *m*]*a-na* kù-babbar rev. ^{10}[*i-š*]*a-qá*$^!$(BI)*-lá* ^{11}*šu-ma ša ú*$^!$(WA)*-ba*$^!$(ŠÍ)-

dí-/ni [12]*ma-ma-an* [13]*i-tù-ra-am* [14]1 *ma-na* kù-babbar [15]*a-na* dam : *A-šur-mu-/ta-pì-il*$_5$ [16]*Na-ki-il*$_5$*-wi-iš-we* [17]*i-ša-qú-lu* u.e. [18]igi *A-zu* igi *Pè-ru-/wa-ah-/šu* le.e. [19]igi *Wa-la-[a]h-šu* igi [20]*A-li-l[i]*

[1-4]Niwalka received 15 shekels of silver, price of his female slave. [5-7]Nakilwišwe, wife of Aššur-mūtappil, bought (her). [7-10]The one who would raise a claim [shall] pay [one m]ina of silver (to Nakilwišwe). [11-13]If anyone from the *ubadinnum* raises a claim, [14-17]they shall pay 1 mina of silver to the wife of Aššur-mūtappil, Nakilwišwe.

[18-20]In the presence of Azu, Peruwahšu, Walahšu, and Alili.

Bibliography: Text of the tablet published in copy by Hrozný as ICK 1, 123; text of the envelope published in copy by Matouš as ICK 2, 182; edited by Kienast (1984, no. 13); translated by Hecker (2004b, 52–53).

Comments: Both parties of this sale contract are Anatolian women. The purchaser of the female slaves is married to an Assyrian merchant. The anonymous slave, object of the contract, is also a woman. The *ubadinnum* refers to land and tenants, granted by the king of Kaneš to high officials, acting here as a legal corporate body; see Dercksen 2004b.

The Anatolian writer did not use the feminine verbal forms for the verbs in lines 7 and 8 of the tablet and 8′ of the envelope.

Envelope, line 11′: this reading is suggested by Veenhof (2003a, 462 n. 154).

---

145. Bad Conduct of a Female Slave

Envelope

Obv. [1](seal) [2]*a-na Ma-ma-la* kišib *A-šur*-utu^{ši} [3]géme *lá ta-ší-im-tum* [4](seal A) [5]*a-wa-sà* : *a-ga-mar-ma* lo.e. [6](seal upside down) rev. [7](seal) [8]*a-ṭá-ra-sí* : *a-tí šé-ṭù-tí* [9]*tal-qé-e ma-nu-um i-bi*$_4$*-[sà-e]* [10]*lá e-mar* [11](seal) u.e. [12](seal) le.e. [13](seal) r.e. [14](seal)

[2]To Mamala, seal of Aššur-šamšī.

[3]The female slave has no sense. [5]I will have done with her and [8]send her away.

[8-10]You held me in contempt. Who does not experience losses?

Tablet

Obv. [1]*a-na Ma-ma-la qí-bi-ma* [2]*um-ma A-šur-*^{d}utu^{ši}*-ma* [3]*ha-ra-ni a-mì-ša-ma* [4]kù-babbar 1 *ma-na* dam-gàr$^{ru-/um}$ [5]*i-ta-áš-a-ni wa-ar-/kà-sú* [6]*ú-kà-ší-dam a-ni* [7]10 *u*$_4$*-me a-lá-kam šu-ma* [8]*lá a-tal-kam* urudu *lu* 5 *ma-na* [9]*lu* 6 *ma-na ú-še-ba-lam* [10]1½ *ma-na A-šur-*sipa [11]*sà-ku-ku-um ub-lá-ki-im* lo.e. [12]*lá ta-áš-ta-na-me-/i* [13][*k*]*i-ma* : *ma-at* rev. [14]*Ku-na-na-mì-it* [15]*sà-ah-a-at-ni-ma* [16]*lá na-aṭ-ú-ma a-šar* [17]10 *ma-na* urudu^{am} *ha-bu-/lu-ni* [18]*lá né-ri-iš* [19]*um-ma «be» a-na-ku-ma* [20]*ma-lá du-lá-am ta-mu-/ru* [21]*du-um-qám* : *lu ta-mu-ur* [22]*a-tí šé-ṭù-tí ta-al-qí-i-/ma* [23]*ṣú-ha-ar-tám ta-ta-/ad-ni* [24]*ú ṣú-ha-ra-am* [25]*lá ta-ší-ri a-*[*n*]*a* u.e. [26]*a-wa-tù-ki A-šur* [27]*lu i-de*$_8$ le.e. [28]*um-ma a-na-ku-ma a-na* [29]*um-mì-*<*a*> : *a-tí* [30]*ta-za-ri-ni*

[1–2]Say to Mamala: thus (says) Aššur-šamšī.

[3–5]As I was on my way toward there, the merchant took away from me silver, at least a whole mina. [5–6]I had to chase after him. [6–7]Now I will come within 10 days. [7–9]If I do not come, I will send copper, either 5 or 6 minas. [10–11]Aššur-rē'ī, the deaf man, brought you 1½ mina.

[12–15]Do you not keep hearing that the land of Kunanamit is in a state of anarchy? [16–18]So it is not convenient for us to ask for payment from people who owe (as much as) 10 minas of copper.

[19]I (said) as follows: [20–21]"May you see good as much as you have seen misery!" [22–23]You, you held me in contempt, and you even sold the female slave. [24–25]And you did not take care of the boy! [25–27]Aššur certainly knows your actions! [28–30]I (said) as follows: "As my mother, would you hate me?"

Bibliography: Text published by Dercksen (2010b) as LB 1209A (envelope) and LB 1209B (tablet).

Comments: The family connection between Mamala and Aššur-šamšī is unknown. Mamala sold a female slave without Aššur-šamšī's consent. But from the envelope of this letter, we learn that this female slave had no sense and that Aššur-šamšī intends to get rid of her.

Lines 20–21 may be understood as an ironic statement: "You will get what you deserve!"

Women at Home

Assyrian women were responsible for keeping up the house as well as managing their domestic staff. The house, *bētum*, was more than just a shelter for the night; it stood for all the life that was lived there and the people who made it their home: the couple, their children, the household slaves. The house was also the locus for certain family traditions. At Aššur, as at Kaneš, the basement could be used as a place for interments. Ownership of a house brought with it maintenance of the ancestor cult, because forgotten ancestors could come back to haunt the inhabitants of the house.[49]

At Aššur, houses were built of unbaked brick, a material ill suited for extremes of weather, so frequently in need of repair. At Kaneš, mud brick walls rested on stone foundations. Floors were of packed earth. The roof was held up by wooden beams, which had to be replaced regularly, and the plaster roofing redone.[50] Women who lived alone at Aššur stocked up on bricks, and bought timbers to strengthen the walls and redo the roof, but might wait for their husbands' return to carry out any work (**146**).

The house was the woman's domain. She wanted to own as large and handsome a house as possible, to symbolize the couple's social success (**147**). Some women at Aššur bought houses for themselves or for joint ownership with their husbands, often the property next door, so they could enlarge their own home (**129, 147**).

The archives found at Kaneš contain contracts for the purchase of real estate in which women sometimes appear, either as buyers or sellers.[51] Some bought, after some years, the house they resided in; others, widowed, were allowed to live in a house sold to a third party (**51, 52, 150**). Sale contracts for houses were drawn up either from the standpoint of the seller or that of the buyer. Women, Assyrian or Anatolian, married or not, could purchase assets on their own (**148, 149, 150, 151, 152**). The prices for houses purchased by women range from about 30 shekels to 2½ minas of silver. Purchase of a house by an Anatolian couple is also attested (**153**). Several texts mention women as owners of houses: "Have the scribe of the *kārum* search the house of Šāt-Ea."[52]

49. Michel 2009a, and chapter 5 of this book, pp. 354–75.

50. Michel 1997b; Veenhof 2011, 213–15.

51. Kienast 1984. Add to the samples given in this chapter Kt v/k 52 (Günbattı 1989), which reports the purchase of a house by the woman Ala.

52. ATHE 34:23–25 (letter to Aššur-nādā from Aššur-idī) dub-sar: *ša kà-ri-im*,

At Kaneš, merchants' houses were built in the lower town, generally on two levels. The residences excavated in the commercial quarter have an average size of 70 to 90 square meters; larger houses could exceed 150 or 200 square meters.[53] The kitchen was located on the ground floor, with an oven, a servants' room, one or several storage rooms, and a sealed strong room (*huršum*, *maṣṣartum*, *maknukum*). The different areas of the house could be ranged around a principal room (*ekallum*, **154**). The sealed room was used for storage of merchandise, especially tin and textiles, and for archives, of which the debt notes were among the most valuable possessions of the couple. The family lived on the upper floor.

Women who lived alone had to see that their house was secure from thieves, especially at night. Their husbands would send them letters about this, urging them to ward off intruders (**140**, **154**, **155**, **156**, **305**, **307**). Women also protected the couple's assets against moneylenders or investors and hostile associates who were tempted to avail themselves of a house abandoned by their debtor or partner. When they themselves were absent, women had to take steps to have their house watched throughout their absence (**303**). Texts do in fact refer to robberies committed in houses inhabited by merchants and their wives in the lower town (**311**).[54]

---

146. Getting Together Bricks and Beams to Repair the House

Obv. ^{1}*a-na* ^{d}*En-líl-ba-ni* ^{2}*qí-bi-ma* : *um-ma* ^{3}*Ta-ri-iš-ma-tum-ma* ^{4}*a-šu-mì* é^{tim} *ša wa-áš-ba-ni-/ni* ^{5}*ki-ma* : é^{tum} *an-hu-ni* ^{6}*áp-lá-ah-ma li-bi-tám* ^{7}*i-na dá-áš-i-im* : *uš-tal-bi-in-/ma* ^{8}*e-me-ra-am* : *e-té-me-er* : *a-šu-mì* ^{9}*gu*$_{5}$*-šu-ri* : *ša ta-áš-pu-ra-ni* ^{10}kù-babbar *ša šé-bu-lim*$^{!}$ *šé-bi-il*$_{5}$ ^{11}*a-na-kam* : *gu*$_{5}$*-šu-ri* : *li*$^{?}$-[*iš-ú-mu-kum*] (lacuna)
Rev. $^{1'}$[*š*]*a*$^{?}$*-pá-ru-*[*um*] *i-*[x-x-x] $^{2'}$*ú-sà-pá-ah-ma* : *ta-áš-*[*ta-pu*] $^{3'}$*a-hi a-ta* : *a-na-ku* : *a-na* [*ma-nim a-ta-kál*] $^{4'}$*ù a-ta* : *a-na ma-nim t*[*a-ta-kál i-na*] $^{5'}$*a-lá-ki-kà* : kù-babbar : *zi-tám ša* é $^{6'}$*a-bi-ni* : *ta-lá-ma-ad-ma* : *li-ba-kà* $^{7'}$*ù li-bi*$_{4}$: *i-nu-a-ah* : *a-na* $^{8'}$*ta-ki*$^{!}$*-li ù li-ša-nim* $^{9'}$*lá ta-la-ak* : *i-na pá-ni* : *wa-*

é *Ša-té-a* : dumu-munus *Sú-e-ta-ta*, *na-hi*$^{!}$(DÍ)*-id*. Sometimes, the formulation is ambiguous and might be interpreted as "the house in which ^{f}PN lives." For example, Nuhšatum lived in the house of her husband; see Veenhof 2015c and Michel 2016d.

53. T. Özgüç 1986, 1–15, 115–17; 2003, 77–98.

54. The best documented example is the theft of two chests of previously stolen tablets from the house of a merchant, see CTMMA 1, 84, a dossier analysed by Michel 2000a, 135–38.

ṣa-i-kà [10']*a-šu-mì : kà-li-tí-ni tù-na-hi-/da-ni* [11']*um-ma a-ta-ma : a-na* é [12']*a-bi-ša : lá tù-šé-ri-ší qá-dí-ki-ma* [13']*i-na* é^{tim} *lu tù-šé-ší-ib-ma* é^{tám} [14']*bar-kà-at-ki : lu ta-ṣur : ki-ma tù-uṣ-ni* [15']*ma-tí-ma : ba-za-ša ù šé-la-sà : ú-lá* [16']*ib-ší : a-ni : iš-tù* iti-8-kam [17']*iš-tí-a wa-*[*š*]*a-ba-*[*am ú-lá*] *ta-mu-wa* le.e. [18']*tù-uš-té-ṣa-ma : a-na* é *a-bi-ša-*[*ma*] [19']*mu-ší-a-tim ta-ta-na-la-ak-m*[*a*] [20']*lá dam-qá-tim áš-ta-na-me-ší-ma* [21']*a-wa-tí : ša-ma-a-am ú-lá* (erasure) [22']*ta-mu-wa*

[1–3]Say to Enlil-bāni: thus (says) Tarīš-mātum.

[4]Concerning the house in which we live, [5–8]I was afraid because the house has fallen into disrepair, so, in the spring, I had mud bricks made, and I stacked (them) in piles. [8–10]Concerning the beams about which you wrote me, send me the necessary amount of silver [11]so that they [will buy] beams [for you] here (lacuna).

[1'–2']He wastes […] and you have k[ept silent]. [3'–4']You are my brother, in [whom else should I trust]? And you, in whom else should y[ou trust? [4'–7']On] your arrival, you will learn how much the share in silver of our father's house is, and then you and I may be at ease. [7'–9']Don't pay heed to slander and gossip!

[9'–10']Before your departure, you gave me instructions concerning our daughter-in-law [11'–12']as follows: "Do not let her go to the house of her father; [12'–13']it is with you that she must be made to live in the house, and [13'–14']she must keep watch on the house after you (have left)." [14'–16']When you left, there had never been any instance of misconduct or misdeed on her part. [16'–17'](But) now, for 8 months she [re]fuses to sta[y] with me, [18'–19']she fights with me, and at night she always goes to her father's house, and [20'–22']I keep on hearing bad things about her; now she refuses to listen to me!

Bibliography: Text published in copy by Pinches (1908, 1); collated by Kawasaki (1998, 85); translated by Michel (2001a, no. 320; 2014b, 207). Lines 4–11, 9′–22′ cited by Michel (1997b, 287 n. 3; 290 n. 14).

Comments: Tarīš-mātum, sister of Pūšu-kēn, son of Sue'a, was married to Aššur-malik, son of Šu-Kūbum, and lived in Aššur. In the absence of her husband, who was probably deceased, she writes to her son, Enlil-bāni, about the maintenance of her house and about her new daughter-in-law, wife of Enlil-bāni, who was supposed to be living with her for the time.

147. A Bigger House to Show Off Social Success

Obv. [1]*a-na Pu-šu-ke-en*$_{6}$ [2]*qí-bi-ma* : *um-ma Lá-ma-sí-ma* [3]*ta-ša-me-ma* : *ta-ni-iš*$^{!}$*-/tum* [4]*il*$_{5}^{!}$*-té-mì-in* [5]*a-hu-um* : *a-na a-hi-im* [6]*a-na ha-lá-tim* : *i-za-az* [7]*ku-ta-bi-it-ma* [8]*ù al-kam-ma* : *ku-ur-ṣí-/kà* [9]*pá-ri-ir* : *ṣú-ha-ar-/tám* [10]*a-na sú-un A-šùr* [11]*šu-ku-un* : *i-na A-lim*^{ki} [12]síg$^{\text{hi-a}}$: *wa-aq-ra-at* [13]*i-nu-mì* : kù-babbar 1 *ma-na* [14]*ta-ša-kà-na-ni* [15]*i-na qé-ra-áb* lo.e. [16]síg$^{\text{hi-a}}$: *šu-uk-nam* [17]kù-babbar 1 *ma-na* rev. [18]*ša wa-ṣí-tí-kà* [19]*ša tù-šé-bi*$_{4}$*-lá-ni* : *mu-ṣí-/um* [20]*e-ri-šu-ni-ma* [21]*a-šu-mì-kà* : *pá-al-ha-ku-/ma* [22]*ù-lá a-<dí>-in* [23]*um-ma a-na-ku-ma* [24]*li-mu-um le-ru-ba-/ma* [25]é$^{\text{bé-tám}}$: *li-pu-/ug* [26]*a-ha-at-kà* (erasure) [27]géme : *a-na ší-mì-im* [28]*ta-dí-in-ma* : *a-na-ku* [29]*a-na* 14 gín *áp-ṭù-ur-/ší* [30]*Ša-lim-a-hu-um* [31]2$^{\text{šé-na}}$: é$^{\text{be-té-en}}$ [32]*iš-tù a-ta* : *tù-uṣ-ú* u.e. [33]*e*$^{!}$*-ta-pá-áš* [34]*né-nu-ma* : *a-na ma-tí* le.e. [35]*né-pá-áš* : túg : *ša A-šur-ma-lik* : [36]*i-na pá-ni-tim* : *ub-lá-ni* : kù-babbar [37]*mì-in* : *lá tù-šé-ba-lam*

[1–3]Say to Pūšu-kēn: thus (says) Lamassī.

[3–6]You hear that people are behaving badly, one tries to gobble up the other! [7–9]Be an honorable man, break your obligations, and come here! [9–11]Consecrate our young (daughter) to the god Aššur. [11–12] (Here), in the city (of Aššur), wool is expensive. [13–16]When you put silver at my disposal, (about) 1 mina, put it in with the wool.

[17–20]The *mūṣû*-official asked me for the silver, (about) 1 mina, for your export tax that you sent me, [21–22]but I was afraid for you, and I did not give (anything); [23]I (told him) as follows: [24–25]"The eponym may come in and confiscate (my) house, (but I will not give anything)!" [26–29]Your sister sold a female slave, but I myself released her for 14 shekels (of silver).

[30–33]Since you left, Šalim-ahum has built two houses; [34–35]when will we be able to do (the same)? [35–36]As for the textile(s) that Aššur-malik brought you previously, [36–37]could you not send the silver?

Bibliography: Text published by Garelli as *RA* 59, 159 (MAH 16209); translated by Michel (2001a, no. 306; 2014b, 208–9).

Comments: Lamassī urges her husband to pay his duties to Aššur authorities because an official put pressure on her asking for the money: the *mūṣû*-official was involved in the levy of the export tax in Aššur.

At the end of the letter, she expresses her wish to enlarge her house. Veenhof (2011, 213–14), suggests that the first and second houses were connected with each other (see ICK 1, 128). According to Sch. 22, Pūšu-kēn's respresentatives in Aššur bought for him Ilum-malik's house, next to his house; this house was previously rented by Pūšu-kēn and Lamassī (**260**). We may conclude that Lamassī was finally satisfied.

Line 20: the verbal form should be singular and not plural.

Line 37: according to Kouwenberg (2017, 348 n. 4), *mì-in* would be an error for *mì-šum*.

---

148. An Assyrian Woman Buys a House from an Assyrian Couple

Obv. ^{1}é *ša Ištar-lá-ma-/sí* ^{2}*ù A-šùr*-du$_{10}$ ^{3}*a-na* 2½ *ma-na* ^{4}kù-babbar *a-na* ^{5}*Ša-lim-ma i-dí-nu-ma* ^{6}kù-babbar *ší-im* é-*šu-nu* ^{7}*A-šùr*-du$_{10}$ *ù Ištar-lá-/ma-sí* ^{8}*ša-bu-ú* ^{9}é$^{bé-tù}$ lo.e. ^{10}*ša Ša-lim-ma* rev. ^{11}*šu-ma* : *ma-ma-an* ^{12}*a-na* é *be-tí i-tù-a-ar-/*[*ší*]*-*im* ^{13}*A-šùr*-du$_{10}$ *ù Ištar-lá-ma-/sí* ^{14}*ú-bu-bu-ší* ^{15}*ṭup-pá-am ša ší-im* ^{16}é$^{bé-tí}$ *a-ni-ú-tim* ^{17}*ša ku-nu-uk nu-a-im* ^{18}*be-el* é *pá-nim A-šur-/*du$_{10}$ ^{19}*a-na Ša-lim-ma i-dí-in* ^{20}igi ^{d}utu-*ba-ni* ^{21}[igi] *A-šur-ma-lik* ^{22}[igi] *Sú-en*$_{6}$-sipa

$^{1-5}$The house of Ištar-lamassī and Aššur-ṭāb, for 2½ minas of silver, they sold to Šalimma; and $^{6-8}$with the silver, price of their house, Aššur-ṭāb and Ištar-lamassī are satisfied. $^{9-10}$That house belongs to Šalimma. $^{11-12}$If anyone raises a claim against her for the house, $^{13-14}$Aššur-ṭāb and Ištar-lamassī shall clear her.

$^{15-19}$Aššur-ṭāb gave to Šalimma the contract recording the sale of this house, with the seal of the Anatolian, its previous owner.

$^{20-22}$In the presence of Šamaš-bāni, Aššur-malik, and Suen-rē'ī.

Bibliography: Text published by Veenhof (2003b, 693–95) as no. 1 (Kt 91/k 522), then as AKT 8, 210; collated May 2012.

Comments: There are at least two other women named Ištar-lamassī: one married to Puzur-Ištar (**23**), and another who is a consecrated woman (**171**; TC 3, 128); in this text, Ištar-lamassī is presumably the wife of Aššur-ṭāb. Šalimma, the buyer of this house, is well-known from the archives excavated in 1991 and studied by Veenhof. Daugther of Lamassatum and Elamma, sister of Ummī-Išhara, she married Ir'am-Aššur (Kt 91/k 386). Šalimma left her husband alone with their child in Aššur and traveled to Kaneš, where she lived with her mother, already a widow

(Veenhof 2007). According to this contract, she bought a house while she was in Kaneš.

The contract mentions at the end the deeds of the previous transactions concerning this building, which are transferred to Šalimma, the buyer. In Old Babylonian documentation, at the sale of a house, letters and judicial records concerning earlier transactions of the building were transferred to the new owner (Charpin 1986).

Line 16: both plural *bētū* and *bētātu* are attested in Old Assyrian texts. The second corresponds to different houses belonging to various people. According to Veenhof (2011, 216–17), the first plural form could refer to a large complex and thus should be translated as a singular (see also in the following texts).

---

149. A Woman Buys from an Anatolian a House Previously Belonging to an Assyrian

Envelope

Obv. ^{1}(seal A) ^{2}kišib *Puzur*$_{4}$*-e-na* dumu *E-li*$^{!}$*-a* ^{3}kišib *I-dí-Sú-en*$_{6}$ dumu *I-dí-Ištar** ^{4}kišib *Pè-ru-a* dumu *Wa-lá-ah-ší-na* ^{5}kišib *Da-lá-áš* dumu *Ha-ma-ra-a* ^{6}kišib *Šu-pì*-ú-ma-an* dumu *Ha-mu-ri-/a*$^{!}$ ^{7}(seal B) ^{8}é^{tám} *ša iš-tí I-ku-nim* lo.e. ^{9}(seal B) ^{10}dumu *Sà*-ma-a Pè-ru-a* rev. ^{11}(seal C) ^{12}dumu *Wa-lá-ah-ši-na a-na* ^{13}½ *ma-na* 4 lá ¼ gín ^{14}(seal D) ^{15}*iš-ú-mu a-na* ½ *ma-na* /4 lá ¼ gín ^{16}é^{tám} *iš-tí* ^{17}(seal E) ^{18}*Pè-ru-a Um-mì-na-ra* u.e. ^{19}(seal A) ^{20}*ta-áš-a-am-šu* kù-[b]bbar le.e. ^{21}*ša-bu* ^{22}(seal E) r.e. ^{23}(seal C)

$^{2-6}$Seal of Puzur-Enna, son of Eliya; seal of Iddin-Suen, son of Iddin-Ištar; seal of Peru(w)a, son of Walahšina; seal of Dalaš, son of Hamaraya; seal of Šu[pp]iuman, son of Hamurum.

$^{8-12}$Concerning the house that Peruwa, son of Walahšina, bought from Ikūnum, son of Samaya, for ½ mina and 4 minus ¼ shekel (of silver); $^{12-15}$Umminara bought it from Peru(w)a for ½ mina and 4 minus ¼ shekel (of silver). $^{20-21}$The silver has been paid.

Tablet

^{1}é$^{be\text{-}tám}$ *ša iš-tí I-ku-/nim* ^{2}dumu *Sà*$^{!}$*-ma-a* «*ta*» *Pè-ru-a* ^{3}dumu *Wa-lá-ah-ší-na* ^{4}*a-na* ½ *ma-na* 4 lá ¼ gín ^{5}*iš-ú-mu iš-tí* ^{6}*Pè-ru-a a-na* ½ *ma-na* /4 lá ¼ gín ^{7}*Um-mì-na-ra* ^{8}*ta-áš-a-am-šu* kù-babbar ^{9}*ša-bu* ^{10}igi *I-dí-Sú-en*$_{6}$ ^{11}igi *Da-lá-áš* ^{12}igi *Šu-pí-ú-ma-an*

$^{1-5}$Concerning the house that Peruwa, son of Walahšina, bought from Ikūnum, son of Samaya, for ½ mina and 4 minus ¼ shekel (of silver); $^{5-8}$Umminara bought it from Peru(w)a for ½ mina and 4 minus ¼ shekel (of silver). $^{8-9}$The silver has been paid.

$^{10-12}$In the presence of Iddin-Suen, Dalaš, and Šuppiuman.

Bibliography: Text published in copy by Lewy as KTS 1, 46; edited by Eisser and Lewy (1930, no. 107), and by Kienast (1984, no. 6). Seals are published in ICK 2, pl. CXXVIII, no. 83, A–E; and seal A is reproduced in N. Özgüç 2006, pl. 5 (CS 277). Envelope collated by Donbaz (2015, 63).

Comments: This sale contract concerns the same house and presumably the same transaction as **150**. The Anatolian woman buys a house from an Anatolian man who previously bought it from an Assyrian.

---

150. A Woman Buys a House for Another Woman

Envelope

Obv. ^{1}(seal A) ^{2}kišib *Šu-pì-a-ah-šu* ^{3}kišib *Šé-ṣú-ur* kišib *Áb-ša-lim* ^{4}kišib *Šu-iš-ku-na* ^{5}(seal B) lo.e. ^{6}(seal B) rev. ^{7}(seal C) ^{8}*ša* é^{tí} *ša I-ku-nim* ^{9}*Šu-iš-ku-na a-šu-mì* ^{10}[*U*]*m-mì-na-ra ta-*<*áš*>*-ú-mu* ^{11}[½] *ma-na* 3 gín kù-babbar ^{12}[*Um-m*]*ì-na-ra ta-áš-qú-ul* ^{13}[*la ta-q*]*á-bi*$_{4}$ *Šu-iš-ku-na* ^{14}[é^{tù}*-a*] *wa-ša-bu-tám* ^{15}[*wa-áš-ba*]*-at* u.e. ^{16}(seal A) le.e. ^{17}(seal D) r.e. ^{18}(seal C)

$^{1-4}$Seal of Šuppiahšu; seal of Šēṣur; seal of Ab-šalim; seal of Šuiškuna.

$^{8-10}$Concerning the house of Ikūnum that Šuiškuna bought in the name of Umminara, $^{11-12}$Umminara paid ½ mina, 3 shekels of silver. $^{13-15}$Šuiškuna must not say: "(It is) my house." But she may go on living in (it).

Tablet

Obv. ^{1}½ *ma-na* 3 gín kù-/babbar ^{2}*ší-im* : é *ša I-/ku-nim* ^{3}*Um-mì-na-ra* ^{4}dam *En-nam-A-šur* ^{5}kù-babbar *a-na Šu-iš-kà-/na* ^{6}*ta-dí-na* : é^{tù} ^{7}*ša Šu-iš-ku-na* ^{8}*ta-áš-ú*$^{!}$*-mu* ^{9}*ša Um-mì-na-ra* lo.e. ^{10}*la ta-qá-bi* ^{11}*Šu-iš-ku-na* rev. ^{12}*um-ma ší-it-ma* ^{13}é^{tù}*-a a-na* ^{14}*wa-ša-bu-tim* ^{15}*ki-a-ma* : *wa-áš-ba-at* ^{16}é^{tù} *ša Um-mì-na-/ra* ^{17}kù-babbar *ta-áš-qú-ul* ^{18}igi *Áb-ša-lim* ^{19}igi *Šu-pí-a-ah-šu* ^{20}igi *Šé-ṣú-ur*

[1-6]½ mina, 3 shekels of silver, price of the house of Ikūnum; Umminara, wife of Enna-Aššur, gave the silver to Šuiškuna. [6-9]Concerning the house that Šuiškuna bought, it (belongs) to Umminara. [10-12]Šuiškuna must not say as follows: [13]"(It is) my house." [13-15]But she may go on living in (it) as she has been. [16-17]The house (belongs) to Umminara: she paid the silver.

[18-20]In the presence of Ab-šalim, Šuppiahšu, and Šēṣur.

Bibliography: Text published by Wilcke (1983, 194–96, as *Or* 52, 1) (Prähistorische Staatssammlung 1979.1191, Munich); edited by Kienast (1984, no. 39).

Comments: Umminara, wife of Ennum-Aššur, buys a house through another woman, Šuiškuna, who is living in it. Šuiškuna is allowed to stay in the house after the transaction. We do not know if there was a family connection between these two women.

This sale contract concerns the same house and presumably the same transaction as **149**. The seller of the house is not mentioned in this contract, but it must be Peruwa. The price announced is ¾ shekel less than in the previous contract.

Lines 14–15: these lines mean that she may live in the house only as tenant.

---

151. An Anatolian Woman Buys a House from Anatolians

Obv. [1]kišib *Ni-ni* kišib *A-lá-bi*[?]*-za** [2](seal A) [3]kišib*Tù-hu-na-ra* kišib [4]*I-li-a* kišib *Ha-bi*$_4$*-a* [5]kišib *A-lá-ša-ki* kišib [6]*Ta-mu-ri-a* kišib *Kà-li-a* [7](seal B, stamp seal, 2 times) [8]kišib *Ša-da-ah-šu* lo.e. [9](seal C, stamp seal, 3 times) rev. [10]1 *ma-na* kù-babbar *ší-im* [11](seal D) [12]*é*[be-tí] *ša Ta-mu-ri-/a* [13]*qá*[!](IŠ)-*dí na-dí-ša ù* [14]*ku-nu-ki-ša Ha-ta-šu-šar* [15]*a-na Ta-mu-ri-a* [16]*Ša-da-ah-*<*šu*> *ù Kà-li-a* [17]*ta-áš-*[qú]*qúl šu-ma* [18]*Ma-da-da ú šé-ru-šu* [19]*i-tù-ru-ší-im* [20]5 *ma-na* kù-babbar u.e. [21](seal A) [22]*i-ša-qú-lu-ší-im* le.e. [23](seal E)* r.e. [24](seal F)*

[1-8]Seal of Nini; seal of Alabiza; seal of Tuhunara; seal of Iliya; seal of Habiya; seal of Alašaki; seal of Tamuriya; seal of Kaliya; seal of Šadahšu.

[10-17]1 mina of silver, price of the house of Tamuriya, with her [...] and her seal, Hatašušar paid to Tamuriya, Šadahšu, and Kaliya. [17-19]If Madada

and his children raise a claim against her, [20–22]they shall pay her 5 minas of silver.

Bibliography: Envelope published by Bayram and Veenhof (1992, 96–97, no. 3 [Kt j/k 39]); collated May 2012.

Comments: The house is sold by three people, but only Tamuriya is living in it, since the house is referred to as his. No explanation is offered concerning the possible claim raised by Madada and his (or her) children.

Line 13: the editors proposed the reading $^{\text{giš?}}$DÍ-NA-DÍ-*ša*, but do not give a translation; see Bayram and Veenhof 1992, 97 n. 4.

---

152. An Anatolian Woman Buys a House from Anatolians

Obv. [1]*ší-im* é^{ti} *ša Wa-al-/ha-áš-na* [2]*Kà-ba-šu-nu-wa* : [3]*Lu-lu ù Wa-al-ha-áš-na* [4]*Šu-pì-a-šu-wa* : *tù-ša-bi*$_4$*-šu-nu* [5]*a-na Šu-pì-a-šu-wa* [6]*ma-ma-an lá i-tù-wa-ar* [7]*ša a-na* é$^{be\text{-}té}$ [8]*i-tù-ru-ší-ni* [9]5 *ma-na* kù-babbar lo.e. [10]*a-na Šu-pì-a-šu-wa* rev. [11]*i-ša-qal* [12]igi *Ša-ha-ša-ra* [13]igi *Pè-ru-a* [14]igi *Ša-ha-ša-ra* [15]dumu *Kà-ba-šu-nu-a*

[1–4](With) the price of the house of Walhašna, Šuppiašuwa satisfied Kabašunu(w)a, Lulu, and Walhašna. [5–6]No one shall raise a claim against Šuppiašuwa. [7–8]Anyone who raises a claim against her for the house [9–10]shall pay 5 minas of silver to Šuppiašuwa.

[12–15]In the presence of Šahašara, Peru(w)a, and Šahašara, son of Kabašunu(w)a.

Bibliography: Text published by Bayram and Veenhof (1992, 97–98, no. 4 [Kt 80/k 25]); collated May 2012.

Comments: As in the previous text, an Anatolian buys a house from three Anatolians, but the house seems to be inhabited only by one of them, Walhašna. The penalty in case of claim is very high, as in the previous text: five minas of silver.

There are two people named Šahašara among the witnesses; one is referred to with his patronymic.

153. Sale of a House by an Anatolian Couple

Obv. $^{1'}$[...] $^{2'}$[*be-ta-tim*] *a-ší-mì-im* $^{3'}$*i-dí-in*-(erasure)-*ma* $^{4'}$*a-na* ⅓ [*ma*]-*na* 1 gín $^{5'}$kù-babbar *Zu-wa* $^{6'}$*ú A-ba-ba a-ša-sú* $^{7'}$*iš-ú-mu-šu-nu* $^{8'}$*šu-ma a-ma-tí-ma* $^{9'}$*a-šu-mì* é$^{be\text{-}tim}$ $^{10'}$*lu tù-zi-num* lo.e. $^{11'}$*lu be-el hu-b*[*u-lim*] $^{12'}$*lu ma-ma-an* $^{13'}$*a-na Zu-w*[*a*] rev. $^{14'}$*ú A-ba-ba* $^{15'}$*a-ší-tí-šu i-tù-ar* $^{16'}$1 *ma-na* kù-babbar $^{17'}$*i-ša-qal-šu-nu-tí* $^{18'}$igi *Ha-nu* igi *Ku-ku-ú* $^{19'}$igi *Wa-ší-nu-ma-an* $^{20'}$igi *Ni-wa-ah-šu*

$^{1'}$[...]$^{2'-3'}$sold the ["houses"] and $^{4'-7'}$Zuwa and Ababa, his wife, bought them for ⅓ [mi]na, 1 shekel of silver. $^{8'-15'}$If ever, concerning the house, either the *tuzinnum*, the creditor or any one raises a claim against Zuwa and Ababa, his wife, $^{16'-17'}$he shall pay them 1 mina of silver.

$^{18'-20'}$In the presence of Hanu, Kukū, Wašinuman, and Niwahšu.

Bibliography: Text edited by Kienast (1984, no. 22) as Kay 4369.

Comments: An Anatolian couple bought a house for twenty-one shekels of silver; the name of the seller(s) is broken.

Line 7′: the plural of the verbal form imposes the restitution *bētātim* in line 2′. But this does not necessarily mean that several houses were sold; the small price might refer to rooms gathered to form one house (line 9′; the word is singular); see note to text **244**.

154. Moving into a New Home

Obv. ^{1}*um-ma* ^{d}*En-líl-ba-ni-ma* ^{2}*a-na A-šur*-gal *A-lá-hi-im* ^{3}*Áb-ša-lim* «*ú*» *Ša-ak-ri-el-kà* ^{4}*ú I-dí-*^{d}utu *qí-bi-ma* ^{5}*šu-ma ú-nu-tum i-ta-dí*$^{!}$*-ma* ^{6}*ma ha-ra-nu-um wa-šu-ra-at* ^{7}*ú-nu-tám šu-um-šu*$^{!}$ *ša i-be-tim* ^{8}*i-ba-ší-ú a-na be-tim* ^{9}*e-ší-im šé-ri-ba-ma* ^{10}é-gal^{lim} *ú du-ri-ni* ^{11}*i-ku-nu-ki-ku-nu ku-un-kà-/ma* ^{12}*ma-ma-an lá i-pá-té* ^{13}*lu qé-mu-um lu ar-ša-tum* ^{14}*a-šar še-um i-ba-ší-ú* ^{15}*šé-ri-ba-ma pì-ih-a* rev. ^{16}*ma-lá té-zi-ba-ni* ^{17}*me-eh-ra-am a-na am-/tim* ^{18}*dí-na ú ša-ni-am* ^{19}*i-na* é-gal^{lim} *ez-ba-ma* ^{20}*am-tum iš-tí* : *A-lá-hi-im* ^{21}*lu ta-ta-al-kam* ^{22}1 *am-tam Ki-lá-ri-tám* ^{23}*a-ší-mì-im dí-na-ší* ^{24}*I-dí-*^{d}utu *ú am-tám ra-bi*$_4$*-tám* ^{25}*a-šar be-tim na-hi-da-/ma* ^{26}*ku-nu-ki ša* é-gal^{lim} ^{27}*ú du-ri-ni lu-ša-ṣí-ru a-na* ^{28}*ba-áp*$^{!}$*-pí-ri ša* é *Šu-Ištar* ^{29}*ma-ma-*[*an*] *lá i-ṭá-hi* ^{30}½ *ma-na* kù-babbar *um-ma-ša* ^{31}*ša am-tim ha-bu-lá-at* le.e. ^{32}*ṭup-pá-ša hi-ir-ma-ma a-na Áb-ša-lim* ^{33}*dí-na a-ha-ma* 7½ gín kù-babbar *ha-bu-/lá-*

am [34]*ša-áš-qí-lá-ší šu-ma še-am ta-š*[*a-qá-al*] [35]*a-li-bi*$_4$ *še-im-ma šu-up-kà-šu* an-[na] [36]3 gín kù-babbar *ú ší-it-ra-*[*am*]

[1–4]Thus (says) Enlil-bāni: say to Aššur-rabi, Ali-ahum, Ab-šalim, Šakri-elka, and Iddin-Šamaš.

[5–6]If the goods have been deposited, and the road has been given free, [7–9]then bring all the goods that are in the house into the new house, and [10–11]seal with your seals the main room and the *surrounding rooms*; [12]nobody should open them. [13–15]Either flour or wheat, wherever grain there is, bring it in and lock it up. [16–18]Give the female slave a list of everything you have left behind, and [18–19]leave another (copy) in the main room, [20–21]then let the female slave come with Ali-ahum. [22–23]Sell one Kilarian female slave. [24–27]Instruct Iddin-Šamaš and the senior female slave concerning the entire building that they watch carefully the seals of the main room and the *surrounding rooms*. [27–29]Nobody should approach the beer breads of the house of Šu-Ištar.

[30–31]The mother of the female slave owes me ½ mina of silver; [32–33]draw up her valid sealed record and give it to Ab-šalim. [33–34]In addition, she owes me 7½ shekels of silver, so make her pay! [34–35]If she pays (her debt) in barley, add it to the stock of barley already stored.

[35–36]There is some tin, for an amount of 3 shekels of silver and a shawl.

Bibliography: Text published in copy by Smith as CCT 3, 14; translated by Michel (2001a, no. 339). Lines 5–9 cited by Balkan (1957, 17); lines 10–27 by Michel (1997b, 287).

Comments: This letter, addressed to a woman (Ab-šalim) and her female slave (Šakri-elka) among other addressees, refers to moving from an old to a new home, and reveals the organization of the second one: it comprises a large main room surrounded by smaller rooms. In the household, one female slave was designated as the head of the female domestic staff.

Line 32: literally, "put her tablet into a sealed case."

---

155. Watching the House and Its Contents

Obv. [1]*um-ma Puzur*$_4$*-Ištar-ma* [2]*a-na Ištar-lá-ma-sí* [3]*qí-bi*$_4$*-ma* : *a-ma-kam* (erasure) [4]*a-šar* : é^{tim} *ša-ṣí-ri* [5]8 gú 50 *ma-na* [6]an-na : *ku-nu-ku-ú* [7]*i-na hu-*

ur-ší-im ^{8}*i-na ma-ṣa-ar-tim* ^{9}*ma-hi-ri-im* (*sic*) ^{10}2 *me-at* 30 túg$^{\text{hi-a}}$ lo.e. ^{11}*ša qá-tim* ^{12}1 *me-at* 20 túg$^{\text{hi-a}}$ rev. ^{13}sig$_5$^{tum} ^{14}13 anše$^{\text{hi-a}}$ ^{15}*ṣa-lá-me-ú mì-ma* ^{16}*a-nim* : *i-na* ^{17}é^{tim} *ku-nu-*[*k*]*e-e* ^{18}*e-zi-ba-ki-im* ^{19}*a-pu-tum* : *a-na ki-dim* ^{20}*a-e-ma* : *lá tù-ṣí-i* ^{21}*a-dí* : *té-er-tí za-ku-sà* ^{22}*ta-ša-me-i-ni*

$^{1-3}$Thus (says) Puzur-Ištar: say to Ištar-lamassī.

$^{3-4}$There, watch over the house.

$^{5-9}$(There are) 8 talents, 50 minas of sealed tin in the store of the foremost strong room, $^{10-15}$2 hundred 30 ordinary textiles, 1 hundred 20 good-quality textiles, 13 black donkeys; $^{15-18}$all the (merchandise) I left you in the house under seal.

$^{19-22}$Urgent! Do not leave for anywhere outside before you have heard clear instructions from me (on what you shall do with all this).

Bibliography: Text published in copy by Veenhof as VS 26, 53; translated by Michel (2001a, no. 362).

Comments: Daughter of Aššur-nādā and his Anatolian wife, Šišahšušar, Ištar-lamassī was the *amtum*-wife of Puzur-Ištar, the writer of this letter (**23**). In the house in which she was living in Kaneš, her husband left large amounts of merchandise, tin, and textiles. Because of these, he asks his wife to stay at home and watch carefully his goods. She is presumably also in charge of the donkeys.

Line 9: *ma-hi-ri-im* is a mistake for *mahrīm*.

---

156. Watching the House

Obv. ^{1}*um-ma A-šur-lá-ma-/sí* ^{2}*ù A-šur-*gal*-ma* ^{3}*a-na Áb-ša*$^{!}$*-lim* ^{4}*ù Ší-ik-ri-el-kà* ^{5}*qí-bi-ma šál-ma-ni* ^{6}*mì-ma lá ta-ra-ší* ^{7}*a-pu-tum a-šar* lo.e. ^{8}é$^{be\text{-}tim}$ rev.^{9}*ša-ṣí-ra* ^{10}*šu-ma* dingir-*ták-lá-ku* ^{11}*iš-tù Tí-mì-*<*il*$_5$>*-ki-a* ^{12}*i-tal-kam ú-ul* ^{13}*ma-ma-an i-ṣú-ha-ri* ^{14}*i-li-kam* u.e. ^{15}*lá ta-*[*k*]*à-lá-a* ^{16}*ṭur*$_4$*-da-nim* le.e. ^{17}*a-Ší-ik-ri-il*$_5$*-kà* ^{18}*qí-bi*$_4$*-ma a-pu-tum* ^{19}*ma-ma-an*

$^{1-5}$Thus (say) Aššur-lamassī and Aššur-rabi: say to Ab-šalim and Šikri-elka.

$^{5-6}$We are fine; do not worry. $^{7-9}$Urgent! Watch over the house. $^{10-12}$If Ilī-taklāku arrived from Tim<il>kiya, $^{12-14}$or if any of the servants arrived, $^{15-16}$you should not hinder (him); send (him) here.

$^{17-19}$Say to Šikri-elka. Urgent! Whoever [...]

Bibliography: Text published in copy by Stephens as BIN 6, 5; translated by Michel (2001a, no. 337). Lines 7–9 cited by Michel (1997b, 287).

Comments: Šikri-elka (written Šakri-elka in the previous text, **154**) is the servant of Ab-šalim and lives with her at Kaneš. This letter must have contained a second page that is lost.

Farming Activities of Anatolian Women

Letters sent by Assyrians to their Anatolian wives, along with contracts, permit the reconstruction of certain activities of these women at Kaneš. Unlike the women at Aššur, who were mostly concerned about how their textile production would fare on the international market, the Anatolian women at Kaneš never even mention any weaving activities, but textiles tools have been found in their houses.[55] Among their day-to-day tasks was agriculture, something unattested for women at Aššur, who bought at the market grain and meat needed to feed their children and their household.

The letters sent by Aššur-nādā to his wife Šišahšušar, for instance, refer periodically to fieldwork.[56] She was supposed to supervise the purchase of good quality cattle and collect fodder to feed them (**319**), then prepare them for plowing (**157**). She was also in contact with local peasants, who delivered to her large quantities of grain (**132**). She bought straw, wood, reeds, and various utensils for the house and for the fieldwork. Likewise, Kunnaniya got instructions from her husband, Aššur-mūtappil, about raising pigs, which she was responsible for (**158**).

Anatolian women raised a few cattle and pigs (**161**), the latter probably in their back courtyards. Sheep are not mentioned. The stock was fed on bran and barley; pigs were fed to fatten them (**158**). Women could use the leftovers from their daily beer production, especially the dregs after the wort had been filtered. This was not suitable for human consumption but was an excellent dietary supplement for domestic animals.[57]

Livestock could be bought by the head or in lots (**161**). The sale contract **159** records the purchase by an Anatolian merchant of a number of animals from an Anatolian couple. It was drawn up in the presence of several witnesses who sealed it, among whom was Wašhupa, chief of the

55. Veenhof 1972, 103–23; Michel 2006b.
56. For Šišahšušar, see Michel 2001a, 476–80; Larsen 2002, xxix.
57. Michel 2009d, with previous bibliography.

market. At the market, goods both local and from other places in Anatolia were exchanged, including slaves, livestock, textiles, foods, and metals.

The involvement of Anatolian women in agriculture and husbandry explains why they seldom traveled, unlike the Assyrian wives of merchants who came to live at Kaneš, who tended to go with their husbands on business trips in Asia Minor.[58] A few Assyrian women seem to have owned or managed an ox, used to draw a wagon (**160**).

---

157. Preparing Oxen for Plowing

Obv. ^{1}*a-na A-lá-hi-im* ^{2}*E-me-me ù Ší-ša-ah-/šu-šar* ^{3}*qí-bi-ma* ^{4}⅓ *ma-na* 1 gín kù-babbar ^{5}*ku-nu-ki-a Puzur*$_4$*-A-šùr* ^{6}*na-áš-a-ku-nu-tí* ^{7}*e-ṣí* : *ù qá-nu-e* ^{8}*tí-ša-a-ma ša* gu$_4^{hi-/a}$ ^{9}*ša-da-dim* ^{10}*li-iš-du-du-nim* lo.e. ^{11}*ša a-ma-kam-ma* (erased sign) ^{12}*ša ma-zi-re-e* rev. ^{13}*ma-lá-hi ù ha-ba-/ša-tim* ^{14}*ša-mì* ^{15}*a-pu-tum mì-ma* ^{16}*šu-mì-šu lu er-sú-ma* ^{17}*i-na e-ra-bi*$_4$*-a-ma* ^{18}*lu-ra-ṭí-ib šu-ma* ^{19}túg^{hi-a} *ša Šu-Sú-en*$_6$ ^{20}*ù i-a-tí iš-tù* ^{21}*Ur-šu ub-lu-nim* ^{22}*a-ma-kam-ma dí-na-ma* ^{23}*ší-im-šu-nu zu-za* u.e. ^{24}*a-ni-um* : *a-na-kam* ^{25}*i-ta-an-ki-iš* ^{26}*šu-ma* le.e. ^{27}*Ku-du-bi*$_4$*-iš* : kù-babbar *mì-ma* ^{28}*e-ri-iš dí-na-šu-um*

$^{1-3}$Say to Ali-ahum, Ememe, and Šišahšušar: (thus says Aššur-nādā).

$^{4-6}$Puzur-Aššur is bringing to you ⅓ mina, 1 shekel of silver under my seal. $^{7-10}$Buy wood and reed, and let the oxen haul here as much as they can (in a wagon). $^{11-14}$Buy whatever *mazīrum*-tin, *malāhum*, and *habašātum* (utensils) are available. $^{15-18}$Urgent! Make certain that everything is ready so that when I arrive, I can proceed immediately. $^{18-21}$If they bring the textiles belonging to Šu-Suen and myself from Uršu, $^{22-23}$sell them there and divide the proceeds; $^{24-25}$(all) this was set aside here. $^{26-28}$If Kudubiš asks for any silver, give him (some).

Bibliography: Text published in copy by Veenhof as VS 26, 20; edited by Larsen (2002, no. 58).

Comments: The author of the letter is presumably Aššur-nādā; see Larsen 2002, 83.

The oxen are used here to haul heavy and large materials, wood and reeds, perhaps to repair the house.

---

58. See chapter 1, texts **26–27**.

Lines 12–13: the word *mazīrum* corresponds to a quality of tin, while *malāhum* and *habaštum* are household utensils; they are mentioned together with bowls in BIN 4, 118.

---

158. Pig Breeding

Obv. ^{1}*um-ma A-šur-mu-ta-p*[*í*]*-il*$_5$ ^{2}*a-na Kà-ru-nu-wa ù* ^{3}*Ku-na-ni-a qí-bi*$_4$*-ma* 1 *pá-na-ra-/am* ^{4}*iš-tù Za-al-*[*p*]*á* : *ub-lu-ni-/ki-im* ^{5}2 *pá-ni-ri* 5[+ x *ma*]*-na* síg^{hi-a} ^{6}1 túg *tí-sá-ba-a*[*m Šu-A*]*-šur ub-lá-ki-/im* ^{7}3 gín kù-bab[bar 1 *pá-na-r*]*a-am* ^{8}*A-šur-e-n*[*a-am ub-lá*]*-ki-im* ^{9}2 *pá-ni-*[*ri A-šur-mu*]*-ta-pì-il*$_5$ ^{10}*ub-lá-k*[*i-im* 1 *pá*]*-na-ra-am* ^{11}*Ha-nu a-hu-u*[*m ša A*]*r-ší-ah* ^{12}[*na*]*-pá-hi-im* : *ub-lá-ki-im* ^{13}[2 *p*]*á-ni-ri* : 5 *sí-sí-né-e* ^{14}[x *m*]*a-na* síg^{hi-a} 1 túg ^{15}[*tí-sá*]*-ba-am* 1 túg *ší-it-r*[*i*]*-a* lo.e. ^{16}[*a-š*]*é-ni-šu* : *ma-áš-ku-nam* ^{17}[*ša ṣú*]*-ba-tí-im* 1 *ší-it-ra-am* rev. ^{18}[*r*]*i-ik-sú* 1 *ma-na* 10 gín ^{19}[kù]-ki 1 *mu-ša-lam* ^{20}10 silà ì-giš *ša ša-m*[*a-š*]*a-me* ^{21}1½ silà *re-eš*$_{15}$*-tám ar-za-la-am* ^{22}*mì-ma a-nim* : *ṣú-ha-ru ub-lu-ni-ki-/im* ^{23}1 *pá-na-ra-am* 1 *sí-sí-nam* ^{24}*A-al-*du$_{10}$ dumu *Hu-ra-ṣí* ^{25}*ub-lá-ki-im* 1 *pá-na-ra-am* ^{26}*Ni-mar-Ištar* dumu *Ba-lá* ^{27}1 *pá-na-ra-am* 2 *sí-sí-né* ^{28}*kà-ṣa-ar A-zu-ta-a* dumu *E-me-/me* ^{29}*ub-lá-ki-im* ^{30}1 túg$^{!}$ *ša lu-bu-ší-im* ^{31}*ša ṣú-ùh-ri-im* u.e. ^{32}*Kà-ru-nu-wa* : *a-hu-*[*um ša*] ^{33}*A-li-li* ^{34}*ub-lá-k*[*i-im*] le.e. ^{35}*šu-ma hu-zi-ru* : *lá i-kà-b*[*i*$_4$*-ru*] ^{36}*a-ší-mì-im* : *dí-na-šu-nu šu-ma* ^{37}<*i*>*-kà-bi*$_4$*-ru* : *li-zi-zu*

$^{1-3}$Thus (says) Aššur-mūtappil: say to Karunuwa and Kunnaniya.

$^{3-4}$They are bringing you (fem.) 1 *pannurum* from Zal[p]a. $^{5-6}$[Šu-A]ššur is bringing you 2 *pannurum*, 5 [+ x mi]nas of wool, and 1 *tisābum*-textile. $^{7-8}$Aššur-en[nam has bro]ught you 3 shekels of silv[er (and) 1 *pannur*]*um*. $^{9-10}$[Aššur-mū]tappil is bringing you 2 *panna*[*rum*]. $^{10-12}$Hanu, the brothe[r of A]ršiah, [the met]alworker is bringing you [1 *pa*]*nnarum*.

$^{13-15}$[2 *p*]*annarum*, 5 brooms, [x m]inas of wool, 1 [*tisā*]*bum*-textile, 1 shawl belonging to me, $^{16-19}$[a do]uble *maškunum* [for a te]xtile, 1 shawl, 1 package of 1 mina, 10 shekels of [go]ld, 1 mirror, $^{20-21}$10 silas of sesame oil, 1½ sila of prime oil, 1 *arzallum*-implement; ^{22}all this, the employees are bringing you.

$^{23-25}$Āl-ṭāb, son of Huraṣi, brought you 1 *pannurum* (and) 1 broom. $^{25-26}$Nimar-Ištar, son of Bala, (brought you) 1 *pannurum*. $^{27-29}$The shipper of Azutaya, son of Ememe, brought you 1 *pannurum* (and) 2 brooms.

[30-34]Karunuwa, the broth[er of] Alili, brou[ght you] 1 textile as garment for a child.

[35-37]If the pigs do not become fat, offer them for sale, (but) if they become fat, let them stay.

Bibliography: Text published in copy by Stephens as BIN 6, 84.

Comments: Aššur-mūtappil details for his Anatolian wife the list of objects and foodstuffs he has sent. He gives her advice about the pigs she is breeding. Anatolian women had a few pigs in their courtyard for the consumption of the family (Michel 2006d). For the lady Kunnaniya, see Michel 1997e and chapter 6 of this book, pp. 444–59.

Lines 13, 23: the brooms, *sissinum*, are made of date spadices; see Sturm 1999.

Line 15: the *tisābum* is a native Anatolian textile product; see Michel and Veenhof 2010, 245.

Line 16: the *maškunum* is a textile used as a kind of cover or pouch; see Michel and Veenhof 2010, 236.

Lines 5, 7, 9–10, 13, 23, 25, 27: for *pannurum*, see the comments on text **136**.

---

159. Selling Pigs

Envelope

Obv. [1]kišib *Ku-lá* kišib *Šál-ku-a-ta* [2]kišib *Wa-áš-hu-ba* gal *ma-/hi-ri* [3](seal) [4]kišib *Ma-nu-kà-a* kišib *Du-/du* [5]kišib *Pé-er-wa* kišib *Mu-lá* [6]*a-ší-tí-šu hu-zi-ri* [7]*ša Pè-er-wa ù Mu-lá* [8]*a-ša-sú a-na* [9](seal) [10]*E-ni-ìš-ru i-dí-nu-ni* [11]kù-babbar *ší-im* [12](seal) [13]*hu-zi-ri-šu-nu* [14]*Pé-er-wa ù Mu-lá* [15]*a-ša-sú ša-bu-ú* [16](seal) [17]*a-na šu-mì hu-zí-ri ù ší-mì-šu* [18]*Pé-er-wa ù Mu-lá* [19]*a-ša-sú a-na E-ni-ìš-ru lá i-tù-/ru* [20]*šu-ma i-tù-ru* [21]1 *ma-na* kù-babbar *a-na* [22](seal) [23]*E-ni-ìš-ru i-ša-q*[*ú*]*-lu* [24](seal)

[1-5]Seal of Kulā; seal of Šalkuata; seal of Wašhuba, the chief of the market; seal of Manukaya; seal of Dudu; seal of Per(u)wa; seal of Mula, his *aššutum*-wife.

[6-10]As the pigs that Per(u)wa and Mula, his wife, sold to Eniš(a)ru, [11-15]Per(u)wa and Mula, his wife, have been satisfied with the silver, price of their pigs. [17-19]Concerning the pigs and their price, Per(u)wa and Mula,

his wife, shall not raise a claim against Eniš(a)ru. [20–23]If they raise a claim, they shall pay 1 mina of silver to Eniš(a)ru.

Bibliography: Tablet published in copy by Smith and Wiseman as CCT 5, 26a. Text edited by Kienast (1984, no. 25); lines 6–18 cited by Michel (2006d, 172 n. 12).

Comments: According to this contract, an Anatolian couple sold their pigs to a wealthy Anatolian merchant, Eniš(a)ru, whose business has been studied by Veenhof (1978). The number of pigs and their price is not specified.

---

160. Assyrians Owing Oxen

Obv. [1]*um-ma* [*Bu-za-zu-ma*] [2]*a-na Lá-ma-ša* : *qí-bi-ma* [3]*i-ša-am-ší* : *ṭup-pá-am* [4]*ú-lá-pí-ta-ki-ni* [5]*ku-ṣú*[!](BA)*-um* : *i-pá-ṭá-ar-ma* [6]*a-na* 10 *u$_4$-me-e ú-ṣí-a-am* [7]*ú-ṭá-tám lu ša Tár-ma-na* [8]*lu ša Ha-tí-a-ar* [9]*lu ša Tù-ru-ùh-na* [10]*ma-lá* : *i-dí-nu-ni-ki-ni* [11]*iš-tí* : *Ku-ku-zi úz-ni* rev. [12]*pè-tí* : *ù a-na ší-tí* [13]*ú-ṭí-tim* : *ih-dí-ma* [14]*lá-ma a-li-kà-ni* [15]*ša-dí-ni-šu-nu* : *al-pu* [16]*lá i-re-qú* [17]*Ša-ak-ri-ú-ma-an* [18]*qá-nu-e* : *li-iz-bi$_4$-lam* [19]*šu-ma* kù-babbar 5 gín [20]*ta-ha-ší-hi* : *ú-ul* [21]*Ku-lu-ma-a* : *ú-ul* [22]*Be-lá-num* : *iš-té-en$_6$* [23]*i-*[*na ba-ri-šu-nu*] le.e. [24]*li-dí-na-ki-im* [25]*šu-ma* : *am-tám* : *ša Zi-zi-lim* [26]*ta-ha-ší-hi* : *šu-up-ri-im*

[1–2]Thus (says) [Buzāzu]: say to Lamaša.

[3–5]The very day I am writing this tablet for you, winter is about to end, and [6]I will leave within 10 days. [7–12]Inform me via Kukuzi how much grain, either from Tarmana, Hatī'ar, or Turuhna, they gave you. [12–15]And, take care, before my arrival, to collect the balance of the grain from them.

[15–18]The oxen must not be idle; let Šakriuman bring me reeds.

[19–24]If you need some silver, up to five shekels, either Kulumaya or Bēlānum, one of [them], should give (it) to you. [25–26]If you need a maid from Zizum, (then) write to me.

Bibliography: Text published in copy by Smith as CCT 3, 48b; translated by Michel (2001a, no. 364).

Comments: The author of this letter is presumably the Buzāzu who also sent **134**, **162**, CCT 6, 3b, and TC 3, 98, to Lamaša, his Assyrian wife living in Kaneš. She is, perhaps, the owner of oxen to be used to haul a wagon-load of reeds. Many of the people mentioned in this letter are Anatolians.

---

161. Instructions about Oxen before a Departure

Obv. ^{1}*um-ma Bu-za-zu-ma a-na* ^{2}*Lá-ma-ša qí-bi*$_4$*-ma* ^{3}*ṣú-ha-re-e : a-na N*[*i*$^{!}$*-ih*]*-ri-a* ^{4}*áš-ta-pá-ar a-dí* 5 *u*$_4$*-me-e* ^{5}*i-ma-qú-tù*$^{!}$*-ni-ma* anše$^{\text{hi-a}}$ ^{6}2 *ú-ul* 3 *a-na* [*ṣ*]*é-ri-ki* ^{7}*ú-šé-ru-ú-ni-ki-im* ^{8}*a-mì-ša-am e-ra-bi*$_4$: *lá-šu* ^{9}*ú-ṭù-up-tí ú ma-lá* ^{10}*i-na ṭup-pì-im a-lá-pá-ta-/ki-ni* ^{11}*i-pá-ni-ki* : *tù-šé-ṣa-am* ^{12}gu$_4^{\text{hi-a}}$ *lu ša-al*$^{!}$(A)*-mu-tim* ^{13}*lu ma-ar-ṣú-tim ma-lá* ^{14}*té-er-tí-a ša ṣú-ha-ri* ^{15}*ú-bu-lu-ni-ki-ni* rev. ^{16}*i-nu-mì-šu-ma ep-ší-i* ^{17}*a-dí* 10 *u*$_4$*-me-e lá ta-ha-dá-/*[*r*]*i* ^{18}*lu sú-a-tim lu* ^{19}*ta-as-kà-ri-ni* ^{20}*kà-lá-šu-nu lu it-qú-/ra-<tim>* ^{21}*ša sí-pá-ri-im* ^{22}*lu ša a-šar I-na-a* ^{23}*i-ba-ší-ú er-ší-ma* ^{24}*i-pá-ni-ki bi*$_4$*-lim* ^{25}*ša-hi-ra-tum lu* sig$_5$ ^{26}[*e*]*-ru-ma e-ru-i-a* ^{27}*lu ma-ṭí-a-tim* ^{28}[*a*$^{?}$]*-ha-ra-nim ma-dí-iš* le.e. ^{29}[x]*-nu-sú a-pu-tum mì-ma* ^{30}[*ú*]*-nu-tim lu* [*r*]*a-ku-sà* anše ^{31}*a-dí a-ša-pá-<ra>-ni lu er-sú-a*

$^{1-2}$Thus (says) Buzāzu: say to Lamaša.

$^{3-5}$I just sent the servants to N[ih]riya. They will arrive within 5 days, $^{5-7}$and they will lead 2 or 3 donkeys to you. ^{8}I have not planned to go over there. $^{9-11}$You will move out the furniture and whatever else I will write down for you on a tablet before your departure. $^{12-16}$(Concerning) the oxen, whether sound or sick, act immediately according to my instructions that my servants will bring you. ^{17}Do not delay this over 10 days!

$^{18-23}$Ask the *sûm*-stones, boxwood, all that are available, or bronze ladles, or whatever is with Innaya, and ^{24}bring everything here yourself. ^{25}The shoe straps must be of good quality, $^{26-27}$*the copper as well because my own copper* is really bad! $^{28-29}$For the caravan, (there is) a lot of [...]! $^{29-30}$Urgent! All the merchandise must be packed, (and) $^{30-31}$when I will write, the donkey must be ready!

Bibliography: Text published in copy by Smith as CCT 4, 36b–37a; edited by Michel (1991, no. 252); translated by Michel (2001a, no. 365).

Comments: Lamaša receives instructions in Kaneš concerning oxen, then various objects that she has to bring personally to her husband, Buzāzu. Since she is going to leave her home for a while, she might have to entrust it to someone or to sell the oxen.

Line 25: the *šahirum* might be a part of a shoe or sandal; it is translated here as "shoe straps." The reading of line 26 is not certain.

Line 31: the verbal form is feminine, but it should be masculine, the subject being the donkey(s).

4
Businesswomen

A gendered division of labor was already observed in the ancient world: women confined their work within the house and men without (Xenophon, *Oec.* 7). Since the mid-nineteenth century, a job has been understood to mean a specific activity for which one is compensated; using this definition, Assyrian women had jobs for which they were paid and which they performed at home.[1] In fact, women of Aššur, above and beyond their purely domestic activities, took part in long-distance trade with Asia Minor. They sustained this commerce by making textiles for export and were paid for what they did. This activity took place in the home, in the private sector, and all the women of the household seem to have taken part, including girls and slave women.[2]

Even if the total production of all the women of a wealthy household might amount to twenty-five pieces of fine cloth each year, the aggregate would be insufficient to sustain the Assyrian textile trade in Anatolia, which ran to a few thousands of textiles a year.[3] This would account for the substantial volume of textiles, called "Akkadian," purchased at Aššur from Babylonian merchants to round out the textile shipments to Kaneš. There is no documentation for any textile production centralized in palace or temple workshops, as known, for example, in Mari, on the Middle Euphrates, so there seems little likelihood of institutional production.[4] A not inconsequential portion of the thousands of textiles sold yearly by Assyrians in Anatolia was, therefore, the output of Assyrian women active

1. Lion and Michel 2016, 1–2.

2. Veenhof 1972; Michel 2006b, 2016a; Michel and Veenhof 2010.

3. Michel 2016c.

4. Dercksen (2004a, 15–17) suggests the existence of such an institutional textile production.

in all phases of production, from buying the wool in places nearby the city to sending the finished cloth by transporters whom they paid or to whom they entrusted their textiles on favorable terms as a "good-faith consignment loan" (*tadmiqtum*, i.e., goods entrusted to someone to sell, with the obligation to give the yield to the owner).

Using the compensation they received as capital, women took part in all sorts of financial transactions, purchasing slaves and real estate, loaning money at interest, investing in various commercial undertakings long or short term, buying goods for export, and so on.

Although financially independent of their husbands, Assyrian wives routinely acted as their representatives to their associates and to the Assyrian authorities. Their husbands, for their part, represented them in certain transactions in Anatolia, selling their textiles and goods, and acting in their interest to secure what was due them. The social position and reputation of Assyrian men and women were determined by the success of the family business (*bēt abini*, "our father's house"), the profile of which might be hard to define: there was no clear demarcation between family connections and the commercial network.[5] Assyrian women enjoyed important social status and showed it by having fine, capacious homes built for themselves (**147**).

Since they were generally at home, wives at Aššur and Kaneš were expected to safeguard the goods kept there, especially merchandise and archives, which would include debt notes and various documents of legal import. These archives were kept in strong boxes and sealed rooms. The documents belonged to their husbands and to different members of the family or associates, though they could have their own as well. Because of the nature of their business activities, women would need to execute certain kinds of documents. They drew up contracts and carried on a sometimes-voluminous correspondence with family members and other merchants. They could seal goods and documents, and some of them were capable of writing their own tablets.

Weaving as a Remunerative Profession

On the domestic front, all women took part in the production of textiles. Unfortunately, as with other activities of daily life, we have little docu-

5. Larsen 2007, and above, in the introduction.

mentation for the organization of private textile production. The wives of Assyrian merchants and the other women of the household, including children and slave women, wove the cloth used to clothe the family, but the largest part of their production went for export to Cappadocia.[6] Spinning and weaving were the main activities of all the household women, including girls, elderly women, and female slaves, perhaps in all a dozen weavers in wealthy households.

Although the women's correspondence refers to the production of cloth at Aššur, technical details are seldom given and are normally confined to the amount of wool used to produce a specific textile, the finishing procedures after weaving, and the quality of the resulting cloth (**162**).[7] Finishing of cloth could be done by a professional (**167**). Excavations of houses at Kaneš have yielded numerous spindle whorls for spinning or weights to hold the threads for vertical looms.[8]

The expertise of Assyrian women was highly valued. They could weave various kinds of cloth and could imitate the techniques and fashions used in other cities.[9] Since their work was commercial in nature, they were judged by the skill of their weaving. The merchants in the market places of central Anatolia knew how to evaluate the quality of the cloth they received and, based on supply and demand, advised on production techniques, including the quality and amount of the wool used, the fineness of the weave, and its appearance and size (**162**, **163**, **164**). The recommended dimensions, 4 by 4.5 m, probably corresponded to one textile made of two or three sewn pieces. Merchant accounts dealing with the transport of textiles to Anatolia indicate that each piece weighed about 5 minas (2.5 kg), but letters show that it could be plus or minus one mina of wool. Other sources indicate that a piece of cloth exported to Anatolia 1.5 m long and 3 or 4 m wide weighed between 2 and 3 kg.[10]

---

6. For textile production in Old Assyrian sources, see Veenhof 1972; Günbattı 1992; Michel 2006b, 2014c, 2016c; Michel and Veenhof 2010; Lassen 2010a, 2010b.

7. See for looms and weaving techniques in the Ancient Near East, Breniquet 2008; Michel and Nosch 2010; Breniquet and Michel 2014.

8. Kulakoğlu and Kangal 2010, 236–38, nos. 164–83; Lassen 2013.

9. There are more than a dozen different names for textiles produced by Assyrian women; see Veenhof 1972, 123; Michel and Veenhof 2010, 231–46.

10. Veenhof 1972, 89–97; Michel and Veenhof 2010, 255–56. The Assyrian textile, measuring 4 by 4.5 m, would presumably not be woven in one piece, but in at least two or three pieces, which were then sewn together. Note that there are other dimensions

The archives found at Kaneš give little information about how the wives at Aššur got the wool to make their cloth or where this raw material came from. They bought the wool for money and grain from Suhûm nomads who came to pluck their sheep near the city.[11] The wool called *šurbu'itum*, coming from animals raised in the Hamrin basin, was particularly valued for the weaving of the textiles called *kutānum*, the most common type among those exported to the West.[12] In the letters they sent to Kaneš, women referred to shortages that left them unable to provide cloth for export, for want of wool; they asked their correspondents at Kaneš to send them some from Anatolia (**163**, **147**, **259**). However, these were unusual requests and involved only small quantities. Owing to distance and the cost of transport, the quality of wool from southern Babylonia was especially esteemed. The reputation of Babylonian cloths was based on their weaves, no doubt enhanced by the excellence of their wool.[13] Important wool markets to the southeast of Kaneš, between the Balih and the Anti-Taurus, account for the small quantities of wool sent from Asia Minor to Aššur.[14]

After buying raw wool, women had to clean and prepare it for spinning. According to an Ur III text, a craftsperson would only prepare for spinning about 125 grams of wool a day.[15] To obtain the five minas neces-

---

given for other types of textiles. For example, a thin textile could measure 2 by 5 m, according to AKT 6c, 533:33–34.

11. Michel 2014d, 232–36. At the beginning of the second millennium BCE, sheep were plucked rather than shorn. In a letter sent to the king of Mari, an official proposed that the plucking of the sheep take place, not in Aššur as it used to be, but in the area where the herds were grazing, in Suhûm, south of Mari. This would then force the inhabitants of Aššur to go there to buy the wool they needed to produce their textiles; see Charpin and Durand 1997, texts no. 4 and 5. Usually, wool was imported directly to Aššur on the hoof, the herds being driven close to the town to be plucked. This seasonal movement was documented because it became impossible due to the war between Mari and Ešnunna.

12. Dercksen 2004a, 16 n. 32; Michel and Veenhof 2010, 221.

13. Mukannišum's correspondence found in Mari shows that Babylonian wool was needed to produce luxury textiles; see Durand 1997, texts no. 134 and 136.

14. Southeast of Kaneš, wool was available in the following towns: Balihum, near the sources of the Balih river; Hahhum, north-east of Balihum; Timilkiya, near the modern city of Pazarcık; Mama, south of Timilkiya, in the Gaziantep area; and at Hurrama, in the area of Göksün. The town of Luhusaddiya, between Elbistan and Pazarcık, was an important textile production center; numerous sheep herds were plucked there. See Michel 2006b; Michel and Veenhof 2010; Lassen 2010b, 167–70; 2014.

15. Waetzoldt 1972, no. 32, rev. 1.6–14; and Waetzoldt 2010, 207.

sary for a textile, it would have taken twenty days. Experiments carried out at the Centre for Textile Research (Copenhagen) have shown that it is possible to spin some 35 to 50 m of thread per hour with archaeological tools.[16] To weave a square meter of fabric, one needs some 2 km of thread, plus 2 to 5 percent for the setting of the loom. Thus, a person had to spin for five days (5 × 8 hours) to obtain 2 km of thread. The Assyrian textiles measuring 4 by 4.5 m (18 sq. m) required 36 km of thread for the weaving, and some three months of spinning for a single woman. The setting of the two or three looms required some 1.8 km, and four more days of work.

Again according to the Centre for Textile Research's hands-on experiments, one person is able to weave about 50 cm per day of work; depending, naturally, on the width of the loom.[17] If we suppose that the fabric was woven in two strips of 2 m each, which were then sewn together, two women were necessary to set up the two looms during some four days, and two women would complete the textile in ten days. If we suppose that the fabric was woven in three strips of 1.35 m each, two women were necessary to set up the three looms during some six days, and three women would complete the textile in nine days.[18]

Tasks/number of days of work for one woman	In two strips	In three strips
Cleaning and combing	20	20
Spinning	94	96
Setting of the loom(s)	8	12
Weaving	20	27
Total of working days/woman	142 [4.75 months]	155 [5.2 months]
Textiles/woman/year	2.5	2.33

16. Andersson Strand 2012, 34. This section is a summary of Michel 2016c.

17. Andersson Strand 2012, 35.

18. As a matter of comparison, Firth and Nosch 2012 have made an estimate for the production of an Ur III ^{túg}guz-za fabric, measuring 3.5 by 3.5 m and weighing 2 kg, with the data of the text Waetzoldt 1972, no. 32, rev. 1.6–14: it amounted to 130 days including cleaning and combing. If we scale up to the size of a *kutānum*-textile, supposing a textile of a similar density, then this would become 192 days. For a different interpretation of the same Ur III text, see Andersson Strand and Cybulska 2013.

In the context of private production at Aššur linked to international trade, it seems probable that production ran throughout the year.[19] If this supposition is correct, a woman would have been able to weave at most two and a half textiles a year. A wealthy household could then have been able to produce a maximum of twenty-five textiles a year. Out of these, some five large pieces—corresponding to ten garments—would be necessary to clothe the household members. Thus, at most twenty textiles could be sent to be sold in Anatolia.

In such computations, each parameter is naturally based on assumptions, and we still lack a lot of data. The number of persons per household, and, moreover, the number of active women, is based primarily on archival and prosopographical studies of wealthy households in Aššur, documented by letters discovered in the houses of the male family members settled in Kaneš. Reconstructed family trees often lack some female members, and it is difficult to know the number of slaves per household. Another important parameter is the number of hours women spun and wove each day.[20] The size of the textiles may also be debated. The caravan accounts show that textiles to be exported had a regular weight of 2.5 kg, so commercialized textiles may have been of standard size. But those produced for internal consumption could have been smaller, and thus faster to produce. Last but not least, the density of a textile varies widely; the proposed data are based on an average of the results of the experiments conducted by the Centre for Textile Research. According to the Old Assyrian letters, it was possible to add one mina of wool per textile without

19. Traditionally, weaving is considered a seasonal activity; Breniquet 2008. However, nowadays in Central Anatolian villages we find both situations, yearly or seasonal activity.

20. Visiting traditional handcraft villages in Jordan in March 2014 together with Eva Andersson Strand, I had the opportunity to interview a widow of Bani Hamida, mother of five children, who said that she weaves six hours per day. The next summer, visiting a traditional weaver in the village of Çavdar, east of Kayseri, she explained that, during wintertime, she used to start weaving at 8:00 in the morning and stop around midnight, thus more than twelve hours a day. I conducted similar interviews, together with Eva Andersson Strand, in Central Anatolian villages in 2014 and in 2018, thanks to the help of Fikri Kulakoğlu and the members of Kültepe excavation team. Women who weave on traditional looms and sell the product of their work—kilims and knotted carpets—to merchants from Kayseri, work frequently throughout the year, starting in the morning as soon as the children have left for school.

changing its size. So according to the type of the textile, the thickness of the thread varied, and the weaving was more or less dense.

Despite these uncertainties, the estimated number of textiles produced per household is realistic since it can be confirmed by the textile shipments made by Lamassī to her husband Pūšu-kēn. These can be summarized as follows:

Text	Shipments of textiles by Lamassī and names of transporters			
165	Kulumaya, 9 textiles	Iddin-Suen, 3 textiles		
166	Kulumaya, 9 textiles	Iddin-Suen, 3 textiles		
163	Done: Kulumaya, 3 *kamsum* + 6 *kutānum*	Done: Aššur-malik, 5 *kutānum*	Urani, 8 (before adding wool)	Ia-šar, (later on + ½ mina)
164		Done: Aššur-malik, 1 heavy + 1 *kamdum* + 3 *kutānum*		

The first three texts (**165**, **166**, **163**) deal with the same shipment transported by Kulumaya. In the first two letters, it is announced; according to the third letter, the shipment has been made. Texts **163** and **164** deal with the same shipment transported by Aššur-malik. The shipments of textiles alluded to in these texts were made in a limited period of time, presumably a caravan season; in all they concern twenty-five textiles sent by Lamassī to her husband. We do not know the origin of these textiles, but it is most probable that they were produced by her household.

The Aššur households' textile production exceeded their needs; the surplus was sent to Anatolia, thus contributing to the international trade. Women were not always able to balance the time needed to maintain their households, including making clothing for the family and servants, with that required for producing textiles for export. For this, they would justify themselves in letters but got back peevish replies from their husbands complaining about the small number or indifferent quality of the textiles they had received (**164**, **165**, **166**, **167**, **207**).

The sale of their textiles by relatives in Anatolia assured an income to these women of Aššur, who were paid by piecework in precious metals, gold or silver, or sometimes jewelry. Some letters give detailed accounts between husband and wife concerning the sale of textiles (**168**). Part of the payment they received for their textiles increased the personal capital of women. It is almost impossible to give an estimate of the percentage spent on food and household commodities and what they kept for themselves or reinvested in financial transactions (**128**, **168**, **169**, **170**). But it is possible to compute the income per garment.

Once the textiles were ready, the women sent them to Asia Minor. They could sometimes entrust them to men of their family who regularly traveled between Aššur and Kaneš, or they could work out arrangements with different transporters who agreed to transport small quantities (**163**, **165**, **166**, **168**, **169**). They could also turn over some textiles to a merchant as a *tadmiqtum*-loan. He would sell them in Asia Minor at a profit to himself (**165**), while they, on the other hand, were guaranteed the sale of their products, preferably at a good price.

Some letters give an indication of the amount of silver women hoped to receive or did receive for the textiles they sent (**170**: 20 shekels per textile; **171**: 17 shekels per textile; **14**: 10 shekels per textile). The standard *kutānum*-textile was sold for fifteen shekels at Kaneš. In Anatolia, the textiles had to go through customs with the local authorities, who often retained the finest of them, then stored them until they offered them for sale, in competition with cheaper, locally produced merchandise.[21] After taxes were deducted from the price of the textiles, women could hope to get back ten to twelve shekels a piece.[22]

From this price, one has to deduce the cost of the wool. A royal inscription of Šamšī-Adad (eighteenth century) indicates that for 1 shekel of silver, one could buy in Aššur 15 minas of (raw) wool. This corresponds to the price given by Mari archives for Upper Mesopotamia.[23] Taking into account that during the cleaning process, there could be a loss of 30 percent of the original wool, with 1 shekel of silver it might have been possible

21. Long-term storage and large quantities of textiles could be problematic, owing to possible moth damage; see Michel 1998b. Text VS 26, 9 (Michel 2001a, no. 199); Veenhof 2003c, 89–94.

22. An import tax corresponding to 5 percent of the textiles was levied by the palace, which could also impose a tithe of 10 percent. A transport tax on the silver proceeds of textiles was levied by the *kārum* authorities at the rate of 1/60, and an import tax by Aššur City Hall amounting to 4 percent of the precious metal.

23. Grayson 1987, A.0.39.1:59–72; Michel 2014d, 244–46.

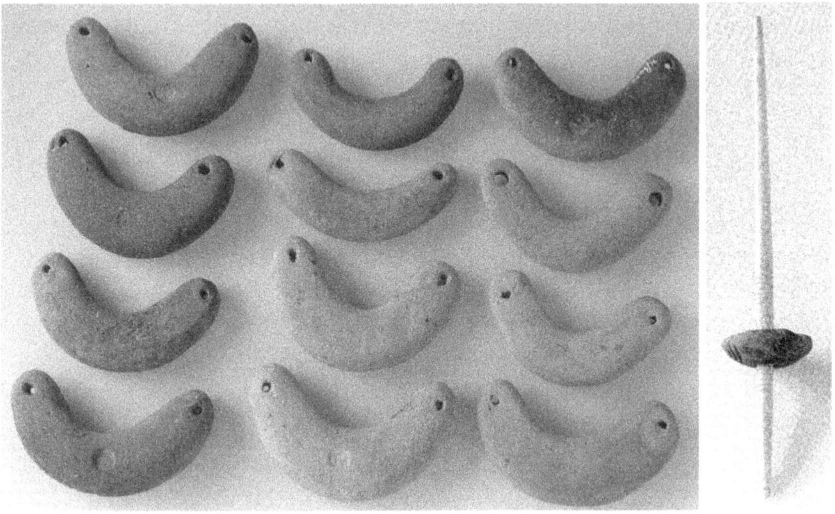

Fig. 11. Textile tools excavated at Kültepe: (left) crescent loom weights; (right) spindle with a spindle whorl. © Archaeological Mission of Kültepe.

to acquire about 10 minas of cleaned wool, which could be used to weave two textiles.[24]

With the income of one textile, corresponding to 10–12 shekels of silver, a woman could buy wool to produce 20 to 24 textiles. But usually, at most, a third of the sale price of a textile was invested in the purchase of wool to produce some 6 or 7 pieces (**171**).

According to these computations, a household producing yearly some 20 textiles sent for trade in Anatolia would receive between 3½ and 4 minas of silver per year as gross income, which corresponded to the price of a small house in Aššur.[25]

Estimation of the production of textiles per household and of the resulting income for Aššur women, even if it needs to be adjusted, is very important for evaluating the role of women in the economy of ancient Aššur. Regular shipping of textiles guaranteed them a steady income. Assyrian women took part in international trade, worked, and were paid for what they did.[26] A few texts from Late Bronze Age Aššur show that

24. According to an Ur III tablet, when the raw wool was very dirty, the losses in cleaning could go up even to 50 percent; see Waetzoldt 1972, no. 32, rev. 1.6–14.

25. Veenhof 2011.

26. Michel 2006b.

comparable for-profit business was carried on during the Middle Assyrian period as well.[27]

---

162. Technical Advice for Weaving and Finishing a Textile

Obv. [1]*um-ma Puzur*$_4$*-A-šur-ma* [2]*a-na Wa-qá-ar-tim qí-bi-ma* [3]1 *ma-na* kù-babbar *ni-is-ha-sú* [4]diri *ša-du-wa-sú ša-bu* [5]*ku-nu-ki-a A-šur-i-dí na-áš-a-ki-/im* [6]*ṣú-ba-tám qá-at-na-am* [7]*ša tù-šé-bi-li-ni* [8]*ša ki-ma šu-wa-tí ep-ší-ma* [9]*iš-tí A-šur-i-dí šé-bi*$_4$*-li-ma* [10]½ *ma-na* kù-babbar *lu-šé-bi*$_4$*-lá-ki-/im* [11]*ša ṣú-ba-tim pá-na-am* [12]*iš-té-na-ma li-im-šu-du* [13]*la i-qá-tù-pu-šu* [14]*šu-tù-šu lu ma-da-at* lo.e. [15]*i-ṣé-er pá-ni-im* [16]*ṣú-ba-tim ša tù-šé-bi*$_4$*-li-/ni* [17]*ša-áp-tám* 1 *ma-na*-ta rev. [18]*ra-dí-i-ma lu qá-at-nu* [19]*pá-na-am ša-ni-a-am* [20]*i-li-la li-im-šu-du-šu* [21]*šu-ma ša-ar-tám i-ta-áš-ú* [22]*ki-ma ku-ta-nim li-iq-tù-/pu-šu* [23]*A-ba-ar-ni-a-am*! [24]*ša tù-šé-bi-li-ni* [25]*la ta-tù-ri-ma ša ki-ma* [26]*a-mì-im la tù-šé-bi*$_4$*-li-im* [27]*šu-ma té-pí-ší ša ki-ma* [28]*a-ma-kam al-ta-áb-šu*! *ep-ší* [29]*šu-ma ṣú-ba-tí qá-at-nu-tim* [30]*la ta-kà-ší-dí a-ša-me-ma* [31]*a-ma-kam a-ší-mì-im* u.e. [32]*ma-du ša-mì-ma* [33]*šé-bi-li-im ga-am*!*-ra-am*! [34]*ṣú-ba-ta-am*! le.e. [35]*ša té-pí-ší-ni tí-šé i-na-mì-tim* [36]*lu ú-ru-uk-šu ša-ma-né* [37]*i-na a-mì-tim lu ru-pu-šu*

[1–2]Thus (says) Puzur-Aššur: say to Waqqurtum.

[3–5]1 mina of silver—its import tax added, its transport fee paid—Aššur-idī brings you under my seal. [6–7]The thin textile you sent me, [8–9]make (more) like it and send (them) to me with Aššur-idī, and [10]I will send you ½ mina of silver (apiece). [11–13]They should *strike* one side of the textile, and not *pluck* it. [14]Its warp should be close. [15–18]Process per piece 1 mina more wool than you used for the previous textile you sent me, but they must remain thin! [19–20]Let them *strike* its second side only slightly. [21–22]If it is still hairy, they should pluck it like a *kutānum*. [23–26]As for the Abarnian-textile you sent me, you must not send me another one like that again. [27–28]If you make (one), make (it) like the one I wore there. [29–33]If you cannot (make) thin textiles, I hear that there are plenty for sale over there. Buy (them) and send them to me! [33–37]A finished textile that you make must be 9 cubits long and 8 cubits wide.

---

27. Postgate 2014.

Bibliography: Text published in copy by Lewy as TC 3, 17; edited by Veenhof (1972, 103–9); Michel (2001a, no. 318); Michel and Veenhof (2010, 250–52).

Comments: Puzur-Aššur, who is in the market in Kaneš and knows what kinds of textiles are appreciated, gives technical advice to Waqqurtum to improve her textile production. This advice is not totally clear and has been interpreted in different ways.

Lines 12, 20: it does not seem possible to translate *mašādum* by "to full" since it applies to only one side of the textile, not both.

Lines 13, 22: the verb *qatāpum* means here "to create a smooth, flat surface that is not hairy" (Michel and Veenhof 2010, 252).

The writer gives here the size of a textile, 4 by 4.5 m, which is very wide and cannot be woven in one piece.

Puzur-Aššur ends by saying that, if Waqqurtum is unable to weave thin textiles, she will have to buy some (though her profits will be smaller).

---

163. Lack of Wool; Addition of Wool in Each Coupon

Obv. ^{1}*a-na Pu-šu-ke-en*$_6$ *qí-bi*$_4$*-ma* ^{2}*um-ma Lá-ma-sí-ma ta-áš-pu-ra-/am* ^{3}*um-ma a-ta-ma* 5 *ma-na*-ta ^{4}síg^{hi-a} : *A-hu-qar ù* ^{5}*I-a-šar* : *na-áš-ú-ni-ki-*<*im*> ^{6}*mì-ma* : *lá i-dí-nu-nim* ^{7}*um-ma I-a-šar-ma* : *a-na-ku-ma* ^{8}1 túg *e-pá-šum* 8 túg^{hi-a} ^{9}*Ú-ra-ni* : *na-áš-a-ku-um* ^{10}*ša* ½ *ma-na*-ta : *ú-ṣú-bu-ni* ^{11}ki *I-a-šar ú-šé-ba-lá-ku-*<*um*> ^{12}*ša Ú-ra-ni na-áš-a-ku-ni* lo.e. ^{13}*pá-ni-ú* : *lá-ma ta-áš-pu-/ra-ni* rev. ^{14}*e-pu*$^{!}$(EP)*-šu-nu* ^{15}*a-dí a-ma-kam* : *wa-áš-ba-tí-ni* ^{16}*i-na ba-áš-tí-kà* ^{17}*nu-*[x-x]*-ni* : *li-iš-bi*$_4$*-ú* ^{18}*i-nu-mì* : *ki-sà-am* ^{19}*tù-šé-ba-lá-ni* : síg^{hi-a} ^{20}*šu-uk-na*[*m*] *ṣú-ha-*[*a*]*r-tum*$_8$ ^{21}*ir-tí-bi*$_4$: *ku-ta-bi*$_4$*-it-ma* ^{22}*al-kam-ma* : *a-na sú-un* ^{23}^{d}*A-šùr* : *šu-ku-ší* ^{24}3 túg *kam-sú-tim* 6 túg *ku-ta-nu* ^{25}*Ku-lu-ma-a* : *ub-lá-ku-*<*um*> u.e. ^{26}1 túg *kà-áb-tum* 5 túg *ku-ta-ni* ^{27}*A-šùr-ma-lik ub-lá-ku-*<*um*> le.e. ^{28}2 gín kù-babbar *ša* síg^{hi-a} *I-a-šar* ^{29}*i-dí-nam* 1 gín *A-hu-qar* ^{30}*i-dí-nam*

$^{1-2}$Say to Pūšu-kēn: thus (says) Lamassī.

$^{2-5}$You wrote me as follows: "Ahu-(wa)qar and Ia-šar are each bringing you 5 minas of wool." ^{6}(But) they gave me nothing! $^{7-8}$Ia-šar (said) as follows: "I will myself make 1 textile for him." $^{8-9}$Urani is bringing you 8 textiles. $^{10-11}$Those to which I am adding ½ mina (of wool) each, I will send you with Ia-šar. $^{11-14}$Those that Urani is bringing you, I made them earlier, before you wrote to me. [15–17]As long as you are staying there, out of respect for you, […] let them be satisfied. [18–20]When you send the purse, enclose some wool.

[20–23]The (little) girl has grown up. Be a man of honor, come here, and consecrate her to the god Aššur. [24–25]Kulumaya brought you 3 *kamsum*-textiles (and) 6 *kutānum*-textiles. [26–27]Aššur-malik brought you 1 heavy textile (and) 5 *kutānum*-textiles. [28–29]Ia-šar gave me 2 shekels of silver for wool. [29–30]Ahu-(wa)qar gave me 1 shekel.

Bibliography: Text published in copy by Clay as BIN 4, 9; translated by Michel (2001a, no. 304). Collated on photo.

Comments: Lamassī explains to her husband that, according to his instruction to her in the previous letter (**164**), she added ½ mina of wool in each textile. But she has some difficulties with the supply of wool and asks Pūšu-kēn to send some from Anatolia.

Lines 5, 11, 25, 27: the writer of this letter omits the mimmation ending of suffixed pronouns attached to verbal forms.

Lines 22–23: literally: "Put her in the lap of divine Aššur"; see the other texts mentioning the consecration of Ahaha, that is, the "little girl," to the god Aššur: **147**, **163**, and **166**.

---

164. Dispute about the Quality and Size of Produced Textiles

Obv. [1]*a-na Pu-šu-ke-en*$_6$ *qí-bi*$_4$*-ma* [2]*um-ma Lá-ma-sí-ma i-nu-mì* [3]*a-na-kam : wa-áš-ba-tí-ni : a-na* [4]*A-šùr-ma-lik* 1 túg *kà-áb-tám* [5]*a-dí-šum : ù i-na tù-wa-ri-/šu* [6]1 túg *kám-dam* 3 túg *ku-ta-ni* [7]*a-dí-šum : mì-šum :* túg^{hi-a} [8]*ša uš-té-[ni]-ba-lá-ku-ni* [9]*ub-lu-ni-ku-<um> [l]á ub-lu-ni-ku-um* [10]*té-er-ta-kà : li-li-kam-ma* [11]*li-bi*$_4$ *: lu i-dí* [12]*ù a-na šu-mì :* túg^{hi-a} [13]*ša ta-áš-pu-ra-ni* lo.e. [14]*um-ma a-ta-ma : ṣa-hu-ru* [15]*lá dam-qú lá i-pì-kà-ma* rev. [16]*ú-ṣa*$^!$*-he-er-šu : ù u*$_4$*-ma-am* [17]*ta-áš-pu-ra-am : um-ma a-ta-ma* [18]½ *ma-na-ta : a-na ṣú-ba-tí-ki* [19]*ra-dí-i : ur-ta-dí* [20]*ù Ú-ra-ni a-na ša ki-ma* [21]*ku-a-tí : a-šu-mì gu*$_5$*-šu-ri* [22]*ú-kà-i-nu : gam-ra-am* [23]*ma-dí-iš : iš-ta-kà-an* [24]*ú-lá ag-ra-am e-gu*$_5$*-ur* [25]*a-ba-áš-tí-kà ni-ta-ri-iš lá at-/kam* [26]*iš-am : lá ip-ra-am* [27]*ša* 10 gín urudu : *il*$_5$*-qé* [28]*ù gu*$_5$*-šu-ri* 8 *ša a-hi-kà il*$_5$*-qé* [29]urudu *ša a-na ma-ri ta-dí-nu-/šu-ni* u.e. [30]*mì-ma lá i-dí-nam* [31]1 túg *na-ma-šu-ha-am* [32]*ša A-ha-ha* le.e. [33]*a-na ṣú-ha-ri-im Ì-lí-ba-ni* [34]*na-ší-šum i-na wa-ar-ki-ú-/tim* [35]1 túg *ni-ib-ra-ra-am* [36]*ú-šé-ba-lá-šum*

[1-2]Say to Pūšu-kēn: thus (says) Lamassī.

[2-5]When you were still here, I gave to Aššur-malik 1 heavy textile, and [5-7]upon his return, I gave him 1 *kamdum*-textile (and) 3 *kutānum*-textiles. [7-11]What (happened)? Did he or did he not bring you the textiles that I had been sending to you? May a message from you arrive here so I will know!

[12-15]As for the textiles about which you wrote to me as follows: "They are (too) small, they are not good!" [15-16]Was it not at your own request that I reduced the size? [16-19]And now you write (again), saying as follows: "Process ½ mina (of wool) more in each of your textiles." Well, I have done so.

[20-24]As for Urani, he charged a high fee to your representatives for the roof beams that he put in place, but he has not hired a man. [25-27]We thus appeal to your sense of honor! The 10 shekels of copper he took correspond neither to [...] nor to a ration (for worker). [28]And as for the beams, he took 8 (beams) from your brother. [29-30]He gave me nothing of the copper that you gave him for the spades. [31-34]Ilī-bāni is bringing him 1 *namašuhhum*-textile from Ahaha for the servant, [34-36]and later, I will send him 1 *nibrārum*-textile.

Bibliography: Text published in copy by Clay as BIN 4, 10; translated by Michel (2001a, no. 303). Collated on photo.

Comments: Lamassī complains about her husband's reproaches concerning the quality and size of the textiles she made and sent. This suggests that profits on the sale of textiles could have been for the husband after having compensated his wife. She also wishes that her husband acknowledge the receipt of textiles she is sending.

Line 6: the *kamdum* textile is a *hapax legomenon*; it could be an error for a *kamsum*-textile, "a finished textile."

Line 31: the *namašuhhum*-textile is usually considered as an expensive piece of garment, but here it is for a boy.

Line 35: *nibrārum*-textiles were valuable textiles that could be made into garments; see Michel and Veenhof 2010, 237.

165. Criticism of the Quality of Textiles Sent

Obv. ^{1}*a-na Pu-šu-ke-en*$_6$ *qí-bi-ma* ^{2}*um-ma Lá-ma-sí-ma* 9 túg$^{hi\text{-}a}$ ^{3}*Ku-lu-ma-a na-áš-a-ku-um* ^{4}3 túg$^{hi\text{-}a}$ *I-dí-Sú-en*$_6$ *na-áš-a-kum* ^{5}*E-lá* túg$^{hi\text{-}a}$ *lá-qá-a-am lá i-mu-a* ^{6}*I-dí-Sú-en*$_6$ 5 túg$^{hi\text{-}a}$ *lá-qá-a-am* ^{7}*lá i-mu-a mì-šu ša ta-áš-ta-na-/pá-ra-ni* ^{8}*um-ma a-ta-ma* túg$^{hi\text{-}a}$ ^{9}*ša tù-uš-té-né-bi-li-ni* ^{10}*lá dam-qú* : *ma-nu-um* lo.e. ^{11}*za-ak-ru-um* rev. ^{12}*ša i-na* é$^{bé\text{-}tí}$*-kà* ^{13}*wa-áš-bu-ni-ma i-lá-ku-ma* ^{14}*ma-ah-ri-šu* : túg$^{hi\text{-}a}$ ^{15}*ú-nu-hu-ni* : *a-na-ku* ^{16}*a-šu-mì i-na ha-ra-an* ^{17}*ha-ra-ma* kù-babbar 10 gín ^{18}é$^{bé\text{-}tí}$*-kà li-im-qú-tám* ^{19}túg$^{hi\text{-}a}$ *uš-té-kà-ap-ma* ^{20}*e-pá-aš-ma* : *ú-šé-ba-lá-kum*

$^{1-2}$Say to Pūšu-kēn: thus (says) Lamassī.

$^{2-3}$Kulumaya is bringing you 9 textiles. ^{4}Iddin-Suen is bringing you 3 textiles. ^{5}Ela refused to accept textiles (for transport). $^{6-7}$Iddin-Suen refused to accept 5 textiles more (for transport). $^{7-10}$Why do you write to me every time as follows: "The textiles that you keep sending me are not good?" $^{10-15}$Who is this man who lives in your house and who is criticizing the textiles when they get to him? $^{15-18}$As for me, in order that from each caravan trip at least 10 shekels of silver accrue to your house, $^{19-20}$I try my best to make and send textiles to you!

Bibliography: Text published in copy by Stephens as BIN 6, 11; translated by Michel (2001a, no. 302; 2014b, 206). Collated on photo.

Comments: The number of textiles sent by Lamassī to her husband by two different transporters is the same as in the next letter **166**; she has trouble finding merchants who will agree to transport more pieces to Anatolia. Lamassī has received criticism from her husband about the quality of the textiles she previously sent; she is doing her best to maintain a regular production of good quality textiles.

166. Difficulties Weaving Textiles for Both the Household and the Trade

Obv. ^{1}*a-na Pu-šu-ke-en*$_6$ *qí-bi-ma* ^{2}*um-ma Lá-ma-sí-ma* 9 túg$^{hi\text{-}a}$ ^{3}*Ku-lu-ma-a na-áš-a-kum* 3 túg$^{hi\text{-}a}$ ^{4}*I-dí-Sú-en*$_6$ *na-áš-a-kum* ^{5}2 *sú-pá-ni ša* zabar *Dan-na-A-šùr* ^{6}*ub-lam* : 1 *sú-pá-nam ša* zabar ^{7}*ú it-qú-ra-am ša* zabar *I-a-šar* ^{8}*ub-lam* 2 *it-qú-ra-tim ša* zabar ^{9}*I-dí-Sú-en*$_6$ *ub-lam* : 1 *it-qú-ra-am* ^{10}*ša* zabar *A-hu-wa-qar ub-lam* [11]1 *sú-pá-nam ša* kù-babbar *I-ku-pí-a ub-lam* [12]<1> *sú-pá-nam ša* kù-babbar dumu *I-bi-sú-a ub-/lam* [13]*sà-ma-lá-tim it-qú-ra-tim* [14]*ú ṣí-ba-tim ub-lu-nim šu*$^{!}$*-ma be-lí a-ta* [15]*a-šu-mì* : túg^{hi-a} *ša ta-áš-pu-ra-ni* [16]*lá ú-šé-bi-lá-ku-ni li-ba-kà* [17]*lá i-lá-mì-in ki-ma ṣú-ha-ar-*[*tum*] [18]*i-ir-ta-bi-ú-ni* : túg *iš-té-en*$_6$ *ú šé-na* rev. [19]*kà-ab-tù-tim a-na na-ar-kà-ab*$_1$*-/tim* [20]*e-ta-pá-áš*$^{!}$ *ú a-na ni-ší bé-/tim* [21]*ú a-na ṣú-ùh-ri-im* [22]*e-pu-uš ú-lá ak-ta-ša-ad-ma* [23]túg^{hi-a} *lá uš-té-bi-lá-kum* túg^{hi-a} [24]*ma-lá qá-tí i-kà-šu-du iš-tí* [25]*wa-ar-ki-ú-tim ú-šé-ba-lá-kum* [26]é *A-bu-um*-dingir *i-na i-ga-ar-tim* [27]*ku-a-tim I-ku-pí-a ša* é *A-ta-a* [28]*i-ga-ar-tám šu-a-tám iš-ta-kán* [29]*ú a-na-ku a-ṣa-al-ma um-ma šu-ut-ma* [30]*ta-pá-ú-tum-ma ú-ta-pá-šu mì-ma-ma* [31]*ú-lá ú-ta-pá-šu* : *it-bé-a-ma* (erased sign) [32]*i-ta-ṣa-am a-ta a-ma-kam qí-bi-šu-um* [33]*um-ma a-ta-ma mì-šu-um i-ga-ar-ta-kà* [34]*i-na* é$^{bé-tí}$*-a* : *ta-áš-ku-un* [35]*ki-ma* é *lá a-ší-ri-im* : *té-pu-uš* [36]*ù a-šu-mì ba-pí-ri ša ta-áš-pu-ra-ni* [37]*ba-pí-ru-um wa-dí e-pí-iš ša-ak-/lu-ul* [38]*ú ṣú-ha-ar-tum da-ni-iš* le.e. [39]*ir-tí-bi tí-ib-a-ma a-tal-kam a-na sú-ni A-šùr* [40]*šu-ku-ší ù šé-ep ì-lí-kà ṣa-ba-at*

[1–2]Say to Pūšu-kēn: thus (says) Lamassī.

[2–3]Kulumaya is bringing you 9 textiles. [3–4]Iddin-Suen is bringing you 3 textiles. [5–6]Dān-Aššur brought me 2 bronze *supānum*-bowls. [6–8]Ia-šar brought me 1 bronze *supānum*-bowl and a bronze ladle. [8–9]Iddin-Suen brought me 2 bronze ladles. [9–10]Ahu-waqar brought me 1 bronze ladle. [11]Ikuppiya brought me 1 silver *supānum*-bowl. [12]The son of Ibbi-sū'a brought me 1 silver *supānum*-bowl. [13–14]They brought me cups, ladles, and *ṣibtum*-objects.

[14–17]If you are my master, do not be angry on account of the garments about which you have written me and (which) I have not sent you. [17–20]Since the girl has grown up, I have now made a few heavy textiles for (wearing on) the wagon. [20–22]And I also made garments for the household personnel and for the children; [22–23](this is why) I could not manage to send you some textiles. [23–25]I will send you with later caravans whatever textiles I can manage (to make).

[26–28]Concerning the house of Abum-ilī, Ikuppiya, from the house of Ataya, placed his wall against your wall, [29–30]so I contested, but he (said) as follows: "I will reach an agreement with him." [30–32]But he did not do so in any way; he set out and left. [32–34]You, over there, tell him as follows: "Why have you placed your wall against my house? [35]You just acted as (someone would) with a property without a protector!"

[36-37]Concerning the beer bread you wrote to me about—the beer bread is certainly made and ready! [38-40]The (little) girl has quite grown up; set out and come here. Consecrate her to (the god) Aššur and touch the foot of your god!

Bibliography: Text published in copy by Smith as CCT 3, 20; translated by Michel (2001a, no. 307).

Comments: Lamassī is sending a dozen textiles to her husband and acknowledges the receipt of various bronze and silver vessels. She has trouble combining the production of textiles to clothe the children and servants with that of textiles she has to make for her husband's trade. Besides a substantial textile production, she has to deal with everyday activities, such as the preparation of beer, and to represent her husband's interest in a quarrel with the neighbor. Lamassī urges her husband to come back home in order to consecrate their daughter Ahaha (see **163**).

---

167. A Specialist Finishes a Garment for the Husband to Wear

Obv. [1]*a-na Pu-šu-ke-en*$_6$ [2]*qí-bi-ma um-ma* [3]*Lá-ma-sí-ma* [4]2 túg : *A-šùr-ba-áš-tí* [5]*na-áš-a-kum a-šu-mì* [6]túg *ša Šu-ur-bu-i-a-tim* [7]*ša ta-áš-pu-ra-ni* [8]*um-ma a-ta-ma* lo.e. [9]1 túg *a-na li-ta-ab-ší-a* rev. [10]*šé-bi-li-im* [11]túg *wa-dí e-pí-iš* [12]*iš-tí áš-lá-ki-im-ma* [13]*a-dí-ni ú-lá ú-šé-li-/šu* [14]*iš-tí* [15]*wa-ar-ki-ú-tim* [16]túg *ša Šu-ur-bu-i-a-tim* [17]*a-na li-ta-ab-ší-kà* [18]*ú-šé-lá-kum*

[1-3]Say to Pūšu-kēn: thus (says) Lamassī.

[4-5]Aššur-bāšti is bringing you 2 textiles. [5-8]As for the textile (made of wool) from Šurbu, about which you wrote me as follows: [9-10]"Send me 1 garment for me to wear"; [11-13]the garment has indeed been made, but (it is) now with the washerman, so I have not yet sent (it) up to you. [14-18]I will send up to you by a later (caravan) the textile (made of wool) from Šurbu for you to wear.

Bibliography: Unpublished text in the possession of K. Rendell, lines 5–13 of which are cited by Michel and Veenhof (2010, 249); lines 1–5 and 14–18 given here by courtesy of Veenhof.

Comments: After the weaving was done by women, some textiles were finished by professionals (*ašlākum*, "washerman") before being used as garments by merchants; this raised the cost of the textile.

Separate Assets for Men and Women

Assyrian women were paid for their textiles (**128**); they kept accounts of the pieces of cloth that they sent to Asia Minor and waited for what they were owed for them. The letters they exchanged with the merchants at Kaneš regularly refer to accounts maintained between spouses and among brothers and sisters or members of the same family. Assyrian women, in their letters, drew up detailed lists of the pieces of cloth they had sent by different shippers, and asked for the prices realized for them (**169**, **172**, **173**). The merchants acknowledged receipt of the cloth, deducted the taxes paid on them, accounted for the pieces sold, and stated the sums of money being sent in return (**162**, **168**). Some private accounts note small sums of silver paid to women, no doubt from the sale of their cloth (**174**). Even if they were not on the spot in the Anatolian markets, these women knew quite well what prices their textiles should fetch and had no scruples about bargaining, even at long range, over sale prices and even asking for more than the customary amount. Thus Tarām-Kūbi told her brother that he should not sell her *kutānum*-textiles for less than twenty shekels of silver each, though they usually went for about fifteen shekels apiece (**170**). With a dozen shekels of silver realized from the sale of a textile in Anatolia, a woman could buy at Aššur what was needed to weave six or seven new pieces, so one can easily imagine the margin of profit she could realize (**171**).

Assyrian women therefore had their own property, independent of her husband's or of their joint assets, and also distinct from her dowry. Husband and wife managed their own assets separately, as can be seen with other family matters.[28] In fact, family connections formed the basis for professional connections within family enterprises (*bēt abini*), but even there, ownership was strictly individual: there was no joint capital.[29] This is why one finds sale contracts or loans at interest between father and son or husband and wife (**138**).[30] Thus a father explains to his son the source of the capital that he gave him: "For each shekel of silver that I gave you,

28. Michel 2006b.
29. Larsen 2007.
30. Note that this text concerns an Anatolian couple.

as well as what I gave you that belongs to your mother, I gave the equivalent to your mother."[31] The assets belonging to each spouse were clearly identified, and if a third party erroneously used a wife's funds to pay her husband's debts, the matter could be brought to court (**175**). This did not prevent a husband from making a purchase in his wife's name nor a wife from representing her husband in a transaction (**176**, and below).

---

168. Account of Textiles between Husband and Wife

Obv. ^{1}*um-ma Pu-šu-ke-en*$_{6}$*-ma* [*a-na*] ^{2}*La*$_{1}$*-ma-sí qí-bi-ma ší-i*[*m*] ^{3}túg$^{\text{hi-a-}\textit{tí}}$*-ki pá-ni-ú-ti*[*m*] ^{4}*gám-ra-ki-im* 20 túg$^{\text{hi-a}}$ *ša* [*a-na*] ^{5}*Puzur*$_{4}$*-A-šùr ta-dí-ni-ni* ^{6}1 túg *ni-is-ha-tum* 2 túg *ší-mu-um* ^{7}*ší-tum* 17 túg$^{\text{hi-a-}\textit{tù}}$*-ki* 6 túg ^{8}*A-hu-qar* : *ub-lam* 6 túg *I-a-šar* ^{9}*ub-lam* 2 túg *I-dí-Sú-en*$_{6}$ *ub-lam* ^{10}šà-ba 3 túg *a-na Puzur*$_{4}$*-A-šùr* ^{11}*ú-ra-dí-ma* 20 túg *ú-pì-iq-šum-m*[*a*] ^{12}*a-qá-tí-šu* : *a-dí-in ší-tí* t[úg$^{\text{hi-a}}$*-ki*] ^{13}11 túg *i-li-bi-a* : šà-[ba] ^{14}1½ *ma-na* kù-babbar *ni-is-*[*ha-sú*] ^{15}diri : *ša-du-a-sú* [*ša-bu*] lo.e. ^{16}*ku-nu-ki-a* : *Ku-lu-m*[*a-a*] ^{17}*na-áš-a-ki-im ta-*[*áš-pu-ri-im*] rev. ^{18}*um-ma a-tí-ma i-l*[*i-bi*] ^{19}túg$^{\text{hi-a}}$ *ša ú-šé-bi*$_{4}$*-l*[*á-ku-ni*] ^{20}2 túg *ša Šu-bu-ul-tim* 1[½ *ma-na*] ^{21}kù-babbar *ša Ku-lu-ma-a na-áš-*[*a-ki-ni*] ^{22}1 *ma-na* kù-babbar *ku-wa-um* ½ *m*[*a-na*] ^{23}*a-na Šu-bu-ul-tim dí-ni-*[*im*] ^{24}*ší-im* 1 túg *kab-tim ša*$^{!}$ *Šu-b*[*u-ul-tim*] ^{25}*iš-tù Bu-ru-uš-ha-tim* ^{26}*ú-bu-lu-nim-ma** 7 gín kù-babbar ^{27}*ša Il*$_{5}$*-ba-ni ša* dumu *Ku-za-ri* ^{28}*iš-qú-lá-ni ù i-na ší-i*[*m*] ^{29}*ší-tí* túg$^{\text{hi-a-}\textit{tí}}$*-ki* kù-babbar ^{30}*uš-ta-ṣa-ba-at-ma* ^{31}*I-dí-Sú-en*$_{6}$ *ú-šé-b*[*a-lá-ki-im*] ^{32}*a-na Lá-ma-sí qí-*[*bi-ma*] ^{33}5-ta túg$^{\text{hi-a}}$ sig$_{5}^{[\textit{tim}]}$ u.e. ^{34}*a-ṣú-ha-ri dí-ni-*[*ma*] ^{35}*lu-ub-lu-nim-*[*ma*] le.e. ^{36}*li-ik-šu-du-ni mì-šu ša e-ma-am* ^{37}*ta-ah-tí-ri-ni* : *a-na-ku a-na-kam* ^{38}*ki-ma i-qá-bi*$_{4}$*-ú-ni i-ṣé-er*$^{!}$ ninda kaš$^{!}$(KÀ) *a-ku***-lu*$^{?}$ ^{39}*e-na-a e-ra-ba ú-ṣí-a*

$^{1-2}$Thus (says) Pūšu-kēn: say [to] Lamassī.

$^{2-4}$The full pri[ce] of your previous textiles has been paid to you. $^{4-7}$Concerning the 20 textiles that you gave [to] Puzur-Aššur: 1 textile for the import tax, 2 textiles as purchase, 17 textiles of yours remain. $^{7-9}$Ahu-(wa)qar brought me 6 textiles; Ia-šar brought me 6 textiles; Iddin-Suen brought me 2 textiles; $^{10-11}$to these, I added 3 textiles for Puzur-Aššur. $^{11-12}$I made for him an *upqum*-load of 20 textiles, and I put (it) at his disposal.

---

31. KTS 1, 2b:7–10: *a-šu-mì* kù-babbar 1 gín *ša a-dí-na-ku-ni, lu ša um-mì-kà, a-dí-na-ku-ni me-eh-ra-tim, a-na um-mì-kà a-dí-in.*

[12-13]The remainder of [your textiles], 11 textiles, are on my account. [13-17][For] these, Kulumaya is bringing you under my seal 1½ minas of silver—its import [tax] added, its transport fee paid for. [17-20]You w[rote me] as follows: "In[cluded with] the textiles that I sent [you] are 2 textiles from Šūbultum." [20-23](So) of the 1[½ minas] of silver that Kulumaya is bringing [to you], 1 mina of silver is yours, (and) give ½ m[ina] to Šūbultum. [24]As payment of 1 heavy textile from Šūb[ultum], [25-31]they brought me from Burušhattum 7 shekels of silver from Ilī-bāni, which the son of Kuzari paid me, and the silver from the sale of the rest of your textiles, I will combine and send [(it) to you] by Iddin-Suen.

[32]Sa[y] to Lamassī. [34-36]Give to the servants good quality textiles in lots of 5 to carry so that they reach me. [36-37]Why did you choose a son-in-law for me? [37-39]As for me, here, as they say, "My eyes come (home) and go out again (still looking) at the bread (and) beer I (should have) eaten."

Bibliography: Text published in copy by Garelli as CCT 6, 11a; translated by Michel (2001a, no. 300). Collated by Veenhof.

Comments: Lamassī entrusted textiles to several transporters, and her husband acknowledges their receipt. He sends back the price in silver for several pieces made both by Lamassī and Šūbultum.

The end of the letter concerns family matters. The expression used by Pūšu-kēn may refer to a proverb ("as we used to say") that is not totally clear for us. Pūšu-kēn is overworked; he cannot keep an eye on everything and also think about eating, the expression "bread and beer" meaning "food and drink."

Line 6: "two textiles as purchase" correspond to the preemption by the palace.

---

169. Asking for Payment for a Textile Sent to Anatolia

Obv. [1]*a-na Pu-šu-ke-en*$_6$ [2]*ú A-šùr-ma-lik qí-bi-ma* [3]*um-ma Lá-ma-sí-ma* [4]*a-na A-šur-ma-lik /qí-bi*$_4$*-ma* túg *kà-ab*$_1$*-/tá-am* [5]*ša i-na* ellat [6]*A-šur-iš-ta-ki-il*$_5$ dumu *Sú-kà-li-/a* [7]«*ša*» *ú-šé-bi-lu-kà* [8]*i-li-kam-ma Pu-šu-ke-en*$_6$ [9]*um-ma šu-ut-ma* [10]*ú-lá i-dí-nam* [11](erasure) *šu-ut a-ma-kam* [12]*ku*[!]*-ta-i-na-ma* [13]kù-babbar *ú ší-a-ma-tí*[!]*-šu* [14]*ša iš-tù ma-al*[!]*-e** [15]*ša-na-tim šé-bi-lá-nim*

[1-4]Say to Pūšū-kēn and Aššur-malik: thus (says) Lamassī. Say to Aššur-malik.

[4-8]Concerning the heavy textile that I made you bring with the caravan of Aššuriš-takil, son of Sukkalliya, it has arrived, [9-10](but) Pūšu-kēn (said) as follows: "He did not give (it) to me!" [11-15]There, make him acknowledge it and send me silver or the (equivalent of the) merchandise that is (due since) for years!

Bibliography: Text published in copy by Smith as CCT 4, 21b; translated by Michel (2001a, no. 299).

Comments: Lamassī has entrusted a heavy textile to a transporter traveling with a caravan that arrived in Kaneš, but her husband has not acknowledged receipt of the textile and has not paid her for it.

---

170. Sister Protests the Low Price Paid by Her Brother for Her Textiles

Obv. [1]*a-na Im-dí-lim qí-bi-ma* [2]*um-ma Ta-ra-am-Ku-bi* [3]*ù Ší-ma-at-A-šùr-ma* [4](line erased) [5]6 túg *i-na šé-pí-šu* [6]*pá-ni-tim Ku-tal-lá-num* [7]*ub-lá-kum* 1 *ma-na* 10 gín [8]kù-babbar *tù-šé-bi-lam ù* [*iš*]*-tù* [9]*tù-uṣ-ú ma-tí-ma* [10]*šé-bu-ul-tám ú-lá* [11]*tù-šé-bi-lam a-na-ku* [12]*a-na ma-nim-ma a-na* [13]6 túg[hi-a] 1 *ma-na* 10 gín [14]kù-babbar *tù-šé-bi-lam* [15]6 túg *ku-ta-ni* rev. [16]*Ku-tal-lá-num na-áš-a-kum* [17]*šu-ma a-hi a-ta* [18]⅓ *ma-na-ta lá ta-ba-ta-qám* [19]1 túg *a-na Ištar-ba-áš-tí* [20]1 é *Ri-mì-ì-lí-a* [21]*a-na* 20 *ma-na* kù-babbar [22]*iš-ú-mu-ni-kum-ma* [23]kù-babbar *e-ri-šu-ni-ma* [24]*a-na ša ki-ma ku-a-tí* [25]*a-dí-in a-dí-ni* [26]*ú-lá ú-ta-e-ru-nim* [27]*um-ma šu-nu-ma ší-ma-am* [28]*ni-ša-am šu-ma a-hi a-ta* [29]*a-ma-nim a-da-kál* [30]igi *i-li-a a-kà-ra-/ba-kum* [31]*Ku-tal-lá-nu-um i-li-kam-ma* [32]*mì-ma ú-lá tù-šé-bi*$_4$*-lam* [33]7 gín kù-babbar *a-na Ku-tal-lá-nim* [34]*áš-qúl*

[1-3]Say to Imdī-ilum: thus (say) Tarām-Kūbi and Šīmat-Aššur.

[5-7]Kutallānum brought you 6 textiles in his previous transport. [7-8]You sent me 1 mina, 10 shekels of silver; [8-11]but [si]nce you left, you have never sent me any other consignment. [11-14]To whom else but me would you send (only) 1 mina, 10 shekels for 6 textiles? [15-16](Now) Kutallānum is bringing you 6 *kutānum*-textiles. [17-18]If you are my brother, you should not send me (less) than ⅓ mina per (textile)!

[19-22]They bought for you 1 textile for Ištar-baštī (and) a house (belonging to) Rīm-iliya for 20 minas of silver, and [23-25]they asked me for the silver, so I gave (it) to your representatives. [25-28]Until now, they have not returned (it) to me, (saying) as follows: "We want to make purchases!" [28-29]If you (really are) my brother, whom else could I expect help from? [30]I will pray for you before my god! [31-32]Kutallānum came here, but you sent me nothing (by him). [33-34]I paid 7 shekels of silver to Kutallānum.

Bibliography: Text published and edited by Moren (1980, 101, as *Or* 50, 2); translated by Michel (2001a, no. 347).

Comments: Tarām-Kūbi was the sister of Imdī-ilum, and Šīmat-Aššur was a relative. Even if both are mentioned as authors of the letter, it is written in the singular, and so only Tarām-Kūbi is speaking. She complains about the very low price paid by her brother for the 6 textiles she has sent: little more than 11½ shekels, and she asks for 20 shekels for each *kutānum*-textile she is sending. Tarām-Kūbi was rich enough to lend 20 minas of silver to Imdī-ilum's representatives to buy a house for him.

---

171. Production of Seven Textiles from the Sale Price of One

Obv. [1]*a-na A-šur-lá-ma-sí* [2]*qí-bi-ma um-ma* [3]*Ištar-lá-ma-sí-ma* [4]*ṣú-ba-tám E-na-Sú-en*$_6$ [5]*na-áš-a-kum* 12 gín [6]kù-babbar *Šu-a-nim* dumu *Ha-nu* [7]*ub-lam* 12 gín kù-babbar [8]*E-na-Sú-en*$_6$ *ub-lam* [9]*ù* 5 gín *a-ha-ma* [10]*šu-ut-ma ub-lam* [11]*i-na* kù-babbar [12]*ša* dumu *Ha-nu ub-lá-ni* rev. [13]1 *A-ba-ar-ni-um* [14]2 *qá-at-nu-tum* [15]4 *ša qá-tim* [16]*e-pu-uš-ma i-na* [17]*DÍ-tim na-ad-ú* [18]*mu-zi-zu ša a-hi-kà* [19]*qú-a-tim ip-ta-na-té-ú-ma* [20]ì-giš *uš-té-né-bu-lu* [21]*ù a-na-ku a-na* [22]*ša ki-ma ku-a-tí* [23]*aq-bi*$_4$*-ma* u.e. [24]*ša-pá-am* ì-[giš] [25]*ma-li-a-n*[*im*] le.e. [26]*lu-šé-bi*$_4$*-il*$_5$ [...]

[1-3]Say to Aššur-lamassī: thus (says) Ištar-lamassī.

[4-5]Enna-Suen is bringing you a textile. [5-7]Šu-Anum, son of Hanu, brought me 12 shekels of silver. [7-10]Enna-Suen brought me 12 shekels of silver, and he also brought me another 5 shekels separately. [11-16]From the silver that the son of Hanu brought, I made 1 Abarnian-textile, 2 fine (textiles) and 4 standard-quality (textiles), [16-17]and they are deposited in the [...]

[18–20]The representatives of your brother keep on opening *qûm*-vessels and sending off oil, [21–26]so I said to your representatives (as follows): "Fill for me a *šappum*-vessel with oil, let me send [...]"

Bibliography: Text edited by Böhl (1934, 41–43 [LB 1201]); translated by Michel (2001a, no. 363).

Comments: With the twelve shekels of silver presumably resulting from the sale of a textile in Anatolia, Ištar-lamassī managed to produce seven textiles of various qualities.

Line 17: *DÍ-tim* is unknown in this context. The words *dittum*, "court of justice," or *ṭīdum*, "clay," make no sense in this text.

---

172. A Woman Sends Textiles to Kaneš and Receives Various Amounts of Metal

Obv. [1]*a-na A-šur-na-da qí-bi*$_4$*-/ma* [2]*um-ma Ša-ra-at-/Ištar-ma* [3][2?] túg! *Zu-pá* : *na-áš-a-ku-um* [4]1 *iš-ra-am* : *ku-a-tí* [5]1 *iš-ra-am* : *a-na* [x (x)]-/*a*-[*r*] *i*-a** [6]4 *ša-ku-kà-tim* [7]*iš-té-na dí-in* [8]*ší-it*!(DA)*-ra-am a-na am-tí*-[*kà*] [9]*ša Kà-ne-eš* [10]2 túg 37 *ma-na* urudu [11]*it-bu-lu* : *i-na* [12][x tú]g *áš-a-am-šu-nu* [13]1 túg *a-na* k[ù-bab]bar *mu*?-[x (x)] lo.e. [14]*a-*<*dí*>*-in ma-lá im-tal*-[x (x)] [15]*Kur-ub-Ištar pá na bi* [x] [16]*iš-tí-kà* : *ša-ki-in* [17]*mì-ma* : *lá aq-bi-šu*-[*ma*] [18]*a-wi-lam*$_5$: *ar-tí-bi*$_4$ [19]*tí*!(BE)*-ib*!*-a-ma* : *a-tal-kam* [20]*mì-ma a-nim* : *Zu-pá* [21]*na-áš-a-ku-um* [22]½ *ma-na* 5 gín kù-babbar [23]*En-nam-A-šur u*[*b-lam*] [24]5 gín kù-babbar 3 gín kù-[gi] [25]*Puzur*$_4$*-Ištar ub-lam* [26]5 gín kù-babbar 5 *ma-na* /urudu [27]du$_{10}$*-ṣí-lá-A-šur* /*ub-lam* le.e. [28]*a-ma*-[*a*]*t-kà ša* <*Kà*>*-ni-iš* [29]*i-na* [*p*]*á-ni-kà lá*!*-ar-ta*!(RI)*-a-am*

[1–2]Say to Aššur-nādā: thus (says) Šarrat-Ištar.

[3]Zupa is bringing you [2?] textiles. [4–5]1 belt for you, 1 belt for [X-x]-aria. [6–7]Sell the 4 metal belts one by one. [8–9]The shawl? is for [your] *amtum*-wife of Kaneš. [10–11]2 textiles cost 37 minas of copper; [11–12]I bought them from the [x] textiles. [13–14]I sold 1 textile for s[ilver x x]. [14–16]As much as [x x] Kurub-Ištar [x x x] is deposited with you, [17]I have told him nothing. [18]I have [...] the man. [19]Set out and come here. [20–21]All this, Zupa is bringing you. [22–23]Ennum-Aššur br[ought me] ½ mina, 5 shekels of silver. [24–25]Puzur-Ištar brought me 5 shekels of silver (and) 3 shekels of gol[d]. [26–27]Ṭāb-ṣilli-Aššur brought me 5 shekels of silver (and) 5 minas

of copper. [28–29]Did I not always love your *amtum*-wife who is with you in Kaneš?

Bibliography: Text published in copy by Clay as BIN 4, 88; edited by Larsen (2002, no. 72).

Comments: According to Larsen (2002, xxv n. 35), for chronological reasons, Šarrat-Ištar could be a daughter of Aššur-nādā and of his Assyrian wife. She is living in Aššur and lists the textiles that she sent to her father. She also sent a shawl to the Anatolian *amtum*-wife of her father, Šišahšušar. She lists the amounts of metal that she received: forty-five shekels of silver, three shekels of gold, and five minas of copper.

Line 6: the word *šakkukum* probably refers to a belt made of metal, sometimes ornamented with precious stones; see Michel 2001a, 72a.

---

173. A Woman Waits for Payment for Her Textiles to Repay a Debt

Obv. [1]*a-na Ma-nu-ki-A-šur qí-bi*$_4$*-/ma* [2]*um-ma Ší-ma-Sú-en*$_6$*-ma* [3]1 *ku-ta-nam* sig$_5$ [4]*a-na ta-ad-mì-iq-/tim* [5]*a-na Šu-*^{d}*En-líl* [6]*a-dí-in* ½ *ma-na* kù-babbar [7]*iq-bi*$_4$*-am ra-qá-tám* sig$_5$ [8]*A-šur-i-dí* dumu *A-mur-A-šur* lo.e. [9]*ú-bi*$_4$*-il*$_5$*-šu-um* túg rev. [10]*ša ṣú-ùh-ri-im* [11]*Puzúr-e-na ú-bi*$_4$*-il*$_5$*-šu-um* [12]*be-lí a-ta Šu-*^{d}*En-líl* [13]*ṣa-ba-at-ma* kù-babbar *ší-im* [14]túg$^{hi\text{-}tí}$*-a* : *ša-dí-šu-ma šé-bi*$_4$*-/lam* [15]*hu-bu-li ša a-ša-du-/uš-tim* [16]*ah-bu-lu lá-ak-šu-ur*

[1–2]Say to Mannum-kī-Aššur: thus (says) Šīmat-Suen.

[3–6]I gave 1 fine *kutānum*-textile to Šu-Enlil as a *tadmiqum*-trust. [6–7]He promised me ½ mina of silver. [7–9]Aššur-idī, son of Amur-Aššur, brought him a thin and fine (textile). [9–11]Puzur-Enna brought to him a textile for a child.

[12–14]You are my master; seize Šu-Enlil, make him pay the silver, price of my textiles, and send (it) to me! [15–16]I want to pay my debt that I incurred to the committee-of-six.

Bibliography: Text published by Bilgiç and Bayram as AKT 2, 52 (Kt n/k 588); collated May 2012.

Comments: Šīmat-Suen sent three different textiles to Šu-Enlil and is waiting for payment for her textiles in order to pay her own debt.

Line 4: the word *tadmiqtum* corresponds to a consignment, often made by women, in which merchandise, often textiles, was entrusted to a relative to sell without guaranteed profit.

Line 15: *šaduštum* is used here for *šedištum*, "a group-of-six," an ad hoc committee of six members set up for special legal matters; see Larsen 1976, 166.

---

174. Women in Aššur Receive Small Amounts of Silver

$^{1'}$[1$^{?}$] *ri-ik-*[*sú* x x x] $^{2'}$10 gín kù *ší-im* an-na *ša* [x x]-*im* $^{3'}$1 *ri-ik-sú* 15 gín kù-babbar $^{4'}$*ší-im* túg *ša Ma-nu-ba* gudu$_4$ *ša A-šur* $^{5'}$1 *ri-ik-sú* 13 gín kù-babbar $^{6'}$*a-Lá-ma-sí ú A-ha-ha* 1½ gín kù $^{7'}$*a-Šu-bu-ul-tim* 1½ gín kù $^{8'}$*a-Ta-ri-iš-ma-tim ú Be-lá-tim* $^{9'}$1½ gín *a-Lá-ma-sí-tim* $^{10'}$2 *né-pí-ša-an* 20 *ma-na* kù-babbar lo.e. $^{11'}$*ša* dam-gàr *a-qá-ra-be-tim* /1 *ri-ik-sú* $^{12'}$*a-ha-ma ni-is-ha-sú* $^{13'}$1 *né-pí-šum* 15 *ma-na* kù-babbar rev. $^{14'}$*ku-nu-ku-a ú ku-nu-uk Ás-qú-dim* $^{15'}$*a-ru-ba-im* 1 *né-pí-šu-um* $^{16'}$5 *ma-na* kù *ku-nu-ki-a ší-im* $^{17'}$an-na *ša a-bi$_4$-šu a-ru-ba-im* $^{18'}$1 *né-pí-šu-um* $^{19'}$5 *ma-na* kù *ša-du-a-sú* $^{20'}$*i-ra-mì-ni-a áš-qúl a-na* $^{21'}$*T*[*a-ri-iš-ma-t*]*im ú Be-lá-tim* $^{22'}$[…] *na* x (lacuna)

le.e. $^{1''}$[… *Bu*]-*zu-ta-a ú Be-lá-nim* $^{2''}$[…] ½ *ma-na a-wi-tum* $^{3''}$[…]-*a* igi *Iš-ma-A-šur* dumu $^{4''}$[PN$_1$ igi PN$_2$ dumu] *Bu-da-tim*

$^{1'-2'}$[1] pack[age …] 10 shekels of silver, price of tin from […].$^{3'-4'}$1 package of 15 shekels of silver, price of a textile from Manuba, priest of Aššur; $^{5'-6'}$1 package of 13 shekels of silver for Lamassī and Ahaha; $^{6'-8'}$1½ shekels of silver for Šūbultum; 1½ shekels of silver for Tarīš-mātum and Bēlātum, (and) $^{9'}$1½ shekels for Lamassatum. $^{10'-11'}$2 bags of 20 minas of silver belonging to the *tamkārum* for the storeroom; $^{11'-12'}$1 package separately, its import tax; $^{12'-15'}$1 bag of 15 minas of silver under my seal and the seal of Asqudum for the king (of Aššur); $^{15'-17'}$1 bag of 5 minas of silver under my seal, price of his father's tin, for the king; $^{18'-20'}$1 bag of 5 minas of silver; I personally paid its transport fee. $^{21'}$For T[arīš-māt]um and Bēlātum […]

$^{1''-4''}$[… Bu]zutaya and Bēlānum […] ½ mina, the value of the caravan […]. In the presence of Išme-Aššur, son of [PN$_1$, and PN$_2$, son of] Budatum.

Bibliography: Text published in copy by Garelli as CCT 6, 27b; edited by Andrea Marie Ulshöfer (1995, no. 176).

Comments: Lamassī, wife of Pūšu-kēn, and her daughter Ahaha receive together 13 shekels of silver; the other ladies, Šūbultum and Lamassatum, each received 1½ shekels; Tarīš-mātum and Bēlātum together received 1½ shekels. Such amounts or silver are inferior to the price of an exported textile.

Line 14′: Asqudum is known as a servant of Aššur palace (*wardum ša ekallim*) according to KTS 1, 55b:3; see Michel 2015c.

---

175. Separate Accounts for Spouses

Envelope

Obv. [1](seal A) [2]*a-na A-t*[*a*]*-ta* dumu [3]*Ma-num-ba-lúm-A-šùr* [4]*ù Qá-nu-tim* dumu-munus [5]*En-na-Sú-en*$_6$ [6](seal A) [7]kišib *A-na-ah-ì-lí* lo.e. [8](seal A) rev. [9]dumu du$_{10}$-*ṣí-lá-A-šùr* [10](seal A) u.e. [11](seal A) le.e. [12](seal A) r.e. [13](seal A)

[1-5]To At[a]ta, son of Mannum-balum-Aššur and Qannuttum, daughter of Enna-Suen.

[7-9]Sealed by Ānah-ilī, son of Ṭāb-ṣilli-Aššur.

Tablet

Obv. [1]*a-na A-ta-ta ù Qá-nu-tim* [2]*qí-bi*$_4$*-ma um-*[*ma*] *A-na-ah-ì-lí-/ma* [3]½ *ma-na* kù-[ki] *ù* 1½ *ma-na* [4]kù-babbar *ša Qá-nu-tim ša* [5]*Il*$_5$*-ba-ni ki-ma Qá-nu-tim* [6]kù-babbar *ip-qí-da-ni : a-na-/kam** [7]*A-lá-bu-um ú-ni-hi-ma* [8] kù-babbar 1 *ma-na ú-ša-ag-me-/er* [9]*a-na A-lim*^{ki} *im-ta-ša-ra-ni-/ma* [10]*i-na dí-in A-lim*^{ki} [11] kù-babbar *ú* kù-ki : *A-lá-bu-um* [12]*i-lá-qé-ma a-na a-wa-at* [13]*Qá-nu-tim A-lá-bu-um* [14]*i-za-az šu-ma Qá-nu-tum* [15]*a-*[*na A-n*]*a-ah-ì-lí* lo.e. [16]*ta-t*[*ù*]*-wa-ar A-lá-bu-/um* rev. [17]*ú-ša-ha-sú-ú* [18] kù-babbar *ú* kù-ki *šu-ut a-na* [19]é *A-lim*^{ki} *a-na hu-bu-ul* [20]*Il*$_5$*-ba-ni i-ší-qí-il*$_5$ [21]*a-ma-kam : a-li : té-er-tí* [22]*Il*$_5$*-ba-ni i-ba-ší-ú* [23]*ša* ½ *ma-na* kù-ki *pá-ša-lam*$_5$ [24]*ù* 1½ *ma-na* kù-babbar [25]*ú ší-a-ma-tí-šu ṣa-áb-ta-/ma* [26]*mì-ṣí-a-ma le-qé-a* [27]*ṭup-pá-am ša A-lim*^{ki} *da-nam* [28]*ša ki-ma* kù-ki *ú* kù-babbar [29]*ša Qá-nu-tí-ni* [30]*ú-kà-al ú šu-ma* u.e. [31]*Ku-li-a i-lá-kà*-ma* [32]*a-wa-tim ú-ga-mar* [33]*a-dí a-lá-kà-ni* le.e. [34]*i-ta-ba-lá-šu a-*[*w*]*a-tim lá tù-ga-/ma-ra*

[1-2]Say to Atata and Qannuttum: thus (says) Ānah-ilī.

[3-6](Concerning) ½ mina of gold and 1½ minas of silver, belonging to Qannuttum; Ilī-bāni, representing Qannuttum, entrusted the silver to

me. [6–8]Here Ali-abum has troubled me and caused me to spend silver, up to 1 mina! [9]He has then dragged me before the city (of Aššur), and [10–12]according to the verdict of the city (of Aššur), Ali-abum can take that silver and gold, and [12–14]Ali-abum shall be responsible for Qannuttum's interests. [14–16]Should Qannuttum raise a claim again[st An]ah-ilī, [16–17]then Ali-abum shall clear him. [18–20]That silver and gold have been paid to the City Hall for Ilī-bāni's debt. [21–22]There, wherever goods ordered by Ilī-bāni are available, [23–25](then) seize to an amount of ½ mina of *pašallum*-gold and 1½ minas of silver or goods bought for (that amount), and [26–26]take them under your own reponsibility. [27–30]I hold a binding tablet from the city (of Aššur) stating that the silver and gold belong to Qannuttum. [30–32]And if Kuliya comes in order to settle the affair, [33–34]until I arrive, string him along, you should not settle the affair!

Bibliography: Text published by Veenhof as AKT 5, 30 (Kt 92/k 191); collated May 2012.

Comments: Qannuttum, daughter of Enna-Suen, was the wife of Ilī-bāni (AKT 5, 28a:4–5; 51:13; 62:2; 63:16). According to Veenhof (AKT 5, 19), her husband might have been an older brother of Kuliya, messenger of the *kārum* and owner of the archives published in AKT 5. For the writing of her name, see Sturm 1995. Another possible reading is Kannūtum, from *kunnûm*, "to honor."

Qannuttum owned substantial amounts of gold and silver personally; some of the silver has been used in Aššur by Ānah-ilī to pay a debt of her husband. But the silver belonged to her and not to her husband, so she had to be indemnified by the sale of Ilī-bāni's goods. This implies that Qannuttum had her own capital separate from her husband's, and so husband and wife had separate accounts.

Line 34: Veenhof takes the form *i-ta-ba-lá-šu* as an imperative Gtn of *wabālum*.

176. A Man Buys Goods for His Wife with Her Own Silver

Obv. [1]*um-ma Im-dí*-dingir-*ma* : *a-na* [2]*Ištar-ba-áš-tí* : *ù A-mur*-dingir [3]*qí-bi-ma* : *a-ma-lá* : *té-er-tí-a* [4]*ṭup-pí-a* : *ší-ta*$^{!}$*-me-a-ma* [5]*lu* an-na^{ki} : *lu* túg^{tí}-*a* : *lu e-ma-ri* [6]*dí-na-ma* : *lu ba-áb-tí* : *ma-*[*l*]*á*$^{!}$ [7]*qá-at-ku-nu* : *ik-šu-du* [8]*lu ša ki-ma* : *i-a-tí* : *me-eh-ra-tim* [9]*i-na-dí-ú* : *ù a-dí* : 10 *ma-na* kù-babbar [10]*ša* *ta-áš-pu-ri-ni : um-ma a-tí-ma* [11]*ša ki-ma : ku-a-tí : ú-lá i-mu-ú* [12]*šé-bi-lim-ma : ša* kù-babbar*[pí]-ki* [13]*ší-ma-am : a-ša-a-ma* [14]*A-mur-*dingir *: ú-šé-ṣa-a-ki-im* [15]*A-mur-*dingir *: a-ma-kam : lá i-sà-hu-ur* [16]*ší-ma-am : áš-a-ma lu* an-na*[kam]* [17]*lu* túg[hi-a] *: i-ba-ší* [18]*ù a-na-ku : lá kà-ṣú-da-ku* rev. [19]*A-mur-*dingir *: u_4-ma-kál*[!] *: lá i-bi-a-at* [20]*li-it-bé-a-ma* [21]*li-tal-kam : maš-kà-tám* [22]*ú-lá a-ša-kà-nam : A-mur-*dingir [23]*ú-qá-a : a-dí : A-mur-*dingir [24]*i-lá-kà-ni : lá ta-ha-dí-ri* [25]*ki-ma : A-mur-*dingir *: e-ru-ba-ni-ni* [26]*u_4-ma-kál : lá uš-bi-a-sú* [27]*i-tù-a-ri-šu : a-tí : al-ki-im* [28]1 túg *A-bar-ni-am : ⅓ ma-na* kù-babbar [29]*áš-qúl : a-na Ištar-ba-áš-tí* [30]*E-lá : na-ší : ú-za-an* [31]*A-mur-*dingir *: pí-tí : pá-lá-ha-am* [32]*lu i-de_8 : a-na* ninda *: ù* kaš [33]*lá i-da-gal lu a-wi-il_5* [34]*ta-ah-sí-is-tum* [35]*ša Ú-ṣur-ší-Ištar* 10½ *ma-na* /5½ gín kù-babbar le.e. [36]*ša* igi *E-na-Be-lim : ù A-šur-*sig_5 [37]*i-na li-bi : ṭup-pè-a-ma : li-ib-ší* [38]kù-babbar *: a-na-kam : i-ta-aq-ra-ni* [39]*i-ṭup-pí : ṭup-pí-ma : uš-tám-ṭí-ku-nu*

[1–3]Thus (says) Imdī-ilum: say to Ištar-baštī and Amur-ilī.

[3–4]According to my instructions, listen carefully to my tablet and [5–6]sell my tin, my garments, and my donkeys, and [6–7]all that you have obtained from my outstanding deliveries, [8–9]or what my representatives will deposit as equivalent. [9–11]And, as for the 10 minas of silver, about which you (fem.) wrote to me as follows: "Your representatives refuse!" [12–13]send it to me, and for the silver (which is) yours (fem.), I will make a purchase and [14]will let Amur-ilī export it to you. [15]Amur-ilī should not stay over there! [16–17]I already made a purchase, and the tin and textiles are (already) available (for shipment). [18]For my part, I will not be delayed. [19–21](Therefore) Amur-ilī should not stay overnight; let him set out and come! [21–22]I will not make (another) deposit. [22–23]I am waiting for Amur-ilī. [23–24]Do not be worried concerning the fact that Amur-ilī has to travel. [25–27]When Amur-ilī arrives here, I will not let him stay overnight. Come yourself here as soon as he returns!

[28–29]I paid ⅓ mina of silver for one Abarnian-textile; [29–30]Ela is bringing (it) to Ištar-baštī.

[30–33]Tell Amur-ilī that he should know how to respect (people); he should not be looking (only) at bread and beer! He must (be) a gentleman!

[34–37]The memorandum of Uṣur-ša-Ištar (concerning) the 10½ minas, 5½ shekels of silver, witnessed by Ennam-Bēlum and Aššur-damiq, should stay with my tablets. [38–39]Here, silver is now difficult for me to obtain, (this is why) letter after letter I have warned you!

Bibliography: Text published in copy by Smith as CCT 4, 28a; edited by Ichisar (1981, 229–31); translated by Michel (2001a, no. 354).

Comments: Imdī-ilum writes from Aššur to his wife and his son in Kaneš. Ištar-baštī owns ten minas of silver; her husband intends to make purchases for her, and their son Amur-ilī will transport her goods to Kaneš for sale. Meanwhile, they are asked to sell Imdī-ilum's tin and textiles, and to send him his silver. Ištar-baštī is supposed to travel back to Aššur. Letter TC 3, 57, is sent to the same recipients but is mainly addressed to Amur-ilī.

Lines 31–32: literally, "he should look for bread and beer."

Women Lend, Buy, and Invest

With the money gained from their work, Assyrian women took part in all sorts of transactions in their own names, such as sales or purchases of slaves, and put their money to work by making interest-bearing loans. Numerous women drew up contracts in which they were creditors. The amounts loaned by women were generally smaller than those loaned by men, often a few shekels, though occasionally much more. Some women's loans exceeded a mina of silver (1 mina, or 500 g: **183**; 1½ minas, or 750 g: **177**; 1½ minas, 3½ shekels; or 780 g: **187**). Women, whether Assyrian or Anatolian, made loans to men as well as to women; practically every combination is attested. One Assyrian woman made a loan to an Assyrian man (Ahattum: **177, 178**; Musa: **182**), another, Šāt-Anna, made several loans to men, both Assyrian and Anatolian (**179–181**). An Assyrian women could make a loan to another Assyrian woman (**80**; Šāt-Ea: **183, 184**) or to an Anatolian woman (**185**). An Anatolian woman could loan money to another Anatolian woman (**189**). A woman could also loan a substantial sum of money to several men (Zizizi: **186, 187**; Kušan: **188**).

Some women's personal circumstances allowed them to stand as guarantors for debtors, especially for members of their own family; they were thus executors for creditors (**193**). An Assyrian woman stood as guarantor for her brother for a debt of fifteen shekels of silver. When he was unable to repay, he gave a small piece of land to the creditor and to his sister; perhaps it was she who paid her brother's debt to the creditor (**194**)? Women could also stand as guarantors for commercial transactions of various kinds (**138**).

Like men, women used their resources to buy slaves or real estate (see above, chapter 3).[32] Various slave sales, often of women and girls, were ini-

32. Kienast 1984; Michel 2008a, 2016d.

tiated by women; these records documented the payment of the price and the transfer of the slave to the buyer. They belonged to Assyrian women (**103**), such as Ahattum, who bought in several instances a girl from her parents (**94**, **107**); to Ištar-baštī (**103**); or to Anatolian women, such as Zaza (**108**), Waliwali (**143**) or Nakilwišwe (**144**). Women such as Ummī-nara (**149**, **150**) likewise became owners of houses. These contracts were found in their archives at Kaneš; most likely similar documents were kept in women's residences at Aššur.

Women invested, just as men, in long-distance trade, buying goods that they sent to sell in Anatolia (**195**, **217**). Text **196**, which lists a woman's goods—silver, textiles, wool, slaves, copper, and donkeys—shows her involvement in international trade. As owners of merchandise brought by caravans to Asia Minor, they, just as men, could be obliged to declare under oath any losses they had incurred (**243**; see chapter 5). And Assyrian women tried to increase their wealth through financial activities of various kinds, by investing in a trader's joint-stock company (**282**, **284**); the details of these transactions are known from letters they sent to members of their families at Kaneš.[33]

Women's involvement in commerce sometimes compelled them to travel. Some made the long journey from Aššur to Kaneš; others visited different commercial settlements in Asia Minor.[34] Their letters explain the reasons, family or business, that took them away from home.[35] Ennum-Ištar, widow of Šalim-Aššur, wrote to her eldest son reminding him of transactions she had carried out at Burušhattum and Kaneš (**198**). Other women made journeys at the request of their husbands in order to transact business (see **200**, and below).

---

177. An Assyrian Woman Lends Silver to an Assyrian Merchant for Three Months

Obv. [1]1½ *ma-na* kù-babbar *ṣa-ru-pá-/am* [2]*i-ṣé-er Šu-Ku-bi$_4$-/im* [3]*A-ha-tum tí-šu* [4]*iš-tù ha-mu-uš-/tim ša* [5]*Im-dí-lim ú A-šur-ṣú-lu-/li* [6]*a-na* 3 iti-

---

33. Michel 2014f.

34. Michel 2008d.

35. For example, the journey of Kunnaniya from Kaneš to Aššur (chapter 6; Michel 1997e; 2001a, 493–99), or that of Šalimma from Aššur to Kaneš (chapter 5; Veenhof 2007).

kam ^{7}*i-ša-qal šu-ma* ^{8}*lá ìš-qú-ul* rev. ^{9}*ki-ma a-wa-at* ^{10}*kà-ri-im ú-ṣa-áb* ^{11}[igi] *Lu-lu* ^{12}[dumu] *A-ra-na-áp-šu*

$^{1-3}$Ahattum has loaned 1½ minas of refined silver to Šu-Kūbum. $^{4-7}$From the week of Imdī-ilum and Aššur-ṣululī, he shall pay in 3 months. $^{7-10}$If he has not paid, he shall add (interest) according to the rate of the *kārum*.

$^{11-12}$In the presence of Lulu, [son] of Aranapšu.

Bibliography: Text published in copy by Clay as BIN 4, 153; edited by Eisser and Lewy (1930, no. 75); Ichisar (1981, 94).

Comments: The amount of silver object of the loan is substantial, 1½ minas, and the debtor, Šu-Kūbum, bears a quite well-known name. If it is the same lady, Ahattum is also creditor in **178**. There is only one witness.

---

178. An Assyrian Woman Lends Silver to an Assyrian Merchant for One Month

Envelope

Obv. ^{1}kišib *A-la$_1$-hi-[im]* ^{2}(seal A) ^{3}dumu *Du$^!$-dí-ki* kišib *Šu-Ku-bi$_4$-lim* ^{4}dumu *Nu-ur$^!$*(NI)*-Ištar* ^{5}½ *ma-na* kù-babbar *ṣa-ru-pá-am* ^{6}(seal B) ^{7}*i-ṣé-er Šu-Ku-bi$_4$-im* lo.e. ^{8}(seal B) ^{9}*A-ha-tum tí-šu* rev. ^{10}*iš-tù ha-mu-uš-tim* ^{11}(seal B) ^{12}*ša Ì-lí-iš-tí-kál* ^{13}*ù Puzur$_4$*-sa-tu ^{14}*a-na* iti-1-kam *i-ša-qal* ^{15}*šu-ma lá iš-qú-ul* ^{16}(seal A) ^{17}1½ gín-ta *a-na ma-na-lim* u.e. ^{18}*ṣí-ib-tám ú-ṣa-áb* ^{19}(seal A) ^{20}iti-kam *A-lá-na-tim* ^{21}*li-mu-um* le.e. ^{22}*Bu-zu-zu* ^{23}(seal B) r.e. ^{24}(seal A)

$^{1-4}$Sealed by Ali-ahu[m], son of Dudiki; sealed by Šu-Kūbum, son of Nūr-Ištar.

$^{5-9}$Ahattum has loaned ½ mina of refined silver to Šu-Kūbum. $^{10-14}$From the week of Iliš-tikal and Puzur-šadu'e, he shall pay in one month. $^{15-18}$If he has not paid, he shall add interest of 1½ shekels per mina. $^{20-22}$Month Allānātum (xii), eponym Buzuzu (REL 87).

Tablet

Obv. ^{1}½ *ma-na* kù-babbar ^{2}*ṣa-ru-pá-am* ^{3}*i-ṣé-er Šu-Ku-bi-im* ^{4}*A-ha-tum tí-šu-ú* ^{5}*iš-tù ha-muš-tim* ^{6}*ša Ì-lí-iš-tí-kál* ^{7}*ù Puzur$_4$-ša-du-e* ^{8}*a-na* iti-1-kam ^{9}*i-ša-qal šu-ma* lo.e. ^{10}*lá iš-qúl* ^{11}1½ gín-ta ^{12}*i*-iti-kam^{im} ^{13}*a-na* 1 *ma-na-im* ^{14}*ṣí-ib-tám ú-ṣa-áb* ^{15}igi *A-la-hi-im*

[1-4]Ahattum has loaned ½ mina of refined silver to Šu-Kūbum. [5-9]From the week of Iliš-tikal and Puzur-šadu'e, he shall pay in one month. [9-14]If he has not paid, he shall add interest of 1½ shekels per mina.

[15]In the presence of Ali-ahum.

Bibliography: Text published in copy by Lewy as TC 3, 228; edited by Rosen (1977, 133).

Comments: Creditor and debtor are the same as those of the previous text; the amount of silver is less, as well as the length of the loan. It takes place during another week period, perhaps of the same year (ca. 1886).

---

179. An Assyrian Woman Lends a Small Amount of Silver to a Man for Three Weeks

Obv. [1]16 gín kù-babbar *ṣa-ru-pá-am* [2]*i-ṣé-er* [3]*Ha-nu* : *Ša-ta-na* [4]*tí-šu iš-tù ha-mu-uš-/tim* [5]*ša Kar-wa-a* [6]*ù Kur-ub-Ištar* [7]*a-na* 3 *ha-am-ša-/tim* [8]*i-ša-qal* [9]*šu-ma lá iš-qú-ul* [10]1 gín-ta *ṣí-ib-/tám* [11]*i*-iti-kam *ú-ṣa-áb* [12]igi *A-šur-*[d]utu[*ši*] [13]igi *Im-li-kà-a* [14]igi *En-na-nim*

[1-4]Šāt-Anna has loaned 16 shekels of refined silver to Hanu. [4-8]From the week of Karwaya and Kurub-Ištar, he shall pay in 3 weeks. [9-11]If he has not paid, he shall add interest of 1 shekel per (mina and) per month.

[12-14]In the presence of Aššur-šamšī, Imlikaya, and Ennānum.

Bibliography: Text published in copy by Smith and Wiseman as CCT 5, 20c; edited by Rosen (1977, 107–8).

Comments: The refined silver is loaned for a short period and an interest of 1 shekel per month—lower than the usual interest of 1½ shekels—is added. The witnesses are two men.

---

180. An Assyrian Woman Lends Silver to an Assyrian Merchant for Two Months

Obv. [1]⅔ *ma-na* 1 gín kù-babbar [2]*ṣa-ru-pá-am i-ṣé-er* [3]*Šál-mì-hi-im* dumu *Ma-áš-hi-li Ša-ta-na* [4]*tí-šu* : *iš-tù* [5]*ha-muš-tim* : *ša me-ra* [6]*En-um-A-nim a-na* [7]iti-2-kam *i-ša-qal* [8]*šu-ma* : *lá iš-qú-ul* [9]*ki-ma a-wa-at* [10]*kà-ri-im* :

i-na iti-kam [11]*ṣí-ib-tám ú-ṣa-ab* iti-kam lo.e. [12]*Ma-hu-ri-lu* [13]*li-mu-um* rev. [14]*ša qá-tí* [15]*En-na-Sú-en*$_6$ (erased sign) [16]dumu *Šu-A-šùr* [17]igi *Ma-sà-A-šùr* [18]dumu *A-al*-du$_{10}$ [19]igi *A-mur-Ištar* dumu [20]*Pí-lá-ah-Ištar*

[1–4]Šāt-Anna has loaned ⅔ mina, 1 shekel of refined silver to Šalim-ahum, son of Mašhi-ilī. [4–7]From the week of the son of Ennam-Anum, he shall pay in 2 months. [8–11]If he has not paid, he shall add interest per month according to the rate of the *kārum*. [11–16]Month Mahhur-ilī (iv), the eponym who followed Enna-Suen, son of Šu-Aššur (REL 107 + 1).

[17–20]In the presence of Massa-Aššur, son of Āl-ṭāb, and Amur-Ištar, son of Pilah-Ištar.

Bibliography: Text published in copy by Lewy as TC 3, 235; edited by Rosen (1977, 141).

Comments: The creditor is the same woman as that of the previous text; she lends forty-one shekels of refined silver for two months to a merchant bearing an Assyrian name but whose father has an Anatolian name. The loan is dated to REL 107 + 1 (ca. 1865). The transaction is witnessed by two Assyrians.

---

181. An Assyrian Woman Lends Silver to a Man

Envelope

Rev. [1'](seal A) [2']½ *ma-na* kù-babbar [3']*i-ṣé-er Zi-*[*ki-ki*] [4'][*Š*]*a-at-A-na* [5'][*tí*]-*šu* : *iš-tù* [*ha-muš-tim*] [6']*ša E-lá-m*[*a ù Šu-Ku-/bi-im*] [7']1 gín-t[a *i*-iti-kam] [8']*ú-ṣa-áb* [9'](seal B) u.e. [10'](seal B?) le.e. [11'](seal C?)

[2'–5'][Š]āt-Anna has loaned ½ mina of silver to Zi[kiki]. [5'–8']From the [week] of Elamm[a and Šu-Kūbum], he shall add 1 shekel (of interest) [per month].

Tablet

Obv. [1]½ *ma-na* kù-babbar [2]*i-ṣé-er* [3]*Zi-ki-ki* [4]*Ša-at-A-na* [5]*tí-šu iš-tù* [6]*ha-mu-uš-tim* [7]*ša E-la-ma* lo.e. [8]*ù Šu-Ku-bi-im* rev. [9]1 gín-ta *i-na* [10]iti-kam : *ú-ṣa-áb* [11]igi *La*$_1$*-ma-sí* [12]igi *Šu-Ku-bi*$_4$*-im*

[1–5]Šāt-Anna has loaned ½ mina of silver to Zikiki. [5–10]From the week of Elamma and Šu-Kūbum, he shall add 1 shekel per month (as interest).

$^{11-12}$In the presence of Lamassī and Šu-Kūbum.

Bibliography: Text published in copy by Lewy as TC 3, 220; edited by Rosen (1977, 126–27).

Comments: The text is concise; no due date is mentioned. Interest of 1 shekel per month—lower than the usual interest of 1½ shekels—is added. The *hamuštum* of Elamma and Šu-Kūbum is attested during month four (iv) of year REL 85 (Kt c/k 799).

---

182. An Assyrian Woman Lends Silver to an Assyrian Merchant

Envelope

Obv. ^{1}kišib [*A-šù*]*r-i-dí* ^{2}dumu [*A*]*-šur-ma-lik* ^{3}(seal A) ^{4}[kišib] *Ás-qú-dim* dumu ^{5}[*A-šur*]*-re-ṣí* ^{6}[3⅔ g]ín 15 še kù-babbar ^{7}*li-tí i-ṣé-er* ^{8}(seal A) ^{9}*Ás-qú-dim* dumu *A-šur-re-ṣí* ^{10}*Mu-sà tí-šu iš-tù* lo.e. ^{11}(seal B) ^{12}*ha-muš-tim ša* ^{13}*Ú-ṣú-ur-ša-Ištar* lo.e. ^{14}(seal B) ^{15}iti-kam *Ṣí-pí-im li-mu*-/um* ^{16}*I-dí-a-hu-um a-na* ^{17}iti-2-kam *i-ša-qal* ^{18}*šu-ma lá ìš-qúl* ^{19}*i*-iti-kam^{im} ⅙ gín-ta ^{20}[*ṣ*]*í-ib-tám* ^{21}*ú-ṣa-áb* u.e. ^{22}(seal A) le.e. ^{23}(seal A) r.e. ^{24}(seal B)

$^{1-5}$Sealed by [Aššu]r-idī, son of [A]ššur-malik; [sealed by] Asqudum, son of [Aššur]-rēṣī.

$^{6-10}$Musa has loaned [3⅔ sh]ekels, 15 grains of *litum*-silver to Asqudum, son of Aššur-rēṣī. $^{10-17}$From the week of Uṣur-ša-Ištar, month Ṣip'um (vii), eponym Iddin-ahum (REL 110), he shall pay within 2 months. $^{18-21}$If he has not paid, he shall add interest of ⅙ shekel per month.

Tablet

Obv. ^{1}3⅔ gín 15 še ^{2}kù-babbar *li-tí i-ṣé-/er* ^{3}*Ás-qú-dim Mu-sà* ^{4}*tí-šu iš-tù ha-muš-/tim* ^{5}*ša Ú-ṣú-ur-ša-/Ištar* ^{6}iti-kam *Ṣí-pì-im* lo.e. ^{7}*li-mu-um* rev. ^{8}*I-dí-a-hu-um* ^{9}*a-na* iti-2-kam *i-ša-/qal* ^{10}*šu-ma lá ìš-qúl* ^{11}⅙ gín-ta *ṣí-ib-/tám* ^{12}*i*-iti-1-kam^{im} ^{13}*ú-ṣa-áb* ^{14}igi *A-šur-i-dí*

$^{1-4}$Musa has loaned 3⅔ shekels, 15 grains of *litum* silver to Asqudum. $^{4-9}$From the week of Uṣur-ša-Ištar, month Ṣip'um (vii), eponym Iddin-ahum (REL 110), he shall pay within 2 months. $^{10-13}$If he has not paid, he shall add interest of ⅙ shekel per month. ^{14}In the presence of Aššur-idī.

Bibliography: Text published by Bilgiç, Sever, Günbattı, and Bayram as AKT 1, 46 (Kt a/k 895); collated May 2011.

Comments: Musa lent a small amount of silver to Asqudum for a short period; there is only one witness. The date REL 110 corresponds to circa 1863. The interest amounts to two shekels per year.

---

183. An Assyrian Woman Lends Silver at Interest to an Assyrian Woman

Envelope

Obv. [1](seal A) [2]ki[šib Zu-zu-a d]umu *Ì-lí-dan* [3]kišib *Šu-B*[*e-l*]*im* dumu *Zu-ur-zu-ur* [4]kišib *Ša-té-a* dumu-<munus> *Sú-e-ta-ta* [5]1 *ma-na* kù-babbar *li-tí* [6](seal B) [7]*i-ṣé-er Ša-té-a* dumu-<munus> lo.e. [8](seal B) rev. [9]*Sú-e-ta-ta Ištar-lá-ma-sí* [10]*tí-šu iš-tù* [11](seal C) [12][*ha*]-*mu-uš-tim ša* ^{d}mar-tu-*ba-ni* [13]*ù A-šùr-na-da* 2 gín-ta [14][*i*]-*na* iti-kam *ṣí-ib-tám tù-ṣa-áb* [15][i]ti-kam *A-lá-na-tim* [16](seal C) u.e. [17][*li-mu-um* d]u$_{10}$-*A-šur* [18](seal A) r.e. [19](seal C)

[1–4]Se[aled by Zuzua, s]on of Ilī-dān; sealed by Šu-B[ēl]um, son of Zurzur; sealed by Šāt-Ea, dau<ghter> of Su'etata.

[5–10]Ištar-lamassī has loaned 1 mina of *litum*-silver to Šāt-Ea, dau<ghter> of Su'etata. [10–14]From the [w]eek of Amurru-bāni and Aššur-nādā, he shall add as interest 2 shekels [p]er month. [15–17][M]onth Allānātum (xii), [eponym] Ṭāb-Aššur (REL 91).

Tablet

[1]1 *ma-na* kù-babbar *li-tí i-ṣé-/er* [2]*Ša-té-a Ištar-lá-ma-sí* [3]*tí-šu iš-tù ha-mu-uš-tim* [4]*ša* ^{d}mar-tu-*ba-ni* [5]*ù A-šur-na-da* [6]2 gín-ta *i-na* [7]iti-kam *ṣí-ib-tám* [8]*ú-ṣa-áb* iti-kam lo.e. [9]*A-lá-na-tim* rev. [10]*li-mu-um* [11]du$_{10}$-*A-šur* [12]igi *Zu-zu-a* [13]igi *Šu-be-lim*

[1–3]Ištar-lamassī has loaned 1 mina of *litum*-silver to Šāt-Ea. [3–8]From the week of Amurru-bāni and Aššur-nādā, he shall add as interest 2 shekels per month. [8–11]Month Allānātum (xii), eponym Ṭāb-Aššur (REL 91).

[12–13]In the presence of Zuzua and Šu-Bēlum.

Bibliography: Text published in copy by Matouš as ICK 2, 11; edited by Rosen (1977, 155).

Comments: A woman lends 1 mina of silver to a woman; the transaction is witnessed by two men. No date is indicated for repayment; an interest of 2 shekels per month—higher than the usual interest of 1½ shekels—is added. The two witnesses and the debtor have sealed the envelope, which gives the names of their fathers. The contract is dated to circa 1882.

Lines 4 and 7 of the envelope: the writer wrote "dumu," "son," instead of "dumu-munus," "daughter."

Line 8 of the tablet: the writer has used by mistake the masculine form *uṣṣab* instead of the feminine *tuṣṣab* (line 14 of the envelope).

---

184. An Assyrian Woman Lends Silver to Another Assyrian Woman

Obv. ^{1}12 gín kù-babbar ^{2}*i-ṣé-er* ^{3}*Lá-ma-sí-tim* ^{4}*Ša-at-E-a* ^{5}*tí-šu iš-tù* ^{6}*ha-mu-uš-tim* ^{7}[*š*]*a* ^{d}mar-tu-*ba-ni* ^{8}[*ú Šá*]*l-ma-A-šur* lo.e. ^{9}[x gín-ta] rev. ^{10}[kù-babbar *ṣí-ib-t*]*ám* ^{11}[*i*]*-na* iti-kam ^{12}*tù-ṣa-áb* iti-kam ^{13}*Ma-hu-ri*$^{!}$*-li* ^{14}*li-mu-um* ^{15}*Šu-Hu-bu-ur* ^{16}igi *Ku-ra* ^{17}[ig]i *I-ku-pì-a*$^{!}$(IM)

$^{1-5}$Šāt-Ea has loaned 12 shekels of silver to Lamassatum. $^{5-12}$From the week of Amurru-bāni [and Ša]lim-Aššur, she shall add [as interest x shekels of silver per (mina) p]er month. $^{12-15}$Month Mahhur-ilī (iv), eponym Šu-Hubur (REL 88).

$^{16-17}$In the presence of Kura [an]d Ikuppiya.

Bibliography: Text publish by Bilgiç, Sever, Günbattı, and Bayram as AKT 1, 1 (Ank. 4669).

Comments: This loan of Šāt-Ea is dated to REL 88 (ca. 1885); perhaps the same lady appears as indebted in several other documents, among them 74 and CCT 6, 1b.

---

185. An Assyrian Woman Lends a Small Amount of Silver to an Anatolian

Obv. ^{1}7½ gín kù-babbar ^{2}*i-ṣé-er A-ta-li* ^{3}*Ištar-ba-áš-tí* : *tí-šu* ^{4}*i-na ša Be-lim* ^{5}*i-ša-qal šu-ma* ^{6}*lá iš-qú-ul* ^{7}4 lá ¼ gín kù-babbar ^{8}*ṣí-ib-t*[*ám*] ^{9}*i-na* iti-[kam] ^{10}*ú-ṣ*[*a-áb*] ^{11}igi *Tù-*[*tù-pì-a-lá*] ^{12}igi *Kà-pì-ú-m*[*a-an*] ^{13}igi *Šu-pu-nu-ma-an* ^{14}igi *I-lu-ra-áš* ^{15}igi *Ha-ar-lá* ^{16}igi *A-du-wa*

[1-3]Ištar-baštī has loaned 7½ shekels of silver to Atali. [4-5]He shall pay at (the festival of) Bēlum. [5-10]If he has not paid, he shall a[dd] intere[st] of 3¾ shekels of silver per month.

[11-16]In the presence of Tu[tupiala], Kapium[an], Šuppunuman, Iluraš, Harla, and Aduwa.

Bibliography: Text published by Bayram (1990, 458 [Kt a/k 335]). Its envelope, Kt a/k 931, is unpublished; it is sealed by the six witnesses and the debtor; collated May 2011.

Comments: The amount of silver is small, but no fewer than six Anatolians witnessed the transaction. The due date is given by means of a religious event. The interest corresponds to 50 percent of the borrowed amount. The divine name Bēlum might be a translation in Akkadian of an Anatolian deity.

---

186. A Woman Lends Silver to Two Men

Envelope

Obv. [1](seal A) [2]kišib *A-[zu]-ú** kišib *Na-qí-[du]* [3]kišib *Ištar-um-mì* kišib [4]*Na-ki-le-ed* [5](2 square stamp seals) lo.e. [6][kišib] *Ma-na-ma-na* [7](seal B) [8][*ša*] *hu-bu-ul* rev. [9](seal C) [10][*N*]*a-ki-le-ed ù* [11]*Ma-na-ma-na ša* [12]½ *ma-na* 4½ gín kù-babbar [13]*i-ṣé-ri-šu-nu* [14]*Zi-zi-zi tí-šu-ú* [15](seal C) [16][*a-n*]*a ša A-na* u.e. [17](seal A) le.e. [18][*i*]*-ša-qú-lu* [19](seal B) r.e. [20](seal D)

[1-6]Sealed by A[z]u; sealed by Naqi[du]; sealed by Ištar-ummī; sealed by Nakile'ed; [sealed] by Manamana.

[18-14][Concerning] the debt of [N]akile'ed and Manamana, which amounts to ½ mina, 4½ shekels of silver that Zizizi has loaned to them, [16-18][th]ey shall pay [at] the (festival) of Anna.

Tablet

Obv. [1]½ *ma-na* 4½ gín [2]kù-babbar *i-ṣé-er* [3]*Na-ki-le-ed* [4]*ù Ma-na-ma-na* [5]*Zi-zi-zi* [6]*tí-šu a-na* lo.e. [7]*ša A-na* [8]*i-ša-qú-lu* rev. [9]igi *A-zu-ú* [10]igi *Na-qí-du* [11]igi *Ištar-um-mì*

[1-6]Zizizi has loaned ½ mina, 4½ shekels of silver to Nakile'ed and Manamana. [7-8]They shall pay at the (festival) of Anna.

[9-11]In the presence of Azu, Naqidu, and Ištar-ummī.

Bibliography: Text published by Bilgiç, Sever, Günbattı, and Bayram as AKT 1, 60 (Kt a/k 811); collated May 2011.

Comments: A woman lent silver to two men; the deadline of the loan is a religious festival. The document has been sealed by the two debtors and three witnesses; among these is an Assyrian woman, Ištar-ummī.

---

187. A Woman Lends an Important Amount of Silver to a Man

Envelope

Obv. [1]kišib *Zu-mu* kišib *Ga-zu-ba* [2](seal A) [3]kišib *Šu-ra-ma* [4]*ša hu-bu-ul Šu-ra-/ma* [5]1½ *ma-na* 3½ gín [6]kù-babbar *i-ṣé-er* [7]*Šu-ra-ma Zi-zi-zi /tí-šu-ú* [8](seal A) [9]2 túg[hi-a] *e-ru-ba-tù-šu* lo.e. [10](seal B) rev. [11]*i-n[a ha-a]r-pè* [12]*i-š[a-qal]* [13]*šu-ma lá iš-qú-ul* [14]3 gín-ta *i-na* [15]iti-kam *ú-ṣa-áb* [16](seal B) u.e. [17](seal C) le.e. [18](seal B) r.e. [1](seal D)

[1-3]Sealed by Zumu; sealed by Gazuba; sealed by Šurama.

[4-7]Concerning the debt of Šu-Rama, corresponding to 1½ minas, 3½ shekels of silver that Zizizi has loaned to Šu-Rama, [9-12](and for which) 2 textiles are his pledge, he sha[ll pay] by the [summ]er. [13-15]If he has not paid, he shall add 3 shekels per (mina and) per month (as interest).

Bibliography: Text published by Bilgiç, Sever, Günbattı, and Bayram as AKT 1, 72 (Kt a/k 925a); collated May 2011. The tablet Kt a/k 925b (published as AKT 1, 71) does not match this envelope; there may have been an error while giving inventory numbers to these documents.

Comments: The same creditor as the previous text, Zizizi, lends 1 mina and 33½ shekels to a man, who deposited as pledge two textiles. The interest imposed on this loan is very high.

---

188. A Woman Lends Silver to Three People

Obv. [1]⅓ *ma-na* 5½ gín kù-babbar [2]*ṣa-ru-pá-am* : *i-ṣé-er* [3]*A-ba-a* : *Lá-ma-sà-tim* [4]*ù Ku-zi-a* : *Ku-ul-ša-/an* [5]*tí-šu* : *iš-tù ha-muš-/tim* [6]*ša A-šùr-i-dí* [7]*ù Šu-Ištar* lo.e. [8]2 *ha-ra-né-en*$_6$ rev. [9]*ú-kà-šu-du-ma* [10]kù-babbar : *i-ša-qú-lu*

^{11}iti-kam *Áb-ša-ra-ni* ^{12}*li-mu-um Ku-bi*$_4$*-a* ^{13}*šu-ma lá iš-qú-lu* ^{14}2 gín-ta *i-* iti-kam^{im} ^{15}*ú-ṣú-bu* : šà-ba *ša* ^{16}10 gín kù-babbar 6 *ma-na*-ta* ^{17}síg^{hi-a} *na-ar-ba-tim* / *i-du-nu-nim* le.e. ^{18}kù-babbar *i-qá-qá-ad* ^{19}*šál-me-šu-nu* : *ke-ni-šu-nu* ^{20}*ra-ki-is* : igi ^{21}*Da-lá-áš*

$^{1-5}$Kulšan has loaned ⅓ mina, 5½ shekels of refined silver to Abaya, Lamassatum, and Kuziya. $^{5-10}$From the week of Aššur-idī and Šu-Ištar, they shall make 2 round trip caravans, and they shall pay the silver. $^{11-12}$Month Ab-šarrāni (v), eponym Kubiya (REL 97). $^{13-15}$If they have not paid, they shall add 2 shekels per month (as interest). $^{15-17}$For it, for each 10 shekels of silver, they shall give 6 minas of soft wool. $^{18-20}$The silver is charged to them as a joint responsibility.

$^{20-21}$In the presence of Dalaš.

Bibliography: Text published by Uzunalimoğlu (1992, 53–54 [Kt n/k 860]); collated May 2011.

Comments: Among the three debtors is the woman Lamassatum. The duration of the loan is based on two round trip caravans, but we do not know in which direction; perhaps inside Anatolia? The interest, which is made partly in wool, is very high. The contract is dated to REL 97 (ca. 1876).

---

189. An Anatolian Woman Lends Silver to Another Anatolian Woman

Envelope

Obv. ^{1}kišib *I-dí-Sú-en*$_6$ ^{2}(seal A, four times) ^{3}kišib *Mu-sà* (erasure) ^{4}kišib *Ša-ta-ah-šu-ša-ar* ^{5}11 (*sic*) gín kù-babbar *i-ṣé-er* ^{6}*Ša-ta-ah-šu-ša-ar* ^{7}*A-na-na* : *tí-šu* ^{8}(seal A, four times) ^{9}*a-na ša Ha-ri-ha-ri* lo.e. ^{10}(seal B) rev. ^{11}(seal C) ^{12}*ta-ša-qal* u.e. ^{13}(seal C)

$^{1-4}$Sealed by Iddin-Suen; sealed by Musa; sealed by Šatahšušar.

$^{5-7}$Anna-anna has loaned 11<¼> shekels of silver to Šatahšušar. $^{9-12}$She shall pay (at the festival of) Harihari.

Seal C Inscription

^{1}*En-na-na-tum* ^{2}dumu-munus *Puzur*$_4$*-/ša-da*

Tablet

Obv. [1]11¼ gín kù-babbar [2]*i-ṣé-er* [3]*Ša-tá-ah-šu-ša-ar* [4]*A-na-na* : *tí-šu* [5]*a-na ša Ha-ri-ha-ri* [6]*ta-ša-qal* [7]igi *I-dí-Sú-en*$_6$ lo.e. [8]igi *Mu-sà*

[1-4]Anna-anna has loaned 11¼ shekels of silver to of Šatahšušar. [5-6]She shall pay (at the festival of) Harihari.

[7-8]In the presence of Iddin-Suen and Musa.

Bibliography: Text published in copy by Hrozný as ICK 1, 24; edited by Rosen (1977, 48). The reverse is not inscribed.

Comments: Anna-anna is the creditor, and Šatahšušar will pay back the silver at the time of the festival of Harihari. This is the unique mention of this Anatolian deity; see Veenhof 2008a, 236, no. 4. The amount of the silver involved in this loan is not certain: 11¼ shekels on the tablet, and 11 shekels on the envelope. There are two witnesses, but the only sealing on the envelope bearing an inscription gives the name of a woman who is not attested in the transaction: Ennanatum, daughter of Puzur-šada; it is not possible to know who used this seal.

---

190. Witness Deposition Relating to a Debt Owed to a Woman

Obv. [1]*i-Kà-ne-eš*$_{15}$ ^{d}nin-šubur-*du-ni* [2]*a-na a-ša-at Dam-qá-a* [3]*iṣ-ba-at-ni-a-tí-ma um-ma* [4]^{d}nin-šubur-*du-ni-ma a-na* [5]*a-ša-at Dam-qá-a-ma* [6]*am-tí a-na* 17 gín kù-babbar [7]*iš-tí-ki wa-áš-ba-at* [8]*li-bi*$_4$ *am-tí-a lá tù-lá-mì-ni* [9]*iš-tù Wa-ah-šu-ša-na* [10]*lá-tù-ra-ma tù-dí-tám* lo.e. [11]*i-na ir-tí-ki a-ša-kán* rev. [12]*ù* kù-babbar^{áp}-*ki ú-ta-ra-ki-/im* [13]*a-na a-wa-tim a-ni-a-tim* [14]*kà-ru-um Wa-ah-šu-ša-na* [15]*ṣa-he-er* gal *i-dí-na-ni-ma* [16]igi *šu-ga-ri-a-im ša A-šur** [17]*ší-bu-tí a-dí-in* [18]igi dingir-*re-ṣí* dumu *Ba-al-/ṭù-a* [19]*Na-na-a* dumu *Ha-na-nim* [20]*tap-pá-i*

[1-3]In Kaneš, Ilabrat-dunnī seized us against the *aššutum*-wife of Damqaya, and [4-5]Ilabrat-dunnī (said) as follows against the wife of Damqaya: [6-8]"My female slave is staying with you (as security) for the 17 shekels of silver. You must not make her unhappy. [9-11]When I return from Wahšušana, I will fix a garment pin on your breast and [12]give you back your silver."

[13-15]For these proceedings, the *kārum* of Wahšušana, (the whole assembly) small and big, appointed me (as arbitrator), and [16-17]I have

given my testimony before Aššur's sword. [18–20]In the presence of Ilī-rēṣi, son of Balṭua; Nanaya, son of Hannānum was my partner.

Bibliography: Text published by Bilgiç and Günbattı as AKT 3, 51 (Kt v/k 135); collated May 2012.

Comments: The female slave of Ilabrat-dunnī has been taken as pledge by the wife of Damqaya for a loan of seventeen shekels of silver. He promises to repay his debt as soon as he comes back from Wahšušana, and, to be sure that in the interim his female slave is well treated, he promised his female creditor a jewel as gift.

---

191. A Woman Lent Silver at Interest to Another Woman, Who Contested It

Obv. [1]*da-a-a-nu dí-nam* [2]*i-dí-nu-ma* 6 gín kù-babbar / *ša* [3]*Kà-áp-sí-a* : dam-munus [4]*A-lá-bí-im* : *a-na* [5]*Bu-ṣí* dumu-munus *I-dí-*^{d}im [6]*ta-dí-nu iš-tù li-mì-im* [7]*A-šùr-i-mì-tí ma-lá-hi-im* [8]1 *ma-na-um* ½ *ma-na* [9]*i-na ša-tim* [10]*ṣí-ib-tám tù-ṣú-bu* [11]*a-na* kù-babbar *ú ṣí-ba-tí-šu* lo.e. [12]*Kà-áp-sí-a* rev. [13]dam-munus *A-lá-bi*$_4$*-im* [14]*Bu-ṣí* dumu-munus *I-dí-*^{d}im [15]*ta-še-e*$^{!}$(ŠU)* : *A-gi*$_5$$^{!}$*-a* [16]dumu *Puzur*$_4$*-A-šùr* [17](erased sign)* ^{d}utu-*ba-ni* [18]dumu *En-na-Sú-en*$_6$ [19]*Ma-num**-*ki-A-šùr* [20]dumu *A-hu-wa-qar* [21]*a-wi-lu a-ni-ú-tum* [22]*da-a-nu*

[1–2]The judges gave the following verdict: [2–6]concerning the 6 shekels of silver that Kapsiya, wife of Ali-abum, had given to Buṣi, daughter of Iddin-Adad, [6–10]and for which she was (supposed) to add an interest of ½ mina per mina per year, beginning with the eponym Aššur-imittī, the boatman (REL 106), [11–15]for the silver and its interest, Kapsiya, wife of Ali-abum may sue Buṣi, daughter of Iddin-Adad.

[15–22]Agiya, son of Puzur-Aššur; Šamaš-bāni, son of Enna-Suen; Mannum-kī-Aššur, son of Ahu-waqar: these gentlemen (were) the judges.

Bibliography: Text published by Veenhof as AKT 5, 70 (Kt 92/k 210); collated May 2012.

Comments: This verdict, which is dated to circa 1867, confirms the loan of six shekels of silver, which the wife of Ali-abum made to the daughter of Iddin-Ištar, which the latter must have contested. Kapsiya has presented sufficient evidence for a formal proceeding resulting in a verdict that allows her to sue her debtor. According to the editor of the text, Ali-abum's wife, Kapsiya, was the mother of Kuliya, owner of a group of texts discovered in 1992 and messenger of the *kārum*.

---

192. Loan by a Woman Linked to the Departure of a Girl

Obv. ^{1}*um-ma Ištar-ba-áš-tí-ma* ^{2}*a-na A-nu-wa Puzur*$_{4}$*-Ištar* ^{3}*Ištar-ba-áš-tí ù A-na-na* ^{4}*qí-bi*$_{4}$*-ma a-na* ^{5}*Ištar-ba-áš-tí* ^{6}*ù A-nu-wa qí-bi*$_{4}$*-ma* ^{7} ⅓ *ma-na* 5 gín kù-babbar ^{8}*ṣa-ru-pá-am i-na* ^{9}*ṣé-ri-ku-nu iš-tù* ^{10}*me-er-at-ku-nu* lo.e. ^{11}*té-kà-ma-ni i-šu* ^{12}kù-babbar^{pì} *a-na* rev. ^{13}*ṣí-ib-tim i-na* ^{14}*qá-qá-ad mu-tí-ki*$^{!}$(ŠU) ^{15}*ku-a-tí ù me-er-e-šu* ^{16}*lá-pì-it šu-ma* ^{17}*a-ha-tí a-tí ki-ma* ^{18}*ṭup-pì ta-áš-me-ú-ni* ^{19}kù-babbar^{pì} *ù ṣí-ba-sú* ^{20}*a-na Puzur*$_{4}$*-Ištar* ^{21}*ù A-na-na* ^{22}*ša ki-ma i-a-tí* u.e. ^{23}*šu-uq-lá-ma* ^{24}*lu-še-bi*$_{4}$*-lu-nim* le.e. ^{25}*a-na Puzur*$_{4}$*-Ištar ù A-na-na* ^{26}*qí-bi*$_{4}$*-ma a-pu-tum ih-da-ma* ^{27}kù-babbar^{pì} *ú ṣí-ba-sú* ^{28}*ša-áš-qí-lá-šu-nu-tí*

$^{1-6}$Thus (says) Ištar-baštī: say to Annuwa, Puzur-Ištar, Ištar-baštī, and Anna-anna; say in particular to Ištar-baštī and Annuwa.

$^{7-11}$I loaned you ⅓ mina, 5 shekels of refined silver, since (the time) you took your daughter away from me. $^{12-16}$My silver is recorded as interest-bearing on the head of your husband, yourself, and his children. $^{16-18}$If you are my sister, when you hear my tablet, $^{19-24}$pay my silver and its interest to Puzur-Ištar and Anna-anna, my representatives, so they can send (it) to me.

$^{25-28}$Say to Puzur-Ištar and Anna-anna. Urgent! Be sure to make them pay my silver and its interest!

Bibliography: Text published in transliteration by Lewy (1965, 273 n. 8) as LB 1217, and by Ichisar (1981, 23 n. 26); translated by Michel (2001a, no. 356).

Comments: Ištar-baštī, presumably the wife of Imdī-ilum, held, probably as pledge, the daughter of her homonym. But the parents of the girl took her back, though still indebted to Ištar-baštī for twenty-five shekels of refined silver.

Line 14: the pronoun might refer to the husband of the Ištar-baštī, addressee of this letter, and thus has to be corrected.

193. Woman Acts as Guarantor in a Loan Contract

Obv. ^{1}3 *ma-na* kù-babbar *ṣa-ru-pá-am* ^{2}*a-na* dam-gàr$^{ri\text{-}im}$ ^{3}*Šál-ma-A-šur* ^{4}*ù A-ta-ta* ^{5}*ha-bu-lu Ša-té-a* ^{6}*qá-tá-tum* ^{7}*A-na-na ù Ṣí-li-Ku-ba-ba-at* ^{8}é^{tù}-*šu-nu* ^{9}[*e-r*]*u-ba-tù-a* lo.e. ^{10}[*iš-tù h*]*a-mu-uš-tim* rev. ^{11}*ša Lá-qé-pì-im* ^{12}*ù Bu-zu-ta-a* ^{13}*a-na* 6 *ha-am-ša-tim* ^{14}*i-ša-qú-lu* ^{15}*šu-ma lá iš-qú-lu* ^{16}1½ gín kù-babbar *a*-1 *ma-na* ^{17}*ṣí-ib-tám ú-ṣú-bu* ^{18}iti-1-kam *A-lá-na-tim* ^{19}*li-mu-um* ^{20}dingir-šu-gal u.e. ^{21}igi *A-šùr-e-mu-qí* ^{22}dumu *E-dí-na-a* le.e. ^{23}igi *En-nam-A-šur* ^{24}dumu ^{d}im-*re-ṣ*[*i*]

$^{1-6}$Šalim-Aššur and Atata owe 3 minas of refined silver to the (Assyrian) creditor; Šāt-Ea is the guarantor. $^{7-9}$Anna-anna and Ṣilli-Kubabat, (as well as) their houses are my pledges. $^{10-14}$[From the w]eek of Laqēpum and Buzutaya, they shall pay within 6 weeks. $^{15-17}$If they have not paid, they shall add 1½ shekels of silver per mina (and per month) as interest. $^{18-20}$Month Allānātum (xii), eponym Ilšu-rabi (REL 89, ca. 1884).

$^{21-24}$In the presence of Aššur-emūqi, son of Edinaya, and Ennum-Aššur, son of Adad-rēṣi.

Bibliography: Text published in copy by J. Lewy as TC 3, 232; translated by Veenhof (2001, 99); discussed by Kienast (1976).

Comments: Šāt-Ea is guarantor for a debt of a substantial amount of silver owed by two Assyrians to an anonymous creditor. Their presumed wives and houses are pledged. We do not know if there is any family link between the guarantor Šāt-Ea and the two debtors.

194. A Woman, Guarantor in a Loan Contract, Receives a Plot of Land

Envelope

Obv. $^{1'}$kišib *E*[*n-um-A-šùr* dumu *Šál-ma*-^{d}im] $^{2'}$kišib *A*-[*dí-a* dumu *A-mur*-dingir] $^{3'}$kišib *I*-[*dí-Sú-en*$_6$] $^{4'}$dumu [PN] $^{5'}$15 [gín kù-babbar] $^{6'}$*ša* [*I-dí-Sú-en*$_6$] lo.e. $^{7'}$(seal A) $^{8'}$*a-na nu-a-em ha-bu-lu-ma* rev. $^{9'}$(seal A) (lacuna) le.e. $^{1''}$[*a*]-*na nu-a-em ù Mu-sà i-tù-a-a*[*r*] $^{2''}$(seal B) $^{3''}$[*I*]-*dí-Sú*-[*en*$_6$] *ú-ba-áb-šu-nu*

$^{1'-4'}$Sealed by E[nnum-Aššur], son of [Šalim-Adad]; sealed by A[diya, son of Amur-ilī]; sealed by I[ddin-Suen], son of [PN].

$^{5'-8'}$(Concerning the) 15 [shekels of silver] that [Iddin-Suen] owes to the Anatolian (creditor) and [for which Musa, his sister, is guarantor] (lacuna)

$^{1''-3''}$[...] raises a claim against the Anatolian (creditor) or Musa, [I]ddin-Su[en] shall clear them of financial claims.

Tablet

Obv. ^{1}15 gín kù-babbar *ša I-dí-/Sú-en*$_6$ ^{2}*a-na nu-a-em ha-bu-/lu-ma* ^{3}*Mu-sà* : *a-ha-sú* ^{4}*qá-ta-tù-ni ki-ma* ^{5}15 gín kù-babbar *qá-qí-ri-/šu-nu* ^{6}*ša ur-ki bé-tim* ^{7}*a-na nu-a-e-em* «*im*» lo.e. ^{8}*ù Mu-sà i-dí-in* rev. ^{9}*šu-ma ma-ma-an* ^{10}*a-na qá-qí-ri a-na* ^{11}*nu-a-e ù Mu-sà i-tù-ar* ^{12}*I-dí-Sú-en*$_6$ *ú-ša-ha-sú-nu* ^{13}igi *En-um-A-šùr* ^{14}dumu *Šál-ma-*^{d}im ^{15}igi A-dí-a dumu *A-mur-/*dingir

$^{1-4}$(Concerning the) 15 shekels of silver that Iddin-Suen owes to the Anatolian (creditor and for which) Musa, his sister, is guarantor; $^{5-8}$as the equivalent of the 15 shekels of silver, he gave to the Anatolian (creditor) and Musa their plots of land behind the house. $^{9-11}$If anyone raises a claim against the Anatolian (creditor) and Musa for the plots of land, ^{12}Iddin-Suen shall clear them of liability.

$^{13-15}$In the presence of Ennum-Aššur, son of Šalim-Adad, and Adiya, son of Amur-ilī.

Bibliography: Text published in copy by Veenhof as VS 26, 97; edited by Eisser and Lewy (1930, no. 215).

Comments: Musa is the guarantor for her brother, who owes silver to an Anatolian creditor. She receives, together with the Anatolian creditor, a plot of land, which means that she had to pay the silver to the creditor on her brother's behalf.

Tablet, line 2: for the word *nuā'um*, see D. O. Edzard (1989).

Tablet, line 12: the verb *šahātum* II, "to clear of obligations," of the tablet (line 12) is replaced on the envelope (line 3″) by the verb *ebābum* II, "to clear a person or property of legal or financial claims"; see Hecker 1980, 69.

195. A Woman Wishes to Recover Her Silver to Repay a Debt

Obv. ^{1}*a-na Pu-šu-ke-en*$_{6}$ ^{2}*qí-bi-ma um-ma* ^{3}*Šu-bu-ul-tum-ma* ^{4}*Ì-lí-ba-ni* : *iš-tù* ^{5}*iš-tí* : *Ú-ṣú-ur-ša-A-šùr* ^{6}*uš*$_{10}$*-bu* : *ar-bi-i-šu* ^{7}*ha-ra-nam* : *i-li-kam* ^{8}5 gín kù-babbar *i-na* ^{9}*bé-ú-lá-tí-šu* ^{10}*ú-lá al-qé* ^{11}*ú-lá šu-ut* : *i-na lá ma-/ṣí* ^{12}*um-me-a-ni-šu* lo.e. ^{13}kù-babbar 1 gín *ú-lá ir-/ší* ^{14}*ú-lá a-na-ku* rev. ^{15}kù-babbar 5 gín ^{16}*ú-lá aṣ-*<*ba*>*-at šu-ma* ^{17}*a-bi* : *a-ta* : *bé-ú-lá-/tí-šu* ^{18}*ta-e-er-ma* ^{19}*a-na ṣé-ri-kà* ^{20}*ṭá-hi-šu* : *ṣú-ha-ru-um* ^{21}*li-il*$_{5}$*-qé ki*$^{!}$*-ma* ^{22}*ṣú-ha-ri-kà* ^{23}*sí-ni-iq-šu* ^{24}*bé-ú-lá-tí-šu* ^{25}*a-na qá-tí-šu* ^{26}*lá tù-ša-ar* ^{27}*i-ga-ma-ar* ^{28}*a-dí qá-sú* u.e. ^{29}*ta-mu-ru-ni* ^{30}*šu-ma* : *da-mì-iq* le.e. ^{31}*ú da-mì-iq-ma* : *a-na hu-bu-/li-a* ^{32}*bé-ú-lá-tù-šu* : *li-tù-ra*

$^{1-3}$Say to Pūšu-kēn: thus (says) Šūbultum.

$^{4-6}$Since Ilī-bāni has been staying with Uṣur-ša-Aššur, $^{6-7}$he has come four times (to Aššur) with a caravan. $^{8-10}$I have not received (even) 5 shekels of silver from his working capital. $^{11-13}$Nor did he, from sheer negligence, obtain any silver from his investors, not even 1 shekel. $^{14-16}$I myself also got no silver, not even 5 shekels.

$^{17-18}$If you are my father, transfer his working capital and ^{19}bring him (again) in contact with you yourself. $^{20-23}$Let a servant take (it), but check him just like your (other) servants. $^{24-27}$Do not release his working capital to him; it would be spent. $^{28-32}$Until you find out whether or not his business is really all right, his working capital should become part of my debt.

Bibliography: Text published in copy by Lewy as TC 3, 27; edited by Łyczkowska (1978, 133–35); translated by Michel (2001a, no. 372).

Comments: Šūbultum gave some silver as working capital to Ilī-bāni, perhaps to pay the transport of some textiles or goods to Anatolia, thus investing in long-distance trade. She is waiting to get back silver from the sale of her merchandise. But it seems that Ilī-bāni was not reliable, and she did not receive any silver.

196. Consigned Merchandise Belonging to a Woman

Obv. ^{1}⅔* *ma-na* 5 gín kù-babbar ^{2}6 túg^{hi-a} *ku-ta-nu* ^{3}2 gú 5 *ma-na ša-áp-tám* ^{4}1 *am-tám* 4 *pì-ri-kà-/ni* ^{5}1 gú 5 *ma-na* urudu ^{6}*ma-sí-a-am* ^{7}3 *e-ma-re-e* ^{8}*ṣa-lá-«ma»-me-e* ^{9}*mì-ma a-nim* ^{10}*ša Ba-za-a* lo.e. ^{11}*me-er-a-at* rev.

[12]*Id-na-A-šur* [13]*a-na* ^{d}im-gal [14]dumu *Ki-ga-zu* [15]*a-be-a-lim a-dí-in* [16]igi *A-šur-ma-lik* [17]dumu *Li-pá-a* [18]igi *Ú-ṣur-pá-kà* [19]dumu *Puzur*$_{2}$*-Ištar* igi *Pè-ru-/wa* [20]igi* *A-šur-mì-tí*

[1–8]⅔ minas, 5 shekels of silver; 6 *kutānum*-textiles; 2 talents, 5 minas of wool; 1 female slave; 4 *pirikannum*-textiles; 1 talent, 5 minas of refined copper; 3 black donkeys—[9–15]I put all those things belonging to Bazaya, daughter of Iddin-Aššur, at the disposal of Adad-rabi, son of Kigazu to manage (them).

[16–20]In the presence of Aššur-malik, son of Lipaya; Uṣur-pāka, son of Puzur-Ištar; Peruwa; and Aššur-imittī.

Bibliography: Text published by Bayram and Çeçen (1996, no. 5 [Kt 76/k 2]); collated May 2012.

Comments: Bazaya owns all these goods—Assyrian and Anatolian textiles, silver, wool, copper, a female slave, and donkeys—which are entrusted to Adad-rabi as consignment, or *tadmiqum*-trust. Thus, she participates in long-distance trade.

Line 4: the four wedges of the number four are written side by side.

---

197. Intense Business Activity and Mobility of a Woman but without Results

Obv. [1]*a-na A-šur-mu-ta-pì-il*$_{5}$ *qí-bi*$_{4}$*-ma* [2]*um-ma Wa-qúr-tum-ma* 2 *ṭup-pè* [3]*ṣú-ha-ru-um ub-lá-kum* [4]*a-ta mì-ma-ša-ma lá tù-ta-e-/ra-am* [5]*mì-nam e-pu-uš-kà-ma* [6]*a-ni-tám lá a-ni-tám úz-ni* [7]*lá ta-pá-té : šu-ma a-hi a-ta* [8]*a-ma-kam ki-ma i-a-tí ú ṣú-ha-ar-/tim* [9]*a-ta i-zi-iz ú-za-ni* [10]*i-na a-wa-tim pè-té* [11]*i-na* kù-babbar 10 *ma-na* [12]*e-ru-ub-ma u*$_{4}$*-ma-am e-ri-tum* [13](erasure) *ú-ṣa-am* [14]*a-ma-kam a-ṭup-pì-im* [15]*ša hu-bu-li-šu-nu* rev. [16]*ša a-bu-ni ih-ri-mu* [17]*ki-ma* kù-babbar *A-šur uš-ta-bi*$_{4}$*-ú* [18]*a-ta ší-tám a-ṭup-pì-šu-nu* [19]*ha-ar-mì-im ṣa-ba-at* [20]*be-lí a-ta iš-tù* mu-1-šè [21]*ki*$^{!}$*-da-tim ar-ta-na-pu-/ud* [22]*lá*$^{!}$ *me-er-um* kù-babbar 1 gín [23]*šu-mì i-za-kàr lá a-hu-um* [24]*ša* kù-babbar *be-lí-a ú-sà-pu-/hu* [25]*šu-mì iz-ku-ur* [26]*šu-ma a-hi a-ta iš-tí* [27]*ba-tí-qí-im a-wa-at-/kà* [28]*li-li-kam-ma* [29]*úz-ni pè-té šu-ma a-t*[*a*] le.e. [30]*a-ma-kam lá ta-ṣa-ba-at a-wa-at-/kà* [31]*li-li-kam-ma a-na-kam* [32]*ša e-pá-ší-im le-pu-uš*

$^{1-2}$Say to Aššur-mūtappil: thus (says) Waqqurtum.

$^{2-3}$A servant brought you 2 tablets, ^{4}but you never returned anything to me. $^{5-7}$What have I done to you that you do not inform me one way or the other? $^{8-10}$If you are my brother, stand there as representative for me and the girl, (and) give us some word.

$^{11-12}$I went in (to the business) with 10 minas of silver, but $^{12-13}$today I have come out empty-handed. $^{14-16}$There, with respect to the tablet of their debt that our father certified, ^{17}since the silver of the (god) Aššur has been paid back, $^{18-19}$you must seize what remains (after paying the debt) on the basis of their certified tablet.

$^{20-21}$You are my master. For one year, I have been roaming back and forth through uninhabited territories. $^{22-23}$One who is no son of mine invokes my name for every shekel of silver; $^{23-25}$one who is no relative of mine, who squanders my master's silver, (also) invoked my name! $^{26-29}$If you (truly are) my brother, let a word from you come to me by the (next) departing messenger to inform me. $^{29-33}$If you, there, cannot take (the matter in hand), let (just) a word from you come to me, so that here I can do whatever is necessary.

Bibliography: Text published in copy by Smith as CCT 3, 41b–42a; translated by Michel (2001a, no. 317).

Comments: Waqqurtum writes to her brother about unsuccessful financial activities. She has been moving a lot but could not recover the silver she invested. She asks her brother to intercede for her as a representative would do.

---

198. A Widow Traveling in Anatolia on Business

Obv. ^{1}*um-ma En-nam-Ištar-ma* ^{2}*a-na En-nam-A-šùr* ^{3}*qí-bi-ma ma-ah-ri-kà-ma* ^{4}*i-na Bu-ru-uš-ha-tim* ^{5}10 gín kù-babbar : *a-na A-šùr*-du$_{10}$ ^{6}*a-dí-in i-na Kà-ne-eš*$_{15}$ ^{7}*iš-té-en*$_{6}$ túg *ku-ta-nam* ^{8}*a-dí-šu-um* 2 gín kù-babbar ^{9}*aṣ-ba-sú*$^{!}$*-ma* : *ma-lá* ^{10}*ú* 2 *ší-ni-šu* : *um-ma šu-ut-ma* ^{11}*me-ra-ki* : *il*$_{5}$*-qé* ^{12}*šu-ma* : kù-babbar : *tal-qé* lo.e. ^{13}*lá tal-qé* : *té-er-ta-kà* ^{14}*li-li-kam* rev. ^{15}*ma-ah-ri-kà-ma* ^{16}*a-na Be-lu-ba-ni* géme ^{17}*lá e-zi-ib* kù-babbar ^{18}10 gín : *a-hu-ur* ^{19}*ṣa-ba-sú-ma* : kù-babbar ^{20}*ša-áš-qí-il*$_{5}$*-šu* ^{21}*um-ma Na-hi-iš-tum-ma* ^{22}*a-na En-um-A-šùr* ^{23}*Ku-da-*[*tum*] *ra-qá-tám* ^{24}*na-áš-a-k*[*um*] kù-babbar ^{25}*da-mì-qá-am ší-im* ^{26}*ra-qí-tim* : *i-ší-ma-tim* ^{27}*ša a-bi-kà* : *a-ta* u.e. ^{28}*A-lá-*

hu-um ú Lá-ma-/s[í] [29]*a-dí* : *Lá-ma-sí* [30]*ba-al-ṭá-at-ni z*[*i**-x-/x] [31]*lá i-ša-ku-nu* : túg *ku-ta-nam* [32]*ú iš-té-et* : *iš-ra-am A-šùr*-du$_{10}$ [33]*ub-lá-kum*

[1–3]Thus (says) Ennum-Ištar: say to Ennum-Aššur.

[3–6]In your presence, in Burušhattum, I gave 10 shekels of silver to Aššur-ṭāb. [6–8](Then) in Kaneš, I gave him a single *kutānum*-textile. [8–9]I managed to seize only 2 shekels of silver, and [9–11]at least twice, he replied as follows: "Your son took (it)." [12–14]Let your report come whether or not you took the silver. [15–17](Also) in your presence, did I not leave a female slave with Bēlum-bāni? [17–20]But 10 shekels of silver are still to be paid; seize him and make him pay the silver.

[21–22]Thus (says) Nahištum to Ennum-Aššur.

[23–24]Kudātum is bringing you a thin textile; [24–25]do give me a good price (for it) in silver! [25–31]You, Ali-ahum, and Lamassī should not deposit! the price of the thin textile in your father's estate during Lamassī's lifetime. [31–33]Aššur-ṭāb has brought you a *kutānum*-textile and a single belt.

Bibliography: Text published by Larsen as AKT 6a, 223 (Kt 94/k 614). Lines 1–8 cited by Michel (2008d, 34). Collated 2016.

Comments: According to the editor of the text, Ennum-Ištar is the mother of Ennum-Aššur, son of the deceased Šalim-Aššur; she is a widow. She may live in Kaneš but happens to travel as far as Burušhattum, to the west, for some commercial purposes.

Line 23: for *raqqatum*, a "thin (textile)," see Michel and Veenhof 2010, 239–40.

Line 31: according to Larsen (AKT 6a, 365), *išakkunū* could be an error for *tašakkanā*.

Women Representing Their Husbands

Besides managing their own personal property, women were involved in their husbands' business and financial affairs. The Assyrian women who lived alone at Aššur represented their husbands' interests while they were absent for long stays in Anatolia. So too wives at Kaneš represented their spouses when they were away at other commercial settlements in Asia Minor or if they had gone back to Aššur to take care of their interests there. They were expected to look after and protect the goods of absent merchants (**199**, **201**). Since they were in regular contact with their husbands' local agents, they sometimes got copies of letters addressed to them so they could follow ongoing transactions or check on how instructions were being carried out and were supposed to keep them informed about various matters going forward (**129**, **205**, **220**, **313**). They stood up to the demands of their husbands' associates (**128**, **209**), and turned down offers of help from them as well, to avoid laying themselves under any obligation to them (**206**, **207**). In Anatolia, some wives were asked to go on journeys to settle business or family affairs, sometimes at the request of their husband (**200**).

Assyrian and Anatolian women were sometimes called upon to see that unpaid debts were collected and to send the amounts collected to their husbands (**202**, **203**). In some instances they were asked to advance the necessary funds to pay off overdue debts (**204**, **205**), in which case they made sure to note the amount to be repaid to them. Wives sometimes had to deal with their husbands' financial obligations to the authorities, such as unpaid taxes or fines (**207**, **208**); they did not, however, always agree to take on this task. Some women, intimidated by the pressure put on them by the authorities, sold their slaves to pay their husbands' debts (**313**). Also, the eponym or another representative of the Assyrian government could sometimes take a female slave as collateral, thus forcing the woman to pay up (**141**). Other women objected strenuously, refusing to pay sums owed by their husbands. Many of these women were careful accountants, keeping accurate records, documenting their expenses and claiming what was due them (**128**). Women could also ask other women or merchants to represent their interests as intermediaries (**210**) or agents for their own affairs (**211**).

The archives of Kaneš show that Assyrian, and to a lesser extent Anatolian, women were bona fide businesswomen, eminently capable of managing their own affairs and routinely acting as agents or partners for their husbands.

---

199. Safekeeping of the House and Its Contents

Obv. [1]*um-ma A-šùr-*gal*-ma a-na* [2]*Ma-ga-ni-kà qí-bi-ma* [3]*mì-šu : ša ta-áš-pu-ri-ni* [4]*um-ma a-tí-i-ma : ma-ak-na-kam* [5]*a-pá-té-ma ba-pì-ra-am a-na* [6]*ší-mì-im a-da-an be-tum* [7]*ša-áp-li-ú!-um e-li-ú*-um* [8]*lá i-na ku-nu-ki-a kà-ni-ik* [9]*a-pu-tum a-dí : a-lá-kà-ni* [10]*be-tám mì-ma ku-nu-ki-a* [11]*lá ta-pá-té-ma ku-nu-ki-a* lo.e. [12]*ša-ṣí-ri : e-mì-iq-tum* [13]*ta-bu-tá-ni-ma* rev. [14]*a-dí* *u$_4$-mì-im a-nim sà-ah-ra-/ku* [15]*a-pu-tum ki-ma-ma ša-ṣú-ra-tí-/ni* [16]*lu ša-ṣú-ra-tí* : *a-dí* [17]*e-né-e-a* : *ta-me-ri-ni ki-ma lá* [18]*a-dí ma-lá ú šé-ni-šu* an-na [19]*ú-šé-bi$_4$-lá-ki-ni-ma i-dí-nu-ni-ki-/ni* [20]*a-ší-a-tí mì-ma lá ú-šé-ba-lá-ki-im* [21]*iš-tí Wa-ar-dí-im* dumu *I-ku-nim* [22]*ú-šé-ba-lá-ki-im mì-šu* : *ša ú-ša-bi$_4$* [23]*i-na be-tim tù-šé-ší-bi$_4$-ni* [24]*ú a-na mu-tim ta-li-ki-ni* [25]*šu-ma me-er-i-tí* : *a-tí-i* u.e.[26]*be-tám ša-ṣí-ri* : *a-dí* 10 *u$_4$-me* [27]*ni-ta-lá-kam mì-ma ša ta-ša-me-i-*[*ni*] [28]*iš-tí Ke-na-A-šur* le.e. [29]*té-er-tí-ki li-li-ki-im* [30]*qí-iš-tám ú ša-hi-re-e*[*n$_6$*] [31]*ku-nu-ki-ma iš-tí Ke-na-A-šùr* [34]*šé-bi$_4$-li-im*

[1-2]Thus (says) Aššur-rabi: say to Maganika.

[3-6]Why have you written me as follows: "I will open the storeroom and sell the beer bread"? [6-8]Are the lower as well as the upper floors not sealed with my seal? [9-12]Urgent! Until my arrival, do not open any of my seals in the house, and keep my sealings intact!

[12-14]The nanny ran away from me, and thus I have been delayed until today. [15-17]Urgent! Until you have seen me personally, be as watchful as you always are. [17-20]It is not because I sent you tin several times but they did not give (it) to you that I do not send you any more? [21-22]I am (now) sending you (some) with Wardum, son of Ikūnum.

[22-24]Why did you let tenants live in the house while you went (to live) with a husband? [25-27]If you are my daughter, keep watch on the house until we arrive in 10 days! [27-29]Let your report come with Kēna-Aššur concerning all that you hear. [30-34]Seal the gift and a pair of shoe straps, and send (them) with Kēna-Aššur.

Bibliography: Text published in copy by Stephens as BIN 6, 20; translated by Michel (2001a, no. 334).

Comments: Aššur-rabi writes to his daughter, asking her to watch over his house and its contents while he is away. He forbids her to sell any goods from the house, and he is unhappy to hear that she has left it, presumably to rent it to others to earn some money, and has gone to live somewhere else.

---

200. Taking Care of Her Husband's Merchandise

Obv. [1]*a-na Ha-šu-ša-ar-na* [2]*qí-bi-ma um-ma* [3]*A-šur-ták-lá-ku ù* [4]*I-dí-*[d]u-tu-*ma i-ša-am-ší* [5]*na-áš-pé-er-tí-ni* [6]*ta-ša-me-i-ni* [7]*tí-ib-e-ma* : *a-na* [8]*Té-*

ga-ra-ma a-ta-al-/ki-im [9]*i-na Té-ga-ra-ma* lo.e. [10]*i-ša-ha-at* rev. [11]*té-er-tí-a lu uš*-ba*-tí* [12]*a-dí e-tí-qá-ni* [13]*i-ša-am-ší ta-ta-li-/ki-ni* [14]*té-er-tí-ki* [15]*li-li-kam* [16]*a-ta-al-ki-im-ma* [17]x[x-x]x : *i-na Wa-ah-šu-ša-na* [18]*kà-i-li* : *a*-ma*-sú** u.e. [19]*I-dí-*^{d}utu *i-ta-m*[*ar*$^{?}$] [20]*a-ki*-ma e*-na**-[x]-*wa-am** le.e. [21]*I-dí-*^{d}u-tu dam-[gàr] [22][x x]-*ni*

[1-4]Say to Hašušarna: thus (say) Aššur-taklāku and Iddin-Šamaš.

[4-8]The day you hear our letter, set out and come to Tegarama. [9-12]In Tegarama, oversee my goods until I come through. [13-15]Let a report come from you the very day you will leave. [16-18]Then come and offer [...] in Wahšušana. [18-22]Iddin-Šamaš has seen his *amtum*-wife, and according to [...] Iddin-Šamaš, the cre[ditor ...]

Bibliography: Text published in copy by Lewy (1969–1970, 55 [L 29-586]); edited by Gwaltney as POAT, 27; translated by Michel (2001a, no. 395). Collated on photo online on the CDLI as P361140.

Comments: Hašušarna was first married to Taliya; after their divorce (**40**), she seems to have married Aššur-taklāku (Michel 2001a, 505), who asks her in this letter to travel to Tegarama in order to take care of his goods there while he is away, then to go to another town, Wahšušana, to fulfill an obligation.

---

201. A Woman Receives Silver for a Merchant in Her Family

Obv. [1]*um-ma A-šur*-gal-*ma a-na* [2]*Ab-ša-lim qí-bi-ma* [3]1 *ma-na* kù-babbar *ku-nu-ki-a* [4]*a-na na-an-d*[*u*]*-im* [5]*Šu-A-šur* dumu *Kur*$^{!}$*-ub-Ištar* [6]igi *A-lá-hu-um* [7]igi [*En-na*]-*Sú-en*$_{6}$ dumu *I-dí-Ku-/bi-im* [8]*a-dí-in-šu-ma* [9]*na-áš-a-ki-im* kù-babbar [10]*i-ku-nu-ki-a a-dí* lo.e. [11]*a-lá-kà-ni li-bi-ší* rev. [12]10 gín kù-babbar *ku-nu-ki-a* [13]*šé-bu-ul-tí-ki šu-ut-ma* [14]*na-áš-a-ki-im* [15]*ri-ik-sà-am ša Lá-qé-ep* [16]*šu-ma* : an-na : *ta-áš-a-ma* [17]*ṭur*$_{4}$*-da-ni-šu* : *šu-ma* : an-na [18]*lá ta-áš-a-ma ra-qá-ma* [19]*ṭur*$_{4}$*-da-ni-šu* : *a-pá-ni-a* [20]*mì-ma* : an-na : *lá ta-ša-a-ma* [21]*a-dí a-lá-kà-ni qé-mu-um* [22]1 dug *ù* 2 dug [23]*li-im-hu-ra-ni* le.e. [24]*ù še-a*[*m a*]*-ší-mì-im* [25]*dí-na*

[1-2]Thus (says) Aššur-rabi: say to Ab-šalim.

[3-9]In the presence of Ali-ahum and [Enna]-Suen, son of Iddin-Kūbum, I gave 1 mina of silver under my seal to Šu-Aššur, son of Kurub-Ištar, to be

deposited, and he is bringing (it) to you. [9–11]Until I arrive, the silver should remain under my seal. [12–14]He is (also) personally bringing you 10 shekels of silver under my seal, (representing) your consignment.

[15–17](Concerning) the package (with silver) of Laqēp(um), if you bought some tin, send him to me (with it); [17–19]if you did not buy any tin, send him empty-handed to me; [19–21]do not buy any (more) tin before my arrival. [21–25]Let 1 or 2 *karpatum*-measures of flour be ready for me. And sell the barley.

Bibliography: Text published in copy by Lewy as KTS 1, 2a; translated by Michel (2001a, no. 336).

Comments: Ab-šalim, who lives in Kaneš, must keep safe silver sent by Aššur-rabi; besides this mina of silver, she receives a small amount for herself. She undertakes purchases and sales of tin and barley.

---

202. Asking for the Payment of Silver Due Her Husband

Obv. [1]*um-<ma> Lá-qé-pu-um-ma* [2]*a-na Ha-ta-lá qí-bi*$_4$*-ma* [3]3 gín kù-babbar *ú a-lá-num* [4]dub *ku-nu-ki-a I-dí-Ku-bu-um* [5]*na-áš-a-ki-im* [6]*ša*$^!$*-al-ma-ku* [7]*a-na-kam ša-am-n*[*a-am*] [8]du$_{10}$$^{bu-um}$ *lá-šu*$^!$-«*um*»*-ma* lo.e. [9]*a-dí ki-a-am* rev. [10]*wa-*[*áš-b*]*a-a-ku* [11]*a-ma-*[*kam* k]ù-babbar [12]*ša* dam-gàr^{ru-um} [13]*ha-bu-lu-ni* [14]kù-babbar *ša-áš-qí-lá-áš** [15]*lá a-kà-ša-áš* [16]*ú li-bi*$_4$ (*lá** erased) [17]*lá i-ma-ra*$^!$-[*aṣ*] [18]kù-babbar *ša*$^!$*-áš-qí-li* :*

[1–2]Th<us> (says) Laqēpum: (say) to Hatala.

[3–5]Iddin-Kūbum is bringing you 3 shekels of silver and hazelnuts, (as well as) a tablet under my seal. [6]I am fine. [7–8]There is no good-quality oil here. [9–10]Until now, I am st[aying] (here) for the present. [11–15]As for the silver the merchant owes me there, make him pay the silver so that I will not be under pressure for debt and [16–17]be unhappy! [18]Make (him) pay the silver!

Bibliography: Text published in copy by Clay as BIN 4, 228; translated by Michel (2001a, no. 388).

Comments: Hatala was married to Laqēpum (**24**). She receives goods from her husband and has to get back silver owed to him by a colleague because Laqēpum needs that silver to repay his own debt.

Line 3: for the translation of *allānum* as "hazelnut," see Sturm 2008.

---

203. Recovering a Debt

Obv. [1]*a-na Ha-tí-tim qí-bi*$_4$*-ma* [2]*um-ma Šu-Sú-en*$_6$*-ma* [3]*ṭup-pá-am ša* ½ *ma-na* [4]kù-babbar *ša* dam-gàr *e-zi-ba-/ki-im* [5]*um-ma a-na-ku-ma* [6]kù-babbar *ú ṣí-ba-sú* [7]*li-iš-qú-lá-ki-ma* [8]*ú ṭup-pá-am ú-šé-ri-šu-/*[*um*] [9]*a-ha-tí a-tí a-ma-kam* [10]⅓ *ma-na* 5 gín [11]kù-babbar *ṣa-ru-pá-am* lo.e. [12]*li-iš-qú-lá-ki-m*[*a*] rev. [13]*ṭup-pá-am ú-šé-r*[*i*]*-/šu-*[*um*] [14]*šu-ma* kù-babbar [15]*ša-qá-lam lá i-mu-a* [16]*i-na na-áb-ší-i-šu* [17]*ki-ma-ma i-ba-ší-ú* [18]*li-ib-ší-ma* [19]*ú té-er-tí-ki iš-tí* [20]*a-li-ki-im pá-ni-im-ma* [21]*li-li-kam šu-ma* [22]kù-babbar *iš-qú-lá-ki-im* [23]*ki-lá-lá-ku-nu ku-un-kà-ma* u.e. [24]kù-babbar *a-Hu-ra-ma* [25]*li-ik-šu-da-ni* le.e. [26]*lá-ma ha-ra-ni* [27]*iš-ni-ú ih-dí*

[1–2]Say to Hattītum: thus (says) Šu-Suen.

[3–4]With respect to the tablet concerning (a debt of) ½ mina of silver, which the agent left you, [5–8]I (said) as follows: "Let him pay you the silver and its interest, then hand over the tablet to him." [9–13]You are my sister; there, let him pay you ⅓ mina, 5 shekels of refined silver, and hand over the tablet to him.

[14–15]If he refuses to pay the silver, [16–18](the tablet) should remain in safekeeping as it has been (up to now), and [19–21]let your report come to me by the next traveler. [21–23]If he does pay you the silver, seal (it), both of you, and [24–27]let the silver reach me in Hurrama before I will travel elsewhere; see (to it)!

Bibliography: Text published in copy by Lewy as TC 3, 116; translated by Michel (2001a, no. 331).

Comments: An agent (*tamkārum*) bought a credit and issued a debt note. The tablet has been entrusted to Hattītum, and she is supposed to recover the debt and its interest and to send the silver to Šu-Suen in Hurrama.

204. Advancing Money to an Indebted Brother

Obv. ^{1}*a-na A-ha-tim* ^{2}*ù Ma-nu-ki-e-ni-*<*a*> ^{3}*qí-bi*$_4$*-ma um-ma* ^{4}*Puzur*$_4$-dingir-*ma* ^{5}*um-mì a-tí be-el-*<*tí*> *a-tí* ^{6}*a-ma-kam* kù-babbar ^{7}*ša Ma-nu-ki-a* ^{8}*šu-qú-li-ma* ^{9}*ma-lá ta-ša-/qí-li-ni* ^{10}kù-babbar *ù ṣí-ba-sú* ^{11}*ṣa-áb-ta-ma* ^{12}*šu-up-ra-ni-ma* ^{13}kù-babbar *lu-šé-bi*$_4$*-lam* ^{14}⅓ *ma-na* lá 1 gín ^{15}kù-babbar *ku-nu-ki-a* ^{16}*ší-im* anše$^{\text{hi-a}}$ ^{17}*Ma-nu-ki-a* le.e. ^{18}*na-áš-a-ki-im* ^{19}*a-ma-kam Ma-nu-ki-/e-ni-a* ^{20}*ša-i-li*

$^{1-4}$Say to Ahattum and Mannum-kī-ēnia: thus (says) Puzur-ilī.

$^{5-8}$You are my mother; you are my mistress. There, pay the silver of Mannukkiya, and, $^{6-11}$as much silver you pay, charge (to me) the silver and interest on it, $^{12-13}$(then) write me so I can send you (the equivalent) silver. $^{14-18}$Mannukkīya is bringing you ⅓ mina minus 1 shekel of silver under my seal, price of the donkey. $^{19-20}$Ask there Mannum-kī-ēnia (for it).

Bibliography: Text published in copy by Smith as CCT 4, 15a; translated by Michel (2001a, no. 394). Collated on photo online on the CDLI as P361142.

Comments: Puzur-ilī could be a younger brother of Ahattum, a consecrated woman, daughter of Ilī-bāni (**56**). He asks her to repay his debt and to tell him the amount—silver and interest—that he owes her.

Line 7 and 17: Mannukkiya could be a nickname for the Mannum-kī-Aššur mentioned in the next text (**205**) as creditor of Puzur-ilī. However, in line 17 it might refer to the Mannum-kī-ēnia to whom the letter is also addressed.

205. Sister Pays a Debt for Her Brother

Obv. ^{1}*a-na A-ha-tim* ^{2}*qí-bi*$_4$*-ma um-ma Puzur*$_4$-/dingir-*ma* ^{3}*a-dí* kù-babbar *ša Ma-nu-/um-*<*ki*>*-A-šur* ^{4}*um-mì a-tí be-el-tí a-tí* ^{5}*a-na Ša-lá-du-wa-ar* ^{6}*ú-lá ú-šu-ru* ^{7}*a-wa-tum da-na* ^{8}kù-babbar *šu-qú-li-ma* ^{9}*a-wi-lam*$_5$ *lam-na-am* lo.e. ^{10}*i-ṣé-ri-a us*$_{10}$*-hi* rev. ^{11}*a-dí* iti-kam *iš-té-en*$_6$ ^{12}*a-wa-tum i-za-ku-a-ni* ^{13}*i-nu-mì ša a-lá-kà-ni* ^{14}kù-babbar *ù ṣí-ba-sú* ^{15}*ša Ha-ṣa-áb-ṣí-li-im* ^{16}*lá ta-ga-mì-li-ni* ^{17}*i-ṣé-ri-a le-qé* ^{18}*ší-im pì-ri-kà-ni* ^{19}*a-na-kam ba-at-qú* ^{20}*ma-hi-ir Kà-ne-eš lá ma-/ṣí* u.e. ^{21}*a-na* «*a*» *u*$_4$*-um* / *ma-lá-kà* le.e. ^{22}*a-šu-mì* anše *ta-áp-qí-da* ^{23}*lá ta-áp-qí*$^{!}$*-da* ^{24}*úz-ni pè-té té-er-tí-ki* ^{25}*a-ni-tum lá a-ni-tum* ^{26}*lí-lí-kam*

[1-2]Say to Ahattum: thus (says) Puzur-ilī.

[3-6]Concerning the silver of Mannum-kī-Aššur—you are my mother; you are my mistress—they should not deliver it to Šaladuwar, [7]things are difficult; [8]pay the silver and (so) [9-10]deliver me from that evil man! [11-12]In one month things will become clearer for me. [13-17]When I come, you will not have to do me (another) favor for Haṣabṣillum's silver and its interest. Collect (it) at my expense.

[18-20]Trade in *pirikannum*-textiles is slack here; the rate (for them) in the market of Kaneš is too low (to make them profitable): [21]so it is still time (for you) to save me! [22-26]As for the donkey, inform me whether or not you consigned it; let your report come to me, one way or the other.

Bibliography: Text published in copy by Lewy (1969–1970, 57–58 [L 29-588]); edited by Gwaltney as POAT, 29; translated by Michel (2001a, no. 393).

Comments: Puzur-ilī asks his sister to pay one of his debts, promising that he will be able to pay another one himself. She must inform him concerning another transaction dealing with a donkey.

---

206. Informing Her Husband and Awaiting a Verdict of the City Hall

Obv. [1]*a-na I-na-a qí-bi-ma* [2]*um-ma I-ku-pí-a* [3]*«I-ku-pí-a» ù Ta-ra-am-/K[u-bi-ma]* [4]*a-šu-mì : ri-ik-sí* [5]*ša ik-ri-bi : ša Ni-k[à$^?$-ra$^?$-ak$^?$]* [6]*ša ta-áš-pu-ra-ni* [7]*A-šùr-*^{d}utu^{ši} dumu *Am-/r[a-a]* [8]*ni-iṣ-ba-at-ma* [9]*um-ma šu-ut-ma : ri-ik-[sí]* [10]*a-na-ku ù A-šùr-ṣú-lu-[li]* [11]*a-na E-lá-lí* dumu *Šu-Ku-bi-[im]* [12]*ni-dí-in-ma :* an-na [13]*iš-a-am-ma : na-ší-šum* [14]*A-šùr-ṣú-lu-li* [15]*i-na A-lim*^{ki} *: lá wa-ša-/áb* lo.e. [16]*i-na a-lá-ki-šu* [17]*ni-ṣa-ba-sú a-š[u]-mì* rev. [18]*ša hu-sà-ri-im* [19]*dí-nu : na-ak-šu-ma* [20]*a-dí-ni : a-wa-at-ni* [21]igi *A-lim*^{ki} *: lá i-ší-k[i-in]* [22]*i-nu-mì : dí-num : i-[dí-nu]* [23]*ù né-nu : nu-ta-ar*$^{!}$*-ma* [24]*a-na sà-bi-tim : n[i-da-an]* [25]*ma-lá : dí-num : i-[dí-nu]* [26]*iš-tí : bar*$^{!}$*-ki-ú-t[im]* [27]*té-er-tí-ni : za-k[u-tum]* [28]*i-lá-kà-kum* [(x-x)] [29]*a-ma-kam : lá ta-[ha-da-ar]* [30]*ší-bi-kà : da-[ni-in]* [31]*ṭup-pí-kà : ha-[ri-ma]* [32]*i-na pá-[ni-im-ma]* [33]*šé-bi-[lam iš-té-en*$_6$*]* [34]*i-na ṣú-ha-ri /ṭur*$_4$*-dam* [35]*é*$^{be\text{-}et!}$*-kà ù ṣú-h[u-ur-kà ša-li-im]*

[1-3]Say to Innaya: thus (says) Ikuppiya and Tarām-K[ūbi].

[4-6]Concerning the packages of votive offerings of Nik[karrak?] about which you wrote to me, [7-9]we seized Aššur-šamšī, son of Amraya, and he

(said) as follows: [10–13]"Aššur-ṣululī and I, we gave the packages to Elālī, son of Šu-Kūbum, and he bought tin that he is bringing to him." [14–17]Aššur-ṣululī is not in the city (of Aššur at the moment); we will seize him when he comes.

[17–19]Concerning (the) lapis lazuli: The cases have been deferred (by court order), and [20–21]until now our case has not yet been brought before the city (assembly of Aššur). [22–24]When the verdict has been passed, we too will return (the lapis lazuli) and pay the *sab/pit(t)um*. [25–28]Our detailed report about which verdict was passed will come to you as soon as possible.

[29–30]There, do not be im[patient]; re[inforce] your witnesses, [31–33]cer[tify] your tablets, and send (them) [to me] by the [very] ne[xt caravan]. [33–35]Send me [one] of your servants. Your house and [your] children [are well].

Bibliography: Text published in copy by Clay as BIN 4, 91; edited by Michel (1991, no. 7); translated by Michel (2001a, no. 287).

Comments: Tarām-Kūbi, together with her son Ikuppiya, informs Innaya concerning several affairs in which he is involved in Aššur. She awaits the verdict of the City Hall concerning some irregularity in the trade of lapis lazuli by Innaya. The text CCT 4, 24a, sent by Tarām-Kūbi alone to her husband mentions the payment to the City Hall of the price of the lapis lazuli (lines 1′–4′; Michel 2001a, no. 346). It is also perhaps linked to the next letter (**207**).

Line 4: the restoration of the goddess Ninkarrak is suggested by Dercksen (1997, 88 n. 47).

Line 24: according to Veenhof (1995, 1730), *ina sab/pit(t)im* is "an expression describing a person's ability to pay or to collect the money" (to take the silver from one's *sabittum*); it would correspond to "assets on hand." However, Dercksen (2004a, 22) notes that, in this text, the word *sab/pit(t)um* is preceeded by *ana* and not *ina* and lacks a pronominal suffix; thus it should mean something else.

207. Paying Taxes for Her Husband to the City Hall

Obv. [1]*a-na I-na-a qí*[!]*-b*[*i-ma*] [2]*um-ma Ta-ra-am-Ku-b*[*i*$_4$]*-ma* [3]*šé-bu-lá-tim* : *ki-a-ma* [4]*tù-uš-té-né-ba-lam* [5]*a-na-kam* : túg^{hi-a} *ša i-kà-bu-/tù* [6]*lá uš-*

té-né-ba-lá-ku-um ^{7}1 *ma-na* kù-babbar : *ša tù-šé-ba-lá-/ni* ^{8}*a-na* 15 gín-ta kù-babbar ^{9}*ša a-na* é *A-lim*^{ki} *ú-ša-/qú-lu*$^{!}$ ^{10}*lá ma-ṣí ša ki-ma ku-a-/tí* ^{11}*um-ma šu-nu-ma* : *né-nu* ^{12}*lu ni-iš-qúl* ^{13}*a-na-ku-ma* : *a-ší-i* rev. ^{14}*qá-tí-a* : *ú-lá-qí-it-ma* ^{15}5 *ma-na* kù-babbar : *a-na* ^{16}é *A-lim*^{ki} *aš*$^{!}$*-qúl* ^{17}*a-dí* : *ma-lá ù* 2$^{šé-ni}$*-šu* ^{18}*áš-pu-ra-kum* 5 *ma-/na* ^{19}kù-babbar *šu*$^{!}$*-qúl* ^{20}*a-ṣé-er* 1 túg* [x x-*u*] *m* ^{21}*šé-bu-lá-*[*tim* x x x] ^{22}*a-na* [x x x]*-ri* ^{23}*be-tim* [x x]*-tám* ^{24}*a-šu-mì* [x x x] ^{25}*ša i-ba-*[*ší-ú* x x] ^{26}*ša taš-pu-r*[*a-ni mì-ma*] le.e. ^{27}*lá i-dí-nam* : *um-ma šu-ut-ma* ^{28}1 *ma-na* kù-ki : *iš-tí* ^{29}*um-me-a-ni* : *a-lá-pá-at*$^{!}$*-ma*$^{!}$

$^{1-2}$Say to Innaya: thus (says) Tarām-Kūbi.

$^{3-6}$You keep just sending me consigments (of silver), but, here, I cannot send you (in return) each time textiles that are weighty. $^{7-10}$(Concerning) the mina of silver that you are sending me, it is not enough for each 15 shekels of silver that I have to pay to the City Hall. $^{10-12}$Your representatives (said) as follows: "We will certainly pay!" $^{13-16}$(But) for my part, I collected the *aši'um*-iron available to me, and I paid 5 minas of silver to the City Hall.

$^{17-19}$I wrote to you at least twice: "Pay the(se) 5 minas of silver!"

$^{20-25}$In addition to one textile [...] consigments [...] for [...] the house [...] concerning [...] that are [...] $^{26-27}$for which you wrot[e me], he gave me [nothing]. $^{27-29}$He (said) as follows: "I will register 1 mina of gold with the investors."

Bibliography: Text published in copy by Smith as CCT 3, 23b; edited by Michel (1991, no. 2); translated by Michel (2001a, no. 343).

Comments: Innaya owed a substantial amount of silver to the City Hall. Tarām-Kūbi, his wife, did not get help from her husband's representatives and paid the silver from her assets. She now asks Innaya to pay her back the five minas of silver.

Line 8: the word "each" might refer to a payment to the City Hall due in several installments.

208. Paying Her Husband's Debts to the Eponyms

Obv. ^{1}*a-na Pu-šu-ke-en*$_{6}$ ^{2}*qí-bi-ma um-ma Lá-ma-sí-/ma* ^{3}*li-mu-um Šu-da-a* ^{4}kù-babbar *e-ri-ša-ni* : *um-ma šu-/ut*$^{!}$(NU)*-ma* ^{5}*ša wa-ṣí-tí-šu* kù-babbar ^{6}1 *ma-na ha-bu-ul* ^{7}kù-babbar 1 *ma-na* 10 gín ^{8}*ša a-na li-mì-im* lo.e. [9]*Bu-zu-zu : tù-šé-bi-lá-ni* [10]*a-na li-mì-im* rev. [11]*Šu-da-a* (erasure) 1 *ma-na* [12]*a-ša-qal* : 5 gín kù-babbar [13]*ša tù-šé-bi-lá-ni* [14]*Ú-ra-ni : ú-lá i-dí-/nam* [15]*um-ma šu-ut-ma* 5 gín [16]kù-babbar *i-dí-nam a-na* [17]*pá-šu-ri-im* [18]*pá-šu-ra-am ú-lá i-dí-nam*

[1-2]Say to Pūšu-kēn: thus (says) Lamassī.

[3-4]The eponym Šudaya (REL 82) asked me for silver, (saying) as follows: [5-6]"He owes 1 mina of silver as his export tax." [7-12]So I will pay 1 mina to the eponym Šudaya from the 1 mina and 10 shekels of silver that you sent me for the eponym Buzuzu (REL 87).

[12-14]Urāni did not give me the 5 shekels of silver that you sent me; [15-17]he (said) as follows: "He gave me 5 shekels of silver, (but it is) for a table!" [18](But) he did not give me the table!

Bibliography: Text published in copy by Stephens as BIN 6, 3; translated by Michel (2001a, no. 308). Collated on photo.

Comments: Pūšu-kēn owes money to at least two eponyms. The eponym Šudaya, son of Ennānum, is REL 82 (ca. 1891), and eponym Buzuzu, son of Ibbi-Suen, is REL 87 (ca. 1886); Veenhof 2003d. His wife, Lamassī, had to use silver he had sent for the second eponym to pay the first one.

---

209. Leaving a Transaction to Her Husband's Representatives

Obv. [1]*[a]-na Pu-šu-ke-en*$_6$ *qí-bi*$_4$*-ma* [2]*um-ma Lá-ma-sí-ma ṭup-pu-/um* [3]*ta-ah-sí-is-tám* [4]*ša ba-a-ba-tim ša i-na* [5]*bé-tí-kà té-zi-bu : mu-zi-zu-/kà* [6]*ú-šé-ṣí-ú-ma qá-sú-nu-ma* [7]*ú-kà-al a-na-ku a-mì-ma ú-lá aṭ-/hi* [8]*ù a-na* dam-gàr^{ri}*-kà iš-qú-lu* [9]*la iš-qú-lu mì-ma ú-lá i-de*$_8$ *a-ta* [10]*ma-lá-kà : ù ki-ma áš-pu-ra-ku-ni* [11]*mì-ma šu-mì lá ta-za-kár-šu-nu-tí* [12]6½ *ma-na* kù-babbar ki *A-šùr-*^{d}utu$^{!/ši}$ [13]dumu *Lá-qé-ep* šà-ba (erasure) rev. [14]*ša-du-a-tám ù ni-is-ha-tim* [15]*ú-ṣa-hu-ru* 3⅔ *ma-na* 5 gín [16]kù-babbar ki *Ú-ṣú-ur-ša-A-šur* dumu *Ì-lí-/a* [17]½ *ma-na* 5 gín ki *Ša-lim-A-šur* [18]šunigin 8½ *ma-na* kù-babbar *a-na A-šur-i-/mì-tí* [19]dumu *En-na-nim i-ša-qal* [20]*i-na* 4 *ma-na* kù *ša a-na Ì-lí-/iš-tí-kál* [21]*ha-bu-lá-ku-ni* 2 *ma-na* [22]kù-babbar ki *I*$^{!}$*-ku-pí-a* 2 *ma-na a-hu-/ur* [23]9 gín *Ur-da-Na-na* [24]1*½ *ma*$^{!}$*-na* kù-babbar *ša* dingir-*ma-lik* [25]*[me]-he-er ṭup-pì-im ša té-zi-bu* [26][x]x gín *a-na wa-ṣí-<tí>-im* [27]*šé-bi*$_4$*-lam*

[1–2]Say to Pūšu-kēn: thus (says) Lamassī.

[2–5]The tablet that is the memorandum of the outstanding claims that you left in your house, [5–7]your representatives removed (it), and they themselves are holding (it). [7]As for me, I did not interfere in any way, and [8–9]I do not know whether or not they paid something to your creditors. [9–11]It is up to you, and according to what I wrote you, do not mention my name to them at all!

[12–15](There are) 6½ minas of silver (owed) by Aššur-šamšī, son of Laqēp; from it they will deduct the transport fee and the import tax. [15–17](There are) 3⅔ minas, 5 shekels of silver (owed) by Uṣur-ša-Aššur, son of Iliya, (and) ½ mina, 5 shekels (owed) by Šalim-Aššur. [18–19]All together, he shall pay 8½ minas of silver to Aššur-imittī, son of Ennānum.

[20–21]Of the 4 minas of silver that I owe to Iliš-tikal, [21–22]2 minas of silver are with Ikuppiya; 2 minas are still (to be paid). [23–24]9 shekels: Urad-Nana, [x +]1½ mina of silver from Ilī-malik. [25–27]Send me a copy of the tablet that you left (and) [x]x shekels for an outgoing messenger.

Bibliography: Text published in copy by Smith as CCT 3, 19b; translated by Michel (2001a, no. 309). Tablet collated on photo online on CDLI website as P358577.

Comments: Lamassī refuses to get involved in one of her husband's transactions and leaves that to his representatives, but she informs him secretly about the situation. Then she gives details about accounts that she and her husband have with other merchants; these involve several minas of silver.

Line 2: the word *ṭuppum*, as *tahsistam*, should be in the accusative.

---

210. Asking a Woman to Give Various Objects to a Merchant

Obv. [1]*a-na Mu-sà ú Pu-šu-ke-en*$_6$ [2]*a-na Mu-sà qí-bi-ma* [3]*um-ma Lá-ma-ša-ma* [4]3 *a-lu-na-tum ša sí-pá-ri* [5]*a-ša-lá-ší-šu šu-ga-ri-a-ú* [6]*a-ša-lá-ší-šu ma-az-lu-gu*$_5$ [7]*ší-ta it-qú-ra-tum* : *ša sí-pá-ri* [8]2 *sú-pá-nu* 1 *ma-mì-ri* [9]3 *ha-ṣí-nu* : 1 *kà-lá-pu* [10]4 *ar-za-lu* : *ù* 1 *zi-ru* [11]*ša* 20 *ma-na mì-ma* [12]*a-nim a-dí-na-ki-im* [13][*a*]*-ha-tí* : *a-tí-i* : *a-ma-kam** rev. [14]*Pu-šu-ke-en*$_6$ *pí-qí-sú-nu* [15]*a-šu-mì* : *ú-nu-tim a-mì-tim* [16]*iš-tù* 8-mu-šè : *iš-tí-a* [17]*a*[!]*-ni* : *a-ha-ma* 7 *ú-kà-pu* [18]*ša-pí-ú-tum* šà 3 *ú-kà-pu* [19]*a-na Pé-ru-a* : *ta-dí-ni* [20]*ší-tí ú-kà-pì a-na Ar-na-*[x] [21]*ú a-šé-ni-šu ta-ma-lá-ki* [22]*ku-nu-ki-a a-na Pu-šu-ke-en*$_6$ [23]*dí-in ú* 1 *zi-ru sà-he-er*[!]*-tum* [24]*e-lá-nu-ma e-zi-ba-ki-šu* [25]*ú šu-a-tí* :

dí-in ^{26}*a-ha-t[í] a-tí-i mì-ma* le.e. ^{27}*ú-ṭù-up-tim ša ta-/du-nu-šu-ni* ^{28}*i-na-[áš-pè-e]r*$^{!}$*-tí-ki* ^{29}*lu-up-tí-im*

$^{1-3}$Say to Musa and Pūšu-kēn; say to Musa: thus (says) Lamaša.

$^{4-7}$3 bronze pincers, 3 knives, 3 forks, 2 bronze ladles, $^{8-11}$2 *supānum*-bowls, 1 *mamirum*, 3 *haṣṣinnum*-axes, 1 *kalappum*-axe, 4 *arzallum*-implements, and 1 cauldron weighing 20 minas; $^{11-12}$all this I gave to you. $^{13-14}$You are my sister; entrust these items there to Pūšu-kēn. $^{15-16}$Concerning these goods, (they have been) with me for 8 years. $^{17-19}$Now, (there are) besides (these) seven thick saddlecloths, out of which you should give 3 saddlecloths to Peru(w)a; $^{20-23}$give the rest of the saddlecloths to Arna[x], and to Pūšu-kēn the 2 *tamalakkum*-chests with my seal. $^{23-25}$As for the 1 cauldron and small goods that I left you besides, give (them) to him as well. $^{26-29}$You are my sister; write down for me whatever furniture you will give to him.

Bibliography: Text published in copy by Smith as CCT 4, 20a; translated by Michel (2001a, no. 369).

Comments: We do not know if there is any family link between Musa and Pūšu-kēn, but we may note that Musa is mentioned first; they both live in Kaneš. Lamaša was married to Buzāzu, a son of Pūšu-kēn (Kt 87/k 314). She entrusted various objects to Musa intended for Pūšu-kēn, her father-in-law. Among these were two *tamalakkum*-chests sealed by her; such containers often contained tablets, but were sometimes used to hold silver and various objects. Text **232** deals with the same matter.

Line 8: the word *ma-mì-ri*, according to Bilgiç (1954, 69), could be "ein Kochgeschirr."

Line 18: *ukāpum*, "saddlecloth," is a blanket made of felt; see Dercksen 2004a, 272.

---

211. A Man Represents His Sisters' Interests

Obv. ^{1}*a-na Pu-šu-ke-en*$_{6}$ *qí-bi-ma* ^{2}*um-ma Ta-ri-iš-ma-tum* ^{3}*ù Ištar-lá-ma-sí-ma* ^{4}*a-bu-ni be-el-ni a-ta* ^{5}*ma-ma-an i-na ṣú-ha-re-e* ^{6}kù-babbar *e e-ri-iš-kà-ma* ^{7}kù-babbar *a-na qá-tí-šu-nu* ^{8}*e tù-ší-ir* kù-babbar *ku-nu-ki-kà* ^{9}*a-na A-lim*^{ki} *lu-ub-lu-nim-ma* ^{10}*mì-ma a-bi-ni lá i-ha-li-/iq* ^{11}*a-ma-kam ki-ma ni-a-tí* ^{12}*a-ta e-ru-ma lu ṭup-pu-ú* ^{13}*ša a-bi*$_{4}$*-ni i-ba-ší-ú* ^{14}*lu* kù-babbar *i-ba-ší* lo.e. [15]*lu na-ru-qám a-na ma-ma-*/*a*[*n*] rev. [16]*i-dí-in a-ma-ka*[*m*] [17]*ša-il*$_5$*-ma ù té-er-ta-k*[*à*] [18]*li-li-kam-ma ú-za-ni pé-té* [19]*a-na-kam* kù-gi *ša Hu-ra-ṣa-*/*nim* [20]*nu-šé-li-ma a-na ṣí-ib-*/*tim* [21]*i-ta-áb-lu-šu ù* kù-babbar *šu-ut* [22]*uk-ta-al a-pu-tum* [23]*i-hi-id-ma* kù-babbar *ša um-me-a-nim* [24]*šé-bi-lam ku-a-tí ni-tá-kál* [25]2 *ma-na* kù-babbar *a-na qá-qí-ri* [26]*ša I-dí-Ištar ni-iš-qú-ul* [27]*a-ma-kam* kù-babbar *ša-áš-qí-il*$_5$*-šu-ma* [28]*šé-bi-lam a-šu-mì Ú-ṣur-ša-A-šùr* [29]*lá-šu-ú ni-iš-me-ma ku*[?]*-lu-kà* [30]*na-áš-a-ni šu-ma a-bu-ni a-ta* u.e. [31]*a-šar qá-qí-dí-šu ša-lá-hi-im* [32]*mì-li-ik* le.e. [33]*a-na a-bi-šu«-ú» i-ta-kà-al ma-lá* [34]*qá-qá-sú ta-ša-lá-ha-ni mì-li-ik*

[1–3]Say to Pūšu-kēn: thus (say) Tarīš-mātum and Ištar-Lamassī.

[4]You are our father (and) master. [5–8]None of the boys should ask you for any silver, and you must not hand over any silver over to them. [8–10]Let them bring the silver to the city (of Aššur) under your seal, lest anything that belonged to our father be lost.[11–18]You yourself must enter there on our behalf, make inquiries if either tablets of our father or silver are there, or he gave (silver for) a joint-stock company to someone there, then let your report come here and inform us. [19–22]Here, we produced Huraṣānum's gold, and they took it at interest, but he himself has retained the (principal in) silver. [22–24]Urgent! Be sure to send the investor's silver; we trust you! [25–28]We paid 2 minas of silver for Iddin-Ištar's plot of land; have him pay the silver there and send (it) to me.

[28–30]As for the fact that Uṣur-ša-Aššur was not present, we heard it, and we are bringing all your (merchandise). If you are our father, [31–34]think of some way he can disengage. He trusts in his father, think of some way you can get him disengaged.

Bibliography: Text published by Garelli as *ArOr* 47, 42. Translated by Michel 2001a, no. 321.

Comments: Tarīš-mātum is the sister of Pūšu-kēn; Ištar-Lamassī cannot be identified because several women bear this name (Michel 2001a, 480–82). She could be another sister. This letter, sent from Aššur to Pūšu-kēn at Kaneš, seems to follow the death of their father, Sue'a. All the deceased's affairs have to be closed out and taken to Aššur.

Line 15: for *naruqqum*, a joint-stock company, see Larsen 1977, 1999, and Hecker 1999.

Line 29: the reading *ku*[?]*-lu-kà* is tentative because *naš'anim* implies a feminine plural subject (*luquātum*).

WOMEN, ARCHIVES, AND SEALS

The women of Aššur and Kaneš led a more sedentary life than their husbands, who were always on the road. One room in their house was set aside for storing merchandise and for archives. The tablets were arranged on wooden shelves along the walls or in wooden chests or in baskets, which have now disappeared, or sometimes in clay vessels. The size of these archives varied considerably. If some households had several dozen tablets, others have produced more than a thousand, so they had to be kept in some sort of order. The tablets were stored in groups, sometimes with clay labels (bullae) that could be inscribed or sealed. To judge from the labels, archives were arranged by the kind of document: letters, legal documents, and so on, or by their owner (addressee of letters, creditor), or comprised texts pertaining to the same matter.[36]

As guardians of the house and its strongroom with the tablets, wives were sometimes directed to provide the men of the family with specific tablets that they needed. Nuhšatum, custodian of the tablets of her husband and their sons, received letters from the latter, in one instance asking her to retrieve specific sealed documents, in another requiring the summaries of expenses for outfitting a caravan (**212**, **213**). Nuhšatum, however, does not seem to have looked for the documents herself; rather, business associates came to help her do this (**214**).[37] Some women found themselves entrusted with containers of tablets (**169**, **215–217**, **219**, **306**) and supervised any access to the archives in their houses (**323**). The primary role of these women was to ensure that their husbands' colleagues did not make off with any other tablets (**218**).[38] When that did happen, they discreetly informed their husbands (**209**).

Women have their own part in the written record, being responsible for more than a hundred of the letters sent from Aššur. Women such as Lamassī, the wife of Pūšu-kēn, Tarīš-mātum, the wife of Aššur-malik, and Tarām-Kūbi, the wife of Innayā, each are sender of more than fifteen

36. Michel 1998a, 2000b, 2008e; Veenhof 2003e; Larsen 2008.

37. Veenhof 2015c.

38. As shown by the texts translated below, there is good reason to modify the view of Larsen (2008), who thinks that when merchants needed documents retrieved from their archives, they generally turned to their male agents who could read texts. Wives gave access to room and monitored what happened.

letters to their husbands and brothers at Kaneš.[39] Their letters deal with the everyday matters of housewives, the concerns of business women, as well as right conduct and religion. They are cast in the vernacular, and their grammar and syntax are sometimes incorrect, but they exhibit strong feelings.[40] No doubt the houses at Aššur still hold many letters sent to these women in return.

The women at Kaneš received letters sent by their fathers, brothers, or husbands, which dealt with both everyday matters and business transactions. One such a woman was Tariša, sister of Aššur-taklāku, who belonged to a family whose archives were discovered in 1993 in two houses in the lower town (fig. 6); she kept there twenty-three letters that her brother sent her after their father's death. But when she was in Aššur, she herself sent various letters to her brother in Kaneš, which were kept in the same house as those she had received.[41]

Along with their correspondence, women kept various legal documents they had initiated or which recorded their transactions, including loans, purchases, sales, and investments. These files belonged to them, even if they were more modest in scope than those of men, and they were kept together with those belonging to other members of the family, sometimes in separate containers. Women's archives eventually contained documents of transactions they had witnessed, such as loans and purchases, especially those to which one or more women were party.[42] For example, Ab-šalim, daughter of Aššur-rēṣi, witnessed a loan taken by an Anatolian woman, Nimahšušar, from an Anatolian couple.[43]

Ištar-ummī, along with two men, witnessed an Anatolian couple's loan from a woman, Zizizi; the four sealings on its envelope cannot be identi-

39. Letters sent by Lamassī, wife of Pūšu-kēn: **67**, **68**, **147**, **163–167**, **169**, **208–209**, **211**, **246**, **259**, **260**; by Tarīš-mātum, wife of Aššur-malik: **146**, **211**, **254–256**; and by Tarām-Kūbi, wife of Innayā: **128–129**, **170**, **207**, **252**, **286–287**, **289**.

40. Larsen 2001; Michel 2010d.

41. Michel 2008e.

42. Women rarely witnessed legal documents. They did, however, seal such documents when they represented one of the parties or were personally involved. Women's seals occasionally appear on the envelopes of marriage contracts. Contract **19** was drawn up to certify the payment of the bridegift, a sum of fifteen shekels of silver, from the groom, Aššur-malik, to his mother-in-law, Šuppī-elka. She rolled her seal over the envelope of the contract. Unfortunately, only about half of the envelope, sealed by four people, is still extant.

43. Prag I, 584:15–16; the corresponding envelope is lost.

fied (**186**). Lamassī, daughter of Masaya, along with a man, witnessed a woman's debt to another woman, the daughter of Zupa (**80**).[44] Another Lamassī, daughter of Ah-šalim, witnessed a loan in which both creditor and debtor are men (AKT 6b, 472). And presumably a third Lamassī witnessed the loan contract of a woman (**181**), for which a fragment of an envelope is preserved. Ištar-lamassī, daughter of Elamma, sealed, presumably as a witness, a contract in which her sister Šalimma appears as buyer (Kt 94/k 181). Šāt-Anna, daughter of Dadanum, witnessed her mother's sale of a slave.[45] It seems most likely that documents of this type were far more numerous in the archives of the merchant families at Aššur, but these have not yet been discovered. These women, like male witnesses, may have occasionaly kept a copy of documents they witnessed in their own archives.

Whether they were parties to marriage contracts as wives or mothers, writing letters, incurring debts, selling property, or serving as witnesses (**86**), women certified the relevant documents by sealing the envelopes, either with their own seal or someone else's. Possession and use of a seal suggests that these women were regularly involved in matters that generated written documents.[46] In the case of loans, the debtor, together with the witnesses, sealed the envelope to acknowledge receipt of the sum indicated and the terms and conditions of the loan. Female debtors sealed the envelope of the creditor's copy of the debt note, using a seal or signet ring (**76, 79, 81**). Some women, writing letters to Kaneš, rolled their seals on the envelopes to show who had sent them.[47]

Such cylinder and stamp seals as have been found in the lower town of Kaneš are of metal (gold, silver, bronze), stone (haematite, steatite, lapis lazuli, rock crystal), ivory, and bone. There are far fewer of them than the numerous impressions known from envelopes and envelope fragments, bullae, and other sealings. Some seals bear the names of their owners and their patronyms. This is the case, for example, with the seal of Ennanatum, daughter of Puzur-šada, impressed on envelope **189** (seal C; fig. 12). Yet, according to the text on the envelope, this seal was not used by its owner.

44. For this contract, only an uninscribed fragment of the envelope survived with a sealing.

45. Kt 88/k 1003:19–20 published by Bayram and Çeçen 1996, text no. 11. The text **106** indicates that it has been sealed by Ennum-Ištar, the concubine of Laqēpum.

46. Michel 2009c. See also McCarthy 2016.

47. Michel 2008g.

Fig. 12. Imprints of inscribed seals used by women: (left) Ennanatum, daughter of Puzur-šada (**189**, seal C; I. Cukr) and (right) Rubātum, daughter of Amur-ilī (N. Özgüç 2006, CS 357).

The envelope for this document was actually sealed by two women, Musa and Šatahšušar, and one man, Iddin-Suen, whose seal is also inscribed with his name (seal A).[48] Enannatum's seal was therefore used either by the debtor, Šatahšušar, or by the female witness, Musa.

Rubātum, whose name means "queen," had a seal in her own name, which identifies her as daughter of Amur-ilī (fig. 12).[49] But it seems that this seal was regularly used by a man, Usānum, son of Amur-Aššur, who may have inherited it.[50]

Most seals, however, were not inscribed, which makes it difficult to identify the owners of seals impressed on envelopes, which normally carried three or more seal impressions. The placement of the seal impressions on an envelope did not necessarily follow the order of the people mentioned as having sealed the envelope, according to the expression "kišib PN_1 (dumu PN_2)," "sealed by PN_1 (son of PN_2)." Three people sealed the envelope of the woman's debt note **74**, one of whom must be the debtor, Šāt-Ea, daughter of Su'etata. But none of the three seal impressions on the envelope can be identified. The same is true for the debt note **75**, which the debtor Ištar-Lamassī sealed, along with two other people. The contract for the sale of a house (**150**) has four seal impressions, of which the only

48. Seal ICK 1, Kultépé 24a, pl. 60; Teissier 1994, no. 247; the name of the lady has been erroneously read *Ha-na-na-tum*. See also the seal used by Ennum-Ištar (**106**) has her name inscribed on it.

49. Donbaz 2005; Veenhof 2008a, 109; see also N. Özgüç 2006, 105, pl. 21 (CS 357); photo, pl. 128, seal on the envelope Kt n/k 1700, and other references. Rubātum sent the letter Kt 94/k 377 (courtesy Larsen) to Šalimma.

50. Hypothesis of Donbaz 2005.

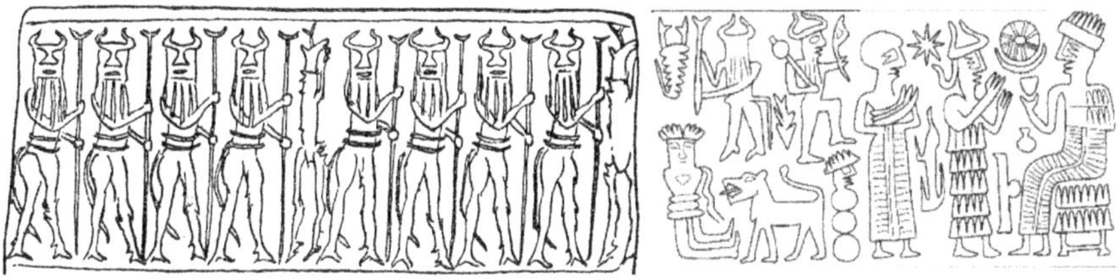

Fig. 13. Imprints of uninscribed seals used by women: (left) Seal of Ištar-baštī (**241**; I. Cukr) and (right) Seal of Waqqurtum (KKS, 46, seal no. 124; Marie Matoušová-Rajmová).

inscribed one identifies Šuppiahšu as seal owner. Two of the other three impressions were made by women: Šuiskana, who made the purchase on another woman's behalf, and Ab-šalim, one of the witnesses.

It sometimes happens that the number of seal impressions on an envelope does not always match the number of people listed as having sealed it (kišib PN). For example, text **97**, concerning the possible redemption of a girl from distraint, records the names of six Anatolians who were supposed to have sealed the document, among them Šuppianika, daughter of Kurukuru; but the envelope, fully preserved, has only five impressions. Likewise, the slave sale **98** has only five impressions, though six are mentioned as having sealed, last among them Šišawada, daughter of Maliahšu. Since this applies to other contracts as well, Veenhof concluded that mention of a woman after kišib, "sealed by," need not mean that the woman's seal was in fact impressed on the envelope.[51]

Systematic analysis of envelopes with seal impressions does sometimes allow uninscribed seals owned by women to be identified, since the presence of of the mention "kišib PN" on envelopes can indicate who used the seals.[52]

For example, the impression of the seal used by Ištar-baštī appears twice on the envelope of a letter she addressed to two men (fig. 13; **241**); the short note concerns a heavy textile that she sold and for which she is awaiting payment; the letter closes with a blessing. Waqqurtum's seal is also well known; it appears on the surviving half of an envelope for a letter,

51. Veenhof 2008a, 109.

52. In her book dated to 1994 (49–50), Beatrice Teissier listed very few seals used by women. The catalogue of Agnete Wisti Lassen's unpublished dissertation (Copenhagen, 2012) gives a few more (even if she does not specify the gender of seal owners).

Fig. 14. Imprint of the seal used by Tariša (photo by Cécile Michel).

now lost, addressed to Puzur-Aššur (fig. 13).[53] The same seal appears on a broken envelope on which various names can be partially deciphered, but not Waqqurtum's.[54] Walawala's seal has been identified on a fragment of an envelope for a letter addressed to Hanunu.[55] The envelope, however, is inscribed: "To Hanunu, seal of Tū'itū'i. I beg that you pay attention to the words of this tablet."[56] This means that Walawala borrowed the seal of a certain Tū'itū'i, unless this name was Walawala's nickname because she was a twin sister (*tū'imtum*). The seal of Tariša appears regularly on the fragments of envelopes addressed to her brother, Aššur-taklāku, whose archives were found in1993 (figs. 6, 14).[57]

Impressions of seals used by women are also found on the envelopes of contracts. The fully preserved envelope of a debt note (**81**) has four sealings.[58] The fourth is of a button-shaped stamp seal with four holes, which

53. ATHE 25:2–3: *a-na Puzur₄-A-šùr*, KIŠIB *Wa-qúr-tim*; seal no. 12, Teissier 1994, no. 129. See also Kt n/k 1735A, the Old Assyrian style seal CS 397, published by N. Özgüç (2006, pl. 27, photo pl. 142).

54. KKS, 46, seal no. 124; identical to ICK 2, seal no. 494.

55. Pinches 1908, 13 (Michel 2001a, no. 387); Teissier 1994, no. 222.

56. Envelope of Pinches 1908, 13: *a-na Ha-nu-nu*, KIŠIB *Tù-ú-i-tù-ú-i*, *a-pu-tum a-na-wa-at, ṭup-pì-im i-hi-id*. See the commentary by Michel 2001a, 500, note.

57. Michel 2008e. Tariša's seal imprint is visible, for example, on the envelope Kt 93/k 372 + 380.

58. TC 3, 239 (Larsen 2002, no. 147) bears four seal imprints whose identification would be the following according to Teissier 1994, 47: KIŠIB *A-ta-ta* (seal TC 3, no. 64), KIŠIB *Me-zi-[ni]* (seal TC 3, no. 99).

must have been impressed by the debtor, Nini, who borrowed from an Assyrian sacks of wheat and barley to be paid back at harvest time.

Women's use of seals is confirmed by letters, in which they are asked to seal a document (**220**) or in which they state that they have sealed merchandise (**221**), silver (**224**), multiple documents (**222**), chests of tablets (**223**), or even a kitchen (**311**). Not all women who used seals to certify documents or goods necessarily owned the seals they used, but this is also true of men who sealed envelopes; they could, for instance, borrow the seal of a brother. Testaments show that women sometimes inherited a seal.[59] This was the case, for instance, with the consecrated daughter of Puzur-ilī. Her father, before he died, turned a lapis lazuli seal over to one of her brothers to give it to her (**64**, **65**). So, too, the widow Ištar-lamassī willed to her consecrated daughter 2¼ shekels of gold, 7½ shekels of silver, and a seal (**59**, **60**). Besides being objects of value, these seals were useful for women to certify their letters and business transactions. Thus, women used seals just as men did. There was no special iconography for women's seals.

212. A Woman Is in Charge of Sealed Containers of Tablets

Obv. [1]*a-na A-šùr-ma-lik* [2]*Šu-A-nim ú Nu-ùh-ša-/tim* [3]*ú Šu-Ištar a-na* [4]*Nu-ùh-ša-ti*-im** [5]*qí-bi-ma um-ma* [6]*A-ni-na-ma* [7]*um-mì-«a»* : *a-tí-i* [8]*i-na* ^{d}utu^{ši} lo.e. [9]*na-áš-pé-er-tí* [10]*ta-ša-me-i-ni* rev. [11]*ta-ma-lá-ki* [12]*ša ṭup-pé-e* [13]*ha-ru-mu-tim* [14]*ša A-šùr*-gal *e-zi-ba-ki-ni* [15]*um-mì-i a-tí-i* [16]*ha-ra-ni a-na* [17]*A-lim*^{ki} *ṣú-ha-re-/e* [18]*ú-qá-a a-ma-/kam* u.e. [19]*ú-ma-kál lá tù-*<*ša*>*-as-/hi-ri* [20]*mì-ma ṭup-pé-e* le.e. [21]*a-na Šu-A-nim Bu-bu-/a-ar* [22]*Áš-ha-a-ni ú Šu-Ištar* [23]*pì-iq-dí-ma ar-hi-iš* [24]*ṭù-ur-da-šu-nu*

[1-6]Say to Aššur-malik, Šu-Anum, Nuhšatum, and Šu-Ištar, (and) in particular to Nuhšatum: thus (says) Anīna.

[7-14]You are my mother. The very day you hear my letter, (send me) the *tamalakkum*-chests with certified tablets that Aššur-rabi left you. [15-19]You are my mother. I (am) traveling to the city (of Aššur); I am waiting for the servants, (so) you should not delay them there one single day. Entrust all the tablets to Šu-Anum, Bubuar, Ašhāni, and Šu-Ištar, and send them quickly!

59. Michel 2009c.

Bibliography: Text published by Bilgiç and Günbattı as AKT 3, 106 (Kt v/k 55); translated by Michel (2001a, no. 290). Collated 2016.

Comments: Anīna, possibly the son of Nuhšatum, asks his mother to hand over to his servants the containers with tablets left behind by Aššur-rabi. This text is linked to TPAK 1, 63, in which Anīna asks merchants to enter his mother's house, break the seals on the tablet containers, and take out some tablets belonging to his father, Ennum-Aššur, then seal the containers again (Veenhof 2015c, 281–82).

---

213. A Woman Is to Seal Tablet Containers and Transfer Them

Obv. ^{1}*a-na A-šur-ma-lik* ^{2}*Nu-ùh-ša-tim ú Dan-A-šur* ^{3}*a-na Nu-ùh-ša-tim* ^{4}*qí-bi*$_4$*-ma um-ma Šál-mah-ma* ^{5}*um-mì a-tí : i-nu-mì a-na A-lim*$^{/ki}$ ^{6}*a-ta-al-ku i-na ba-áb* ^{7}*ha-ra-ni-a ta-ma-lá-ki* ^{8}*ša ṭup-pì ra-bi*$_4$*-ú-tim* ^{9}*ša ha-ra-nim* (end of line erased) ^{10}IGI *A-mur*-dingir *ša e-zi-ba-ki-/ni* ^{11}*a-ṣé-er ku-nu-ki-a* ^{12}*ú a-tù-nu* ^{13}*ku-un-kà-ma* ^{14}*a-na A-bu-qar* lo.e. ^{15}*ṣú-ha-ri-a* ^{16}*pì-iq-da-ma* rev. ^{17}*a-ṣé-ri-a* ^{18}*a-na Ša-mu-ha* ^{19}*lu-ub-lam pá-na-ra-am* ^{20}*ku-nu-ki-a A-bu-qar* ^{21}*na-áš-a-ki-im* ^{22}*a-na A-šur-ma-lik ú Dan-A-šur* ^{23}*qí-bi*$_4$*-ma a-na na-áš-pè-ra-tí-/a* ^{24}*ša a-ṣé-er ša-zu-za-tí-a* ^{25}*ú a-ṣé-ri-ku-nu* ^{26}*lá-pu-ta-ni ih-da* ^{27}*lá ta-ša-lá-ṭá* ^{28}*a-ha-ma* 5 *gu*$_5$*-ur-šu* ^{29}*ša a-šar ú-ṭù-up-tí* ^{30}*i-ba-ší-ú* u.e. ^{31}*i-ku-nu-ki-a-ma* ^{32}*«a» li-bi*$_4$*-ší-ú* (one sign erased)

$^{1-4}$Say to Aššur-malik, Nuhšatum, and Dān-Aššur, (and) in particular to Nuhšatum: thus (says) Šalim-ahum.

$^{5-10}$You are my mother. When I went to the city (of Aššur), I left to you, before my departure (and) in the presence of Amur-ilī, *tamalakkum*-chests with large tablets about caravan (journeys). $^{11-19}$Add your seals to mine, and entrust (them) to Abu-(wa)qar, my servant, so that he may bring (them) to me to (the town of) Šamuha. $^{19-21}$Abu-(wa)qar is bringing you a *pannurum*-utensil under my seal.

$^{22-23}$Say to Aššur-malik and Dān-Aššur.

$^{23-27}$Pay attention to my letters that have been written to my representatives and to you; do not act independently. $^{28-32}$In addition, the five *guršum*-objects that are with my furniture, let them remain under my seal.

Bibliography: Text published by Bilgiç and Günbattı as AKT 3, 77 (Kt v/k 17); translated by Michel (2001a, no. 398). Lines 5–19 cited by Günbattı (1992, 233); collated May 2012.

Comments: Šalim-ahum asks his mother, Nuhšatum, to seal containers of caravan tablets that are in her house, and to send them to the town of Šamuha with his servant.

Line 21: for the word *pannurum*, see **136**:7.

Line 28: the word *guršum* is unknown; it might correspond to a valuable object, perhaps in metal.

---

214. Man and Woman to Remove a Sealed Tablet from a Tablet Container at the Gate of the God

Obv. ^{1}*a-na A-lá-ku* ^{2}*ú Nu-ùh-ší-tim qí-bi*$_4$*-/ma* ^{3}*um-ma En-um-A-šùr-ma* ^{4}*ṭup-pá-am* :* *ša ší-bi*$_4$*-a* ^{5}*ša A-šùr*-du$_{10}$:* dumu *Ki-i-ki* ^{6}*ú En-na-Sú-en*$_6$ ^{7}dumu *I-lá-nim* : *i-na* ^{8}ká dingir *ah-ri-im-ma* ^{9}*i-na li-bi*$_4$ *ṣí-li-/a-nim* ^{10}*a-šar* : *ṭup-pu-ú* ^{11}*ša ba-áb* dingir *ša-ak-/nu-ni* ^{12}*am-ra-ma ṭup-pá-am* lo.e. ^{13}*ša ku-nu-uk* : *A-šur*-du$_{10}$ ^{14}*ú En-na-Sú-en*$_6$ ^{15}*šé-li-a-ma* rev. ^{16}*i-na ma-áš-ki-im* ^{17}*ki/qí-i-ša-šu-ma* ^{18}*dá-ni-na-ma* ^{19}*ku-un-kà-šu-ma* ^{20}*a-na Ha-áš-ta-i-li* ^{21}*ú-lá* : *a-na* ^{d}utu-sipa ^{22}*pì-iq-dá-šu-ma* ^{23}*lu-ub-lam* : *ih-da* ^{24}*a-šu-mì* : dumu *I-da-a* ^{25}*a-na a-wa-tí-a* : *lá-qá-im* ^{26}*ú-qá-a* : *ṣú-ha-ri* 3 *šu-nu-/tí* ^{27}*ṭù-ur-dá**-*nim* : *a-na* ^{28}*sà-ra-dim* : *ú-qá-a-šu-/nu* u.e. ^{29}*áb-nam sú-a-am sí-sí-/ni* ^{30}*ṣí-pá-ra-tim iš-ra-tim* ^{31}*šé-na-tim* : ì-giš *ša i-é*^{tim} le.e. ^{32}*ṭá-ú-bu* : *ub-lu-nim šu-ma Ša-lim-a-hu-um* ^{33}*a-ni-ša-am* : *e-ra-ba-am-ma mì-ma* ^{34}*e-ri-iš-ku-nu* : *mì-ma lá ta-da-na-šu-um* ^{35}*um-ma a-tù-nu-ma a-ṣé-er a-bi*$_4$*-kà* ^{36}*a-na A-lim*^{ki} *at-lá-ak a-na* ^{37}*ma-lá áš-pu-ra-ni-ni ep-ša* ^{38}*ih-da*

$^{1-3}$Say to Alaku and Nuhšatum: thus (says) Ennum-Aššur.

$^{4-8}$I have drawn up a certified tablet at the Gate of the God with the (names of) my witnesses: Aššur-ṭāb, son of Kīki, and Enna-Suen, son of Ilānum, and $^{9-11}$it is placed in the *ṣiliānum*-container with the tablets of the Gate of the God. $^{12-14}$Look for (this) tablet, sealed with the seal of Aššur-ṭāb and Enna-Suen. ^{15}Take out it out (of it), $^{16-23}$wrap it securely in leather, and seal it, then entrust it to Hašta'ili or to Šamaš-rē'ī to bring (it) to me; take care (to do it)!

[24–26]Concerning the son of Idaya, I am waiting for my case to be accepted. [26–28]Send me all three of the servants; I am waiting for them to pack (merchandise). [29–32]They brought me a *sûm*-stone, brooms, nails, belts, sandals, (and) oil that has been refined in the house. [32–34]If Šalim-ahum arrives there and asks you for something, you must not give him anything, [35–36]but (say) as follows: "Go to your father in the city (of Aššur)!" Take care to act according to what I wrote you.

Bibliography: Text published by Bilgiç and Günbattı as AKT 3, 84 (Kt v/k 29). Lines 4–23 cited by Günbattı (1992, 232–33) and Veenhof (2013a, 56); collated May 2012.

Comments: Ennum-Aššur asks a colleague Alaku and his (Ennum-Aššur's) wife to find a tablet that he sealed and is deposited in a container with other tablets that have been as well certified at the Gate of the God. It may be that Nuhšatum is supposed to assist Alaku. The second part of the letter is concerned with the couple's servants and their son Šalim-ahum, who has to go to his father's house at Aššur. For other letters addressed by Ennum-Aššur to his wife, see Veenhof 2015c.

Line 17: the verb *kīāšum* or *qīāšum* means "to wrap" (a tablet).

Line 29: the *sûm*-stone could be used as a millstone.

---

215. Two Women to Seal Tablet Containers

Obv. [1]*a-na Ha-tí-tim ú Ša-ša-/ma-a* [2]*qí-bi-ma um-ma* [3]*Šu-Sú-en*$_6$*-ma a-na* [4]*Ha-tí-tim : qí-bi-ma* [5]*ṭup-pá-am ha-ar-ma-am* [6]*ša ½ ma-na* kù-babbar [7]*ša* dam-gàr *ša i-na* [8]*ṣí-li-a-ni ku-nu-ki-a* [9]igi *Kur-ub-Ištar* dumu *I-dí-Ištar* [10]igi *A-šùr-mu-ta-pí-il*$_5$ [11]*kà**$^{!}$*-ṣa-ar I-na-a* [12]*ú I-dí-a-bi-im* lo.e. [13]*áp-qí-da-ki-ni a-ma-/kam* rev. [14]*ṣí-li-a-ni* [15]*ku-nu-ki-a a-na* [16]^{d}utu*-ub-lam ú Ku-zi* [17]*dí-na-ma lu-ub-lu-nim* [18]*ú té-er-tí-ki*$^{!}$ *li-li-kam* [19]*a-ha-tí a-tí šu-ma* [20]*ṣí-li-a-nu ú* [21]*ku-nu-ku-a pá-aṭ-ru* [22]*a-tí ú Ša-Ša-ma-áš* u.e. [23]*ku-un-kà-ma* [24]*šé-bi-lá-nim* [25]*a-pu-tum ṭup-pu-um* [26]*ša ta-hi***-tim*

[1–4]Say to Hattītum and Ša-Šamaš: thus (says) Šu-Suen. Say in particular to Hattītum.

[5–13]I have entrusted to you a certified tablet of the creditor concerning ½ mina of silver, (which is) in one of the *ṣiliānum*-containers under my seal, in the presence of Kurub-Ištar, son of Iddin-Ištar, Aššur-mūtappil, harnessor of Innaya and Iddin-abum. [13–18]Give the *ṣiliānum*-containers under my seal there to Šamaš-ublam and Kuzi to bring to me, and let your report come to me (that you have done this).

[19–24]You are my sister. If the *ṣiliānum*-containers and my seal (impressions) are open, seal (them), you and Ša-Šamaš, and send (them) to me. [25–26]Urgent! This tablet is an (urgent) message.

Bibliography: Text published in copy by Clay as BIN 4, 55; edited by Michel (1991, no. 183); translated by Michel (2001a, no. 330).

Comments: This letter is addressed to two women but more specifically to Hattītum. The other woman, Ša-Šamaš, has her name abbreviated as Ša-Šama in line 1. They are both asked to reseal a container of tablets in case the original seals have been broken.

Lines 8 and 14: the *ṣiliānum*-container, usually considered as a storage jar, seems to be smaller here since it can be transported.

---

216. A Woman Should Deny That She Has Been Entrusted with Tablets

Obv. [1]*[um-ma] A-šur*-gal-*/ma* [2]*a-na Ha-tí-tim* [3]*qí-bi-ma* [4]*šu-ma ṭup-pé* [5]*mì-ma Ma-num-ba-/lúm-A-šur* [6]*e-zi-ba-/ki-im* lo.e. [7]*ik-ri* rev. [8]*a-na ma-ma-/an* [9]*lá tù-šé-ri* [10]*a-dí a-hu-ki* [11]*i-lu-ku-ni-ni* [12]*ú a-na-ku* u.e. [13]*a-lá-kà-ni* [14]*hu-ša!-e!-ki* [15]*ša-ṣí-ri* [16]*šál-ma-ku*

[1–3]Thus (says) Aššur-rabi: say to Hattītum.

[4–6]If Mannum-balum-Aššur left you any tablet, [7]deny it! [8–9]Do not release (anything) to anyone! [10–11]Until your brother arrives [12–13]or I arrive myself, [14–15]keep an eye (even) on your scraps! [16]I am fine.

Bibliography: Text published in copy by Lewy (1969–1970, 70a [L 29-607]); edited by Gwaltney (POAT, no. 43); translated by Michel (2001a, no. 328).

Comments: Hattītum gets an injunction not to give anything to anyone.

217. Archives to Be Kept Safe

Obv. [1]*um-ma* : *Im-dí-lúm-ma a-na* [2]*Ištar-ba-áš-tí qí-bi-ma* [3]*a-pu-tum ba-ab-tí-ki* [4]*za-ki-i* : kù-gi *ša* dumu [5]*Li-mì*$^{?}$*-šar*$^{!}$: *ša-dí-ni-/ma* [6]*šé-bi-lim* [7]*A-mur-dingir ki-ma* [8]an-na *ù* túg$^{hi\text{-}a}$ lo.e. [9]*i-na* é-gal^{lim} [10]*ú-ṣa-ni* rev. [11]*a-na Bu-ru-uš-/ha-tim* [12]*li-ta-lá-ak-/ma* [13]*a-ma-kam* : *lá i-sà-hu-/ur* [14]*na-hi-dì-šu-ma* [15]*a-ma-ma-an* [16]*lá ú-šar* [17]ì-giš du$_{10}$-ga [18]*šé-bi-lim* u.e.[19]*a-pu-tum mì-ma* [20]*ṭup-pí-a lu ša* dumu le.e. [21]*Ì-lí-dí-na-šu lu ša /Bu-ṣí-a* [22]*ša-ṣí-r*[*i*]

[1-2]Thus (says) Imdī-ilum: say to Ištar-baštī.

[3-4]Urgent! Clear your outstanding merchandise. [4-6]Collect the gold of the son of Limiššar and send (it) to me. [7-12]When tin and textiles leave the palace, let Amur-ilī go to Burušhattum, [13]but he should not linger there. [14-16]Instruct him not to deliver (it) to anyone. [17-18]Send me some good-quality oil.

[19-22]Please, put all my tablets in safekeeping, both those concerning the son of Ilī-iddinaššu and those concerning Buṣia.

Bibliography: Text published in copy by Lewy as TC 3, 56; edited by Ichisar (1981, 251); translated by Michel (2001a, no. 353).

Comments: Ištar-baštī is asked to fulfill various tasks linked to the international trade and to send her husband good oil from Kaneš. She has to archive several important documents.

218. A Woman Is to Supervise Access to Tablets

Obv. [1]*um-ma* ^{d}*En-líl-ba-ni-ma* [2]*a-na Áb-ša-lim qí-bi*$_{4}$*-/ma* [3]*té-er-tí a-ṣé-er ša ki-ma* [4]*i-a-tí i-li-kam* [5]*a-ma-kam ṭup-pè-a* [6]*li-ip-té-ú-ma* [7]*a-lá-an* 2 *ṭup-pè-e* [8]*ša ú-šé-lu-ni* [9]*mì-ma ṭup-pá-am* [10]*ša-ni-am lá ú-šé-lu* [11]*i-zi-zi ki-ma* [12]*ṭup-pè-e ú-šé-li-ú* [13]*i-na ma-ah-ri-ki* [14]*li-ik-nu-ku-ma* [15]*ku-nu-ki-šu ša-ṣí-ri-i* [16]*ki-ma pá-ni-ú-tí-ma* [17]*ṭup-pè-e a-na k*[*à*]*-ri-im* [18]*šé-li-i-šu-nu* [19]*ha-ra-ni a-me-ša-am* [20]5 gín kù-babbar *ku-nu-ki* [21]*Ištar-pá-li-il*$_{5}^{!}$(LU) *ub-lá-ki-im* [22]5 gín kù-babbar le.e. [23]*A-ta-a ub-lá-ki-im* [24]3 gín kù-babbar *Nu-ur-ki-ì-/lí* [25]*na-áš-a-ki-im*

[1-3]Thus (says) Enlil-bāni: say to Ab-šalim.

[3-4]My instructions have gone to my representatives. [5-10]Let them open my tablets (container) there, and apart from the 2 tablets that they will take out, they should not take out any other tablet. [11-15]Stand (by them), and after they have taken out the tablets, have them (re)seal (the container) in your presence and keep its sealing intact. [16-19]In the same way as for the previous ones, take out the tablets for the *kārum*. I am traveling there.

[20-21]Ištar-pālil brought you 5 shekels of sealed silver. [22-25]Ataya brought you 5 shekels of silver. Nūr-kī-ilī is bringing you 3 shekels of silver.

Bibliography: Text published in copy by Smith as CCT 4, 13b; translated by Michel (2001, no. 342); collated 1987.

Comments: Ab-šalim was married to a member of the family of Enlil-bāni, Aššur-rabi, and Aššur-lamassī. She is in charge of the archives of Enlil-bāni and is asked to be sure that his representatives do not take any more tablets than they are allowed to.

---

219. A Woman Is to Place a Tablet in Safekeeping

Obv. [1]*um-ma Ku-zu-um-ma* [2]*a-na Šu-ma-a-bi*$_4$*-a* [3]*ú Ma-kà qí-bi*$_4$*-ma* [4]1 túg *tí-sà-ba-am* 2 *na-ah*$^{!}$(HI)*-lá-pá-té* [5]*a-na ṣú-ha-ri ú ṣú-ha-ar-ti* [6]*Sí-in*-gal *na-áš-a-ku-nu-tí* [7]1 túg *a-na ší-mì-im* : *dí-na-ma* [8]*i-na ší-im* túg 3 gín kù-babbar [9]*a-na e-mì-iq-tim* [10]*dí-na-ma ṣú-ha-ra-am* [11]*šé-ṣí-a-ni* 2 gín kù-babbar [12]*a-na Ma-kà dí-in* lo.e. [13]*ší-tí* kù-babbar *sà-he-er-tám* [14]*le-qé-a-ni* rev. [15]*a-na Šu-ma-bi*$_4$*-a qí-bi*$_4$*-ma* [16]*a-hi a-ta ṣú-ha-ra-am* [17]*lá té-zi-ba-am ṣú-ha-ra-am* [18]*i-na pá-ni-kà šé-ṣí-am* [19]*a-na Ma-kà qí-bi*$_4$*-ma* [20]*ṭup-pá-am ša ší-im* é$^{be\text{-}tí}$ [21]*ša šu-um a-bi*$_4$*-a* «*tí*» : *ú-du-ú* [22]*um-mì a-tí ṭup-pá-am* [23]*šu-a-tí* : *a-tí ú Šu-ma-bi*$_4$*-a* [24]*ṭup-pé-e-a pè-té-a-ma* [25]*i-na li-bi*$_4$ *ṭup-pè-e-a* [26]*šu-uk-na-ma* : *Šu-ma-bi*$_4$*-a* [27]*li-ik-nu-uk* u.e. [28]*šu-ma ṭup-pá-am i-na* [29]*li-bi*$_4$ *ṭup-pè-e-a* le.e. [30]*lá ta-áš-ta-ak-ni* : *lá um-mì*/*-i* «*a*» [31]*a-tí* : *pá-na-ra-am I*-dingir-*ku* [32]*na-áš-a-ki-*<*im*> *iš-tí Ha-du-a* : *lu-be-ri* [33]*ú ša-áp-ta-am* 5 *ma-na*

[1-3]Thus (says) Kuzum: say to Šumi-abiya and Maka.

[4-6]Suen-rabi is bringing you a *tisābum*-textile and 2 tunics for the boy and the girl. [7-11]Sell 1 textile and give from the price of the textile 3 shekels of silver to the nanny, and get the boy free. [11-12]Give 2 shekels of

silver to Maka. [13–14](With) the remainder of the silver, take for me small wares.

[15]Say to Šumi-abiya. [16–18]You are my brother; you must not abandon the boy, get the boy free personally.

[19]Say to Maka. [20–26]Concerning the tablet of the house sale on which my father's name is written, as you are my mother, that very tablet, you yourself and Šumi-abiya open the tablet (container) and place (it) with my tablets, and [26–27]have Šumi-abiya seal (the container). [28–31]If you haven't put the tablet with my tablets, you are no longer my mother! Iluku is bringing you 1 *pannurum*. [32–33]With Hadua, the *lubērū*-garments and the wool, 5 minas, […]

Bibliography: Text published by Michel and Garelli as TPAK 1, 32 (Kt 90/k 236).

Comments: The woman Maka is asked by Kuzum to place a document of his father in his archives. Then Šumi-abiya must reseal the tablet container. This suggests that Maka had no seal of her own.

Line 4: for other references to the native Anatolian *tisābum*-textile, see Michel and Veenhof 2010, 245.

Line 32: the *lubērum*-garment would be of low quality according to CTMMA 1, 79:19–23; see Michel and Veenhof 2010, 234.

Line 33: the verb of the sentence is missing.

---

220. A Woman Is Asked to Seal a Document with Her Husband's Agents

Obv. [1]*a-na Ku-li-a qí-bi-ma* [2]*um-ma A-ba-ba-a-a-ma* [3]*a-na-kam* 1⅓ *ma-na* kù-babbar [4]*ša a-na mu-lá-e-i* [5]*ša* é *Sá*-ba-sí-a* [6]*ni-il*$_5$*-qé-ú* : *be-el* [7]*qá-ta-tí-a ša iš-tí-a* [8]*i-zi-zu-i-ni* 5-*šu-nu* [9]*i-na-zu-mu-ú* [10]*um-ma šu-nu-ma* [11]*ṭup-pá-am ša ku-nu-ki-ki* [12]*dí-ni-ni-a-tí* [13]*ša* kù-babbar *a-na* rev. [14]*ṣí-it* : *Ku-li-a* [15]*i-ší-iq-lu-i-ni* [16]kù-babbar 1 *ma-na-um* [17]7 gín *ni-il*$_5$*-qé* [18]*a-pu-tum* 5 gín kù-babbar [19]*a-bu-kà* : *a-šu-ur* [20]*ù ni-ší-kà* 1 gín kù-babbar-ta [21]*a-šu-ur* [22]*ù ta-zi-ma-tí-ší-na* [23]*lá áš-ta-na-me-e* [24]*a-pu-tum ša a-wi-lu-tí-/kà* u.e. [25]*e-pu-uš* le.e. [26]*a-pu-tum* kù-babbar *a-na A-šùr-/ṣú-lu-li* [27]*dí-in-ma lu-ub-lam* [28]*a-na-kam lá* ú-ša-ah-du-ru-ni*

[1–2]Say to Kuliya: thus (says) Ababaya.

[3–10]Here, (concerning) the 1⅓ mina of silver which we took to supplement (the cost) of Sabasiya's house, my guarantors, who assisted me, all 5 of them are complaining as follows: [11–15]"Give us a tablet with your seal (showing) that the silver has been paid for Kuliya's expenses. [16–17]We have borrowed the silver (at an interest of) 7 shekels per mina." [18–19]Urgent! Provide your father with 5 shekels of silver. [20–23]Also, provide each of your people with 1 shekel of silver so that I have no longer to listen to their complaints! [24–25]Urgent! Act as the gentleman you are! [26–27]Urgent! Give silver to Aššur-ṣululī so he can bring it to me. [28]Here they should not cause me anxiety.

Bibliography: Text published by Veenhof as AKT 5, 10 (Kt 92/k 214); collated May 2012.

Comments: Ababaya, an Assyrian lady, was married to Kuliya, messenger of the *kārum* of Kaneš.[60] She is living in Aššur and has had to deal with the complaints of guarantors asking her for a document bearing her seal confirming that the borrowed silver has been applied to Kuliya's expenses. They may have succeeded since we learn from another letter that "your wife has sealed (the debt-note) together with us" (AKT 5, 13:20–21). This matter is also mentioned in texts AKT 5, 14–15 and 30.

---

221. Various Textiles Shipped to Anatolia Are Sealed by the Writer and a Woman

Obv. [1]*a-na Šu-pì-a-ah-šu-šar* [2]*ù Ha-tí-tim qí-bi*$_4$*-ma um-ma* [3]*Šu*$^!$*-Lá-ba*$^!$*-a[n ù] A-sà-a-ma* [4]1 túg *ku-ta-nam qá-áb-li-am* [5]*a-na Šu-pì*$^!$*-a*$^!$*-ah-šu-šar* [6]1 túg *ší-it-ra-a[m] ša A-ki-dí-e* [7]*a-na Um-mì-na-ra* 1 *ší*-it*-ra*-a[m]** [8]*ša*$^!$ *A-ki-dí-e a-na Ha-tí-tim* [9]*ku-nu-ki-a-ma*$^!$(E) *ù ku-nu-ki* [10]*A-ni-ni : me*$^!$*-er-i-tí-ki-na* [11]*Ma*$^!$*-ṣí-li kà-ṣa-ar* [12]*Ma-nu-ba-lu-um-A-na* [13]*na-áš-a-ki-na-tí* : *ù a-na* [14]*Wa-ar-dim ù Me-me-e* [15]*iš-tí wa-ar-ki-ú-tim* [16]*ú-šé-ba-lam* kù-babbar [17]*a-ma-kam ša ub-lá-ni* rev. [18]*a-wi-il*$_5$*-tum ta-ta-ba-al-ma* [19]*ša* ⅓ *ma-na* kù-babbar [20]*tù-dí-tám té-pu-ša-am* [21]*re-eh-tám ta-ta-ba-al* [22]kù-ki *mì-ma Šu-Ku-bu-um* [23]*lá i-dí-nam mu-tù-um* [24]*i-a-tù-ma : En-na-ma-num* [25]*mì-ma lá i-dí-nam* [26]*um-ma šu-ut-ma* ⅔ *ma-na* kù-babbar [27]*i-na wa-ar-ki-tí-a* [28]*a-da-na-ki-im* 1½ gín kù-babbar [29]*A-lá-hu-um ub-lam*

---

60. Veenhof, AKT 5, pp. 20–21.

1 *mu-uš-ṭum* ^{30}2$^{!}$ *ší-kà-tum*$_{8}$ ì-giš *ma-al-a-/ší-na-ma* ^{31}*ší-kà-tám šu-ma na ar*$^{?}$ kù-gi ^{32}*i-qé-er-bi*$_{4}$*-im ša-ak-nu-ni** ^{33}*lá i-de*$_{8}$ *i-be-tí-ni* ^{34}*ih-tí-li-iq* : *pá-ar-ší-gám* ^{35}dumu *Ha-na-na-ri-im ub-lá-ki-<im>* le.e. ^{36}*na-ah-lá-áp-tám En-um*$^{!}$*-ì-lí* : *ni-a-um** ^{37}*ub*$^{!}$(SÍ)*-lá-ki-im ší-kà-tám ša* kù-babbar 2 *tù-dí-na*-tim** ^{38}*i-ṣa-ba-tim* : [x x x]*-ku-ur*-tám* ^{39}*mu-ša-am mì-ma e*-zi*-bu šé-bi*$_{4}$*-lim*

$^{1-3}$Say to Šuppiahšušar and Hattītim: thus (say) Šu-Labā[n and] Asaya.

$^{4-5}$1 middle-quality *kutānum*-textile for Šuppiahšušar, $^{6-7}$1 Akkadian shawl for Umminara, $^{7-8}$1 Akkadian shawl for Hattītum, $^{9-10}$under my seal and the seal of Anini, your daughter, $^{11-13}$ Mannum-balum-Anna's harnessor, Maṣi-(i)lī, is bringing you. $^{13-16}$Also, I will send (things) for Wardum and Memē by a later (caravan).

$^{16-21}$The lady appropriated the silver that he brought there, and made me a garment pin for ⅓ mina of silver. ^{21}She (also) appropriated the remainder (of the silver). $^{22-25}$Šu-Kūbum did not give me any gold. Nor did my own husband, Ennam-Anum, give me any, $^{26-28}$(saying) as follows: "I will give you ⅔ mina of silver after my departure." $^{28-29}$Ali-ahum brought me 1½ shekels of silver. $^{29-34}$1 comb, 2 *šikkatum*-bottles that have been filled of oil, and concerning the *šikkatum* in which a golden [...] was put inside, have (all) disappeared from our house; I don't know how.

$^{34-37}$The son of Hannanārum brought you a sash. Our Ennum-ilī brought you a tunic. $^{37-39}$A silver *šikkatum*-bottle, 2 garment pins, earrings [...], a *muššum*-jewel—send me all that I left.

Bibliography: Text published in copy by Smith as CCT 3, 31; translated by Michel (2001a, no. 332).

Comments: This letter, addressed to two women, mentions the shipment of various textiles from Aššur sealed by a man and a woman, Anini; she is referred to as the "daughter" of the two recipients of the letter.

Line 30: *šikkatum* is not attested as a container but may here be a kind of bottle, since it is filled with oil.

Line 34: note that the verb *ihtiliq* is a singular, but it is translated by a plural form. For the *paršīgum*, "a sash, often used as headdress," see Michel and Veenhof 2010, 238.

222. A Woman Sends a Document Bearing Her Seal

Obv. [1]*a-na Pu-šu-ke-en*$_6$ [2]*qí-bi-ma um-ma* [3]*Šu-bu-ul-tum-ma* [4]7 túg *ku-ta-ni* [5]dub *ku-nu-ki-a* [6]*Dan-A-šur* [7]*na-áš-a-kum* [8]*da-tám* [9]*ù ni-is-ha-tim* [10]*ú-lá i-lá-mu-du*$^{!}$(UD) [11]*šu-ma a-bi a-ta* [12]*iš-tí pá-ni-ú-tim* [13]*ṣú-ha-ra-am* [14]*ṭù-ur-da-šu*

[1–3]Say to Pūšu-kēn: thus (says) Šūbultum.

[4–7]Dān-Aššur is bringing you 7 *kutānum*-textiles (and) a tablet with my seal; [8–10]they are not liable to *dātum*-toll and import tax. [11–14]If you are my father, send me the servant with the earliest (caravan).

Bibliography: Text published in copy by Clay as BIN 4, 85; edited by Łyczkowska (1978, 132–33); translated by Michel (2001a, no. 371).

Comments: A document bearing her seal impression is added to the textile consignment sent by Šūbultum to Kaneš. The identity of this woman remains unknown; she is also the sender of letter **195**, addressed to Pūšu-kēn.

223. A Woman Seals Boxes of Tablets

Obv. [1]*a-na Mu-sà ú Pu-šu-ke-en*$_6$ [2]*qí-bi-ma um-ma Lá-ma-ša-ma* [3]3 *ku-sí-a-tum* : *ší-ta sú-a-tum* [4]2 *me-at ba-pí-*<*ri*> 20 *na-ru-uq* [5]*ú-ṭá-tum* : 7 *ar-ha-lu* [6]šà-ba 2 *ba-du-tum* 2 *ba-áb-ru-/um* [7]15 *e-ṣú-ú ša-áp-lá-nu-/um* [8]*i-ba-ší-ú* : 17 *e-ṣí I-dí-Ku-*<*bu*>*-/um il*$_5$*-/qé* [9]*a-ša-be-šu qá-áb-li-a-/tum* [10]*ša* kù-babbar *ší-ta* [11]*qá-áb-li-a-tum ša* urudu lo.e. [12]11 *sà-ma*$^{!}$*-lá-tu[m] ú iš-té-/en*$_6$ [13]*ta-as-k[à-r]i-n[um]* [14]*a-ša-lá-ší-šu* rev. [15]*ta-ma-lá-ku ša ṭup-pè* [16]*i-na ṣí-li-a-ni kà-an-ku* [17]*ku-nu*$^{!}$*-ki-a* 1 *it-qú-ru-um* [18]*a-na ki-ší-ni a-na ša-pár-tim* [19]*i-ni-dí-ma ší-im ki-ší-né-e* [20]*e-zi-ba-ki-ma it-qú-ru a-na* (*sic!*) [21]*qá-tí-ki e-zi-ib-šu a-ha-tí* [22]*a-tí* : *a-ma-kam i-ša-ha-at* [23]*Pu-šu-ke-en*$_6$ *i-zi-*<*zi*>*-ma* [24]*a-na* é$^{\text{bé-tim}}$ *er-bi*$_4$*-ma* [25]*mì-ma a-nim ú-nu-tim* u.e. [26]*pá-qí-d[í-š]u*$^{!}$*-um šu-ma* [27]*ṭup-p[í] ša li-bi*$_4$ [28]*ṣí-li-a-nim* [29]*ša-ak*$^{!}$*-nu*$^{!}$*-ni a-na* é^{tí} [30]*tù-uš-té-ṣí ṭup-pì-ki* [31]*a-na Pu-šu-ke-en*$_6$ *dí-n[i]*

[1–2]Say to Musa and Pūšu-kēn: thus (says) Lamaša.

[3–5]3 *kusītum*-textiles, 2 *sûm*-stones, 2 hundred beer breads, 20 sacks of grain, 7 *arhalum*-utensils, [6–8]including 2 *badutum*, 2 *babrum*, (and)

15 logs are still down there. [8]Iddin-Kūbum took 17 logs. [9–17]7 *qablītum*-containers of silver, 2 *qablītum*-containers of copper, 11 cups, plus 1 piece of boxwood (and) a set of 3 *tamalakkum*-chests with tablets are in the *ṣilianū*-containers, sealed with my seal. [17–19]A ladle was given as pledge for the vetch; I left you the price of the vetch, and I left the ladle at your disposal. [21–23]You are my sister; assist there Pūšu-kēn; [24–26]enter the house and entrust all these utensils to him. [26–30]If you have removed the tablets that have been placed inside the *ṣilianum*-container to the house, give your tablets to Pūšu-kēn.

Bibliography: Text published in copy by Clay as BIN 4, 90; translated by Michel (2001a, no. 368). Lines 9–16 cited by J. Lewy (1950, 4–5).

Comments: The letter has been sent by Lamaša from Aššur. As for the addressee, Musa is cited before Pūšu-kēn, perhaps because the letter is clearly addressed to her: all the second-person forms are feminine. Letter **210**, which concerns the same correspondents and deals with the same topics, is specifically addressed to Musa. Lamaša has sealed three chests (*tamalakkum*) containing tablets that are kept inside *ṣilianū*-containers.

Lines 5–7: the *arhalum* and its two subcategories, *b/pad/tutum* and *b/pab/prum*, are unknown objects.

Lines 9, 11, 15–16, 28: if *qablītum* is some kind of metal container, the *tamalakkum* is a wooden chest, and the *ṣilianum* could be made of clay.

Note that this tablet expresses quantities both with numerals and by words (lines 3, 9–10, 12, 14).

---

224. A Female Servant Seals Silver

Obv. [1]1 *šé-bu-<ul>-ta-am* [2]3 gín kù-babbar *ku-nu-ki-a* [3]*a-na Áb-ša-lim ù* [4]*Na-na-a a-na <Šu>-Hu-bur* [5]1 *šé-bu-ul-ta-am* [6]3 gín kù-babbar lo.e. [7]*ku-nu-ki-a* rev. [8]*a-na A-ha-ha* [9]1 *šé-bu-ul-ta-am* [10]1 gín kù-babbar *ku-nu-ki* [11]*ša am-tim a-na* [12]*Na-na-a* dumu *Bu-du-/du* [13]*a-na A-bi*$_4$*-a-a* [14]dumu *En-na-nim* u.e. [15]*áp-qí-id* le.e. [16]igi *A-du-da*

[1–4]1 consignment of 3 shekels of silver under my seal for Ab-šalim and Nanaya (I have entrusted) to Šu-Hubur. [5–8]1 consignment of 3 shekels of silver under my seal for Ahaha, [9–12]1 consignment of 1 shekel of silver under the seal of the maid for Nanaya, son of Bududu, [13–15]I entrusted to Abiaya, son of Ennānum.

[16]In the presence of Aduda.

Bibliography: Text published in copy by J. Lewy as KTS 1, 50a; edited by Eisser and Lewy (1930, no. 117).

Comments: This short text refers to small consignments of silver sent from Kaneš for men and women (Ab-šalim, Ahaha) living in Aššur. Among these, a consignment of one shekel of silver has been sealed by a female servant or a wife (*amtum*).

Line 4: Donbaz (2015, 68) suggests to read after collation *Na-na-a* du[mu *P*]*u-šu-hu-šu*.

Women and Writing

Considering the number of letters women at Aššur sent to their husbands at Kaneš, one may suppose that they in turn received as many or more letters from Kaneš and other Assyrian commercial settlements in Asia Minor. Likewise, women at Kaneš receive numerous letters sent either from Aššur or from other places in the Anatolian interior. When a merchant sent instructions to his agents, he sometimes sent a duplicate to his wife. Did she have to ask a scribe or a literate member of her family to read it to her? No scribe is ever mentioned whom she would have to employ to write her correspondence. While it is possible that some letters sent by women from Aššur were written by their eldest sons still at home, who, in some cases, got scribal training, the broader question of who wrote their tablets may be put this way: how many people, men or women, did it take to produce, in the span of some sixty years, the more than twenty-two thousand tablets so far found at the site of Kultepe?[61]

61. For a catalogue of Old Assyrian tablets, see Michel 2003a, 2006c, 2011a, 2015e. For the chronological distribution of the documentation, see Veenhof 2003d; Kryszat 2004; Barjamovic, Hertel, and Larsen 2012. Michel 2009c takes up the issue of how much women wrote. This topic is dealt with more generally for the ancient Near East in the work from which this section has been extracted, Briquel-Chatonnet et al. 2009, as well as Lion 2011.

The archives at Kaneš give the names of several scribes (dub-sar).[62] Their tablets are well made and covered with careful writing, and they sometimes make use of unusual cuneiform signs. Most of these scribes' work was for the day-to-day administration of the trade bureau, and no doubt also for the larger business enterprises, and some of them hired out their services to the Anatolian chancelleries. Unlike Old Babylonian practice, scribes are rarely mentioned among the witnesses to contracts. No woman's name figures among those of a few dozen known scribes. These scribes, presumably paid for their secretarial work, produced documents that can be readily distinguished from those written by educated merchants who could write their own tablets. The merchants' tablets use a simplified syllabary containing somewhere between eighty and one hundred twenty syllabic signs, and a few dozen word signs.[63] The great mobility of the merchants and the sheer volume of the correspondence found at Kaneš strongly suggest that a substantial proportion of the Assyrian population were ready to take up a stylus without worrying too much about mistakes in syntax, grammar, or spelling.

Certain women evidently did learn to read. They were able to arrange documents in their archives and could write tablets. Although their grammar and syntax may sometimes be rather wobbly, as those of uneducated men, their choice of words sometimes reveals their personalities. Some Assyrian women's letters show their hopes for a harmonious and prosperous life in society. Their letters often have a high emotional content and seem to use everyday speech.[64] Certain expressions seem to be more typical of women that of men. For example, women's letters often refer to intemperate comments that they have heard or read; the expression used is (*awātim*) *himṭātim*, literally, "heated words."[65] This phrase is generally used with the verb *šapārum*, "send (a tablet)," as in the letter of Tarām-Kūbi to her husband, Innaya: "Why do you always pay attention to slander and keep writing me angry words?" (**128**). In another instance, Aššur-taklāku's sister, Tariša, writes, "Why do you write me angry words?"[66] The expression occurs also sometimes in men's letters, directed at women (**225**).[67]

62. Larsen 1976, 304–7; Dercksen 2004a, 74.

63. Michel 2008b.

64. Larsen 2001; Michel 2001a, ch. 7; 2010d.

65. Hirsch 1967; Larsen 1971, 2001.

66. Kt 93/k 198:3–4: *a-wa-tim, hi-im-ṭá-tim ta-áš-pu-ra-ni*.

67. ATHE 41:20; CCT 2, 6:7; VS 26, 4:7; VS 26, 52:5–6.

Sending a tablet need not mean, of course, that it was actually written out by the sender.[68] There is a verb, *lapātum*, which, in Old Assyrian, when used with the word *ṭuppum*, means to "write out" or "draw up" a tablet.[69] Its use may be significant; when someone says that he has sent a letter, that does not imply that he wrote it himself, unless he uses *lapātum*. Hence, the use of this verb in her letter to Zikri-elka should mean that Hattītum herself wrote her rather indignant message (**226**). And Abaya explains to her brother-in-law that she knows how to draw up the accounts that concern him (**227**).

A summons relating to a lawsuit between Hanunu, son of Ṣilli-Ištar, and Laqēp, son of Wardum, refers specifically to documents drawn up by a woman. Hanunu mentions certain measures he had taken previously, "Obtain for me the tablets concerning 1 mina of silver that Šāt-Ištar, the wife of Aššur-taklāku, drew up."[70] Šāt-Ištar is unfortunately poorly attested elsewhere. She was the mother of Walawala, according to the latter's divorce record (**35**), and the mother of Maruru (TC 3, 246). She may well be the same woman who, according to an anonymous account, sends small sums of silver from Kaneš to Aššur (BIN 6, 175).

Finally, among the rare Old Assyrian tablets found at Aššur is a letter from a woman to the goddess Tašmētum (**242**). Letters to gods, or letter-prayers, could, in the Old Babylonian period, be placed in front of a cult statue in a temple, with a gift. Such letters were generally written by kings or queens or members of the elite.[71] The Old Assyrian letter to Tašmētum, of which only the opening line is preserved, came from a woman named Akatiya, well attested in documents found at Kaneš in 1962; she may well have been related to the Assyrian royal family (see chapter 6).[72] This letter could have been written by Akatiya herself, since she was a member of the Assyrian nobility.

---

68. Veenhof 2008d. The recipient of the letter is aware of "someone who hears it" (*šēmum*), cf. Wilcke 2000; Charpin 2008.

69. Its meaning corresponds to the Old Babylonian verb *šaṭārum*; see Wilcke 2000.

70. TC 3, 269:9–12: *ṭup-pí-i, ša* 1 *ma-na* kù-babbar, *ša Ša-at-Ištar* dam *A-šur-ták-lá-ku, tal-pu-ut*[!](TÙ)*-ni šé-ṣí-a-am*.

71. There is, for example, the draft of a letter sent by Zimrī-Lîm, king of Mari, to the river god (ARMT 26, 191). For this type of letters, see Hallo 1981.

72. Her brother, Uṣur-ša-Ištar, son of Aššur-imittī, exchanged letters with the king of Aššur; see Michel 2015c and chapter 6, pp. 397–410.

225. A Man Answers Two Women Who Rebuked Him by Letter

Obv. ^{1}*um-ma E-ni-ba-áš-ma a-na* ^{2}*Ha-tí-tim ú Ba-ba-ar-Ší-ma-lá* ^{3}*qí-bi-ma mì-nam* ^{4}*hi-im-ṭa-tí-im ta-áš-ta-na-pá-ra-n*[*im*] ^{5}*a-na-ku : a-na-kam* ^{6}*a-na ší-a-ma-tim wa-áš-ba-ku ú* ^{7}kù-babbar *ša a-ma-kam a-na nu-a-im* ^{8}*a-hi-ib*$^{!}$(BI)*-lu-ni a-na-nu-um* ^{9}kù-babbar *ú-šé-bi-lá-ma* ^{10}*E-ri-ri-a : iš-qú-ul-šu* ^{11}*ba-pí-ra-am* rev. ^{12}*ú bu-qú-lá-am* ^{13}*ša e-zi-ba-ki-na-tí-ni* ^{14}*a-na ší-ta :* ^{15}*ki-na-tí : lá ma-ṣí*$^{!}$ ^{16}*ú* 5 gín kù-babbar *šé-bu-lá-tí-im* ^{17}*uš-té-bi*$_{4}$*-lá-ki-na-tí* ^{18}1½ gín kù-babbar *Tù-na* ^{19}ir *ša A-hu-qar* ^{20}*na-áš-a-ki-na-tí* ^{21}*Nu-ur-ki-li šé-bu-ul-tám* ^{22}*mì-ma lá ub-lam*

$^{1-3}$Thus (says) Ē-nibâš: say to Hattītum and Babbar-Šimala.

$^{3-4}$Why do you keep writing me angry words? $^{5-6}$As to me, I am here to make purchases, and $^{7-9}$I sent from here the silver that I came to owe there to the Anatolian (creditor), and ^{10}Eririya paid it. $^{11-15}$The beer bread and the malt that I left for you (fem. pl.) was not enough for the two of you, $^{16-17}$so I sent you, (in several) consignments, 5 shekels of silver. $^{18-20}$Tuna, Ahu-(wa)qar's slave, is bringing you 1½ shekels of silver. $^{21-22}$Nūr-kī-ilī has not brought me any consignment.

Bibliography: Text published by Jankovskaja as KTK, 67.

Comments: Ē-nibâš answers a letter that Hattītum and Babbar-Šimala, two women, wrote to him in which they rebuked him. He is aware that he did not leave them enough food and several times sent some silver.

Babbar-Šimala is attested here for the first time. Eririya occurs also in Kt o/k 113:17.

226. A Woman Writes Her Own Letter to Another Woman

Obv. ^{1}*a-na Ha-tí-tim* ^{2}*qí-bi-ma um-ma* ^{3}*Zi-ik-ri-el-kà-ma* ^{4}*li-lu-tí-i* ^{5}*ta-áš-me-i-ma* ^{6}*a-wa-tim* (erasure) ^{7}*ha-am-ṭá-tim* ^{8}*tù-lá-pí-tim* lo.e. ^{9}[*m*]*a*$^{?}$*-a um-ma a-tí-/ma* ^{10}[x x x-*i/u*]*š-tum* rev. ^{11}x [x x x x] ^{12}*ù a-hi iš-tù* ^{13}mu-5-šè *lá-šu* ^{14}*a-ni-a-tim* ^{15}<*tù*>*-lá-pì-tí-im* ^{16}*iš-tù a-na Wa-ah-šu-ša-/na* ^{17}*a-li-kà-ni li-bi*$_{4}$ ^{18}[*a*]*-di ha-am-ší-šu* u.e. ^{19}*im-*[*r*]*a-aṣ* ^{20}*a-ma-kam ša-il*$_{5}$*-tám* ^{21}*ša-li-ma*$^{!}$ le.e. ^{22}*té-er-tí-*[*ki*] ^{23}*li-l*[*i-kam*]

$^{1-3}$Say to Hattītum: thus (says) Zikri-Elka.

[4-8]You heard of my foolishness and wrote me angry words! [9-13]Indeed, you (wrote) as follows: "[...] and my brother has been absent for 5 years!" This is what you wrote out to me.

[16-19]Since I came to Wahšušana, I have had heartache 5 times over! [20-23]Consult a female dream interpreter there and send me your report.

Bibliography: Text published in copy by Stephens as BIN 6, 93; translated by Michel (2001a, no. 333).

Comments: Zikri-Elka answers a letter from Hattītum. She twice uses the verb *lapātum*, "to write down, write out," with reference to her, implying that Hattītum wrote the letter herself. "Foolishness" may refer to irresponsible behavior.

---

227. A Woman Draws Up Some Accounts

Obv. [1]*a-na I-na-a qí-bi-ma* [2]*um-ma A-ba-a-a-<ma>* 3 *ku-ta-nu* [3]*A-ba-ta-na-nu-um* [4]*na-áš-a-kum* 1 túg *kà-áb-tám* [5]*Šu-mì-a-bi-a na-áš-a-kum* [6]*é a-hi-kà a-ta-ma* [7]*tí-de*$_{8}$*-e* : *ki-ma* 1 gín [8]kù-babbar *a-šar lá-qá-im* [9]*lá i-ba-ší-ú* : *mì-nam* [10]*a-na* 10 *ma-na* kù-babbar [11]*a-ni-ša-am ta-áš-ta-na-pár* [12]*i-hi-id-ma* kù-babbar [13]*a-ma-kam le-qé* [14]*ma i-na a-lá-ki-kà* [15]*ṣú-lu-um pá-ni* [16]*lá tù-kà-lá-ma-ni* rev. [17]*šu-ma be-lí a-ta* [18]kù-babbar *ša Puzur*$_{4}$*-Sú-en*$_{6}$ [19]*ša il*$_{5}$*-qé-ú* [20]*lá i-ga-ma-ar-ma* [21]*i-hi-id* kù-babbar^{áp}-*kà* [22]*a-ma-kam-ma le-qé* [23]*i-na ša iš-tí-šu* [24]*ba-tí*$^{!}$*-iq-tám* [25]*ú wa-ta-ar-tám* [26]*a-lá-pá-ta-ku-ni* [27]*li-ba-kà lá i-lá-mì-in*$^{!}$ [28]*um-ma a-na-ku-ma* [29]*a-dí li-hi-id-ma* [30]kù-babbar *li-dí-na-kum-ma* le.e. [31]*hi-im-ṭá-tim ú-lá-pí-tám* [32]*mì-nam ša-zu-uz-tí-kà lá-áš-pu*$^{!}$ [33]*a-ma-kam a-ta-ma ša-il*$_{5}$

[1-2]Say to Innaya: thus (says) Abaya.

[2-4]Abatanānum is bringing you 3 *kutānum*-textiles. [4-5]Šumi-abiya is bringing you 1 heavy textile. [6-9](Concerning) your brother's house, you know perfectly well that there is not a shekel, no silver to be had there. [9-11]Why do you keep writing me here for 10 minas of silver here? [12-13]Be sure to get silver there. [14-16]Also, when you do come, don't show me a dark face!

[17-22]If you are my lord, the silver that Puzur-Suen took, he should not spend it, so see to it that you get your silver there. [23-27]Do not blame me for the fact that I might write down for you as owed by him more or less!

[28]I (thought) as follows: [29–31]"Let him anyhow take care to give you the silver, although he wrote me angry words." [32]Why should I *approach* your agents? [33]Ask (them) yourself there!

Bibliography: Text published in copy by Smith as CCT 4, 8a; edited by Michel (1991, no. 56); translated by Michel (2001a, no. 272).

Comments: Abaya was the wife of Šu-Kūbum, an older brother of Innaya. When she wrote this letter, she was presumably a widow.

Line 32: the translation of this sentence is very tentative.

5
Religion and Social Mores

The Old Assyrian archives being mostly concerned with commercial matters, information about religion is both infrequent and incidental. Some texts mention merchandise belonging to temples and deities, such as gold and silver dedicated as votive offerings.[1] Priests (*kumrum*) of Adad, Aššur, Ištar, Suen, Šamaš, and Šarra-mātēn are, most of the time, referred to as witnesses. Some of them are mentioned in connection with their business activities, but nothing is said of their cultic responsibilities.[2] For example, a priest of Suen owned one of several houses where one could buy tin and textiles to export to Anatolia.[3] Among the Aššur eponyms are Elālī, the temple administrator (*sangûm*), and Iddin-Aššur, son of a priest.[4] Deities were invoked as witnesses and as guarantors of oaths. A list of the gods and goddesses worshiped at Aššur would include: Adad, Amurrum, Aššur, Aššurītum, Bēlum, Ilabrat, Išhara, Ištar the Star, Ištar-ZA-AT, Ninkarrak Nisaba, Suen, Šamaš, Šarra-mātēn, and Tašmētum.[5] Some of these were family or personal deities, such as Amurrum, Ilabrat, or Ištar-ZA-AT.[6] Most of these deities occur as theophoric elements in personal names.[7]

---

1. Dercksen 1997.

2. Hirsch 1961. According to Dercksen (2015b, 45–46), in the absence of priest, the care for the goddess of Ištar—her statue and jewelry kept in the house of the priest in Kaneš—was temporarily performed by his wife.

3. TC 3, 129.

4. Veenhof 2003d; Kryszat 2004.

5. According to an oral suggestion of L. Colonna d'Istria, Ištar-ZA-AT could perhaps be read Ištar-4^{at} for Ištar-erbat. Larsen, on the other hand, proposes to read *manzat*, a name for the rainbow; Larsen 2015a, 268. On the deities, see Garelli 1962; Eidem 2004, 2011; Dercksen 2005a, 2011b; Kryszat 1995, 2003, 2006b, 2007b.

6. Kryszat 2006a; Michel 1991, 85–88; Veenhof 2014. This book was already finished when Veenhof 2018b appeared; its conclusion could not be taken into account.

7. Veenhof 2008a, 102–5.

The temples of Adad, Aššur, Ištar, and Išhara could have served as self-managing storehouses for merchandise and votive offerings, whereas the treasury (*maṣṣartum*) of the principal god, Aššur, with whom the Assyrian king had a special relationship, may well have been kept in the City Hall, because it was under the responsibility of the steward (*laputtā'um*).[8]

At Aššur, the temple of Aššur, first built in the third millennium and situated on the extremity of a rocky promontory, was restored successively by Šalim-ahum and Erišum I. Ištar and Adad likewise had temples in the city. The former, founded in the third millennium, was restored by Ilušuma; the latter was constructed by Erišum I and his son Ikūnum.[9] The god Aššur furthermore had a temple or chapel at Kaneš, and in other places the Assyrians frequented, such as Uršu, on the western bank of the Uppper Euphrates.[10] There were also altars in private houses with statues of deities on them (**252**, **258**). One text gives an inventory of such a chapel: "[x] tables that were before his gods, one chair that was before Aššur, one cup that was before Šarru-mātēn, two salt-*haweru*, one silver cup, and a flask that was before Uqur (Nergal's vizier); five weapons, two *qablītum*-containers, one heart of silver, one computing tool(?), and one wax tablet—all this belonging to Kura's son. When Ennum-Aššur opened his main house, he left Kura's […]."[11]

We know little of Assyrian religious practice, especially because the archives of the merchants at Aššur have not been found. The archives at Kaneš have yielded several incantations, mostly having to do with childbirth and childhood illnesses.[12] They say nothing about the rituals performed when these incantations were recited. The few mentions of religious matters occur primarily in women's letters. Indeed, women's letters

---

8. Matouš 1974; Dercksen 2004a, 77–79.

9. Larsen 1976, 56–60.

10. Kaneš: Matouš 1974; Dercksen 2004a, 101. For the temples excavated at Kaneš, see T. Özgüç 1999. Uršu: letter known as SUP 7 (Sayce 1912, 191), translated or cited by Larsen 1976, 261; Kryszat 1995; Michel 2001a, no. 251; 2016b.

11. AKT 6b, 468:1–18, published as Kt 94/k 670 in Barjamovic and Larsen 2008, 153–54: [x *p*]*á-šu-ru sa* igi *i-li-šu*, 1 *ku-sí-um ša* igi, *A-šùr* 1 *kà-sú-um*, *ša* igi *Ša-ru-ma-té-en*, 2 *ha-we-ru ša ṭá-áb-té-en*, 1 *kà-sú-um ša* kù-babbar, *ú ší-ku-tù-um*, *ša* igi *Ú-qú-ur*, 5 *kà-ku-ú*, 2 *qá-áb-li-a-tum*, 1 *li-bu-um ša* kù-babbar, 1 *ni-kà-sú ú* 1 *ṭup-pu-um*, *ša is-ku-ri-im*, *mì-ma a-nim ša* dumu *Ku-ra*, *i-nu-mì e-kál-lu-šu*, [*En*]-*um-A-šur ip-té-ú*, [x x x]-*ta-at Ku-ra*, [*e-zi*]-*ib* (witnesses). For the translation of *nikkassū* as a calculating instrument, see Dercksen 2015c.

12. See chapter 3, pp. 197–203.

show their strong concern for religion: they made offerings in temples, honored the gods, and reminded their husbands of their religious obligations. In Assyrian public life women from the commercial elite were mostly active in the sphere of religion, in such occupations as dream interpreter (*šā'iltum*), diviner (*bārītum*), and the "consecrated" women (*gubabtum, qadištum*). These last, often consecrated to the god Aššur, were not personnel of a temple but lived independently, perhaps nearby, no doubt devoting themselves to prayer, though we know almost nothing of their religious duties. The letters they sent to their relatives show their high status within their families (**238**, **264**). In general, women's influence was most palpable in family matters. Concerned about the father's house and what people might say, they sometimes gave the men of their families veritable lectures on morality, motivated by their profound regard for the gods and the spirits of their ancestors, not to mention their desire to keep up the best possible appearances for the neighbors.[13] They did not hesitate to keep men mindful of their religious duties, and prayed to the gods on their behalf.

Women's Feelings and Advice on Behavior

Ancient Near Eastern textual sources rarely say much about the expression of feelings.[14] Marten Stol, in an article on private life in Mesopotamia, suggests that private correspondence was the only written medium for such expression, but even there it is the exception because, according to him, letters were drafted by professional scribes: "No one wrote a love letter; illness was a rare subject. What the ideal life was to a Babylonian man is clear, however: he felt happiest within the context of his family, watching his sons growing up, reaching a good old age, free from debts of servitude."[15] The Babylonian concept of the good life was thus built on such moral values as being a good father of a family and a good steward of the family patrimony. But what about the Assyrians, especially Assyrian women?

---

13. Michel 2008f, 2009a.

14. For the expression of feelings in the Sumerian literature, see Jacques 2006. An unpublished dissertation concerns the idea of happiness in the Sumerian and Akkadian literature (Lion 1993).

15. Stol 1995b, 499.

The correspondence discovered at Kaneš, although mostly dealing with commerce and business matters, reveals various aspects of private life, especially in the case of women who had to run their households alone. Emotions were all the more expressed because many men and women wrote their own letters, even though, as Larsen has observed, they do show a certain reserve in that regard.[16]

Negative feelings were most often expressed because letters were mostly motivated by difficult material or financial circumstances or loneliness. Letters sent to relatives, close or distant, were often emotionally charged, closeness being invoked by actual or rhetorical kinship ties: "You are my father; you are my brother." On rare occasions, men or women even dared to deify their addressee to push their case, "You are my god," as did Kunnaniya, addressing Šēṣur (**310**); or Amur-ilī, writing to his father, Imdī-ilum, to plead his irreproachable sense of duty, "You are the only one: my god, my trust, and my dignity. Let your father be healthy, and pray for me so that I can see face to face the god Aššur and you!"[17]

These letters reveal the code of conduct women upheld, including traditional values such as devotion to family and propriety. Assyrian women profiled the portrait of the perfect gentleman (*awīlum*): the respectable man was above all honest in business, founded a family, and owned a home (**228**); the mere appearance of respectability was not enough. The good man was one who loved his relatives and home life more than money (**252**). Thus Aššur-taklāku defended himself against suspicion of avarice to his sister Tariša: "Would I love only silver and not love the house of our father, you, and my brothers?"[18]

The less frequent references to values upheld by men in their relations with other men include respect for others; a gentleman should not succumb to good food: "Tell Amur-ilī that he should know how to respect (people); he should not be looking (only) for bread and beer! He must (be) a gentleman!" (**176**).[19] For men, wives should be attentive, act as a good, caring wife

---

16. Men and women writing letters: Michel 2008b, and in this volume chapter 4, pp. 333–38. Reserve in writing letters: Larsen 2001, 275.

17. KTS 1, 15:38–42, translated by Michel 2001a, no. 161. This letter shows that some men could, like the women, express their feelings in their correspondence.

18. KTK 18:9′–10′: *a-na-ku* kù-babbar : *ar-ta-a-ma* é *a-bi*$_4$*-ni*, *ku-a-tí ú a-hi-a* : *lá ar-ta-am.*

19. This recalls the ideal lifestyle of the warrior and nomadic chief; see Lion 2003; Cooper 2016, 118–20.

(**3**), and above all be faithful. A merchant warned an associate of his wife's indiscreet behavior and, at the same time, asked him to report on his own wife: "You are my brother! Keep an eye there on my *amtum*-wife. I keep hearing here that your *aššutum*-wife has left (you) for (another) husband. Send me reliable information concerning her (my *amtum*-wife), and then I may also come (home). Because of that, I am so depressed (that) I don't want to come (home)! Send me reliable information about her with the very next traveler."[20] Unmarried daughters were expected to stay at home in their parents' absence to guard it against theft. Thus Aššur-rabi reproaches his daughter for having let outsiders live in the parental home while she took up residence with a man (**199**). Daughters, like sons, were supposed to honor and respect their parents and grandparents. Aššur-idī complained to his son about the ingratitude of his grandchildren, whom he had raised but who decided to go their own ways: "I raised your son, but he said to me, 'You are no father to me,' and got up and left. I raised your daughters too, but they said, 'You are no father to us.' Three days later they got up and left to go to you, so let me know what you think."[21]

To judge from their letters, the core values of Assyrian women were family solidarity and harmony; these could be disturbed insofar as business connections got in the way of family ties.[22] To please his father, a son was supposed to respect him, obey his instructions, and safeguard his interests (**229**). In situations of financial ruin, he was expected to put his father's affairs in order and to save the women of the family (**234**). A daughter likewise owed respect and obedience to her father and mother and was to show her solidarity with her brothers; if she did not, her parents could disown her (**50**). A married daughter who had left home could still expect her parents' attention, support, and encouragement: Zizizi, left isolated by a contagious disease making the rounds of her family circle, wrote a sad letter to her father and mother asking for their love and a kind word from them (**230**). Occasionally young women sought the consider-

20. Chantre 15:11–24, letter to Ennum-Aššur from Enna-Aššur (*sic*!): *a-hi a-ta a-ma-/kam, a-ṣé-er a-am-tí-a, e-en$_6$-kà, li-li-kam, a-na-kam áš-ta-na-me-ma, a-ša-at-kà a-na mu-tim, ta-ta-lá-ak a-ma-/kam, zu-ku-sà šé-bi$_4$-lam-ma, ú le-ru-ba-am,* šà-ba *pá-nu-ú-<a> kà-áb-tù-/ma, e-ra-ba$^!$-am$^!$ lá a-mu-a, iš-tí a-li-ki-im, pá-né-e-ma, zu-ku-sà šé-bi$_4$-lam-ma*. Collated.

21. CCT 3, 6b, edited by Larsen 2002, no. 22, and translated by Michel 2001a, no. 254.

22. See Larsen 2007 and the introduction of chapter 4 in the present volume.

ation of their parents' business partners, such as Šāt-Aššur, daughter of Šalim-ahum, who, feeling lonely and excluded, asked Pūšu-kēn for moral support and news (**124**).

A good mother was never slow to give moral advice to her children or to reprimand her son if he was not acting like a gentleman. She supervised the management both of her husband's household and that of a son who had set up on his own (**229**). If a son was married and was going abroad for business, he could leave his young wife in his mother's care, though she might not take her mother-in-law's authority in good part (**146**).

Assyrian women preached harmony among brothers and sisters and worried about their children's future after they had become young adults and had gone off to live in Asia Minor, where political troubles could endanger their lives. Ištar-baštī reprimanded her two sons for their constant quarrels over money rather than heeding their parents' instructions. As she saw it, such disputes could damage the reputation of the family (**231**). Sisters were supposed to love and stand up for each other no matter what (**232**, **312**); brothers and sisters should likewise be able to count on each other and to share news (**170**). Brothers should be ready when needed to offer material assistance to their sisters (**235**). It was not uncommon for an Assyrian woman to scold her brother, charging him with neglect or bringing the family into disrepute, even mistreating his sisters and forgetting his religious duties (**237**).

Thanks to women's strong sense of family, as well as business networks based on kinship connections, we have letters sent by women at Aššur to their brothers living abroad in Anatolia. In other social contexts, once they were married, girls left the paternal home to live with their husbands and so often disappeared from the archives of their own families.

The women at Aššur, despite the peculiar circumstances of their lives that kept them separated from their husbands for long months, even years, wanted to build their family as a lifetime couple. Tarām-Kūbi wrote her husband a long letter informing him of matters in progress, housekeeping problems, and making what one might call an indirect declaration of love: "The beer bread I made for you has become too old.… Please, when you hear (this) letter, come, look at Aššur, your god, and your home hearth, and let me see you in person while I am still alive!" (**129**). A merchant stresses the loneliness he feels when his fiancée's arrival is delayed: "Please, the day you hear my tablet, there, turn to your father (so that he agrees); set out and come here with my servants. I am alone. There is none to serve me and set my table" (**3**). A man expected of his wife that besides just being there and keeping him company, she should look after him and prepare his meals. Most letters were to complain or criticize. Women upbraided their husbands for going away and leaving the house empty and them unprovided for (**128**). Disputes carried on by letter were frequent and sometimes led to separation; if not legal, at least physical (**27**, **233**).

Assyrian women were particularly sensitive about their social standing and other people's opinion of them as a couple and as a family, starting off with the neighbors. They sought to show off their families' social and economic success by purchasing fine, spacious houses in Aššur, teeming with slaves and servants (**147**). Conscious of what people might say, Lamassī insists repeatedly that her husband come as soon as possible to fulfill his paternal and religious obligations: "You hear that people have become bad; one tries to swallow up the other! Be an honorable man, break your obligations, and come here!" (**147**). They feared gossip (**128**, **146**), a frequent source of disputes between family members: "Your sister talks a lot to your father; she tries to push you out of your father's mind!" (**228**). To sum up, these women stood up for harmony in human relations and a certain code of behavior informed by their deeply held religious beliefs, all traits markedly less apparent in men's letters.

---

228. A Trustworthy Man Is One Who Has Built a Family

Obv. [1]*a-na Ku-li-a qí-bi-ma um-ma* [2]*A-ba-ba-a-ma a-na ma-lá* [3]*pì-i na-áš-pa[r-t]í-kà : pá-ni-tim* [4]3 *ma-na* kù-bab[bar] *a-na E-na-/na-/tim* [5]*a-dí-in [a]-pu-tum* [6]*mì-nu-u[m] ša a-na E-na-na-at-/A-šùr* [7]kù-babbar *tù-ší-ru-ú* [8]*a-na lá-ni-šu ta-tí-ki-il*$_5$ [9]*lá* é-^{tám} : *lá ša-ra-am* [10]*[i]-šu ú* kù-babbar *tù-ší-ir* [11]*[a-p]u-tum a-na me-ra u[m-m]ì-a-/nim* lo.e. [12][x] x [x x x x x x x] (lacuna of four lines on the bottom of the obverse and the lower edge) [17][x x x x x x x] x-*bi*$_4$ rev. [18][x x x *m*]*a-na-ah-tí* [19]*[B]ur-Ištar ša-i-il*$_5$ [20]*mì-ma ša a-dí-nu-šu-i-ni* [21]*a-na A-šùr**-*ṣú-lu-li i-na ṭup-/pì-im* [22]*ša i-is-ku-ri-im* [23]*lá-pu-ut a-pu-tum lá ta-ša-/lá-aṭ* [24]*ṭup-pá-am ša* é *Bé-lúm-ba*$^{!}$*-/ni* [25]*na-áš-par-ta-kà li-li-/kam* [26]*lu nu-šé-ṣí-šu : a-ha-at-kà* [27]*a-na a-bi-kà ma-da-tí-ma* [28]*ta-ta-wu : i-na li-bi* [29]*a-bi-kà tù-šé-ṣa-kà* [30]*lá ta-ša-lá-aṭ : mì-ma* [31]*lá ta-pá-lá-ah e-lá-nu-kà* lo.e. [32]*[a-b]u-kà mì**-*ma** *lá i-šu* le.e. [33]*[a-pu]-tum a-ni-qí ša a-mu-tim* [34][x x (x)] *ù* KI/SÁ-DU-*ra-am A-šùr-ṣú-lu-/li* [35][x x x x x] *lu-ub-lam*

[1–2]Say to Kuliya: thus (says) Ababaya.

$^{2-5}$Following the orders of your previous lett[er], I gave 3 minas of silv[er] to Ennanatum. $^{5-7}$[Ur]gent! Why did you release silver to Ennanat-Aššur? ^{8}You put trust in his outward appearance, $^{9-10}$but [he] has neither house nor child, and still you released the silver! ^{11}[U]rgent! To a recognized tr[ad]er [... *broken lines* ...] ^{18}concerning my misery, ^{19}ask [B]ūr-Ištar. $^{20-23}$All that I gave him for Aššur-ṣululī has been registered on a wax tablet. ^{23}Urgent! Do not act on your own.

$^{24-25}$As for the tablet of the house of Bēlum-bāni, let your letter arrive here, ^{26}(then) we will obtain its release. $^{26-28}$Your sister talks a lot to your father; $^{28-29}$she is trying to make him forget you. $^{30-31}$Do not act on you own; do not be afraid. $^{31-32}$Your [fath]er has nobody (and) nothing but you. ^{33}[Urg]ent! The rings of meteoritic iron [...] and the [...], $^{34-35}$let Aššur-ṣululī [...] bring (them) here.

Bibliography: Text published by Veenhof as AKT 5, 11 (Kt 92/k 233). For philological comments, see AKT 5, 99–101; collated May 2012.

Comments: Ababaya, wife of Kuliya, was presumably living in Aššur (see **133**), near Kuliya's relatives. As her husband is away, she protects his interests vis-à-vis his father against his sister's machinations. Acting as a representative of Kuliya in the city, she gives him advice about how to recognize honest traders: the outward appearance does not make the man, but one who has built a family should be trustworthy.

---

229. A Good Son Looks after His Father's Interests

Obv. ^{1}*um-ma Ištar-ba-áš-tí-ma* ^{2}*a-na Puzur*$_4$*-Ištar* ^{3}*qí-bi-ma mì-nam*$^{!}$ ^{4}*ma-da-tim : a-wa*$^{!}$*-tim* ^{5}*lu-lá-pí-tá-kum* ^{6}*šu-ma : lá ku-a-tí : ma-nam* ^{7}*a-ma-kam ni-šu : šu-ma* ^{8}*lá ku-a-tí : a-na ma-ma-an* ^{9}*ša-nim : a-ma-kam* ^{10}*a-bu-kà : ú-lá i-šu* ^{11}*lu a-wi-lá-tí-ma : a-na* lo.e. ^{12}*té-er-tí : a-bi*$_4$*-kà* ^{13}*i*-hi-id-ma ṭup-pè* rev. ^{14}*ša a-bi*$_4$*-kà : ša-ṣí-ir** ^{15}*ù mì-ma ba-áb-tí-šu* ^{16}*ša-áš-qí-il*$_5$ *ù lu-qú-ut* ^{17}*a-bi-kà : a-na* kù-babbar ^{18}*ta-e-er-ma : tí-ib-a-/ma* ^{19}*a-tal-kam-ma e-en*$_6$ ^{20}*A-šùr ù e-en*$_6$ ^{21}*a-bi*$_4$*-ka : a-mur-ma li-bi*$_4$ ^{22}*a-bi*$_4$*-ka ha-dí : a-ta* ^{23}*lá tí-de*$_8$*-e : ki*$^{!}$(ŠU)*-ma* ^{24}*ú-ma-am lá a-na-zu-<ru>-kà* ^{25}*ar-hi-iš : al-kam* u.e. ^{26}*ù iš-tí-kà lu-ṣí-/ma* ^{27}*i-na Kà-né-eš*$_{15}$ le.e. ^{28}*é a-bi*$_4$*-kà ù ku-a-tí* ^{29}*lá-ṣú-ur-ma : ma-ma-an* ^{30}*i-ṣé-er* é *a-bi*$_4$*-ku-nu* ^{31}*lá i-ša-lá*

$^{1-3}$Thus (says) Ištar-baštī: say to Puzur-Ištar.

[3-5]Why must I write you so many words? [6-7]If not you, who else do we have over there? [7-10]If not you, your father has nobody else over there! [11-13]Be a gentleman, pay heed to the instructions of your father, [13-14]keep the tablets of your father safe, [15-16]and make (the persons concerned) pay all his outstanding claims. [16-18]And exchange for silver your father's merchandise, [18-19]then get ready and come here [19-21]so you may look at (divine) Aššur and your father in person [21-22]and thus please your father!

[22-24]Do you not know that today I will not scold you? [25]Come quickly [26]so that I can depart with you and [27-29]watch over yours and your father's house in Kaneš, [29-31]and thus no one will make trouble for your father's house.

Bibliography: Text published in copy by Lewy as KTS 1, 1b; translated by Michel (2001a, no. 352; 2014b, 208).

Comments: Ištar-baštī, wife of Imdī-ilum, writes to their son Puzur-Ištar, urging him to take care of his parents' interests. Her moral advice concerns her son's behavior, as well as the respect he should show to his father and his piety toward the god Aššur. She awaits his arrival so she can travel with him to Kaneš and take care of the family household there.

---

230. A Lonely Daughter Asks for Her Parents' Moral Support

Obv. [1]*a-na Im-dí*-dingir [2]*ù Ištar-ba-áš-tí qí-bi*$_4$*-ma* [3]*um-ma Zi-zi-zi-ma* [4]*Ší-du-na a-ha-tí* [5]*me-ta-at* [6]*ù a-ni* : *A-al*-du$_{10}$ [7]*ma-ri-iṣ* [8]*ú-lá a-le-e-ma* [9]ki *ma-ma-an* [10]*ú-lá a-ta-w*[*u*] [11]*ú ma-ma-an* [12][*l*]*i-ba-am ú-lá* lo.e. [13]*i-da-nam* rev. [14]*a-bi*$_4$ *a-ta be-lí a-ta* [15]*um-mì a-ti* [16]*i-na u*$_4$*-mì-im* [17]*ša ṭup-pì ta-ša-me-a-ni* [18]*ṭup-pá-am lá-pí-ta-ma* [19]*ṭup-pá-am* : *a-wa-tim* [20]*dam-qá-tim lá-pí-ta-ma* [21]*iš-té-en*$_6$ *i-na* [22]*ṣú-ha-ri-kà lu-ub-lá-ma* [23]*li-bi*$_4$*-kà dì-nam* [24]*e-na-an ṣú-ha-ri-kà* [25]*lá ta-lá-qé* u.e. [26]*e-na-né-a le-qé-ma* [27]*ṭup-pá-kà li-li-kam-ma* le.e. [28]*li-ba-am dì-na*[*m*] [29]*šu-ma e-ṣí-iš ṭup-p*[*á-kà*] [30]*lá i-li-kam a-mu-a-at*$^{!}$

[1-3]Say to Imdī-ilum and Ištar-baštī: thus (says) Zizizi.

[4-5]Šiduna, my sister, died, [6-7]and now Āl-ṭāb is ill. [8]I can't manage anymore. [9-10]There is no one with whom I can speak [11-13]and no one to give me satisfaction. [14]You are my father and my master; [15]you are my mother. [16-17]The very day you hear my tablet, [18]write (pl.) a tablet; [19-20](please)

write (me) a tablet with friendly words, and $^{21–22}$let one of your servants bring it here and ^{23}give me your encouragement!

$^{24–25}$You should not accept the pleas of your servant, ^{26}but do accept my (own) entreaties; ^{27}thus let your tablet come here and ^{28}give me courage. $^{29–30}$If your tablet does not come soon, I will die!

Bibliography: Text published by Hecker, Kryszat, and Matouš as Prag I, 688; edited by Kryszat (2007a, 211–12); translated by Hecker (2006, 97).

Comments: Zizizi was the daughter of Imdī-ilum and Ištar-baštī. This letter gives the name of another daughter of the couple not attested elsewhere: Šiduna. There seems to be an epidemic, since we know from another letter that Āl-ṭāb, Zizizi's husband, also died (**50**). In the present letter, she feels lonely and thus asks for the moral support of her parents. Later on, she married an Anatolian in Kaneš and, according to her father, neglected her family (**50**).

The word *ennānum*, lines 24 and 26, refers to precisely the plea that Zizizi addresses to her parents.

---

231. Brothers Should Not Quarrel over Money

Obv. ^{1}*um-ma Ištar-ba-áš-tí-ma* ^{2}*a-na Puzur*$_4$*-Ištar qí*$^{!}$*-bi-ma* ^{3}*a-bu-kà iš-tù* iti-5-kam ^{4}*a-na ší-ip-kà-tim a-na* ^{5}*Qá-áb-ra i-lik-ma a-dí-ni* ^{6}*ú-lá i-li-kam* : *i-na u*$_4$*-mì-im* ^{7}*ša a-bu-kà* : *i-lá-kà-ni* ^{8}*ù a-ha-kà «ha-kà» i-ṭa-ra-/dam* ^{9}*mì-šu-ú ša a-ta ù a-/hu-kà* ^{10}*«ša» i-na ba-ri-ku-nu-ma* ^{11}*a-na* kù-babbar^{pì}*-ku-nu ù* kù-gi*-ku-/nu* ^{12}*tù-uš-té-ṣa-a-ni ma-nu-um* ^{13}*iš-tí ma-nim-ma tù-uš-té-ṣa-a* lo.e. ^{14}*a-na-ku ú-ba*$^{!}$(ŠU)*-lá-aṭ-ku-nu-/ma* ^{15}*mì-šu-um* : *a-hu-um* rev. ^{16}*ša a-hi-im* : *lá i-ša-me-ma* ^{17}*ša-li-um i-ṣé-er* ^{18}é *a-bi*$_4$*-ku-nu i-ša-lá* ^{19}*a-ṣé-er mur-ṣí-a ù* ^{20}*a-tù-nu ša tù-uš-té-ṣa-a-/ni* ^{21}*ù sí-hi-tám ša ma-tim* ^{22}*áš-me-ma da-ni-ša-ma* ^{23}*li-bi*$_4$ *im-tár-ṣa-ku-nu-tí* ^{24}kù-babbar *ù* kù-gi *lu ku-nu-tù*$^{!}$(TÍ)*-ma* ^{25}*a-tù-nu-ma* : *a-na* ^{26}*a-bi*$_4$*-ku-nu* : *na-pá-áš-ta-/ku-nu* ^{27}*lu šál-ma-at* : *a-dí* ^{28}*ma-tum i-ša-li-mu* ^{29}*i-n*[*a* x x] *a-i-ma* u.e. ^{30}*lá t*[*a*-x-x-*i*]*d/t iš-tù* ^{31}*ma-tum* : *i-ša-li-mu* ^{32}*ù ma-lá té-er-tí* le.e. ^{33}*a-bi*$_4$*-kà-ma e-pu-uš-ma tí-ib-a-ma* ^{34}*a-tal-kam li-bi*$_4$ *a-bi*$_4$*-kà lá i-ma-ra-aṣ* ^{35}*ù iš-tí a-hi-kà lu ṭá-ba-tí-ma* ^{36}*lá tù-uš-té-ṣa-a*

$^{1–2}$Thus (says) Ištar-baštī: say to Puzur-Ištar.

[3–6]5 months ago, your father left for Qabrā for investments, and so far, he has not come back. [6–8]The day your father comes back, he will send your brother. [9–12]Why are you and your brother quarreling among each other about your silver and your gold? [12–13]Who is quarreling with whom? [14]Am I then the one who is going to cure you (of this behavior)? [15–16]Why does one not listen to the other, [17–18]so that a troublemaker might cause harm to your father's house? [19–20]On top of my heartsickness and you quarreling, [21–22]I also heard about the rebellion of the country, [22–23]and I became worried about you. [24]The gold and silver do indeed belong to you, [25–27]and (therefore) your lives must be safe for your father's (sake)! [27–28]Until the country is peaceful (again) [29–30][…], wherever it is, you (sg.) should not […]. [31]When the country is peaceful (again), [32–33]act according to your father's instructions, [33–34]get ready and come here; your father should not be worrying. [35–36]You must be friendly with your brother, and you should stop quarreling!

Bibliography: Text published in copy by Lewy as TC 3, 112; translated by Michel (2001a, no. 350).

Comments: Ištar-baštī writes to her son Puzur-Ištar from Aššur as she is alone there, waiting for the return of her husband. She lectures him on his behavior and his ongoing disputes with his brother: good sons should not quarrel over money.

Line 5: the city of Qabrā is located north of the lower Zab, probably at Tepe Yaʿqub; see Deller 1990. Larsen (1976, 90, n. 17), suggests an alternative reading, *kà-áp-ra-<tim>*, "the villages."

Line 14: here Ištar-baštī uses figurative language. Larsen (1982) proposes to read this line: *ú ki-lá-la-ku-nu-ma*, thus translating the passage as follows: "As for me, and you both, why doesn't one listen to what the other says"; but it seems rather strange that the writer would have use two different signs for *la* consecutively.

Lines 21–22: the rebellion might have taken place in an Anatolian kingdom (*mātum*), perhaps Kaneš, since Ištar-baštī writes from Aššur.

232. Sisters Must Love Each Other

Obv. ^{1}*a-na Mu-sà qí-bi*$_{4}$*-ma* ^{2}*um-ma Lá-ma-ša-ma* ^{3}*šu-ma a-ha-tí : a-tí* ^{4}*šu-ma be-el-tí : a-tí* ^{5}*a-na-ku : ù a-tí* ^{6}*ni-ir-té-'a*$_{x}$(HA)*-am mì-ma* ^{7}*ú-nu-tim : ša a-na* ^{8}*Pu-šu-ke-en*$_{6}$ ^{9}*ta-pá-qí-dí-ni* ^{10}*té-er-tí-ki : li-li-kam-/ma* ^{11}*úz-ni : pè-tí-i* lo.e. ^{12}*ṭup-pá-am ša um-mì* ^{13}*ta-dí-na-ni -ni ú a-na* ^{14}*a-*[x x x x] rev. ^{15}[x x (x)]*-tám : Ì-lí-x-*[(x)] ^{16}*a-tí a-na* dumu *um-me-a-nim* ^{17}*ke-nim : pì-iq-dí a-n*[*é*]*-/ma* ^{18}*lu-ub-lá-am : ú a-šar* ^{19}*ta-pá-qí-dí-ni : i-na* ^{20}*na-áš-pè-er-tí-ki lu-ub-lá-am* ^{21}*ki-ma : ṭup-pá-am : a-mì-a-am* ^{22}*tù-šé-bi*$_{4}$*-lá-ni* ^{23}*a-té-be-a-ma : a-ta-lá-kam* ^{24}*a-ṣé-ri-ki : a-ta-lá-kam* ^{25}*ta-ma-lá-ke-en*$_{6}$ *ša i-na* ^{26}*ma-aṣ-ar-tim* ^{27}*i-ba-ší-ú-ni : a-na* ^{28}*Ì-lí-iš-*<*ta*>*-ki-il*$_{5}$ *lá ta-dí-/ni* u.e. ^{29}*šu-ma Pu-šu-ke-en*$_{6}$ ^{30}*e-ri-iš-ki* le.e. ^{31}*dí-ni : šu-ma : lá ki-a-am : a-dí : e-né-a* ^{32}*ta-me-ri*$^{!}$*-ni : a-ma-ma-an lá ta-dí-ni*

$^{1-2}$Say to Musa: thus (says) Lamaša.

$^{3-4}$If you are my sister (and) if you are my mistress, $^{5-6}$ (then), you and I, we should love each other! $^{6-10}$Let your report come here concerning all the goods that you entrusted to Pūšu-kēn, and ^{11}inform me.

$^{12-13}$Concerning the tablet that my mother gave me, and for $^{14-15}$[...] Ilī-[x-x], $^{16-18}$you, entrust it to a recognized trader, so he brings (it) here now. $^{18-20}$Let him bring (it with) a letter from you (indicating) to whom you have entrusted (it). $^{21-22}$As soon as you have sent me this tablet over there, $^{23-24}$I will get ready and depart to come to you.

$^{25-28}$You should not give to Iliš-takil the *tamalakkum*-chests that are in the strong room. $^{29-31}$If Pūšu-kēn asks you, give (them); $^{31-32}$if not, do not give (them) to anyone until you see me personally!

Bibliography: Text published in copy by Stephens as BIN 6, 14; translated by Michel (2001a, no. 370).

Comments: Musa lives in Kaneš and has close ties to Pūšu-kēn there. She received several letters from Lamaša, wife of Buzāzu, one of Pūšu-kēn's sons (**210**). There is, unfortunately, no clue about their relationships: they could be real sisters or related by some other family connection. This connection, according to the writer, entails feelings of friendship. Lamaša is about to leave Aššur to travel to Kaneš to join Musa there.

233. Complaints about the Husband's Behavior

Obv. ^{1}*a-na A-na-lí* ^{2}*qí-bi-ma um-ma* ^{3}*Ša-at-ì-lí-ma* ^{4}*Ì-lí-a-lim* ^{5}*i-na* é$^{bé\text{-}tim}$ ^{6}*it-ta-ni-a-ma* ^{7}*i-na ki-dim* ^{8}*wa-áš-ba-ku* : *šu-ma* ^{9}*a-ta* : *lá ta-šu-ra-ni* ^{10}*ma-nu-um li-šu-r*[*a-n*]*i* ^{11}*a-hi* : *a-ta* : *Ì-lí-*[*a-lim*] lo.e. ^{12}*lá-am-ni-iš* ^{13}*e-ta-na-pá-áš-ni* rev. ^{14}*sú*$^{!}$*-ba-ar-am* ^{15}*a-na hu-bu-li-im* ^{16}*al-qé-ma* : *sú*$^{!}$*-ba-ar-*/ *ri-*/*a* ^{17}*ta-dá-na-am* ^{18}*ú-lá i-«a»-mu-a* ^{19}*ma-ah-ri-«a»-kà-ma* ^{20}*ke-e* : *e-ta-pá-áš-a-ni* ^{21}*a-hi a-ta* : *té-er-tí-kà* ^{22}*li-li-kam* : *pá-ni-*/*a* ^{23}*i-na me-at* (erasure) ^{24}urudu : *ša* : *té-zi-ba-n*[*i*] u.e. ^{25}*70 ma-na* urudu *a*[*l-q*]*é* le.e. ^{26}*am-tám* : *al-qé* : *am-tá*[*m*] ^{27}*Ì-lí-a-lim* : *e-ta-ha-a*[*z*] ^{28}*am-tim a-ni me-ta-a*[*t*]

$^{1-3}$Say to Annali: thus (says) Šāt-ilī.

$^{4-6}$Ilī-ālum has thrown me out of the house, and $^{7-8}$I am living in the open. $^{8-10}$If you do not take care of me, who could take care of me? $^{11-13}$You are my brother. Ilī-[Anum] keeps treating me badly. $^{14-16}$He$^{?!}$ took a servant as debt (collateral$^{?}$) and $^{16-18}$refuses to give me (back) my servant. $^{19-20}$If you had been present, would he have done that to me? $^{21-22}$You are my brother; let your instructions come here. $^{22-24}$Previously, from the 1 hundred (minas) of copper that you left me, ^{25}I took 70 minas. ^{26}I bought a female slave. $^{26-27}$Ilī-Anum had taken (as concubine) the female slave. ^{28}Now the female slave is dead!

Bibliography: Text published by Biggs (1996).

Comments: Šāt-ilī is not well known from the Old Assyrian sources; in **73**, she might be the mother of Kititi, who married Šalim-bēlī. A woman with this name might have been the widow of Šu-Ištar (Kt c/k 1301 + 1347; Albayrak 2015, 19). In this letter, she writes to her brother complaining about the behavior of her presumed husband: he threw her out of the house and took one of her female slaves as a concubine; for this meaning of *ahāzum*, see text **23**.

This letter is full of spelling and grammar errors; it was written by a nonprofessional writer. There are superfluous signs, wrong verbal persons on lines 16 and 18, and a strange writing for the word *subrum*, "servant, domestic," on lines 14 and 16, if the reading is correct.

234. A Son Must Rescue His Father's House

Obv. [1]*a-na Im-dí-*dingir *ù Ú-zu-a qí-bi*$_4$*-ma* [2]*um-ma Lá-ma-sà-tum-ma* [3]*ù Na-ar-am-tum-ma* [4]*du-lu-um i-na A-lim*^{ki} [5]*ik-tí-bi*$_4$*-id mì-šu a-ni-um* [6]*ša ta-áš-pu-ra-ni mì-šu-um* [7]é *a-bi*$_4$*-kà ù a-ma-*[*a*]*t a-bi*$_4$*-/kà* [8]*a-na hi-lá-tim i-ta-bu-lu* [9]*a-na Ú-zu-a qí-bi*$_4$*-ma* [10]*a-ma-nim ta-áš-ta-na-pár-ra-am* [11]*a-hu-ú-kà ma-du* [12]*ma ta-áš-ta-na-pár-ra-am* [13]*a-hu-kà ú-kà-lu ù ni-a-/tí* [14][x] *a-hu-hu* dam-gàr^{ru} lo.e. [15]*a-hu-kà i-na kà-ú-lim* rev. [16]*i-mu-at ù né-nu i-bu-bu-tim* [17]*a-ṣé-er du-li-ni : ni-mu-at* [18]*al-kam-ma* é *a-bi*$_4$*-kà e-ṭí-/ir* [19]*a-na hi-lá-tí-ma* é *a-bi*$_4$*-kà* [20]*ù a-ma-at a-bi*$_4$*-kà : lá i-ta-bu-lu* [21]*šé-ší-ir a-na šé-ep* [22]*um-mì-*<*a*>*-ni-kà mu-*<*qú*>*-ut-ma* [23]*al-kam-ma* é *a-bi*$_4$*-kà e-ṭí-ir* [24]*šu-ma lá ta-le-e* é^{tám} [25]*ú a-ma-at a-bi*$_4$*-kà té-ni* [26]*um-mì-a-nu i-na ni-a-tim* [27]*a-ni-tim ha-bu-lu a-bu-kà-ma* [28]*qá-tám iš-ku-un a-pu-tum* [29]é *a-bi*$_4$*-kà lá i-ha-li-iq* u.e. [30]*lá ta-ak-šu-dam* le.e. [31]*al-kam*$^{!}$(HI)*-ma e-ṭí-ir ma-ma-an* [32]*šé-šú-ur* é *a-bi*$_4$*-kà lá i-mu-a* [33]*al-kam-ma šé-ší-ir a-ma-nim né-nu* [34]*ni-ta-kál ku-a-tí ni-da-gal*

[1–3]Say to Imdī-ilum and Uzua: thus (say) Lamassatum and Narāmtum.

[4–5]There is now serious misfortune in the city (of Aššur); why is it that you have written this (news) to me? [6–8]Why does one take in distraint your father's house and your father's *amtum*-wife?

[9]Say to Uzua. [10]To whom do you keep writing here? [11]You have many brothers. [12]Even so you keep writing here! [13–14]They hold your brother, and *Ahuhu*(?) the merchants […] us. [15–16]Your brother will die from being held (in distraint), [16–17]and as for us, to top off our misfortune, we will die of hunger, too! [18]Come here and rescue your father's house! [19–20]Your father's house and *amtum*-wife should not be taken in distraint. [21–22]Straighten this matter out! Fall at the feet of your investors; [23]come here and rescue our father's house! [24–25]If you cannot, then transfer (ownership) of your father's house and *amtum*-wife! [26–28]While the investors are in debt because of our affair, your father has levied a distraint! Urgent! [29–30]Your father's house must not be ruined; you've been unsuccessful (so far), [31–32]so come here and rescue it. Nobody wants to straighten out your father's house; [33–34]you yourself must come and straighten (it) out. As for us, whom can we trust? We look to you!

Bibliography: Text published by Hecker, Kryszat, and Matouš as Prag I, 467. Collated on photo online on the CDLI as P359077.

Comments: Lamassatum and Narāmtum are two women living in Aššur. They seem to be quite close to Imdī-ilum and Uzua, but the ruined father and the *amtum*-wife would be those of Uzua. Lamassatum is a homonym of the wife of Elamma, whose archives were excavated in 1991. She wrote also letters to Pūšu-kēn, to whom she writes, "You are my father" (**239**, CCT 4, 40a). Narāmtum (written *Na-ra-am-tum*) is the author of letter **235**, addressed to Akatiya and Adad-bāni. The tablet is well shaped and the writing quite regular, but there are mistakes in its language.

Line 8: the word *hi-lá-tim* would come from *halālum*, "to detain."

---

235. A Woman Asks for News and Help from Relatives

Envelope Fragment

(a) Obv. ^{1}[… x]x kišib$^{?}$ […] ^{2}[*Na-ra-a*]*m*$^{?}$*-tum* […] ^{3}[^{d}]im-[*ba-ni*]

Tablet

(b) Obv. ^{1}*a-na A-ki-ta-a* ^{2}*ù* ^{d}im-*ba-ni qí-bi*$_{4}$*-ma* ^{3}*um-ma Na-ra-am-tum-ma* ^{4}*mì-nu-um* : *a-ni-tum* ^{5}*ša ṭup-pá-am* 2 *ú-ba-an* ^{6}*šu-lu-um-ku-nu* ^{7}*lá tù-šé-ba-lá-ni-ni* ^{8}*a-ṣé-er a-na iš-ri-šu* ^{9}*ha-al-qá-ku-ni-ma* ^{10}*ù li-bi*$_{4}$*-i* : *na-as-/hu* ^{11}*ù a-tù*$^{!}$*-nu šu-lu-um-/ku-nu* ^{12}*lá tù-šé-ba-lá-ni-/ni* ^{13}*mì-nu-um* : *a-ni-tum* ^{14}*ša lu-qú-ut* : *a-hi-ku-nu* ^{15}*sà-pu-ha-at-ni-ma* lo.e. ^{16}*ù ki-ma a-hu-ku-nu* rev. ^{17}*a-šé-ra-am* : *lá i-šu-ú* ^{18}*té-ta-na-pá-ša-ni-*<*ni*> ^{19}*ù-lu* : *ṭup-pá-am* ^{20}*šé-bi-lá-nim-ma* : maškìm ^{21}*lá-hu-za-ku-nu-tí lu*$^{?}$ *a-hu-/ku-/nu* ^{22}*lu ur-dum* : *iš-tí* kù-babbar ^{23}*ta-ṣ/za-ni-a hu-bu-lam* ^{24}*ma-num* : *i-ša-qal* ^{25}*a-pu-hi-ku-nu* : *a-na-kam* ^{26}*ki-ma a-hu-ku-nu ù a-bu-ku-nu* ^{27}kù-babbar *a-na* é *A-lim*^{ki} ^{28}*ha-bu-lu lá tí-de*$_{8}$*-a* : *i-ṣé-er* ^{29}*ša A-šùr* kù-babbar dam-gàr^{ru-tim} ^{30}*ir-tí-bi-ma* : *i-ma-šu-hu-ku-nu* ^{31}*ù ta-áš-ta-pu-a-ma* ^{32}*kà-ra-am lá ta-ma-ha-/ra* u.e. ^{33}[kù]-babbar *lá tù*$^{!}$*-pá-ha-ra* ^{34}*ù šu-ma a-ta* le.e. ^{35}*a-hu-ra-tí* : *I-ku-pì-a ṭur*$_{4}$*-da-am* ^{36}*ma-ma-an ša e-ṣí ù še-am* ^{37}*i-ša-a-ma-ni lá-šu*$^{!}$ (c) ^{38}*še-um ša-qí-il*$_{5}$ ^{39}*ù ta-ak-ši-tum* ^{40}*lá-šu-ma* : ninda ^{41}*i-na qá-ta-tim* ^{42}*e-ta-na-ṭí-ir* ^{43}*ší-im* túg-hi-a *šé-bi*$_{4}$*-lá-nim* ^{44}*e-né-a* : *pè-té-a*

$^{1-2}$Say to Akitaya and Adad-bāni: thus (says) Narāmtum.

$^{4-7}$What is this that you do not even send me a tablet 2 fingers wide with good news from you? $^{8-9}$Not only am I lost ten times over, $^{10-12}$so that my heart is broken, but you also send me no good news of yourself! $^{13-15}$What is this that your (pl.) brother's merchandise has been squandered, $^{16-18}$and that you act as if your (pl.) brother has no one to take care (of him)? $^{19-21}$Just send a tablet, and I will hire an attorney for you! [21–24](If you have) either a brother or a slave, (and) with the silver […] who will pay the debt (instead of you)? [25–28]Don't you know that here, your brother and your father owe silver to the City Hall? [28–30]The (amount of) silver (owed) to the creditors has now become even bigger than that owed to Aššur; they rob you! [31]But you remain silent, [32]and do not approach the *kārum* (authorities). [33]Do not collect the [si]lver. [34]And if you are late, send Ikuppiya!

[36–37]There is nobody to buy wood or barley for me. [38]Barley is scarce, and there is no profit (to be made), and [39–42]bread is snatched away from (our) hands! [43]Send me the price of the textiles. [44]Cheer me up!

Bibliography: Text published by Hrozný as ICK 1, 17b + c, for the letter, which is written on a tablet, and a supplement; and ICK 1, 17a, for the fragment of envelope.

Comments: Narāmtum, who is known only from this letter and **234**, writes from Aššur to Akitaya and Adad-bāni, presumably two men, asking for news. She may have married the brother of one of the two, since she is pleading for this unnamed brother and their father. She feels lonely and needs their support.

Line 23: the first word is not understood.

Line 44: the expression *e-né-a pè-té-a* must be translated literally, "open my eyes"; it is a metaphor for "bring me to life again." It is also attested in BIN 4, 72:23.

Women's Religion and the Spirits of the Dead

We know little about Assyrian religious practices. For women, their beliefs, behavior, and social mores were closely interconnected. Thus, adhering to a code of good conduct, as women defined it in their letters, was first of all directed toward keeping the favor of the gods and the spirits of the dead (**236**, and see below). One was supposed to pray to and to praise the gods regularly, and make offerings in the temple. In their letters, women frequently mention their intention to pray to the god Aššur on behalf of their correspondents (**170, 238, 239**).[23] In the same spirit, women call for

23. Šīmat-Suen, one of the sisters of Uṣur-ša-Ištar, announces to her brother: "I will pray for you before my god" (Kt n/k 530:26–27, courtesy Çeçen). Note that,

their male relatives to come back to Aššur, not just to visit their families but to carry out their religious obligations and to present themselves at the temple of Aššur to worship the god (**129**, **229**, **265**).

Letters mentioning deities worshiped by Assyrian men and women mostly identify them as family gods: "the god of my father," "my/your god" (**129**, **166**, **170**, **240**).[24] Certain gods can be associated with specific merchant families. In the letters Tarām-Kūbi sends to her husband, she mentions offerings to Amurrum; out of respect for Innaya's special devotion to Amurrum, "your god and the god of your household," she invokes the love of the god Aššur to ask Innaya to come back home (**129**).[25] Tariša, in a letter to her brother Aššur-taklāku, gives the name of the family god, Ilabrat, as follows: "May Aššur, our god Ilabrat, and our fathers' spirits act as witnesses! I have no one but you!"[26] The goddess Ištar-ZA-AT was specially venerated by Aššur-imittī and his sons Uṣur-ša-Ištar and Hunniya, whose archives were excavated in 1962 (Kt n/k), and by Imdī-ilum's family, as shown by a letter of Ištar-baštī to her brother: "I will pray for you before Ištar and Ištar-ZA-AT" (**241**).[27] She likewise prays for them to Ištar. Women not only venerated the god Aššur but were also particularly attentive to female deities: thus Akatiya writes a letter to the goddess Tašmētum (**242**).

---

besides women's letters, the mention of "praying to god" appears in royal correspondence; see Michel 2015c.

24. Van der Toorn 1996, 72–74; see also Veenhof 2014, 365–68. Note that besides Mesopotamian deities, the Assyrians respected and worshiped also the goddess of Kaneš, Anna (Michel 2014a, 2016b). Anatolians too occasionally swore by the symbol of the god Aššur (Dercksen 2008a).

25. Matouš 1982; Michel 1991, 85–87; and Kryszat 2006a. The other correspondents of Innaya invoke Amurrum when they write to him, for example, in the following letters: Michel 1991, nos. 96 (CCT 5, 1a), 96 (BIN 6, 99), and 177 (*RA* 60, 34, and its duplicate AKT 3, 62). And when Innaya writes, he mentions "Aššur and Amurrum, the god of my father"; Michel 1991, no. 99 (BIN 6, 99):8–9

26. Kt 93/k 198:25–28: [^{d}A]-*šùr* ^{d}NIN.ŠUBUR *i-l*[*i*]-*ni*, [*ù*] *e-ṭé-mu a-bi-ni* [*li-ṭù-la*], [*šu-ma*] *lá ku-a-tí* : *ma-*[*nam*], [*ša-n*]*i-a-am* : *lá i-šu-ú*. Aššur-taklāku replied in the same manner: "May the god of our father and the spirits of our father watch (over you)"; Kt 93/k 527:12–13: DINGIR^{lu} *a-bi*$_4$*-ni ú e-ṭá-mu a-bi*$_4$*-/ni*, *li-ṭù-lá*; texts cited by Michel 2008f, 196–97 nn. 71–72. For this archive, unearthed in 1993, see Michel 2008e.

27. Kryszat 2006b. Archive studied by Günbattı, Bayram, and Çeçen; see Veenhof 2014, 365–68.

Gods could be invoked on various occasions, singly or along with spirits of ancestors (see below), or as witnesses to an oath. Depending upon whether the oath was sworn by a woman or a man, the deity called upon was not the same: men had to take oaths on the weapon of Aššur (*patrum*, *šugariā'um*), which was kept in the sacred precinct (*hamrum*) or gate of the god, whereas women took oaths on the frame drum of the goddess Ištar (*huppum*; **243**, **244**).[28]

Women's letters mention fundraising for the temple, offerings made to the gods in the form of emblems, statuettes (**128**, **245**), and votive offerings (*ikribū*), though the last were more often the responsibility of men (**246**, **247**). Indeed, temples invested in commerce by making funds derived from offerings or merchandise available to merchants as long-term loans (**124**, **206**, **252–255**, **265**).[29]

Besides gods, spirits of the dead (*eṭemmū*) were regularly invoked, especially by women.[30] Ancestors were venerated after their deaths; their descendants prayed to them and made them offerings. Tombs (*quburum*) were dug under family homes, as shown by one text, "the house of Hinnaya, where Ilī-bāni lies buried."[31] Some were built of stone, with a marker set up over them.[32] Sometimes the cost of a tomb is mentioned: "We spent for the grave of our father ½ mina, 4 shekels of silver from our father's silver" (**64**:13–15); "⅓ mina, 3 shekels of silver for the grave of our father"; "I paid 1½ shekels for a stone when she died"; or "7 talents of copper was used for our father's grave."[33]

When the woman was a widow, her eldest son, as heir to the family home, was obligated to pay his mother's funeral expenses, including construction of a tomb: "The house in Kaneš and the furniture belong to Iddin-Ištar.… For the burial of Puzur, their mother, for expenses, and for the debt of their mother, Puzur, Iddin-Ištar alone is responsible" (**49**).

---

28. Michel 1997a.

29. Dercksen 1997.

30. Almost half of the letters mentioning the spirits of the dead were written by women.

31. AKT 5, 38:2–4: é$^{be\text{-}et}$ *Hi-na-a, ša a-šar Il$_5$-ba-ni, na-lu-ni*.

32. AKT 6a, 273:33′–35′ mentions the building of "a house" in front of a grave; see the comments to this text by Larsen; Heffron 2016.

33. TPAK 1, 212:1–3: ⅓ *ma-na* 3 gín, kù-babbar *a-na qú-bu-ri-im, ša a-bi-ni*. CCT 5, 37a:28–29: 1½ gín *a-na, ab-nim i-mu-tí-ša áš-qúl*. This personal memorandum also lists various payments in favor of an anonymous woman. AKT 6a, 251:6–7: 7 gú urudu *a-qú-bu-ur*, [*a*]*-bi-ni ga-me-er*.

Some tombs excavated under the house in the Kanesh lower town have yielded clay pots, some of them specially made to be interred with the dead. Tombs also contained pots, weapons, and other objects of bronze. Women's skeletons could be adorned with jewelry in gold, silver, electrum, and semiprecious stones.[34] Other ornaments included thin leaves of gold to cover the eyes and mouth of the deceased to prevent the spirit of the dead from coming out and demons from getting in.

Sometimes valuables such as statuettes of deities, cosmetic boxes of ivory, faience, or stone were placed in burials, as well as amulets in the shapes of animals.[35] Although the Old Assyrian residential area at Aššur has not been discovered, some tombs have been found, such as tomb number 37, east of the temple of Suen-Šamaš.[36] In this burial, the skeleton of a woman lay surrounded by extremely rich funerary goods: weapons and vessels of bronze, extensive jewelry in gold and precious stones, as well as three lapis lazuli cylinder seals. Certain objects, such as gazelle figurines, three in bronze and three in lead, were made and buried on the occasion of the interment as part of a ritual associated with life after death; other Old Assyrian tombs at Aššur have also produced this type of amulet.

All these objects clearly had some special purpose in the funerary rites, about which little is known. Some texts could mention certain procedures, such as perhaps pouring water, which could be related to some purification (**248**, **249**), but their interpretation remains difficult because they appear in broken contexts. The small group of documents pertaining to the death of a woman, Ištar-Lamassī, and of her sons, mentions funeral expenses, including a ceremony in which a chair was used in some way in connection with the dead person (**60**, **250**). The deceased mother's chair (*kussium*) was meant to replace her soul between the time of her death and her burial.[37] A ceremony was performed in which the ghost of the dead mother participated through her chair. Removing the chair of the dead woman would then symbolize her departure, though it might simply have referred to the burial of the chair along with the body (**60**). Expenses were incurred for food and drink consumed during the ceremony. In total, 19½

34. T. Özgüç 2003, 242–51. A group of ten metal vessels was excavated in a cist grave of level Ib (M6, located in LVI-135), published by Emre 2008.

35. T. Özgüç 2003, 233–41

36. Number according to Hockmann 2010; see also graves 36 and 53.

37. Scurlock 2002.

shekels of silver were spent for the ceremony for the mother and her two sons (**59, 60**).[38] A textile turned over to a relative of the deceased woman may have been used as a shroud (**251**).[39]

There is extensive Mesopotamian documentation on the matter of whether, the body of the deceased having decayed after burial, its "spirit" (*eṭemmū*) simply mingled with others in the land of the dead or was believed to join those of different generations of the same family (*eṭemmū ša abini*, "the spirits of our father"; *eṭemmū bēt abini*, "the spirits of our father's house").[40] Actions of these spirits could be beneficent or malignant. They were mostly invoked along with gods (**236, 310**) but sometimes together with demons (*utukkū*, **253**). These spirits could intercede on behalf of the living with the netherworld deities in the kingdom of the dead. Some women, moreover, believed that the spirits of the dead, knowing the future through their interaction with netherworld deities, could be consulted and questioned about it. Some women, living in the house where their parents-in-law were buried, were fearful that their ghosts would come to haunt them when the regular ritual for the family dead could not be carried out in their husbands' absence.

Women seem to have been more engaged with popular beliefs than men. It is therefore no surprise that the rare instances of specialists in divination referred to in the Kaneš archives concern women, consulted by women, in matters of everyday life: dream interpreters (*šā'iltum*) and diviners (*bārītum*).[41] The former interpreted the symbolism of messages communicated by spirits and divinities, often in dreams (**253**); the latter carried out divinatory procedures but without reference to the written materials available to their male counterparts (**226, 252, 256**). Impetus for

38. Veenhof 2008b. See also Kt 91/ 369 (AKT 8, 188) which mentions two shekels for bewailing, and many expenses for funerals over two days. According to unpublished texts cited by Dercksen 2015a, 53–54, commemorative rituals for the dead performed regularly through the year are also attested, such as *nasbītum* (Kt c/k 737, previously considered to be mourning) and *tamrum* (Kt c/k 127); see below.

39. See also *RHA* 18, 39:23–26: 1 túg *ša qá-tim i-nu-mì, a-ša-at Du-du me-ta-at-/ ni, a-Šu-<I>-la-áb-ra-at, a-šu-mì Du-du a-dí-in*, "I gave 1 textile of normal quality to Šu-Ilabrat in the name of Dudu when Dudu's wife died."

40. Michel 2008f; 2009a; Veenhof 2014; Hertel 2015. For the Mesopotamian documentation, see, for example, Alster 1980; Bottéro 1980, 1983; Katz 2003; Bachelot 2005; Van der Stede 2007; Lion 2009a.

41. Hirsch 1961, 72; Michel 2009b. This is quite exceptional, because female diviners are very rare in the cuneiform sources.

a consultation was provided by illness or a financial misfortune, scourges sent by the gods to punish dishonest businessmen (**124**), or perhaps by the spirits of ancestors who felt they had been neglected (**117**, **118**).[42] One needed to ask of the gods or spirits the reason for their disfavor, then do what was required to appease them and be healed (**254–256**).

---

236. Being Honest Is Pleasing to the Gods

Obv. [1]*a-na Bu-za-zu* [2]*qí-bi-ma um-ma* [3]*Wa-qur-tum-ma* 4 túg-hi-a *ku-nu-ki-a* [4]*a-na A-sà-nim* : [5]*a-dí-in-ma* : *a-na a-wi-lim* [6]*ú-šé-bi-il*$_5$*-ma*$^!$ [7]*a-hi a-ta* : *be-lí a-ta* [8]*e-ni-kà* : *lá ta-na-ší-ma* [9]*lá tù-ha-lá-qá-ni* [10]*ki ma-ṣí* [11]*lu ki-iš-da-tù-kà* [12]*tí-de*$_8$*-e* : *a-ta-ma* [13]*ki-ma i-na* é^{tim} [14]*e-ri-im* : *e-zi-bi*$_4$*-ni* [15]*a-hi a-ta* : túg-hi-a [16]*a-na* kù-babbar : *ta-er-ma* [17]kù-babbar *ku-nu-uk-ma* u.e. [18][*š*]*é-bi*$_4$*-lam ki-ma* [19]dingir *ù e-ṭé-me* le.e. [20]*ta-ga-mì-lu-ma* [21]*lá a-ha-li-qú* [22]*e-pu-uš*

[1–3]Say to Buzāzu: thus (says) Waqqurtum.

[3–6]I gave 4 textiles under my seal to Asānum to send them to the gentleman. [7]You are my brother and my master; [8–9]don't be so greedy that you ruin me! [10–11]How much are your revenues? [12–14]You well know that he has left me in an empty house! [15–18]You are my brother; exchange the textiles for silver, then seal the silver and send (it) to me. [18–22]Act so that you please the god(s) and the spirits of the dead, and that I not be ruined!

Bibliography: Text published in copy by Clay as BIN 4, 96; translated by Michel (2001a, no. 316).

Comments: Waqqurtum writes to her brother Buzāzu concerning textiles she sent him for sale and for which she is awaiting the proceeds in silver. She appeals to the presumed religious feelings of her brother lest he forgets her interests.

Line 8: literally: "You should not look intentionally, and you should not ruin me."

---

42. Scurlock 2002.

237. The God Warns a Merchant via His Sister

Obv. [1]_a-na Ú-ṣur*-ša-Ištar_ [2]_qí-bi_$_4$_-ma um-ma A-kà-tí-a_ [3]_ù Ší-ma-at-Sú-en_$_6$_-ma_ [4]_mì-nam_ : _é a-bi-kà_ [5]_té-ta-pá-áš_ : _a-ha-at-kà_ [6]_lam-ni-iš_ : _té-ta-pá-áš_ [7]_ù a-ma-kam_ : _mu-ta-am_ [8]_iš-te_$_9$_*-en_$_6$ _ú_ $2^{\text{šé-na}}$ [9]_tù-uš-té-mì-it_ [10]A-_šùr_ : _a-šu-mì_ lo.e. [11]_šé-pé-kà_ : _uš-ta-na-ad-/kà_ rev. [12]_tí-ib-a-ma_ : _a-tal-kam_ [13]_ù i-a-tí_ : _a-ṣé-er_ [14]_ṣú-ru-up-tim_ : _ša be-lí-a_ [15]_ù a-ta_ : _lá ta-lá-kam-ma_ [16]_ki-ma_ : dumu-munus : _lá a-ší-ri_ [17]_a-ba-ší_ : _a-šu-mì_ : _ša_ [18]_É-a-šar ù Šu-Lá-ba-an_ [19]_ša áš-ta-na-pá-ra-ku-ni_ [20]kù-babbar 10 gín _ša e-ṭá*-ri-im_ [21]_eṭ*-ra-šu-nu_ : _lá ku-a-tí_ u.e. [22]_ki-ma a-bi_$_4$_-a_ : _a-da-gal_ [23]_tí-ib-a-ma_ : _a-tal-kam_ le.e. [24]_iš-tí A-šur_ : _na-pá*-áš*-ta-kà*_ [25]_e-ṭí-ir_

[1–3]Say to Uṣur-ša-Ištar: thus say Akatiya and Šīmat-Suen.

[4–5]What have you done to your father's house? [5–6]Your sister you have treated badly, [7–9]and, moreover, there you have caused the death of one or two! [10–11](Divine) Aššur keeps on warning you concerning your moves! [12]Get ready and come here. [13–15]As for me, despite my master's burning anger, you just don't come to me. [16–17]I am like a daughter without a protector! [17–19]Concerning Ea-šar and Šu-Labān, about whom you keep writing to me, [20–21]save them by (supplying) 10 shekels of silver needed to save them! [21–22]Do I not look at you as my father? [23]Get ready and come here. [24–25]Save your life with the help of (divine) Aššur!

Bibliography: Tablet published by Çeçen and Gökçek (2017, 464–65, 471–74) as Kt n/k 1336. Lines 1–11 cited by Kryszat (2003, 257, n. 22); lines 4–17 by Çeçen (1996b, 14, n. 19); collated May 2011.

Comments: Akatiya and Šīmat-Suen are sisters of Uṣur-ša-Ištar, whose archives were unearthed in 1962 (see pp. 397–410). Akatiya warns her brother about his behavior and his endangered associates; she urges him to come back to Aššur to fulfill his religious and family obligations.

Line 14: the word _ṣuruptum_ is unknown; it could be formed on the verbal root ṢRP, "to burn"; see **264**:6.

238. Sisters Pray to Aššur for Their Brothers

Obv. [1]_a-na A-du-ma qí-bi_$_4$_-ma_ [2]_um-ma Ší-ma-at-A-šùr-ma_ [3]_ša iš-tí_ : _a-hu-a-tí-šu-nu_ [4]_i-za-ni-ú-ni_ : _a-dí_ [5]_du-ri-ma_ : _i-za-ni-ú_ [6]_mì-nam e-pu-uš-kà-ma_

[7]*iš-tù* : *tù-ṣú-ni* [8]*iš-tù* 10 *ša-na-tim* lo.e. [9]*šu-mì-ma lá ta-za-kàr* rev. [10]*i-na* é$^{be_4\text{-}et}$ [11]*ra-mì-ni-a uš-ba-ku-ma* [12]*li-ba-kà* : *tù-lá-ma-nam* [13]*a-hi a-ta i-na* kù-babbar [14]1 gín *áš-ra-ni-ma* igi *A-šùr* [15]*ì-lí-a* : *lá-ak-ru-ba-kum*

[1–2]Say to Aduma: thus (says) Šīmat-Aššur.

[3–5]Do those who become angry with their sisters stay angry forever? [6]What have I done to you? Indeed, [7]since you left [8]10 years ago, [9]you have not even given me any present! [10–12]I am living alone in my house, but you are still angry at me! [13–14]You are my brother; help me with some silver, even a single shekel; [14–15]then I will pray for you to my god Aššur.

Bibliography: Text published by Albayrak as AKT 4, 63 (Kt o/k 79). Collated May 2012.

Comments: Šīmat-Aššur, who is living alone in her house in Aššur, asks Aduma, presumably her brother, the reason for his anger against her. According to her, brothers and sisters should help each other: if he provides her some silver, she intends to pray for him. The fact that she lives alone, the last sentence, and the name she bears suggest that she could have been a consecrated woman.

239. A Woman Prays to Aššur for Her Correspondent

Obv. [1]*a-na Pu-šu-ke-en*$_6$ [2]*qí-bi-m*[*a*] *um-ma* [3]*Lá-ma-sú-tum-ma* [4]^{d}im-*ba-ni* [5]*ur-du-um* [6]*wa-ra-ad-kà* [7]*šu-ma a-bi a-ta* lo.e. [8]*i-na a-he-a* rev. [9]*ma-ma-an* [10]*lá ú-pá-ra-sú* [11]*ma-áš-kà-na-tù-kà* [12]*kà-a-na* : *wa-ar-dam* [13]1 gín-ta kù-babbar [14]*i-ma-áš-kà-na-tí-kà* [15]*ša-dí-šu-ma* [16]*šé-bi-lam* u.e. [17]*a-b*[*i*] *a-ta* le.e. [18]igi *A-šur lá-ak-ru-ba-kum*

[1–3]Say to Pūšu-kēn: thus (says) Lamassatum.

[4–5]The slave Adad-bāni is your slave. [7]If you are my father, [8–10]no one among my relatives should frighten him! [11–12]Your deposits (arrive here) regularly. [12–15]As to the slave, make him collect each shekel of silver of your deposits, and [16]send (the silver) here. [17]You are my father; [18]I will pray to Aššur for you.

Bibliography: Text published by Hecker as KUG, 39; translated by Michel (2001a, no. 391).

Comments: We do not know the relationship between Pūšu-kēn and Lamassatum. This lady, who is living in Aššur, intends to pray to the god Aššur for him.

---

240. A Man Asks His Sister to Pray for Him

Obv. ^{1}*um-ma Ú-ṣur-ší-Ištar-ma* ^{2}*a-na A-kà-tí-a* ^{3}*qí-bi-ma mì-nu-um* ^{4}*ṭup-pé-e lá dam-qú-tim* ^{5}*ša ta-áš-ta-na-pì*-ri-ni* ^{6}*a-dí ša* é *Šu-Be-lim* ^{7}*lu i-gi*$_5$*-ir-ú* ^{8}*lu mì-ma i-pí-šu-nu* ^{9}*ta-ša-me-i* lo.e. ^{10}*úz-ni pí-tí-i* rev. ^{11}*a-ha-tí a-tí e-lá-nu-ú*-ki*$^{?}$ ^{12}*ma-nam i-šu* ^{13}igi *A-šur ú i-li-ki* ^{14}*ku-ur-bi-im* ^{15}*I-ku-pí-a ù Šál-ma-A-/šur* ^{16}kù-ki-*sú-nu* ^{17}*il*$_5$*-táq-qé-ú* ^{18}*ù I-dí-A-šur* u.e. ^{19}*lá-qá-a-am e-ta-wu*

$^{1-3}$Thus (says) Uṣur-ša-Ištar: say to Akatiya.

$^{3-5}$Why do you keep sending me bad letters? $^{6-10}$As to the house of Šu-Bēlum, inform me whether they have been quarreling, $^{8-10}$or whatever you hear they have said. $^{11-12}$You are my sister; without you, whom have I? $^{13-14}$Pray for me to Aššur and your god!

$^{15-17}$Ikuppiya and Šalim-Aššur have been collecting repeatedly their gold, and they have told Iddin-Aššur that (he should) collect (as well).

Bibliography: Text published by Bilgiç and Bayram as AKT 2, 40 (Kt n/k 571); collated May 2011.

Comments: This text could be a copy of a letter sent to Aššur. Uṣur-ša-Ištar relies on his sister for his business, and asks her to pray for him to the god Aššur and her own goddess, Tašmētum (**242**).

Line 7: the verb might be *garā'um*, "to attack, to exert pressure on," in the N-stem; see Veenhof 2015a, 247.

---

241. A Woman Prays to Ištar and Ištar-ZA-AT for Her Correspondent

Envelope

Obv. ^{1}(seal) ^{2}*a-na A-šùr*-dùl ^{3}*ù A-mur*-dingir ^{4}kišib *Ištar-ba-áš-tí* ^{5}(seal)

$^{2-4}$To Aššur-ṣululī and Amur-ilī. Seal of Ištar-baštī.

Tablet

Obv. ^{1}*a-na*$^{!}$ *A-šùr*-dùl *ù* ^{2}*A-mur*-dingir *qí*$^{!}$*-bi-ma* ^{3}*um-ma Ištar-ba-áš-tí-ma* ^{4}1 túg *kà-áb-tám* ^{5}*ša a-na ta-ad-mì-iq-/tim* ^{6}*a-dí-na-ku-ni šu-ma* ^{7}*be-lí a-ta* kù-babbar ^{8}*ší-im* 1 túg *kà-áb-tim* ^{9}*da-mì-iq-ma* ^{10}*a-na A-mur*-dingir ^{11}[*dí*]*-in-ma* lo.e. ^{12}[*A-m*]*ur*-dingir *lu-ub-/lam* rev. ^{13}[igi] *Ištar* ^{14}*ù Ištar*-ZA-AT ^{15}*lá-ak-ru-ba-/kum*

$^{1-3}$Say to Aššur-ṣululī: thus (says) Ištar-baštī.

$^{4-6}$Concerning the heavy textile that I gave you as a *tadmiqum*-trust, $^{6-7}$if you are my master, $^{7-11}$be so kind as to give the price of 1 heavy textile to Amur-ilī so that ^{12}Amur-ilī brings (it) to me. $^{13-15}$I will pray for you to Ištar and Ištar-ZA-AT.

Bibliography: Text published in copy by Hrozný as ICK 1, 28; translated by Michel (2001a, no. 349).

Comments: Ištar-baštī prays to two goddesses, Ištar and Ištar-ZA-AT.

The envelope of this letter bears the seal of Ištar-baštī; see chapter 4.

---

242. Letter Prayer by a Woman to the Goddess Tašmētum

Obv. ^{1}*a-na Taš-me-tim be-*[*el*]*-*[*tí-*(*a*)] ^{2}*qí-bi*$_{4}$*-ma um-ma A-kà-tí-a-*[*ma*] ^{3}gémé*-ki-ma a-wi-lu-tum* <*ša*> ^{4}*tù*$^{!}$*-da-ba-ba-ni-*[*ni*] ^{5}*li-ik-šu-*[*du-nim*] ^{6}*e-lá-nu-ki* [*ma-ma-an*] ^{7}*lá i-šu* [...] ^{8}*ù du-x-*[...]

$^{1-3}$Say to Tašmētum, [my] lady: thus (says) Akatiya, your servant.

$^{3-5}$Let the gentlemen you told me about com[e here]; $^{6-7}$I have [no one] but you! [...]

Bibliography: Text discovered in a large house at Aššur and published by Donbaz (1985, 15) as Ass 13058h; edited by Kryszat (2003).

Comments: Akatiya was the sister of Uṣur-ša-Ištar, son of Aššur-imittī, whose archives were excavated in 1962 at Kaneš. She may have been married to a member of the Assyrian royal family: letter-prayers to gods were often written by members of the elite.[43] In this very fragmentary letter,

43. We may note that, half a century later, one of the wives of the great king

Akatiya suggests that she had a message from the goddess announcing someone's arrival.

---

243. Men Take Oaths before Aššur, Women before Ištar

Obv. [1]*kà-ru-um* [2]*ṣa-he-er* gal igi gír [3]*ša A-šùr dí-nam* [4]*i-dí-in-ma* [5]*a-dí ša Ir-ma-A-/šùr* [6]*a-na hu-lu-qá-/e-šu* rev. [7]*i-pá-li-lu-ni* [8]*šu-ma za-kà-ar* [9]*i-na* gír *ša A-šur* [10]*sí-ni-iš-tum* [11]*i-na hu-pì-im* [12]*ša Ištar* u.e. [13]*ú-ta-ma* le.e. [14]*ù ší-be-šu ša* [15]*ṭup-pì ha-al-/qú-tim* [16]*i-šé-e*

[1–4]The *kārum*, (the whole assembly) small and big, gave the following verdict before the dagger of Aššur. [5–7]Concerning the affair of Ir'am-Aššur, as they proceeded to a formal trial on account of his losses, [8–13]if it is a man, he shall swear by Aššur's dagger, if it (is) a woman, (she shall swear) by the frame drum of Ištar; [14–16]then he shall seek out his witnesses who (know of) the lost tablets.

Bibliography: Text published by Michel (1997a, 112, photo 123) as Kt 94/k 131.

Comments: This verdict shows that both men and women could initiate a legal procedure and swear under oath. The only difference is that they did not swear by the same divinity: men by the god Aššur, through his symbol, the dagger, and women by the goddess Ištar, through her symbol, presumably a frame drum.

Line 7: the verb *palālum* used in juridical context is to be understand as "to interrogate someone under oath"; see Hertel 2013, 355, 465.

---

244. Men Take Oaths before Aššur, Women before Ištar

Envelope

Obv. [1](seal A) [2]kišib *kà-ri-im Kà-ni-iš* [3]*kà-ru-um dí-nam* [4]*i-dí-in-ma* [5]*i-t[a-m]a A-mur-Ištar* [6](seal B) [7]*i-n[a* gír] *ša A-šùr* lo.e. [8](seal C) [9]*b[é]-tù i-na* kù-babbar^{áp} rev. [10]*Ša-lim-ma lu ša-mu-ni* [11](seal D) [12]*li-bu-šu* la_1 *i-*de_8*-ú* [13]*ki-ma* kù-babbrar^{áp*} La_1*-ma-sí-tí-/ni* [14]*šu-ma A-mur-Ištar i-ta-ma*

Šamšī-Adad, perhaps the mother of Išme-Dagan, was also named Akad/tia (Ziegler 1999, 120).

[15]*bé-tù ša Ša-lim-ma* [16]*šu-ma la*$_1$ *i-ta-ma* [17]*ta-ta-ma La*$_1$*-ma-sú-tum* [18]*i-na hu-pí-im ša Ištar* [19]*bé-tù i-na* kù-babbar^{áp} [20]*I-dí-Sú-en*$_6$ *la*$_1$ *ša-mu-ni* [21]*i-na* kù-babbar^{pì}*-ša lu ša-mu-ni* [22]*šu-ma ta-ta-ma bé-tum* u.e. [23]*bé-sà* [24](seal E, upside down) [25]*šu-ma A-mur-Ištar ù La*$_1$*-ma-sú-tum* [26]*la*$_1$ *i-ta-am-ú-ma* le.e. [27]*i-ta-am-gu*$_5$*-ru* 4 *ma-na* k[ù-babbar] [28](seal F) [29]*i-ší-im bé-tí kà-ru-um* [30]*i-la-qé* r.e. [31](seal G)

[1-2]Seal of the *kārum* of Kaneš. [3-4]The *kārum* (authorities) gave the following verdict: [5-8]Amur-Ištar will swear by Aššur's dagger (that) [9-11]the houses have been bought with Šalimma's silver, [12-13](that) he honestly did not know that the silver belonged to Lamassatum. [14]If Amur-Ištar swears, [15]the houses belong to Šalimma; [16]if he does not swear, [17-18]Lamassatum will swear by the frame drum of Ištar [19-20]that the houses were not bought with Iddin-Suen's silver [21](but) were bought with her own silver. [22-24]If she swears, the house is her house. [25-26]If Amur-Ištar and Lamassatum do not swear but [27-30]reach a compromise, the *kārum* will take four minas of silver from the price of the houses.

Tablet

Obv. [1]*kà-ru-um dí-nam* [2]*i-dí-in-ma* [3]*i-ta-ma A-mur-Ištar* [4]*i-na* gír *ša A-šùr* [5]*bé-tù* :* *i-na* kù-babbar^{áp} [6]*Ša-lim-ma lu* * *ša-mu-ni* [7]*li-bu-šu la*$_1$ *i-de*$_8$*-ú* [8]*ki-ma* kù-babbrar^{áp} [9]*Lá-ma-sí-tí-ni* [10]*šu-ma A-mur-Ištar i-ta-ma* [11]*bé-tù ša Ša-lim-ma* [12]*šu-ma la*$_1$ *i-ta-ma* [13]*ta-ta-ma La*$_1$*-ma-sú-tum* lo.e. [14]*i-na hu-pì-im ša Ištar* rev. [15]*bé-tù i-na* kù-babbar^{áp} [16]*I-dí-Sú-en*$_6$ [17]*la*$_1$ *ša-mu-ni* [18]*i-na* kù-babbar^{pì}*-ša* [19]*lu ša-mu-ni* [20]*šu-ma ta-ta-ma* [19]*bé-tum : bé-sà* [20][*šu*]*-ma A-mur-Ištar* [21]*ù La*$_1$*-ma-sú-tum* [22]*la*$_1$ *i-ta-am-ú-ma* [23]*i-ta-am-gu*$_5$*-ru* [24]4 *ma-na* kù-babbar *i-ší-im* u.e. [25]*bé-tí kà-ru-um* [26]*i-lá-qé*

[1-2]The *kārum* (authorities) gave the following verdict: [3-4]Amur-Ištar will swear by Aššur's dagger (that) [5-6]the houses have been bought with Šalimma's silver, [7-9](that) he did not know that the silver belonged to Lamassatum. [10-11]If Amur-Ištar swears, the house belongs to Šalimma; [12]if he does not swear, [13-14]Lamassatum will swear by the frame drum of Ištar [15-17]that the house (was not bought) with Iddin-Suen's silver [17](but) was bought (with her own silver). [18-19]If she swears, the house is her house. [20-22]If Amur-Ištar and Lamassatum do not swear but [23]reach a compromise, [24-26]the *kārum* will take 4 minas of silver from the price of the houses.

Bibliography: Text published by Veenhof as AKT 8, 210 bis (Kt 86/k 155a–b). Collated October 2017.

Comments: This verdict concerns the dispute between two women of the same family, Lamassatum, wife of the deceased Elamma, son of Iddin-Suen; and Šalimma, her daughter and niece of Amur-Ištar, brother of Elamma, over ownership of a house. It is not impossible that the house in question had been bought by Šalimma, as stated in the contract **148**. This shows, once more, that men swore by the dagger of Aššur, while women had to swear by the symbol of the goddess Ištar: the frame drum.

The envelope bears seven sealings of men representing the *kārum* of Kaneš.

Lines 11 and 15: the word *bētum* is most of the time used as a plural, referring, presumably, to the rooms of the house; but it also appears in the singular, confirming that the dispute concerns one entire house.

---

245. Gifts for Ištar and Išhara

Obv. ^{1}*a-na A-du-e qí-bi*$_4$*-ma* ^{2}*um-ma Wa-lá-wa-lá-ma* ^{3}2 gín kù-babbar *ku-nu-ki-a* ^{4}*Pu-šu-ke-en*$_6$: *ub-lá-ki-im* ^{5}*a-na Iš-ta-ar* ^{6}*ú Iš-ha-ra* : 2 *ri-mu* ^{7}1 *kà-sú-um a-na Iš-ha-ra* ^{8}*ku-nu-ki-a* : *Pu-šu-*<*ke*>*-en*$_6$ lo.e. ^{9}*ub-lá-ki-im* rev. ^{10}*lá ub-lá-ki-im* ^{11}*té-er-tí-*[*ki*] *li-li-kam* ^{12}2 gín kù-babbar *i*-šà-ba ^{13}[k]ù-babbar *ša* : *Zu*$^{!}$*-pá* ^{14}*i-dí-na-ki-im* ^{15}*lá i-dí-na-ki-im* ^{16}*té-er-tí-ki ar-hi-iš* ^{17}*li-li-kam* u.e. ^{18}*Pu-šu-ke-en*$_6$ le.e. (upside down)^{19}*mì-ma ṭup-pá-am* ^{20}*lá ub-lam*

$^{1-2}$Say to Adue: thus (says) Walawala.

$^{3-4}$Pūšu-kēn brought you 2 shekels of silver under my seal. $^{5-11}$Let your report come here whether Pūšu-kēn brought you or not 2 bull (figurines) for Ištar and Išhara (and) 1 cup for Išhara under my seal. $^{12-17}$Let your report come quickly here whether or not he gave you 2 shekels of silver from the silver of Zupa. $^{18-20}$Pūšu-kēn did not bring me any tablet.

Bibliography: Text published in copy by Lewy as TC 3, 106; translated by Michel (2001a, no. 386).

Comments: Walawala has sent to Adue, perhaps her sister-in-law, some bull figurines and a cup for the goddesses Ištar and Išhara; we do not know the status of these objects. But it is interesting to note that it was women who made such gifts to female deities.

Line 5: the writing *Iš-ta-ar* for the goddess Ištar is unusual.

---

246. Votive Offerings for Tašmētum

Obv. [1]*a-na Pu-šu-ke-en*$_6$ [2]*qí-bi-ma um-ma Lá-ma-sí* [3]*ù A-ha-ha-ma* 10 gín [4]kù-gi : *ša a-na ú-ṭá-tim* [5]*ša-pá-ki-im tù-še-bi-lá-ni* [6]*ki-ma ša-tum a-na* [7]*pá-ni-ša i-lu-ku-ni* [8]*a-dí-ni : ša ki*$^{!}$*-ma ku-a-tí* [9]*ú-ṭá-tám : ú-lá iš-pu-ku-/ma* [10]*ù té-er-tí-ni ú-lá* [11]*i-li-kà-kum* lo.e. [12]*u*$_4$*-ma-am : ú-ṭa-tám* [13]*ma-lá i-ša-pu-ku-ni* rev. [14]*ù za-ku-sà ni-ša-pá-ra-kum* [15]*ù ik-ri-ba-am* [16]*ša a-na Ta-áš-me-tim* [17]*ta-ak-ru-bu-ni* [18]*a-pu-tum lá ta-ma-ší* [19]*i-il*$_5$*-tum : i-ir-tí-bi* [20]*i-pá-ni-kà bi-lam* [21]*ú-ul i-pá-nim-ma* [22]*a-li-ki-im šé-bi-lam*

[1–3]Say to Pūšu-kēn: thus (say) Lamassī and Ahaha.

[3–5]As for the 10 shekels of gold that you sent us in order to store up grain, [6–7]since the season is still running, [8–9]so far your representatives have not stored up any grain; [10–11]this is why our report did not reach you. [12–14]Today, we will send you precise information about the quantity of grain that they will be storing.

[15–17]As to the offering that you have vowed to (the goddess) Tašmētum—[18]urgent!—do not forget (it)! [19]The obligation (to fulfill the vow offering) has become pressing! [20]Bring it here personally, [21–22]or send it with the first traveler.

Bibliography: Text published in copy by Lewy as TC 3, 35; translated by Michel (2001a, no. 311).

Comments: Lamassī and her daughter Ahaha are concerned about the votive offerings that Pūšu-kēn promised to the goddess Tašmētum; the temple may have asked for them.

---

247. Votive Offerings and Gifts for the Gods Bēlum and Anna

Obv. [1]*um-ma Pu-šu-ke-en*$_6$*-ma* [2]*a-na La-ma-sí qí-bi-m*[*a*] [3]1 *ma-na* 15 gín kù-babbar *ni-<is-ha-sú>* [4]diri *ša-du-a-sú ša-bu* [5]*ku-nu-ki-a Dan-A-šùr na-áš-a-ki-im* [6]*lu ší-im* 1 túg *ù* 2 túg *ša Šu-bu-ul-/tim* [7]*ša a-na ṣé-ri-a tù-šé-bi*$_4$*-/li-/ni* [8]kù-babbar ^{áp}*-ki : gám-ra-ki-im* [9]30* *ma-na* urudu sig$_5$: *ik-*

ri-bu [10]*ša Bé-lim* 2 *sú-p*[*á*]*-na-an ša* zabar [11]14-*e-šu* : *i-na maš-qal-tim* [12]*a-la-n*[*u*] : *mì-iš-lúm* : *kà-bu-tù-/tum* [13]*mì-iš-lúm* : *ta-sí-ki* [14]*pá-šu-ru-um ša A-na* [15]*ki-ta-um* 5 *e-pá-da-tum* [16]*tal-ha-dí-a-tum* ⅓ *ma-na* kù-babbar [17]*lu ša-wi-ru* : *lu mu-sà-/ru-um* rev. [18]*ša ṣú-ha-ri-im* [19]ki-lá-bi ⅔ *ma-na* 2½ gín [20]*a-ha-ma* : *a-nu-qú*[!]*-šu* : *ṣú-ha-*<*ra*>*-am* [21]*ú am-tám* [*mì*]*-ma a-nim* [22]*Dan-A-šùr i-ra-de*$_8$*-a-ki-im* [23]*a-pu-tum ṣú-ha-ra-am* [24]*a-na ma-ma-an* : *lá tù-šé-ri-/ma* [25]*i-na qé-ra-be-tim* [26]*li-ir-bi* : *i-nu-mì Dan-A-šùr* [27]*a-ni-ša-am* : *ú-ṣí-a-ni* [28]*ša-wi-ri-šu* : *ù mu-sà-ra-am* [29]*a-ṣé-er* ⅓ *ma-na* kù-babbar [30]*ša a-dí-nu-šu-ni a-na Dan-A-/*[*šur*] [31]*dí-ni-ma* : šunigin *ša* 1 *ma-*[*na*] [32]*ší-ma-am* : *li-iš-am* [33]*lu-šé-ṣí-am*

[1-2]Thus (says) Pūšu-kēn: say to Lamassī.

[3-5]Dān-Aššur is bringing you 1 mina, 15 shekels of silver—its import tax added, its transport fee paid—under my seal. [6-7](It comprises also) the price of the few textiles of Šūbultum that you sent to me. [8]All your silver has herewith been paid out to you.

[9-10]30 minas of copper of good quality for the votive offering to Bēlum, 2 bronze *supānum*-bowls, [11-13]14 measuring cups with hazelnuts, half of them complete/heavy ones, half of them *crushed* (?), [14]an altar for (the goddess) Anna, [15-16]linen, 5 *epattum*-cloaks from Talhad, [16-18]⅓ mina of silver, bracelets or a belt for the child, [19]their weight: ⅔ minas, 2½ shekels; [20-21]moreover, rings for him, a young slave and a female slave; [21-22]all this Dān-Aššur is bringing along to you. [23-24]Urgent! You should not give up the child to anyone else; [25-26]he should grow up in the house. [26-27]When Dān-Aššur leaves for here, [28-31]give Dān-Aššur his bracelets and the belt in addition to the ⅓ mina of silver that I gave him, [31-33]so that he makes purchases for an amount totaling 1 mina, (and) export (them) out (of the city).

Bibliography: Text published in copy by Smith as CCT 2, 36a; translated by Michel (2001a, no. 301).

Comments: Besides silver as payment for textiles, Pūšu-kēn informs his wife of the shipment of various goods, including copper for votive offerings to the god Bēlum and an altar for the goddess Anna. Lamassī was living in Aššur, so this letter should be a copy of a letter sent there. The shipment of hazelnuts and of silver as the price for textiles would confirm this hypothesis. But the shipment of copper from Anatolia to Aššur is exceptional, and the mention of an altar for the Anatolian goddess Anna to Aššur is also very unsual.

248. Ritual for a Woman's Funeral

Obv. [1]*a-na A-šur-e*$^{?}$-[x-x] [2]*qí-bi-ma um-m*[*a*] [3]*I-lá-áb-ra-*<*at*>*-ba-n*[*i-ma*] [4]*lá i-li-bi*$_4$ dingir-[*ma*] [5]*um-ma-ša ša am-*[*tí-a*$^{?}$] [6]*me-ta-at e-za-dam* (line erased) [7]*le-qé-ší-ma* lo.e. [8]*ma-e-e i-na* rev. [9]*kà-nu-nim lu ta-at-/bu-uk* [10]*ú ki-ra-am* [11]1 *ú ší-ta dí-in-ší* [12]*a-wi*^{o}*-lá-tí dan-na* [14]*ṭup-pí-im lá tù-ša-*[(x)] [15]*a-dí Šu-Sú-en*$_6$ 6[(+ x) gín] [16]kù-ki *ša ú-šé*$^{!}$*-bi-lu-k*[*u*$^{?}$*ni*] [17]*i-hi-id-ma š*[*a*/ *u*$^{?}$-(x)] u.e. [18]*a-dí E-lá-lí ú* [x x /*a-ma-lá*$^{?}$] [19]*na-áš-pè-ra-tí-*[*a*] [20]*ša A-šur-ṣú-*[*lu-li*] le.e. [21]*ni-iš-a-ku-nu-tí-ni* [22]*A-šur-mu-ta-pì-il*$_5$ [23]*i-na ša-ha-tí-kà* /«kù-babbar$^{?}$» [24]*li-zi-iz-ma*

[1-3]Say to Aššur-e[x-x]: thus (say) Ilabrat-bāni.

[4-6]Unfortunately, the mother of [my$^{?}$] *amtum*-wife has died! [7-9]Take the *ezadum* for her, and let her pour water on the brazier. [10-11]Then, give her one or 2 pitchers of beer. [12]My ladies should be strong!

[14]You should not [...] a tablet. [15-17]Until Šu-Suen sends to you the 6[+ x shekels] of gold, be sure to [...]. [18]As to Elālī and [PN, according to] [19-21]my message that Aššur-ṣululī brought to you, [22-24]assist Aššur-mūtappil.

Bibliography: Unpublished letter excavated in 1993 in square LVIII/128 of Kültepe's lower town (Kt 93/k 916). Lines 1–14 cited by Michel (2008f, 186, n. 26).

Comments: Ilabrat-bāni announces to his correspondent the death of his mother-in-law. He should help his wife with the funeral. Among the gestures to perform, there is a libation with water on the brazier, and an offering of beer. The translation of the reverse is tentative.

Line 6: the word *e-ZA-DAM* could be an offering or a cultic vase. It is also attested in TuM 1, 7c; Kt 94/k 432 and 462 (courtesy Barjamovic), where it is linked to the goddess Ištar.

Line 9: the word *kanūnum*, "brazier," is attested in the incantation Kt 94/k 520:5–6, published by Barjamovic and Larsen (2008, 148). Note that Charpin (2009, 133, n. 12) suggested that the Sumerian word gá-nun, corresponding to *ganūnum* in Akkadian, could refer to the main room of a house under which the tomb was situated.

249. Death of a Female Servant

Obv. [1]*um-ma Ištar-lá-ma-sí-/ma* [2]*ù Ra-bi-tum* [3]*a-na I-ku-pì-a qí-bi$_4$-ma* [4]*ša-ta-am : lá ta-me-a* [5]*ku-a-am : lá e-ri-iš-/kà* [6]*ta-ad-mì-iq-tí-ma* [7]*šé-bi$_4$-lam a-ta* lo.e. [8]*ú a-hu-kà : am-tám* rev. [9]*šé-ri-a-nim : am-tám* [10]*me-ta-at : i-na wa-ar-/ki-«wa-ki»-a-/tim* [11]*Ha-za-ba a-lá-qé* [12]*be-ta-at* diri^{tim} [13]*a-ma-e a-sà-hu-ur* [14]*me-er-at-kà* [15]*a-ni šé-ri-am* lo.e. [16]*ki-a-me /mì\-ma lu-šé-bi$_4$-/lam* le.e. [17]*ṣú-ùh-ru-um* [18]*ma-ad li-bu-um*

[1-3]Thus (says) Ištar-Lamassī and Rabītum: say to Ikuppiya.

[4]You refuse *that*! [5]I did not ask you for what is yours! [6-7]Send me only (the amount of) my *tadmiqum*-trust.

[7-9]You and your brother (said$^?$): "You must bring the female slave here," [9-10]but the female slave died. Later on, [11]I will take Hazaba, [12](since) there are extra rooms. [13]I will go around for water. [14-15]Have your daughter brought here instantly. [16]Likewise, send everything (I have asked for)! [17-18]The little boy is depressed.

Bibliography: Text published in copy by Lewy as TC 3, 103.

Comments: This letter, sent by two women, has numerous mistakes, and several sentences are difficult to understand; this could suggest that Ištar-Lamassī wrote it herself. The text mentions the death of a female slave, who presumably had a little boy. There is something to do with water, which could be part of a funerary ritual, but the sentence is unclear.

Line 12: the word *be-ta-at* could be the plural of *bētum*, "house, room," but it is also possible to read *pè-ta-at* (*pêtum*, "to open").

Line 4: the writing *ta-me-a* must be understood as *tamu'ā*. *Ša-ta-am* is a mistake for *šu-a-tám*, which does not contract in Old Assyrian.

Line 16: the word *ki-a-me* would be an error for *kīamma*.

250. Death of a Female Servant

Obv. [1]*Puzur$_4$-A-šur* dumu *I-ku-/pì*-a* [2]*En-um-A-šur* dumu *I-dí-/Sú-/in* [3]*ù a-hu-šu* [4]*I-dí-Ištar* dumu *Ah-ša-lim* [5]*Ištar-ba-ni* [6]*Ma-ṣí-ì-lí* [7]*En-nam-A-šur* [8]dumu *A-šur-dan* lo.e. [9]*Šu-ma-a-bi$_4$-a* [10]*ša ki-ma* [11]dumu-e *Ku-ni-lim* [12]*i-pu-ùh-ri-šu-nu* [13*]*gam-ra-am a-na* [14]*bi$_4$-ki-tí-šu-nu* [15]*ù ku-sí-im ša*

Ištar/-lá-ma-/sí [16]*i*-kù-babbar *ša i-é* u.e. [17]dam *E-lá-ma ib-ší-/ú* [18]*ig-mu-ru* le.e. [19]*hu-ša-li* dumu *A-šur-/dan* [20]*ù Šu-ma-a-bi*$_4$*-a* [21]*ik-nu-ku*

[1–3]Puzur-Aššur, son of Ikuppiya; Ennum-Aššur, son of Iddin-Suen; and his brother, [4–8]Iddin-Ištar, son of Ah-šalim; Ištar-bāni; Maṣi-ilī; Ennum-Aššur, son of Aššur-dān; [9–11]Šumi-abiya—representing the sons of Kūn-ilum—[12–18]collectively paid the expenses for bewailing them and of Ištar-lamassī's chair, from the silver that was in the house of Elamma's wife. [19–21]The son of Aššur-dān and Šumi-abiya sealed the pouches.

Bibliography: Text edited by Veenhof as AKT 8, 185 (Kt 91/k 446). Collated October 2017. Line 13 omitted by the editor.

Comments: In this memorandum found in Elamma's archive, eight people paid for the bewailing of Ištar-lamassī and her two sons and for the chair of the mother; there is no mention of chairs for the sons. For this dossier, see also texts **59** and **60**.

---

251. Textile Gift for the Funerals of a Woman

Obv. [1]½ túg *i-nu-mì* [2]dumu-munus-*sú* [3]*me-ta-at-/ni* [4]*a-na Um-/ma-na* rev. [5]*ú-šé-bi*$_4$*-/il*$_5$

[1–5]I sent ½ of a textile to Ummana when his daughter died.

Bibliography: Text published in copy by Clay as BIN 4, 141; edited by Ulshöfer (1995, no. 397).

Comments: The text is very brief. The piece of textile was presumably used for the burial of the girl; she might have been young and a half-size textile enough for her shroud.

---

252. Consulting Female Diviners about a Brother's Conduct

Obv. [1]*a-na Im-dí*-dingir *qí-bi-ma* [2]*um-ma Ta-ra-am-Ku-bi*$_4$*-ma* [3]*ú Ší-ma-at-A-šùr-ma* [4]*a-na-kam ša-i-lá-tim* [5]*ba-ri-a-tim ù e-ṭé-me* [6]*nu-ša-al-ma* [7]*A-šùr uš-ta-na-ad-/kà* lo.e. [8]kù-babbar *ta-ra-am* [9]*na-pá-áš-ta-kà* rev.

[10]*ta*[!](ZA)*-ze-ar i-na* [11]*a-lim*[ki] *A-šùr ma-ga-ra-/am* [12]*ú-lá ta-le-e* [13]*a-pu-tum ki-ma ṭup-pá-am* [14]*ta-áš-me-ú al-kam-ma* [15]*e-en A-šùr : a-mu-ur-ma* [16]*na-pá-áš-ta-kà* u.e. [17]*e-ṭé-er ší-im* túg[ti]*-a* le.e. [18]*mì-šu-um* [19]*lá tù-šé-ba-lam*

[1-3]Say to Imdī-ilum: thus (speak) Tarām-Kūbi and Šīmat-Aššur.

[4-6]Here (in Aššur) we consulted the women dream interpreters, the women diviners, and the spirits of the dead, and (their answer was: [7]the god) Aššur keeps on warning you; [8-10]you love money (so much that) you despise your own life! [10-12]Can't you comply with (the god) Aššur's (wishes here) in the city (of Aššur)? [13-14]Urgent! When you have heard the letter, (then) come here, [15]meet (the god) Aššur face to face, and [16-17]save your life!

[17-19]Why don't you send to me the proceeds from my textiles?

Bibliography: Text published in copy by Contenau as TC 1, 5; translated by Larsen (1982, 214) and by Michel (2001a, no. 348; 2014b, 208). Collated March 2018.

Comments: Tarām-Kūbi and Šīmat-Aššur, presumably two sisters of Imdī-ilum, rebuke him for his conduct: spending all his time to make profits, he forgets his religious obligations.

---

253. Female Diviners and Demons in Aššur

Obv. [1]*a-na Ša-lim-m*[*a*] *a* [(x x)] [2]*qí-bi-ma um-ma* [3]*Be-lá-tum-ma mì-š*[*u ša*] [4]*ta-ta-na-ri-*[*ší-im i-na A-lim*[ki]] [5]*A-šur : ba-ri-a-ti*[*m*] [6]*ù ú-tù-ki* : [x x x igi] [7]dingir *ša ak-ta-*[*na-ru-bu*] [8]*a-na A-lim*[ki] [*A-šur*] [9]*e-lá : a-bi-kà* [x x] [10]*a-bu-ni i-*[x x (x)]

[1-3]Say to Šalimm[a …]: thus (says) Bēlātum.

[3-6]Wh[y do] you keep reques[ting from me that *I consult* in the city of] Aššur the female diviners [6]and the demons? [6-7]The god to whom I keep [praying], [8]for the city of [Aššur], [9]apart from your father […] [10]our father […].

Bibliography: Text published by Larsen as AKT 6d, 786 (Kt 94/k 1759).

Comments: This very broken letter was sent by Bēlātum, who could be the daughter of Tāriš-mātum, and thus the niece of Pūšu-kēn (**256**). In texts **254–255**, her illness is connected to the visits of demons and spirits of the dead. Šalimma is the daughter of Elamma; she went to visit her mother in Kaneš, leaving her husband and child in Aššur (**264**).

---

254. Demons and Spirits of the Dead Plague the Family

Obv. [1]*a-na Pu-šu-ke-en*$_6$ [2]*qí-bi-ma um-ma Ta-ri-iš-/ma-tum* [3]*ù Bé-lá-tum-ma* [4]*a-šu-mì* kù-babbar *ša ik-ri-be* [5]*a-na-kam Bé-la-tum* [6]*ta-am-ra-aṣ i-na ú-tù-/ke* [7]*ù i-na e-ṭá-me* [8]*ša-am-ṭù-a*$^{!}$(ZA)*-ni* : *a-bu-ni* [9]*a-ta be-el***-ni a-ta* kù-babbar [10]*a-na ṣú-ha-re lá tù-wa-ša-/ar* [11]*a-šu-mì ma-za-zi-im* [12]dingir *lam-ni-iš* é *a-bi*$_4$*-ni* [13]*e-pá-áš a-pu-tum* [14]*šu-ma a-bu-ni a-ta* lo.e. [15]*ki-ma ta-le-e-ú* rev. [16]*mì-it*$^{!}$(DA)*-ha-aṣ-ma* [17]*šu-um-kà šu-ku-un-ma* [18]*ṣú-ha-ru a-šu-mì ik-ri-be* [19]*ki-a-am i-né-pì-šu* [20]*a-pu-tum ma-ma-an* [21]*i-na ṣú-ha-re-e*$^{?}$ [22]*lá um-ta-ṣa-ma* kù-babbar [23]1 gín *lá i-lá-qé* [24]«1» anše-hi-a *ša I-šar-be-lí* [25]*i-ra-de*$_8$*-a-ku-ni* : *ni-iš-me-ma* [26]*Ú-ṣur-ša-A-šùr* [27]*i-ṭá-ar-dam e um-ta-ṣí-ma* [28]kù-babbar 1 gín *e il*$_5$*-qé šu-ma* [29]*I-šar-be-lí* : *a-dí-ni* [30]*lá e-ru-ba-am šu-pur-ma* [31]*a-na pá-ni-šu* 1 anše-hi-a u.e. [32]*a-šar ku-a-tí le-ru-bu* [33]*ki-ma* túg-hi-a le.e. [34]*ta-dí-nu* kù-babbar *ku-nu-uk-ma šé-bi*$_4$*-lá-ma* [35]*na-pá-áš-tí-ni iš-té-ni-iš e-ṭé-er a-bu-ni* [36]*a-ta a-lá-nu-kà ma-nam ni-šu*

[1–3]Say to Pūšu-kēn: thus (say) Tarīš-mātum and Bēlātum.

[4–6]Here, Bēlātum fell ill because of the silver of the votive offerings! [6–8]We are plagued by the demons and spirits of the dead! [8–10]You are our father, you are our master; you must not deliver the silver to the boys! [11–13]Because of the divine statuette, the god plagues our father's house! [13–14]Urgent! If you are (truly) are our father, [15–17]do what you can to repair your reputation [18–19](by seeing to it) that the boys are treated in this way because of the votive offerings. [20–23]Urgent! None of the boys should take on his own accord any silver, even 1 shekel!

[24–25]We heard that Išar-bēlī is driving the donkeys to you, but [26–28]Uṣur-ša-Aššur has just been sent down here, let him not *dare to take* even 1 shekel of silver! [28–30]Write me if Išar-bēlī has not yet arrived; [31–32]I hope the donkeys reach you before he arrives. [33–34]When you have sold the textiles, seal the silver, send (it) to me, and [35–36]save our lives at the same time! You are our father; we have no one except you!

Bibliography: Text published in copy by Lewy as KTS 1, 24; translated by Michel (2001a, no. 323). Lines 4–36 cited by Hirsch (1961, 385).

Comments: Tarīš-mātum, the sister of Pūšu-kēn, and her presumed daughter, Bēlātum, claim they are being persecuted by demons, spirits of the dead, and the god because Pūšu-kēn has not provided the silver for the votive offerings to the temple. The divine statuette might have been a promise made by Pūšu-kēn to the temple.

Line 8: the reading of the verb form needs correction. Here, the reading *ša-am-ṭù-a*$^{!}$(ZA)*-ni* proposes an Š-stem form of *maṭûm*. Another possible reading is *ša-am-ru*$^{!}$(DU)*-ṣa-ni* for an Š-stem form of *marāṣum*.

---

255. Illness as a Punition Sent by the God

Obv. ^{1}*a-na Pu-šu-ke-en*$_6$ ^{2}*Puzur*$_4$*-Ištar Ú-ṣur*$^{!}$(ELLAT)*-ša-A-šur* ^{3d}Nin-šubur*-ba-ni ù I-dí-Ištar* ^{4}*qí*$^{!}$*-bi-ma a-na Puzur*$_4$*-Ištar* ^{5}*Ú-ṣur-š*[*a-A*]*-šur* ^{d}Nin-šubur-/*ba-ni* ^{6}*ù I-dí-Ištar qí-bi-ma* ^{7}*um-ma Ta-ri-iš-ma-tum* ^{8}*ù Be-lá-tum-ma* [*a-h*]*u-ni* ^{9}*a-tù-nu a-šu-mì* k[ù]-babbar ^{10}*ik-ri-bi*$_4$ *ša a-bi*$_4$*-ni* ^{11}*Be-lá-tum a-na-kam* lo.e. ^{12}*ta-am-ra-aṣ* ^{13}*ù i-na ú-tù-ki* rev. ^{14}*ù i-na e-ṭá-me* ^{15}*ša-am-ṭù-a-ni a-ma-kam* ^{16}*a-na Pu-šu-ke-en*$_6$ *pu-nu-a-ma* ^{17}an-na *ù* túg$^{ba\text{-}tí}$: *a-ma-lá* ^{18}*i-le-e-ú* : *li-dí-ma* ^{19}kù-babbar *li-ik-nu-uk-ma* ^{20}*lu-šé-bi*$_4$*-lá-ma na-pá-áš-ta-ak-nu* ^{21}*ù na-pá-áš-tí-ni* ^{22}*li-ṭé-er a-na-kam* ^{23}*lam-ni-iš* : *i-lu-um* ^{24}é *a-bi*$_4$*-ku-nu* : *e-pá-áš* ^{25}*ma-ma-an a-ma-kam a-na* ^{26}kù-babbar 1 gín *i-na ba-ri-ku-*/*nu* u.e. ^{27}*lá i-ṭá-hi* lo.e. ^{28}an-na *ù* túg$^{ba\text{-}tù}$ ^{29}*ša nu-šé-bi*$_4$*-lá-ni a-dí a-na* kù-/babbar ^{30}*i-tù-ru* é *Pu-šu-ke-en*$_6$ ^{31}*li-ib-ší*

$^{1-8}$Say to Pūšu-kēn, Puzur-Ištar, Uṣur-ša-Aššur, Ilabrat-bāni, and Iddin-Ištar; say to Puzur-Ištar, Uṣur-ša-Aššur, Ilabrat-bāni, and Iddin-Ištar: thus (say) Tarīš-mātum and Bēlātum.

$^{8-9}$You are our brothers. $^{9-12}$Because of the silver for the votive offerings of our father, here, Bēlātum fell ill, $^{13-15}$and we are plagued by the demons and spirits of the dead! $^{15-18}$Turn there to Pūšu-kēn so that he sells as much tin and textiles as he can, $^{19-22}$and seals the silver and sends it here, thereby saving your lives and ours! $^{22-24}$Here, the god plagues your father's house! $^{25-27}$Over there, nobody should touch a single shekel of silver of your common fund, not even one shekel! $^{28-31}$As for the tin and textiles that we sent, until they can be converted into silver, they should remain in the house of Pūšu-kēn!

Bibliography: Text published in copy and edited by Garelli as *RA* 59, 165 (MAH 19612); translated by Michel (2001a, no. 324).

Comments: Uṣur-ša-Aššur, Ilabrat-bāni, and Iddin-Ištar may be the sons of Aššur-malik, husband of Tarīš-mātum, and thus nephews of Pūšu-kēn (KTH 19); Puzur-Ištar would be an employee of Pūšu-kēn. Puzur-Ištar and Uṣur-ša-Aššur are called "boys" in **254** and **256**. Thus, in these three texts, Pūšu-kēn is concerned that his household, in the broadest sense, is affected: the girls are ill because of his negligence toward the gods (**256**).

---

256. Consulting Female Dream Interpreters

Obv. ^{1}*a-na Pu-šu-ke-en*$_6$ ^{2}*qí-bi-ma um-ma Ta-ri-iš-ma-/tum* ^{3}*ù Bé-lá-tum-ma* ^{4}*ṣú-ha-ra-tum ša Puzur*$_4$*-Ištar* ^{5}*ú Ú-ṣur-ša-A-šur* ^{6}*im-ra-ṣa-ma mu-a-tí-iš* ^{7}*i-li-kà a-na ša-i-lá-tim* ^{8}*ni-li-ik-ma um-ma* ^{9}*i-lu*$^{!}$*-um-ma ik-ri-bé* ^{10}*lá tù-qá-i-a* lo.e. ^{11}(erasure) *ek-ma-ší-na* rev. ^{12}*a-na ha-ar-pé* ^{13}*nu-uš-té-re-sà* ^{14}*e-kà-ma-am* ^{15}*lá e-kà-ma-am ṣú-ha-ri* ^{16}*ša-al-ma té-er-ta-kà* ^{17}*li-li-kam-ma* ^{18}*lu né-ki-im-ší-na lu ší-im* ^{19}an-na *lu ša* túg-hi-a kù-babbar ^{20}*ku-nu-uk-ma šé-bi-lam* ^{21}10 *ku-ta-ni ša a-na* maškim ^{22}*ni-dí-nu* kù-babbar *ša-áš-qí-il*$_5$*-ma* ^{23}*šé-bi-lam* 1 túg *ku-ta-nam* ^{24}*a-na A-šur-i-mì-tí ù Šu-Ištar* ^{25}*ni-dí-in-ma i-na* ellat ^{26}*I-na-a I-dí-Sú-en*$_6$ le.e. ^{27}*ú-šé-bi*$_4$*-lu-ni-kum Šu-Ištar* kù-babbar ^{28}*né-ri-iš-ma um-ma šu-ut-ma* 1 túg ^{29}*šu-a-tí I-dí-Sú-en*$_6$ *a-Pu-šu-ke-en*$_6$ ^{30}*i-dí-in* kù-babbar *ší-im* 1 túg *šé-bi*$_4$*-lam*

$^{1-3}$Say to Pūšu-kēn: thus (say) Tarīš-mātum and Bēlātum.

$^{4-7}$The girls of Puzur-Ištar and Uṣur-ša-Aššur have fallen ill and are dying. $^{7-8}$We went to the women dream interpreters, $^{8-9}$and the god (said) as follows: $^{9-11}$"Take the votive offerings away from them without delay!" $^{12-13}$We will be ready not later than the summer; $^{14-17}$ask the boys whether or not (we should) take (them) away, and let your instructions come here if ^{18}we are to take (them) away from them.

$^{18-20}$Seal the silver, price of the tin or the textiles, and send (it) here. $^{21-23}$Get paid for the 10 *kutānum*-textiles that we sold to the attorney, and send (it) here. $^{23-25}$We gave 1 *kutānum*-textile to Aššur-imittī and Šu-Ištar, $^{25-27}$and they sent (it) to you via the caravan of Innaya and Iddin-Suen. $^{27-28}$We asked Šu-Ištar for silver, but he (said) as follows: $^{28-30}$"Iddin-Suen has actually given this textile to Pūšu-kēn." (So) send me the silver, price of the textile.

Bibliography: Text published in copy by Lewy as KTS 1, 25a; edited by Michel (1991, no. 253); translated by Michel (2001a, no. 325).

Comments: The disease from which the young women suffer has a divine origin, as can be seen from the questioning of the god by the dream interpreters. The votive offerings must be taken away from them, perhaps because they cannot fulfill the obligations they entail. The offense is not theirs but the one of their relatives.

Women Consecrated to Gods

The best-attested women with religious titles in the Kaneš archives are merchants' daughters consecrated to a deity (*gubabtum* or nin-dingir, which corresponds to the Akkadian *ugbabtum*, and *qadištum*).[44] These are often considered to be "priestesses," but that implies specific religious functions not yet documented in the texts. The translation "consecrated women" preferred here is inspired by the Assyrian expression "put a girl under the protection of a god."[45]

The existence of consecrated women (*gubabtum*) at Aššur is indirectly documented by brief and mostly uninformative references to them in the Kaneš archives. More often than not, we do not know who they were, and the few references to them are mostly restricted to business matters. Among the few *gubabtum* known by name, some are quite prominent in the archives: Ahaha, daughter of Pūšu-kēn and Lamassī; Ahattum, daughter of Ilī-bāni; Ummī-Išhara, daughter of Elamma and Lamassatum; and Šīmat-Ištar, daughter of Kūn-ilum and Ištar-Lamassī, and granddaughter of Elamma.[46] Some fifteen consecrated women are known by name; their status as *gubabtum* being noted for some special reason, such as the death of their parents. Another fifteen are known through the names of relatives.

44. For studies of consecrated women in Old Babylonian sources, see Renger 1967, 1969; Harris 1975; Jeyes 1983; Stol 2000a; Barberon 2012. Stol 1995a; 2016, 586–605, equates the *nadītum* of Šamaš to a nun; and 608–14, the *qadištum* to a holy woman.

45. Michel 2009b is focused on the Old Assyrian consecrated women.

46. We sometimes suppose that a woman was consecrated to a god, though she never appears with this title in the texts. When these women are recipients or senders of letters, they are mentioned by name, like Ištar-lamassī, one of the recipients of the letter TC 3, 128B:1; thanks to a piece of the envelope, we learn that she was consecrated to a god: *a-na Ištar-lá-ma-sí ug-ba-áb-tim*.

The great majority of these women lived at Aššur, and many were consecrated to the god Aššur, but two of them are known to have been living at Zalpa and Hurrama.[47] One consecrated woman, Ilališkan, has an Anatolian name,[48] but the document gives no indication about which deity she was consecrated to.[49] And there were also women consecrated to the goddess Ištar, as suggested by a votive inscription written on a bronze plaque in the shape of a female sex: "For the Assyrian goddess Ištar, her mistress, has Ab-šalim, the consecrated woman (*gubabtum*), for her life and for the life of PN [... en]ter."[50]

None of these *gubabtum* seems to have been married, so we suppose that, like the *nadītum* of Šamaš at Sippar, they had to remain celibate.[51] The *qadištum*, on the other hand, could marry, so they can be compared to the *nadītum* of Marduk at Babylon.[52]

In Old Babylonian sources, the *qadištum*, once considered a prostitute, has more recently been understood as a woman associated with the temple.[53] There were numerous *qadištum* at Sippar; the best known of these, Ilša-hegalli, a native of Babylon, was married to the first lamentation singer of Annunītum at Sippar-Amnānum.[54] To provide her husband with offspring, she had to buy a female slave or to adopt a child.[55] Thus, *qadištum* could be women of high status who could marry but were not supposed to bear children.

---

47. At Zalpa: AKT 3, 103:15–18: an-na [...] *i-na Za-al-pá*, *<a>-gu$_5$-ba-ab-tim* : *li-ip-qí-du-šu*, "the tin [...] they must entrust to the consecrated woman in (the town of) Zalpa." At Hurrama: Kt m/k 125 (courtesy Hecker):10–14: 7 *ma-na*, an-na *i-na*, *Hu-ra-ma*, é *gu$_5$-ba-áb-tim*, *e-zi-ib*; "I left 7 minas of tin in Hurrama, in the house of the consecrated woman."

48. Kt 94/k 804, 14–15 (courtesy Larsen).

49. Kryszat 2006b, 105. The title nin-dingir (once written dingir-nin in **258**) is later also used in Anatolia, in the Hittite texts; see Taggar-Cohen 2006.

50. Assur 19624a/VA 8365 (Kyrszat 2017):1–7: *a-na* ^{d}inanna, *A-šu-ri-tim*, *be-el-ti-ša*, *Áb-ša-lim* ni[n-dingir *a-n*]*a*, *ba-lá-tì-ša ú*, *ba-lá-*[*a*]*t* dingir-*x*-[x], [x x *tù-šé-r*] *i-ib*. See also text **14**.

51. Harris 1975. But contrary to the *nadītum* of Šamaš, the *gubabtum* of Aššur were not living in a *gagûm* but in their family homes.

52. Barberon 2012.

53. Renger 1967; Stol 2000a.

54. Barberon 2012, 44, quotes an unpublished text from Sippar (Di 1805:29), which mentions a head of the *qadištums*. See also Stol 2016, 611, who notes that *qadištum* not consecrated to the god Adad, had a much lower status.

55. Barberon 2012, 78–79.

Four Old Assyrian texts mention *qadištum*; two of them are marriage contracts setting the terms for second wives, and one is a will. In one of the contracts, for a marriage at Kaneš, the woman's status is not specified, but she could be a *qadištum* because of the provision that a second wife could not also be a *qadištum*. Assyrian merchants could have two wives, one at Aššur and the other in Anatolia, but they could not be of the same legal status (**15**). In the other contract, a man who marries a primary wife (*aššutum*) at Kaneš already has a *qadištum*-wife at Aššur, who would therefore be his secondary wife (**24**). An additional clause stipulates that if she does not provide her husband with offspring, he can buy a slave woman to bear his children. This clause and the rather short time it allows to take another woman, two years, leads one to suppose that the man had no other children with his *qadištum*, and to conclude that the Old Assyrian *qadištum* could marry, like the Old Babylonian ones, but could not have children.[56] *Qadištum* are known at Aššur and Kaneš, but they are presumably always Assyrian women. In an unpublished letter, several people undertake to pay the travel expenses of a young *qadištum*-woman who is supposed to go to Kaneš, perhaps to marry.[57] Document **14**, which lists the expenses for a wedding, may apply to a consecrated woman, perhaps a *qadištum*, because the text states that the young woman has shaved her head for the goddess Ištar.[58] The reference to the "uncovered" head of the bride in text **15** could also pertain to consecration in connection with a marriage.

The *qadištum* could inherit from her husband if there were no other heirs. For example, Lamassī, a *qadištum*, inherited from her husband, Amur-Ištar, their house at Kaneš as well as the slaves and furniture (**55**). One may suppose that, like other women, she had also received her portion of the family assets at her marriage.

The *gubabtum*, who had to be able to live independently, inherited a share of her father's estate along with her brothers.[59] Most wills include

56. According to the world order established in the myth of Atra-hasīs, there were women who gave birth and women who did not, among them, the consecrated women who were forbidden to bear children; see Lambert and Millard 1969.

57. Kt n/k 259:5–8 (courtesy Çeçen): *ṣú-ha-ar-tám, ša A-šùr-re-ṣí, qá-dí-iš-tám i-na : a-li-ki-im, šé-ri-a-ší*.

58. The shaving of the woman's head during her consecration ceremony is known for the high priestess (nin-dingir) at Emar; Fleming 1992, 11.

59. See chapter 2, p. 114.

among the beneficiaries the wife of the testator and his consecrated daughter. She is often the one first mentioned and receives promissory notes, gold, silver, tin, copper, and female slaves (**54–56, 59–60, 258**); sometimes her father's seal (**64–65**), gold figurines of deities (**258**), or real estate, the last jointly with male relatives (**58, 62**). The consecrated woman Ahattum received an annual allowance from her brothers: 6 minas of copper and a cut of breast from their offerings (**56**). Another received ⅓ mina of silver (**258**). A consecrated woman could also inherit from her mother.[60]

Some consecrated women owned the houses they lived in. The reading of the will and distribution of the assets could take place there.[61]

Consecration of women to a god seems to have been a regular practice in Old Assyrian society. Merchants tended to consecrate their first daughters, to give thanks for their success in business, and to demonstrate their high social status. Most Assyrian families had a consecrated daughter (**257, 258**). Some *gubabtum* came from the richest families in Aššur.

A nice metaphor was used to symbolize the act of consecration: "to place in the lap (of the god)" (*ana sūnim šakānum*), which means "to place under the protection (of the god)." Consecration, decided by the parents, took place before the girl reached the age of marriage; in one instance, the consecrated girl might still be quite young, since she still has a nanny (*ēmiqtum*; **263**).[62] Thus, Lamassī, from Aššur, wrote to her husband in Kaneš: "The little girl has quite grown up, set out and come here. Consecrate her to (the god) Aššur and touch the foot of your god!" (**166**); or: "You hear that people have become wicked, one tries to swallow up the other! Be an honorable man; break your obligations and come here! Consecrate our young (daughter) to the god Aššur" (**147**; see also **163, 259**).[63] Lamassī wished to consecrate her daughter to the main divinity of her city: Aššur. She was satisfied since Ahaha became a *gubabtum*.

60. AKT 8, 179:9–12, will of Ištar-lamassī: 2¼ gín kù-g[i], *ù* 7½ gín kù-babbar [*ù*], *ku-nu-kam a-na* dumu-munus-[*i-a*], *gu*$_5$*-ba-ab-tim ú-šé-b*[*u-lu*]; "they will send to my consecrated daughter 2¼ shekels of gol[d], 7½ shekels of silver and the seal."

61. AKT 6a, 227:23–28: *ù a-na, A-lim*^{ki} : *a-ṣé-er* : *a-ha-tí-ni, gu*$_5$*-ba-áb-tim* : *lu ni-li-ik-ma, a-na ma-lá* : *ší-ma-at, a-bi-ni* : *ša A-lim*^{ki}, *lu ni-iz-ku*; "and let us go to the city (of Aššur) to our consecrated sister, and clear the matter in accordance with our father's testament, which is in the city (of Aššur)." See Hertel 2013, 288, no. 65, and also AKT 6b, 355, which mentions a consecrated woman living opposite Kura's house.

62. The consecration, even if it had been decided at the birth of the girl, was performed later, according to Barberon 2012, 195–96.

63. For Ahaha, see also chapter 6, pp. 411–26

We know nothing about the ceremony during which the girl was consecrated to the god, other than that the father had to be present. Perhaps on this occasion she received a jewel (**260**), and possibly her head was shaved (**14**).

The religious activities of consecrated women are rarely mentioned. Like other women, they surely prayed to the gods. They made offerings or arranged offerings for other members of their families. Ahattum, for example, made offerings in silver to the god Aššur (**261**). Their consecration to the city god Aššur did not prevent them from honoring other deities. Ahaha, the daughter of Pūšu-kēn and Lamassī, took charge of her father's votive gift to the goddess Tašmētum, along with her mother (**246**). Some unpublished texts show the involvement of consecrated women in certain rituals.[64] Šīmat-Ištar, daughter of Ali-ahum, was consecrated to the god Adad and lived at Aššur; in a letter to her father, she mentions one of her cultic activities, "providing for my god and the spirits of the dead."[65] In another of her letters, the matter at hand is using barley to carry out a ritual (*naspittum*) that took place twice a year.[66] Finally, in another letter, this consecrated women explains that she has gone to the temple of Adad to do homage in the *tamrum*-ritual, no doubt in connection with the preceding one and having to do with the dead.[67]

Some of the references to consecrated women provide information about their business activities. Ahaha, daughter of Pūšu-kēn, lived first with her mother at Aššur, where she had been consecrated to the god Aššur. Later on her own, she writes to her brothers and manages her own affairs, investing silver in several commercial partnerships. At her father's death, she takes part in settling his estate and informs her brother about the parlous state of the family (see pp. 411–26). Ahattum, daughter of Ilī-bāni, lends small amounts of silver to several Assyrian merchants (**177**, **178**) and pays a debt of her brother (**204**), and it is perhaps the same lady involved with votive offerings in text **261**. Unnamed *gubabtum*, clearly

---

64. Dercksen 2015a, 53–54; these texts belong to the archive of Ali-ahum (1950).

65. Kt c/k 266 :19–20: *ù i-li ù e-ṭá-me, a-za-na-an*.

66. Kt c/k 737:14–17: *i-nu-mì na-as-/pí-tim, ra-bi-tí-im lu i-na, na-ar-ma-ak-A-šùr, lu i-na qá-ra-a-tim*; "at the time of the great *naspittum* either in the month Narmmak-Aššur (ii) or in the month Qarrātum (viii)."

67. Kt c/k 127:6–8: *i-na ta-am-ri-im, a-dí a-na-ku a-na* é ^{d}im, *a-na šu-kà-ú-nim a-li-ku*; "during the *tamrum*-ritual, while I had gone to the temple of Adad to prostrate myself."

involved in the family business, receive several amounts of silver (**262**, **263**, AKT 3, 103; cited above, n. 50).[68] The daughter of Naplis sells a slave belonging to her father's estate (**105**), and the daughter of Ilī-dān borrows silver from a merchant to free her brother from debt slavery (Kt 91/k 148). A house of a consecrated woman could be used for storing merchandise.[69] They sometimes appear as witnesses to business transactions.[70]

---

257. Agreement between Two Families, Each Having a Consecrated Woman

Envelope

Obv. [1]kiš[ib *Ú-s*]*à-n*[*im* dumu] *A-m*[*ur*]-*A-šur* kišib *Ku-lu-ma-a* [2](seal A) [3][dumu] *A-šur-i-mì-tí* : ki[šib *Hu-ni-a* dumu *A-šu*]*r-i-mì-tí* [4]kišib du$_{10}$-*ṣí-lá-A-šur* dumu *A*-[*šur-i-dí*] : kišib *A-šur-ták-lá-ku* [5]dumu *A-lá-hi-im* kišib *Be-lá-ni*[*m* du]mu *Šu-A-šur* [6](seal B) [7]kišib *Puzur-A-na* dumu *En-n*[*a-A-šur*] kišib *I-dí-A-š*[*ur* d]u[mu *Da*]*n-A-šur* [8]kišib *A-šur-pì-lá-ah ra-bi-ṣí-im* [*ša*] *A-mur-Ištar* [9](seal C) [10]kišib *S*[*ú-e*]*n*$_6$-sipa kišib *Ì-lí*-[*b*]*a-ni* kišib *A-šur-ni-šu* [11]kišib *Š*[*u-Lá-b*]*a-an* : *me-er-e* : *A-mur-Ištar* : kišib *A-šur-mu-«mu»-ta-pí-il*$_5$ [12](seal D) [13]kišib *Bu-za-zu* k[iši]b *I-ku-pá-šá me-er-e Pu-šu-ke-en*$_6$ [14]*A-šur-pì-lá-a*[*h* maš]kim *ša* é *A-mur-Ištar* : *Sú-en*$_6$-sipa *Ì-lí-ba-ni* [15](seal E) [16]*A-šur-ni-šu* : *ú Šu-Lá-ba-an* : *ki-ma rá-mì-ni-šu-nu ú ki-ma* lo.e. [17]*Áb-ša-lim* dumu-munus *A-mur-Ištar ú I-dí-in-*^{d}im *a-hi-šu-nu* [18]*A-šur-mu-«mu»-ta-pì-il*$_5$ *Bu-za-zu I-ku-pá-ša* [19](seal F) [20][*me-er*]-*ú* [*Pu-šu-k*]*e-en*$_6$ *ki-ma r*[*a-mì-ni-šu*]-*nu ú ki-ma A-ha-ha* [21][*gu*$_5$-*ba-ab-t*]*im ú a-hi-*[*š*]*u-nu S*[*ú-e-a*] *i-*[*n*]*a mì-ig-ra-tí-šu-nu* [22][*iṣ-bu-tù-ni*]*-a-tí-ma ni-iš A-lim*^{ki} *i*[*t-m*]*u-*[*ú-m*]*a* rev. [23]*a-wa-tí-šu-nu nu-g*[*a-m*]*e-er-ma lu A-mur-Ištar ša-zu-ú*[*z-tí*] [24](seal G) [25]*Pu-šu-ke-en*$_6$: *i-zi-iz lu Pu-šu-ke-en*$_6$ *ša-zu-úz-tí* [26]*A-mur-Ištar i-zi-iz lu a-hu-um a-na a-hi-im* [27](seal H) [28]*ma-aš-kà-tám ú-šé-bi*$_4$*-il*$_5$: *lu a-hu-um* : *ša a-hi-im* [29]kù-babbar : *i-na ba-áb-tim* :

---

68. See also the unpublished text Kt 93/k 598:8–11: 3 gín, [*a-n*]*a Ší-ma-at-A-šùr*, dumu-munus *I-ku-pí-Ištar*, nin-dingir; "3 shekels of silver [fo]r Šīmat-Aššur, daughter of Ikuppī-Ištar, the consecrated woman."

69. See Prag I, 558:5–7: *a-dí* 41 túg^{hi-a}, *ša* é *gu*$_5$-*ba-áb-tim*, *Puzur*$_4$-*A-šùr* : *e-zi-bu*; "As for the 41 textiles which Puzur-Aššur left in the house of the consecrated woman." This woman seems to own a house in Kaneš.

70.CCT 5, 12a:12: igi *gu*$_5$-*ba-áb-tim*; "in the presence of the consecrated woman"; AKT 6a, 207:29–30: igi *me-er-i-tí-šu*, *gu*$_5$-*ba-áb-tim*; "in the presence of his consecrated daughter."

il$_5$*-qé* : *lu ṭup-pu-um* [30](seal I) [31]*ha-ar-mu-um* : *ša ku-nu-ki-šu-nu lu ša ší-be-e* [32]*lu ši-ip-[k]à-tim* : *a-hu-um a-na a-hi-im* [33]*iš-pu-uk* : *lu i-na A-lim*^{ki} *lu i-na* gán^{lim} [34](seal K) [35]*me-er-ú A-mur-Ištar ú me-er-at A-mur-Ištar gu*$_5$*-ba-áb-tum* [36]*me-er-ú Pu-šu-ke-en*$_6$: *ú* dumu-munus *Pu-šu-ke-en*$_6$ *gu*$_5$*-ba-áb-tum* [37](seal L) [38]*a-hu-um a-na a-hi-im a-na mì-ma šu-um-šu* [39]*lá i-tù-ar* : *a-wi-lu a-ni-ú-tum* u.e. [40](seal M) [41][*ga-me-er a-w*]*a-tim* le.e. [42](seals N, O) r.e. [43](seals P, Q)

[1–3]Seal[ed by Us]ān[um, son of] Am[ur]-Aššur; sealed by Kulumaya, [son] of Aššur-imittī; seal[ed by Hunniya, son of Aššu]r-imittī; [4–6]sealed by Ṭāb-ṣilli-Aššur, son of A[ššur-idī]; sealed by Aššur-taklāku, son of Ali-ahum; sealed by Belānu[m, so]n of Šu-Aššur; [7]sealed by Puzur-Anna, son of Enn[u(m)-Aššur]; sealed by Iddin-Ašš[ur, s]o[n of Dā]n-Aššur; [8]sealed by Aššur-pilah, the attorney [of] Amur-Ištar; [10–11]sealed by S[î]n-rē'ī, sealed by Ilī-[b]āni; sealed by Aššur-nīšu; sealed by Š[u-Lab]ān, sons of Amur-Ištar; [11–13]sealed by Aššur-mūtappil; sealed by Buzāzu; s[ea]led by Ikuppaša, sons of Pūšu-kēn.

[14–17]Aššur-pila[h, the att]orney for the house of Amur-Ištar, Suen-rē'ī, Ilī-bāni, Aššur-nīšu, and Šu-Labān, on behalf of themselves and as representative of Ab-šalim, daughter of Amur-Ištar, and Iddin-Adad, their brother (on the one side), [18–22]Aššur-mūtappil, Buzāzu, (and) Ikuppaša, [the son]s of [Pūšu-k]ēn, as their [own rep]rensentatives and as representative of Ahaha, [the consecrated wom]an, and [t]heir brother S[ue'a] (on the other), by mutual agreement, [seized u]s (as arbitrators) and s[wore] the oath of the city (of Aššur), and [23–25]we p[u]t an end to their dispute: whether Amur-Ištar acted as the agent of Pūšu-kēn, [25–28]or whether Pūšu-kēn acted as the agent of Amur-Ištar, whether one sent the *maškattum*-deposits to the other, [28–31]whether one collected outstanding claims for the other, either (on the basis of) a certified tablet with their seals or (on the basis of) witnesses, [32–33]whether one has made investment deposits for the other, be it in the city (of Aššur) or abroad; [35]the sons of Amur-Ištar and the consecrated daughter of Amur-Ištar (and) [36]the sons of Pūšu-kēn and the consecrated daughter of Pūšu-kēn, [38–39]one shall not raise a claim against the other about anything whatsoever. These men [settled the] case.

Tablet

Obv. [1]*A-šur-pí-lá-ah* maškim *ša* [2]é *A-mur-Ištar Sú-en*$_6$-sipa [3]*Il*$_5$*-ba-ni* : *A-šur-ni-šu* [4]*ù Šu-Lá-ba-an me-er-ú* [5]*A-mur-Ištar ki-ma ra-mì-ni-šu-nu* [6]*ù ki-ma* : *Áb-ša-lim* dumu-munus [7]*A-mur-Ištar ù I-dí-in-*^{d}im [8]*a-hi-šu-[n]u*

A-šur-mu-ta-pí-il$_5$ [9]*Bu-za-zu ù I-ku-pá-ša me-er-ú* [10]*Pu-šu-ke-en*$_6$ *ki-ma ra-mì-ni-šu-nu* [11]*ù ki-ma A-ha-ha : a-ha-tí-šu-nu* [12]*gu*$_5$*-ba-áb-tim ú Sú-e-a a-hi-šu-nu* [13]*«Sú-e-a» : i-na mì-ig*$^!$*-ra-tí-šu-nu* [14]*iṣ-bu-tù-ni-a-tí-ma* [15]*ni-iš : A-lim*^{ki} *: it-mu-ú-ma* [16]*a-wa-tí-šu-nu : nu-ga-me-er-ma* [17]*lu A-mur-Ištar ša-zu-ú[z-tí]* [18]*Pu-šu-ke-en*$_6$ *i-[zi-iz]* lo.e. [19]*lu Pu-šu-ke-en*$_6$ *: š[a-zu-úz-tí]* [20]*A-mur-Ištar i-zi-[iz]* rev. [21]*lu a-hu-um a-na a-h[i-im]* [22]*ma-áš-kà-tám : ú-šé-bi-i[l*$_5$*]* [23]*lu a-hu-um ša a-hi-im* [24]kù-babbar *i-na ba-áb-tim* [25]*il*$_5$*-qé : lu ṭup-pu-um* [26]*ha-ar-mu-um ša : ku-nu-ki-šu-nu* [27]*lu ša ší-be lu ší-ip-kà-tum* [28]*a-hu-um a-na a-hi-im* [29]*iš-pu-uk : lu i-na* [30]*A-lim*^{ki} *lu i-na eq-li-im* [31]*me-er-ú A-mur-Ištar me-er-at* [32]*A-mur-Ištar gu*$_5$*-ba-áb-tum* [33]*me-er-ú Pu-šu-ke-en*$_6$ [34]*ù me-er-at Pu-šu-ke-en*$_6$ [35]*gu*$_5$*-ba-áb-tum a-hu-um* [36]*a-na a-hi-im a-na mì-ma* [37]*šu-mì-šu lá i-tù-ar* u.e. [38]*Ú-sà-nu-um* dumu *A-mur-A-šùr* [39]*Ku-lu-ma-a* dumu *A-šur-i-mì-tí* le.e. [40]*Hu-ni-a* dumu *A-šur-i-mì-tí* du$_{10}$-*ṣí-lá-A-šur* dumu [41]*A-šur-i-dí : Puzur*$_4$*-en-na* dumu *En-na-A-šur* [42]*A-šur-ta-ak-lá-ku* dumu *A-lá-hi-im Be-lá-nu-um* dumu [43]*Šu-A-šur I-dí-A-šur* dumu *Dan-A-šur a-wi-lu a-ni-ut-tù-um* [44]*ga-me-er a-wa-tim*

[1–8]Aššur-pilah, the attorney for the house of Amur-Ištar, Suen-rē'ī, Ilī-bāni, Aššur-nīšu, and Šu-Labān, the sons of Amur-Ištar, on behalf of themselves and as representatives of Ab-šalim, daughter of Amur-Ištar, and Iddin-Adad, th[ei]r brother (on the one side), [8–12]Aššur-mūtappil, Buzāzu, and Ikuppaša, the sons of Pūšu-kēn, as their own reprensentatives and as representatives of Ahaha, their sister, the consecrated woman, and their brother Sue'a (on the other), [13–15]by mutual agreement, seized us (as arbitrators) and swore the oath of the city (of Aššur), and [16]we put an end to their dispute: [17–20]whether Amur-Ištar ac[ted] as the age[nt] of Pūšu-kēn, or whether Pūšu-kēn acte[d] as the a[gent] of Amur-Ištar, [21–22]whether one sen[t] the *maškattum*-deposits to the ot[her], [23–27]whether one collected outstanding claims for the other, either (on the basis of) a certified tablet with their seals or (on the basis of) witnesses, [27–30]whether one has made investment deposits for the other, be it in the city (of Aššur) or abroad; [31–32]the sons of Amur-Ištar and the consecrated daughter of Amur-Ištar (and) [33–35]the sons of Pūšu-kēn and the consecrated daughter of Pūšu-kēn, [35–37]one shall not raise a claim against the other about anything whatsoever.

[38–43]Usānum, son of Amur-Aššur; Kulumaya, son of Aššur-imittī; Hunniya, son of Aššur-imittī; Ṭāb-ṣilli-Aššur, son of Aššur-idī; Puzur-Enna, son of Enna-Aššur; Aššur-taklāku, son of Ali-ahum; Belānum, son of Šu-Aššur; Iddin-Aššur, son of Dān-Aššur. [43–44]These men settled the case.

Bibliography: Text edited by Kienast as ATHE, 24; analyzed by Hertel (2013, 279–80).

Comments: This long document, whose envelope is preserved, is an agreement between the children of Amur-Ištar, five boys and a consecrated woman named Ab-šalim, and those of Pūšu-kēn, four boys and a consecrated woman named Ahaha. In both families, only the consecrated women are mentioned, the other girls, being married, having left their families. Since Amur-Ištar and Pūšu-kēn, who were partners and had represented each other's interests, had died, this agreement is intended to settle any dispute that might arise between the two families.

Since the text was written in Kaneš, both consecrated women are represented. The envelope bears seventeen different seal impressions of the members of the two families and the witnesses.

---

258. A Consecrated Woman Is Supported by Her Anatolian Brother-in-Law

Envelope

Obv. ^{1}[*Ha-ma-lá Ma-da-i-um* ^{2d}utu-*ba-ni A-mur-Ištar* ^{3}*Šu-ma-A-šùr ú A-šùr-*^{d}utu^{ši} ^{4}dumu^{ú} *Šál-lim-A-šùr* ^{5}*ú Zi-ki* du]mu-mu[nus *Šál-lim-A-šùr* dingir-nin] ^{6}*i**-*na mì-ig-r*[*a-tí-šu-nu*] ^{7}*iṣ-bu-tù-ni-a-t*[*í-ma a-na* é *Šál-lim-A-šùr*] ^{8}*né-ru-ub-ma a-*[x x x x] ^{9}é$^{be\text{-}tum}$ gal *š*[*a Š*]*ál-li*[*m-A-šùr*] ^{10}[*š*]*a Ha-ma-lá* [*Ma-d*[*a*]-*i-*[*im ú*] *Ha-ar-šu-me-e*[*l-kà*] ^{11}(seal A) ^{12}[*a*]-*ší-tí-šú Zi-ki* dingir-nin dumu-munus ^{13}*Šál-lim-A-šùr ki-ma um-mì-šu* lo.e. ^{14}(seal B) ^{15}[*š*]*a Ha-ma-lá ú a-ší-tí-šu* ^{16}[*u*]*š-ba-at ak-lá-at* ^{17}(seal C) rev. ^{18}*ú pá-ša-at iš-tí-šu-nu-ma šu-m*[*a*] ^{19}*Ha-ma-lá ú a-ša-sú Zi-ki ú-lá-mu-nu* ^{20}*ú-lu ar-ha-lúm ša-num e-ra-áb* ^{21}dingir^{le} *ša* kù-gi *ša Šál-lim-A-šùr* ^{22}*a-bi*$_4$*-ša šu-ku-ta-ša i-na* 3 *ṣú-h*[*a-re*] ^{23}*mu-uš-té-bi*$_4$*-le*$^{!}$(LAM) 1 *ṣú-ha-ra-am dan-*[*nam*] ^{24}[1] géme 1 anše *ú mì-ma ú-nu-ut qá-tí-*[*ša*] ^{25}[*Ha-m*]*a-*[*lá*] *a-*(seal A)*-na Zi-ki* ^{26}[*i-da-ši*]-(seal A)*-ma a-ṣé-er* ^{27}[*a-he-e-ša t*]*ù-ṣí* ^{d}utu-*ba-*[*ni* ^{28}*A-mur-Ištar Šu-ma-A-š*]*ùr ú A-šùr-*^{d}[utu^{ši} ^{29}dumu^{ú} *Šál-lim-A-šùr e-lu-t*]*um šu-*[*nu*] ^{30}[*a-šar li-bi-šu-nu i-lu-ku* …] (lacuna)

Le.e. $^{1'}$[*Šál-lim-A*]*-šur ṭup-*[*pu* …]

$^{1-6}$[Hamala from (the town of) Mada, Šamaš-bāni, Amur-Ištar, Šuma-Aššur, and Aššur-šamšī, the sons of Šalim-Aššur, and Ziki, the da]ught[er of Šalim-Aššur, the consecrated woman], $^{6-8}$by [common] agreement seized us (as arbitrators), [and] we entered [the house of Šalim-Aššur (with this outcome)]:

8–10[...] Šali[m-Aššur]'s large house [be]longs to Hamala [from (the town of) Mada] 10–12[and] Haršum-e[lka], his [w]ife. 12–18Ziki, the consecrated daughter of Šalim-Aššur, shall live, eat, and be anointed together with them, like Hamala's mother and his wife (Haršum-elka). 18–20If Hamala and his wife maltreat Ziki, or (if) another *arhālum* enters (the household), 21–26[Ham]a[la will give] her, Ziki, the golden figurines of the gods of Šalim-Aššur, her father, her jewelry, from the three b[oys] active in trade$^{?}$, one stro[ng] slave boy, [one] female slave, one donkey, and all [her] belongings, and 26–27then [she] will leave to go to [her brothers]. 27–29Šamaš-bā[ni, Amur-Ištar, Šumi-Aššur, and Aššur-šamšī, sons of Šalim-Aššur, are free of cl]aims. 30[They can go wherever they want...]

1′[Šalim-A]ššur [...] tabl[ets...]

Tablet

Obv. 1*Ha-ma-lá Ma-da-i-um* 2^{d}utu-*ba-ni A-mur-Ištar* 3*Šu-ma-A-šùr ú A-šùr-*^{d}utu^{ši} 4dumu^{ú} *Šál-lim-A-šùr* 5*ú Zi-ki* dumu-munus : *Šál-lim-A-šùr* 6dingir-nin *i-na mì-ig-ra-tí-šu-un* 7*iṣ-bu-tù-ni-a-tí-ma a-na* 8é : *Šál-lim-A-šùr n*[*é*]*-ru-ub-ma* 9é$^{be\text{-}tám}$ gal$^{!}$: <šà> *Šál-lim-A-*[*š*]*ùr* 10*ša ru-ba-um Kà-ni-ší-i-um* 11*qá-dum du-um-qí-šu a-na* 12*Ha-ma-lá Ma-da-i-um i-dí-nu* 13*a-na Ha-ma-lá-ma i-za-az* 14*Ha-ar-šu-me-el-kà* du[mu-m]unus : *Šál-lim-A-šùr* 15*i-ta-ru Zi-ki* dumu-munus *Šál-lim-A-šùr* 16dingir-nin *ki-ma um-mì-*[*šu š*]*a Ha-ma-lá* 17*ú a-ší-*[*t*]*í-šu uš-b*[*a-a*]*t* 18*a*[*k*]*-lá-at ú pá-ša-a*[*t*] 19*iš-t*[*í*]*-šu-nu šu-ma Ha-ma-lá* 20*ú a-ša-sú Zi-ki ú-lá-mu-nu* 21*ú-lu ar-ha-lúm ša-num* lo.e. 22*a-na* é$^{be\text{-}tim}$ *e-ra-áb* 23dingir^{le} *ša* kù-gi 24*ša a-bi$_4$-ša šu-ku-ta-ša* rev. 25*i-na* 3 *ṣú-ha-re mu-uš-té-bi$_4$-le* 261 *ṣú-ha-ra-<am>* 1 géme 1 anše 27*ú mì-ma ú-nu-ut qá-tí-ša* 28*i-na* é : *a-bi$_4$-ša Ha-ma-lá* 29*i-da-ší-ma a-ṣé-er a-he- e-ša* 30*tù-ṣí* ^{d}utu-*ba-ni A-mur-Ištar* 31*Šu-ma-A-šùr ú A-šùr-*^{d}utu^{ši} 32dumu^{ú} *Šál-lim-A-šùr e-lu-tum šu-nu* 33*a-šar li-bi$_4$-šu-nu i-lu-ku ù*$^{*!}$ 34*a-na ar-ha-lim lá ṭa-hu-ú* 35é$^{be\text{-}tám}$ *ṣa-ah-ra-am* é : *ša ki-dí* 36[*a*]*t-hu-ú i-lá-qé-ú-ma* mu-3-šè 371 *ṣú-ba-tám* 1 *ší-it-ra-am* 38*a-na Zi-ki a-ha-tí-šu-nu i-ta-na-dí-nu* 39*iš-tù* mu-3-šè *i-ma-lu-ú-ni* 40*ṣú-ba-tám ú ší-it-ra-am* 41*ú-ṭá-bu-ú-ma* ⅓ *ma-na* kù-babbar 42*ša-na-sú-ma a-na Zi-ki a-ha-tí-šu-/nu* 43*i-ta-na-dí-nu ur-kà-at* 44*Zi-ki a-*[*ha*]*-tí-šu-nu* dingir-nin 45^{d}utu-*ba-ni A-mur-Ištar* 46*Šu-ma-A-šùr ú A-šùr-*^{d}utu^{ši} 47dumu^{ú} *Šál-lim-A-šùr* 48*lu ṭup-pu lu ta-ah-sí-sá-tum* u.e. 49*lu da-na-tù ša*$^{!}$ *Šál-lim-A-šùr* 50*a-bi$_4$-šu-nu Ha-ma-lá ú-šar-šu-nu-tí* 51*a-na hu-bu-lim ša Šál-lim-A-šùr* 52*ha**-*ar**-*x-x-a**-*tim** 53*i-dí-na-tí-šu-nu* le.e. 54*Ha-ma-lá lá ṭa-hu-ú* iti-1-kam *ša ke-na-*

tim li-mu-um [55]*ša qá-tí A-hi-a-a dumu A-du-*[*n*]*a-a* igi *Šu-ul-mu-ša-A-šùr* [56]dumu *Da-da-a* igi *A-zi-ri-im* dumu *Ku-ra-r*[*a*] igi *Šu-Ra-ma* [57]dumu *Ša-ru-Sú-en*$_6$ [58]igi *Šu-Iš-ha-ra* dumu *Uš-he-er* igi *Lá-qé-ep* dumu *Šu-Ištar* [59]igi *Da-ku-ú* [60]igi *Wa-du-ú*

[1–6]Hamala from (the town of) Mada, Šamaš-bāni, Amur-Ištar, Šuma-Aššur, and Aššur-šamšī, the sons of Šalim-Aššur, and Ziki, the daughter of Šalim-Aššur, the consecrated woman, [6–8]by common agreement seized us (as arbitrators), and we entered the house of Šalim-Aššur (with this outcome):

[9–12] The large house <of> Šalim-Aššur that the king of Kaneš, by his goodness, gave, together with its valuables, to Hamala from (the town of) Mada; [13]it will stand for Hamala himself. [14–15]Haršum-elka (his wife) will take Šalim-Aššur's (young) daughter along. [15–19]Ziki, the daughter of Šalim-Aššur, the consecrated woman, shall live, eat, and be anointed together with them like Hamala's mother and his wife (Haršum-elka).

[19–22]If Hamala and his wife maltreat Ziki, or (if) another *arhālum* enters the household, [23–29]Hamala will give her the golden figurines of the gods of her father, her jewelry, one of the three servants active in trade?, one female slave, one donkey, and all her belongings in her father's house, and [29–30]then she will leave to go to her brothers. [30–32]Šamaš-bāni, Amur-Ištar, Šumi-Aššur, and Aššur-šamšī, sons of Šalim-Aššur, are free of claims. [33–34]They can go wherever they want, and they are not liable for the *arhālum*. [35–38]The brothers will receive the small house outside the city, and, for the next 3 years, they will give to their sister Ziki 1 textile (and) 1 shawl. [39–43]After 3 years have passed, they will stop providing a textile and an shawl, and they will annually give to Ziki their sister ⅓ mina of silver. [43–50]After (the death) of their sister Ziki, the consecrated woman, Šamaš-bāni, Amur-Ištar, Šumi-Aššur, and Aššur-šamšī, sons of Šalim-Aššur—Hamala will release to them tablets, memoranda, and valid deeds of their father Šalim-Aššur. [51–54]Hamala is not liable for the debts of Šalim-Aššur […] in case? of a lawsuit about them.

[54–55]Month ša Kēnātim (iii), eponym that succeeded Ahiaya, son of Adunaya (REL 227a + 1). [55–58]In the presence of Šulmu-Aššur, son of Dadaya; Azirum, son of Kurara; Šu-Rama, son of Šarru-Suen; Šu-Išhara, son of Ušher; Laqēp, son of Šu-Ištar; Dakū; and Wadū.

Bibliography: Text edited by Albayrak (2004) as Kt 01/k 325. Lines 9–19, 40–41 cited by Kogan and Koslova (2006, 589–90). Collated May 2011.

Comments: This text dates to level Ib. Ziki, the consecrated daughter of a deceased Assyrian merchant, was living in her father's house, where she kept his archive. But the house was confiscated by the local king, who gave it to an Anatolian named Hamala. Hamala was obliged to take care of Ziki as a member of his household. The brothers of Ziki, who inherited another, smaller house, had to give their sister first textiles and, after three years, an allowance in silver. Among the objects that Ziki received from her father were golden figurines of gods.

Line 15: literally, "take away."

Lines 21 and 34: *arhālum* is a general term for a service obligation attached to the possession of a house, to be performed by an inhabitant of the house; see Dercksen 2004b, 155. Line 21: one has to understand that if someone else than Hamala takes possession of the house and performs the *arhālum* obligation, then Ziki will have to leave the house. Line 34: the brothers of Ziki are not living in the house, and thus are not liable for the *arhālum* service.

Lines 24: the word *šukuttum* refers to a woman's jewelry; see Dercksen 2015b, 40.

Line 55: Ahiaya, son of Adunaya, was eponym in the middle of the eighteenth century BCE.

---

259. A Wife Asks Her Husband to Be an Honorable Man

Obv. ^{1}*a-na Pu-šu-ke-en*$_6$ ^{2}*qí-bi-ma : um-ma* ^{3}*Lá-ma-sí-ma : šu-ma a-hi a-/ta* ^{4}*šu-ma : be-li a-ta : a-na ma-/nim* ^{5}*ta-na-ṭá-al* ^{6}*ku-ta-bi-it-ma* ^{7}*ku-ur-ṣí-kà : pá-ri-ir* ^{8}1 túg *kà-áb-ta-am* ^{9}*a-na A-šur-ma-lik* ^{10}*i-na pá-ni-tim* lo.e. ^{11}*ha-ra-ni-šu : a-dí-in-/*[*š*]*u-um* rev. ^{12}kù-babbar ^{pí}*-šu : mì-ma* ^{13}*ú-lá ub-lá-am* ^{14}*ku-nu-kam : ša* $^{\text{na}_4}$-za-gìn ^{15}diri^{um} *: na-áš-a-kum* ^{16}*i-nu-mì : ki-sà-am* ^{17}*tù-šé-ba-lá-ni* ^{18}síg$^{\text{hi-a}}$ *šu*$^{!}$*-uk-/nam* ^{19}*ša-áp-tù-um* ^{20}*i-na A-lim*^{ki} ^{21}*wa-aq-ra-at*

$^{1-3}$Say to Pūšu-kēn: thus (says) Lamassī.

$^{3-5}$If you are my brother and my master, to whom do you look? ^{6}Be an honorable man and ^{7}break your obligations.

$^{8-11}$I gave 1 heavy textile to Aššur-malik at the time of his previous journey. $^{12-13}$He in no way brought me back (the price in) silver. $^{14-15}$He is bringing you a seal of lapis lazuli of extra quality. $^{16-17}$When you send me the purse, $^{18-21}$place wool (inside): wool is expensive in Aššur.

Bibliography: Text published in copy by Stephens as BIN 6, 7; translated by Michel (2001a, no. 305).

Comments: Although not explicitely stated, this letter is linked to the consecration of Ahaha, the daughter of Lamassī and Pūšu-kēn (**163**, **166**). Indeed, in the letter **147**:9–11, Lamassī wrote: "Be an honorable man, break your obligations and come here! Consecrate our young (daughter) to the god Aššur."

Line 7: literally, "break your fetters"; this expression means: "give up what you are doing."

---

260. Jewelry for the Consecrated Daughter

Obv. [1]*a-na Pu-šu-ke-en*$_6$ *qí-bi-ma* [2]*um-ma Lá-ma-sí-ma* [3]kù-babbar 1½ *ma-na ša ig-ri* [4]é*bé-tim* ša dingir-*ma-lik* [5]*i-ba-ab ha-ra-ni-kà ta-am-ší-/ma* [6]*i-na ta-ah-sí-is-tí-kà* [7]*ú-lá ta-al-pu-ut mu-zi-zu-/kà* [8]*il*$_5$*-ta-qé-ú-šu i-na* 70 áš [9]*ša li-bi Ab-ba-a-im* [10](erasure) 20 baneš *še-am* [11]*im-du-ud ší-tí še-im* [12]*i-ma-da-ad-ma té-er-tum* [13]*i-lá-kà-kum* (erasure) lo.e. [14]*a-pu-tum i-hi-id-ma* [15]*pu-ùh a-né-qé ša ṣú-ha-/re* rev. [16]*ša ta-áp-ṭù-ru* [17]kù-gi *šé-bi*$_4$*-lam-ma a-ni-qé* [18]*lá-áš-ku-šu-nu-ma li-ba-šu-nu* [19]*lá i-lá-mì-in* kù-gi [20]*ša Bu-za-zu ša té-zi-bu* [21]*hi-dí : a-na A-ha-ha e-pu-uš* [22]*a-na mu-zi-zi-kà* [23]*lá ta-ša-lá-aṭ* [24]*ṣú-ha-ra-am ṭur*$_4$*-dam-ma* [25]*ip-ra-am lu-pá-hi-ir*

[1–2]Say to Pūšu-kēn: thus (says) Lamassī.

[3–7]At the beginning of your journey, you forgot to record the silver—1½ minas, corresponding to the rent for the house of Ilī-mālik—in your memorandum. [7–8]So your representatives are trying to collect it.

[8–11]From the 70 *ṣimdum*-measures owed by Abbayaum, he measured out 20 *ṣimdum*-measures of barley. [11–13]When he measures out the rest of the barley, a report will come to you.

[14–18]Urgent! Be sure to send me gold in place of the children's rings that you removed, so I can give them rings to wear, [18–19]and they will not be angry! [19–20]From the the gold of Buzāzu that you left, [21–23]I had beads made for Ahaha; [22–23]you should not make it available to your representatives. [24–25]Send me a servant so that he can collect food (to store).

Bibliography: Text published in copy by Veenhof as VS 26, 42; translated by Michel (2001a, no. 310).

Comments: Among various expenses, Lamassī mentions a piece of gold jewelry that she had made for her consecrated daughter, Ahaha.

Line 8: the *ṣimdum* measure alternates with the *karpatum*; it amounted to about 30 liters. Thus, 70 *ṣimdum* is between 1,680 and 2,100 liters.

Line 21: the word *hiddum* corresponds to a piece of jewelry made of gold. It is often associated with garment pins (*tudittum*; CCT 3, 29:24–26; TC 1, 30:12–13) and could be attached to them as a decorative element. At Mari, it was a metal or stone bead (Ilya Arkhipov 2012, 45).

---

261. A Consecrated Woman Owns Votive Offerings Loaned to a Merchant

Obv. [1]½ *ma-na* kù-babbar [2]*ṣa-ru-pá-am i-ṣé-er* [3]*Lá-li-im A-ha-tum* [4]*tí-šu* iti-kam *Ku-zal-li* [5]*li-mu-um* [6]*A*[!]*-šur-i-dí* 1 gín-ta [7]*i-na* iti-kam[!] lo.e. [8]*ṣí-ib-tám* rev. [9]*ú-ṣa-áb* [10]*a-ha-ma* 2 gín [11]kù-babbar 6 gín kù-babbar [12]*a-ta-ad-mì-iq-tim* [13]*a-ha-ma* 1½ gín [14]kù-babbar *ik-ri-b*[*u*] [15]*ša A-šur mì-m*[*a*] [16]*a-nim a-na* u.e. [17]*Lá-li-im* le.e. [18]*a-dí-in*

[1–4]Ahattum has loaned ½ mina of refined silver to Lālum. [4–6]Month Kuzallum (xi), eponym Aššur-idī (REL 95). [6–9]He will add interest of 1 shekel per (mina) per month. [10–12]As a separate item, 2 shekels of silver (and) 6 shekels of silver as a *tadmiqum*-trust; [13–15]as a separate item, 1½ shekels of silver as votive offerings for Aššur—[15–18]all this I gave to Lālum.

Bibliography: Text published in copy and edited by Garelli as *RA* 59, 34.

Comments: Ahattum, who is presumably a consecrated woman, owns 1½ shekels of silver for votive offerings. For other loans of Ahattum, see **177** and **178**.

---

262. A Consecrated Woman Owns Jewelry as Pledge

Obv. [1]⅔ gín 15 še [2]kù-babbar *a-na* [3]*gu*$_5$*-ba-áb-tim* [4]*ša a-ni-qe* [5]*ša A-na-ah-Ištar* lo.e. [6]*tù-kà-i-lu* [7]*áš-qúl* rev. [8]2 gín kù-babbar [9]*i-na tap-hi-ri-im* [10]*ša Be-lim* [11]é *A-la-hi-im* [12]*ni-a-im áš-qúl*

[1–7]I paid ⅔ shekels, 15 grains of silver to the consecrated woman who held the rings of Ānah-Ištar (as pledge). [8–12]I paid 2 shekels of silver from the goods for the temple collection of (the god) Bēlum (in?) the house of our Ali-ahum.

Bibliography: Text edited by Kienast as ATHE, 8.

Comments: This text lists two transactions that could be related. In the first one, an unnamed consecrated woman held jewelry as pledge; in the second one, a payment is done for the collection of Bēlum's temple.

Line 9: the word *taphirum* is also attested in text **128**:19; it corresponds to goods collected for a temple.

---

263. A Consecrated Woman, Together with Her Nanny, Receives Silver

Obv. ^{1}10 gín kù-babbar *A-mur*-dingir ^{2}1 gín kù-babbar *a-na qá-tí-šu* ^{3}10 gín kù-babbar *a-na* dumu-munus ^{4}*Ú-ṣú-ur-ša-A-šur* nin-dingir ^{5}[x g]ín kù-babbar *a-na e-mì-iq-tí-ša* ^{6}1 gín kù-babbar : (°erasure) ^{7}*I-dí-A-šùr* dumu *A-šur-i-mì-tí* ^{8}3 gín kù-babbar ^{9}*A-la-hu-um* dumu *Zu-ku-hi-im* ^{10}1 gín kù-babbar *a-na me-er-i-šu* ^{11}2 gín kù-babbar lo.e. ^{12}*Ì-lí-iš-tí-kál* ^{13}2 gín kù-babbar rev. ^{14}*En-um-A-šùr* dumu *I-bi*$_4$*-sú-a* ^{15}3 gín kù-babbar ^{16}*Šu-Nu-nu* 1 gín kù-babbar ^{17}*a-na me-er-i-šu* ^{18}1½ gín kù-babbar ^{19}*En-na-Sú-en*$_6$ dumu *Ku-ra-ra* ^{20}⅓ *ma-na* kù-babbar ^{21}*Puzur*$_4$-[*A-šur*] dumu *Šu-Lá-ba-an* ^{22}2 gín kù-babbar ^{23}*Ku-tal-lá-nu-um*

^{1}10 shekels of silver: Amur-ilī; ^{2}1 shekel of silver at his disposal. $^{3-4}$10 shekels of silver for the consecrated daughter of Uṣur-ša-Aššur. ^{5}[x sh]ekels of silver for her nanny. $^{6-7}$1 shekel of silver: Iddin-Aššur, son of Aššur-imittī. $^{8-9}$3 shekels of silver: Ali-ahum, son of Zukuhum. ^{10}1 shekel of silver for his son. $^{11-12}$2 shekels of silver: Iliš-tikal. $^{13-14}$2 shekels of silver: Ennum-Aššur, son of Ibbisu'a. $^{15-16-17}$3 shekels of silver: Šu-Nunu; 1 shekel of silver for his son. $^{18-19}$1½ shekel of silver: Enna-Suen, son of Kurara. $^{20-21}$⅓ mina of silver: Puzur-Aššur, son of Šu-Labān. $^{22-23}$2 shekels of silver: Kutallanum.

Bibliography: Text published by Hecker, Kryszat, and Matouš as Prag I, 542. Collated on photo online on the CDLI as P359148.

Comments: Anonymous distribution list of small quantities of silver to various persons. Among these, a named consecrated woman receives ten shekels; her nanny gets some silver as well. This might suggest that she was still young when consecrated to the god.

---

264. A Consecrated Woman Gives Advice to Her Sister to Help Save Her Marriage

Envelope

Obv. [1][kišib *Um-mì-Iš-ha-ra*] [2][*a-na Lá-ma-sà-tim*] [3][(seal)] rev. [4][(se]al) [5]*ù Ša-lim-ma* [6]*a-ša-at* [7]*Ir-ma-A-šur* [8](seal)

[1][Sealed by Ummī-Išhara.] [2–7][To Lamassatum] and Šalimma, wife of Ir’am-Aššur.

Tablet

Obv. [1]*a-na Lá-ma-sà-tim ú Ša-lim-ma qí-bi-ma* [2]*um-ma Um-mì-Iš-ha-<ra>-ma a-dí-i na-áš-pé-er-tim* [3]*ša ta-áš-pu-ri-ni* : *um-ma a-tí-ma mì-šu-um* [4]*ma-ma-an lá i-ṭa-ra-dam ší-pá-ar-šu* [5]*i-li-kam-ma* : *a-na-ku aṭ-ru-ud* : *a-dí ma-lá* [6]*ú ší-ni-šu aq-bi-šu-ma li-bu-šu* : *i-ta-na-aṣ-/ra-áp* [7]*um-ma šu-ut-ma* : *a-dí* : *ma-lá* : *ú ší-ni-šu* [8]*na-áš-pé-er-tí* : *i-li-ik-ší-im-ma a-lá-kam* [9]*lá ta-mu-a* : *ša a-ša-pá-ru-ší-ni-*BA *i-ṣé-er* [10]*na-áš-pé-ra-tí-a iš-té-et* : *ú ší-ta* : *ša i-li-kà-/ší-ni* [11]*a-wi-lúm* : *a-wa-tim* : *i-ta-ah-dar* [12][*u*]*m-ma šu-ut-ma iš-tù* : *a-lá-kam lá ta-mu-ú* [13]*lá ta-tù-ri-ma* : *lá ta-qá-bi-im* [14]*šu-ma* : *a-ha-tí* : *a-tí* : *a-wa-tim* : *sà-ra-tim* [15]*lá ta-áš-ta-na-pá-ri-im* : *a-na* kù-babbar *mì-ma* [16]*lá ta-ša-pá-ri-šu-um* : *a-šu-mì* kù-babbar *aq-bi-šu-ma* [17]*um-ma šu-ut-ma* : *ma-lá-ma-a* : kù-babbar ½ *ma-na* [18]*gám-ri-ša* : *gi*$_5$*-mì-lam*$_5$: *i-ṣé-er um-mì-ša* [19]*ú-ul a-hi-ša lá-áš-ku-un ú-ul* lo.e. [20]*i-na ba-áb-tí-a* : kù-babbar 10 gín *lá i-ba-ší* [21]*ú šu-ma* : *i-na ba-áb-tí-a lá-šu* rev. [22]kù-babbar 10 gín : *ma-lá* : *gám-ri-ša* [23]*iš-tí um-mì-ša* : *ú-ul** : *a-hi-ša* [24]*lu té-ri-iš-ma* : *a-na-ku a-na-kam* : *lu-ta-er-šu-ma* [25]*lu ta-ta-al-kam* : *mì-ma* : *a-wa-tim* [26]*ú na-áš-pé-ra-tim* : *lá ta-áš-ta-na-pá-ri-im* [27]*i-na pá-ni* : *a-wi-lim* : *tù-uš-ta-zi-zi* [28]*um-ma šu-ut-ma iš-tù-ma lá am-tí-ni* : *ší-it* [29]*a-lá-kam lá ta-am-tù-a-ni* : *lá ta-tù-ar-ma* [30]*šu-um-ša* : *lá ta-za-kà-ri-im* : *ú a-tí* [31]*lá a-ha-tí* : *mì-šu-um šé-ri-ki ú* é *bé-et-ki* [32]*ša-ni-ú-tum* : *i-bé-e-lu* : *ú a-tí* : *a-ma-kam* [33]*wa-áš-ba-tí* : *a-pu-tum* : *šé-ri-ki* : *lá tù-ha-li-qí* [34]*ú i-a-tí i-na* é *a-wi-lim* : *lá tù-re-qí-ni* [35]*šu-ma* : *a-lá-ki* : *i-ba-ší* : *tí-ib-e-ma a-tal-ki-im* [36]*lá-ma a-wi-lúm li-bu-šu* : *iš-ni-ú* [37]*i-na* ^{d}utu^{ši} : *Pí-lá-ah-Ištar* : *e-ru-ba-ni* [38]*ki-ma iš-tí-šu lá ta-li-ki-ni* : *li-bu-šu* [39]*im-ra-aṣ-ma* : 5 *u*$_4$*-me-e* : *a-na ki-dim* [40]*lá ú-ṣí* : *šu-ma* : *mu-tám* : *ša-ni-a-am* [41]*ta-šé-e-i* : *šu-up-ri-ma* : *lu i-dí* [42]*šu-ma lá ki-*

a-am : *tí-ib-<e>-ma a-tal-ki-/im* u.e. [43]*šu-ma* : *lá ta-li-ki-im* [44]*i-a-tí* : *i-na pá-ni* : *a-wi-lim* [45]*tù-ša-zi-zi* le.e. [46]*ú šé-ri-ki* : *tù-ha-li-qí* : *ú a-na-ku* [47]*lá a-tù-ar-ma* : *šu-um-ki lá a-za-kà-ar* [48]*ú-lá a-ha-tí a-tí ú mì-ma i-a-tí* [49]*lá ta-ša-pí-ri-im*

[1–2]Say to Lamassatum and Šalimma: thus (says) Ummi-Išhara.

[2–3]Concerning the letter that you sent me, in which (you wrote) as follows: [3–4]"Why does he not send me someone?" [4–5]His messenger did arrive, but it was I who sent (him). [5–7]I talked to him several times, but each time he became angry, saying: [7–9]"Several times a letter of mine went to her, but she refused to come here! [9–10]What I could write her now really goes beyond all the several letters of mine that have already reached her."

[11–12]The gentleman has become very annoyed by the matter saying: [12–13]"Since she refuses to come, you must not speak to me again!" [14–16]If you are my sister, do not keep writing me lies, (and) do not write to him for any silver. [16–17]I wrote to him concerning the silver, and he (said): [17–19]"Should I really oblige her mother or her brothers for all the ½ mina of silver for her expenses? [19–20]Or is there no silver available from my outstanding claims, (at least) 10 shekels? [21–24]And if there is not, let her ask for 10 shekels of silver for her expenses from her mother or her brothers, [24–25]and as for myself, here I will give it back (only if) she comes here."

[25–26]Do not keep on sending to me all sorts of words or letters. [27–28]You have brought me into conflict with the gentleman, (and) he (keeps telling) me: [28–31]"Since, not (acting as) my *amtum*-wife, she refuses to come here, you must not mention her name again to me, or you will no longer be my sister!" [31–33]Why are others managing your children and your household (in Aššur) while you are staying over there (in Kaneš). [33–34]Urgent! Do not let your children waste away, and do not take me away from the gentleman's house! [35–36]If there is a possibility for you to come here, get ready and leave for here before the gentleman changes his mind! [37]The day Pilah-Ištar arrived here, [38–40]since you did not come with him, he (the gentleman) felt very unhappy, and for 5 days he did not go out (of his home). [40–41]Write me if you are looking for another husband, so I know it. [42]If not, then get ready and leave for here.

[43–45]If you do not come here, you will bring me into conflict with the gentleman, [46–47]and you will let your children waste away, and I, I will never mention your name again! [48–49]You will no longer be my sister, and you must not write me any more.

Bibliography: This tablet was published by Veenhof (2007) as Kt 91/k 385; then as AKT 8, 206. The envelope, Kt 91/k 386, was omitted in AKT 8 (see fig. 15 below). Text translated by Michel (2014b, 209–10). It is very small and presents a microscopic regular script. Collated May 2012.

Comments: Ummī-Išhara, the consecrated daughter of Elamma, sent her letter from Aššur to her sister, Šalimma, in Kaneš. Šalimma stayed with their mother, Lamassatum, there, refusing to go back to Aššur to join her husband. Ummī-Išhara writes as a wise older sister, giving advice to Šalimma to save her marriage. The so-called gentleman was Šalimma's husband, Ir'am-Aššur, who felt very lonely in Aššur. Ummī-Išhara used several arguments to convince her sister to come back home: she is afraid that if, after a while, Ir'am-Aššur might ask to divorce, such a separation would then estrange her from her brother-in-law's house. Her lack of children might have made her especially sensitive to her sister's disregard of them. Ummi-Išhara's advice to her sister either to divorce or to come back to Aššur and take up her duties.

Fig. 15. Imprint of the seal used by Ummī-Išhara on the envelope 264e (Kt 91/k 386). Photograph by Cécile Michel. © Kültepe Archaeological Mission.

6
Portraits of Assyrian and Anatolian Women

As is clear from preceding chapters, the Old Assyrian archives offer a considerable body of information about women. Women in Aššur are better documented than those in Anatolia. Living for long periods without their husbands, they wrote them and other relatives living in Kaneš many letters, rich in detail, about their day-to-day activities and business dealings. We lack their marriage and divorce documents or any other contracts to which they would have been parties, because these were kept in their houses in Aššur. The Assyrian and Anatolian women living in Kaneš, on the other hand, sent letters to other commercial settlements in Anatolia and to Aššur, so this correspondence is not found in Kaneš. Rather, they kept in their houses there any letters they received from their spouses traveling to central Anatolia and all their contracts, whether familial or commercial. Some of the letters they sent to their husbands might have been taken back home by them. Thus the nature of the sources documenting women in Aššur and women in Kaneš is quite different.

Drawing a portrait of these women is often challenging, because whereas some are well known and have names not in common use, such as Akatiya, Tarām-Kūbi, or Kunnaniya, others have relatively common names, and it is difficult to distinguish among them.[1] Moreover, some used two names, such as Ištar-baštī, daughter of Imdī-ilum, who was also called by the nickname Zizizi.

Thanks to their vivid letters found in their husbands' archives in the lower town of Kaneš, the lives of some Assyrian women living in Aššur can be reconstructed. Certain activities of Assyrian women residing at Kaneš, having followed their husbands or having traveled to Kaneš to get married

1. For a tentative list of some of these women with their cities of residence, see Hecker 1978.

there, are also documented, through the letters they sent while traveling or received from their relatives.[2] Women in Aššur could belong to prominent families, such as Akatiya and Šīmat-Suen, the sisters of Uṣur-ša-Ištar, who was in direct contact with the ruler of Aššur (**127, 142, 173, 237, 240, 242, 265–274**). Akatiya may have been married to a member of the royal family.[3] Tarām-Kūbi's letters were found in the houses of her husband, Innaya, and of her brother, Imdī-ilum, together with a few letters sent by their sister, Šīmat-Aššur (**128–129, 170, 206–207, 252, 286–290, 292, 295-297**). Both houses were excavated by illicit diggers and by Hrozný in 1925.[4] These women managed their households with the help of female slaves, brought up their young children, participated in long-distance trade by producing textiles, and represented their husbands' and brothers' interests in the city of Aššur. Ahaha, the daughter of Pūšu-kēn and Lamassī, is also well documented because she remained single, consecrated to the god Aššur (**130, 141, 246, 275–284**). She exchanged letters with her brothers after their father's death in the course of settling his affairs. She also invested in various partnerships along with her male investors.

By contrast, the lives and concerns of Anatolian women living in Kaneš are still poorly known.[5] Since they seldom left the town, they hardly had the opportunity to write letters that would turn up at Kaneš. Furthermore, only those married to Assyrian merchants are documented; the others appear only in loan contracts. One may imagine that they were happier in their conjugal lives compared to the Assyrian women living in Aššur, if only because they were closer to their Assyrian spouses during the period those were active in Anatolia. These women often stayed at home in Kaneš. Such was the case, for example, of Hatala, Laqēpum's wife (**140, 202, 322–324**); Šišahšušar, who was married to Aššur-nādā (**132, 157, 313–321**); or Anna-anna, Ennum-Aššur's wife (**22, 189, 192–193, 325–334**). There, they lived with their children, some servants, and sometimes other mem-

---

2. Some of the Assyrian women were the subject of various publications: Veenhof 1972, 111–18 (Lamassī) and 111–23 (other women); Garelli 1979 (Tarīš-mātum and Ištar-Lamassī); Michel 1991, 1:76–88 (Tarām-Kūbi); Günbattı 1992 (Waqqurtum, Lamassī, Ištar-baštī, and Nuhšatum); Łyczkowska 1978 (Šūbultum); Matouš 1982 (Tarām-kubi); Michel 2001a, 465–70 (twenty-five different women); Veenhof 2015c (Nuhšatum).

3. Michel 2015c.

4. Hrozný 1927.

5. Hecker 1978, Michel 1997e, Albayrak 1998, Donbaz 2008, Michel 2008c, Dercksen 2015b.

bers of the family, as well as visitors, including their husband's business associates. Unlike the women at Aššur, they rarely mention textile production. Their occupations were largely restricted to domestic chores and to their participation in their spouses' commercial activities. Their involvement with animal husbandry probably explains why they were not very mobile compared to the Assyrian women residing in Kaneš. If, however, their husbands died without having made a formal arrangement for their future, such as a will, Anatolian women could face difficult circumstances, as shown by the case of Kunnaniya, the wife of Aššur-mūtappil, son of Pūšu-kēn (**107**, **158**, **299–312**).

Akatiya and Šīmat-Suen, Sisters of Uṣur-ša-Ištar

Akatiya and Šīmat-Suen were sisters of Uṣur-ša-Ištar, son of Aššur-imittī, whose large archive was excavated in 1962 in squares C–D/11–12 of the lower town at Kültepe.[6] They had two other brothers, Iddin-Aššur and Hunniya.[7] Both sisters were living in Aššur and sent jointly the letter **237** to

6. T. Özgüç 1986, 5–6, fifth building, 116, fig. 10; and for the seals, N. Özgüç 2006, 10–44; the seal of Akatiya has not been identified. This section concerns above all Akatiya; Šīmat-Suen's letters are studied only as they mention Akatiya and her death; she may have been married to Mannum-kī-Aššur, to whom she wrote the letters AKT 2, 52, and Kt n/k 720, published by Erol 2010. If this hypothesis is correct, then the Šīmat-Suen who wrote **142** was a homonym married to Aššur-taklāku. This archive is currently being studied by Çeçen.

7. AKT 4, 26:2, 73, 74, 82. The status of Lamassatum, who wrote the unpublished letter Kt n/k 792 to Uṣur-ša-Ištar and Hunniya, is unclear. She could be the wife of the father or of a brother, as suggested in the unpublished letter Kt n/k 204:39–40: *Lá-ma-sà-tum i-nu-mì a-na*, é *a-bi*$_4$*-ku-nu* : *té-ru-bu mì-ma* : *lá tù-šé-ri-ib*, "Lamassatum, when she entered your father's house, did not bring anything into it"; lines cited by Veenhof 2012a, 176 n. 20. She could also be an unmarried sister (**270**) or a niece of Akatiya, daughter of Uṣur-ša-Ištar, if she was the one concerned in **265**. In the letter Kt n/k 792:3–4, 12–24, she urged the two men to take care of their father's house: "Why have you neglected your father's house?… Why do you not take care for your father's house, and why do you not let me take care (of it)? Why does the domesticity perish? Your accursed brother is about to destroy your father's house. He keeps on acting badly. He has destroyed your father's reputation! Everywhere, he keeps on doing terrible things!"; *mì-šu-um* é *a-bi-ku-nu*, *ta-dí-a-ma*, … *mì-šu-um* é *a-bi-ku-nu*, *lá ta-ša-ra*, *ú i-atí la ta-ša-ra-ni*, *mì-šu-um* : *áš-tí-pì-ru-um*, *i-ha-liq a-hu-ku-nu*, *ha-al-pu-um*, é *a-bi-ku-nu* : *a-na*, *ha-lu-qí-im i-za-az*, *lá-am-ni-iš e-ta-na-pá-áš*, *šu-mì* : *a-bi-ku-nu* sig$_5$, *a-na mì-ma-ma* : *iš-ta-kán*, *a-na-nu-um* : *ú a-na-nu-um*, *ha-al-pá-tim e-ta-na-pá-áš* (lines cited by Çeçen 1996b, 16 n. 33).

their older brother, Uṣur-ša-Ištar, in Anatolia.[8] Their father, Aššur-imittī, was the uncle of the merchant Imdī-ilum and his sister Tarām-Kūbi, wife of Innaya; both merchants have been the objects of detailed studies (see below, the family tree of Tarām-Kūbi, fig. 17).[9] In one of the unpublished letters Akatiya wrote to her older brother Uṣur-ša-Ištar, she mentions the death of their uncle Šu-Labān, and a debt he owed her (Kt n/k 153).

In the archives excavated in 1962 were two letters sent by the ruler of Aššur, showing close relationships between Uṣur-ša-Ištar's family and the royal family of Aššur. The first letter was addressed by the king to two of his sons, Aduda and Enna-Suen, and to Uṣur-ša-Ištar; it concerned trade matters.[10] In the second letter, addressed to Uṣur-ša-Ištar alone, the king rebuked him in the name of his sister, presumably Akatiya, because of his failure to inform her about a commercial transaction: "You are sending silver to your representatives, but to your sister, you do not send her a letter about a deposit (for her) from your silver. Your sister became very angry with you. If you love me, write, when your report arrives here, to your sister that she must attend to your representatives and watch what they do. Your representatives are not reliable!"[11] The ruler of Aššur was engaged in Uṣur-ša-Ištar's private family affairs, and he was very close to Akatiya. She could have either been married to a member of the Aššur royal family or held an important role in the city of Aššur, perhaps as a high priestess. We may note that, half a century later, one of the wives of the great king Šamšī-Addu, perhaps the mother of Išme-Dagan, was also named Akatiya.[12]

---

8. Text **240**. See also Çeçen 1996b, contra Donbaz 1991, 7–9. For this family and its activities linked to the copper trade, see also Dercksen 1996, 140–49.

9. For Imdī-ilum, see Ichisar 1981 and Larsen 1982; for Innaya and his wife Tarām-Kūbi, see Michel 1991; 2001a, 464–70, and below, pp. 426–34.

10. The letter AKT 2, 22, was edited by Dercksen 2004a, 106–7; for the letters of the rulers of Aššur, see Michel 2015c and Erol 2018, with previous literature.

11. Kt n/k 1538:3–18: kù-babbar *a-na, ša ki-ma ku-a-tí, tù-šé-ba-la-ma máš-kà-at*, kù-babbar^{pí}*-kà* : *ṭup-pá-am, a-na a-ha-tí-kà, ú-la tù-šé-ba-lá-ší-im*, lo.e. *da-ni-iš* : *a-ha-at-kà, tal-mì-na-ku-um* : *šu-ma*, rev. *ta-ra-a-ma-ni i-nu-mì, té-er-ta-kà* : *i-lá-kà-ni, a-na* <*a*>*-ha-tí-kà* : *šu-up-ra-ma, i-na* sag : *ša-zu-úz-tí-kà, lu ta-zi-iz-ma, qá-sú-nu* : *lu ta-ṭù-ul, ša-zu-úz-ta-kà, la da-am-qú*. This text is published by Çeçen 1990, and translated by Michel 2001a, no. 14; 2015c, 51–52 (text 24).

12. Ziegler 1999, 120. Akatiya was the name of Yasmah-Addu's mother, whose correspondence was found in room 110 of the palace at Mari, at the entrance to the women's residence.

Akatiya is the author of the only Old Assyrian letter-prayer thus far found (**242**). It was unearthed at Aššur and is unfortunately very broken; only the beginning remains: "Say to Tašmētum, my lady: thus (says) Akatiya, your servant: Let the gentlemen you told me about come here; I have no one but you! [...]." She seems to have had a message from the goddess announcing the arrival of someone and waits for this person; she was in a difficult situation and asked for help from the goddess. Letter-prayers to gods were often written by members of the elite.[13] Whatever was her position, Akatiya was much concerned by the behavior of her siblings (**270**), and in particular of Uṣur-ša-Ištar. She repeatedly reminded her brother to care for her by praying to the god Aššur and the family god (**237**).[14] She was also worried about the "silver of the god" and votive offerings; she asked her brothers to come back to Aššur, not only because she missed or needed them, but also to go to the temple of Aššur and to fulfill their religious duties (**265**, Kt n/k 153). In a unique letter sent by Uṣur-ša-Ištar, of which we have a copy, he reacted to the "bad letters" of his sister, asking her to pray to Aššur and her god for him (**240**).

Akatiya represented her brothers in Aššur in the business affairs of their deceased father, paying debts to the eponym (**265**); she was owed a *tadmiqum*-trust and asked to be paid back (**267**). She was presumably living in the family house in Aššur, together with her brother Hunniya, and managed the household. She had to look after a young woman, either the daughter of Uṣur-ša-Ištar or wife of Hunniya, and complained about her conduct, which became even worse after Hunniya's departure (**266**, **267**, Kt n/k 212). This young woman finally left the house with her belongings and bronze objects.[15] In a letter addressed to Hunniya, Akatiya explained how her situation had deteriorated, for she lacked money and grain of good quality to prepare the daily beer (**269**). She informed Uṣur-ša-Ištar of the death of a woman called Kanua (**267**) and explained that she was in mourning and thus unable to leave the house (**268**). She asked her brother to come back home, and he himself informed her that he was on his way to

---

13. Kryszat 2003.

14. The family god of Aššur-imittī and his sons, Uṣur-ša-Ištar and Hunniya, was the goddess Ištar-ZA-AT, according to Kryszat 2006b. For this goddess, see above, p. 339 n. 5. But Akatiya's personal goddess might have been Tašmētum (**243**).

15. See the unpublished letter sent by Akatiya to Hunniya, Kt n/k 212:11–14, cited by Dercksen 1996, 78 n. 261.

Aššur (**267**). However, her situation presumably got worse, and she turned to the goddess, asking her support in a letter-prayer (**242**).

The death of Akatiya is documented in several letters exchanged between her brothers (**271**) or sent by her sister Šīmat-Suen to her brother Uṣur-ša-Ištar (**272–274** and Kt n/k 204).[16] According to Iddin-Aššur, there was, among the goods that Akatiya left, one talent of copper that had been used for her grave.[17] She had also left some bronze objects, from which Aššur officials took almost thirty minas to pay the eponym.[18] This could be linked to a debt of one mina of silver that she owed to Aššur City Hall and for which goods were pledged (**271**). Šīmat-Suen complained that the creditors of both their father and sister claimed reimbursement and were harassing her and threatening to ruin the paternal house (**271**, **273**).[19] She urged her brother to come back to Aššur, to settle the whole business himself, and to honor the god Aššur, for the benefit of his own well-being and the reputation of the paternal house (**272**, **274**). The young woman relative Akatiya had in charge was later on the responsibility of her sister, Šīmat-Suen (**273–274**).

16. There are more letters sent by Šīmat-Suen that do not mention Akatiya. For example, in Kt n/k 268 (Çeçen and Gökçek 2017, 466–67, 478–79), she informs her elder brother of the arrival of Hunniya with garments and belts.

17. Kt n/k 204:25–28: 1 gú urudu, *ša A-kà-tí-a* : *té-zi-bu* : *um-ma*, *I-dí-A-šùr-ma* : *a-na qú-bu-ur*, *A-kà-tí-a* : *ga-me-er*; "As for the 1 talent of copper that Akatiya left, Iddin-Aššur said that it has been bent spent on the tomb of Akatiya." These lines are cited by Veenhof 2014, 364 n. 113.

18. Kt n/k 204:15–22: *i-na* zabar, lo.e. *ša A-kà-tí-a* : *té-zi-bu-ni*, 30 lá ½ *ma-na* zabar, é *ku-nu-ki* : *bé-ru* : *ú-šé-ṣí-ú-nim-ma*, rev. *a-na li-mì-im*, *bé-ru ù I-dí-A-šùr iš-qú-lu*, *ší-tí* : zabar *a-na ša-áp-ra-tim*, *i-ta-du-ú*; "the *bērū*-officials took out of the sealed storehouse 30 minus ½ minas of bronze from the bronze (objects) that Akatiya had left, and the *bērū*-officials and Iddin-Aššur weighed it out to the eponym. The remaining bronze (objects) were deposited as pledges." (Lines cited by Dercksen 1996, 80 n. 272). This amount of bronze corresponds to about 1 mina of silver. This is also mentioned in the unpublished letters Kt n/k 107 and Kt n/k 540.

19. An unpublished letter sent by Akatiya to Anīna also refers to threats against the paternal house: "Take all the silver that falls into your hands and come here with the silver, then clear (i.e., remove the claims) on the spirits of our father and on our paternal house"; Kt 93/k 74:36–40: *ma-lá* kù-babbar, *i-na qá-tí-kà* : *ma-aq-tù* : *le-qé-/a-ma*, *iš-tí* kù-babbar : *al-kam-ma* : *e-ṭé-me*, *a-bi-ni ù pu-ú-ut* : é *a-bi-ni*, *za-ki-ma*; lines cited by Michel 2008f, 190 n. 60. The father was presumably buried under the floor of the house, and the children tried to prevent the sale of the house; see Michel 2009a.

265. Akatiya Asks Her Brothers to Come to Aššur to Pay Their Late Father's Debts

Obv. ^{1}*[a]-na Ú-ṣú-ur-ší-Ištar* ^{2}*ù I-dí-A-šùr* ^{3}*ù Hu-ni-a* ^{4}*qí-bi*$_4$*-ma um-ma* ^{5}*A-kà-tí-a-ma a-na* kù-babbar ^{6}*ša ik-ri-be-e* ^{7}*lá ša-al-ṭá-tù-nu* ^{8}*a-ṣé-er* : *ma-ni-ha-tí-a* ^{9}*i-a-a-tí-im* ^{10}*ú ṣú-ha-ar-ku-nu* ^{11}*re-ša-ma* ^{12}*lá i-na-ší-i* lo.e. ^{13}*i-na qá-tí* : dingir rev. ^{14}*šu-ma a-hu-ú-a* ^{15}*a-tù-nu* kù-babbar ^{16}*ša* dingir : *pá-hi-ra-ma* ^{17}*ú ba-a-ba-tí-im* ^{18}*ša a-bi-ni i-na šé-pí-ku-nu* ^{19}*li-ma-am* ^{20}*lu né-pu-ul* ^{21}*al-kà-nim-ma* ^{22}*e-ni-a* : *ú e-en* ^{23}*A-šùr* : *i-na šu-ul-mì-im* ^{24}*am-ra-ma*$^{!}$(AM) : ^{25}*i-na* é$^{be\text{-}et}$ u.e. ^{26}*[l]i-mì-im* ^{27}*i-na-du-ma* le.e. ^{28}*a-ma-tù-a* : *lá ú-ṣí-a* ^{29}kù-babbar : *ša* dumu *I-ku-ni-im* ^{30}*pá-hi-ra-ma* : *re-eq* (*sic*!) ^{31}*i-na pá-ni-ku-nu* : *bi*$_4$*-lá-nim*

$^{1-5}$Say [t]o Uṣur-ša-Ištar, Iddin-Aššur and Hunniya: thus (says) Akatiya.

$^{5-7}$You have no right to claim authority over the silver of the votive offerings. $^{8-13}$In addition to my own misery, also your boy is unable to raise his head due to the "hand of the god." $^{14-16}$If you are my brothers, collect the silver of the god, $^{17-20}$so that we can pay to the eponym our father's outstanding claims from what you ship here. $^{21-24}$Come to see me in person and to see (the god) Aššur in person in good standing, $^{25-27}$and one will deposit (the silver) in the eponym's office, and ^{28}your female slaves have not left. $^{29-30}$Gather (pl.) the silver of the son of Ikūnum and depart (sg.); ^{31}bring (pl.) it personally.

Bibliography: Unpublished text found during the 1962 season; its inventory number is Kt n/k 1189. Lines 1–24 cited by Çeçen 1996b, 13–14 n. 17; lines 14–20 by Günbattı 1990, 128; lines 25–27 by Günbattı 1992, 233; lines 28–31 courtesy of Çeçen.

Comments: Akatiya writes to her brother concerning votive offerings of an unnamed god, presumably Aššur. She accuses them of having abandoned her and of not paying enough attention to the god; thus she asks them to come to visit her and to worship the god.

Line 13: the "hand of the god" means that the boy was seized by disease.

Line 30: the form *re-eq* is an imperative second-person masculine singular of *rêqum*, where a plural form is needed.

266. Akatiya Complains about the Bad Behavior of Her Niece

Obv. ^{1}a-na Ú-ṣur-ší-Ištar ^{2}qí-bi$_{4}$*-ma um-ma A-kà-tí-/a-ma ^{3}mì-šu-um :* ta-ki-li ^{4}ša me-er-i-tí-kà ^{5}ta-áš-ta-na-me :* a-ma ^{6}Hu-ni-a ú* A-mur-dingir ^{7}ša-il$_{5}$:* a-na šu-mì ^{8}a-na ki-dim ak-ta-na-/lá$^{!}$(LU)-ší$^{!}$(ŠU) ^{9}iš-tí-a :* lo.e. ^{10}tù-uš$^{!}$(IŠ)-té-ṣa ^{11}iš-tù Hu-ni-a rev. ^{12}ú-ṣa*-ni :* nu-a-ha-am ^{13}ú pá-ša-ha-am ^{14}lá ta-dí-ni :* um-ma ší-/it-ma ^{15}i-na ú-ri-im ^{16}lu-ší-ib :* mì-nam e-pu-uš ^{17}lu-mu-un li-bi$_{4}$-im ^{18}tí-šu-a-am :* i-lá-an ^{19}ku-a-tí :* ú šé-ri-kà ^{20}a-na-ku :* ma-nam i-šu u.e. ^{21}šu-up-ra-am ^{22}a-dí ta-lá-kà-ni le.e. ^{23}ša ki-ma ku-a-tí ^{24}x-ha-tim lu-na-e-hu-ší$^{?}$

$^{1-2}$Say to Uṣur-ša-Ištar: thus (says) Akatiya.

$^{3-5}$Why do you keep listening to slander from your daughter? Well, $^{6-7}$ask Hunniya and Amur-ilī! $^{7-8}$Because I constantly prevent her from going outside, $^{9-10}$she quarrels with me. $^{11-12}$After Hunniya left, $^{12-14}$she gave me no rest or peace, (saying) as follows: $^{15-16}$"I would rather live on the roof!" What have I done (that) she is angry with me? Apart from you and your child, who else do I have? Write me. Until you come here, … let your representatives calm her!

Bibliography: Tablet published by Çeçen and Gökçek 2016, 248–49, 253–56, as Kt n/k 657. Collations on photos (there is no photo of the right edge).

Comments: In this letter to her brother Uṣur-ša-Ištar, Akatiya complains about the bad behavior of her niece, who lives with her while her father is away. The letter shows several mistakes in signs and grammar. The end of the last line on the left edge is not visible on the photo.

Line 8: the pronominal suffix should be feminine: *aktanallaši*.

Line 15: for a different interpretation of *ūrum*, "nakedness," see the comment to TC 3, 93, in Larsen 2002, 23.

Line 24: the form *luna"ehūši* would be an optative D, 3rd masc. pl., of *na'āhum*. Before the verb, the editors of the text read *ṣú-ha-<ar>-tim*, but a genitive is not possible.

267. Akatiya Asks Her Brother for Help to Clear Their Father's House Debts

[1]*a-na Ú-ṣú-ur-ša-Ištar* [2]*qí-bi-ma um-ma* [3]*A-kà-tí-a-ma* [4]*i-na ṭup-pé-e-kà* [5]*um-ma a-ta-ma : ha-ra-ni* [6]*a-na A-lim*^{ki} *: ša ha-ra-šu-nu* [7]*a-na A-lim*^{ki} :* é *a-bi-šu-nu* [8]*lá e-šu-ru : ṣú-ha-ar-šu-nu* [9]*lá e-šu-ru : áš-ta-na-pá-/ra-kum* lo.e. [10]*iš-tù / Hu-ni-a* [11]*ú-ṣú** *: um-ma* rev. [12]*a-na-ku-ma* [13]*lu ki-na-tám* [14]*iš-té-en*$_6$ *ṭur*$_4$**-da-am* [15]*lu* kù-babbar 1 gín [16]*i-na ša ta-ad-mì-iq-/tí-a* [17]*šé-bi-lám : iš-tù-ma* [18]*dá-ni-ni-ni : ha-ra-kà* [19]*a-na A-lim*^{ki} *áš-ta-na-par-/ma* u.e. [20]*ba-a-ba-tim ša a-bi*$_4$**-/ni* [21]*za-ki-ma* le.e. [22]*i-pá-ni-kà bi-lá-am* [23]*a-na-kam Kà-nu-a : a-na ší-im-tí-ša* [24]*i-ta-lá-ak-ma : a-šu-mì-ša* [25]*lá a-la-kà-am*

[1–3]Say to Uṣur-ša-Ištar: thus (says) Akatiya.

[4–5]In your tablets, (you wrote) as follows: "I am about to travel to the city (of Aššur)." Do those who travel to the city (of Aššur) not care about of their father's house? [8–9]Do they not care about their boys? I have been constantly writing to you. [10–12]When Hunniya left, I (wrote you) as follows: [13–14]"Send me either one menial (servant), [15–17]or send me at least every shekel of silver from my *tadmiqum*-trust." [17–19]If it is true that your travel to the city (of Aššur) *is really imminent*, I keep writing that [20–21]you must clear the outstanding goods of our father, and [22]bring (them) along personally. [23–24]Here, Kanua died, [24–25]and because of her, I will not come.

Bibliography: Tablet published by Çeçen and Gökçek 2016, 249–50, 257–60, as Kt n/k 1065. Collations on photos (photos are distorted; there is no photo of the right and the left edges).

Comments: In this letter, Akatiya reminds her brother that he had promised to come to Aššur. Those she is mentioning, who came to Aššur but did not take care of family affairs, might be their brothers. She has to deal with the debts left behind by their father and asks his brother for some help. As the previous one, the letter shows several mistakes.

Line 13: the word *ki-na-tám* has been interpreted as the defective writing of the Old Babylonian word *kinattum* (*CAD* K, 381/1a).

Line 18: the translation of *dá-ni-ni-ni* is tentative; it could be an imperative from *danānum* II + *ni* as subordinating.

Lines 23–24: literally, "She went to her destiny"; the *-ša* suggests that Kanua is a woman.

268. Akatiya Is in Mourning and Feels Abandoned by Her Brother

Obv. ^{1}*a-na Ú-ṣur-ší-Ištar* ^{2}*qí-bi-ma : um-ma* ^{3}*A-kà-tí-a-ma* ^{4}*mì-šu : ša pá-NU-kà* ^{5}*ta-áš-ta-na-pá-ra-ni* ^{6}*Šu-Be-lúm* : kù-babbar ^{7}*i-nu-mì : ub-lá-ni*$^{!}$(NIM) ^{8}*lá e-ta-wu-kum* ^{9}*i-na bi*$_4$*-ki-tim* ^{10}*wa-áš-ba-ku* ^{11}*i*-iti-kam : *Hu-bur* ^{12}*i-li-kam* lo.e. ^{13}*ba-pí-ru-um ú* še rev. ^{14}*e-pí-iš* : (°erasure) ^{15}*ba-a-ba-tim* ^{16}*ša a-bi*$_4$*-a* ^{17}*za-ki-a-ma : tí-ib-a-ma* ^{18}*a-tal-kam : šu-ma* ^{19}*a-hi a-ta : šu-ma* ^{20}*a-bi a-ta : ma-nam* ^{21}*a-lá-nu-kà : i-šu* ^{22}*mì-šu-um : a-na-ku* ^{23}*i-bi*$_4$*-ki-tim* ^{24}*wa-áš-ba-ku-ma* ^{25}*li-bi*$_4$*-i* u.e. ^{26}*ṣa-ar-pu ú* ^{27}*šé-ṭù-tí : tal-ta-qí-a-/am*

$^{1-3}$Say to Uṣur-ša-Ištar: thus (says) Akatiya.

$^{4-5}$Why is it that you keep writing me …? $^{6-8}$When he brought the silver, Šu-Bēlum did not speak to you. $^{9-10}$I am in mourning. ^{11}When he came in the month Hubur (vi), $^{13-14}$beer bread and barley were ready. $^{15-18}$Clear the outstanding claims of my father, set out and come here. $^{18-21}$If you are really my brother, if you are really my father—whom else besides you do I have?—$^{22-27}$why did you keep showing contempt for me when I was mourning and felt heartache?

Bibliography: Tablet published by Çeçen and Gökçek 2016, 249–50, 257–60, as Kt n/k 1108. Collations on photos.

Comments: In this letter to her brother, Akatiya complains that she has nothing left and none to take care of her. She feels lonely, and he does not check in on her when she has lost a loved one, presumably Kanua, mentioned in the previous letter. Waiting for her brother to come back home, she prepared food and beer for him.

Line 9: for *bikītum*, "bewailing," see Veenhof in AKT 8, 268.

Lines 25–27: the expression *libbī ṣarip* is also attested in AKT 8, 206:6, and *šeṭūtam laqā'um* can be found in AKT 4, 69:17.

269. Akatiya Stored Barley, but Its Quality Is Not Good to Prepare Beer

Obv. ^{1}*a-na Hu-ni-a qí-bi-ma um-ma* ^{2}*A-kà-tí-a-ma tù-úṣ-a-ma* ^{3}*ù ta-am-tí*$^{!}$(TA)*-ší «a» du-lam* ^{4}*ša A-lim ù-ul ma-DU-BA-am* […] ^{12}*šé-am* 10 baneš$^{!}$ *lá-áš-pu-uk-ma* ^{13}é *a-bi*$_4$*-ku-nu* ^{14}*lu-kà-bi*$_4$*-it ú a-na-ku* : ^{15}*lu kà-áb-ta-ku* kù-babbar [16]*ša tù-šé-bi*$_4$*-lá-ni : a-na ú-ṭí-tim* [17]*lá id-mì-iq ù ša i-ba-ší-ú* [18]*šé-um lá da-mì-iq* 20 silà [19]*ší-ma-am i-ša-ú-mu-ni-ku-ma* [20]*ù-šé-bu-lu-ni-kum* [21]*ù a-ba-pì-ri-im* [22]*ša ta-áš-pu-ra-ni šé-um* le.e. [23]*lá da-mì-iq lá e-pá-áš* [24]*i-na da-ma-aq ša-tim* [25]*e-pá-áš*

[1–2]Say to Hunniya, thus (says) Akatiya.

[2–3]You left, then you forgot (me)! As to the misery of the city (of Aššur) or the [...] [12]I wish to store 10 *ṣimdum*-measures of barley, so that [13–15]I can bring respect to your father's house and be respectable myself. [15–17]As for the silver that you sent me for (buying) grain, it proved to be bad, [17–18]and the available barley is also not good. [19–20]They will purchase for you 20 liters (*sic*!), and will send it to you. [21–23]And for the beer bread that you wrote to me about, the barley is not good, (so) I will not prepare (it); [24–25]when the season become favorable, I will make some.

Bibliography: Unpublished text excavated during the 1962 excavation season; its inventory number is Kt n/k 1372. Lines 1–4 and 12–25 cited by Çeçen 1996, 12 and 14 n. 21; lines 21–23 by Günbattı 1992, 232; lines 12, 16–18, 21–25 by Öz 2014, 13, 51. Lines 5–11 remain unpublished.

Comments: Akatiya writes to her brother Hunniya, who was previously living with her and had left for Anatolia. She complains about the bad situation in Aššur: she has not enough money to buy barley, and the grain she bought is of bad quality, and thus she did not prepare beer.

Line 17: the amount of silver is not sufficient to buy grain.

Line 18: the amount of barley purchase is far too little.

---

270. Akatiya Rebukes a Young Man of the Family about His Marriage

Obv. [1]*um-ma A-kà-tí-a-ma* [2]*a-na A-šur-ma-lik* [3]*qí-bi*$_4$*-ma mì-šu* [4]*ša a-ša-tám* [5]*ta-hu-zu* [6]*a-na-ku* lo.e. [7]*a-na-kam* rev. [8]*a-bu-ša* [9]*al-le* [10]*a-bu-ša e-ku-ša-/am* [11]*a-šé-pé-šu* [12]*mu-qú-ut* [13]*ú kà-bi-sú* u.e. [14]*ra-qá-tám dí-šu-um*

[1–3]Thus (says) Akatiya: say to Aššur-malik.

[3–5]Why have you taken a wife in marriage? [6–9]As for me, should I handle? her father here? [10]Her father has gone off. [11–12]Fall at his feet [13]and honor him. [14]Give him a fine (textile).

Bibliography: Tablet published by Larsen as AKT 6d, 742 (Kt 94 k 1722).

Comments: Akatiya addresses her letter to Aššur-malik, who could be her younger brother, her son, or her nephew. This man has just gotten married, and Akatiya, who seems unhappy with this marriage, suggests to him to honor his father-in-law.

---

271. Akatiya Died, Leaving a Debt in Silver and Bronze Objects

Obv. ^{1}a-na Ú-ṣú-ur-ša-Ištar qí-bi$_{4}$-ma ^{2}um-ma I-dí-A-šur-ma A-kà-tí-a ^{3}me-[t]a*-at kù-babbar 1 ma-na ^{4}hu-[b]u-lá-am : té-zi-i[b] :* ú ^{5}sí-pá-ru : a-na ša-áp-ra-tim ^{6}na-du : sí-[pá]-ru* ša Lá-ma-sa-/tim ^{7}1 gín lá i-ba-š[í]-ú [a]-na ^{8}ša-ap$_{1}$-ra-tim : na$^{!}$(A)-du* [a]-na-kam* ^{9}ša ki-ma : E-lá : i-bu-lu-uṭ ^{10}A-kà-tí-a : i-li-ku-nim-ma ^{11}Puzur$_{4}$-ì-lí ú-[š]a*-hi-sú-nu ^{12}i-tù-ru-ma iš-tù A-kà-tí-a lo.e. ^{13}me-ta-at-ni : i-li-ku-nim ^{14}nu-ša-hi-sú-nu a-wi-lu rev. ^{15}ša-ak-ṣú : šu-ma lá ta-li-/kam ^{16}qú-lá-lu é a-bi-ni ^{17}i-ša-ku-nu a-wi-lu-um ^{18}lá da-am-qú-um : ú«-mu-»um ^{19}é a-bi-ni e-ma-ar ^{20}Lá-ma-sà-tum i-na é$^{\text{bé-tí}}$-/kà ^{21}ta-ta-ša-ab$_{1}$ um-ma ^{22}ší-it-ma i-na ší-ma-tim ^{23}a-ha-tum : a-ha-at : ta-bé-/el ^{24}ú ší-ma-tim : a-pá-ta-im ^{25}ta-za-az : šu-ma : lá ta-li-/kam ^{26}qú-lá-lu é a-bi-ni i-ša-ku-nu$^{!}$ ^{27}a-ta ma-lá-kà : a-dí : ša dumu u.e. ^{28}Ì-lí-a-lim : lu ṭup-pá-am il$_{5}$-qé ^{29}lu ší-bé-e a-na ba-ab$_{1}$ dingir-<lu>-/im ^{30}ú-šé-ri-id uz-ni le.e. ^{31}pé-té ta-ah-sí-is-tám ša ^{32}Ú-sà-nim ú ta-pá-e-šu ^{33}lu ša-ṣú-ra-at

$^{1-2}$Say to Uṣur-ša-Ištar: thus (says) Iddin-Aššur.

$^{2-4}$Akatiya is dead. She left a debt of one mina of silver, and $^{5-6}$the bronze objects have been deposited as pledges. $^{6-7}$As for the br[onze objects] of Lamassatum, there is nothing of any value available; $^{7-8}$they have been deposited as pledges. $^{8-10}$Ela's representatives came [he]re while Akatiya was still alive, and ^{11}Puzur-ilī instructed them (that) $^{12-15}$they should come back after Akatiya had died. They did come, and (now) we instructed them. The men were rude. $^{15-17}$If you do not come here, our father's house will be discredited!

$^{17-18}$The man is evil, and $^{18-19}$he is waiting for the day (of ruin) of our father's house. $^{20-21}$Lamassatum has now taken residence in your house. $^{21-23}$She (said) as follows: "On the basis of the will, each sister will manage separately her own (share)." $^{24-25}$And she is ready to open the will! ^{25}If you do not come here, ^{26}our father's house will be discredited!

[27]It is up to you! [27–31]As to the son of Ilī-ālim, inform me whether he acquired a document or (only) made witnesses go down to the Gate of the God. [31–33]See to it that you take good care of the memorandum of Usānum and his associates.

Bibliography: Text published by Albayrak as AKT 4, 45 (Kt o/k 30). Collated October 2017.

Comments: Iddin-Aššur writes to his brother after the death of their sister Akatiya. She left an important debt in silver owned to Ela. Her possessions in bronze, as well as those of her presumed sister, have been pledged.

Line 4: the line is clear, and the restoration of Hakan Erol (2018, 68 n. 58) is not possible.

Line 20: the house of Uṣur-ša-Ištar, in which Lamassatum took up residence, must be the paternal house located in Aššur.

Line 22: depending on the status of Lamassatum within the family, the testament that she wants to open was either her father's or Akatiya's.

---

272. After Akatiya's Death, Šīmat-Suen Urges Her Brother to Salvage Their Father's Affairs

Obv. [1]*um-ma Ší-ma-Sú-en*$_6$*-ma* [2]*a-na Ú-ṣú-ur-ša-Ištar* [3]*qí-bi-ma* : *a-na té-er-tim* [4]*ša a-šu-mì* : *é a-bi-kà* [5]*ša ta-áš-ta-na-pá-ra-ni* [6]*mì-šu-um* : *lá ta-lá-kam-ma* [7]*é a-bi-kà* [8]*lá tù-šé-ša-ar* [9]*ki-ma ṭup-pá-am* : *ta-áš-me-ú-ni* [10]*tí-ib-a-ma a-tal-kam* lo.e. [11]*lá ta-li-kam-ma* [12]*é a-bi-kà* rev. [13]*lá tù-šé-šé-er* [14]*é a-bi-kà* : *ha-lá-aq* [15]*a-ha-at-kà* : *ih-ti-li-/iq* [16]*ù i-a-tí* [17]*ma-lu-a-am* : *a-na* [18]*ma-lu-a-e* : *i-da-nam*!(NI) [19]*ù ku-a-tí* : *šu**-*na-tim* [20]*i-da-gu*$_5$*-lu-ni-ku-um* [21]*šu-ma a-hi a-ta* [22]*tí-ib-a-ma a-tal-kam-ma* [23]*šé-ep A-šùr* : *be-li-kà* u.e. [24]*ṣa**-*ba-at-ma* [25]*na-pá-áš-ta-kà* le.e. [26]*e-ṭé**-*er ù é a-bi-kà* [27]*šé-šé-er-ma* : *lá i-ha-liq*

[1–3]Thus (says) Šīmat-Suen: say to Uṣur-ša-Ištar.

[3–5]For the instructions concerning the house of your father that you have been repeatedly sending me, [6]why don't you come here and [7–8]put the house of your father in order? [9–10]When you heard (my) letter, (you should have) gotten ready and come here. [11–13]You did not come here and did not put in order your father's house! [14–15](Now) your father's house is ruined! Your sister has now passed away! [16]And as for me, [17–18]he gives me an abundance of (misfortunes), $^{19-20}$while you, they see dreams *for* you! $^{21-22}$If you are my brother, get ready and come, $^{23-24}$seize the foot of Aššur, your lord, and $^{25-26}$save your life! $^{26-27}$And put your father's house in order, lest it be ruined.

Bibliography: Tablet published by Çeçen and Gökçek 2017, 464–65, 475–77, as Kt n/k 650. Collated on photos (there is no photo of the lower edge, upper edge, and right edge).

Comments: Šīmat-Suen writes this urgent letter to her brother after her sister's death. He sent her advice, but she prefers that he comes in person to save their father's affairs. She urges him to fulfill his religious obligations and salvage his life.

Line 1: note the defective writing *Ší-ma-Sú-en*$_6$ instead of *Ší-ma-at-Sú-en*$_6$. Her name appears first in the letter heading, before her older brother, which is unusual.

Line 15: the verbal form *ihtiliq* (masc.) is an error for *tahtiliq* (fem.).

Lines 17–20: this sentence is figurative, and the translation is tentative. Its first part means literally, "he gives us full over full." The expression "They see dreams *for* you" means "they see a rosy future for you."

---

273. Šīmat-Suen Takes Over the Tasks of Her Deceased Sister

Obv. ^{1}*um-ma Ší-ma-at-Sú-en*$_6$*-ma* ^{2}*a-na Ú-ṣur-ša-Ištar qí-bi-ma* ^{3}*a-na ša* é *Li-lá* ^{4}3 *ma-na* kù-babbar *ša qá-ta-tí-kà* ^{5}*Puzur*$_4$*-ì-lí* dumu *Ú-ṣur-ší-Ištar* ^{6}*na-al-pu-tù* : *i-pá-na a-ha-at-/kà* ^{7}*ba-al-ṭa-at-ma* :* *ṣí-ib-tám* ^{8}*tù-ša-qí-il*$_5$:* *iš-tù a-ha-at-kà* ^{9}*me-ta-at-ni* 10 *ma-na* urudu *i-na* ^{10}*ig-ri* : *Sí-ra-bi*$_4$* : *I-dí-A-šùr* ^{11}*a-na a-wi-il*$_5$*-tim* :* *i-dí-ší-im* ^{12}*ù a-na-ku* :* *a-dí* 2$^{šé-ni}$*-šu* lo.e. ^{13}*ù šál-ší-šu* : *Puzur*$_4$*-ì-/lí* ^{14}*i-na kà-sí-im a-sí-ma* ^{15}*ú-ša-hi-zu u*$_4$*-ma-am* rev. ^{16}*a-wi-il*$_5$*-tum e-ṭí-ri-ma* ^{17}é^{tám} : *a-na kà-na-ki-im* ^{18}*ta-ta-na-lá-kam a-pu-tum* ^{19}kù-babbar *šé-bi-lam-ma* ^{20}*a-na a-wi-il*$_5$*-tim li-iš-/qú-lu-ma* ^{21}é^{tám} : *lá tù-pá-ra-ar* ^{22}*a-hi a-ta* : kù-babbar *ša I-a-šar* ^{23}*ma-lá tù-ša-dí-nu-ni* ^{24}*šé-bi*$_4$*-lam-ma šé-im* g[ig]* ^{25}*a-na ú-ku-ul-tí-ni* ^{26}*lá-áš-pu-uk* : *ša-tum* ^{27}*ša-na-at me-er-at-kà* u.e. ^{28}*a-ha-at a-bi*$_4$*-ša ta-tí-dí-ší* ^{29}[*m*]*ì-ma lá té-zi-ib-ší-im* ^{30}[*t*]*ù-dí-tám ša tù-šé-bi*$_4$*-lá-ší-ni* ^{31}*ša-ak-na-at* le.e. ^{32}*a-pá-ni-a na-ad-a-at a-na-ku-/ma* ^{33}*ú-lá-ba-ší ù ú-kà-ta-am-ší* ^{34}*ù iš-tí-a-ma* : *ta-ta-na-lá-ak* ^{35}*lá ta-ṣa-ra-áp-ší* :* *a-šu-ur-ší*

1–2Thus (says) Šīmat-Suen: say to Uṣur-ša-Ištar.

3–6As for the house of Lila, the 3 minas of silver for which Puzur-ilī, son of Uṣur-ša-Ištar, has been recorded as your guarantor, previously, when your sister was still alive, she paid the interest. 8–9After your sister's death, 9–11Iddin-Aššur gave the lady 10 minas of copper from the rent of Sirabi. 12–15And as for me, two or three times I called upon Puzur-ilī when (we drank) a cup, and I gave him instructions. 15–18Today the lady is trying to deprive me (of it), and she keeps coming in order to seal the house!

18–20Urgent! Send the silver, so that they can pay the lady, and 21she will not break up the household. 22–24You are my brother; send the silver of Ia-šar, as much as you made (him) pay, 24–26so that I can store barley (and) wheat for our food. 26–27The season is there!

27–28Your daughter, her aunt has rejected her; 29she left her nothing! 30–31She is wearing the garment pin that you sent her. 32–34She is placed before me; I will personally clothe her and cover her, 34and she always will go with me. 35You should not be anxious about her. I will take care of her.

Bibliography: Text published by Bilgiç and Bayram as AKT 2, 31 (Kt n/k 584); collated March 2016.

Comments: In this letter, Šīmat-Suen explains to her brother that Akatiya had paid the interest on a debt, and that the house in which she lives should not be seized. The person who is threatening Šīmat-Suen is a lady, presumably a member of the Assyrian royal family.[20] Akatiya, while she was alive, had charge of Uṣur-ša-Ištar's daughter, presumably also mentioned in **266**, and Šīmat-Suen is now responsible for the girl (line 32: "I am now responsible for her").

Line 14: the expression *ana kāsîm šasā'um* means "to demand payment."

Line 28: the formulation *ahat abiša* means "her aunt"; that is, Akatiya.

The translation of line 35 is tentative; the verbe *ṣarāpum* is also attested in letter **268**, there combined with *libbum*.

20. This lady sent at least three letters to Uṣur-ša-Ištar; they mention votive offerings and textiles for which she asks payment; Aduda, the son of the king, is involved in these letters, see Erol 2018.

274. Šīmat-Suen Urges Her Brother to Come Back Home

Obv. ^{1}*a-na Ú-ṣúr-ša-Ištar qí-bi*$_4$*-ma* ^{2}*um-ma Ší-ma-Sú-en*$_6$*-ma* ^{3}*a-dí ma-at la*$_1$ *ta-lá-kam-ma* ^{4}*a-dí ma-at i-ṣé*-er* é^{tim} ^{5}*ù ú-ṭù*-up-tim* ^{6}*a-zu-a-ab*$_1$** mì-šu-um* ^{7}*la*$_1$** ta-la*$_1$**-kam-ma* é *a-bi*$_4$*-kà* ^{8}*la*$_1$** tù-šé-ša-ar* ^{9}*a-dí :* a-i-e-im* lo.e. ^{10}*u*$_4$*-mì-im* é *a-bi*$_4$*-kà* ^{11}*lu-šé*$^{!}$*-er*$^{!}$(RI)* *ù ṣú*-ha-ar-tám* rev. ^{12}*a-na a-kà-al* ^{13}*kal-bi-tí te*$_9$**-zi-ib* ^{14}*ù a-na-ku a-na ṣú*-ha-ar-tim* ^{15}*a-zu-a-ab*$_1$** :* wa-dí a-ha-at-kà* ^{16}*me-ta-at-ma a-dí : ma-lá* ^{17}*ù šé-ni-šu ṭup-pá-am* ^{18}*áš-pu-ra-k[u]m a*-ma-tí-ma* ^{19}*té-er-ta-kà [la*$_1$ *i]-li-kam* ^{20}*a-pu-tum :* ki-[ma ṭup-p]á-am* ^{21}*ta-áš-me-ú :* tí-ib-a-ma* ^{22}*a-tal-kam*

$^{1-2}$Say to Uṣur-ša-Ištar: thus (says) Šīmat-Suen.

^{3}How long do you fail to come, and $^{4-6}$for how long will I sweat on account of the house and the furniture? $^{6-8}$Why don't you come and put in order the house of your father? $^{9-11}$How long will I have to *keep in order* your father's house? $^{11-13}$Indeed, you left the girl to eat the bitches! ^{14}As for me, I sweat for that girl! $^{15-18}$Truly, your sister is dead, and I sent you a letter several times. $^{18-19}$Your message never came back to me. $^{20-22}$Urgent! When you will hear my letter, set out and come here!

Bibliography: Tablet published by Çeçen and Gökçek 2017, 466–67, 478–79, as Kt n/k 713. Collated on photos (there is no photo of the right edge).

Comments: Šīmat-Suen took over the role of Akatiya in the family house; she manages the household and has to take care of the girl who was previously in the care of her sister. She urges her brother Uṣur-ša-Ištar to come back to Aššur to help her.

Note the repeated use of *la*$_1$ by the writer of this tablet, instead of the more common *lá* used in the previous two letters sent by Šīmat-Suen; this suggests the existence of different writers.

Line 9: the expression *adi ayyēim* means literally: "until which other day."

Line 11: the editors read the first three signs *lu-šé-er*. However, the last sign is a clear *ri* on the photo 479.

Ahaha, a Woman Consecrated to the God Aššur

Ahaha was the daughter of Pūšu-kēn and Lamassī; she had four brothers, Sue'a, Aššur-mūtappil, Buzāzu, and Ikuppaša; and one sister, Waqqurtum, who was little involved in the family affairs, presumably after her marriage (fig. 16).[21] Ahaha was brought up by her mother at Aššur while her father was mostly staying in Kaneš for his business activities. Lamassī wrote several letters to her husband urging him to come back home and consecrate their daughter to the god Aššur (**147**, **163**, **166**, **259**, and above chapter 5). Ahaha was presumably consecrated to the god while she was still young and living with her mother. She received jewelry items such as gold beads (**260**) or garment pins (fig. 8)[22] and small amounts of gold and silver (five shekels of silver in **275**,[23] ten shekels of silver,[24] thirteen shekels of silver in **174**, and four shekels of gold[25]). In a letter sent to her husband, Lamassī

21. For Waqqurtum, sister of Ahaha, see Michel 2001a, 438–42, texts no. 225–226, and Michel 2009b. Veenhof 2014, 361, followed this interpretation, while Larsen 2015a, 287, considered that Ahaha and Waqqurtum are two names of the same woman. There are two texts mentioning both Ahaha and Waqqurtum, suggesting that they are two different women. In TC 3, 210, several women receive goods, among whom, lines 24–28, 35–36: "1 package for Waqqurtum, daughter of Pūšu-kēn, 1 package for Šāt-Aššur, daughter of Šalim-ahum, sealed by Sue'a. Furthermore, 22½ grains of gold under my seal for Ahaha … 2 shekels for Ahaha sealed by the *amtum*-wife"; 1 *ri-ik-sà-am a-na Wa-qur-tim*, dumu-munus *Pu-šu-ke-en*$_6$ 1 *ri-ik-sà-am*, *ša Ša-at-A-šur* dumu-munus *Šál-ma-a-hi-im*, *ku-nu-ku ša Sú-e-a a-ha-ma* 22½ še, kù-ki *ku-nu-ki-a* : *a-na A-ha-ha* … 2 gín *a-na*, *A-ha-ha ku-nu-ki ša am-tim*. And in the letter TC 1, 21, addressed to Aššur-imitti, Ilī-šudu, Buzāzu, and Waqqurtum from Puzur-Aššur, we read lines 34–36: "the rest of my silver, 2⅔ minas and 1⅓ minas of silver, which is on the account of Ahaha"; *ší-tí* kù-babbar^{pì}*-a* 2⅔ *ma-na*, *ù* 1⅓ *ma-na* kù-babbar, *ša li-bi*$_4$ *A-ha-ha*. According to CCT 5, 43:29–30, Waqqurtum received a gift (*iddinū*) of 2 minas of gold (a share in a joint stock company), presumably as a dowry from her father: 2 *ma-na* kù-gi *i-dí-nu ša Wa-qár-tim*, *me-er-i-tí-a*. This suggests that she was married, and thus is not mentioned later on in the texts mentioning the succession of Pūšu-kēn.

22. TC 2, 54 :33–34: 2 *tù-dí-ta-an* ⅓ *ma-na* ki-lá-bi, *a-na Lá-ma-sí ù A-ha-ha*; "2 garment pins—their weight (in silver): ⅓ mina—for Lamassī and Ahaha."

23. See also CCT 5, 41a :14–15: 5 gín kù-babbar *šé-bu-ul-tum*, *ša Lá-ma-sí ú A-ha-ha*; "5 shekels of silver, consignment of Lamassī and Ahaha," among other shipments to Aššur.

24. ICK 1, 120:5–8: 1 *ri-ik-sú* 10 gín kù-babbar, *šé-bu-ul-ta-áš-na*, *a-Lá-ma-sí ú*, *A-ha-ha*; "1 package of 10 shekels of silver, their consingment, for Lamassī and Ahaha."

25. AKT 1, 7:26–27: 4 gín kù-gi *a-Lá-ma-sí ù*, *A-ha-ha*.

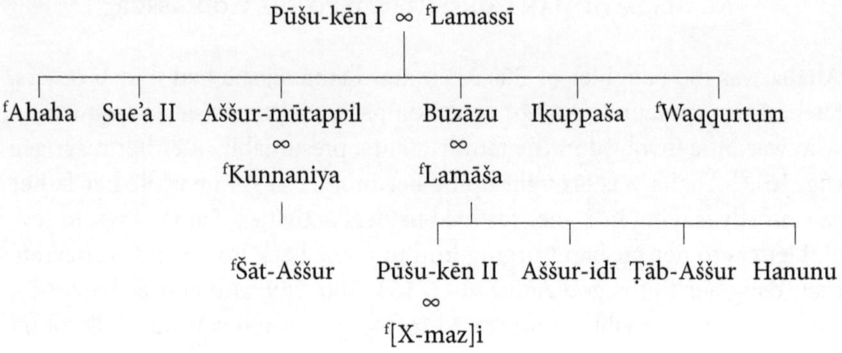

Fig. 16. Family tree of Ahaha, daughter of Pūšu-kēn and Lamassī.

announced the shipment of a garment from Ahaha for a woman in Anatolia (**164**). Mother and daughter wrote together a letter to Pūšu-kēn concerning the purchase and storing of grain for the household, and about votive offerings that he had promised to the goddess Tašmētum but had not yet sent (**246**), suggesting that Ahaha was still living in the paternal home but at the same time was grown up enough to be concerned with financial and religious matters.

It is not entirely clear whether, after her mother's death, she was still living in the family house or on her own, but she took care of the paternal estate.[26] She still appeared as recipient of small amounts of silver (3 shekels in **224**; Prag I, 569[27]) or gold (2½ shekels in Prag I, 824,[28] and 3¼ shekels of good quality gold in TC 3, 204[29]). In a letter presumably sent by one of her brothers, Ahaha was accused of having taken some gold and silver in order to buy grain and refused to give it back (**130**).

Most of the letters sent by Ahaha to her brothers follow the death of their father and concern the settling of his estate, a matter which lasted some six or seven years. These letters reflect a deteriorating conflictual situation, first between the heirs and the former associates of their father,

26. TC 1, 30:3–4, copy of a letter addressed by Pūšu-kēn to representatives in Aššur: "Alas! My wife is dead!"; *la li-bi*, dingir-*ma a-ší-tí me-ta-at.*

27. Prag I, 569:5: [3] gín *a-na A-ha-ha*.

28. Prag I, 824:13–15: 2½ gín, kù-gi *šé-bu-ul-ta-ša, a-na A-ha-ha*; "2½ shekels of gold, consignment for Ahaha."

29. TC 3, 204:1–10: 3¼ gín kù-gi, sig$_5$ *pá-ša-lúm, ku-nu-ki-a a-na, Šál-mì-Ištar*, dumu *Be-za-ni, áp-qí-id, a-ṣé-er, ša ki-ma i-a-tí, ù A-ha-ha*, <*ú*>-*bi*$_4$-*il*$_5$.

then among the heirs themselves through their individual representatives.[30] For example, they made an agreement with the heirs of Amur-Ištar, a former partner of their father, who was also dead (**257**). Pūšu-kēn died in 1871 or 1870 (eponymy years REL 102 or 103), leaving loans and various debts. An attorney named Bēlānum was hired to assist Pūšu-kēn's children in several settlements (**281**). Together with Aššur-mūtappil, he received the forty minas of silver owned by Ikuppiya to the deceased (**276**). Ahaha's letters to her brothers deal with the recovery of silver from various debtors in Aššur, including Kulumaya (**281**), and with the dispute she had with the eponyms.[31] Because of a debt owed by Pūšu-kēn to the City Hall, they put pressure on her as the family representative in Aššur, confiscating her brother's houses and her own slaves as collateral (**141**, **277**, **278**). She asked her father's associate Puzur-Aššur for help in this affair, but with little success (**279**). In Aššur, she also had to deal alone with the claims of her father's individual creditors (**277**, **279**).[32] Tired of being alone to cope with them in Aššur, she threatened her brothers to have them transferred by force to Aššur (**277**), and since she wrote a letter together with them to Puzur-Aššur asking him to recover money from an agent of their father, she may have succeeded (**280**).

Part of her correspondence with her brothers concerns her own transactions, including her investments in several commercial partnerships.[33] A legal text, involving two of her brothers, mentions that Ahaha owned more than six minas of gold.[34] A group of letters, presumably dated around

30. Hertel 2013, 346–349.

31. CCT 5, 21a:1–10: "Concerning the 30 minas of silver that Pūšu-kēn had loaned to Kulumaya in Aššur, silver that went to his joint-stock company, 10 minas of silver, share of Ahaha, daughter of Pūšu-kēn, Puzur-Aššur, and Buzāzu, her brother, have taken"; [*a-šu-mì* 3]0 *m*[*a-na* kù-babbar], [*š*]*a Pu-šu-ke-en*$_6$ [*i-na*], *A-lim*[ki] *i-ṣé-er*, *Ku-lu-ma-a-a i-šu-ú-m*[*a*], kù-babbar *a-na na-ru-qí-šu*, *i-lu-ku-ni* 10 *ma-na* kù-babbar, *qá-tí* : *A-ha-ha* : dumu-munus, *Pu-šu-ke-en*$_6$ *Puzur*$_4$*-A-šùr*, *ù Bu-za-zu a-hu-ša*, *il*$_5$*-qé-ú*.

32. In another broken letter sent to Puzur-Aššur, Buzāzu, and presumably other sons of Pūšu-kēn, Ahaha mentions a matter going on for two years (CCT 6, 44–45).

33. She was at the same time representing her brother Buzāzu in Aššur. In a letter sent by him to a group of persons including Ahaha, he announced the shipment of gold to Aššur and asked her correspondents to buy tin and textiles, and to send him the merchandise with a transporter (CCT 2, 32a).

34. Prag I, 652:4–6: *lu ša* 5 *ma-na* kù-gi *ù a-ha-ma*, 1⅓ *ma-na* kù-gi *šál-ṭim*, *qá-tí-ša ša A-ha-ha*.

1865 (REL 107–109), indicates that she had invested part of her capital in at least two joint-stock companies (*naruqqum*) and that her brother Buzāzu caused problems by collecting his sister's silver. Such a partnership involved several persons investing silver—valued in gold: two minas of gold each—or gold, which was made available to a trader on long term to gain profit from overland trade.[35]

Ahaha owned a share in the capital administered by Dān-Aššur. It seems that it was assigned to her by her father as part of her inheritance, but her brother and her father's associate took her share without her permission (**282–283**).[36]

She had also invested 3½ minas of silver in the joint-stock company administered by Puzur-Aššur, her father's partner. In addition, he owed her 10 minas of silver. Her brother Buzāzu had also invested in Puzur-Aššur's joint-stock company and was apparently in charge of managing his sister's share. But instead, he took out silver belonging to her for his own business. She accused Buzāzu of having appropriated her silver in letters she wrote to Aššur-mūtappil alone (**284**). And in one of his letters, he quotes what Ahaha wrote to him: "Not all the 7 minas of gold in the joint-stock company of Puzur-Aššur, which are booked on Buzāzu's name, do belong to him; note well that 3½ minas of gold belong to me!"[37] She urged her brother to get back her silver. Ahaha was living in Aššur, which explains why she had to ask her brothers to represent her in Anatolia. The fact that she remained single, being consecrated to the god Aššur, could explain why she appears as economically quite active.

---

275. Ahaha and Her Mother Receive a Small Amount of Silver

Obv. [1]5 gín kù-babbar [2]*ša Amur-A-šur* [3]dumu *Sú-kà-lí-a* [4]*iš-qú-lá-ni*$^{!}$ [5]*a-na Lá-ma-sí* rev. [6]*ú A-ha-ha* [7]*A-mur-A-šur-ma* [8]*ú-bi-il*$_5$

[1–4]The 5 shekels of silver that Amur-Aššur, son of Sukkalliya, paid, [5–8]Amur-Aššur himself brought to Lamassī and Ahaha.

---

35. See Larsen 1977 and 1999.

36. See also TC 3, 274:1, 6–10: 10 *ma-na* kù-babbar … kù-babbar *a-ni-um i-na, qá-tí-ša : ša A-ha-ha, ša na-ru-uq Dan-A-šùr, ša a-na-ku ù Puzúr-A-šur, ni-il*$_5$*-qé-ú.*

37. CCT 5, 2b:4–10: *i-na*, 7 *ma-na* kù-gi : *ša na-ru-uq, Puzur*$_4$*-A-šur* : *ša šu-mì* : *Bu-za-zu lá-áp-tù*, kù-gi *ku-lu-šu-ma lá šu-wa-ú-ma ih-d*[*a*$^{!}$*-/ma*], 3½ *ma-na* kù-gi : *i-a-um.*

Bibliography: Text published in copy by Clay as BIN 4, 140.

Comments: Delivery of silver to Lamassī and her daughter Ahaha.

---

276. Ahaha Is Represented in a Family Agreement in Kaneš

Obv. ^{1}kišib du$_{10}$-*ṣí-lá-A-šur* dumu *Šu-Nu-nu* ^{2}kišib *Šu-Lá-ba-an* dumu *A-al*-du$_{10}$ ^{3}kišib *Pí-lá-ah-Ištar* dumu *A-šùr-ba-ni* ^{4}kišib *A-ni-na* dumu *Ú-ṣur-ša-A-šùr* ^{5}kišib *I-dí-a-bi*$_{4}$*-im* dumu *A-šùr-ma-lik* ^{6}kišib *Sú-e-a* dumu *Pu-šu-ke-en*$_{6}$ ^{7}kišib *Bu-za-zu* dumu *Pu-šu-ke-en*$_{6}$ ^{8}kišib *I-ku-pá-ša* dumu *Pu-šu-ke-en*$_{6}$ ^{9}kišib *A-ha-ha* dumu-munus *Pu-šu-ke-en*$_{6}$ ^{10}40 *ma-na* kù-babbar *ša I-ku-pí-a* dumu *A-ta-a* ^{11}*i-na Kà-ni-iš*^{ki} *a-na Pu-šu-ke-en*$_{6}$ ^{12}*i-hi-ib-lu-ma A-šùr-mu-ta-píl* ^{13}*ù Bé-lá-nu-um ra-bi-ṣú-um* ^{14}kù-babbar *il*$_{5}$*-qé-ú-ni a-na* kù-babbar *šu-a-tí* ^{15}*me-er-ú Pu-šu-ke-en*$_{6}$ *ù* dumu-munus ^{16}*Pu-šu-ke-en*$_{6}$ nin-dingir *a-na* ^{17}*A-šùr-mu-ta-pí-il*$_{5}$ *a-hi-šu-nu* ^{18}*ú-lá i-tù-ru ú i-na e-lá-i-šu-ma*$^{!}$ ^{19}*i-na Ka-ni-iš*^{ki} *ṭup-pá-am* ^{20}*ša hu-bu-ul I-ku-pí-a* dumu *A-ta-a* ^{21}*me-er-ú Pu-šu-ke-en*$_{6}$ ^{22}*ù* dumu-munus *Pu-šu-ke-en*$_{6}$ nin-dingir ^{23}*a-na A-šur-mu-ta-pí-il*$_{5}$ *i-du-nu* ^{24}*ma-lá dí-in A-lim*^{ki} kù-babbar lo.e. ^{25}*me-er-ú Pu-šu-ke-en*$_{6}$ ^{26}*ù* dumu-munus *Pu-šu-ke-en*$_{6}$ *ša-bu-ú* rev. ^{27}*I-dí-a-bu-um* dumu *A-šùr-ma-lik* ^{28}*ki-ma A-ha-ha i-zi-iz* (the rest of the reverse in not inscribed)

^{1}Sealed by Ṭāb-ṣilli-Aššur, son of Šu-Nunu; ^{2}sealed by Šu-Labān, son of Āl-ṭāb; ^{3}sealed by Pilah-Ištar, son of Aššur-bāni; ^{4}sealed by Anīna, son of Uṣur-ša-Aššur; ^{5}sealed by Iddin-abum, son of Aššur-malik; ^{6}sealed by Sue'a, son of Pūšu-kēn; ^{7}sealed by Buzāzu, son of Pūšu-kēn; ^{8}sealed by Ikuppaša, son of Pūšu-kēn; ^{9}sealed by Ahaha, daughter of Pūšu-kēn.

$^{10-12}$Concerning the 40 minas of silver that Ikuppiya, son of Ataya, for which he had become indebted to Pūšu-kēn in Kaneš, $^{12-14}$which silver Aššur-mūtappil and Bēlānum, the attorney, took; $^{14-18}$for this silver, the sons of Pūšu-kēn and the consecrated daughter of Pūšu-kēn will not raise a claim against Aššur-mūtappil, their brother. $^{18-23}$And when he comes up, the sons of Pūšu-kēn and the consecrated daughter of Pūšu-kēn will give to Aššur-mūtappil in Kaneš the tablet of the debt of Ikuppiya.

$^{24-26}$According to the verdict of the city (of Aššur), the sons of Pūšu-kēn and the consecrated daughter of Pūšu-kēn have been paid with the silver. $^{27-28}$Iddin-abum, son of Aššur-malik, was present on behalf of Ahaha.

Bibliography: Text published in copy by Contenau as TC 1, 79; edited by Eisser and Lewy (1930, no. 11). Collated on photo online on CDLI as P357414.

Comments: One of Pūšu-kēn's sons recovered an important loan of his deceased father, and the other heirs, including Ahaha, renounce any claim on it. This record is a copy of the envelope text of an agreement that took place in Kaneš. Ahaha is mentioned among the sealers even though she was not there and was represented in the transaction by Iddin-abum, son of Aššur-malik. The text KTH 33 + 34 (join made by Veenhof) deals with the same affair.

---

277. Ahaha Asks Her Brothers to Pay Their Father's Debt to the Eponym

[1]*a-na Sú-e-a A-šur-mu-ta-pì-il*$_5$ [2]*Bu-za-zu ù I-ku-pá-ša* [3]*qí-bi-ma um-ma A-ha-ha-ma* [x *m*]*a-na* [4]kù-babbar *ša a-na li-mì-im* [*ha*]*-bu-lá-ni-ni* [5]*i bi ni ru* é *a-bi*$_4$*-ni* [6]*i i ma nu* 8 *ma-na* kù-g[i] [7][*ù* x] *ma-na* 9 gín kù-babbar é dam-gàr [*a-n*]*a* [8]*ṣí-ib-tim ni-il*$_5$*-qé-ma* [9]*lu ší-im* é X-x-*tí-a lu ší-im* [10]*hu-sà-ri-im lu* <*sú*>*-ub-ru-um ša* [11]*ša-mu lu* kù-babbar *lu ṣí-ba-at* [12]*na-ru-qí-im ša a-na* é *A-lim* [13]*ha-bu-lá-tù-nu-ni* šu-nígin 5 *ma-na* kù-babbar [14]kù-babbar *ša-bu* : *Puzur*$_4$*-Sú-en*$_6$ [15]1 *ma-na* kù-babbar *ša Puzur*$_4$-sa-tu-*e* [16]*ša a-bu-ni qá-ta-tí-šu il*$_5$*-tap-tù* lo.e. [17]*a-ṣé-er hu-bu-li-ni-ma ṭá-hu* [18]šu-nígin 26 *ma-na* kù-babbar *mì-ma* [19]*a-nim a-na li-mì-im i-ší-qí-il*$_5$ [20]2 *ma-na wa-ṣí-tum ú-lá ša-qí-il*$_5$ rev. [21]8 *ma-na* kù-babbar *a-na li-mì-im* [22]*ša-ap-li-im* 2 *ma-na* kù-babbar [23]*ṣí-ba-at na-ru-qí-im ša* é *Šál-mah* [24]*a-ha-ma mì-ma a-nim hu-bu-li-ni* [25]*a-t*[*ù-n*]*u a-ma-kam qá-ta-tí-ku-nu té-ta-ki-ma* [26]*ù* [kù-babbar?] *ma-da-am té-ta-na-pá-ša* [27]*a-na du-li x* é *a-bi-ni* sig$_5$ *ša-ki-in* [28]*a-tù-nu a-ma-kam* [...] *i-a-ti* [29]*a-na-kam sí-ki-a ú-ša-ku-ku a-ma-kam* [30]*lu ší-ip-kà-tum lu ba-áb-tum ša a-bi-ni* [31]*a-dí ṣí-tám a-ni-tám ta-pá-lá-ni* [32]*ma-ma-an lá i-ṭá-hi a-na ha-al-qú-tim* [33]*ra-ma-ku-nu ta-áš-ku-na-ma ša-zu-uz-tám* [34][*ša-zi*]*-za-ma i-na ša-ha-tí-a la i-za-zu* [35]*e-ir-tám lá i-né-ú šu-ma a-li-ma* [36]*wa-ás-ma-at-*[*ni*] é *a-bi*$_4$*-ku-nu* [37]*la té-pá-ša a-ša-pá-ra-ma ú-ša-sú-hu-ku-nu-ma* [38]é *a-bi*$_4$*-ku-nu šé-ší-ra mì-num* [39]*ša ta-áš-ta-na-pá-ra-ni-ni me-er-ú* [40]*A-mur-Ištar i-dí-nim il*$_5$*-e-ú-ni-a-tí* [41]*ki-iš-da-tí-ki lu* an-na *lu* túg$^{hi\text{-}a}$ [42]*šé-bi*$_4$*-li-ma lu nu-ša-bi*$_4$ [43]14 *ma-na it-ra-tim i-li-bi*$_4$*-ku-nu* [44]*i-šu i-nu-mì qá-ta-tí-ku-nu* le.e. [45]*ta-na-dí-a* [x x x x *i*]*t-ra-tí-a li-iṣ-hi-ra-am* [46]*ša a-bi-ku-nu ir-*[...] *i-zi-bu* [47]*hu-bu-ul a-bi-šu-nu lá ik-šu-*[...]

[1-3]Say to Sue'a, Aššur-mūtappil, Buzāzu, and Ikuppaša: thus (says) Ahaha. [3-4]As for the [x m]inas of silver which we [o]we to the eponym, [5-6]... our father's house... [6-8]We borrowed 8 minas of gol[d and x] minas, 9 shekels of silver at interest at a money lender's house, and [9-11]be it the price of the house of X-x-tiya, the price of the lapis lazuli and the slaves that were bought, or silver, [11-13]or contribution to a join-stock company, which you owe to the City Hall—[13-14]in all: 5 minas of silver—he (the eponym) has been satisfied with the silver. [14-17]As for Puzur-Suen, 1 mina of silver from Puzur-šadue, for whom our father was recorded as guarantor, has been added to our own debt. [18-19]In all: 26 minas of silver. All this was paid to the eponym. [20]But 2 minas export tax has not been paid. [21-22](There are) 8 minas of silver (more) for the lower eponym, [22-23](and) 2 minas of silver as the addition to the joint-stock company of the house of Šalim-ahum [24]—all this is also our debt.

[25](And) y[o]u, there, you have constantly taken away your shares, [26]and you are making a lot of [silver]! [27]Has good come about for the misery of our father's house? [28]You, there [...]. As to me [29]here, they are tearing the hem (of my garment) to shreds. [29-32]Until you pay this expenditure, there, nobody shall approach the investments and outstanding merchandise of our father. [32-33]You have wrought your own destruction, [33-35]by [ins]talling representatives who do not support me! They cannot stop (my adversaries). [35-37]If you do not treat your father's house what is appropriate, I will write, and have you transferred by force (to Aššur). So [38]put your father's house in order!

[38-39]Why are you constantly writing to me: [39-40]"The sons of Amur-Ištar prevailed over us in the lawsuit. [41-42]Send what accrues to you, be it tin or textiles, and we will repay (them) in full." [43-44]There is a surplus of 14 minas in your account. [44-45]When you deposit your share [...] my surplus must be deducted for me. [46-47]As for what your father left behind, they *do not match* the debts of your father.

Bibliography: Unpublished letter known by a transliteration of Benno Landsberger as Ankara 1938; Veenhof, who provided me the text, suggested many readings. Lines 1–24 follow restitutions by Dercksen (2004a, 45–46 n. 147). The transliteration is, in many cases, uncertain, and several signs remain unread; untranslated passages are marked by "...."

Comments: Ahaha writes to three of her brothers—Sue'a, the oldest one being not involved—about her father's estate, asking them to come back to

Aššur and settle it. Indeed, Pūšu-kēn left an important debt in silver owed to the eponym. In order to repay this debt, the children borrowed gold and silver at interest and sold a house, merchandise, and slave in order to pay back part of the amount. There were still ten minas of silver to be paid (**141**). Ahaha complains that she receives no help from her brothers and threatens them to force their transfer to Aššur.

Line 33: the plural form *šazzuzātum* would be better since both verbs on lines 34 and 35 are in the plural.

Line 43: the surplus mentioned here might be the same as the one belonging to Ahaha in Prag I, 680.

---

278. Ahaha Brothers' Houses Have Been Seized as Collateral

[1]*a-na Sú-e-a A-šur-mu-ta-/pí-il*$_5$ [2]*Bu-za-zu* [3]*ú I-ku-pá-ša : qí-bi-ma* [4]*um-ma A-ha-ha-ma a-ma hu-bu-/ul* [5]*a-bi*$_4$*-ku-nu ta-al-ta-am-/da* [6]*lu ší-ip-kà-tim lu tám-kà-/ra-am* [7]*tí-šu-a : ma-ma-an qá-sú* [8]*lá i-lá-qé : a-na hu-bu-li-ku-/nu* [9]*ku-nu-im bé-ta-ku-nu* [10]*ú i-ší-tí* : é$^{\textit{bé-ta}}$*-ku-nu* [11]*i-ta-aq-nu : i-na* é *li-mì-/im* [12]*ší-im* é$^{\textit{ta}}$*-ku-nu i-ba-ta-/aq-ma* [13]*ma-lá hu-bu-lá-ak-nu* [14]*i-ší-tù-ni a-ša-pá-ra-ku-/nu-tí* [15]é [*A*]*-šur ú : ú-*[16]*ṭù-up-tù-šu* [17](erasure) *a-na* 30 *ma-/na* [18][*š*]*a qá-ta-tí-šu* [19][*n*]*a-al-pu-ta-tí-ni* [20][*a-w*]*a-tum i-za-ku-w*[*a*] *ú ší-a-/tí* [21]*za-ku-sà a-ša-pá-r*[*a-k*]*um* [22]*i-na* 2 *ma-na* 50 gín kù-ki [23]*ú* 1 *ma-na* kù-babbar *ša aṣ-bu-tù*$^{!}$(UT) [24]7½ *ma-na* kù-babbar *a-na* [25]*ṣí-ba-at* 30 *ma-na* [26]*ša qá-ta-tim na-al-/pu-ta-/tí-ni* [27]*i-na* kù-babbar$^{\textit{pì}}$*-kà* [28]*i-ší-qí-il*$_5$ 6½ *ma-na a-na* [29]*ší-im* é *Ú-ki-da* (erasure) [30]*i-ší-qí-il*$_5$ 5 *ma-na a-na* [31]*ší-im* é *na-gi*$_5$*-ri-im* [32]*i-ší-qí-il*$_5$ *šu-ma-me-en*$_6$ [33] kù-babbar *a-ni-um* le.e. [34]*lá ib-ší-ma lá i-ší-qí-il*$_5$ [35]*a-wa-tù-me-en*$_6$ *i-bi-ší-*[*a*] [36]*hu-bu-lá-ak-*<*nu*> *iq-tí-li-i*[*l*$_5$]

[1–4]Say to Sue'a, Aššur-mūtappil, Buzāzu, and Ikuppaša: thus (says) Ahaha.

[4–5]Look! You have been informed about the debt of your father. [6–8]Whatever investments or (outstanding claims on) agents you may have, no one must take his share. [8–11]For your own debt, your houses and the stocks of your houses have been threatened to be seized! [11–12]In the office of the eponym, the price of your houses will be deducted, and [13–14]I will write to you how much of your debt remains.

[15–19]As for the house in Aššur and its furniture (serving as security) for the 30 minas (of silver) for which you have been recorded as his guarantors, [20–21]when the [mat]ter will be clarified, I will write to you a detailed report about it. [22–23]As to the 2 minas, 50 shekels of gold and 1 mina of silver which I seized, [24–28]7½ minas of silver—the interest on the 30 minas for which you have been recorded as guarantors—have been paid from your silver. [28–30]6½ minas for the price of the house of Ukida have been paid. [30–32]5 minas for the price of the house of the herald have been paid.

[32–35]If this silver had not been available and had not been paid, there would have been a lawsuit! [36](The burden of) your debt has (now) become lighter.

Bibliography: Text published in copy by Smith and Wiseman as CCT 5, 8a; translated by Michel (2001a, no. 312) and Dercksen (2004a, 48). Text commented by Veenhof (1999b).

Comments: Ahaha alerts her four brothers, informing them that all their transactions are frozen, and their houses in Aššur, including their furniture, have been seized. Concerning the debt left by their father, part of it has been repaid with her brothers' silver, and she justifies herself by explaining that having made these payments, she avoided a trial.

---

279. Ahaha Urges Her Father's Associate to Help Her Pay the Eponym

Obv. [1]*a-na Pu[zur*$_4$*-A-šùr qí-bi-ma]* [2]*u[m-ma A-ha-ha-ma]* (rest of the obverse and lower edge destroyed).
Lo.e. [1']*t[ù* x x x x x] [2']*ta-áš-pu-r[a-am* x x x x] rev. [3']*na-áš-pè-er-ta-k[à]* [4']*ša-ma-am : lá i-mu-a* [5']*A-šur-i-mì-tí : ú A-ma-m[a*?] [6']*ú a-na-ku : i-na qá-tí* [7']*A-šur-ma-lik* : dumu *A-lá-hi-im* [8']*ú I-na-a* : dumu *A-mu-ra-a* [9']*i-na bé-tí : kà-tù-im* [10']*uš*$_{10}$*-ta-am-ṭí-ú-ni : ú a-na-/ku* [11']*a-ba-ki-šu-nu-tí-ma : ba-ṣa-ma* [12']*ša-zu-za-tù-kà : lá i-du-/nu-nim* [13']kù-babbar *pá-ni-a-am* [14']*ša tù-šé-bi*$_4$*-lá-šu-nu-tí-ni* [15']*a-na ṣí-tí-šu : ša Bu-za-zu* [16']*a-na* é : *na-gi-ri-im* u.e. [17']*iš-ta-aq-lu-šu* : 1 gín kù-[babbar] [18']*lá i-ba-ší : ú ku-a-tí : ša i-*[x (x)] [19']*a-na ṣí-ib-tim* [20']*i-lá-kà-ku[m]* le.e. [21']*ú* 2 *ma-na* kù-babbar : *li-mu-um a-hu-/ur* [22']*lá iš-qú-lu : be-lí a-ta : mì-šu-um* [23']*ta-ad-mì-qá-tí-a : a-na šé-bu-lá-tim* [24']*tù-uš*$_{10}$*-té-né-ba-lam*

[1–2][Say] to Pu[zur-Aššur]: th[us (says) Ahaha].

[...]

[1'–2']You wrote [me ... but] [3'–4']he refuses to hear your message. [5'–6']Aššur-imittī and Amama and I, [6'–10'](who was) in the hands of Aššur-malik, son of Ali-ahum, and Innaya, son of Amuraya, they put pressure on me by taking the house$^?$ as collateral. $^{10'-12'}$Although I have been crying before them, your representatives did not give me as much as a grain of sand! $^{13'-14'}$As for the previous (consignment of) silver that you sent them, $^{15'-17'}$they pay it to the house of the herald for Buzāzu's expenses. $^{17'-18'}$There is not a single shekel of silver available. $^{18'-20'}$And as for you, they [...] is running at interest at your expense. $^{21'-22'}$And they did not pay the 2 minas of silver, still due to$^?$ the eponym. You are my master. $^{22'-24'}$Why do you always send my *tadmiqtum*-trusts as consignments?

Bibliography: Text published in copy by Stephens as BIN 6, 178; edited by Michel (1991, no.184) and Dercksen (2004a, 49 n. 154).

Comments: Pūšu-kēn left some debts to the Aššur City Hall. The eponym REL 103 (ca. 1870) was not able to collect an old debt and was later helped by eponym REL 105 (ca. 1868); together, the eponyms took the houses inherited by the children as collateral. Ahaha complains to her father's associate Puzur-Aššur that, even though she has been crying to her father's associate's representatives, no one was willing to help her. The debt of Pūšu-kēn to the eponym is already mentioned in letter **147**, sent to him by his wife Lamassī. The end of the letter is not clear: Ahaha's *tadmiqtum*-trusts were probably textiles, which her brother would sell for her in Anatolia and whose yield he would send back as consignment. Are the consignments he is sending too few to cover the price of her textiles, or is he sending the proceeds to Aššur as if they were part of his own business proceeds?

---

280. Ahaha and Her Brothers Ask Their Father's Associate to Have a Loan Repaid

Obv. ^{1}*a-na Puzur$_4$-A-šùr qí-bi$_4$-ma* ^{2}*um-ma A-ha-ha Sú-e-a* ^{3}*Bu-za-zu ù I-ku-pá-ša* ^{4}*a-dí ša Ku-lu-ma-a ša ta-áš-pu-ra-ni* ^{5}*a-ma-la na-áš-pé-er-ti-kà* : *qá-tám* ^{6}*la ni-ma-ha-aṣ ù-la nu-ba-áš-kà* ^{7}*ù u$_4$-mu-šu* 3 *ša-na-tim lu e-ta-at-*[*qú*] ^{8}*ù iš-tù úṣ-ú-ni* : *e-ṭé-me* ^{9}[*ša é a-b*]*i-ni lu ú-qá-li-il$_5$* ^{10}[*ù*] *ni-a-tí* : *a-na ṣa-hu-ru-tim* ^{11}[*lu iš-ku-ni-a-tí*]*-ma* : *ma-tí-ma* ^{12}[x x x x x x]-*tù-šu a-n*[*a*]

(end of obverse, lower edge, and beginning of reverse broken)

Rev. $^{1'}$[*e*]*-ba-ru* [x x x x x] $^{2'}$*li-zi-i*[*z* x x x x x x] $^{3'}$*Ša-at-A-šùr ù* [*a-ta-ma a-na*] $^{4'}$*é a-wi-lim* : *er-ba-ma* : *i*[*-šu*] $^{5'}$*a-wi-lim* : *li-im-da-ma* [*mì-ma ša*]

6' *i-ba-ší-*[*ú*?] *ku-un-k*[*à-ma*] 7' an-na *ù* túg^{hi-a} : *a-na* [*ma-ma-an*] 8' *lá tù-ša-ra* kù-babbar *le-*[*ru-ub-ma*] 9' an-na *ù* túg^{hi-a} *lu-úṣ-ú i-*[*hi-id*]*-ma* 10' *ba*?*-lu-kà* : *mì-ma la*$_1$ *e-pu-šu* 11' *lu ṭup-pu ha-ru-mu-tum* : *ša* dam-gàr-*ru-tim* 12' *lu ša nu-a-e lu na-áš-pu-ku-um* 13' *a-na* kù-babbar *ta-e-ra-ma* : *an-nu-ku* u.e. 14' *a-na-kam wa-aq-ru* 14 gín-ta 15' *ù*! *ša-ap-li-iš* : *i-za-az* 16' *a-dí* iti-1-kam *ù* iti-2-kam *a-wa-tum* 17' *lá i-za-ku-wa* : *šu-ma* 10 *ma-na* [k]ù?-b[abbar] le.e. 18' *na-ad-am* : *tí-šu* : *Ba-zi-*[*a*] 19' *ù* ^{d}im-sig$_5$ *ha-bu-lu-ni* 20' [k]i *Ištar-pì-lá-ah* dumu [*I*?-x-x-x] 21' *i-zi-iz-ma* [x x x x]

1–3 Say to Puzur-Aššur: thus (say) Ahaha, Sue'a, Buzāzu, and Ikuppaša.

4–6 As to what you wrote me concerning Kulumaya, we will not disobey your instructions and will not shame you, 7 although his term is overd[ue] by 3 years 8–9 and he has really slighted the spirits of our father's house since he left. 10–11 [Even] us, [he has treated us] as unimportant people, and never [...] (lacuna)

3'–4' [You] and Šāt-Aššur enter the house of the man, 4'–6' and get to know ab[out the situation] of the man, then se[al everything that] is available (there), but 7'–8' do not deliver [anyone] the tin and textiles. Only when the silver [comes in, then] 9' the tin and textiles may leave! Pay [attention], 10' I cannot do him anything without your help! 11'–13' Turn (everything) into silver, either from certified debt-notes of Assyrian agents or of native Anatolians, or stores of barley. 13'–15' Tin is expensive here (in Aššur); (the rate) stands at 14 shekels (of tin) each (shekel of silver), or even less. 16'–17' These matters will not improve in 1 or 2 months.

17'–18' If you have 10 minas of [silver] in deposit, 18'–21' (which) Baziya and Adad-damiq owe, 20' [assi]st Ištar-pilah, son of [I-x-x-x], and [...]

Bibliography: Text published in copy by Stephens as BIN 6, 59; translated by Michel (2001a, no. 313); lines 1–11 cited by Larsen (1976, 288 n. 8).

Comments: The position of Ahaha in the heading of this letter, in the first place before her brothers, reflects the important role she has in the family, presumably because of her status as a consecrated woman. Aššur-mūtappil is not among the senders; he might be in Anatolia, where he had married Kunnaniya (see below). Pūšu-kēn's children complain in this letter about a debtor, Kulumaya, who not only did not pay back his debt, but even dishonored whole family, including its ancestors. In the letter CCT 5, 21a, we learn that from the thirty minas of silver, Ahaha was entitled to a share of ten minas, which was taken by Puzur-Aššur and her brother Buzāzu.[38] Pūšu-kēn's children ask their father's associate to sell the tin and textiles stored in his house in order to get back their silver.

Lines 13′–15′: "lower" means that even less tin is available at this high price.

---

281. Ahaha Gives Orders to Her Brother to Recover the Payment of a Substantial Debt

[1]*a-na Bu-za-zu qí-bi-ma* [2]*um-ma A-ha-ha-ma* [3]kù-babbar *ša Ku-lu-ma-a* [4]*a-ma-lá ší-ma-tim* [5]*a-ma-kam a-ma-ma-an lá ta-da-/an-ma* [6]*lá i-ṭá-hi* kù-babbar (two signs erased) [7]*[l]i-ki-ni-ik-ma a-na A-lim*^{ki} [8]*[šé]-bi-lam* : *i-na* 40 *ma-na* [9][k]ù-babbar *lu qá-tí* : *lu i-li-bi* [10]*Puzur*$_4$*-A-šùr ta-ad-mì-iq-/tum* [11]*i-ba-ší* kù-babbar 10 *ma-na* [12]*ku-un-kà-ma e-né-a pé-té* [13]*a-na Puzur*$_4$*-A-šùr* lo.e. [14]*ša-am-ri-iṣ a-le-BA* [15]*a-wa-tù-šu ki-ma* kù-babbar [16]10 *ma-na ší-bu-tí-ma* rev. [17]*ga-ma-lim* : *tí-ṭá-am* [18]*[x x]-ba-am* : (erasure) [19][x x x x x k]ù-babbar [20][x x x x x]*-it-ma* [21][x x x x]*-x-ru-ba-/am* [22][x x x x x x x]*-um* [23][x (x) *Puzur*$_4$*-A*]*-šur iš-pu-/ra-am* (sign erased) [24][*um-ma šu-ut-ma*] : [25]kù-babbar *le-qé-ma lá ú-kà-lá-/ku-nu-tí* (sign *ni* erased) [26]*šu-up-ra-am-ma* [27]*úz-ni pé-té-ma lu i-de*$_8$ [28]*a-na Be-lá-nim ša ta-áš-pu-ra-/ni* [29]*um-ma a-ta-ma an-na* [30]*li-dí-na-ki-im e-ri-šu-ma* u.e. [31]*um-ma Be-lá-num-ma* an-na *lá*$^!$*-\šu* [32]*a-na gám-ri-im ša* é *a-bi*$_4$*-ku-/nu* [33][*lu*] *a*[*g*]$^?$*-dá-mar*$^?$ *a-ta ma-lá-kà*$^!$(AK) le.e. [34][*m*]*i-š*[*u š*]*a ta-ki-l*[*i ta-áš-t*]*a-na-me-*[*ú*] [35]*i-n*[*a*] *ša* : x [x x x]*-kà-ku-ma* [36]x x x *ma* x [x x x x *t*]*a-zi-iz*

[1–2]Say to Buzāzu: thus (says) Ahaha.

[3–6]As for the silver of Kulumaya, accoding to the testamentary disposition, there, do not give (it) to anyone, and nobody shall approach it! [6–8]Let the silver be sealed, and [se]nd it to the city (of Aššur). [8–11]Of the 40 minas of silver, or what is in the account of Puzur-Aššur, there is a *tadmiqum*-trust. [11–12]Seal (and send me) 10 minas of (that) silver and make me happy! [13–15]Put pressure on Puzur-Aššur: what then about his promise? [15–18]Instead of obliging the elders (of the city by paying) the 10 minas of silver, [you only send] me clay (tablets)! [18–22][…] silver […] [23–24][Puzur-

---

38. CCT 5, 21a:1–4, 6–10: 10 [*a-šu-mì* 3]0 *m*[*a-na* kù-babbar], [*š*]*a Pu-šu-ke-en*$_6$ [*i-na*], *A-lim*^{ki} *i-ṣé-er, Ku-lu-ma-a-a i-šu-ú-m*[*a*], … 10 *ma-na* kù-babbar, *qá-tí* : *A-ha-ha* : dumu-munus, *Pu-šu-ke-en*$_6$ *Puzur*$_4$*-A-šùr, ù Bu-za-zu a-hu-ša, il*$_5$*-qé-ú.*

A]ššur wrote me [as follows]: [25–27]"Take the silver; I will not offer it to them." [26–27]Write me and inform me so that I know (about it).

[28–29]About Belānum, what you wrote me as follows: [29–30]"Let him give you the tin"; I asked him, but [31]Belānum (replied) as follows: "I do not have the tin. [32–33]I have spent it to cover the expenses of your father's house." (Now) it is up to you!

[34][W]h[y is it that you ke]ep listening to slander [35–36][...]

Bibliography: Text published by Hecker, Kryszat, and Matouš as Prag I, 437. Lines 31–33 cited by Hertel (2013, 348 n. 1111).

Comments: Ahaha gives instructions to her brother Buzāzu concerning the silver representing the debt of Kulumaya, in which she owes a share of ten minas (**280**; CCT 1, 17b). From line 18 on, the text is very broken. Puzur-Aššur, their father's partner, is still in contact with them. Ahaha was supposed to get back some tin from Belānum, but he had already spent it for their family.

Line 12: literally, "Open my eyes."

Line 33: *atta ma-lá-ak* stands probably for *malaka*.

---

282. Ahaha Tries to Recover Her Silver from Two Joint-Stock Companies

Obv. [1]*a-na A-šùr-mu-ta-pì-il*$_5$ [2]*qí-bi-ma um-ma A-ha-ha-ma* [3]kù-babbar *ša na-ru-uq* [4]*Dan-A-šùr aṣ-ba-at-ma* [5]*um-ma šu-nu-ma Puzur*$_4$*-A-šur* [6]*Bu-za-zu ú I-ku-pá-ša* [7]*il*$_5$*-qé-ú : a-ma-kam* kù-babbar [8]*ša-áš-qí-il*$_5$*-šu-nu-ma [ku-u]n-kà-m[a]* [9]*a-šu-mì-šu-nu-ma e[q]*$^!$*-la[m]* [10]*le-tí-qám : šu-m[a i]-ša-q[ú*$^!$*-lu]* [11]*i-pá-ni-im-ma na-áš-[pé-er]-/ta-kà* [12]*za-ku-tum l[i-l]i-kam-/ma* [13]*a-na-kam a-[šar]* lo.e. [14]*ma-lá-ki-im [la]m-lik* [15]3½ *ma-na* kù-babbar [16]*a-na Puzur*$_4$*-A-šùr* rev. [17]*ad-ma-ku : a-ha-ma* [18]kù-babbar 10 *ma-na : a-na-kam* [19]*ší-bi*$_4$ *i-šu-šu-um* [20]*ša ki-ma i-na* [21]*e-ra-bi*$_4$*-šu-ma ú-šé-ba-/lá-ni* [22]*i-nu-mì a-na* [23]é *Puzur*$_2$*-A-šur té-ru-bu* [24]igi *um-me-a-ni a-wa-/tám* [25]*a-ni-tám i-dí-ší* [26]*a-hi a-ta : šu-ma lá ku-a-tí* [27]*ma-ma-an lá i-šu* [28]*ta-ki-li : ša ma-ma-an* u.e. [29]*lá ta-ša-me a-na* [30]*ú-um «tí» ga-ma-lim* [31]*ú ú-um e-ṭá-ri-im* le.e. [32]*i-hi-id-ma* kù-babbar 10 *ma-na* [33]*ša-am-qí-tám-ma : ma-ma-an ú-mì* [34]*lá e-mar-šu iš-ra-am A-ba-*silim *na-áš-a-ku-um*

[1–2]Say to Aššur-mūtappil: thus (says) Ahaha.

[3–5]I tried to seize silver from the joint-stock company administered by Dān-Aššur, but they (said) as follows: [5–7]"Puzur-Aššur, Buzāzu, and Ikuppaša have (already) taken (it)." [7–10]Make him pay the silver there, seal it, and let it go overland in their name. [10–12]Let a detailed letter from you come to me by the very next (caravan, saying) if they do pay (the silver), [13–14]so that here I can make the correct decision.

[15–17]I have invested 3½ minas of silver with Puzur-Aššur. [17–21]Furthermore, concerning the 10 minas of silver, I have here witnesses against him (who can confirm) that he should send (it) to me as soon as he arrives. [22–25]When you enter Puzur-Aššur's house, raise this matter in the presence of the investors.

[26–27]You are my brother; I have no one except you. [28–29]Do not listen to anyone's slander. [29–31]Now is the time to do me a favor and to save (me from financial stress)! [32–34]Be sure to dispatch to me at least 10 minas of silver. Nobody shall see the day of my (ruin).

[34]Abu-šalim is bringing you a belt.

Bibliography: Text published by Lewy as KTH, 7; translated by Michel (2001a, no. 225).

Comments: Ahaha could not recover her shares in two joint-stock companies. According to TC 3, 274, she held 10 minas of silver in the joint-stock company administered by Dān-Aššur. This silver could refer to her father's investment in the latter's joint-stock company, or to a share to which she was entitled. She also owned 3½ minas in the joint-stock company administered by her father's associate Puzur-Aššur, to whom she also loaned 10 minas of silver. She asks her brother to help her recover all these amounts.

---

283. Ahaha Claims Her Share in a Joint-Stock Company

Obv. [1]*a-na A-šur-mu-ta-pí-[il*$_5$ *qí]-bi-/ma* [2]*um-ma A-ha-h[a]-ma* 10 *ma-na* [3]kù-babbar *Ku-ra-ra ub-lam* kù-babbar *šu-[a]-/tí*[!](TIM) [4]*ša* [x x x x x x] kù-/gi [5]*ša [i-na na-ru-uq Da]n-*^{d}*A-/šur* [6]*il*$_5$*-q[é* x x x x kù]-gi [7]*ša* [x x x x x x-*m*]*a* [8]*qá-sú* [x x x] [9]*ša-áš-qí-il*$_5$ x (x)] [10]*šu-ma [lá i-mu-a n]a*[!]*-pá-al-/tám* [11]*i-na-áš-[pé-er-tí-kà lá-pí-it]* [12]*na-áš-pè-er-ta-kà šé*[!]*-bi*$_4$*-lá-ma* rev. [13]*a-na wa-bi*$_4$*-il*$_5$ *ṭup-pì-im* [14]1 gín kù-babbar *dí-in-ma a-na-ku* [15]*lu-ma-li a-na-kam* kù-babbar [16]*ša na-ad-ú ša na-ru-uq* [17]*Dan-A-šur* : *qá-tí ša-ak*[!](AD)-

na-at ^{18}*a-na-kam-ma* : *a-lá-qé a-hi a-ta* ^{19}*šu-ma lá a-ni-im* : *bu-lá-tí mì-ma* ^{20}«*mì-ma*» *lá i-šu i-hi-id-ma ma-/lá* ^{21}*lá a-ha-li-qú* : *e-pu-uš* ^{22}*a-šu-mì ša Puzur*$_2$*-A-šur iš-tí* ^{23}*A*$^?$*-du-ša a-ša-pá-r*[*a-kum* x x x] ^{24}*za-ku-ú* : *ú ba* [x x x *ù*] ^{25}*ša ta-áš-pu-*[*ra-am*] le.e. ^{26}*um-ma a-ta-ma* : *a-wa-tum*$^!$(AT) *ša na-áš-pè-er-/tim* ^{27}*i-ma-tim na-ad-a* ^{28}dingir-*ma i-ba-ri-tí-ni* ^{29}*i-da-gal*

$^{1-2}$[S]ay to Aššur-mūtappi[l]: thus (says) Ahah[a].

$^{2-3}$Kurara brought 10 minas of silver. $^{3-4}$This silver is that of [...] $^{4-6}$[...] the gold which he took from [the join-stock company of Dā]n-Aššur. $^{6-9}$[...] gold, who [*took somebody else's*] share, and make [him$^?$] pay back [...] $^{10-12}$If [he refuses], [write (his)] answer in [your] let[ter], and send it to me, then $^{13-14}$give to the bearer of the tablet 1 shekel of silver, $^{14-15}$and I myself will compensate it (to you).

$^{15-17}$Here, I have established a claim on the silver that has been deposited from the joint-stock company administered by Dān-Aššur. ^{18}I will take it right here! You are my brother; $^{19-20}$I have nothing else apart from these funds. $^{20-21}$Take care to act so that I will not be ruined!

$^{22-23}$As for the matter of Puzur-Aššur, I will writ[e you] with Aduša. [*When it*] has been cleared [... $^{24-26}$And] as for the [...] about which you wrote [me] as follows: $^{26-27}$"The words of the letters lie in the country (Anatolia). $^{28-29}$Only god will be witness between us."

Bibliography: Text published in copy and edited by Donbaz as Sadberk, 14; lines 3, 5, 11, 20, 26–29 cited by Michel (2001b, 176–81; citation, 180).

Comments: Ahaha urges her brother Aššur-mūtappil to help her recover her silver, representing her share in the joint-stock company administered by Dān-Aššur. She also mentions the matter concerning Puzur-Aššur.

---

284. Ahaha Accuses Her Brother of Having Appropriated Her Invested Silver

Obv. ^{1}*a-na* [*A-šur-mu-ta-pí-il*$_5$] ^{2}*ù I-ku-pá-*[*ša qí-bi-ma*] ^{3}*um-ma A-ha-ha-ma a-n*[*a* kù-babbar] ^{4}*ša a-na na-ru-uq* ^{5}*Puzur*$_2$*-A-šur ad-ma-ku-ni áš-ta-*[*na*]*-/me-m*[*a*] ^{6}*ší-ip-kà-tí-a Bu-za-zu* ^{7}*a-šu-a-tí-ma* : *ša-ak-na* ^{8}*ú* kù-babbar *ma-dam* : *il*$_5$*-ta-na-qé* ^{9}*i-zi-za-ma*$^!$ *ih-da-ma* ^{10}*iš-ti* (erased sign) *Bu-za-zu a-wa-tí-/a* ^{11}*gu*$_5$*-um-ra-ma ki-ma* ^{12}*iš-té-en*$_6$ *ú šé-na* ^{13}*il*$_5$*-qé-ú-ni ú a-tù-/nu* ^{14}*le-qé-a a-dí-i* ^{15}*ta-ad-mì-iq-tí-a* ^{16}[*a-šar*] *ta*$^!$*-da-ga-lá-ma*

Rev. (The reverse is illegible and has not been copied.)

[1–3][Say] to [Aššur-mūtappil] and Ikuppa[ša]: thus (says) Ahaha.

[3–5][As for the silver] that I invested in the (joint-stock company administered) by Puzur-Aššur, [5–8]I keep hearing that Buzāzu has joined my investments to his own and is constantly taking out substantial amounts of silver! [9–11]Come into action and take care to settle my case with Buzāzu, and, [12–14]just as a few others collected (their silver) once or twice, you too must collect (it)!

[14–16]As to my *tadmiqum*-trust, [wherever] you see [...]

Bibliography: Text published in copy by Smith as CCT 4, 31b; translated by by Michel (2001a, no. 226).

Comments: Ahaha and her brothers owned shares in the joint-stock company administered by Puzur-Aššur, presumably inherited from their father. However, Buzāzu managed to record all the silver under his own name and withdrew silver several times. Ahaha claims her share back. She urges another brother, Aššur-mūtappil, who also owns a share, to help her recover some of the silver by acting the same way Buzāzu did, that is, by withdrawing amounts of silver.

Tarām-Kūbi, Wife of Innaya, and Her Sister, Šīmat-Aššur

Tarām-Kūbi was married to Innaya (**285**), a well-known merchant, with whom she had five sons—Aššur-rēṣī, Aššur-taklāku, Puzur-Aššur, Šu-Suen, and Ikuppiya—and presumably some daughters, but we do not know how many or their names.[39] She was the sister of another famous Assyrian merchant from Kaneš, Imdī-ilum, with whom she exchanged several letters, together with her sister, Šīmat-Aššur.[40] The latter is less documented than her sister; she was presumably younger, since she appears regularly after her in letter headings.[41]

39. Michel 1991, 1:76–88; 2001a, 465–70. It is impossible to decide if the Tarā(m)-Kūbi, daughter of Aššur-ṭāb, attested in the 1993 archives is the same woman: Kt 93/k 402:9–10: 1 túg : *a-na Ta-ra-Ku-bi*, dumu-munus *A-šùr*-du$_{10}$; she sent the letter Kt 93/k 658, addressed to Ištar-lamassī, together with Pilah-Ištar.

40. Ichisar 1981, Larsen 1982, Kryszat 2007a, and the following footnote.

41. Note that there are several women named Šīmat-Aššur. Among these are

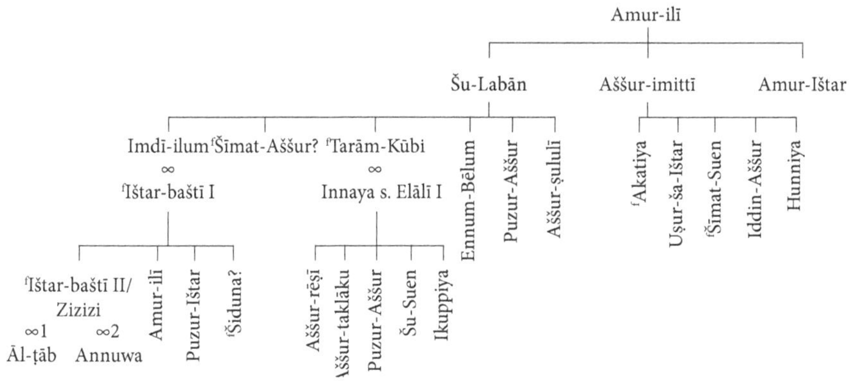

Fig. 17. Family tree of Tarām-Kūbi and Ištar-baštī.

Tarām-Kūbi lived in Aššur while her husband was active in Kaneš for at least twenty years and traveled from time to time to Aššur to visit his wife. Their sons left home, one after the other, in order to participate in the family business, transporting goods between Aššur and Kaneš, or within Anatolia, and acting as agents for their father. They regularly visited their mother and helped her to settle some affairs in Aššur.

Tarām-Kūbi managed her household and sent a dozen emotional letters, mainly to her husband in Kaneš. She gave him news of their house and children while some of them were still with her in Aššur (**206**). But later on, she was feeling lonely and regularly asked Innaya to come back home, presenting herself as a model wife who made beer for her husband (**129**). She also repeatedly complained that she was living in an empty house, without money to buy food (**128**). While claiming silver from her husband, she rejected his accusations that she had expensive tastes and urged him not to listen to slander about her (**128**). However, she asked for more female slaves (**129**, **206**) and wished to enlarge their house in Aššur by buying their neighbor's house (**129**).

Like most of the women in Aššur, Tarām-Kūbi wove textiles and sent part of her production to her husband in Kaneš (**128**, **286**), sometimes having difficulties in fulfilling his demands (**207**).[42] She asked him in return for the proceeds of her textiles, as well as for various goods (**286**),

the sister of Adu (**238**) and the consecrated daughter of Ikuppī-Ištar attested in Kt 93/k 598:8–11: 3 gín, [*a-n*]*a Ší-ma-at-A-šùr*, dumu-munus *I-ku-pí-Ištar*, nin-dingir; "3 shekels of silver [fo]r Šīmat-Aššur, daughter of Ikuppī-Ištar, the consecrated woman."

42. See also CCT 4, 46a:25–27 (letter to Innaya by Aššur-ṭāb, edited by Michel

and received even gold (**285**). Some of the precious metals were not for her own use but to be offered to divinities; for example, no less than fifteen minas of silver (7.5 kg) to be deposited in the Aššur temple as Innaya's votive offerings (**287**). She also paid for an emblem for the god (**128**) and worried about votive offerings for Ninkarrak that had been withheld by a colleague (**206**) or linen and a belt for the god Amurrum, the family god of Innaya (**129**).[43] Tarām-Kūbi was particularly devoted to religion and did not fail to remind her husband to come to Aššur to fulfill his religious duties toward the god Aššur (**129**).

Tarām-Kūbi also acted as a representative of her husband, in contact with both his investors and collaborators and the authorities of the City Hall (**128**, **206**). She sent several letters alone or together with her husband's representatives in Aššur concerning his current business (**128**, **129**).[44] Innaya owed a substantial debt in silver to the eponym, but she lacked silver to pay the debt (**207**).[45] Together with their son Ikkupiya, she also asked for certified tablets in order to defend in the City Hall his case concerning trade in lapis lazuli (**206**).[46] In a copy of a message sent to both of them and to a collaborator, Innaya complained about their lack of effectiveness in answering his letters and settling his affairs (**289**).

Interestingly, Tarām-Kūbi was in contact not only with other women living in Aššur, such as Lamassī, the wife of Pūšu-kēn, but also with women staying in Kaneš: she received silver from Tariša, the daughter of Ali-ahum, who lived in the house excavated in 1993 (**288**).[47] She might have met her when Tariša stayed for a while in Aššur, since Tarām-Kūbi herself seems to have never traveled to Anatolia.

Tarām-Kūbi also stood in contact with her brother Imdī-ilum, to whom she wrote several letters, often together with their possible sister,

---

1991, no. 60): 1 túg *šu-ru-am*, 1 túg *za-ku-am*! *ša Ta-ra-am-Ku-bi*, *na-áš-a-ku-um*; "he is bringing you 1 dark textile and 1 light-colored textile from Tarām-Kūbi."

43. Lewy 1961, 47–50, Michel 1991, 1:86 and Kryszat 2006a, 53–56.

44. See also *RA* 81, 7, edited by Michel 1991, no. 90, which is a copy of a letter sent by Innaya to his representatives and to Tarām-Kūbi. The first half of this broken tablet is addressed to his wife, while the reverse concerns all the recipients of the letter.

45. A very fragmentary letter of Tarām-Kūbi to her husband, *RA* 81, 15, edited by Michel 1991, no. 6, also deals with a debt in silver that Innaya owed to the eponym.

46. The text CCT 4, 24a, sent by Tarām-Kūbi alone to her husband, mentions the payment to the City Hall of the price of the lapis lazuli (lines 1′–4′; Michel 2001a, no. 346).

47. Michel 2015b.

Šīmat-Aššur. However, even if the latter appears in the headings, the letters are regularly formulated in the first person singular, which gives the impression that only Tarām-Kūbi was writing or dictating the message. They consulted female diviners and warned Imdī-ilum about possible terrible consequences of his bad behavior: spending all his time on earning more silver, he neglected the god Aššur and his religious duties (**252**). They sent him textiles to be sold in Anatolia and contested the low prices he sent in return, expecting at least twenty shekels apiece (**170**, **252**). They informed him about the purchase of a house, which was arranged by his representatives (**170**).

Both sisters received various objects sent by their brother from Kaneš: jointly, one mina of silver in the form of bracelets and for each of them a pair of sandals (**295**), and twice, jointly, three shekels of silver from their sister-in-law, Ištar-baštī (**296**).[48] Tarām-Kūbi was the recipient of some silver sent by Imdī-ilum to various people in Aššur.[49] Šīmat-Aššur also received silver from her brother, along with other men and women in Aššur.[50] Alone, she occasionally acted with representatives of her brother in Aššur, paying salaries of employees or giving silver for the purchase of a house.[51]

Tarām-Kūbi and Šīmat-Aššur were thus regularly in contact with their brother Imdī-ilum, receiving silver from him and working with his representatives in Aššur, and, at the same time, Tarām-Kūbi exchanged many letters with her husband Innaya, managing their household, producing textiles, and representing him or attending to his affairs in Aššur. Even though Tarām-Kūbi had left the family home by marrying Innaya, she kept in contact with them and was still involved in the business of her own siblings.

---

48. Bracelets: Prag I, 495:1–3: 1 *ma-na* kù-babbar *ša-wi-re, Ta-ra-am-Ku-bi, ù Ší-ma-at-A-šùr*. Three shekels of silver: Prag I, 556:15–16: 3 gín kù-babbar *a-na*, *[T]a-ra-am-Ku-bi ù Ší-ma-at-A-šur.*

49. Unpublished text, Kayseri 1831; transliteration by Landsberger (Kayseri 30):14–15, 1 *ri-ik-sú-um ša* [...], *ù Ta-ra-am-Ku-bi*.

50. CCT 5, 40:12–13 // TC 2, 58:6′–7′: 1 *ri-ik-sà-am, a-na Ší-ma-*<*at*>*-A-šur*; text edited by Ulshöfer (1995, no. 46). ICK 2, 87:20′–21′, text edited by Ulshöfer (1995, no. 333), [x *ma*]*-na* 3 gín kù-babbar, [*Ší-ma-a*]*t-A-šùr.*

51. CTMMA 1, 75:23–24, 42–45, letter sent by Aššur-imittī, Šu-Ištar, Ennānum, and Puppurānum to Imdī-ilum: 7⅓ gín kù-babbar, ^{d}utu-du$_{10}$ *Ší-ma-at-A-šùr tal-qé* ... *a-na* 3 *ma-na* 5 gín kù-babbar é, *Šu-Be-lim ni-iš-a-ma-kum* kù-babbar *iš-tí, Ší-ma-at-A-šùr ni-il*$_{5}$*-qé-ma*, [*ni-iš*]*-qúl.*

285. Tarām-Kūbi Receives Gold from Her Husband

Obv. [1]⅓ *ma-na* kù-ki *p*[*á*]*-ša-*/[*l*]*am* [2]s[i]g$_5$ di[r]i *ni-i*[*s-h*]*a-*[*sú* /d]iri [3]*ku-nu-ki ša* dingir-*ba-ni* [4]dumu *Ma-ni-a a-na A-lim*^{ki} [5]*a-na Ta-ra-am-Ku-bi*$_4$ [6]*a-ša-at I-na-a* [7]*ki-ma* dingir-*ba-n*[*i*] [8]*Lu-zi-*[*n*]*a a-n*[*a*] [9]*A-ta-ta ší-i*[*p-ri-im*] lo.e. [10]*ip-q*[*í*]*-id-ma* rev. [11]*ú-bi-il*$_5$ [12](uninscribed line) [13]igi *Ku-da-tim* [14]igi *Šu-mì-a-bi*$_4$*-a* [15]igi *Sú-en*$_6$-sig$_5$

[8–10]Luzina entrusted to Atata, the mes[enger], [1–2]⅓ minas of extra-fine *pašallum*-gold—its import tax added—[3–4]sealed by Ilī-bāni, son of Manniya, [7]on behalf of Ilī-bāni [10–11]and he brought (it) [4]to the city (of Aššur) [5–6]to Tarām-Kūbi, wife of Innaya.

[13–15]In the presence of Kudātum, Šumi-abiya, and Suen-damiq.

Bibliography: Text published by Hecker as KUG, 5; edited by Eisser and Lewy (1930, no. 138) and Michel (1991, no. 131).

Comments: Tarām-Kūbi, Innaya's wife, is the recipient of 20 shekels of extra-fine gold, which has been sent by Ilī-bāni. This echoes letter **128**, in which she acknowledges receipt from her husband of ½ mina of gold brought by Ilī-bāni.

286. Tarām-Kūbi Sends Various Textiles to Her Husband

Obv. [1]*a-na I-na-a* [2]*qí-bi-ma um-ma* [3]*Ta-ra-am-Ku-bi-ma* [4][x] túg$^{\text{hi-a}}$ sig$_5$^{tim} diri [5][x +] 2 túg$^{\text{hi-a}}$ *qá-áb-li-*[*ú*]*-tim* [6]5 túg$^{\text{hi-a}}$ *ša A-ki-dí-e* [7][x +] 26½ *ma-na* an-na [8][x *a*]*t*$^?$ *a-*[x x x x] lo.e. [9][x] x [x] *šu* [x x] x [10][x] gí[n k]ù-babbar [x x x] rev. [11]*mì-šál* anše [12]*ù mì-šál* kù-babbar [13]anše$^{\text{hi-a}}$ *il*$_5$*-qé* [14]10 gín k[ù-k]i *ku-bu-ur-/ší-nim* [15]*ù na-áb-ri-tám* [16]*a-ṣú-ha-ar-tim* [17]*šé-bi*$_4$*-lam na-áb-ri-/tum* [18][*lu*] *ra-bi*$_4$*-a-at* :

[1–3]Say to Innaya: thus (says) Tarām-Kūbi.

[4][x] textiles of top quality, [5][x +]2 textiles of standard quality, [6]5 Akkadian textiles, [7][x +] 26½ minas of tin, [8–9][…] [10][x] sh[ekels of silver…] [11–12]half a donkey (load), and half of the silver; [13]he took the donkeys.

[14–17]Send me 10 shekels of *kupuršinnum*-gold and a *nabrītum* for the girl; the *nabrītum* must be of large size.

Bibliography: Text published in copy by Stephens as BIN 6, 90; edited by Michel (1991, no. 1).

Comments: In this letter, addressed by Tarām-Kūbi to her husband, she lists different types of textiles that she presumably sent him. She asks in return for some gold and an unknown object.

Line 10: *kupuršinnum* is a low-quality gold, according to Veenhof, in AKT 8, 286.

Lines 15, 17: according to this text, the *nabrītum* mentioned here might be a piece of garment. For a detailed study of this word, see Veenhof 2015a, 253–59.

---

287. Tarām-Kūbi Receives Silver to Be Deposited in the Aššur Temple

Obv. [1]*a-na I-na-a* [2]*qí-bi-ma um-ma* [3]*Hu-sà-ru-um* : *ù* [4]*Ta-ra-am-Ku-bi-ma* [5]15 *ma-na* kù-babbar [6]*ša ik-ri-bi-k*[*à*] [7]*A-šùr*-du$_{10}$ *ub-lá*-[*ni-/a-tí*] lo.e. [8]*é*$^{bé-et}$ *A-šur* [9]*na-dí-i*

[1–3]Say to Innaya: thus (say) Husārum and Tarām-Kūbi.

[5–7]Aššur-ṭāb brought [us] 15 minas of silver as your votive offering. [8–9]It is deposited in the Aššur temple.

Bibliography: Text published by Larsen as AKT 6d, 770 (Kt 94/k 935).

Comments: Husārum and Tarām-Kūbi acknowledge the receipt of a substantial amount of silver (7.5 kg), which has been deposited in the Aššur temple as votive offerings.

---

288. Tarām-Kūbi Receives Silver from a Woman in Kaneš

Obv. [1]10 gín kù-babbar [2]*ku-nu-ki ša Ta-ri-ša* [3]*a-na Ta-ra-am-Ku-bi*$_4$ [4]*ù La-ma-sí* [5]*a-na A-sà-nim* [6]*kà-ṣa-ar I-dí-Ku-bi*$_4$*-im* [7]*áp-qí-id-ma* [8]*a-na A-lim*^{ki} [9]*ú-bi-il*$_5$ rev. [10]igi *En-na-nim* [11]*ší-ip-ri-im* [12]igi Tí-tí-na-tal [13]igi *I-dí-Ku-bi*$_4$*-im* [14]*um-me-a-ni-šu*

[5–7]I entrusted to Asānum, Iddin-Kūbum's harnessor, [1–2]10 shekels of silver sealed by Tariša, [3–4]for Tarām-Kūbi and Lamassī, [7–9]and he brought (it) to the city (of Aššur).

[10–11]In the presence of Ennānum, the messenger, [12]Titinatal, [13–14]and Iddin-Kūbum, his investor.

Bibliography: Text edited by Donbaz (1998, 417) as Kt z/t 13; collated on photo.

Comments: This transport contract was found on Kültepe mound, in the fortifications of the Old Palace. Tariša, presumably the daughter of Ali-ahum—whose archive was excavated in 1993 (fig. 6; Michel 2008e)—sends a small amount of silver to Tarām-Kūbi and Lamassī, the wife of the well-known merchant Pūšu-kēn. These two women appear several times together as recipients of small amounts of silver; for example, in the very damaged tablet VS 26, 162:9′. They are also mentioned sequentially in the transport contract Prag I, 736:21–24: 1 *ma-na* kù-babbar *ša* x [x], *ù* 3 lá ¼ gín kù-ki *a-nu-qú-a*, *a-na La-ma-sí* 1 *ma-na* kù-babbar, *a-na Ta-ra-am-Ku-bi*, "1 mina of silver of […] and 3 minus ¼ shekels of gold, (weight of) my rings, for Lamassī; 1 mina of silver for Tarām-Kūbi."

---

289. Tarām-Kūbi Has to Make Sure That Her Husband's Associates Settle His Affairs

Obv. [1]*um-ma I-na-a-ma a-na* [2][*Ú*]*-ṣur-ša-A-šùr I-ku-pì-a* [3][*ù Ta-ra*]*-am-Ku-bi*$_4$ *qí-bi*$_4$*-ma* [4]*a-dí* 20 [x x] *a-dí* é *Ku-ra* [5]*áš-pu-ra-ku-nu-tí* : *té-er-ta-*[*a*]*k-nu-*[*m*]*a* [6][*l*]*á i-tù-ra-am* : *a-na-ku* [7]*a-na ku-nu-a-tim* : *ki-a-a*[*m*] [8]*a-ša-lá-aṭ a-h*[*u-a*] *a-*[*tù-nu*] [9][*b*]*e-lu-a a-tù-*[*nu* x x] [10][x x] *ší-na* [x x x x] [11][x x *z*]*i-zu-m*[*a* x x x] [12][x x x x x x x x] lo.e. [13][x x x x x x x] [14][x x x x x x] rev. [15][x x x x x x x x] [16][x x x]*-im* x [x x x] [17]*ù šu-ma i-ga-ri-*[*ú-ku-nu*] [18][*k*]*i-ma ta-le-e-a-ni* [19][*a*]*-wa-tám* : *gu*$_5$*-um-ra a-hu-ú-*[*a*] [20][*a*]*-tù-nu ki-ma ma-ma-an* [21]*šu-ma-nam* : *lá áš-ku-na-ku-nu-tí* [22][*bu*]*-lá-tí-a ú i-bi*$_4$*-sà-e-a* [23]*tí-de*$_8$*-a a-na ú-um ga-ma-lim* [24]*ù e-ṭá-ri-im lam-ni-ìš* [25]*i-qá-tí* du-mus-munus *Ku-ra* [26]*ep-ša-kum* a-na kù-babbar u.e. [27]2 *ma-na mì-ma ú-lá* [28][*t*]*a-ša-a-lá-ni i-na* le.e. [29][…]

[1–3]Thus (says) Innaya: say to [U]ṣur-ša-Aššur, Ikuppiya, [and Tarā]m-Kūbi.

[4–6]I wrote you up to 20 [times?] concerning the house of Kura, (but) no report from you has ever came back to me. [6–8]As for me, do I act presumptuously in any way over you? [8–9]Y[ou] are [my] brothers; yo[u] are my [l]ords […]

[17]And if he quarrels [with you], [18–19]bring to an end the affair as you can. [19–20]You are [my] brothers. [20–21]I have not tethered you like anybody else. [22–23]You know (everything) about my [ca]pital and my losses! [23–26]Now it is the time to do a favor and to save (me from financial distress); I am badly treated by the daughter of Kura. [26–28]As for the silver, you never asked me for 2 minas. In […]

Bibliography: Text published by Hecker, Kryszat, and Matouš as Prag I, 547. Collated on photo.

Comments: Tarām-Kūbi receives this letter from Innaya, together with her son and one of her husband's associates, presumably to urge them to act and settle the matter of the house of Kura.

Line 21: the reading was suggested to me by Veenhof. The word *šummannum*, "rope, tethering rope," is also attested in BIN 6, 51:20; see *CAD* Š/3, 280a. This sentence means "I left you your freedom."

Line 26: the verbal form *ep-ša-kum* has been understood as an error for *epšāku*, stative 1st person singular.

---

290. The Sisters Receive Silver Bracelets from Their Brother, Who Asks for Textiles

Obv. [1]*[um-ma] Im-dí-*dingir*-ma* [2]*[a]-na Ta-ra-am-Ku-bi* [3]*ù [Š]í-ma-at-A-šur qí-bi-ma* [4]*li-*[x x x] *šu-pu-ur-ma* [5]*ša-wi-re ša*$^{!}$ *qá-tí-a* [6]*šu-qúl*$^{!}$*-ta-áš-nu* 1 ma-na kù-babbar [7]*ku-nu-ki-a Puzur*$_4$*-A-šùr* [8]*na-áš-a-ku-nu-tí a-hu-ú-a* [9]*a-tí-n[a ṭu]p-pá-am ša a-na* [10]*ša ki-[ma ki-na-tí] ù ša ki-ma* [11]*i-a-tí áš*$^{!}$*-pu-[r]u : šé-me*$^{!}$(EM)*-a-ma* [12]*a-ma-lá té-er-t[í-a]* [13]*a-ṣé-er* [x x x x] [14]*ša a-na ší-tí* [x x x] [15]*a-na ša-*[x x x] [16]*ša ah-bu-[lu* x x x] [17]kù-babbar *ṣí-ba-s[ú* x *m]a-/na* [18]kù-babbar *ṭup-pá-áš*$^{!}$*-nu* [x x] [19]*gi-im-lá-ni a-dí a-lá-ak* [20]*Pu-šu-ke-en*$_6$ [kù-babbar]^{ap}*-ki-na* [21]*li-bé-e-el-ki-na Pu-šu-ke-en*$_6$ [22]*a-na* 1 iti-kam : *ú-ṣí-a-am* [23]*a-na-kam : ú-um ga-ma-li-im* [24]*gi-im-lá-ni* : túg$^{hi\text{-}a}$ *a-na* [25]*[q]á-tí-a la i-šu* túg$^{hi\text{-}a}$ [26][x]*-x-ak* 10 túg$^{hi\text{-}a}$ *šé-bi-lá-nim-ma* [27]*[a*$^{?}$*-ṣí]-ib-tí-ki-na* [28]*[a-g]a*$^{?}$*-mì-il*$_5$*-ki-na* [29][x x *a-ha]-tù-a : a-tí-na* [30]*[a-na] té-er-tí-a : la* [x x (x)] [31][x x]*-x-e ki-ma i-a-tí* [x x] [32][x x]*-x-x e ma-am-*[x x] le.e. [33][…] *té-er-tí-a li-iš-ú-mu* [34][…] *x ṣí-ib-tim* [35][…]

[1–3][Thus (says)] Imdī-ilum: say [t]o Tarām-Kūbi and [Š]īmat-Aššur.

[4][...] write, and [5-8]Puzur-Aššur is bringing you, under my seal, bracelets at my disposal; their weight is 1 mina of silver. [8-9]You are my sisters. [9-11]The tablet that I sent to [your] repre[sentatives] and my representatives, listen to it and, [12-16]according to [my] instructions, to [...], that [...] for the remainder [...] for [...] that I owe[d...] [17-19]the silver, its interest [x m]inas, the silver [...] their tablet, do me a favor, [19-21]until the arrival of Pūšu-kēn, let your silver be at your disposal. [21-22]Pušū-kēn will leave in 1 month. [23-24]Here, now it is the time to do a favor, so do me a favor! [24-25]I have no textiles at my disposal, [25-26][...] textiles, send me [...] 10 textiles, and [27-28][I will] do you a favor [for] your [in]terest. [29][...] you are my [sis] ters. [30][For] my instructions [...] [31][...] in my name [...] [33][...] let them listen to my instructions [34][...] interest [...]

Bibliography: Unpublished text known from a transliteration by Matouš as 50a (K926); lines 1–8 cited by Matouš (1982, 270) under the text reference Ka 1044.

Comments: This text is presumably a copy of a letter sent by Imdī-ilum to his sisters in Aššur. The silver bracelets weighing one mina are also mentioned in **297** and Prag I, 495:1–3, cited above, note 48 in this chapter. Imdī-ilum asks his sisters for help and for textiles.

Line 8: the pronominal suffix of the verb is in the masculine plural form; it should be feminine plural.

There is another broken letter, LB 1296, edited in Ichisar 1981, 339, sent by Šīmat-Aššur to Imdī-ilum, which mentions silver and textiles; at the end, it is sent by both Tarām-Kūbi and Šīmat-Aššur.

Ištar-baštī I, Wife of Imdī-ilum, and Her Daughter, Ištar-baštī II/Zizizi

Ištar-baštī is a name regularly found in the family of Imdī-ilum, a well-known merchant who worked first in Kaneš then retired to Aššur.[52] Ištar-

52. Ichisar 1981; Larsen 1982; 2015a, 207–8. For the family tree of Ištar-baštī I and II, see fig. 6.2. Imdī-ilum is attested during the years REL 81–104, mainly in Anatolia. There are presumably other women named Ištar-baštī; one of them could be the corecipient of the letter BIN 6, 4, also addressed to Puzur-Adad by Edin-Aššur. It is impossible to identify the Ištar-baštī who buys a slave in the contract Kt a/k 898, published by Sever 1998, 486–87, or the one who appears as creditor in **185**. A text men-

baštī was the name of both the wife and the daughter of Imdī-ilum, which causes to some confusion in the interpretation of a few letters (fig. 17).[53] Imdī-ilum and Ištar-baštī had two sons: Amur-ilī, who had the same name as his grandfather, and Puzur-Ištar, as well as a daughter, Ištar-baštī, named after her mother, who also used the nickname Zizizi, and perhaps another daughter, Šiduna (**230**).

Ištar-baštī wrote several letters from Aššur to Puzur-Ištar, who was living in the family house in Kaneš and was in charge of his father's business there; these letters illustrate aspects of her life in Aššur (**229**, **231**). While she was staying there, her husband traveled in upper Mesopotamia and Anatolia, leaving her alone for long periods (**231**). Her second son, Amur-ilī, traveled between Aššur and Anatolia. She urged her sons to stop quareling and to act as good children and to send news to reassure their mother (**231**). Ištar-bāšti prayed to two goddesses, Ištar and Ištar-ZA-AT (**241**).

Like most of the women in Aššur, Ištar-baštī produced textiles, which she sold or gave on *tadmiqum*-trust to merchants (**241**, **294**, **297**).[54] Thus she appears in a memorandum as the sender of six *kutānum*-textiles (**291**), and, in return, she received small amounts of silver together with her husband and in-laws, as, for example, a silver bowl of fourteen shekels (**292**).

When her second son, Puzur-Ištar, was supposed to make a visit to Aššur, she waited for him in order to travel with him to Kaneš, intending to take care of the family affairs there (**229**). And indeed, she lived for some time in Kaneš, together with her husband, or alone when he was traveling either in Anatolia or back to Aššur. In Kaneš, she received textiles from her sisters-in-law, Tarām-Kūbi and Šīmat-Aššur (**170**), and she sent back silver and other goods, such as pairs of sandals, to Aššur (**294**–**297**).

In Kaneš, she received letters from her husband, alone or with their son Amur-ilī, in which he asked her or them to supervise his business there: clearing or selling his merchandise, collecting gold and silver, entrusting

tions the death of a woman named Ištar-baštī: Kt 94/k 432:8–9 (courtesy Barjamovic): *i-nu-m*[*i*] *Ištar-ba-áš-tí*, *i-mu-tù*. In the text AKT 6b, 445, Ištar-baštī seems to be the wife of the author of the letter, Bēlia.

53. According to Kryszat 2007a. This goes against the previous interpretations of Ichisar 1981, 14; Larsen 1982, 219; Michel 2001a, 464; and previous literature, which suggested that Imdī-ilum was married to Šīmat-Aššur; and also against Barjamovic, Hertel, and Larsen 2012, 62, who noted that Tarīš-mātum was the wife of Imdī-ilum.

54. For her cylinder seal, see fig. 13.

goods to agents, and safeguarding his archive (**176**, **217**, **293**). Thus, she acted as representative of her husband when he was away and their son Amur-ilī was traveling and maintained the connection between them. For his part, Imdī-ilum represented his wife: when he was in Aššur, he bought goods for her to be sold in Anatolia (**176**). He also wrote her advice concerning the education to be given to their son, who was supposed to behave as a gentleman. In Kaneš, she received letters from her husband's collaborator, who informed her about her *tadmiqum*-trust (**294**).

Imdī-ilum and Ištar-baštī had a daughter named after her mother, Ištar-baštī, but who also was nicknamed Zizizi.[55] She was first married to Āl-ṭāb, who died in an epidemic, and took as second husband the Anatolian Annuwa (**298**).[56] If the pathetic letter (**230**) she sent to her parents to announce the illness of her (first) husband is not a copy, then she first lived in Aššur, where her Assyrian husband died, and later on moved to Kaneš, where she received letters from her parents. Her parents complained that her two marriages cost them the substantial sum of ten minas of silver and that, since they were back in Aššur, she did nothing to help their business in Kaneš (**50**)!

In a letter addressed to his wife and son, Imdī-ilum indicated that he bought an Abarnian-textile for his daughter (**176**). Her mother, Ištar-baštī, sent a letter to her husband, Annuwa, to her brother, and to her concerning a debt she had to repay (**192**). And Ištar-baštī received a letter from a certain Ikuppiya, who announced his intention to travel with her husband, Annuwa.[57]

---

55. There is at least one other woman named Zizizi, who married Atata, the son of Mannum-balum-Aššur, who was the mother of Uṣur-ša-Aššur according to TC 3, 250:6. It is impossible to identify the Zizizi mentioned in AKT 1, 60, who lent ½ mina, 4½ shekels of silver to a couple of Anatolians, and, in AKT 1, 72, silver to an Assyrian. Furthermore, it is difficult to identify the Zizizi who figures, together with Ištar-lamassī, as addressee of the letter AKT 6c, 646.

56. TC 2, 28:6–7, 9–11, 24–25: 2 *me-at* 13 túg$^{hi\text{-}a}$, sig$_5$ … é *Ištar-ba-áš-tí*, *a-ša-at A-al*$^!$(TAL-A)-du$_{10}$, [*i-b*]*a-ší-ú* … [*a*]*-šar Ištar-ba-áš-tí*, [*ku-nu*]*-ku-šu* : *i-ba-ší-ú* (edited by Michel 1991, no. 64; correction of line 10 already proposed by Lewy 1950, 374 n. 49): "213 good-quality textiles … are in the house of Ištar-baštī, wife of Āl-ṭāb … they are with Ištar-baštī under his [se]al."

57. It is not impossible that the daughter of Imdī-ilum is concerned in the unpublished text Kt n/k 1385:15′–21′: 10 *pì-ri-kà-nim*, *na-ar-bu-tim*, *ša Ištar-ba-áš-tí ší-im-šu-nu*, urudu sig$_5$ *Ta-ri-ta-ra-i-am*, *a-na U-zu-a* : *dí-in-ma*, ki urudu^{-i}*-a a-na Bu-ur-ha-tim*, *lu-šé-ri-bu*; "As for the 10 soft *pirikannum*-textiles of Ištar-bastī, give their

291. Ištar-baštī, Together with Her Husband, Sends Tin and Textiles to Kaneš

Obv. [1]8 gú an-na [2]40 túg *ku-ta-nu* [3]*a-ší-a-ma-tim* [4]*ša Im-dí-lim* [5]*a-ha-ma* 14 túg *ku-ta-nu* [6]12 túg *šu-ru-tum* [7]2 túg *A-bar-ni-ú* [8]*ša Im-dí-lim* [9]10 *ma-na* an-[n]a lo.e. [10]6 túg *ku-ta-n*[*u*] rev. [11]*ša Ištar-ba-áš-*[*tí*]

[1]8 talents of tin, [2]40 *kutānum*-textiles, [3-4]for purchases of Imdī-ilum. [5]In addition, 14 *kutānum*-textiles, [6]12 dark texiles, [7]2 Abarnian-textiles [8]from Imdī-ilum; [9]10 minas of ti[n], [10]6 *kutānum*-textiles from Ištar-baštī.

Bibliography: Text published in copy by Stephens as BIN 6, 230; edited by Ichisar (1981, 90–91) and Ulshöfer (1995, no. 311).

Comments: Ištar-baštī sends merchandise to Anatolia: 5 kg of tin and six *kutānum*-textiles, together with a consignment of her husband.

292. Ištar-baštī Is the Recipient of a Silver Bowl

Obv. [1]5 *né-pì-šu* 50 *ma-na* [2]kù-babbar *ṣa-ru-pu-um* [3]1 *ri-ik-sú-um* [4]⅚ *ma-na* 2 gín kù-gi [5]*pá-šu-lu-um* sig$_5$ [6]1 *ri-ik-sú-um* 1⅓ *ma-na* [7]kù-babbar 1 *ri-ik-sú-um* [8]1⅔ *ma-na* kù-babbar [9]*mì-ma a-ni-um* [10]*ku-nu-ki-a a-na* [11]*ṣé-er Im-dí-lim* [12]*a-na I-dí-*[d]im lo.e. [13]*áp-qí-id* [14]⅓ *ma-na* 6 gín kù-babbar rev. [15]*kà-sú-um ša* [16]*a-na Im-dí-lim* [17]⅚ *ma-na* 5 gín kù-babbar [18]*ú ša* 10 gín *kà-sú-um* [19]*a-na Ší-ma-at-A-šur* [20]14 gín kù-babbar *kà-sú-um* [21]*a-na Ištar-ba-áš-tí* [22]1½ gín *a-na Ni-na-lá* [23]1½ gín *a-na Lá-ma-ša* [24]*mì-ma a-ni-im ša-du-a-sú* [25]*ša-bu a-na Im-dí-*[d]im [26]igi *A-hu-qar* [27]dumu *Šu-Ištar* u.e. [28]igi *Šu-A-nim* [29]dumu *Ha-da-a* le.e. [30]igi *Šu-Ištar* dumu *Ì-lí-iš-tí-kál*

[1-2]5 packets with 50 minas of refined silver, [3-5]1 package of ⅚ minas, 2 shekels of good-quality *pašallum*-gold, [6-7]1 package of 1⅓ minas of silver, [7-8]1 package of 1⅔ minas of silver; [9-13]all this I entrusted under my seal to Iddin-Adad to deliver it to Imdī-ilum.

proceeds in fine Taritar copper to Uzua, so that they may bring it together with my copper to Bur(uš)hattum." Lines cited by Bayram 1997, 56; and Dercksen 1996, 129 n. 402.

$^{14–16}$A silver cup of ⅓ mina, 6 shekels of silver for Imdī-ilum, $^{17–19}$a silver cup of ⅚ minas, 5 shekels of silver for Šīmat-Aššur, $^{20–21}$a silver cup of 14 shekels of silver for Ištar-baštī, ^{22}1½ shekels for Ninala, ^{23}1½ shekels for Lamaša; $^{24–25}$all this, its transport fee paid, for Imdī-ilum.

$^{26–30}$In the presence of Ahu-(wa)qar, son of Šu-Ištar; Šu-Anum, son of Hadaya; and Šu-Ištar, son of Iliš-tikal.

Bibliography: Text published in copy by Smith and Wiseman as CCT 5, 41b; edited by Ichisar (1981, 105–6).

Comments: In this transport contract concerning quantities of silver to be sent from Anatolia to various recipients in Aššur, Ištar-baštī receives a silver bowl of fourteen shekels of silver. The shipment is made in the name of her husband. Among the other recipients are several women, including her sister-in-law, Šīmat-Aššur.

Lines 15, 18, 20: the cup, *kāsum*, corresponds to a form of "concrete money" here.

---

293. Imdī-ilum Makes His Wife, Ištar-baštī, Witness a Letter Addressed to Their Son

Obv. ^{1}[*u*]*m-ma Im-dí-lúm-ma* ^{2}*a-na Ištar-ba-áš-tí* ^{3}*ù A-mur*-dingir : *qí-bi-ma* ^{4}*a-na A-mur*-dingir : *qí-bi-ma* ^{5}*i-ṭup-pí* : *ṭup-pí-ma* ^{6}*uš-ta-am-ṭí-kà* : *um-*[*ma*] ^{7}*a-ta-ma* : *ta-ma-a*[*r*] ^{8}*a-wi-lu-tí* : *lu ba-áb-t*[*a-kà*] ^{9}*lu lu-qú-ut-kà* : *ša šé-p*[*í-kà*] ^{10}*za-ki-a-ma* : *tí-ib-a-ma* ^{11}*a-tal-kam* : 4⅔ *ma-*[*na*] ^{12}8 gín kù-babbar *iš-*[*tí*] lo.e. ^{13}*I-dí-Sú-en*$_6$ dumu *A-*[*lá-hi-im*], ^{14}1⅓ *ma-na* 4[+ x gín kù-babbar] ^{15}[*iš*]*-tí* : Ku-ra-[ra] rev. ^{16}1⅓ *ma-na* 2[+ x gín] ^{17}kù-babbar *iš-tí Ištar-*[x x (x)] ^{18}1½ *ma-na* 6 gí[n kù-babbar] ^{19}*ší-im* 1 *ša-am-*[*ší-im*] ^{20}*iš-tí* : *Pu-šu-ke-en*$_6$ ^{21}*ù ša* 2 *ša-na-a*[*t*] ^{22}*ṣí-ba-sú* 2 *ma-na* k[ù-babbar] ^{23}*a-na-kam* : *a-na Pu-šu-ke-e*[*n*$_6$] ^{24}*ah-bu-ul* : *iš-té-ni-iš* ^{25}*li-ik-nu-uk-ma* ^{26}[*lu*]*-šé-bi*$_4$*-lam* : *i-re-eš*$_{15}$ ^{27}[*š*]*a ki-ma* : *i-a-tí* u.e. ^{28}[*li-zi*]*-iz-ma* kù-babbar ^{29}[*ù ṣ*]*í-ba-sú* le.e. ^{30}*A-šùr-*du$_{10}$ *ša-áš-qí-lá-šu* (erasure) ^{31}[*ù*] : *a-šu-mì* : *ša* dumu *Ì-lí-dí-n*[*a-šu*] ^{32}[*šu*]*-ma* : *ú-sà-lá-a-ku-nu-tí* : *a-ma-lá* ^{33}*ta-le-e-*<*a*>*-ni gu-um-ra*

$^{1–4}$Thus (says) Imdī-ilum: say to Ištar-baštī and Amur-ilī; say to Amur-ilī.

$^{5–6}$In letter after letter I have warned you! $^{6–8}$You (reacted) as follows: "You will see that I am a gentleman!" $^{8–10}$Clear [your] outstanding claims and your merchandise of [your] transport, then $^{10–11}$set out and come here.

[11–13]4⅔ mi[nas], 8 shekels of silver is [with] Iddin-Suen, son of A[li-ahum]; [14–15]1⅓ minas, 4[+ x shekels of silver fr]om *Kura*[*ra*]; [16–17]1⅓ minas, 2[+ x shekels] of silver from Ištar-[x-x-(x)]; [18–20]1½ minas, 6 sh[ekels of silver], price of 1 sun di[sk] from Pūšu-kēn. [21–24]And I became indebted here to Pūšu-kēn for 2 minas of s[ilver] plus the interest on it for 2 years. [24–26]Let him seal (it) altogether, and [let] him send it to me. [26–28][Let hi]m assist my representatives, and [28–30]make Aššur-ṭāb pay the silver [and] its [in]terest.

[31–33][And] as for the son of Ilī-iddin[aššu, i]f he begs you, settle (the affair) as best you can.

Bibliography: Text published in copy by Lewy as TC 3, 57; edited by Ichisar (1981, 251–53).

Comments: Ištar-baštī is corecipient of a letter from her husband mainly addressed to their son. Imdī-ilum has her witness his instruction to the son, Amur-ilī, to clear his merchandise and come to meet him. There follows a list of silver items from various people. Letter **176** is addressed to the same people and uses the same expression as lines 5–6 of this letter; it must have been sent to Kaneš from elsewhere in Anatolia. This suggests that Imdī-ilum's wife must have traveled and stayed in Kaneš for a while.

---

294. Ištar-baštī Has a *Tadmiqum*-Trust of Fifteen Shekels of Silver

Obv. [1]*a-na Ištar-ba-áš-tí* [2]*ù A-šùr-be-lí qi-bi*$_4$*-ma* [3]*um-ma Ku-tal-lá-num-ma* [4]*a-na Puzur*$_4$*-A-šùr* [5]15 gín kù-babbar *ta-ad-mì-iq-/ti*-ki* [6]igi *En-na-nim a-dí-in* [7]igi *Pu-pu-ra-nim* [8]*a-na Puzur*$_4$*-A-šur* [9]*áp-qí-id* lo.e. [10]*ša A-šur-be-lí* rev. [11]12 [gín] kù-babbar [12]*a-*[*na*[?] x x] *kà-ṣa-ri-k*[*à*] [13]*á*[*p-qí-i*]*d* [14]*lá* [x x x x] [15][x-x-x-*n*]*im* [16]*a-ha-tí* : *a-tí* [17]*li-bi*$_4$*-ki lá* u.e. [18]*i-lá-mì-in*

[1–3]Say to Ištar-baštī and Aššur-bēlī: thus (says) Kutallānum.

[4–6]I gave Puzur-Aššur 15 shekels of silver, (representing) your *tadmiqum*-trust, in the presence of Ennānum. [7–9]I entrusted (it) to Puzur-Aššur in the presence of Puppurānum. [10–13]As for Aššur-bēlī, I [entrust]ed 12 [shekels] of silver t[o…] yo[ur] harnessor, [14–15]not […]. [16]You are my sister; [17–18]do not be angry!

Bibliography: Text published in copy by Veenhof as VS 26, 41. Collated on photo online on CDLI as P358206. The surface of most of the reverse has been smoothed, and signs are erased.

Comments: Kutallānum, the sender of this letter, also addressed the letter TC 3, 45, to Imdī-ilum; we do not know from where he sent these letters, but the destination is presumably Kaneš. Ištar-baštī owes a *tadmiqum*-trust, for which silver has been entrusted to a transporter, who is bringing it to her.

---

295. Ištar-baštī Sends Footgear from Kaneš to Her Sisters-In-Law

Obv. $^{1'}$1 *ša-hi-re-*[*en a-na* x x x] $^{2'}$1 *ša-hi-re-e*[*n*] *a-*[*na* x x x] $^{3'}$1 *ša-hi-re-en a-na A-šur-*^{d}utu$^{/ši}$ $^{4'}$dumu *La-qé-pì-im ù* 10 gín kù-/babbar $^{5'}$*a-na am-tí-šu ú šé-bu-lá-tim* $^{6'}$*ša* é *e-mì-šu ša A-šur-*^{d}utu^{ši} $^{7'}$2 *ša-hi-re-en a-na um-me-a-ni-/šu* $^{8'}$dub-sar *ša A-mur-*dingir lo.e. $^{9'}$1 *ša-hi-re-en* rev. $^{10'}$*a-na um-me-a-ni-šu* $^{11'}$*ša iš-tí-šu* : *a-na* é *A-šur* $^{12'}$*A-mur-*dingir *i-ta-n*[*a*$^{!}$]*-lu-ku* $^{13'}$*šé-né-en a-na Ší-ma-at-/A-šur* $^{14'}$*šé-né-en a-na* $^{15'}$*Ta-ra-am-Ku-bi* $^{16'}$*šé-né-en a-na Ha-tí-a* (lacuna)
Le.e. $^{1''}$[x] *A-mur-*dingir : *mì-ma a-nim* $^{2''}$[*šé-b*]*u-lá-tim Ištar-ba-aš-tí* $^{3''}$[*t*] *a-áp-qí-dam*

$^{1'}$1 pair of shoe str[aps for x x x], $^{2'}$1 pair of shoe stra[ps] f[or x x x], $^{3'-6'}$1 pair of shoe straps for Aššur-šamšī, son of Laqēpum, and 10 shekels of silver for his *amtum*-wife, and also consignments from the house of Aššur-šamšī's father-in-law, $^{7'-8'}$2 pairs of shoe straps for his investor, the scribe of Amur-ilī, $^{9'-12'}$1 pair of shoe straps for his investor who always goes with him—Amur-ilī—to the temple of the god Aššur, $^{13'}$a pair of sandals for Šīmat-Aššur, $^{14'}$a pair of sandals for Tarām-Kūbi, $^{15'}$a pair of sandals for Hattiya […] $^{1''}$[x] Amur-ilī.

$^{1''-3''}$All these consigments, Ištar-baštī [e]ntrusted to me.

Bibliography: Text published in copy by Matouš as ICK 2, 310; edited by Ulshöfer (1995, 71–72, no. 51).

Comments: This anonymous memorandum mentions several members of Imdī-ilum's family: his sisters, Tāram-Kūbi and Šīmat-Aššur, who receive pairs of sandals, his wife Ištar-baštī, who entrusted all the goods to the author of the text, and his son Amur-ilī. This text is linked to **297** and Prag I, 495.

Line 16′: the name Hattiya is attested in AKT 8, 9:12, and ATK 8, 42:12.

---

296. Ištar-baštī Sends Silver to Her Sisters-In-Law

Obv. 1′[x x] *A-lá-hi-i*[*m ú A*]*-mur-Iš*[*tar*] 2′[x *ma-n*]*a* 8 gín kù-[babbar *ša*] *Ištar-ba-áš-tí* 3′[*ša*]*-du-*<*a*>*-sú ša-bu ku-nu-ki-a* 4′[*a-na*] *En-na-nim Pu-pu-ra-nim* 5′[*ù A-m*]*ur-Ištar* 1 *né-pi-šu-um* 6′[x *ma-na*] kù-babbar *ni-is-h*[*a-sú* DIRI] 7′[*ša-du*]*-a-sú š*[*a-bu* x x x] 8′[x x]*-ni E-na-*[x x x x] 9′[*a-na*] *Ištar-*DU*-ma* [x x x] 10′[1 *r*]*i-ik-su-um* [x gín kù-babbar *a-na*] 11′[*A-sù*]*r*-sig$_5$ *ù E-n*[*a*-x-x] 12′[1 *ri-i*]*k-su-um* 3 gín kù-[babbar] 13′[*a-na*] *Ta-ra-am-Ku-bi*$_4$ *ù Ší-m*[*a-A-/šùr*] 14′[1 *ri-i*]*k-sú-um* 1½ gín kù-ba[bbar] 15′[*ša I*]*štar-ba-áš-tí a-na a-wi-lá-*[*tim*] 16′[1 *ri-i*]*k-sú-um* 1 gín *a-na Il*$_5$*-ba-n*[*i*] 17′[x x *a-na*] *A-mur-Ištar* 18′[x x x x x 1 *ri-ik-sú*]*-um*

(lacuna)

[…] 1′Ali-ahu[m and A]mur-Ištar, 2′[x min]as, 8 shekels of sil[ver from] Ištar-baštī—3′its [tran]sport fee paid for—under my seal, 4′[for] Ennānum, Puppurānum, [and Am]ur-Ištar, 1 bag [of] 6′–7′[x minas] of silver—[its] import tax [added], its [tran]sport tax p[aid for—…] 8′–9′Enna-[x-x … for] Ištar-DU […] 10′[1 bu]ndle of [x shekels of silver for] 11′[Aššu]r-damiq and Enn[a-x-x], 12′[1 bu]ndle of 2 shekels of sil[ver] 13′[for] Tarām-Kūbi and Šīm[at-Aššur], 14′[1 bu]ndle of 1½ shekels of silv[er] 15′[from I]štar-baštī for the ladi[es], 16′[1 bu]ndle of 1 shekel of silver for Ilī-bān[i 17′[… for] Amur-Ištar, 18′[… 1 bun]dle […]

Bibliography: Text published in copy by Matouš as ICK 2, 311; edited by Ulshöfer (1995, 176).

Comments: This partly broken, anonymous memorandum lists items—mainly small packages of silver—for various people in Aššur. An amount of silver is sent by Ištar-baštī to colleagues of her husband, and another one to the ladies (line 15′), presumably Imdī-ilum's sisters, mentioned previously.

297. Ištar-baštī Has a *Tadmiqum*-Trust and Sends Silver to Her Husband's Sisters

Obv. ^{1}3 *ma-na* 15$^{!}$ gín [k]ù-babbar ^{2}*ta-ad-mì-iq-tám* ^{3}*ša Ištar-ba-áš-ti*$_{1}$ ^{4}*a-na Puzur*$_{4}$*-A-šùr a-dí-in* ^{5}igi *Ú-ṣú-ur-ša-A-šur* dumu *A-šùr-/ma-lik* ^{6}igi *Ah-ša-lim* dumu *Šu-A-nim* ^{7}1 *ma-na* kù-babbar *ša-wi-re-e* ^{8}*a-na Ta-ra-am-Ku-bi* ^{9}*ù Ší-ma-at-A-šùr tù-bi-il*$_{5}$ ^{10}[x] 5 gín kù-babbar *ša Ištar-ba-áš-*<*tí*> lo.e. ^{11}[*a-n*]*a Ta-ra-am-Ku-bi-ma* ^{12}[*ù*] *Ší-ma-at-A-šùr* rev. ^{13}[x gín] kù-babbar *A-šùr-i-mì-tí* ^{14}[x gín] kù-babbar *Šu-Ištar* ^{15}6 gín kù-babbar *A-šùr-*^{d}utu^{ši} nu-/bandà ^{16}1½ gín kù-babbar *Pu-pu-ra-num* ^{17}1½ gín kù-babbar *En-na-num* ^{18}15 gín kù-babbar (erasure) ^{19}*ša ta-ad-mì-iq-ti*$_{1}$*-ša*$^{!}$(ŠU) ^{20}*Na-ni-a* 2 gín kù-babbar *Ì-lí-dan* ^{21}2 gín kù-babbar *A-mur-A-šùr ni-a-um* ^{22}2 gín kù-babbar *Ha-tí-a* 2 gín kù-babbar ^{23}*La*$_{1}$*-ma-ša* 1 gín kù-babbar *A-dí-ma-tum* u.e. ^{24}1 gín k[ù-babbar *a-n*]*a um-me-a-ni-šu* ^{25}*ša* A-[*mur-*dingir *mì-ma a-nim*] le.e. ^{26}*šé-bu-la*$_{1}$*-tim a-na Puzur*$_{4}$*-A-šùr* ^{27}*ap-qí-id* igi *Ú-ṣur-ša-A-šur* ^{28}igi *Ah-ša-lim* dumu *Šu-Anim*

$^{1-4}$I gave to Puzur-Aššur 3 minas, 15 shekels of [s]ilver, the *tadmiqum*-trust of Ištar-baštī, $^{5-6}$in the presence of Uṣur-ša-Aššur, son of Aššur-malik, and Ah-šalim, son of Šu-Anum.

$^{7-9}$She brought 1 mina of silver bracelets to Taram-Kūbi and Šīmat-Aššur. $^{10-12}$[x +]5 shekels of silver from Ištar-baštī also [t]o Tarām-Kūbi [and] Šīmat-Aššur. ^{13}[x shekels] of silver: Aššur-imittī. ^{14}[x shekels] of silver: Šu-Ištar. ^{15}6 shekels of silver: Aššur-šamšī, the steward. ^{16}1½ shekels of silver: Puppurānum. ^{17}1½ shekels of silver: Ennānum. $^{18-20}$15 shekels of silver from her *tadmiqum*-trust: Naniya. ^{20}2 shekels of silver: Ilī-dān. ^{21}2 shekels of silver: our Amur-Aššur. ^{22}2 shekels of silver: Hattiya; 2 shekels of silver: ^{23}Lamaša; 1 shekel of silver: Adimātum. $^{24-25}$1 shekels of s[ilver fo]r the investor of A[mur-ilī]. $^{25-27}$I entrusted [all these] consignments to Puzur-Aššur, $^{27-28}$in the presence of Uṣur-ša-Aššur, and Ah-šalim, son of Šu-Anum.

Bibliography: Text published in copy and edited by Donbaz as Sadberk, 24 (ARK 168-9476).

Comments: This text lists consignments of silver to be sent to Aššur. A *tadmiqum*-trust of three minas, fifteen shekels of silver belonging to Išatr-baštī has been entrusted to Puzur-Aššur. This, or another such *tadmiqum*-trust is also mentioned in the text **294**; however, the amount of silver is much smaller. She sends silver to her sisters-in-law, who also receive silver bracelets weighing a total of one mina, are also mentioned in text **290**.

---

298. A Merchant Announces to Ištar-baštī (II) His Intention to Travel with Her Husband

Obv. [1]*a-na Ištar-ba-áš-tí* [2]*qí-bi-ma um-ma* [3]*I-ku-pì-a-ma a-na-kam* [4]*A-ki-ta-a ù-ṣa-ri-/pá-ni* [5]*iš-tí-šu : a-ta-lá-ak* [6]*iš-tí : A-nu-a : a-lá-kam* [7]*a-dí* 10 u_{4}*-me-e* [8]*a-ma-kam : wa-áš-ba-ni* [9]17 *ma-na ší-pá-tim* lo.e. [10]*A-mur-A-šùr na-ší* rev. [11]ir : *i-ša-ha-tí-šu* [12]*A-mur-A-šùr li-zi-iz-ma* [13]*ší-im ší-pá-tim* [14]*lu a-na* urudu *lu : a-na* [15]kù-babbar *ma-lá uš-ta-ra-ni* [16]*lu-up-ta-nim* [17]*ù ší-im pá-li-tim* [18]*lu-be-ri-im ma-lá* [19]*i-du-nu lu-up-ta-ni*

[1-3]Say to Ištar-baštī: thus (says) Ikuppiya.

[3-4]Here, Akitaya irritated me! [5]Should I leave together with him? [6]I will come with Annuwa. [7-8]We will stay there for 10 days.

[9-10]Amur-Aššur is bringing 17 minas of wool. [11-12]Let Wardum stay with Amur-Aššur, and [13-16]write down the price of the wool, either for copper or for silver, whatever *is feasible.* [17-19]Write down the price of the *palītum*-garment, as much as they will offer (for it).

Bibliography: Text published by Michel and Garelli as TPAK 1, 59 (Kt 90/k 182).

Comments: Ikuppiya writes to the daughter of Imdī-ilum, Ištar-baštī, announcing that he will travel with her second husband, Annuwa. He is sending her wool and a garment and asks her to record their proceeds. The connection between Ikuppiya and Ištar-baštī is unknown, but it is worth noting that she appears first in the letter heading.

Line 15: the translation of the verb is tentative, taken for *uš-ta-ri*, from *wuššurum*, Š perfect.

Line 17–18: for *lubērum pālitum*, see Michel and Veenhof 2010, 232.

Kunnaniya, a Lonely Anatolian Woman

Kunnaniya is one of the best-known Anatolian women, thanks to the volume of her correspondence, some fifteen letters received or sent by her.[58] Her name would be formed on the Hittite element kunna-, "right, good, straight," and anni, "mother."[59]

Kunnaniya had two older sisters with whom she exchanged letters: Walhišna/Walhašna (**309**), and Azu-elka (**311**, **312**), who was married to Išpunuman (TC 3, 254:5). She also had a brother, Šēṣur, who was married to Adue (**310**; fig. 18). To judge from the content of the six letters that she received from Aššur-mūtappil, she was his wife.[60] Aššur-mūtappil was the son of Pūšu-kēn—by that time dead—and brother of Buzāzu (**307**; fig. 16).[61] He might have had a wife in Aššur.

---

58. For this woman, see Michel 1997e, which gives the previous literature; and Veenhof 2015c, 283–84.

59. Goetze 1954, 77 n. 58; and Laroche 1966, 98. Indeed, most of the citations refer to a woman, except a few debt notes in which Kunnaniya would be a man. Kunnaniya, son of Ikua? (ICK 1, 5:10–11); Kunnaniya, debtor of Laqēp(um) (Kayseri 71:7); and Kunnaniya, debtor of Laqēpum, son of Šabahanum, are the subjects of verbs conjugated in the 3rd person masc. singular (Prag I, 594:3, 8–9). The same Kunnaniya is witness of a debt of Laqēpum, son of Šabahanum (ICK 1, 112:5). He might be the same person who is witness in the contract TC 2, 72:16. This masculine name would originate from the synthesis of the feminine name Kunnaniya and the masculine name Kunnananiya, formed with the elements kunna-, "good," and naniya, "brother." In three other purchase contracts, Kunnaniya is a woman. The first one concerns the sale of a slave to Ahattum by Kunnaniya and Nakišduar (**107**); there is no indication about possible family relationships between the persons involved. The second contract, partly broken, refers to the sale of Kunnaniya, daughter of Tamuriya, to Ali-ahum (Kt 87/k 554, unpublished text courtesy Hecker). The third text relates to the sale of Kunnaniya by Šihišnuman and by her mother (Ank. 14-1-80, Günbattı 1987, 189–99, no. 2). It is probable that, in this contract, Kunnaniya serves as a pledge in a debt contracted by her parents. Kunnaniya also appears, togther with two other Anatolians, as a seller of a house to Ela for 5 minas of silver (Kt 94/k 519, unpublished text courtesy Barjamovic). The individuals mentioned in all these contracts do not match those found in Kunnaniya's correspondence. This is also the case for the letter CCT 6, 7b, sent to Kupidahšu by Kunnaniya, which concerns exclusively Anatolians.

60. The letter **310** would confirm the matrimonial link between Kunnaniya and Aššur-mūtappil.

61. According to his seal impression on CTMMA 1, 78c (Teissier 1994, no. 634), which is identical with the seal E of **257**, Aššur-mūtappil is one of the sons of Pūšu-kēn.

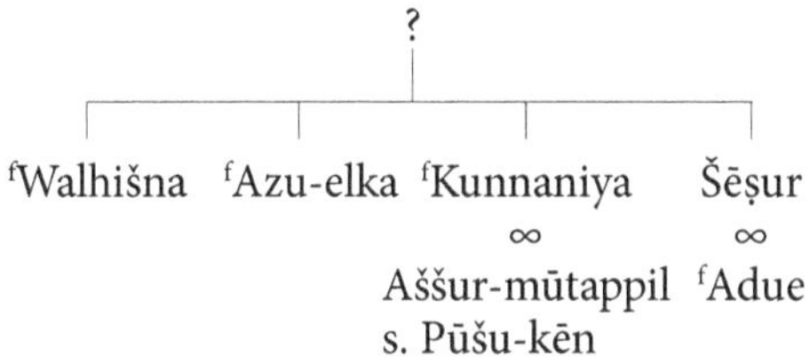

Fig. 18. Family tree of Kunnaniya.

The texts reveal two phases in this woman's life. The letters she exchanged with her husband reflect the usual activities of a merchant's wife living in Kaneš who actively participated into the family business, while the majority of the other letters of this dossier, characterized by the absence of the mention of Aššur-mūttappil, portray a woman who has been abandoned and was confronted with family conflicts.

Kunnaniya lived in Kaneš, together with her husband (**141**, **303**). She kept in the house the letters he sent her as he was traveling to Aššur or inside Anatolia. Aššur-mūtappil supplied his wife with various products, sending her from Aššur tin and textiles (**299**), as well as various utensils (**158**, **301**). The goods traveled with colleagues or servants of the couple (**300**, **302**). In exchange, Aššur-mūtappil asked his wife to send him local products, like Kaneš oil (**300**).

In the absence of her husband, Kunnaniya managed her household, including slaves (**303**, **304**). She also had some agricultural tasks, receiving instructions from her husband about pigs she was raising (**158**). Part of Aššur-mūtappil's archives was stored in his house in Kaneš, together with tablet containers belonging to others (**305**, **306**), and Kunnaniya had, among other tasks, to keep an eye on the strong room. On several occasions, her husband asked her to take care of Šāt-Aššur, presumably their daughter (**307**). At some point, Kunnaniya planned to meet with her husband, perhaps in another Anatolian town, but had to postpone her travel because of troubles in Kaneš and because it was dangerous to leave the town (**303**).

Lacking silver, her husband took from her property in Aššur and gave her two female slaves in exchange in Kaneš, which must have been part of Pūšu-kēn's inheritance, since one of his sons who was in Kaneš took the slaves. She was encouraged by her husband to go to court for them (**307**).

In a second phase, after Aššur-mūtappil had disappeared from the texts—he had presumably died—conflicts with Aššur-mūttappil's brothers and sister after their father's death (TC 1, 79) confronted Kunnaniya. Her in-laws took steps to retrieve valuable documents stored in her house (**308**). She shared her concerns with her sister, Walhišna (**309**). She was worried, and complained to her siblings that her husband's nephew, Pūšu-kēn, son of Buzāzu and grandson of Pūšu-kēn, took for himself the rent for a house that should have been hers (**310**). Her daughter, Šāt-Aššur, was on her side and claimed a right to her father's estate (**311**).

In order to defend her interests, Kunnaniya left Kaneš for Aššur, and entrusted her house and her goods to her older sister Azu-elka and to her sister-in-law, Adue, who was living there with her husband (**311**). She did not succeed, and she came back and accused them of having stolen her furniture (**310**). She refused to pay a rent for the house in which she was living, especially since someone else who had lived there for a decade had never paid her any rent. Desperate and feeling abandoned by all, Kunnaniya wrote a pathetic letter to her sister Azu-elka (**312**).

This small epistolary record recounts the disappointments of a woman, happy at the beginning of her life, then abandoned and at odds with her powerful in-laws and with her own family.

---

299. Kunnaniya Receives Goods and Buys Food

Obv. [1]*um-ma A-šur-mu-ta-pì-il*$_5$*-<ma>* [2]*a-na Ku-na-ni-a* [3]*qí-bi-ma* 10 gín an-na [4]*ku-nu-ki-a* [5]*En-um-ì-lí* dumu *Ku-za* [6]*iš-tí A-hu-ni* [7]*wa-áš-bu*[?] *x-tim* [8]*na-[áš-a]-ki-im* [9]1 túg *ša ṣú-ha-ar-tim* [10]2 gín kù-babbar 5 *kà-sà-tim* [11]*Kà-ru-nu-wa a-hu-ú* [12]*A-li-li* [13]*li-dí-na-ki-im* [14]10 *na-ru-uq mì-iš-lam* [15]*ar-ša-tim* [16]*ša-a-mì-ma* [17]*li-bi*$_4$*-ší* [18]*a-dí e-ra-ba-ni*

[1–3]Thus (says) Aššur-mūtappil: say to Kunnaniya.

[3–8]Ennum-ilī, son of Kuza, is br[ing]ing you 10 shekels of tin under my seal with Ahuni.... [9–13]Karunuwa, the brother of Alili, should bring you 1 garment for the girl, 2 shekels of silver, (and) 5 cups. [14–18]Buy 10 sacks, half of them with wheat, so that they are available at my arrival.

Bibliography: Unpublished text known by a transliteration by Landsberger under the reference "Kalley C36," courtesy Veenhof.

Comments: Kunnaniya receives silver, tin, and various commodities from her husband and has to buy grain for her household. Lines 9–13 deal with the same topic as the next text, **300**. The garment for the girl could be for Šāt-Aššur, the presumed daughter of the couple.

Line 7: the reading of this line is uncertain; it could also be a mistake for *išti ahhēni wašbūtim*, "with our brothers, those who are present."

---

300. Kunnaniya Receives Goods from Her Husband and Sends Him Oil in Return

ki-im [12]<1> túg *ku-sí-tam*[!](IM) [13]*lá-be-er-tám* : *En-um-A-šur* [14]*ù Ṣú-li-a* [15]*na-áš-ú-ni-ki*[!]*-im*[!] [16]*a-dí ma-áš-ke-e* : *ša-pá-tí-im* [17]*ša ta-áš-pu-ri-ni* [18]*a-ša-a-ma* : *ú-šé-ba-lam* [19]½ silà ì-giš : *ša Kà-ni-iš* u.e. [20][*i*]*-na ša-am-ni-im* [21]*ša Wa-al*[!]*-hi-iš-na* [22]*šu-pá-i-li-ma* le.e. [23]*šé-*bi_4*-lim ṣú-ha-ru* [24]*ú-ma-kál* : *lá i-*bi_4*-tù* [25]*li-tal-ku-ni-im*

[1–2]Thus (says) Aššur-mūtappil: say to Kunnaniya.

[3–6]I gave him 1 textile as a garment for a youngster, and 15⅓ shekels of tin, equivalent to 2 shekels of silver. [7–11]Karunuwa, the brother of Alili, is bringing you 5 cups from Haburā. [12–15]Ennum-Aššur and Ṣulliya are bringing you 1 old *kusītum*-textile. [16–17]As to the woolen fleeces about which you wrote to me, [18]I will buy (them) and send (them) to you.

[19–22]Exchange the oil of Walhišna for ½ sila of oil from Kaneš and send (it) to me. [23–25]The servants should not stay, not even one night; they should come (back) here.

Bibliography: Text published in copy and edited by Donbaz as KTS 2, 31; translated by Michel (2001a, no. 379).

Comments: Kunnaniya receives various goods from her husband, together with some tin that she can spend for her household. She is asked to send some oil from Kaneš, which was known for its good quality. Servants working for Aššur-mūtappil are in charge of transporting the goods between husband and wife.

301. Kunnaniya Receives Various Items and Textiles from Her Husband

Obv. ^{1}*um-ma A-šur-mu-ta-pì-il*$_5$ ^{2}*a-na Ku*$^{!}$*-na-ni-a qí-bi*$_4$*-ma* ^{3}*«qí-bi*$_4$*-ma»* 1 *pá-na-ra-am* ^{4}*I-ku-pì-a* dumu *A-zu-ú-a* ^{5}*ub-lá-ki-im* 1 túg *tí-sà-ba-/am* ^{6}*ša Ha-qá 5 ma-na* síg$^{hi-/a}$ ^{7}*ša-kà-ki-iš* : 2* *pá-ni-ri* ^{8}*ša* gu$_4$: *ku-nu-ki-a* ^{9}*A-mur-A-šur* [du]mu *Zi-ku-ur-/ì-lí* ^{10}*ub-lá-ki-im* lo.e. ^{11} 2 gín kù-babbar rev. ^{12}*ù ší-it-ra-am* ^{13}*A-šur-e-na-am* ^{14}dumu sig$_5$ *ub-lá-ki-im* ^{15}1 túg *šu-ra-am ù* 2 sìla ^{16}*re-eš-tám* ^{d}utu-*ta-ak-lá-<ku>* ^{17}*ù Zu-li-a* ^{18}*ub-lu-ni-ki-im* 1 túg *qá-tí* ^{19}*ša a-li-ta-ab*$_1$*-ší-im* ^{20}*e-zi-bu* : *Wa-lá-wa-lá* ^{21}*lu la-bu-ša-at* u.e. ^{22}*tí-sà-ba-am ù šu-ra-am* ^{23}*a-tí-i lu la-bu-ša-tí* ^{24}*iš-tí ur-ki-ú-tim* ^{25}*ma-áš-ke-e* le.e. ^{26}*ù* sà-áp-dí*-nam* ^{27}*ú-šé-ba-lam li-bi*$_4$*-ki* ^{28}*lá tù-lá-mì-in*

$^{1-2}$Thus (says) Aššur-mūtappil: say to Kunnaniya.

$^{2-5}$Ikuppiya, son of Azūa, brought you 1 *pannurum*. $^{5-10}$Amur-Aššur, son of Zikur-ilī, brought you, under my seal, 1 *tisābum*-textile from Haqqa, 5 minas of wool for making the weft, 2 *pannurums* of/for oxen. $^{11-14}$Aššur-ennam, son of Damqum, brough you 2 shekels of silver and a shawl. $^{15-18}$Šamaš-taklāku and Zuliya brought you 1 dark textile and 2 liters of top-quality (oil).

$^{18-21}$Let Walawala be dressed in a textile of current quality for clothing that I left. $^{22-23}$You yourself, you may wear the *tisābum*-textile and the dark textile. $^{24-27}$I will send the hides and the *sapdinnum*-textile with the next (travelers). $^{27-28}$You must not be angry!

Bibliography: Text published by Hertel (2017, 14). Collated on photo online on CDLI as P250550.

Comments: Several of the items sent to Kunnaniya are also mentioned in letter **158**, addressed by Aššur-mūtappil to Karunuwa and Kunnaniya. The *tisābum* and *sapdinnum*-textiles were made in Anatolia, which would suggest that Aššur-mūtappil travels within Anatolia.

Lines 3 and 7: for the word *pannurum*, see comments to text **136**:7.

Lines 5–6: for *tisābum*-textiles from Haqqa, see Michel and Veenhof 2010, 222 n. 96.

Line 7: *šakākiš* is discussed by Michel and Veenhof 2010, 214.

302. Kunnaniya Receives Tin and Textiles to Be Converted into Copper and Silver

Obv. [1]*um-ma A-šur-mu-ta-pì-i*[*l*$_5$-*ma*] [2]*a-na Ni-mar-Ištar Ku-na-ni-a* [3]^{d}utu-*ta-ak-lá-*<*ku*> *En-um-A-šur* [4]*ù Zu-li-a qí-bi*$_4$*-ma* [5]*i-na* ^{d}utu^{ši} *ṭup-pì-i* [6]*ta-ša-me-a-ni* [7]*a-na* 2 *ma-na* an-na [8]*ù* 3 túg *pì-ri-kà-ni* lo.e. [9] *ša a-dí-na-ku-nu-tí-ni* rev. [10]35 *ma-na* urudu [11]*ma-sí-am ša Tí-iš-mu-ur-*/[*n*]*a* [12]*ù* 5 gín kù-babbar [13]*sà-he-er-tám* [14]*li-il*$_5$*-qé-ú-ni-ma* [15]*li-tal-ku-ni-im* [16]*a-Ha-hi-im : e-li-i* [17]*ù zi-ra-tim ša qá-*/*tí* [18]*Ir*$^{!}$*-ma-A- šur ù A-du-da* lo.e. [19] *ša-ak-na-at-ni* [20]*lu-ub-lu-ni-im* [21]*a-na Ni-mar-Ištar* le.e. [22]*qí-bi*$_4$*-ma šu-ma ṣú-ha-ru* [23]*a-ma-kam i-sà-hu-ru* [24]*té-er-ta-kà lí-lí-kam*

[1–4]Thus (says) Aššur-mūtappil: say to Nimar-Ištar, Kunnaniya, Šamaš-taklāku, Ennum-Aššur, and Zuliya.

[5–6]The day you hear my letter, [10–14]let them take 35 minas of refined copper from Tišmurna and 5 shekels of silver small wares [7–9]for the 2 minas of tin and 3 *pirikannum*-textiles that I gave you, and [15]let them come here.

[16]Go up to Hahhum, [17–20]and let them bring here the cauldrons on which Ir'am-Aššur and Aduda have established a claim.

[21–22]Say to Nimar-Ištar: [23–24]let your report come if the servants are still staying there.

Bibliography: Text published by Lewy as KTBl, 5.

Comments: Kunnaniya, together with four merchants, receives instructions from her husband concerning various purchases. He sent them tin and textiles and asks them to buy copper, perhaps to make cauldrons and small items. We do not know what role Kunnaniya plays among the other recipients of the letter: checking that the others obey her husband's orders or acting together with them.

303. Kunnaniya to Travel with Goods to Join Her Husband

Obv. [1]*um-ma A-šùr-mu-ta-pì-il*$_5$*-ma* [2]*a-na Ku-na-ni-a* <*qí-bi*$_4$*-ma*> ½ sìla [3]*kà-mu-ni* 2 *ri-ik-sí* [4]*ṣú*$^{!}$*-um-lá-le-e ša* 1 gín [5]kù-babbar *sí-pá-ra-tim* [6]30 *i-lá-tim* 3 túg *me-nu-ni-a-*/*ni* [7]*ša* 1 gín-ta kù-babbar (erasure) [8]*a-ṣú-ha-ri ša-a-mì-ma* [9]*tí-ib-e-ma : a-tal-ki-im* [10]*šu-ma : i-nu-mì* lo.e. [11]*Ku-du-du i-li-kà-ni*

^{12}*ma kà-ru-um* rev. ^{13}*a-na iš-ri-šu* ^{14}*i-tù-a-ar : ú-ma-am* ^{15}*iš-té-en*$_{6}$ *: ki-il*$_{5}$*-i-šu-ma* ^{16}*tí-ib-e-ma : a-tal-ki-im* ^{17}*Ša-at-A-šur : i-na* ^{18}*ša-ha-at Wa-lá-w[a-l]á* /ìr$^{dí\text{-}im}$ ^{19}*ez-bi*$_{4}$*-i-ší :* ^{20}*lá ú-šu-ru-ší : šu-ma* ^{21}*a-wa-tum : da-na-a* ^{22}ì-giš sig$_{5}$: *ú ṭup-pá-am* u.e. ^{23}*iš-tí Ku-du-du* ^{24}*šé-bi*$_{4}$*-lim ú a-dí-i* ^{25}*nu-a-ah : kà-ri-im* le.e. ^{26}*tí-ib-e-ma : a-tal-ki-im* ^{27d}utu-*ta-ak-lá-<ku> a-šar* ^{28}*da-al-tim lu na-al*

$^{1-2}$Thus (says) Aššur-mūtappil: <say> to Kunnaniya.

$^{2-8}$Buy for the servants ½ liter of cumin, 2 bundles of *ṣumlālû*-aromatic plants for 1 shekel of silver, nails, 30 bags and 3 *menuniānum*-textiles at 1 shekel of silver each, then ^{9}get ready and come here. $^{10-14}$If, when Kududu has arrived, the *kārum* (district) has returned to normal again, ^{15}detain him for one day, then ^{16}get ready and come here. $^{17-19}$Leave Šāt-Aššur in the care of the slave Walawala. ^{20}One should not leave her alone.

$^{20-21}$(But) if matters remain difficult, $^{22-24}$send good-quality oil and a tablet with Kududu. $^{24-25}$And as soon as the *kārum* (district) has quieted down, ^{26}get ready and come here. $^{27-28}$Let Šamaš-taklāku sleep near the door!

Bibliography: Text published by Lewy as KTH, 6; translated by Michel (2001a, no. 378). Lines 2–24 cited by Michel (1997e, 247–49, nn. 28, 30, 31, 35).

Comments: Kunnaniya is supposed to travel to meet her husband, but there is no indication of his location. Her travel might need to be postponed because of troubles in Kaneš.

Šāt-Aššur, according to this text, would be the daughter of Aššur-mūtappil and Kunnaniya. She is still young since she cannot live alone; a slave must take care of her while her mother is away.

Line 6: the *menuniānum*-textile was produced locally in Anatolia; see Michel and Veenof 2010, 236. They are here very cheap.

Line 12: for the reading *ma kārum*, see Veenhof 1992.

Lines 20–21: Aššur-mūtappil asks Kunnaniya to send goods by a transporter if it is forbidden to travel.

---

304. Kunnaniya Has to Watch Over the House

Obv. ^{1}*um-ma En-um-A-šur-/ma* ^{2}*a-na Ku-na-ni-a* ^{3}*qí-bi-ma ha-ra-ni* ^{4}*a-dí* : 5 *u*$_{4}$*-me-e : a-ma-/kam* ^{5}*wa-áš-ba-ni : a-na* /kù-babbar ^{6}5 gín (°signs erased) [7]*ša* tù-ùh-ta-bi*$_4$*-/li-/ni* lo.e. [8]*lá ta-ra-ší-i* [9]*ni-lá-kam-ma* rev. [10]*nu-ša-ba : a-lá-nu-ki* [11]*ma-ma-an : lá ni-/šu* [12]*é*$^{\text{be-tám}}$ [13]*ú ṭup-pè-e* [14]*ša-ṣí-ri-i* [15]*lá ta-ha-dí-ri* [16]*ṣú-ha-ra-am* [17]*lá tù-mì-ṣí* u.e. [18]*qá-at-ki* [19]*lu*-bi*$_4$*-il*$_5$*-ma* le.e[20]*a-dí : e-ni-ni* [21]*ta-mì-ri-n[i] a-na-<kam>* [22]*ú-sà-he-er-ma*

[1-3]Thus (says) Ennum-Aššur: say to Kunnaniya.

[4-5]For 5 days we are staying over there. [5-7]About the 5 shekels of silver that you borrowed, [8]do not worry! [9-10]We will come, and we will pay (it). [10-11]We have no one except you! [12-15]Watch over the house and the tablets; do not be afraid. [16-17]Do not let the boy starve! [18-21]Support (him) until you see us! [21-22]Let him be around here, and....

Bibliography: Text published in copy by Albayrak as AKT 4, 62 (Kt o/k 77). Tablet collated in May 2012 and 2016.

Comments: Ennum-Aššur represents here a group of two or more people since he writes in the first-person plural, except in the last sentence. The letter ends with the enclitic *-ma*, suggesting that there was a second page on which the text ended. The letter indicates that the situation is not easy for Kunnaniya in Kaneš, and that she has to manage things on her own.

---

305. Kunnaniya Is Entrusted with Tablets

Obv. [1]*um-ma A-šùr-mu-ta-pì-/il*$_5$*-ma* [2]*a-na Ku-na-ni-a* [3]*qí-bi*$_4$*-ma ṭup-pè-e* [4]*ša Na-zi ù* [5]dingir-*ba-ni ú-bu-lu-ni-/ki-ni-ma* [6]*i-pá-qí-du-ni-/ki-ni* [7]*a-šar ta-tí-ni-li-ni* [8]*šu-uk-ni-šu-nu-/ma* lo.e. [9]*ša-ṣí-ri*

[1-3]Thus (says) Aššur-mūtappil: say to Kunnaniya.

[3-6]The tablets that Nazi and Ilī-bāni will bring you and entrust to your care, [7-9]put them wherever you sleep, and so guard them!

Bibliography: Text published in copy by Stephens as BIN 6, 1; translated by Michel (2001a, no. 377).

Comments: Kunnaniya is in charge of tablets sent by her husband, Aššur-mūtappil.

306. Kunnaniya Is in Charge of Tablet Containers

Obv. [1]*um-ma En-nam-A-šùr-ma* [2]*a-na Ku-na-ni-a* [3]*ù A-lá-hi-im a-na* [4]*Ku-na-ni-a* [5]*qí-bi*$_{4}$*-ma ta-ma-lá-ki* [6]*ku-nu-ki ù* 2 *ṭup-pè-e* [7]*ha-ru-mu-tim* [8]*ša e-zi-ba-ki*$^{!}$(KU)*-ni* [9]*a-ma-kam ta-ma-lá-ki* [10]*ku-nu-ki a-na* [11]*A-lá-hi-im dí-ni* [12]*ù ṭup-pu-ú* [13]*li-ib-ší-ú* [14]*a-dí : té-er-tí* [15]*i-lá-kà-ni*

[1-3]Thus (says) Ennum-Aššur: say to Kunnaniya and Ali-ahum. [4-5]Say to Kunnaniya.

[6-8]As for the sealed *tamalakkum*-chests and the 2 certified tablets that I left you, [9-11]give the sealed *tamalakkum*-chests there to Ali-ahum, and as for the tablets, let them stay (where they are) [14-15]until my instructions arrive.

Bibliography: Text published in copy by Smith as CCT 4, 21a; translated by Michel (2001a, no. 382).

Comments: Kunnaniya is in charge of the transfer of tablet containers entrusted to her by Ennum-Aššur, presumably identical to the author of another letter addressed to her (**304**). He might be a member of her family.

307. Kunnaniya Has to Get Her Slaves Back and Buy Food for Her House

Envelope

Obv. [1]*a-na Ir-ma-A-šùr* [2](seal A) [3]*Wa-al-hi-iš-na ù* [4]*Ku-na-ni-a* kišib *A-šur-mu-ta-pì-il*$_{5}$ [5](seal A) lo.e. [6](seal A) rev. [7](seal A) u.e. [8](seal A) le.e. [9](seal A) r.e. [10](seal A)

[1-4]To Ir'am-Aššur, Walhišna, and Kunnaniya. Seal of Aššur-mūtappil. (Several impressions of the seal used by Aššur-mūtappil.)

Tablet

(a) Obv. [1]*a-na Wa-al-hi-iš-na* [2]*ù Ku-na-ni-a qí-bi-ma um-ma* [3]*A-šùr-mu-ta-pì-il*$_{5}$*-ma a-na* [4]*Wa-al-hi-iš-na : qí-bi*$_{4}$*-ma* [5]1 *ma-na* kù-babbar : *lu a-nu-qú-ša* [6]*lu tù-dí-na-tum : i-na A-lim*^{ki} [7]*A-šur : ša a-ha-tí-ki : al-qé-e* [8]*ù a-ma-kam : ú-ša-hi-sí*$^{!}$ [9]*um-ma a-na-ku-ma a-*kù-babbar^{pì}*-ki* [10]*ša al-qé-ú : a-ma-tum* [11]*ki-lá-al-ta-ma : lu ku-a-a-tum* [12]*áš-ta-na-me-ma : Bu-za-zu*

^{13}*a-ma-tí-ki* : *iṣ-ba-at* lo.e. ^{14}*i-ṭá-ba-tim* : *a-ma-tí-im* rev. ^{15}*pu-nu-a-ma* : *lu-ší-ru-ni-ki-na-tí* ^{16}*šu-ma* : *e-mu-qí* ^{17}*e-ta-wu-ú* : *ma* : *a-ma-tim* ^{18}*lá ú-ša-ar* : *a-dí-ni-im* ^{19}*ku-uš-da* : *a-ma-tum* : *ku-a-a-/tum* ^{20}⅓ *ma-na* 5 gín kù-babbar ^{21}*e-zi-ba-ki-im* : 5 gín kù-babbar ^{22}*Ni-ša-šar* : géme *ša* é *a-bi*$_4$*-ki* ^{23}*ú-šé-bi*$_4$*-lá-ki-im* : *iš-té-ni-iš* ^{24}½ *ma-na* kù-babbar : *e-zi-ba-ki-im* (sign erased) ^{25}*ša* 7 gín kù-babbar : *še-am* ^{26}*Gal-ga-lí-a* : *li-dí-na-ki-im* u.e. ^{27}*ku-nu-ki* : *ša* é$^{be\text{-}tim}$ ^{28}*ša-ṣí-ri* : *a-ki-dim* ^{29}*lá ta-ta-na-ṣí-i* le.e. ^{30}*be-tám* [*u*]*ṣ-ri* : *Ša-at-A-šur* ^{31}*lá tù-mì-ṣí* : *e-me-ra-am*
(b) ^{32}*ša-a-mì-ma* ^{33}*ma-áš-e-er-tum* ^{34}*a-ṣú-ha-ar-tim* ^{35}*li-bi-ší* : *a-dí* ^{36}*e-ni-a* : *ta-mì-ri-ni* ^{37}*li-ba-am* : *a-li-bi*$_4$*-/ki* ^{38}*dí-ni-i*

$^{1–4}$Say to Walhišna and Kunnaniya: thus (says) Aššur-mūtappil. Say to Walhišna.

$^{5–7}$I took 1 mina of silver belonging to your sister in the city of Aššur, either from her rings or her garment pins, ^{8}and over there, I gave her to understand as follows: $^{9–11}$"For your silver that I took, both female slaves shall be yours."

^{12}I keep hearing that Buzāzu seized your female slaves. $^{14–15}$Take up the matter of the female slaves politely so that one releases (them) to you. $^{16–19}$If he utters threats and does not release the female slaves, (then) go to court! The female slaves are yours.

$^{20–21}$I left you ⅓ mina, 5 shekels of silver. $^{21–23}$I sent you 5 shekels of silver with Nišašar, a female slave of the house of your father. $^{23–24}$All together, I left you ½ mina of silver. $^{25–26}$Let Galgalia sell you 7 shekels of silver worth of barley.

$^{27–28}$Keep a close watch on the seals of the house. $^{28–29}$Do not go out all the time. $^{30–31}$Watch over the house. Do not let Šāt-Aššur starve of hunger! $^{31–35}$Buy a sheep and let it serve as a food supply for the girl. $^{35–38}$Until you see me, keep courage!

Bibliography: Text published in copy by Larsen as CTMMA 1, 78; translated by Michel (2001a, no. 380).

Comments: Aššur-mūtappil explains to Kunnaniya's sister how to recover the female slaves that were taken away from his wife by his brother Buzāzu. The second part of the letter is presumably addressed to Kunnaniya, and it concerns instructions about the management of the house.

The seal CTMMA 29 (Teissier 1994, no. 634), impressed several times on the envelope of this letter, belongs to Aššur-mūtappil, son of Pūšu-kēn:

it is also found on the legal text **257** (seal 31E) that involves all the children of Pūšu-kēn.

---

308. Kunnaniya Must Keep the Strong Room of Her Husband Closed

Obv. ^{1}*a-na Ku-na-ni-a qí-bi*$_4$*-ma* ^{2}*um-ma A-šur-ták-lá-ku-ma* ^{3}*šu-ma a-ma-kam li-bi*$_4$*-ki* ^{4}*mì-ma ú-lá-mu-nu té-er-tí-ki* ^{5}*a-ṣé-ri-a li-li-kam-ma* ^{6}*Hu-ma-da-šu a-na-nu-um* ^{7}*lá-aṭ-ru-dam a-ma-kam* ^{8}*ma-ma-an e ú-wa-er-ki-ma* ^{9}*ma-ak-na-kam ša mu-tí-ki* ^{10}*e ta-áp-té-a : a-dí* lo.e. ^{11}[x x x x] *ú* [x x x] rev. ^{12}*lá* [x x x x] *ma* [x] ^{13}*ba-*[x x x x] *ba-ti*[*m*] ^{14}*Hu-*[*ma-da-šu* x x]*-ba-ki* ^{15}*i-pá-*[x x x x x x x] ^{16}*šé-ṣ*[*í*]-[x] *a* [x x x]*-tám* ^{17}*áš-ku/qú-*[x x x x x-*t*]*im* ^{18}*a-ta-na-dí-in-ma* ^{19}*ṣ*[*ú*]*-ha-ri lá i-sí-ú* ^{20}*i-nu-mì ša ha-ra-na-tim* ^{21}*i-lu-*[*ku*]*-ni-ni iš-tí-šu-nu* ^{22}*ú-še-ba-lá-ki-im mì-ma* u.e. ^{23}*li-bi*$_4$*-ki lá i-pá-ri-id* ^{24}*ṣú-ùh-ru-um ša-lim*

$^{1-2}$Say to Kunnaniya: thus (says) Aššur-taklāku.

$^{3-4}$If they offend you there in any respect, $^{4-5}$let a message from you come to me, then $^{6-7}$I will send Humadašu from here. $^{7-8}$No one should give you orders there, and $^{9-10}$you (pl.) must not open your husband's strong room. $^{10-18}$Until [...] and [...] not [...] Hu[madašu ...] take out [...] I keep giving, but ^{19}my servants have not invited. $^{20-22}$When those of the caravans come, I shall send (goods) to you with them. $^{22-24}$You do not have to worry at all, the child is fine.

Bibliography: Text published in copy by Stephens as BIN 6, 17. Lines 3–10 cited by Michel (1997e, 250 n. 38).

Comments: Aššur-taklāku, whose possible family link to Kunnaniya is unknown, is ready to send someone to help Kunnaniya protect the goods of her husband against her in-laws.

---

309. Walhašna Is Concerned about Her Younger Sister Kunnaniya

^{1}*um-ma Wa-al-ha-áš-na-/ma* ^{2}*a-na Ku-na-ni-a* ^{3}*qí-bi*$_4$*-ma : mì-šu-um* ^{4}*ta-ra-ší-i* ^{5}*a-na-ku : ba-al-ṭá-/ku-ma* ^{6}*a-tí-i* ^{7}*ta-ra-ší-i* lo.e. ^{8}*a-na A-šur-e-na-/am* rev. ^{9}*qí-bi*$_4$*-ma :* (sign erased) ^{10}*iš-ra-am :* ^{11}*ú ša-hi-re-en*$_6$ ^{12}*ú ša-am-nam* ^{13}*ú-šé-bi*$_4$*-lá-kum* ^{14}*e-mì : a-ta* ^{15}*šu-ma a-ha-tí* u.e. ^{16}*té-zi-ib* le.e. ^{17}*ša e-pu-šu-kà* ^{18}*ta-mar*

[1-3]Thus (says) Walhašna: say to Kunnaniya.

[3-4]Why are you worried? [5]Although I am fine, [6-7]you are worried.

[8-9]Say to Aššur-ennam: [10-13]I sent you a belt, a pair of shoe straps, and some oil. [14]You are my brother-in-law. [15]If you divorce my sister, [17]you will see what I will do to you!

Bibliography: Text published in copy by Lewy (1969–1970, 69 [L 29-606]); edited by Gwaltney as POAT, 42; translated by Michel (2001a, no. 381).

Comments: The word *emum* refers to a family relationship by marriage: son-in-law (VS 26, 64; Michel 2001a, no. 300:32–39), father-in-law (BIN 6, 183:8), or even brother-in-law, as proposed for this text by some authors (Gwaltney in POAT, 42) who considered Aššur-ennam to be the husband of Kunnaniya. Whatever his family relationship with Walhašna, he was supposed to take care of her younger sister Kunnaniya. Apart from this letter, Aššur-ennam is mentioned only once in this dossier, together with other transporters, in a letter sent by Aššur-mūtappil to Karunuwa and Kunnaniya (**158**).

---

310. Kunnaniya Complains to Her Brother and His Wife about Their Attitude

Obv. [1]*a-na Šé-ṣú-ur qí-bi*$_4$*-ma* [2]*um-ma Ku-na-ni-a-ma* [3]*a-hi a-ta : i-li : a-ta* [4]*mì-na-am e-pu-uš-kà* [5]*ma-tí-ma : a-na a-hi-i-a* [6]*ú-na-ki-ir-kà : a-ma :* [7]*hu-lu-kà-ni-kà : i-na pu-zu-/ri-im* [8]*ú-šé-bi*$_4$*-lá-ku-um mì-šu-um* [9]*a-ta a-na a-hi-i-a tù-kà-li-/im* [10]*mì-šu-um i-na e-ni-šu* [11]*tù-ba-a-ša-ni : mì-na-am* [12]*e-pu-uš-kà : i-lu-um* [13]*lu i-de*$_8$*-e : ú e-ṭá-mu* [14]*lu i-de*$_8$*-ú a-na A-du-e* lo.e. [15]*qí-bi*$_4$*-ma ma-num* [16]*iq-bi*$_4$*-a-ki-im-ma* rev. [17]*a-pá-ni : Še-ṣú-ur : a-hi-[a]* [18]*ta-zi-zi a-ma : ig-ri* [19]é^{tim} *ki-ma* dumu^{e} *A-šur-mu-/ta*$^{!}$*-pì-il*$_5$ [20]*Pu-šu-ke-en*$_6$ *: il*$_5$*-qé* [21]*ki-a-am : da-mì-iq : ki-ma* [22]*a-na-ku : ig-ri be-tim* [23]*lá-qá-im a-ni Pu-šu-ke-en*$_6$ [24]*il*$_5$*-té-qé : a-na A-du-e* [25]*qí-bi*$_4$*-ma a-ma : me-er-at-ki* [26]*i-ra-de*$_8$*-ú-nim ra-mì-i-ší* [27]*a-na Še-ṣú-ur*$^{!}$(IR) *qí-bi*$_4$*-ma* [28]*a-ma me-er-at-kà i-ra-de*$_8$*-ú-/nim*$^{!}$ [29]*a-ma-kam ra-a-am-ší* [30]*ší-im hi-lu-kà-ni-im* u.e. [31]*a-hi lá té-ri-iš* [32]*a-na A-du-e qí-bi*$_4$*-ma* [33]*a-ma :* é^{tum} le.e. [34]*ù ú-ṭù-up*$^{!}$(IP)*-tum a-ma-kam* [35]*mì-ma : lá-šu-ma ku-a-um* [36]*ar-nu-um*

[1-2]Say to Šēṣur: thus (says) Kunnaniya.

[3]You are my brother; you are my god. [4]What have I done to you? I never disavow you to my brother! [6–8]Look, I sent you your carriage secretly. [8–9]Why did you show it to my brother? [10–11]Why do you shame me in his eyes? [11–12]What have I done to you? [12–14]The god knows well, the spirits know well (that I have done nothing wrong)!

[14–15]Say to Adue: [15–18]Who told you to side against Šēṣur, [my] brother? [18–20]And Pūšu-kēn collected the rent of the house instead of the sons of Aššur-mūtappil! [21–24]Isn't that nice! Instead of me collecting the rent of the house, Pūšu-kēn has now taken it!

[24–25]Say to Adue: [25–26]Look! They will bring you your daughter; treat her with love!

[27]Say to Šēṣur: [28–29]Look, they will bring you your daughter; there, treat her with love! [30–31]You should not ask my brother for the price of the carriage.

[32]Say to Adue: [33–36]Look, over there, there is nothing left of the house and the furniture, and it is your fault!

Bibliography: Text published by Bilgiç, Sever, Günbattı, and Bayram as AKT 1, 14; translated by Michel (2001a, no. 383). Collated March 2016.

Comments: In this emotional letter sent to her brother and his wife, Kunnaniya mentions the existence of another brother, who is not identified. She accuses Šēṣur of having revealed things to this other brother and explains to his wife that she has been deprived of the rent of a house by a nephew of her husband. Because of him, she has lost her house and furniture. The "daughter" that she says is coming to her brother and his wife could perhaps be Šāt-Aššur, her own daughter. The Pūšu-kēn mentioned in this letter could be the son of Buzāzu and grandson of the famous merchant Pūšu-kēn.

Line 7, 20: the *hi/ulukannum* could refer to a light carriage.

Lines 12–14: the reference to the god and spirits of the dead is normally typically Assyrian; this could suggest that Kunnaniya had at least an Assyrian parent, mother or father.

311. Kunnaniya and Her Daughter Complain to Female Family Members

Obv. ^{1}*a-na A-zu-e-el-kà* ^{2}*ù A-du-e a-na* ^{3}*A-zu-e-el-kà qí-bi*$_4$*-ma* ^{4}*um-ma Ku-na-ni-a ú Ša-at-A-šur* ^{5}*i-nu-mì : a-na Kà-ni-iš* ^{6}*e-ru-ba-ni : i-na hu-ur-ší-/im* ^{7}*ba-pì-ir-ki : i-ší-ki-in* ^{8}*ú ú-nu-tám áp-qí-da-/ki-im* ^{9}*um-ma a-na-ku-ma : ki-ma* ^{10}*ba-pì-ir-ki : tù-šé-ṣí-ni* ^{11}*ú hu-ur-ša-am : ku-un-ki* ^{12}*lá aq-bi*$_4$*-a-ki-im um-ma* lo.e. ^{13}*a-na-ku-ma a-na lam-ni-/šu* ^{14}*lá tù-ta-ri-ni* rev. ^{15}*u*$_4$*-ma-am a*-lam-ni-šu* ^{16}*a-tù-wa-ar : e-ma* ^{17}*ta-ma-lá-ku-a : ú šu-nu* ^{18}*li-ih-li-qú-ma* ^{19}*a-na A-du-e qí-bi*$_4$*-ma* ^{20}*um-ma Ša-at-A-šur-ma a-na-ku* ^{21}*a-na um-mì-a áš-ta-na-kà-ki* ^{22}*um-ma «ma» a-na-ku-ma* ^{23}*a-lá : ú-nu-tù i-na* ^{24}*Kà-ni-iš i-ba-ší* ^{25}*a-tí : pá-ta-a-tí-ma* ^{26}*tù-ùh-ta-li-qí* ^{27}*mì-šu-um ṣa-ah-ra-ku-ma* le.e. ^{28}*ú be-tám :* ša a-bi*$_4$*-a* ^{29}*lá ú-ga-ra-ma i-na* ^{30}*i-ga-ri-im sí-kà-tám-ma*

$^{1-4}$Say to Azu-elka and Adue, especially to Azu-elka: thus (say) Kunnaniya and Šāt-Aššur.

$^{5-7}$When I arrived in Kaneš, your beer bread had been deposited in the kitchen storeroom, $^{8-9}$and I had also entrusted you some furniture with the words: $^{9-11}$"When you have taken out your beer bread, seal the kitchen storeroom."

$^{12-14}$Did I not tell you as follows: "Do not make me his enemy"? $^{15-16}$Today, I have become his enemy. $^{16-18}$Wherever my *tamalakkum*-chests are, they too surely will get lost!

$^{19-20}$Say to Adue: thus (says) Šāt-Aššur. $^{20-21}$As for me, I always consider you to be my mother! ^{22}I (must say) as follows: $^{23-24}$"Although my goods are in Kaneš, $^{25-26}$and you, yourself are far away, you have (nevertheless) ruined me! $^{27-30}$Why am I (considered) too young to rent my father's house, while (driving) the peg into the wall?

Bibliography: Text published by Contenau as TTC, 26; republished by Michel (1986, 127–28); translated by Michel (2001a, no. 384). Collated March 2018.

Comments: Kunnaniya accuses her older sister of being responsible for the loss of tablet containers kept in her house, while her daughter, Šāt-Aššur, complains to her aunt that she is responsible for the loss of her mother's goods; she claims the rent of her father's house in Aššur.

Line 30: the peg in the wall somehow proves ownership, and Šāt-Aššur, daughter of the deceased, claims her property rights on the house by driving a peg into the wall. For this expression, see, for example, Meir Malul (1987, 22–23).

---

312. Kunnaniya Asks Her Older Sister for Help

Obv. ^{1}*a-na A-zu-e-el-kà* ^{2}*qí-bi-ma um-ma Ku-na-ni-a-/ma* ^{3}*šu-ma : a-ha-tí : a-tí* ^{4}*ma ke-na-tí-ma ta-ra-i-mì-/ni* ^{5}*lá al-té-e : a*$^{!}$*-mu-wa-/at-ma* ^{6}*qá-qí-ri-i : lá-šu* ^{7}*i-na pá-ni-tim* ^{8}*té-er-tí : lá i-li-kà-kum* ^{9}*u*$_4$*-ma-am : na-áš-pè-er-tí* ^{10}*i-li-kà-kum : ù a-tí* ^{11}*a-wa-tám iš-té-en*$_6$ lo.e. ^{12}*qá-ri-ba-ma ú lá-tal-kam-/ma* ^{13}*a-ni : a-tí : me-ra-ki* rev. ^{14}*ú šu-ma-am : ta-áš-ku-/ni* ^{15}*l[á] tù-l[á]-bi*$_4$*-iš :* ^{16}*Šé-ṣú-ur ša i-na* ^{17}*é*$^{be-tí}$*-a wa-áš-bu-ni : «iš»* ^{18}*ú-lá ú-lá-bi*$_4$*-iš* ^{19}*a-na-ku u*$_4$*-ma-am : ša i-na* ^{20}é *: wa-áš-ba-ku-n[i]-«n[i]»* ^{21}*ig-re-e : lá a-ta-na-/dí-in* ^{22}*Ṭá-ba ša iš-tù* ^{23}mu-10-šè *wa-áš-bu mì-nam* ^{24}*i-dí-nam : a-na :* u.e. ^{25}*A-zu-e-el-kà qí-bi*$_4$*-ma* ^{26}*um-ma A-šur-m[a-l]ik-ma* le.e. ^{27}*Šál*$^{?}$*-ma-lúm : i-na Wa-ah-šu-/ša-na* ^{28}*wa-áš-ba-at-/ma um-mì a-tí* ^{29}*li-bi lá tù-lá-mì-ni* ^{30}*mì-ma lá ú-šé-bi*$_4$*-lá-ki-im*

$^{1-2}$Say to Azu-elka: thus (says) Kunnaniya.

$^{3-4}$If you are my sister and you really love me, (listen) $^{5-6}$I can't cope (any longer); I am going to die, because there is no (other) way out for me! $^{7-10}$No message from me has come to you before, (but) today my letter has come to you. $^{10-12}$So as for you, you have to address only one word to me, and I will come.

$^{13-14}$Now, you, you have your son and you have started a family, ^{15}(but) you did not provide him clothes. $^{16-18}$(Neither) did Šēṣur, who was living in my house, provide (him) clothes. $^{19-21}$As to me, (up to) today, while living in the house, I never paid rent. $^{22-24}$Ṭāba, who has been living (here) for 10 years, what did he give me?

$^{24-26}$Say to Azu-elka: thus (says) Aššur-malik. $^{27-28}$While Šalim-ālum lives in Wahšušana, $^{29-30}$you are my mother, do not blame me for not sending you anything!

Bibliography: Text published by J. Lewy as KTH, 5; translated by Michel (2001a, no. 385). Lines 3–12 cited by Michel (1997e, 253 n. 47).

Comments: Kunnaniya, desperate, begs her sister Azu-elka to help her. She refuses to pay a rent for the house she is living in, arguing that another person living there never paid rent to her.

Lines 8 and 10: twice the writer wrote *-kum* instead of *-kim*.

Šišahšušar, a Housewife Owning Cattle

Šišahšušar (also written Šašahšušar) was the Anatolian *amtum*-wife of Aššur-nādā, son of Aššur-idī, and the mother of a son, Aššur-nēmedī, and a daughter, Ištar-lamassī, whom she married to Puzur-Ištar (**23**; fig. 19).[62] She lived in Kaneš and received there several letters from her husband, either addressed to her alone or to a group of people including her. There is a unique letter sent by Šišahšušar to her husband, which he might have brought back to the house. Since Aššur-nādā traveled frequently within Anatolia for his business, Šišahšušar was supposed to go to meet her husband in another Anatolian town, but her journey was postponed, both because of bad weather and lack of money (**314**).

Šišahšušar was mainly concerned with the management of her household in Kaneš, including her children and slaves. One of her main tasks was the provisioning of food—barley, wheat, lard—and firewood (**319**, **313**, **315**). She had to check the oil stock of the house (**316**). She bought goods herself (**313**), or she received them as payment for debts owed to her husband. The grain was delivered in sacks, from four sacks to thirty-five, both wheat and barley (**132**). Such a large quantity of grain could perhaps suggest that the couple owned fields cultivated by Anatolians peasants who paid in kind.[63]

According to letters sent by her husband, she seems to have been involved in agricultural activities. Together with her husband's associates, she purchased straw, wood, and reeds. She also bought good quality oxen,

62. Larsen 2002 contains the reconstructed archive of this merchant, which comprises several letters addressed to this woman (OAA, 1, nos. 50–58, 73). See also Michel 2001a, 476–80, and Veenhof 2015c, 284. Note that this woman had a namesake mentioned at least twice with her husband Dikšar in texts belonging to the rich Anatolian Peruwa. In AKT 10, 12a–b, together with a group of Anatolians, they owe 6 sacks of barley to Peruwa; and in AKT 10, 55a–b, presumably because they were unable to pay their debts, they are bought by Peruwa for half a mina of silver. It is not clear whether the same woman or a third namesake is indebted, together with Zuzuban, for 8 minus ¼ shekels of silver to Walhišna in AKT 10, 52.

63. Against Dercksen 2008a, 83.

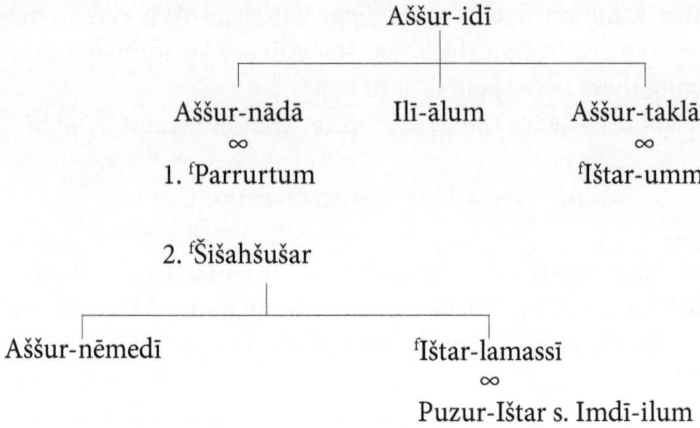

Fig. 19. Family tree of Šišahšušar, wife of Aššur-nādā.

gathered straw to feed them (**319**), or received fodder for them (**315**), and she had to make them ready for ploughing (**157**).

Šišahšušar, as a good housewife, prepared food, and especially beer, for which she soaked malt and beer bread in large quantities (**132**, **319**, CCT 3, 7b, BIN 4, 49). She was certainly also involved in the production of textiles to dress household members and received wool (**321**).

As Aššur-nādā traveled in Anatolia or to Aššur, his wife acted as his representative in Kaneš, sometimes together with their son Aššur-nēmedi (**317**). She sent servants and donkeys to her husband in Wašhaniya (**316**) and supervised anyone wishing access to Aššur-nādā's archives to remove a tablet recording a debt (**316**). She had to inform him about his current financial operations (**132**, **313**) and oversaw the repayment of her husband's loans. She was supposed to receive part of this capital for her own use and reported to her husband when she had not (**313**, **315**, KTS 1, 13a, **318**). Šišahšušar herself owned silver, and sent a small amount to Aššur to buy a bracelet there (**320**).

313. Šišahšušar Reports to Her Husband about Trade Activities of His Associates

Obv. ^{1}*a-na A-šùr-na-da qí-bí-ma* ^{2}*um-ma Ša-ša-ah-šu-šar-ma ki-ma* ^{3}*a-ta : tù-ṣú-ni* ⅔ *ma-na* 5 gín kù-babbar ^{4}*im-hu-ru-ma a-na Ú-ṣú-ur-/ša-A-/šùr* ^{5}dumu *A-šùr-ma-lik i-dí-/nu* ^{6}3 *ku-ta-ni Ú-ṣú-ur-ša-A-šùr* ^{7}*il*$_5$*-qé-ma a-na* é *kà-ri-im i-dí-i* [8]12 gín kù-babbar ki *Ša-ra-bu-nu-wa* [9]*im-hu-ru-ma i-a-tí : i-dí-nu-ni-šu* [10]4 *na-ru-uq še-am* é *Ku-du-bi-iš* [11]*ub-lu-nim a-na-kam am-hu-ur-ma* [12]3* *na-ru-uq e-li-a-am* [13]3 *na-ru-uq* gíg [14]é *Kà-ú-ba-a ub-lu-nim* [15]*ù mì-ma ú-lá i-dí-nu-nim* lo.e. [16]*ki-ma a-ta tù-ṣú-ni* [17]*A-šùr-bé-el-a-wa-tim* rev. [18]*i-li-kam-ma maš-ke-e* [19]*i-zu-a-áz zi-ta-kà-a* [20]*i-ib-ší-ma ù a-ni-i* [21]*i-ta-ab-lu-šu-nu* 15 gín kù-babbar [22]*ša Ta-ar-hu-nu ší-tí* kù! *ha-bu-lu-/ú* [23]šà 8¼ gín kù-babbar *i-dí-nu-nim* [24]*ú mì-ma ú-lá i-dí-nu-nim* [25]*ù iš-tí Ta-ar-hu-nu-ú* [26]5 gín kù-babbar *a-hu-ur* [27]*ù ší-tí* kù-babbar *šu-nu-ú il*$_5$*-qé-ú* [28]*i-ba-áb-tí-kà mì-ma* [29]*ú-lá im-hu-ru-ú a-na* [30]*té-er-tí-kà Ú-ṣú-ur-ša-A-šùr* [31]*na-hi-id u*$_4$*-mu-um iš-tù* [32]*i-ta-at-qú* iti-3-kam u.e. [33]*e-ṣé-e-ma* «*ma*» *ú-lá iš-a-ma* [34]*a-na-ku-ma a-áš-a-am* [35]ki *Ha-bi-i* le.e. [36]1⅔ *ma-na* 5 gín kù-babbar *ni-im-hu-ur** [37]*U-ṣú-ur-ša-A-šùr il*$_5$*-qé-e* ⅔ *ma-na* [38]ki *Ha*-lu*-le-e ni-il*$_5$*-qé-e ù* 5 gín kù-babbar [39]*Ú-ṣú-ur-ša-A-šur*

[1–2]Say to Aššur-nādā: thus (says) Šišahšušar.

[2–5]After you left, one received ⅔ mina, 5 shekels of silver, and gave it to Uṣur-ša-Aššur, son of Aššur-malik. [6–7]Uṣur-ša-Aššur took 3 *kutānum*-textiles, and he made a deposit at the trade bureau. [8–9]They received 12 shekels of silver from Šarabunuwa, and they gave it (the silver) to me. [10–11]The household of Kudubiš brought 4 sacks of barley; I received them here and [12–14]3 sacks came up to me. [13–15]The household of Ka'uba brought 3 sacks of wheat here, but they did not give me anything!

[16–19]After you left, Aššur-bēl-awātim came here and divided the hides. [19–21]There was a share for you, but now they took it away. [21–22](There are) 15 shekels of silver from Tahrunu; they owe the remainder of the silver. [23]They gave me 8¼ shekels of silver of it, [24]but they did not give me anything else, [25–26]and 5 shekels are still owed by Tarhunu. [27]Also, they were the ones who took the remainder of the silver. [28–29]They received nothing from your outstanding claims. [29–31]Let Uṣur-ša-Aššur pay attention to your instruction! [31–32]3 months have passed since his term was over. [33–34]He did not buy even firewood, and I myself had to buy (it)! [35–36]From Habi we received 1⅔ minas, 5 shekels of silver; [37]Uṣur-ša-Aššur took it. [37–39]We took ⅔ minas from Halule, and Uṣur-ša-Aššur (received) 5 shekels of silver.

Bibliography: Text published by Bilgiç, Sever, Günbattı, and Bayram as AKT 1, 15 (Ank. 4668); edited by Larsen (2002, no. 73); translated by Michel (2001a, no. 357). Collated March 2016.

Comments: This unique letter sent by Šišahšušar to her husband might have been brought back to Kaneš by him. She reports to her husband about the activities of his representatives in Kaneš after he had left the town. They gave her part of the silver they have been paid, but not all that corresponded to her husband's share. She also received some barley, either from fields belonging to the couple and cultivated by Anatolians peasants, or for repayment for debts. She had to buy firewood for herself.

---

314. Šišahšušar Had to Postpone Her Travel to Meet Her Husband

Obv. [1]*um-ma A-šur-na-da* [2]*a-na Ší-ša-ah-šu-šar* [3]*qí-bi$_4$-ma a-ša áš-pu-ra-/ki-ni* [4]*um-ma a-na-ku-ma* [5]*a-re-eš$_{15}$ da-áš-e* [6]*a-ša-pá-ra-ki-ma* [7]*ta-li-ki-im li-bi$_4$-ki* [8]*lá tù-lá-mì-ni ku-ṣú-um* [9]*is-ni-iq-ni-a-tí-ma* [10]*ù bu-lá-tí-im* [11]*ša a-da-gu$_5$-lu-ni* [12]*a-na ba-áb-tim* [13]*i-tù-ar-ma* lo.e. [14]*a-ší-a-tí lá áš-pu-ra-ki-<im>* [15]*mì-šu ša um-ma a-tí-ma* rev. [16]*ú-lá al*[!]*-té-e* [17]*bu-lá-tí ša qá-tí* [18]*iṣ-bu-tù-ni-ni* [19]*e-ṣú-ma iṣ-ba-at* [20]*ma-du ha-lá-aq* [21]*a-na Ku-na-na-mì-it* [22]*e-ra-áb-ma ša lá-qá-/e* [23]*a-lá-qé-a-ma i-wa-ṣa-i-/a* [24]*a-ša-pá-ra-ki-im-ma* [25]*a-ṣé-ri-a ta-li-ki-im* [26]*wa-dí a-li-tí-a* [27]*ú-lá i-ṭá-hi-i* [28]*šu-ma i-lá-kam qá-<qár->šu-um* u.e. [29]*lá tù-ṣa-bi$_4$-i-ma* [30]*la ta-da-šu-u[m]* le.e. [31]*ú šu-ma ṣú-ha-ar-tam$_4$ e-ri-iš$_6$-ki* [32]*Sá-a-ma ú šé-ri-šu a-šar li-/bi$_4$-šu* [33]*li-it-ru-šu*

[1-3]Thus (says) Assur-nādā: say to Šišahšušar.

[3-4]As to what I wrote to you as follows: [5-7]"By the beginning of spring, I will write to you, and you will come here"; [7-8]you must not be angry at me! [8-9]Winter has tested us, and [10-13]the funds that I was expecting have turned into outstanding merchandise, and [14]therefore I did not write to you.

[15-16]Why (did) you (write me) as follows: "I can't cope anymore"? [17-20]The working capital that I could seize was only a little; much has been lost! [21-23]When I enter Kunanamit, I will take what can be taken, [23-24]and as soon as I can leave again, I will write you, [25]and you will come to me.

[26-27]Surely, he must not touch my *funds*! [28-30]If he comes, do not be timid, and do not give (it) to him. [31-33]But if he asks you for the girl, let him take along Sāma and *his* children wherever he wishes.

Bibliography: Text published in copy by Smith as CCT 3, 7a; edited by Michel (2001a, no. 361) and Larsen (2002, no. 50).

Comments: Šišahšušar was supposed to join her husband at the beginning of spring in another Anatolian town, but she could not travel because of bad weather conditions in the area where he was staying, and also because he could not recover the silver he was waiting for. This letter seems to be an answer to one sent by her in which she expressed her disappointment. He warns her against an unnamed individual who might ask for silver.

---

315. Šišahšušar Must Recover Grain and Metals from Two Merchants

Obv. [1]*um-ma A-šùr-na-da-ma* [2]*a-na Ší-ša-ah-šu-šar* [3]*qí-bi-ma ú-ṭá-tám* [4]*ù sú-ba-ra-am* [5]*ma-lá Ì-lí-i-šar* [6]*ù Hu-lu-ba ší-im* [7]*ni-ga-li ù* an-na [8]*ša a-dí-nu*-šu-nu-tí-ni-ma* [9]*a-na A-lá-ni* [10]*ub-lu-ni ma-lá* lo.e. [11]*i-dí-nu-ni-ki-ni* [12]*mì-šu-um ma-tí-ma* rev. [13]*té-er-tí-ki lá i-lá-kam* [14]*šu-ma lá i-du-nu-nim* [15]*a-na bé-tí-a* [16]*lá e-ru-bu-nim* [17]*Hu-lu-ba i-na ki-ša-/ar-ší-im* [18]*id-a* [19]*ù Ì-lí*-ša-ar* [20]*ší-im* 30 *ma-na* <urudu> u.e. [21]*ù* 1 gín 22½ <še> kù-babbar [22]*ša ha-bu-lu ša-áš-qí-/lá-šu* le.e. [23]40 *ma-na* urudu 10 túg *ku-ta-/nu* [24]4 *šu-ru-tum ša* túg [25]*ša il*$_5$*-qé-ú-šu-nu-ni*

[1-3]Thus (says) Aššur-nādā: say to Šišahšušar.

[3-4]Concerning grain and *subārum*-fodder, [5-8]as much as Ilī-išar and Huluba (gathered) as the price of the sickles and tin that I gave them, and [9-13]that they brought to Alāni, why did you never report to me about how much they gave you?

[14-16]If they did not give you any, they must not enter my house! [17-18]Throw Huluba in jail, [19-22]and make Ilī-išar pay the price of the 30 minas <of copper> and the 1 shekel, 22½ <grains> of silver he owes. [23-25]40 minas of copper, 10 *kutānum*-textiles, 4 dark textiles they took for themselves.

Bibliography: Tablet from the Rosicrucian Egyptian Museum at San Jose, California, known under the inventory number RC 1749c; edited by Larsen (2002, no. 51). Collated on the photo online on CDLI as P361694.

Comments: Two men are in debt to Aššur-nādā and are supposed to pay Šišahšušar with grain and fodder. He asks his wife to send him a report and tells her to be tough in the negotiations, presumably with the help of his representatives there—verbs are in the imperative plural in the second part of the letter—even threatening one of them with jail.

316. Aššur-nādā Asks His Wife and Associates to See to the Payment of a Debt

Obv. ^{1}*um-ma A-šùr-na-da-ma* ^{2}*a-na A-gu*$_{5}$*-a* ^{3}*Ší-ša-ah-šu-šar* ^{4}*ù A-šùr-*^{d}utu^{ši} ^{5}*qí-bi-ma šu-ma* ^{6d}im-*ba-ni ṭup-pu-/šu* ^{7}*e-ri-iš-ku-nu* ^{8}*ṭup-pì-a pé-té-a-ma* ^{9}*ṭup-pu-šu am-ra-ma* ^{10}*ša i-ša-qú-lu* ^{11}*ṣa-hi-ra-ma ša ší-/tim* ^{12}*ṭup-pu-šu lu-up-/ta-ma* lo.e. ^{13}*ù a-li-am* rev. ^{14}*dí-na-šu-um* ^{15}*ṭup-pá-am : ša* ^{16}½ *ma-na* kù-babbar ^{17}*ša bé-ú-lá-at* ^{18}*A-šùr-i-dí* dumu *Ku-sá-/a* ^{19}*i-nu-mì ra-bi*$_{4}$*-ṣú-um* ^{20}*ša* é *Ku-ra iṣ-bu-tù-/kà* ^{21}*a-na ku-nu-ki ša a-bi*$_{4}$*-kà* ^{22}*wa-du-im a-dí-na-/kum* ^{23}*A-gu*$_{5}$*-a a-na* ^{24}*li-bi*$_{4}$ *ṭù-pì-a* (*sic!*) ^{25}*lu-ta-er-šu* ^{26}ì-giš du$_{10}$-ga u.e. ^{27}*kà-lá-šu-ma sà-ni-/qá-ma* ^{28}anše^{hi-a} le.e. ^{29}*ù ṣú-ha-ri mì*$^{!}$*-ma* *<a>-ṣé-er* ^{30}*Wa-áš-ha-ni-a-ma ṭur*$_{4}$*-[da-nim]*

$^{1-5}$Thus (says) Aššur-nādā: say to Agua, Šišahšušar, and Aššur-šamšī.

$^{6-7}$If Adad-bāni asks you for his tablet, ^{8}open my tablet-container, $^{9-11}$look for his tablet, and deduct (from his debt) what he will pay, $^{11-14}$then write a new tablet of the remainder (of his debt), and give him the other one.

$^{15-22}$As for the tablet of ½ mina of silver, which is the working capital of Aššur-idī, son of Kusaya, that I gave you, when the attorney for the house of Kura seized you in order to identify your father's seal, $^{23-25}$let Agūa put it again among my tablets.

$^{26-30}$Check all of the top-quality oil, and $^{28-30}$send all the donkeys and servants to Wašhaniya.

Bibliography: Tablet from the Rosicrucian Egyptian Museum at San Jose, California, known under the inventory number RC 1749d; edited by Larsen (2002, no. 55). Collated on the photo online on CDLI as P361695.

Comments: The role of Šišahšušar, together with the other adressees of this letter, is to supervise the actions with Aššur-nādā's archives: removal of a tablet recording a debt, partial reimbursement, and production of an updated debt record.

She is also to check the oil stock of the house and to send donkeys and servants to Wašhaniya, where, presumably, her husband was staying when he wrote this letter.

Lines 2 and 23: the proper name Agūa has been corrected by Larsen (2002, no. 55) into Aguza in view of the letter KTS 1, 13a (Larsen 2002, no.

56). The names Agūa and Aguza both exist, and Aššur-nādā is in contact with both (for Agūa, see KTH, 3:5).

Lines 15–22 are adressed to one of the male correspondents, presumably Agūa. In the previous and following lines, the imperatives are in the plural form, and thus orders concern all the addressees.

Line 26: the reading proposed by Larsen (2002, no. 55) is correct according to the photo of the tablet.

---

317. Šašahšušar Acts as Representative for Her Husband

Obv. [1]*um-ma A-šùr-na-da-ma* [2]*a-na Ša-ša-ah-ša-šu-šar* [3]*ú A-šùr-né-me-dí qí-bi-ma* [4]1⅔ *ma-na* kù-babbar [5]*iš-tí* ^{d}im-*ba-ni* [6]dumu *Du-du* ½ *ma-na* 3⅓ gín-ta [7]*i-ša-tim i-ša-qal* [8]*u*$_4$*-mu-šu ma-dí-iš* [9]*e-ta-at-qú ṣa-áb-ta-/šu-ma* [10]*ma-lá ta-al-qé-/a-ni* [11]*lu-ṣa-hi-ra-ku-nu-tí-ma* lo.e. [12]*ší-tí* : kù-babbar *ša-áš-/qí-lá-šu* [13]1 *ma-na* 3 gín rev. [14]kù-babbar *ša A-lá-hi-/im* [15]*ú i-a-tí iš-tí* [16]*Pì-lá-ah-A-a ṣa-áb-ta-šu-/ma* [17]*ša-áš-qí-lá-šu* [18]*a-šu-mì lu-bu-ší-im* [19]*ša a-na A-ha-ar* [20]*lu-bu-ša-am* : *dam-qám* [21]*áš-e-ma ú-lá ú-ta-/ma* [22]*ú-lá ú-šé-bi*$_4$*-lá-ší* [23]*li-ba-ša* u.e. [24]*lá i-lá-mì-in* [25]*i-na a-lá-ki-a* le.e. [26]*ú-ba-lá-ší-im*

[1–3]Thus (says) Aššur-nādā: say to Šašahšušar and Aššur-nēmedī.

[4–7]1⅔ minas of silver are owed by Adad-bāni, son of Dudu; he shall pay ½ mina, 3⅓ shekels per year. [8–9]His term is far overdue! Seize him, and [10–11]he may deduct for you all that you have (already) received, [12]then make him pay the rest of the silver. [13–17]1 mina, 3 shekels of silver belonging to Ali-ahum and myself are owed by Pilahaya; seize him and make him pay. [18–21]As to the garment for Ahar, I looked for a garment of good quality [21–22]but could not find one and did not send her any. [23–26]She must not be angry. I will bring her one when I come.

Bibliography: Text published by Garelli as *RA* 60, 138; edited by Michel (2001a, no. 360) and Larsen (2002, no. 53). Tablet bought by A. Frank and later on, in 1973, by the Musée d'Histoire Naturelle de Blois "Les Jacobins," inventory number 73-7-69. Tablet collated on photo.

Comments: Ša/išahšušar, together with her oldest son, is asked by her husband to recover the silver of two in different loans, thus acting as a representative for her husband. All verbs are in the plural and addressed to both mother and son.

318. Šišahšušar Is to Recover Silver from an Unpaid Debt

^{1}*[u]m-ma A-šùr-na-da-/m[a]* ^{2}*a-na I-dí-Sú-en*$_{6}$ ^{3}*ù Ší-ša-ah-<šu>-ša-ar* ^{4}*qí-bi*$_{4}$*-ma* 17 gín ^{5}kù-babbar *ṣa-ru-pá-am* ^{6}*ší-im A-bar-ni-im* ^{7}*Ku-zu-zi-a iš-tù* ^{8}10 *ša-na-tim ha-bu-lam* ^{9}*mì-šu ša am-tum* ^{10}*ta-li-ku-ma ú-qá-/li-lu-ší*$^{!}$(ŠU) ^{11}*né-ma-al* kù-babbar^{pì}*-a* ^{12}*ša iš-tù* 10 *ša*$^{!}$*-na-/tim* lo.e. ^{13}*i-be-e-lu* ^{14}kù-babbar *ša-áš-qí-/il*$_{5}$*-šu-ma* rev. ^{15}*a-na a-am-tim* ^{16}*dí-in šu-ma mì-ma* ^{17}*i-qá-bi*$_{4}$ *šu-ga-ri-/a-am* ^{18}*ša A-šùr* ^{19}*li-it-ma-ma* ^{20}*ú li-it-ba-al-/šu* ^{21}*a-pu-tum lá ta-ga-/mì-il*$_{5}$*-šu* ^{22}*ú-ul* kù-babbar ^{23}*li-iš-qú-ul* ^{24}*ú-ul ta-mì-šu* ^{25}15 gín kù-babbar *iš-tí* ^{26}*Ha-ar-ta-al* u.e. ^{27}an-na^{ak}*-šu* ^{28}*a-na ša-pá-ar-/tim* ^{29}kù-babbar *ša-áš-qí-il*$_{5}$*-šu-/ma* le.e. ^{30}½* *ma-na* 5 gín kù-babbar ^{31}*ša Du-du* ½ *ma-na* ki ^{32}*Ša-ra-bu-nu-a ša-áš-qí-lá-/ma* ^{33}*a-na a-am*$^{!}$*-tim dí-in*

$^{1-4}$Thus (says) Aššur-nādā: say to Iddin-Suen and Šišahšušar.

$^{4-8}$Kuziziya has owed me 17 shekels of refined silver, price of an Abarnium-textile, since 10 years (ago)! $^{9-10}$Why is it that when the *amtum*-wife (Šišahšušar) went (for it), he insulted her? $^{11-16}$Make him pay in silver the profit (gained) on my silver, which he has been using for 10 years, and give (it) to (my) *amtum*-wife. $^{16-20}$If he protests, let him swear by Aššur's sword, and then take it (the silver) along. ^{21}Urgent! Do not make concessions: $^{22-23}$either he pays the silver, ^{24}or make him take an oath!

$^{25-26}$15 shekels of silver are owed by Hartal; $^{27-28}$his tin has been pledged (for that). ^{29}Make him pay the silver, and $^{30-32}$make pay the ½ minas, 5 shekels of silver from Dudu, (and) ½ mina owed by Šarabunuwa, and ^{33}give (the silver) to the *amtum*-wife.

Bibliography: Text published in copy by Lewy as KTS 1, 13b; edited by Larsen (2002, no. 57). Line 30 collated by Donbaz (2015, 64).

Comments: This letter follows a previous one sent by Aššur-nādā to Aguza, Uṣur-ša-Aššur, and Šišahšušar (KTS 1, 13a), in which the debt of Kuziziya had already been unpaid for eight years. In this letter, Aššur-nādā loses patience. His representatives are asked to collect the silver and to give it to his wife or to make Kuziziya take an oath denying the debt. If Kuziziya swears that he has not spent the corresponding silver, then he does not have to pay. All the silver collected must go to Šišahšušar.

Line 17: the word *šugariā'um* corresponds to a symbol of Aššur; it is an object that can be mentioned by pairs. The word is perhaps attested under the form *šak/q/garum* at Mari, an object in copper or bronze given to soldiers together with weapons and tools; see Arkhipov 2012, 123.

319. Ox Breeding

Obv. ^{1}*um-ma A-šùr-na-da-/ma* ^{2}*a-na Ší-ša-ah-šu-/šar* ^{3}*qí-bi-ma* ^{4}55 *ma-na* ì-kal ^{5}*ša hu-zi-ri-im* ^{6}*nu-hu-um ku-nu-ki-a* ^{7}*ù na-ru-tum* ^{8}*ša e-ru-bu* ^{9}^{d}utu-*ba-ni* ^{10}*na-áš-a-ki-im* rev. ^{11}*a-pu-tum* ^{12}*mu-za-am ù e-wa-za-tim* ^{13}*ša e-zi-bu* ^{14}*ša-ṣí-ri-ma* ^{15}*šé-bi*$_{4}$*-li-ší-na* ^{16}urudu *li-dí-nu-ma* ^{17}*tí-ib-nam* ^{18}*ša-ma* 1 (bán) *tù-hi* ^{19}*ih-da-ma a-bi*$_{4}$*-lá* ^{20}gu$_{4}$$^{hi\text{-}a}$ le.e. ^{21}sig$_{5}$ *A-lá-hu-um* ^{22}*li-iš-a-ma* ^{23}*tí-ib-nam pá-hi-ra*

$^{1-3}$Thus (says) Aššur-nādā: say to Šišahšušar.

$^{4-10}$Šamaš-bāni is bringing you both 55 minas of lard (in) a leather bag under my seal and *narūtum*-malt that has arrived. $^{11-15}$Urgent! Send under guard the *muzum* and the *ewaztum* that he left.

$^{16-18}$Let them sell copper and buy straw. $^{18-19}$Take care to dry 1 seah of bran. $^{20-23}$Let Ali-ahum buy good-quality oxen and gather straw.

Bibliography: Text published in copy by Thureau-Dangin as TC 2, 47; translated by Michel (2001a, no. 358) and Larsen (2002, no. 52).

Comments: The *ewaztum* and the *muzum* might probably refer to foodstuffs.

Aššur-nādā writes to his Anatolian wife in Kaneš about domestic matters, among which is delivery of foodstuffs for her house. The oxen to be purchased refer to agricultural activities that might have been performed by slaves and supervised by Šišahšušar.

320. Šišahšušar Owes Silver to Buy a Bracelet

Obv. ^{1}½ *ma-na* kù-babbar *ṣa-ru-pá-/am* ^{2}*ni-is-ha-sú* ^{3}diri *ša-du-a-sú* ^{4}*ša-bu a-na Ša-ra-at-/Ištar* ^{5}10 gín kù-babbar ^{6}*ṣa-ru-pá-am ša ik-ri-/bi*$_{4}$*-a* ^{7}5 gín kù-babbar *ṣa-ru-/pu-um* ^{8}*ša Ší-ša-ah-šu-šar* lo.e. ^{9}[*a*]*-na ša-wi-ri-*[*i*]*m* ^{10}*ša-a-mì-im* rev. ^{11}5 gín kù-babbar *a-na* ^{12}*ni-qí-šu* : *a-na Kur-ub-/Ištar* ^{13}5 gín kù-babbar ^{14}*ša A-šur-ì-mì-tí* ^{15}*a-na Ša-ra-at-Ištar* ^{16}1½ gín *a-na* 1 udu-*šu* ^{17}*mì-ma a-nim a-na* ^{18}*En-nam-A-šùr* u.e. ^{19}dumu *I-dí-Sú-en*$_{6}$

[20]*áp-qí-id* [igi] *I-dí-/a-bi*$_4$*-im* le.e. [21]igi *A-ni-na* igi [22]*A-ni-na* dumu *Puzur*$_4$*-/A-na*

[1-4]½ mina of refined silver—its import [tax] added, its transport fee paid for—for Šarrat-Ištar; [5-6]10 shekels of refined silver from my votive offerings; [7-10]5 shekels of refined silver belonging to Šišahšušar to buy a bracelet; [11-12]5 shekels of silver for his sacrifices for Kurub-Ištar; [13-15]5 shekels of silver from Aššur-imittī for Šarrat-Ištar; [16]1½ shekels for his sheep: [17-20]all this I entrusted to Ennum-Aššur, son of Iddin-Suen. [20-22]In the presence of Iddin-abum, Anīna, and Anīna, son of Puzur-Anna.

Bibliography: Text published by Lewy in 1930 as KTH, 26; edited by Larsen (2002, no. 155).

Comments: Transport contract giving the list of small quantities of silver belonging to different individuals or from various origins. Among these, there are five shekels of silver belonging to Šišahšušar that she is presumably sending to Aššur for the purchase of a bracelet that will be brought back to Kaneš later on. The anonymous author of this contract might be Aššur-nādā himself.

---

321. Šišahšušar Receives a Certain Quantity of Wool

Obv. [1]14 *áb-ni-im* [2]*i-na ba-li-ša-im* [3]6 *áb-ni-im* [4]*Ši-*[*ša*]*-ah-šu-šar* lo.e. [5]*i-na* rev. [6]síg^{hi-a} [7]*ša i-qa-ra-be-/tim* [8]*ib-ší-a-nim*

[1-2]14 stone-weights (of wool) …, [3-4]6 stone-weights (of wool): Šišahšušar. [5-8]From the wool that was present in the storeroom.

Bibliography: Text published by Lewy in 1930 as KTH, 40; edited by Ulshöfer (1995, no. 464) and Dercksen (2016, 18 n. 26).

Comments: Šišahšušar receives a quantity of wool, which suggests that she is spinning and weaving textiles. The wool is quantified with a stone-weight specific to weighing wool.

Line 2: this word is unkown. It could be a standard of measure. It has been interpreted by J. Lewy and Ulshöfer as a nisbe: "the man of Bališa."

Hatala, a Woman Involved in Trade

Hatala, also written Hutala and Huatala, was the daughter of Eniš(a)ru, an important Anatolian moneylender known from several secured loan and debt-slavery texts.[64] He may also have worked as transporter for the family of Ennum-Aššur, son of Šalim-Aššur.[65]

Hatala was married to Laqēpum, son of Wardum, with the status of *aššutum*-wife. The wedding ceremony took place in Kaneš, and the marriage contract has been preserved (**24**).[66] This contract indicates that Laqēpum had not previously contracted a marriage, so that, after having married Hatala in Kaneš, he was allowed to take a second wife with a different status in Aššur. It also specifies that if Hatala did not gave birth to a child within two years, she was the one to choose and buy a female slave to provide a descendant to her husband. She was afterward allowed to sell this female slave as she wished. Such clauses gave her a considerable power in her marriage. In a letter addressed to her, her husband confirmed that if she did not like her female slave, she could sell her and keep the proceeds for herself (**140**).

As he was traveling, Laqēpum addressed several letters to Hatala, sending her silver and local specialities such as hazelnuts (**202**, **322**). He asked her to keep a close eye on their house and their goods, and to remove loan contracts she herself needed from his archives (**140**, **323**). Hatala also had to contact several debtors, men and women, to make them pay their debts to her, whether the silver belonged to herself (**322**), to her husband, or to an Anatolian creditor to be reimbursed later (**140**, **202**, **323**).

Hatala herself sent a small amount of silver to Aššur to make purchases, thus participating in long-distance trade (**324**).

64. The activities of Eniš(a)ru have been studied by Veenhof (1978). He acted as a creditor of Anatolian couples.

65. See the many references in AKT 6b.

66. Michel 2001a, 501–2. There are at least two other women named Hatala. One homonym is attested during level Ib as the wife of Taha (Kt r/k 19 and perhaps also Kt n/k 14). The other one is mentioned as the wife of Šarnikan in the loan contract Kt 91/k 170:3–4; the date of this text is unknown.

322. Hatala Receives Instructions concerning Various Transactions in Silver

Obv. ^{1}*um-ma Lá-*[*qé-pu-ma a-na*] ^{2}*Hu-a-t*[*a-lá* (…)] ^{3}*qí-bi-*[*ma*] 3 g[ín] ^{4}kù-babbar *En-nam-*[x-(x)] ^{5}dumu *Ba-lá na-áš-a-ki-im* ^{6}1½ gín kù-babbar ^{7}*A-šur-mì-tí* ^{8}dumu *Šu-iš$_{4}$-tár* lo.e. ^{9}*tap-pá-i* rev. ^{10}*li-dí-na-ki-im* ^{11}*a-ma-kam* (erasure) ^{12}*A-šur-iš-ta-ki-il$_{5}$*$^{!}$(IN) ^{13}kù-babbar : *ša ṭup-<pí>-ki* ^{14}*lá-ma* : *a-li-kà-*[*ni*] ^{15}*ša-dí-na-šu* ^{16}*a-na-kam* : *a-n*[*a-ku*] u.e. ^{17}*ú A-bu-ša-*[*lim*] ^{18}*ni-ṣí-bi-i*[*t i-na*] ^{19}*kà-ša-dí-a* le.e. ^{20}*ú-ma-lá*$^{!}$(LÍ) : *mì-ma* : *lá ta-ra-gi$_{5}$-<mì>-šu* ^{21}3 gín kù-babbar *š<a> A-lá-lá* ^{22}*ku-nu-ki-a I-dí-Ku-bu-um* [*na-áš-a-ki-im*]

$^{1-3}$Thus (says) La[qēpum]: say [to] Huat[ala].

$^{3-5}$Ennam-[x-x], son of Bala, is bringing you 3 shekels of silver. $^{6-10}$Aššur-imitti, son of Šu-Ištar, my associate, should give you 1½ shekels of silver. $^{11-15}$Make there, before I come, Aššuriš-takil pay the silver of your tablet. $^{16-18}$Here, I and Abu-šalim, we got into a legal fight (about it), $^{19-20}$so [when] I arrive, I will compensate (it). $^{20-21}$You must in no way raise a claim against him. $^{21-22}$Iddin-Kūbum [is bringing you] 3 shekels of silver from Alala under my seal.

Bibliography: Text published by Hecker, Kryszat, and Matouš as Prag I, 669. Collated on photo online on CDLI as P359265.

Comments: Laqēpum informs his wife about several amounts of silver that she is supposed to receive from different colleagues. It seems that she herself owes some silver that her husband will pay as soon as he comes back.

323. Hatala Is in Charge of Her Husband's Archives

Obv. ^{1}*a-na A-šur-ma-lik* ^{2}*ú Ha-ta-lá* ^{3}*a-na Ha-ta-lá* ^{4}*qí-bi$_{4}$-ma um-ma Lá-qé-pu-ma* ^{5}*ta-ma-lá-ke-en$_{6}$* ^{6}*ša ṭup-pè-a* ^{7}*pè-té-a-ma* ^{8}*ṭup-pá-am* ^{9}*ša hu-bu-ul* rev. ^{10}^{d}im-gal ^{11}dumu *A-šur-ma-lik* ^{12}*šé-li-a-ma* ^{13}⅓ *ma-na* 3½ gín kù-babbar ^{14}*li-iš-qú-lá-ku-nu-tí-ma* ^{15}*ú ṭup-pu-šu* ^{16}*ú-šé-ra-šu-um* ^{17}*ha-mu-uš-tí* ^{18}*lá ta-qí-i*

$^{1-4}$(Say) to Aššur-malik and Hatala; say to Hatala: thus (says) Laqēpum.

[5-7]Open (pl.) the 2 *tamalakkum*-chests containing my tablets and [8-12]take out (pl.) the tablet concerning the debt of Adad-rabi, son of Aššur-malik, and [13-14]let him pay you (pl.) ⅓ mina, 3½ shekels of silver, [15-16]and then release (pl.) the tablet to him. [17]You (fem.) have not *offered* me my fifth share.

Bibliography: Text published in copy by Smith as CCT 3, 50a; translated by Michel (2001a, no. 390).

Comments: As Laqēpum is away, he asks his wife to open his archive's containers and take out a specific loan contract, which could suggest that Hatala was able to read or at least to recognize the seal of the debtor on the envelope. Note, however, that all the imperatives are in the plural, and the letter is addressed to both Hatala and her husband's colleague Aššur-malik. Laqēpum's archives are arranged into two chests; this statement gives some idea of the size of the archive preserved by Laqēpum in his house in Kaneš. Hatala, together with Aššur-malik, had to make the debtor pay the debt and then hand over to him the tablet recording the debt.

Line 18: a verb *naqûm* with a meaning fitting here is unknown. The word *ha-mu-uš-tí* could also be understood as "my *hamuštum*-week"; that is, the *hamuštum*-week bearing my name.

---

324. Hatala Sends a Small Amount of Silver to Aššur for Trade

Obv. [1]6 gín kù-babbar : *ni-is-/ha-sú* [2]diri : *Hu-a-ta-lá* [3]dam : *Lá-qé-ep* [4]dumu IR : *a-na* [5]*Tù-ta-a* : dumu [6]*Šu-A-nim* : *a-na* lo.e. [7]*ší-a-ma-tim* /*ta*$^{!}$-*dí-in* rev. [8]igi *A-šur-i-mì-tí* [9]dumu *Ma-num-ba-lúm-/A-šur* [10]igi *I-dí-sú-en*$_{6}$ [11]dumu *A-šur-lá-ma-/sí*

[1-7]Huatala, wife of Laqēp(um), son of Wardum, has given 6 shekels of silver—its import tax added—to Tutaya, son of Šu-Anum, for purchases. [8-11]In the presence of Aššur-imittī, son of Mannum-balum-Aššur, and Iddin-Suen, son of Aššur-lamassī.

Bibliography: Text published in copy by Hrozný as ICK 1, 67; edited by Larsen (1967, 47).

Comments: In this transport contract, Hatala entrusts a small amount of silver to a transporter who is presumably traveling to Aššur. There, the silver will be used to make purchases for Hatala.

Anna-Anna, Married to Ennum-Aššur

Anna-anna is the *amtum*-wife of Ennum-Aššur, son of Šalim-Aššur, with whom she had a daughter (AKT 6b, 371:14). Thus she had as sisters-in-law Lamassī and Šāt-Anna (married to Šuppunuman), and Ištar-lamassī, the wife of her husband's brother Ali-ahum (fig. 20). The letters sent to her, mainly by her husband, as well as at least eight letters sent by her, were found in a house excavated in 1994, as part of the archives belonging to Šalim-Aššur and his sons (figs. 2–3).[67] These last letters are addressed to her husband, and their context suggests that Anna-anna was living in Kaneš. This means that Ennum-Aššur brought her letters home, when he returned to Kaneš—as she requested in one of her letters (**326**)—or they were taken back to Kaneš after the murder of Ennum-Aššur.[68] Ennum-Aššur was in fact murdered only two years after the death of his father, so it seems that some of the letters exchanged between Anna-anna and Ennum-Aššur are to be placed within this short period of time. Larsen noted that, after the death of his brother, Ali-ahum moved into the house, where he left archives as well.

In Kaneš, Anna-anna was in charge of the household and domestics, buying various goods for the house (**331**; AKT 6b, 302; AKT 6c, 554), and she had to safeguard the tablets and goods of her husband (**325**; AKT 6b, 304, 311, 371). She sent servants, as well as objects and clothes, to her husband, and asked for silver in exchange (**326**; **331**; AKT 6b, 310). She possessed goods on her own, such as silver, gold (**325**; AKT 6c, 554) and textiles (**334**; AKT 6e, 1073), but could also be in debt (AKT 6a, 12).

Anna-anna acted as representative of her husband, receiving silver from his outstanding merchandise and various goods in his name (**329**,

---

67. This archive has been published by Larsen in the volumes of AKT 6a–e; the family tree is given in AKT 6b, p. 7, and Anna-anna is commented on in AKT 6b, p. 13; for all the references to Anna-anna in this archive, see the complete index at the end of AKT 6e. See also Veenhof 2015c, 284–85.

68. Note that the letter AKT 6b, 313 is sent by both Ennum-Aššur and Anna-anna to a group of people. There is no explanation why this letter was found in their house, apart from the possibility that it is a copy.

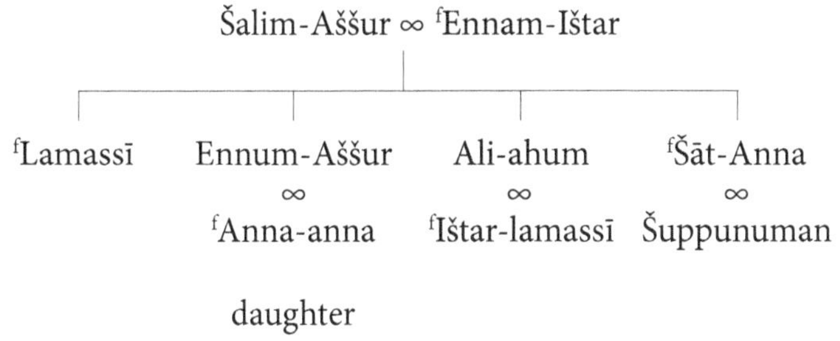

Fig 20. Family tree of Anna-anna, wife of Ennum-Aššur.

330). It seems that the family loaned silver to Anatolians, who repaid in grain (**328**; **326**; AKT 6b, 302). Anna-anna had to negotiate in the name of her husband with the merchants (**327**), but at the same time, Ennum-Aššur urged her to take personal initiatives concerning his outstanding merchandise or his house (**329**), but some of his colleagues preferred to have a man as their interlocutor (**327**). She herself complained that she had no help managing this business (**326**; AKT 6b, 302).

Anna-anna informed his husband about the activities of his representatives in Kaneš (**327**), although he complained that she did not send enough reports (**330**). She also warned her husband against his brother, Ali-ahum, who, after the death of their father, emptied their father's strong room and perhaps made contact with their sister in Aššur (**328**, **325**, **326**).

There is no indication about what happened to Anna-anna after the death of her husband. However, there are a few letters sent or received by Anna-anna in which her husband is not mentioned, and which could have been sent after his death. In these, she gives instructions for the recovery of silver or sends silver to buy textiles (**332**, **333**).

325. Anna-anna Warns Her Husband about His Brother's Behavior

Obv. [1]*[a-]na En-um-A-šùr* [2]*qí-bi-ma um-ma A-na-na-ma* [3]*iš-tù a-b[u-k]à me-tù* [4]*a-hu-kà : a-na [A-li]m*[k[i]] [5]*ṭup-pá-am : ú-šé-b[i-l]á-ma* [6]*mì-ma ú-nu-tám : i-n[a]* é *a-/bi-kà* [7]*i-ba-ší-ú : i-na q[á-at]* [8]*a-hi-kà : a-na ki-d[im]* [9]*tù-uš-té*[!]*-ṣí : a-[t]a a-na* [10]*ú-nu-tim : ša qá-at-kà* [11]*ik-šu-du : a-t[a] ki-ma* [12]*ša-zu-úz-tám* lo.e. [13]*tù-ša-zi-zu-ú* [14]*pá-al-ha-ku-ma : mì-ma* rev. [15]*ú-lá e-pá-áš : ù mì-šu* [16]*ša ta-áš-ta-na-<pá>-ra-ni* [17]*um-ma a-[ta-ma] : a-na* (the remainder of the text is surface damaged)

[1-2]Say [t]o Ennum-Aššur: thus (says) Anna-anna.

[3-5]After your father died, your brother sent a tablet to the [cit]y (of Aššur), and [6-7]all the goods that were in your father's house [8-9]that you have taken outside, out of the grip of your brother! [9-11]As for you, for the goods you could lay your hand on, [11-13]since you yourself have appointed an agent, [14-15]I am afraid and will do nothing! [15-17]Also why do you always write to me as follows: "For [...]." [...]

Bibliography: Text published by Larsen as AKT 6a, 238 (Kt 94/k 1337).

Comments: Anna-anna reports to her husband that his brother is trying to rob him of his share of his father's estate. Anna-anna adds that, concerning his own goods, since her husband has already hired an agent supposed to take charge of them, she does not wish to get involved.

Line 4: it is most probable that the tablet sent to Aššur by Ennum-Aššur's brother was addressed to their sister there, Lamassī.

---

326. Anna-anna Sent Goods to Her Husband and Asks for Silver

Obv. [1]*a-na En-um-A-šur qí-bi*$_4$*-ma* [2]*um-ma A-na-a-na-ma na-áš-pè-er-tám* [3]*ša* é^{tí} *ṣú-ha-ri* : *ú-bi*$_4$*-ku-ni* [4]*lá i-ha-li-iq ta-e-ra-ší* [5]kù-babbar *ša ag-mu-ru* šà-ba [6]*lá-pu-ut* 1 *ta-lá-né-en* [7]2^{-ni}*-šu šu-hu-pá-ta-an* [8]*mu-sà-ra-am* 3*-ší-šu ša-hi-ra-an* [9]2 *iš-ra-an ri-i*[*š*]*-tám* [10]*qá-ar-nam ú* [x]*-i* [11]15 *du-ul-ba-tum* [12]*ú mu-lu-hu-um mì-*[*ma*] [13]*a-nim ṣú-*«ZA»*-ha-ri ú-šé-bi*$_4$*-lam* lo.e. [14]*I-tur*$_4$-dingir *ha-r*[*a-š*]*u* [15]*a-na A-lim*^{ki} *ek-pá-at* rev. [16]*šu-ma mì-ma ri-ik-sú-um* [17]é^{tí}*-šu i-ba-ší* [18]*té-er-tí-kà li-li-kam-ma* [19]*mì-*<*li*>*-ik áš-pu-ra-kum um-ma a-na-ku-ma* [20]*ki-ma ṣú-ha-ru e-ru-bu-ni-ni* [21]*ma-ma-an i-ša-ha-tí-*<*a*> *lá-šu* [22]*a-pu-tum i-na ša-am-ší* [23]*ṭup-pì ta-ša-me-ú* 5 *ma-na* kù-babbar [24]*ku-nu-uk-ma ku-nu-ki-kà* [25]1 *ṣú-ha-ru-um lu-ub-lam* [26]*a-na-kam nu-a-ú a-ṣí-ib-tim* [27]*e-ta-na-ri-šu-ni* u.e. [28]*I-na-Sú-en*$_6$ [29]*i-Hu-ra-ma wa-ša-áb* [30]*A-lá-hu-um a-hu-kà iš*$^{!}$(ŠU)*-tí-kà* le.e. [31]°*a-*[*š*]*a-áp-ru-sí-im i-za-az* [32][*té-er-*]*ta-kà a-wa-tim* sig$_5$*-tim* [33]*a-na A-mur-Ištar šé-bi*$_4$*-lam*

[1-2]Say to Ennum-Aššur: thus (says) Anna-anna.

[2-4]The letter that I dispatched with the servants must not be lost; bring it back (home, because) [5-6]the silver that I spent is noted in it. [6-12]1 pair of *tallānum*-shoes, 2 pairs of boots, 1 *musārum*-belt, 3 pairs of

shoe straps, 2 belts, a horn of first-class (oil), and […], 15 plane logs and *muluhum*-wood: [12–13]all this I sent you with my servants.

[14–15]Concerning Itūr-ilī, his journey to the city (of Aššur) is approaching. [16–19]Let your report come to me whether there is any package in his house, and make up your mind. [19]I wrote you as follows: [20–21]"Since the servants have gone (home), there is no one to assist me." [22–23]Urgent! The day you hear my tablet, [24–25]seal five minas of silver and let one servant bring (it) under your seal. [26–27]Here, Anatolians keep asking for (silver) at interest from me. [28–29]Enna-Suen lives in Hurrama. [30–31]Ali-ahum, your brother, intends to separate (him) from you. [32–33]Send your report with good news to Amur-Ištar.

Bibliography: Text published by Larsen as AKT 6a, 239 (Kt 94/k 1178).

Comments: Anna-anna wrote previously to her husband giving him the details of her expenses; she asks him to send back the tablet with her accounts. She sent him a great variety of objects, including shoes, belt, oil, and wood, with her servants and has nobody left to help her. She also reports about various colleagues and warns him once more about the behavior of his brother.

---

327. Anna-anna Reports on Her Conversation with Her Husband's Representatives

Obv. [1]*a-na En-um-[A-šur]* [2]*qí-bi-ma um-ma A-[n]a-na-ma* [3]*En-na-Sú-en*$_6$ *ni-a-um* [4]*i-li-kam-ma : um-ma šu-ut-ma* [5]*ma-nu-um ki-ma En-um-A-šùr* [6]*a-na-kam wa-ša-áb* [7]*a-na ṣé-e[r] : I-tur*$_4$-dingir [8]*ni-lik-ma : um-ma En-na-Sú-/en*$_6$*-ma* [9]*a-na I-tur*$_4$-dingir*-ma* [10]*lu-qú-tám ša* dam-gàr [11]*ša iš-tí-a : i-lu-k[u-ni]* [12]*mì-nam : ta-am-t[í-ší]* [13]*šu-ma li-ba-kà* [14]*iš-tí-[ma] lu-qú-tí-a* [15]*[lu-qú-tum ša* d]am-gàr lo.e. [16][x x x x x x] [17][x x x x x]*-ma* rev. [18]*ù* [x x x x x] *šu* [19]*a* x [x x x x x] *ni* [20][x x x x x x x] *dí* [21]*tí-*[x x x x x x]*-lá-kà* [x] [22]*u[m-m]a a-na-k[u-m]a a-n[a]* [23]*[En-n]a-Sú-e[n*$_6$*]-ma* [24]*q[á-d]í-m[a] lu-qú-tí-kà ù ša* /da[m-gà]r [25]*li-li-ku i-ṣé-er* [26]*lu-qú-tí-kà : um-ma* [27]*En-na-Sú-en*$_6$*-ma* [28]*za-a[k]-ru-um ša ki-ma* [29]*be-lí-ki li-zi-iz-ma* [30]*ù ší-bé-e lá-áš-ku-ma* [31]*ù iš-[tí-m]a lu-qú-tí-a* [32]*li-[li]-ku [a-l]i-ku* u.e. [33]*lá a-*[x x x x] le.e [34]*ša a-na-ku-/ma\ ša ta-áš-pu-ra-ni* [35]*ša dam-qí-iš : té-[pu]-ší-ni* [36]*a-na-kam lá* kù-babbar 1 *m[a-n]a t[í-šu-a]m* [37]*um-ma a-ta-ma* [x x] *En-um-*[x x x]

[1-2]Say to Ennum-[Aššur]: thus (says) Anna-anna.

[3-4]Our Enna-Suen came here and (said) as follows: [5-6]"Who is living here representing Ennum-Aššur?" [7-9]We went to Itūr-ilī, and Enna-Suen (said) as follows to Itūr-ilī: [10-12]"Why have you forgotten the merchandise of the merchant who travels with me?" [13-15]If you wish, together with my merchandise, [the merchandise of] the merchant (six broken lines).

[22-23]I (said) to Enna-Suen as follows: [24-26]"Let your merchandise and that of the merchant go together in addition to your merchandise." [26-27]Enna-Suen (replied) as follows: [28-29]"Let a man who represents your master (i.e., your husband) take action, and then [30]I will provide witnesses so that [31-32]they go together with my merchandise." [32-34]I must not [...] the travelers [...] that I personally [...] about which you wrote to me, [35]that you treated me well [36]here, you do not have silver for me, even one mina. [37]You (said) as follows: "[...] Ennum-[...]"

Bibliography: Text published by Larsen as AKT 6b, 299 (Kt 94/k 1017); photo presented on AKT 6b, 345–47.

Comments: Enna-Suen, referred to as "our" by Anna-anna, is a cousin of her husband, who has arrived in Kaneš. Anna-anna participates in a conversation involving Ennum-Aššur's representative and concerning the organization of goods to be transported and traded by Enna-Suen. She gives her point of view, but Enna-Suen prefers to have a confirmation by her husband's representative.

---

328. Ennum-Aššur Asks Anna-anna to Protect His Grain Stock

Obv. [1]*a-na Ku-zi-zi-a Lá-qé-ep* [2]*ù A-na-a-na qí-bi-ma* [3]*um-ma En-um-A-šùr-ma* [4]*a-na A-na-a-na qí-bi-ma* [5]*lá-ma a-na Kà-tí-lá a-li-ku* [6]5 *na-ru-uq* gig [7]*ú* 2 *na-ru-uq še-am* [8]*e-lá-nu-ma e-zi-ba-ki-im* [9]*a-ha-ma* 17 *na-ru-uq* 2 dug gig [10]*ú* 17 *na-ru-uq* 2 dug [11]*še-am iš-tù* : *Tù-um-li-a* [12]*iš-du-du-nim* [13]*mì-ma ú-ṭí-tim ú* kù-babbar lo.e. [14]*ša nu-a-e* : *a-bi* [15]*i-a-tí-ma e-ta-aṣ-/ra-am* [16]*a-pu-tum a-na* rev. [17]*a-wi-il$_5$-tim* [18]*lá ta-pá-ṭí-ri ú mì-ma* [19]*lá ta-dí-ni-ší-im ú iš-tí* [20]*E-wa-ri-mu-ša ta-hi-tám* [21]*áš-pu-ur-ší-im a-hu-a a-tù-nu* [22]*a-ma-kam na-hi-da-ší-ma i-na* [23]*hu-ur-ší-a ší-lá-tum* [24]*lá i-ba-ší-ma li-bi lá i-ma-/ra-aṣ* [25]*ṭup-pí-a ú ú-ṭù-up-tí* [26]*lu tù-ša-ṣí-ir ma-lá ú-ṭù-tum* [27]*a-bi-ki-tim i-gi$_5$-im-ru úz-ni* [28]*pé-té-a* : *a-dí bu-lá-tí ša a-bi-a* [29]*a-hi ú-pá-ta-a-ni-ni a-sà-hu-<ur>* [30]*lá-ma a-li-kà-ni ma-ṣa-ar-tám* [31]*A-lá-hu-um ip-té-té-*

e u.e. [32]*ú bu-lá-tí uš-té-ṣí-i* [33]*lu* kù-babbar *i-ba-áb-tí-a* [34]*Lá-qé-ep im-hu-ur lu* [35]*ša šé-ep* le.e. [36]*E-wa-ru-mu-ša i-ri-ih lu* 1½ *ma-/na* [37]kù-babbar *ú* 3⅙ gín kù-gi *ša iš-tí* [38]*am-tí-a i-ba-ší-ú ší-ma-am* [39]*ma-ah-r*[*a*]*-am ša ba-lá-ṭí-a ša-ma-ma* [40]*iš-tí E-wa-ri-mu-ša šé-*bi_4*-lá*

[1–3]Say to Kuziziya, Laqēp, and Anna-anna: thus (says) Ennum-Aššur; [4]say to Anna-anna.

[5]Before I went to Katila, [6–8]besides the 5 sacks of wheat and 2 sacks of barley I left you, [9–12]in addition, they carted (to you) 17 sacks, 2 jars of wheat, and 17 sacks, 2 jars of barley from Tumliya. [13–15]My father had fixed for me the whole amount of grain and the silver from the Anatolians. [16–19]Urgent! Do not open (it) for the lady, and do not give her anything. [19–21]Also, I sent her pressing instructions with Ewarimuša.

[21]You are my brothers. [22–24]There, instruct her so that nothing presumptuous will take place in my storeroom, and I will not get angry. [25–26]Let her watch carefully over my tablets and furniture. [26–28]Inform me how much grain has been spent for the mourning. [28–29]Until my brother discloses to me my father's assets, I will stay around. [30–32]Before I came, Ali-ahum had opened the strong room and had taken out the assets. [33–34]Whether Laqēp received some silver from my outstanding claims, [35–36]or there is some leftover from the transport of Ewarimuša, [36–38]or the 1½ minas of silver and 3⅙ shekels of silver of gold that are with my *amtum*-wife—[38–39]first and foremost make a profitable purchase for me, and [40]send (it) with Ewarimuša.

Bibliography: Text published by Larsen as AKT 6a, 225 (Kt 94/k 1009).

Comments: Ennum-Aššur reminds his wife the huge amounts of grain that have been delivered to him originating from credit loans of his father. After the death of his father, a lady—his mother or sister—wants to get some, as well as gold and silver left with his wife, and he asks Anna-anna to keep anyone from approaching his storeroom. Some grain has been spent for the mourning of his father, and his brother, Ali-ahum, has already taken assets left by their father. He also asks that any remaining cash be invested in profitable merchandise.

329. Anna-anna Is Asked by Her Husband Not to Make Decisions on Her Own

Obv. ^{1}*um-ma En-um-A-š[ur]-ma* ^{2}*a-na A-na-a-na* ^{3}*qí-bi-ma a-na-kam* ^{4}*a-ba-ru-um ša I-tur*$_{4}$-/dingir ^{5}*ih-li-iq-ma* ^{6}1 gín 15 še kù-babbar ^{7}*a-na Ša-lim-bé-lí* lo.e. ^{8}*ṣú-ha-ri-šu a-dí-in* rev. ^{9}*a-ma-kam* kù-babbar ^{10}*Ša-lim-bé-lí li-dí-na-/ki-im* ^{11}*a-pu-tum a-ma-kam* ^{12}*lu a-ba-ba-tí lu a-na* é$^{/be\text{-}tí}$*-a* ^{13}*lá ta-ša-li-ṭí* ^{14}*a-wa-tí ša Ì-lí-dan* ^{15}*I-dí-A-šur ù Šu-Ištar al-/té-qé* ^{16}*ha-ra-ni a-ta-lá-kam* u.e. ^{17}*a-dí En-na-Sú-en*$_{6}$ ^{18}*ša-li-ma šu-ma* le.e. ^{19}*iš-tù A-lim*^{ki} ^{20}*i-ta-ṣa-am úz-ni* ^{21}*pé-té-a*

$^{1-3}$Thus (says) Ennum-Aš[šur]: say to Anna-anna.

$^{4-5}$Here, the lead of Itūr-ilī is lost, and $^{6-8}$I gave 1 shekel, 15 grains of silver to Šalim-bēlī, his servant. $^{9-10}$There, let Šalim-bēlī give you the silver. $^{11-13}$Urgent! Do not act there on your own authority with regard either to my outstanding claims or to my house.

$^{14-15}$I have just accepted the proposal of Ilī-dān, Iddin-Aššur, and Šu-Ištar. ^{16}I will leave for you on my trip.

$^{17-18}$Ask about Enna-Suen, and $^{18-21}$inform (pl.) me whether he has left the city (of Aššur).

Bibliography: Text published by Larsen as AKT 6b, 300 (Kt 94/k 662).

Comments: Ennum-Aššur informs his wife about an amount of silver that has been sent to her. But he urges her not to take any decision on her own; she should just inform her husband about the activities of his relatives.

330. Ennum-Aššur Complains to Anna-anna That She Does Not Keep Him Informed

Obv. ^{1}*um-ma En-um-A-[šur-ma a-na]* ^{2}*Lá-qé-pí-im ù A-[na-a-na]* ^{3}*a-na A-na-a-na qí-bi*$_{4}$*-ma* ^{4}*a-dí* 10 *iš-ri-šu áš-pu-ra-ki-im* ^{5}*um-ma a-na-ku-ma ba-áb-tí za-ki-a-ma* ^{6}*a-dí a-[l]á-kà-ni ší-lá-tum* ^{7}*lá i-ba-ší* : *ú* kù-babbar 1 gín *li-im-hu-ri* ^{8}*a-tí ki-ma ša-pá-ri-ma úz-ni-/a* ^{9}*pá-ta-im té-er-tí-ki ma-tí-ma* ^{10}*ú-lá i-lá-kam* 1 *ma-na* 15 gín ^{11}[kù]-babbar *ú ṣí-ba-tù-šu i-dí ša* ^{12}*H[a]-pí-ah-šu* 1 *ma-na* 10 gín *ú ṣí-[ba-tù-šu]* ^{13}*iš-tí Ta-ar-hi-š[a]-a[n]* ^{14}½ *ma-na* 5 gín kù-[babbar] ^{15}*ú* 18 gín *ṣí-[ba-tù-šu iš-tí]* lo.e. ^{16}*Al-wa-ta* (…)

1-3Thus (says) Ennum-A[ššur to] Laqēpum and A[nna-Anna]: say to Anna-anna.

4-5I wrote you up to 10 times as follows: 5-7"Clear my outstanding claims, so that until my arrival, nothing presumptuous will occur, 7and every shekel of silver should reach me!" 8-9(But) you, instead of writing and informing me—9-10your report never comes to me!

10-121 mina, 15 shekels of silver and its interest: the wages of Happiahšu. 12-131 mina, 10 shekels and [its] in[terest] are with Tarhiš[an]. 14-16½ mina, 5 shekels of si[lver] and 18 shekels [its] in[terest are with] Alwata [...]

(The remainder of the letter is partly broken and presumably addressed to Laqēpum: "I have repeatedly written to my *amtum*-wife...")

Bibliography: Text published by Larsen as AKT 6b, 309 (Kt 94/k 1014).

Comments: Anna-anna is asked to recover her husband's silver from his outstanding merchandise and to inform him by letter. Ennum-Aššur complains that she does not send him regular reports about his business in Kaneš.

In the second part of the letter, addressed to Laqēpum, and which deals with other matters, he insists that he has sent many letters to his wife.

---

331. Anna-anna Has to Perform Domestic Tasks

Obv. 1*a-na M*[*a-n*]*u-ki-A-šùr ù* 2*A-n*[*a-a-n*]*a qí-bi-ma um-ma* 3*En-*[*um-A-šù*]*r-ma*
(Lines 4–8 and 1′–6′ are addressed to both correspondents and are partly broken.)
6′*a-*[*na*] 7′[*A-*]*na-a-na qí-bi-m*[*a*] *ša-am-nam* 8′[*ṭ*]*á-i-bi* : *ù a-na mì-ma* u.e. 9′*ša áš-pu-ra-ki-ni* rev. 10′*ku-un-ki-ma iš-tí Ša-lim-ar-/dí* 11′*šé-bi₄-li-im* le.e. 12′*ú a-dí ša Lá-qé-ep* [x x x] 13′[*š*]*u-up-ri-im a-Ma-nu-ki-*[*A-šur*] 14′[*q*]*í-bi-ma ší-im ṣú-ba-tí-k*[*à*] 15′[*i*]*-na a-lá-ki-a ú-b*[*a-al*]

1-3Say to Mannum-kī-Aššur and Anna-anna: thus (says) Ennum-Aššur. (...)

6′-7′Say to Anna-anna. 7′-8′Make the oil sweet (tasty)! 8′-9′As for all that I have written to you, 10′-11′seal it and send it with Šalim-wardī. 12′-13′And as to Laqēp [...] write me.

[13'–14']Say to Mannum-kī-Aššur. [14'–15']I will bring the proceeds of your textiles when I come.

Bibliography: Text published by Larsen as AKT 6b, 303 (Kt 94/k 1668).

Comments: Ennum-Aššur asks Anna-anna to process the oil and to seal and send goods to him. This could perhaps also be understood as a metaphor with the meaning "do be nice!"

---

332. Anna-anna Travels in Anatolia

Obv. [1]*a-na Ša-at-A-na* [2]*L*[*u*!]*-lu-ú* (erasure) [3]*ù Na-zi qí-bi-ma* [4]*um-ma A-na-na-ma* [5]*šu-ma Lu-lu-ú ù* [6]*Na-bi-*[d]en-líl [7]*iš-tù Za-al-pá* [8]*i-li-ku-nim* [9]*ṣa-áb-ta-šu-nu-ma* lo.e. [10]⅔ *ma-na* 2 gín [11]kù-babbar *ša-áš-qí-lá* rev. [12]*lá a-kà-ša-dam* [13]*li-bi*$_4$ *lá i-lá-mì-/in* [14]*šu-ma Ša-ba-na-tum* [15]dam *Ku-zi-zi-a* [16]*a-na Wa-ah-šu-ša-*[*na*] [17]*ta-ta-lá-ak na-ru-u*[*q*] [18]*še-am* 1 udu *ta-dí-na-ší*?*-/i*[*m*] [19]*iš-tù* kù-babbar ⅔ [*ma*]*-/n*[*a*?] [20]*Lu-lu i-ša-q*[*ú-l*]*u* u.e. [21]*ší-im* udu 3 g[ín] le.e. [22]*li-dí-nu-ni-/ku-nu-tí*

[1–4]Say to Šāt-Anna, [Lu]lu, and Nazi: thus (says) Anna-anna.

[5–8]If Lulu and Nabi-Enlil have arrived from Zalpa, [9]seize them and [10–11]make (them) pay ⅔ minas, 2 shekels of silver, [12–13]lest I will arrive there and get angry! [14–17]If Šabanātum, the wife of Kuziziya, has just left for Wahšuša[na], [18](and) you have given her 1 sack of barley and 1 sheep, [19–20]after Lulu has paid the silver, ⅔ minas, [21]they should give you 3 shekels, price of the sheep.

Bibliography: Text published by Larsen as AKT 6b, 314 (Kt 94/k 682).

Comments: According to this letter, Anna-anna seems to be traveling somewhere in Anatolia and intends to come back to Kaneš. While she is away, she gives instructions to three people to recover silver from traded goods and animals.

333. Anna-anna Sends Silver to Make Purchases

Obv. [1]*um-ma A-šur*-du$_{10}$-*m*[*a*] [2]*a-na A-na-na* [3][*q*]*í-bi-ma* 16 gín [4]k[ù-bab]bar *ša tù-šé-bi-lá-/ni* [5]*ší-i*[*m*] *li-bi*$_4$-*šu* lo.e. [6]*šu-ut-ma* rev. [7]*iš-a-am* [8]*la iš-e-li* [9]*sà-áp-tí-nu-um* [10]*i-na ra-mì-ni-a* u.e. [11]*ú-ba-la-am*

[1-3]Thus (says) Aššur-ṭāb: say to Anna-anna.

[3-4]Concerning the 16 shekels of silver that you sent me, [5-8]he made purchases according on his own without asking me. [9-11]I will bring you, at my own cost, a *saptinnum*-textile.

Bibliography: Text published by Larsen as AKT 6b, 301 (Kt 94/k 642).

Comments: Anna-anna sent silver to make purchases but did not choose the goods to be bought. She will receive an Anatolian textile.

334. Anna-anna Produces Some Anatolian Textiles

Obv. [1][x] *pí-ri-kà-ni* [2]*ša A-na-na* [3]1 *lu-bu-ša-am* [4]1 túg *ra-qá-tám* [5]*a-na A-bu-ša-lim* [6]dumu *Ṣí-lá*-[d]im [7][*a*]-*dí-in* [8][ig]i *Ma-nu-ki-A-/šur* [9]igi *Ku-zi-zi-a*

[1-2][x] *pirikannum*-textiles from Anna-anna; [3-7]1 piece of clothing, 1 thin textile I gave to Abu-šalim, son of Ṣilli-Adad.

[8-9]In the presence of Mannum-kī-Aššur and Kuziziya.

Bibliography: Text published by Larsen as AKT 6b, 471 (Kt 94/k 693).

Comments: This text is a receipt for the delivery of textiles, among them Anatolian textiles from Anna-anna; it is highly possible that she made them.

Texts Edited

Texts Concordance

1. VS 26, 64
2. KTS 2, 55
3. BIN 6, 104
4. Kt 93k236
5. TC 1, 67 + *RA* 76, 170
6. Kt i/k 120
7. Kt 88k625
8. KTP, 17
9. Kt 84/k 281
10. Kt 88/k 97
11. Kt 88/k 651
12. Kt n/k 1138
13. Kt 83/k 164
14. Kt 88/k 71
15. AKT 1, 77
16. AKT 3, 80
17. Kt v/k 147
18. CCT 5, 16a
19. TPAK 1, 161
20. AKT 1, 76
21. KTS 2, 6
22. AAA 1/3, 8
23. Prag I, 490
24. ICK 1, 3
25. Kt 94/k 149
26. Kt a/k 616b
27. Kt h/k 73
28. Kt 88/k 269
29. *RA* 51, 6
30. Kt 91/k 132
31. Kt 94/k 141
32. Kt d/k 29
33. Prag I, 513 + ICK 2, 221 + 237
34. Prag I, 651
35. ICK 1, 32
36. TuM 1, 21 d
37. TC 2, 76
38. Kt n/k 1414
39. TC 1, 100
40. TCL 1, 242
41. KKS, 36
42. Kt r/k 19
43. TC 1, 122
44. TC 3, 214
45. Kt j/k 625
46. Kt k/k 1
47. Kt 91/k 158 + 240
48. Kt 78/k 176
49. AKT 8, 297
50. VS 26, 33
51. Sadberk, 28
52. Kt a/k 1255
53. Kt 89/k 370
54. Kt o/k 196ac
55. BIN 6, 222
56. ICK 1, 12

57. *RA* 60, 133
58. AKT 8, 175
59. AKT 8, 180
60. AKT 8, 184
61. AKT 8, 164
62. KTK, 103 +
63. AKT 3, 94
64. Kt m/k 1
65. Kt m/k 69
66. AKT 6a, 233
67. AKT 6a, 236
68. AKT 6a, 247
69. TC 2, 73 + TC 3, 215
70. CCT 5, 8b
71. ATHE, 22
72. Kt 91/k 200
73. KTS 1, 47a
74. CCT 1, 8c + CCT 6, 1b
75. Adana 237E
76. CCT 5, 48b–c
77. KTH, 20
78. TC 3, 222
79. TC 3, 240 + TC 2, 66
80. AKT 1, 45
81. TC 3, 239
82. TC 3, 266
83. AKT 1, 57
84. TC 3, 237
85. Kt b/k 260
86. Prag I, 475
87. CCT 1, 11b
88. AKT 1, 44
89. KTK, 96
90. CCT 1, 10b
91. Kt n/k 1716
92. Kt 92/k 1033
93. Kt j/k 288/b
94. ICK 1, 27
95. ICK 1, 35
96. *AulaOr* 8
97. TC 3, 252
98. Kt 87/k 99
99. Kt 87/k 275
100. Kt e/k 164
101. BIN 4, 190
102. BIN 6, 225
103. ICK 2, 116
104. TPAK 1, 159
105. Kt n/k 1772
106. Kt 87/k 287
107. BIN 4, 183
108. Kt a/k 554
109. AKT 3, 42
110. TC 3, 183
111. WAG 48-1646
112. AKT 8, 156
113. BIN 4, 68
114. *HUCA* 40, 59
115. TuM 1, 22a
116. AKT 6d, 732
117. Kt 90/k 178
118. Kt 94/k 821
119. Kt a/k 851
120. TCL 1, 240
121. TC 3, 207
122. *AoF* 8, 326
123. TPAK 1, 34A
124. BIN 4, 22
125. BIN 6, 197
126. AKT 6c, 646
127. BIN 6, 124
128. CCT 3, 24
129. CCT 3, 25
130. BIN 6, 118
131. TC 3, 172
132. VS 26, 19
133. AKT 5, 9
134. TC 3, 97

135. Kt h/k 87
136. CCT 4, 15b
137. BIN 4, 75
138. ICK 1, 19
139. CCT 4, 40b +
140. ICK 1, 69
141. TC 2, 46
142. BIN 4, 67
143. ICK 2, 76 + ICK 1, 46a + ICK 2, 77 + KKS, 45b
144. ICK 1, 123 +
145. LB 1209
146. AAA 1/3, 1
147. *RA* 59, 159
148. AKT 8, 210
149. KTS 1, 46
150. Or 52, 1
151. Kt j/k 39
152. Kt 80/k 25
153. Kay 4369
153. Kay 4369
154. CCT 3, 14
155. VS 26, 53
156. BIN 6, 5
157. VS 26, 20
158. BIN 6, 84
159. CCT 5, 26a
160. CCT 3, 48b
161. CCT 4, 36b + 37a
162. TC 3, 17
163. BIN 4, 9
164. BIN 4, 10
165. BIN 6, 11
166. CCT 3, 20
167. Rendell
168. CCT 6, 11a
169. CCT 4, 21b
170. *Or* 50, 2
171. LB 1201
172. BIN 4, 88
173. AKT 2, 52
174. CCT 6, 27b
175. AKT 5, 30
176. CCT 4, 28a
177. BIN 4, 153
178. TC 3, 228
179. CCT 5, 20c
180. TC 3, 235
181. TC 3, 220
182. AKT 1, 46
183. ICK 2, 11
184. AKT 1, 1
185. Kt a/k 335
186. AKT 1, 60
187. AKT 1, 72
188. Kt n/k 860
189. ICK 1, 24
190. AKT 3, 51
191. AKT 5, 70
192. LB 1217
193. TC 3, 232
194. VS 26, 97
195. TC 3, 27
196. Kt 76/k 2
197. CCT 3, 41a
198. AKT 6a, 223
199. BIN 6, 20
200. *HUCA* 40, 55
201. KTS 1, 2a
202. BIN 4, 228
203. TC 3, 116
204. CCT 4, 15a
205. *HUCA* 40, 57
206. BIN 4, 91
207. CCT 3, 23b
208. BIN 6, 3
209. CCT 3, 19b
210. CCT 4, 20a

211. *ArOr* 47, 42
212. AKT 3, 106
213. AKT 3, 77
214. AKT 3, 84
215. BIN 4, 55
216. *HUCA* 40, 70a
217. TC 3, 56
218. CCT 4, 13b
219. TPAK 1, 32
220. AKT 5, 10
221. BIN 4, 85
222. CCT 3, 31
223. BIN 4, 90
224. KTS 1, 50a
225. KTK, 67
226. BIN 6, 93
227. CCT 4, 8a
228. AKT 5, 11
229. KTS 1, 1b
230. Prag I, 688
231. TC 3, 112
232. BIN 6, 14
233. Weir 1 Biggs
234. Prag I, 467
235. ICK 1, 17bc
236. BIN 4, 96
237. Kt n/k 1336
238. AKT 4, 63
239. KUG, 39
240. AKT 2, 40
241. ICK 1, 28
242. Ass 13058h
243. Kt 94/k 131
244. AKT 8, 210 bis
245. TC 3, 106
246. TC 3, 35
247. CCT 2, 36a
248. Kt 93/k 916
249. TC 3, 103
250. AKT 8, 185
251. BIN 4, 141
252. TC 1, 5
253. AKT 6d, 786
254. KTS 1, 24
255. *RA* 59, 165
256. KTS 1, 25a
257. ATHE, 24
258. Kt 01/k 325
259. BIN 6, 7
260. VS 26, 42
261. *RA* 59, 34
262. ATHE, 8
263. Prag I, 542
264. AKT 8, 206
265. Kt n/k 1189
266. Kt n/k 657
267. Kt n/k 1065
268. Kt n/k 1108
269. Kt n/k 1372
270. AKT 6d, 742
271. AKT 4, 45
272. Kt n/k 650
273. AKT 2, 31
274. Kt n/k 713
275. BIN 4, 140
276. TC 1, 79
277. Ankara 1938
278. CCT 5, 8a
279. BIN 6, 178
280. BIN 6, 59
281. Prag I, 437
282. KTH, 7
283. Sadberk, 14
284. CCT 4, 31b
285. KUG, 5
286. BIN 6, 90
287. AKT 6d, 770
288. Kt z/t 13

289. Prag I, 547
290. Ka 1044
291. BIN 6, 230
292. CCT 5, 41b
293. TC 3, 57
294. VS 26, 41
295. ICK 2, 310
296. ICK 2, 311
297. Sadberk, 24
298. TPAK 1, 59
299. Kalley C36
300. KTS 2, 31
301. CUSAS 34, 14
302. KTBl, 5
303. KTH, 6
304. AKT 4, 62
305. BIN 6, 1
306. CCT 4, 21a
307. CTMMA 1, 78
308. BIN 6, 17
309. *HUCA* 40, 69
310. AKT 1, 14
311. TTC, 26
312. KTH, 5
313. AKT 1, 15
314. CCT 3, 7a
315. RC 1749C
316. RC 1749D
317. *RA* 60, 138
318. KTS 1, 13b
319. TC 2, 47
320. KTH, 26
321. KTH, 40
322. Prag I, 669
323. CCT 3, 50a
324. ICK 1, 67
325. AKT 6a, 238
326. AKT 6a, 239
327. AKT 6b, 299
328. AKT 6a, 225
329. AKT 6b, 300
330. AKT 6b, 309
331. AKT 6b, 303
332. AKT 6b, 314
333. AKT 6b, 301
334. AKT 6b, 471

Reverse Texts Concordance

AAA 1/3, 1	146
AAA 1/3, 8	22
Adana 237E	75
AKT 1, 1	184
AKT 1, 14	310
AKT 1, 15	313
AKT 1, 21	21
AKT 1, 44	88
AKT 1, 45	80
AKT 1, 46	182
AKT 1, 57	83
AKT 1, 60	186
AKT 1, 72	187
AKT 1, 76	20
AKT 1, 77	15
AKT 2, 31	273
AKT 2, 40	240
AKT 2, 52	173
AKT 3, 42	109
AKT 3, 51	190
AKT 3, 77	213
AKT 3, 80	16
AKT 3, 84	214
AKT 3, 94	63

Bibliography

For a complete bibliography of the Old Assyrian period, see Michel 2003a and its supplements, Michel 2006c, 2011a, and 2015e.

Albayrak, İrfan. 1998. "Koloni Çağında Yerli Bir Bayan 'Madawada.'" Pages 1–14 in *III. Uluslararası Hititoloji Kongresi bildirileri: Çorum, 16–22 Eylül, 1996 / Acts of the IIIrd International Congress of Hittitology: Çorum, September 16–22, 1996*. Edited by Sedat Alp and Aygül Süel. Ankara: Uyum Ajans.

———. 2000. "Ein neues altassyrisches Testament aus Kültepe." *ArAn* 4:17–27.

———. 2002. "Kültepe'den Değişik Bir Masraf Listesi." *ArAn* 5:1–10.

———. 2004. "'She Will Live, Eat and Be Anointed Together with Them': *Ušbat aklat u paššat ištišunu*." Pages 9–20 in *Assyria and Beyond: Studies Presented to Mogens Trolle Larsen*. Edited by Jan Gerrit Dercksen. PIHANS 100. Leiden: Nederlands Instituut voor het Nabije Oosten.

———. 2010. "The Understanding of Inheritance in Ancient Anatolia according to Testaments from Kültepe." Pages 142–47 in *Anatolia's Prologue: Kultepe, Kanesh, Karum; Assyrians in Istanbul*. Edited by Fikri Kulakoğlu and Selmin Kangal. KMMCP 78. Istanbul: Kayseri Metropolitan Municipality.

———. 2015. "Asurlu Tüccar Šu-İštar'ın Kültepe'de Ele Geçen Vasiyetnamesi." Pages 15–27 in *Cahit Günbattı Armağan: Studies in Honour of Cahit Günbattı*. Edited by İrfan Albayrak, Hakan Erol, and Murat Çayır. Ankara: Ankara Üniversitesi Dil ve Tarih-Coğrafya Fakültesi.

Alster, Bendt, ed. 1980. *Death in Mesopotamia*. CRRAI 26; Mesopotamia 8. Copenhagen: Akademisk Forlag.

Andersson Strand, Eva. 2012. "The Textile *Chaîne Opératoire*: Using a Multidisciplinary Approach to Textile Archaeology with a Focus on the Ancient Near East." *Paléorient* 38:21–40.

Andersson Strand, Eva, Catherine Breniquet, and Cécile Michel. 2017. "Textile Imprints on Bullae from Kültepe." Pages 87–104 in *Movement, Resources, Interaction: Proceedings of the Second Kültepe International Meeting, Kültepe, 26–30 July 2015; Studies Dedicated to Klaas Veenhof*. Edited by Fikri Kulakoğlu and Gojko Barjamovic. KIM 2; Subartu 39. Turnhout: Brepols.

Andersson Strand, Eva, and Maria Cybulska. 2013. "Visualising Ancient Textiles: How to Make a Textile Visible on the Basis of an Interpretation of an Ur III Text." Pages 113–27 in *Textile Production and Consumption in the Ancient Near East*. Edited by Marie-Louise Nosch, Henriette Koefoed, and Eva Andersson Strand. ATS 12. Oxford: Oxbow.

Arkhipov, Ilya. 2012. *Le vocabulaire de la métallurgie et la nomenclature des objets en métal dans les textes de Mari*. ARMT 32. Leuven: Peeters.

Arnaud, Daniel. 1986. *Recherches au pays d'Aštata: Textes sumériens et accadiens*. Emar 6.3. Paris: Editions Recherche sur les Civilisations.

Asher-Greve, Julia M. 2000. "Stepping into the Maelstrom: Women, Gender and Ancient Near Eastern Scholarship." *NIN* 1:1–22.

———. 2002. Women and Gender in Ancient Near Eastern Culture: Bibliography 1885 to 2001 AD." *NIN* 3:33–114.

———. 2006. "'Golden Age' of Women? Status and Gender in Third Millennium Sumerian and Akkadian Art." Pages 41–81 in *Images and Gender: Contributions to the Hermeneutics of Reading Ancient Art*. Edited by Silvia Schroer. OBO 220. Fribourg: Academic Press Fribourg.

Atici, Levent, Fikri Kulakoğlu, Gojko Barjamovic, and Andrew Fairbairn, eds. 2014. *Current Research at Kültepe/Kanesh: An Interdisciplinary and Integrative Approach to Trade Networks, Internationalism, and Identity*. JCSSup 4. Atlanta: Lockwood.

Bachelot, Luc, ed. 2005. *Entre mondes orientaux et classiques: La place de la crémation; Actes du colloque international de Nanterre, 26–28 février 2004*. Ktèma 30. Strasbourg: Marc Bloch University of Strasbourg.

Bahrani, Zainab. 2001. *Women of Babylon: Gender and Representation in Mesopotamia*. London: Routledge.

Balkan, Kemal. 1957. *Letter of King Anum-Hirbi of Mama to King Warshama of Kanish*. TTKY 7.31a. Ankara: Türk Tarih Kurumu Basimevi.

———. 1965. "The Old Assyrian Week." Pages 159–74 in *Studies in Honor of Benno Landsberger on His Seventy-Fifth Birthday, April 21, 1965*. Edited by Hans Gustav Güterbock and Thorkild Jacobsen. AS 16. Chicago: University of Chicago Press, 1965.

———. 1974. "Cancellation of Debts in Cappadocian Tablets from Kültepe." Pages 29–42 in *In Anatolian Studies Presented to Hans Gustav Güterbock on the Occasion of His Sixty-Fifth Birthday*. Edited by Erica Reiner and Kurt Bittel. PIHANS 35. Istanbul: Nederlands Historisch-Archaeologisch Instituut in het Nabije Oosten.

———. 1986. "Betrothal of Girls during Childhood in Ancient Assyria and Anatolia." Pages 1–11 in *Kaniššuwar: A Tribute to Hans G. Güterbock on His Seventy-Fifth Birthday, May 27, 1983*. Edited by Harry A. Hoffner and Gary M. Beckman. AS 23. Chicago: Oriental Institute of the University of Chicago, 1986.

———. 1992. "The Conception of Trinity in the Tablets of Kültepe." Pages 15–44 in *Hittite and Other Anatolian and Near Eastern Studies in Honour of Sedat Alp*. Edited by Heinrich Otten, Ekrem Akurgal, Hayri Ertem, and Aygül Süel. Ankara: Türk Tarih Kurumu Basımevi.

Barberon, Lucile. 2012. *Les religieuses et le culte de Marduk dans le royaume de Babylone*. Archibab 1. Paris: Société pour l'étude du Proche-Orient ancien.

Barjamovic, Gojko. 2011. *A Historical Geography of Anatolia in the Old Assyrian Colony Period*. CNIP 38. Copenhagen: University of Copenhagen; Museum Tusculanum Press.

———. 2014. "The Size of Kanesh and the Demography of Early Middle Bronze Age Anatolia." Pages 55–68 in *Current Research at Kültepe/Kanesh: An Interdisciplinary and Integrative Approach to Trade Networks, Internationalism, and Identity*. Edited by Levent Atici, Fikri Kulakoğlu, Gojko Barjamovic, and Andrew Fairbairn. JCSSup 4. Atlanta: Lockwood.

———. 2015. "Contextualizing Tradition." Pages 48–86 in *Texts and Contexts: The Circulation and Transmission of Cuneiform Texts in Social Space*. Edited by Paul Delnero and Jacob Lauinger. SANER 9. Berlin: de Gruyter.

Barjamovic, Gojko, Thomas Hertel, and Mogens Trolle Larsen. 2012. *Ups and Downs at Kanesh: Chronology, History and Society in the Old Assyrian Period*. OAAS 5; PIHANS 120. Leiden: Nederlands Instituut voor het Nabije Oosten.

Barjamovic, Gojko, and Mogens Trolle Larsen. 2008. "An Old Assyrian Incantation against the Evil Eye." *AoF* 35:144–55.

Bayram, Sabahattin. 1990. "Kültepe Tabletlerinde geçen yeni bir vâde ifâdesi ve çÿkan neticeler." Pages 453–62 in *X. Türk Tarih Kongresi, 22–26 Eylül 1986*. Ankara: Türk Tarih Kurumu Basımevi.

———. 1997. "New and Some Rare Geographical Names in the Kültepe Texts." *ArAn* 3:41–66.

———. 2018. "Asur Ticaret Kolonileri Dönemi'nde Nafaka Ödeniyor Muydu?" *ArAn* 12:31–52.

Bayram, Sabahattin, and Salih Çeçen. 1995. "6 Neue Urkunden über Heirat und Scheidung aus Kaniš." *ArAn* 1:1–12.

———. 1996. "The Institution of Slavery in Ancient Anatolia in the Light of New Documents." *Belleten* 60:606–45.

Bayram, Sabahattin, and Remzi Kuzuoğlu. 2015. "Takı Takma Âdetinin Eski Asur Toplumundaki İzleri." Pages 29–37 in *Cahit Günbattı Armağan: Studies in Honour of Cahit Günbattı*. Edited by İrfan Albayrak, Hakan Erol, and Murat Çayır. Ankara: Ankara Üniversitesi Dil ve Tarih-Coğrafya Fakültesi, 2015.

Bayram, Sabahattin, and Klaas R. Veenhof. 1992. "Unpublished Kültepe Texts on Real Estate." *JEOL* 32:87–100.

Beyer, Wiebke. 2019. "The Identification of Scribal Hands on the Basis of an Old Assyrian Archive." PhD diss., University of Hamburg.

Biga, Maria Giovanna. 1988. "Frauen in der Wirtschaft von Ebla." Pages 159–71 in *Wirtschaft und Gesellschaft von Ebla: Akten der internationalen Tagung Heidelberg, 4.–7. November 1986*. Edited by Hartmut Waetzoldt and Harald Hauptmann. HSAO 2. Heidelberg: Heidelberger Orientverlag.

———. 1997. "Enfants et nourrices à Ebla." *Ktèma* 22:35–44.

———. 2000. "Wet-Nurses at Ebla: A Prosopographic Study." *VO* 12:59–88.

———. 2016. "The Role of Women in Work and Society in the Ebla Kingdom (Syria, 24th century BC)." Pages 71–89 in *The Role of Women in Work and Society in the Ancient Near East*. Edited by Brigitte Lion and Cécile Michel. SANER 13. Berlin: de Gruyter.

Biggs, Robert D. 1996. "A Woman's Plaint in an Old Assyrian Letter." Pages 47–52 in *Festschrift für Hans Hirsch zum 65. Geburtstag: Gewidmet von seinem Freunden, Kollegen und Schülern*. Edited by Arne A. Ambros, Markus Köhbach, and Claudia Römer. WZKM 86. Vienna: Institut für Orientalistik.

Bilgiç, Emin. 1954. *Die Einheimischen Appellativa der Kappadokischen Texte und ihre Bedeutung für die Anatolischen Sprachen*. Ankara: Türk Tarih Kurumu Basımevi.

———. 1992. "'Ebla' in Cappadocian Inscriptions." Pages 61–66 in *Hittite and Other Anatolian and Near Eastern Studies in Honour of Sedat Alp*.

Edited by Heinrich Otten, Ekrem Akurgal, Hayri Ertem, and Aygül Süel. Ankara: Türk Tarih Kurumu Basımevi.

Böhl, Franz M. Theodor. 1934. Vol. 2 of *Mededelingen uit de Leidsche Verzameling van Spijkerschriftinscripties.* Amsterdam: Uitgave van de N. V. Noord-Hollandsche Uitgevers-Maatschappij.

Bottéro, Jean. 1980. "La mythologie de la mort en Mésopotamie ancienne." Pages 25–52 in *Death in Mesopotamia.* Edited by Bendt Alster. CRRAI 26; Mesopotamia 8. Copenhagen: Akademisk Forlag.

———. 1983. "Les morts et l'au-delà dans les rituels en accadien contre l'action des 'revenants.'" *ZA* 73:153–203.

Breniquet, Catherine. 2008. *Essai sur le tissage en Mésopotamie des premières communautés sédentaires au milieu du IIIe millénaire avant J.-C.* TMRG 5. Paris: de Boccard.

Breniquet, Catherine, and Cécile Michel, eds. 2014. *Wool Economy in the Ancient Near East and the Aegean: From the Beginnings of Sheep Husbandry to Institutional Textile Industry.* ATS 17. Oxford: Oxbow.

Brinkman, John A. 1963. "New Evidence of Old Assyrian *hamuštum.*" *Or* 32:387–94.

Briquel-Chatonnet, Françoise, Saba Farès-Drappeau, Brigitte Lion, and Cécile Michel, eds. 2009. *Femmes, cultures et sociétés dans les civilisations méditerranéennes et proches-orientales de l'antiquité.* TopoiSup 10. Paris: de Boccard.

Buccellati, Giorgio, and Marilyn Kelly-Buccellati. 2002. "Mozan/Urkesh: A New Capital in the Northern Djezireh." Pages 127–33 in *The Syrian Jezira: Cultural Heritage and Interrelations; Proceedings of the International Conference Held in Deir ez-Zor April 22nd–25th, 1996.* Edited by Michel Al-Maqdissi, M. A. Karim, A. Al-Azm, and M. D. Al-Khoury. Damascus: République arabe syrienne, Ministère de la culture, Direction générale des antiquités et des musées.

Budin, Stephanie Lynn, and Jean MacIntosh Turfa, eds. 2016. *Women in Antiquity: Real Women across the Ancient World.* London: Routledge.

Cadelli, Danièle. 1997. "Lorsque l'enfant paraît … malade." *Ktèma* 22:11–33.

Çeçen, Salih. 1990. "Kültepe metinlerinde bulunan yeni 'waklum' mektupları." *DTCFD* 34:35–51.

———. 1995. "*Mūtānu* in den Kültepe-Texten." *ArAn* 1:43–72.

———. 1996a. "*Idinnum* Kelimesinin Anlamı Hakkında Yeni Bir Teklif." *ArAn* 2:19–24.

———. 1996b. "Uṣur-ša-Ištar est le fils de Sargon, roi de l'ancienne Assyrie?" *ArAn* 2:11–17.

———. 1998. "Yerli Kralların Mabedleri Ziyareti ve Çıkan Neticeler." Pages 119–24 in *III. Uluslararası Hititoloji Kongresi bildirileri: Çorum, 16–22 Eylül, 1996 / Acts of the IIIrd International Congress of Hittitology: Çorum, September 16–22, 1996*. Edited by Sedat Alp and Aygül Süel. Ankara: Uyum Ajans.

Çeçen, Salih, and L. Gürkan Gökçek. 2016. "Asurlu Bayan Akadia'nın Ağabeyi Uṣur-ša-İštar'a Göndermişğu üç Mektup." *CAHIJ* 7:247–64.

———. 2017. "Uṣur-ša-İštar Ailesinden [f]Šimat-Su'en'e Ait Dört Mektup." *CAHIJ* 9:463–82.

Charpin, Dominique. 1986. "Transmission des titres de propriété et constitution des archives privées en Babylonie ancienne." Pages 121–40 in *Cuneiform Archives and Libraries: Papers Read at the 30e Rencontre assyriologique internationale, Leiden, 4–8 July 1983*. Edited by Klaas R. Veenhof. CRRAI 30. Leiden: Nederlands Historisch-Archaeologisch Instituut te Istanbul.

———. 2000. "Les prêteurs et le palais: Les édits de *mîšarum* des rois de Babylone et leurs traces dans les archives privées." Pages 185–211 in *Interdependency of Institutions and Private Entrepreneurs*. Edited by A. C. V. M. Bongenaar. MOS Studies 2; PIHANS 87. Leiden: Nederlands Instituut voor het Nabije Oosten.

———. 2008. *Lire et écrire à Babylone*. Paris: Presses universitaires de France.

———. 2009. "Chroniques bibliographiques: 12. Archives paléo-babyloniennes." *RA* 103:131–48.

Charpin, Dominique, and Jean-Marie Durand. 1997. "Aššur avant l'Assyrie." *Mari* 8:367–92.

Chavalas, Mark W., ed. 2014. *Women in the Ancient Near East: A Sourcebook*. London: Routledge.

Cooper, Jerrold S. 2016. "Female Trouble and Troubled Males: Roiled Seas, Decadent Royals, and Mesopotamian Masculinities in Myth and Practice." Pages 112–24 in *Being a Man: Negotiating Ancient Constructs of Masculinity*. Edited by Ilona Zsolnay. London: Routledge.

Couto-Ferreira, M. Erica. 2016. "Being Mothers or Acting (Like) Mothers? Constructing Motherhood in Ancient Mesopotamia." Pages 25–34 in *Women in Antiquity: Real Women across the Ancient World*. Edited by Stephanie Lynn Budin and Jean MacIntosh Turfa. London: Routledge.

Darga, Muhibbe. 1994. "The Women of the Assyrian Colony Period

(1950–1700 B.C.)." Pages 26–35 in *Woman in Anatolia: 9,000 Years of the Anatolian Woman*. Exhibition catalog. Istanbul, n.p.
De Graef, Katrien. 2016. "Cherchez la femme! The Economic Role of Women in Old Babylonian Sippar." Pages 270–95 *The Role of Women in Work and Society in the Ancient Near East*. Edited by Brigitte Lion and Cécile Michel. SANER 13. Berlin: de Gruyter.
Deller, Karlheinz. 1958. "Zu einer neuen Veröffentlichung altassyrischer Texte." *Or* 27:59–65.
———. 1990. "*Pullulu*, 'Closely Guard,' in OB Prayers to the Gods of the Night." *NABU*: art. 86.
Dercksen, Jan Gerrit. 1991. "The Old Assyrian Marriage Contract AKT 1 77." *NABU*: art. 28.
———. 1996. *The Old Assyrian Copper Trade in Anatolia*. PIHANS 75. Leiden: Nederlands Instituut voor het Nabije Oosten.
———. 1997. "The Silver of the Gods: On Old Assyrian *Ikribū*." *ArAn* 3:75–100.
———. 1999. "On the Financing of Old Assyrian Merchants." Pages 85–99 in *Trade and Finance in Ancient Mesopotamia: Proceedings of the First MOS Symposium (Leiden 1997)*. Edited by Jan Gerritt Dercksen. MOS Studies 1. Leiden: Nederlands Instituut voor het Nabije Oosten.
———. 2002. "Kultureller und wirtschaftlicher Austausch zwischen Assyrern und Anatoliern (Anfang des zweiten Jahrtausends v. Chr.)." Pages 35–43 in *Bruckenland Anatolien? Ursachen, Extensitat und Modi des Kulturaustausches zwischen Anatolien und seinen Nachbarn*. Edited by Hartmut Blum, Betina Faist, Peter Pfälzner, and Anne-Maria Wittke. Tubingen: Attempto.
———. 2004a. *Old Assyrian Institutions*. MOS Studies 4; PIHANS 98. Leiden: Nederlands Instituut voor het Nabije Oosten.
———. 2004b. "Some Elements of Old Anatolian Society in Kaniš." Pages 137–78 in *Assyria and Beyond: Studies Presented to Mogens Trolle Larsen*. Edited by Jan Gerrit Dercksen. PIHANS 100. Leiden: Nederlands Instituut voor het Nabije Oosten.
———. 2005a. "Adad is King! The Sargon Text from Kültepe." *JEOL* 39:107–29.
———. 2005b. "Metals according to Documents from Kültepe-Kanish Dating to the Old Assyrian Colony Period." Pages 17–34 in *Beiträge des im Oktober 2002 in Bochum veranstalteten Internationalen Symposiums "Anatolian Metal III."* Vol. 3 of *Anatolian Metal*. Edited by Ünsal Yalçin. Bochum: Deutsches Bergbau-Museum, 2005.

———. 2007. "On Anatolian Loanwords in Akkadian Texts from Kültepe." *ZA* 97:26–46.

———. 2008a. "Subsistence, Surplus and the Market for Grain and Meat at Ancient Kanesh." *AoF* 35:86–102.

———, ed. 2008b. *Anatolia and the Jazira during the Old Assyrian Period*. OAAS 3; PIHANS 111. Leiden: Nederlands Instituut voor het Nabije Oosten.

———. 2008c. "Observations on Land Use and Agriculture in Kaneš." Pages 139–57 in *Old Assyrian Studies in Memory of Paul Garelli*. Edited by Cécile Michel. OAAS 4; PIHANS 112. Leiden: Nederlands Instituut voor het Nabije Oosten.

———. 2010a. "Some Varieties of Meat in Old Assyrian: *Umṣu* and *Pannaru*." *NABU*: art. 69.

———. 2010b. "From the NINO Collections: An Unread Letter." Pages 22–25 in *Annual Report 2009: The Netherlands Institute for the Near East [and] the Netherlands Institute in Turkey*. Edited by J. Eidem and Carolien van Zoest. Leiden: Nederlands Instituut voor het Nabije Oosten.

———. 2011a. "Weeks, Months and Years in Old Assyrian Chronology." *BiOr* 68:233–44.

———. 2011b. "The Double God Šarramat(t)ān." *NABU*: art. 75.

———. 2014. "The Old Assyrian Trade and Its Participants." Pages 59–112 in *Documentary Sources in Ancient Near Eastern and Greco-Roman Economic History: Methodology and Practice*. Edited by Heather D. Baker and Michael Jursa. Oxford: Oxbow.

———. 2015a. "The Archive of Ali-ahum (I): The Documents Excavated in N-O-P/20 in 1950, KIM 1." Pages 47–58 in *Proceedings of the First Kültepe International Meeting, Kültepe, 19–23 September, 2013: Studies Dedicated to Kutlu Emre*. Edited by Fikri Kulakoğlu and Cécile Michel. KIM 1; Subartu 35. Turnhout: Brepols.

———. 2015b. "The Goddess Who Was Robbed of Her Jewellery: Ishtar and Her Priest in an Assyrian Colony." *Anatolica* 41:37–60.

———. 2015c. "*Nikkassū*: A Calculating Instrument?" *NABU*: art. 9.

———. 2016. "*Kaspam Lašqul*: 'Let Me Weigh Out the Silver'; Mesopotamian and Anatolian Weights during the Old Assyrian Colony Period." Pages 11–22 in *Silver, Money and Credit: A Tribute to Robartus J. van der Spek on the Occasion of His Sixty-Fifth Birthday on September 2014*. Edited by Kristin Kleber and Reinhard Pirngruber. PIHANS 128. Leiden: Nederlands Instituut voor het Nabije Oosten.

Donbaz, Veysel. 1974. "Four Old Assyrian Tablets from the City of Aššur." *JCS* 26:81–85.
———. 1985. "More Old Assyrian Tablets from Aššur." *Akkadica* 42:1–23.
———. 1988. "The Business of Ašēd, an Anatolian Merchant." *AfO* 35:48–63.
———. 1989. "Some Remarkable Contracts of Ib Period Kültepe-Tablets." Pages 75–98 in *Anatolia and the Ancient Near East: Studies in Honour of Tahsin Özgüç*. Edited by Kutlu Emre, Barthel Hrouda, Machteld J. Mellink, and Nimet Özgüç. Ankara: Türk Tarih Kurumu Basımevi.
———. 1991. "New Evidence for the Expression *Mērūa Attunu*." *NABU*: art. 10.
———. 1993. "Some Remarkable Contracts of Ib Period Kültepe-Tablets II." Pages 131–54 in *Aspects of Art and Iconography: Anatolia and Its Neighbors; Studies in Honour of Nimet Özgüç*. Edited by Machteld J. Mellink, Tahsin Özgüç, and Edith Porada. Ankara: Türk Tarih Kurumu Basımevi.
———. 1997. "Reminder to the Author of 'An Old Assyrian Marriage Contract.'" *NABU*: art. 106.
———. 1998. "Tablets from the Palace of Waršuma." Pages 413–19 in *XXXIVème Rencontre Assyriologique Internationale 6–10; VII. 1987 Istanbul / XXXIV. Uluslararasi Assıryoloji Kongresi 6–10; VII. 1987 Istanbul / XXXIV. International Assyriology Congress 6–10; VII. 1987 Istanbul*. Edited by Hayat Erkanal, Veysel Donbaz, and Ayşegül Uğuroğlu. CRRAI 34; TTKY 26.3. Ankara: Türk Tarıh Kurumu Basımevi.
———. 2003. "*Lamniš ulā ezebši*: 'He Shall Not Leave Her in a Bad Situation (Wickedly).'" Pages 47–50 in *Festschrift für Burkhart Kienast zu seinem 70. Geburtstage dargebracht von Freuden, Schülern und Kollegen*. Edited by Gebhard J. Selz. AOAT 274. Münster: Ugarit-Verlag.
———. 2004. "Some Remarkable Contracts of 1-B Period Kultepe Tablets III." Pages 271–84 in *Šarnikzel: Hethitologische Studien zum Gedenken an Emil Orgetorix Forrer*. Edited by Detlev Groddek and Sylvester Rössle. Desden: Verlag der Technischen Universität Dresden.
———. 2005. "Old Assyrian *Rubātum*, "Queen," or a ^{f}PN Seen on Cylinder Seals." *NABU*: art. 18.
———. 2008. "Three Court Proceedings Concerning Walaliašu'e, an Anatolian Woman." Pages 209–20 in *Muhibbe Darga Armağanı*. Edited by Aksel Tibet, Erkan Konyar, and Taner Tarhan. Istanbul: Sadberk Hanim Muzesi Yayini.
———. 2015. "To Remind the Past: KTS 1 Revisited." Pages 59–69 in *Cahit Günbattı Armağan: Studies in Honour of Cahit Günbattı*. Edited by

İrfan Albayrak, Hakan Erol, and Murat Çayır. Ankara: Ankara Üniversitesi Dil ve Tarih-Coğrafya Fakültesi.

Driel, Govert van. 1999. "Agricultural Entrepreneurs in Mesopotamia." Pages 213–23 in *Landwirtschaft in alten Orient: Ausgewählte vorträge der XLI Rencontre assyriologique internationale, Berlin 4–8.7.1994*. Edited by Horst Klengel and Johannes Renger. Berlin: Reimer.

Durand, Jean-Marie. 1997. Vol 1 of *Documents épistolaires du palais de Mari*. LAPO 16. Paris: Cerf.

Edzard, Dietz-Otto. 1989. "Altassyrisch *Nuwa'um*." Pages 107–10 in *Anatolia and the Ancient Near East: Studies in Honour of Tahsin Özgüç*. Edited by Kutlu Emre, Barthel Hrouda, Machteld J. Mellink, and Nimet Özgüç. Ankara: Türk Tarih Kurumu Basımevi.

Eidem, Jesper. 2004. "In the Names of Aššur!" Pages 191–204 in *Assyria and Beyond: Studies Presented to Mogens Trolle Larsen*. Edited by Jan Gerrit Dercksen. PIHANS 100. Leiden: Nederlands Instituut voor het Nabije Oosten.

———. 2011. *The Royal Archives from Tell Leilan: Old Babylonian Letters and Treaties from the Lower Town Palace East*. PIHANS 117. Leiden: Nederlands Instituut voor het Nabije Oosten.

Eisser, Georg, and Julius Lewy. 1930. *Die altassyrische Rechtsurkunden vom Kültepe*. Parts 1–2. *MVAG* 33. Leipzig: Hinrichs.

———. 1935. *Die altassyrische Rechtsurkunden vom Kültepe*. Parts 3–4. *MVAG* 35.3. Leipzig: Hinrichs.

Emre, Kutlu. 1971. *Anadolu Kurşun Figurinleri ve Taş Kalıpları / Anatolian Lead Figurines and Their Stone Moulds*. Ankara: Türk Tarih Kurumu Basımevi.

———. 2008. "A Group of Metal Vessels from *Kārum* Kültepe/Kaneš." Pages 3–12 in *Old Assyrian Studies in Memory of Paul Garelli*. Edited by Cécile Michel. OAAS 4; PIHANS 112. Leiden: Nederlands Instituut voor het Nabije Oosten.

———. 2015. "Tahsin Ozguc: The Nestor of Anatolian Archaeology." Pages 1–5 in *Proceedings of the First Kültepe International Meeting, Kültepe, 19–23 September, 2013: Studies Dedicated to Kutlu Emre*. Edited by Fikri Kulakoğlu and Cécile Michel. KIM 1; Subartu 35. Turnhout: Brepols.

Erol, Hakan. 2010. "Uṣur-ša-Ištar Arşivinden (Kt n/k) Šimat-Su'en'in Bir Mektubu." Pages 273–84 in *VII. Uluslararasi Hititoloji Kongresi Bildirileri, Çorum 25–31 Agustos 2008 / Acts of the VIIth International Congress of Hittitology, Çorum, 25–31 August 2008*. Edited by Yayina Hazirlayan and Aygül Suel. Ankara: Anit Matbaa.

———. 2015. “The Archives of Šu-Ištar son of Aššur-bāni (Kt 92/k 264–1008).” Pages 59–72 in *Proceedings of the First Kültepe International Meeting, Kültepe, 19–23 September, 2013: Studies Dedicated to Kutlu Emre*. Edited by Fikri Kulakoğlu and Cécile Michel. KIM 1; Subartu 35. Turnhout: Brepols.

———. 2018. “Old Assyrian Royal Families as Private Entrepreneurs in the Anatolian Trade.” *JNES* 77:47–66.

Ezer, Sabahattin. 2014. “Kültepe-Kanesh in the Early Bronze Age.” Pages 5–23 in *Current Research at Kültepe/Kanesh: An Interdisciplinary and Integrative Approach to Trade Networks, Internationalism, and Identity*. Edited by Levent Atici, Fikri Kulakoğlu, Gojko Barjamovic, and Andrew Fairbairn. JCSSup 4. Atlanta: Lockwood.

Farber, Walter. 1989. *Schlaf, Kindchen, Schlaf!: Mesopotamische Baby-Beschwörungen und -Rituale*. MC 2. Winona Lake: Eisenbrauns.

———. 1990. “Hanum kauft Gadagada: Eine altassyrische Selbstverfaufs-Urkunde.” *AulaOr* 8:197–203.

Firth, Richard, and Marie-Louise Nosch. 2012. “Spinning and Weaving Wool in Ur III Administrative Texts.” *JCS* 64:67–84.

Fleming, Daniel E. 1992. *The Installation of Baal’s High Priestess at Emar: A Window on Ancient Syrian Religion*. HSS 42. Atlanta: Scholars Press.

Fontaine, Laurence. 2014. *Le Marché: Histoires et usages d’une conquête sociale*. Paris: Gallimard.

Foster, Benjamin R. 1981. Review of *Death in Mesopotamia: Papers Read at the XXVI*^e^ *Rencontre Assyriologique Internationale*. Edited by Bendt Alster. *BiOr* 38:619–26.

———. 2005. *Before the Muses: An Anthology of Akkadian Literature*. 3rd ed. Bethesda, MD: CDL.

Gadaut, Géraldine. 2009. “Les femmes dans les inscriptions royales de Mésopotamie IIIe-Ier millénaire av. J.-C.” Pages 233–51 in *Femmes, cultures et sociétés dans les civilisations méditerranéennes et proches-orientales de l’antiquité*. Edited by Françoise Briquel-Chatonnet, Saba Farès-Drappeau, Brigitte Lion, and Cécile Michel. TopoiSup 10. Paris: de Boccard.

Garcia-Ventura, Agnès, and Saana Svärd. 2018. “Theoretical Approaches, Gender, and the Ancient Near East: An Introduction.” Pages 1–13 in *Studying Gender in the Ancient Near East*. Edited by Saana Svärd and Agnès Garcia-Ventura. University Park, PA: Eisenbrauns.

Garcia-Ventura, Agnès, and Gioele Zisa. 2017. “Gender and Women in Ancient Near Eastern Studies: Bibliography 2002–2016.” *Akkadica* 138:37–67.

Garelli, Paul. 1957. "Trois tablettes cappadociennes du musée de Rouen." *RA* 51:1–10.

———. 1962. "La religion de l'Assyrie ancienne d'après un ouvrage récent." *RA* 56:191–210.

———. 1963. *Les Assyriens en Cappadoce.* Bibliothèque archéologique et historique de l'institut français d'archéologie d'Istanbul 19. Paris: Maisonneuve.

———. 1965. "Tablettes cappadociennes de collections diverses." *RA* 59:19–48, 149–76.

———. 1966. "Tablettes cappadociennes de collections diverses." *RA* 60:93–152.

———. 1979. "Femmes d'affaires en Assyrie." *ArOr* 47:42–48.

Goedegebuure, Petra. M. 2008. "Central Anatolian Languages and Language Communities in the Colony Period: A Luwian–Hattian Symbiosis and the Independent Hittites." Pages 137–80 in *Anatolia and the Jazira during the Old Assyrian Period.* Edited by Jan G. Dercksen. PIHANS 111. Leiden: Nederlands Instituut voor het Nabije Oosten.

Goetze, Albrecht. 1954. "The Linguistic Continuity of Anatolia as Shown by Its Proper Names." *JCS* 8:74–81.

Gökçek, L. Gürkan. 2003. "Kultepe Metinlerinde Gecen Kaplar." *ArAn* 6, no. 2:73–87.

Gräff, Andreas. 2005. "Thoughts about the Assyrian Presence in Anatolia in the Early 2nd Millennium." *AoF* 32:158–67.

Graslin-Thomé, Laetitia. 2016. "Long-Distance Trade in Neo-Babylonian Mesopotamia: The Effects of Institutional Changes." Pages 167–86 in *Dynamics of Production in the Ancient Near East 1300–500 BC.* Edited by Juan Carlos Moreno Garcia. Oxford: Oxbow.

Grayson, Albert K. 1987. *Assyrian Rulers of the Third and Second Millennia BC (to 1115 BC).* RIMAP 1. Toronto: University of Toronto Press.

Guichard, Michaël. 2005. *La Vaisselle de luxe des rois de Mari.* Vol. 2 of *Matériaux pour le Dictionnaire de Babylonien de Paris.* ARMT 31. Paris: Éditions Recherche sur les civilisations.

Günbattı, Cahit. 1987. "Ankara Anadolu Medeniyetleri Müzesi'nde Bulunan üç Tablet." *DTCFD* 31:189–99.

———. 1989. "Ev Satışı İle İlgili Beş Kültepe Tableti ve Bunlardan Çıkan Bazı Sonuçlar." *Belleten* 53:51–59.

———. 1990. "Kültepe Tabletleri Arasında Aile Haberleşmelerinden Örnekler." Pages 126–32 in *Hititoloji Kongresi; Bildirileri (19–21 temmuz 1990) Çorum.* Vol. 1 of *Uluslararası Hititoloji Kongresi bildirileri*. Edited by Sedat Alp. Ankara: Uluslararasi Çorum Hitit Festivali Komitesi Başkariliği.

———. 1992. "Some Observations about the Commercial Activities of Women in the Light of the Kültepe Tablets." Pages 229–34 in *Hittite and Other Anatolian and Near Eastern Studies in Honour of Sedat Alp*. Edited by Heinrich Otten, Ekrem Akurgal, Hayri Ertem, and Aygül Süel. Ankara: Türk Tarih Kurumu Basımevi.

———. 2004. "Two Treaty Texts Found at Kültepe." Pages 249–68 in *Assyria and Beyond: Studies Presented to Mogens Trolle Larsen*. Edited by Jan Gerrit Dercksen. PIHANS 100. Leiden: Nederlands Instituut voor het Nabije Oosten.

———. 2008. "An Eponym List (KEL G) from Kültepe." *AoF* 35:103–32.

———. 2014. *Harsamna Kralı Hurmeli'ye Gönderilen Mektup ve Kaniš Kralları / The Letter Sent to Hurmeli King of Harsamna and the Kings of Kaniš*. TTKY 5.3. Ankara: Türk Tarih Kurumu.

Hallo, William W. 1981. "Letters, Prayers and Letter-Prayers." Pages 17–27 in *Proceedings of the Seventh World Congress of Jewish Studies: Studies in the Bible and the Ancient Near East, Held at the Hebrew University of Jerusalem, 7–14 August 1977 under the Auspices of the Israel Academy of Sciences and Humanities*. Edited by Israel Gutman. Jerusalem: World Union of Jewish Studies.

Halton, Charles, and Saana Svärd. 2017. *Women's Writing of Ancient Mesopotamia: An Anthology of the Earliest Female Authors*. Cambridge: Cambridge University Press.

Harris, Rikvah. 1975. *Ancient Sippar: A Demographic Study of an Old Babylonian City, 1894–1595 B.C.* PIHANS 36. Istanbul: Nederlands historisch-archaeologisch instituut te Istanbul.

Hecker, Karl. 1968. *Grammatik der Kültepe-Texte*. AnOr 44. Rome: Biblical Pontifical Institute.

———. 1978. "*Tib'imma atalkim*: Assyrerinnen im *kārum* zeitlichen Anatolien." *Or* 47:404–18.

———. 1980. "Zur Beurkundung von Kauf und Verkauf im Altassyrische." *WO* 11:64–75.

———. 1997. "Über den Euphrat… Ortsbezogene Restriktionen in aA Kaufurkunden." *ArAn* 3157–72.

———. 1999. "In nova…" *ArOr* 67:557–65.

———. 2001. "Akkadische Rechts- und Verwaltungsurkunden." Pages 26–30 in *Ergänzungslieferung*. Edited by Manfred Dietrich, Karl Hecker, and Friedrich Junge. TUAT. Gütersloh: Gütersloher Verlagshaus.

———. 2003. "*Kunuk kārim saher rabi*." Pages 183–96 in *Festschrift für Burkhart Kienast zu seinem 70. Geburtstage dargebracht von Freuden, Schülern und Kollegen*. Edited by Gebhard J. Selz. AOAT 274. Münster: Ugarit-Verlag, 2003.

———. 2004a. "Beim Tode unseres Vaters... Der leidige Streit ums Erbe." Pages 281–98 in *Assyria and Beyond: Studies Presented to Mogens Trolle Larsen*. Edited by Jan Gerrit Dercksen. PIHANS 100. Leiden: Nederlands Instituut Voor Het Nabije Oosten.

———. 2004b. "Altassyrische Texte." Pages 43–57 in *Texte zum Rechts- und Wirtschaftsleben*. Edited by Helmut Freydank, Karl Hecker, Andrea Jördens, and Michael Lichtenstein. TUAT NS 1. Gütersloh: Gütersloher.

———. 2006. "Altassyrische Briefe." Pages 77–100 in *Briefe*. Edited by Bernd Janowski and Gernot Wilhelm. TUAT n.s. 3. Gütersloh: Gütersloher.

———. 2008. "Rituale und Beschwörung." Pages 61–127 in *Omina, Orakel, Rituale und Beschwörungen*. Edited by Bernd Janowski and Gernot Wilhelm. TUAT n.s. 4. Gütersloh: Gütersloher.

Heffron, Yağmur. 2016. "Stone Stelae and Religious Space at Kültepe-Kaneš." *AnSt* 66:23–42.

———. 2017. "Testing the Middle Ground in Assyro-Anatolian Marriages of the Kārum Period." *Iraq* 79:71–83.

Hengstl, Joachim. 1992. "'Soll und Haben' in einer altassyrischen familienrechtlichen Urkunde." *ZA* 82: 212–20.

Hertel, Thomas K. 2010. "The Akkadian Noun muttum." *NABU*: art. 35.

———. 2013. *Old Assyrian Legal Practices: Law and Dispute in the Ancient Near East*. OAAS 6; PIHANS 123. Leiden: Nederlands Instituut voor het Nabije Oosten.

———. 2014. "The Lower Town of Kültepe: Urban Layout and Population." Pages 25–54 in *Current Research at Kültepe/Kanesh: An Interdisciplinary and Integrative Approach to Trade Networks, Internationalism, and Identity*. Edited by Levent Atici, Fikri Kulakoğlu, Gojko Barjamovic, and Andrew Fairbairn. JCSSup 4. Atlanta: Lockwood.

———. 2015. "Paternal Estates in Old Assyrian Society." Pages 29–43 in *Proceedings of the First Kültepe International Meeting, Kültepe, 19–23 September, 2013: Studies Dedicated to Kutlu Emre*. Edited by Fikri Kulakoğlu and Cécile Michel. KIM 1; Subartu 35. Turnhout: Brepols.

Highcock, Nancy. 2017. "Assyrians Abroad: Expanding Borders through Mobile Identities in the Middle Bronze Age." *JANEH* 4: 61–93.

Hirsch, Hans. 1961. *Untersuchungen zur altassyrischen Religion*. AfOB 13–14. Graz: Weidner, 1961.

———. 1966. "Eine Kleinigkeit zur Heiratsurkunde *ICK* 1, 3." *Or* 35:279–80.

———. 1967. "Zornige Worte." *ZA* 58:104–9.

———. 2007. "HG 75: Einige Bemerkungen." *NABU*: art. 38.

Hockmann, Daniel. 2010. *Gräber und Grüfte in Assur I: Von der zweiten Hälfte des 3. bis zur Mitte des 2. Jahrtausends v. Chr.* WVDOG 129. Wiesbaden: Harrasowitz.

Hrozný, Bedrich. 1927. "Rapport préliminaire sur les fouilles tchécoslovaques du Kultèpè." *Syria* 8:1–12.

Ichisar, Metin. 1981. *Les archives cappadociennes du marchand Imdīlum.* RGC 3. Paris: Éditions A.D.P.F.

———. 1982. "Un contrat de mariage et la question du lévirat à l'époque cappadocienne." *RA* 76:168–73.

Jacques, Margaret. 2006. *Le vocabulaire des sentiments dans les textes sumériens: Recherche sur le lexique sumérien et akkadien.* AOAT 332. Münster: Ugarit-Verlag.

Jakob-Rost, Liane, and Hermann Freydank. 1981. "Eine altassyrische Votivinschrift." *AoF* 8:325–27.

Jensen, Karen. 1997. "An Old Assyrian Marriage Document." *NABU*: art. 75.

Jeyes, Ulla. 1983. "The *Nadītu* Women of Sippar." Pages 260–72 in *Images of Women in Antiquity*. Edited by Averil Cameron and Amélie Kuhrt. London: Routledge.

Joannès, Francis, and Fumi Karahashi. 2014. *Le rôle économique des femmes en Mésopotamie ancienne (REFEMA) / Women's Role in the Economy of the Ancient Near East: Report December 31, 2011–December 30, 2014.* Nanterre: REFEMA; Tokyo: Japan Society for the Promotion of Science.

Jursa, Michael. 2010. *Aspects of the Economic History of Babylonia in the First Millennium BC.* AOAT 377. Münster: Ugarit-Verlag.

Justel, Josué J. 2008. *La posición jurídica de la mujer en Siria durante el Bronce Final: Estudio de las estrategias familiares y de la mujer como sujeto y objeto de derecho.* Zaragoza: Instituto de Estudios Islámicos y del Oriente Próximo.

———. 2014. *Mujeres y derecho en el Próximo Oriente Antiguo: La presencia des mujeres en los textos jurídicos cuneiformes del segundo y primer milenos a.C.* Zaragoza: Libros Pórtico.

———. 2018. "¿Mujeres al poder? El caso de las mujeres con estatus jurídico masculino en Mesopotamia." Pages 293–309 in *La Mujeres en el Ori-*

ente Cuneiforme. Edited by Josué J. Justel and Agnès Garcia-Ventura. Alcalá de Henares: Universidad de Alcalá, Servicio de Publicaciones.

Katz, Dina. 2003. *The Image of the Netherworld in the Sumerian Sources*. Bethesda, MD: CDL.

Kawasaki, Yasushi. 1994. "Status of Women and Marriage Institution of the Old Assyrian Society" [Japanese]. *Orient* 37:52–70 (English abstract, 52).

———. 1998. "An Unpublished Old Assyrian Tablet in the 'Prof. Garstang Collection,' Housed in Liverpool Museum." *Orient* 33:79–87.

Kienast, Burkhart. 1976. "Bemerkungen zum altassyrischen Pfandrecht." *WO* 8:218–27.

———. 1984. *Das altassyrische Kaufvertragsrecht*. FAOS 1. Stuttgart: Steiner.

———. 2008. "Altassyrisch *Amtum* = 'Zweitfrau.'" *AoF* 35:35–52.

———. 2015. *Das altassyrische Eherecht: Eine Urkundenlehre*. SANTAG 10. Wiesbaden: Harrassowitz.

Kogan, Leonid E., and Natalia V. Koslova. 2006. Review of *Assyria and Beyond: Studies Presented to Mogens Trolle Larsen*. Edited by Jan Gerrit Dercksen. Pages 589–612 in *Babel und Bibel 3: Annual of Ancient Near Eastern, Old Testament, and Semitic Studies*. Edited by Leonid E. Kogan, Natalia V. Koslova, S. V. Lëzov, and Serguei Tishchenko. BabBib 3. Winona Lake, IN: Eisenbrauns.

Kouwenberg, N. J. C. 2017. *A Grammar of Old Assyrian*. HdO 118. Leiden: Brill.

Kouwenberg, N. J. C., and Jeanette C. Fincke. 2013. "A 'New' Old Assyrian Incantation." *JEOL* 44:141–46.

Kryszat, Guido. 1995. "Ilu-šumma und der Gott aus dem Brunnen." Pages 201–13 in *Vom Alten Orient zum Alten Testament: Festschrift für Wolfram Freiherrn von Soden zum 85. Geburtstag am 19. Juni 1993*. Edited by Manfried Dietrich and Oswald Loretz. Kevelaer: Butzon & Bercker; Neukirchen-Vluyn: Neukirchener. AOAT 240. Münster.

———. 2001. "Beobachtungen zum Archiv des Iddi(n)-Ištar." Pages 263–73 in *Veenhof Anniversary Volume: Studies Presented to Klaas R. Veenhof on the Occasion of His Sixty-Fifth Birthday*. Edited by Wilfried Hugo van Soldt, Jan Gerrit Dercksen, N. J. C. Kouwenberg, and Theo J. H. Krispijn. PIHANS 89. Leiden: Nederlands Instituut voor het Nabije Oosten.

———. 2003. "Altassyrischer Brief an die Göttin Tašmētum." Pages 251–58 in *Festschrift für Burkhart Kienast zu seinem 70. Geburtstage darge-*

bracht von Freuden, Schülern und Kollegen. Edited by Gebhard J. Selz. AOAT 274. Münster: Ugarit-Verlag.

———. 2004. *Zur Chronologie der Kaufmannsarchive aus der Schicht 2 des Kārum Kaneš*. OAAS 2; PIHANS 99. Leiden: Nederlands Instituut voor het Nabije Oosten.

———. 2006a. "Die altassyrischen belege für den Gott Amurru." *RA* 100:53–56.

———. 2006b. "Herrscher, Herrschaft und Kulttradition in Anatolien nach den Quellen aus den altassyrischen Handelskolonien, Teil 2: Götter, Priester und Feste Altanatoliens." *AoF* 33:102–24.

———. 2007a. "Eine Dame mit Namen Zizizi." *AoF* 34:210–18.

———. 2007b. "Zur Liste der Schwurgötter im Assur-Apûm-Vertrag." Pages 99–102 in *Assur und sein Umland: Im Andenken an die ersten Ausgräber von Assur*. Edited by Peter A. Miglus and Joaquín Ma Córdobain. Isimu 6. Madrid: Universidad Autónoma de Madrid.

———. 2008a. "The Use of Writing among the Anatolians." Pages 231–38 in *Anatolia and the Jazira during the Old Assyrian Period*. Edited by Jan Gerrit Dercksen. OAAS 3; PIHANS 111. Leiden: Nederlands Instituut voor het Nabije Oosten.

———. 2008b. "Herrscher, Kult und Kulttradition in Anatolien nach den Quellen aus den altassyrischen Handelskolonien, Teil 3/1: Grundlagen für eine neue Rekonstruktion der Geschichte Anatoliens und der assyrischen Handelskolonien in spätaltassyrischer Zeit." *AoF* 35:156–89.

———. 2008c. "Herrscher, Kult und Kulttradition in Anatolien nach den Quellen aus den altassyrischen Handelskolonien, Teil 3/2: Grundlagen für eine neue Rekonstruktion der Geschichte Anatoliens und der assyrischen Handelskolonien in spätaltassyrischer Zeit II." *AoF* 35:195–219.

———. 2017. "Zur altassyrischen Votivinschrift Assur 19624a/VA 8365." *NABU*: art. 66.

Kulakoğlu, Fikri. 2015. "Current Research at Kültepe." Pages 9–21 in *Proceedings of the 1st Kültepe International Meeting, Kültepe, 19–23 September, 2013: Studies Dedicated to Kutlu Emre*. Edited by Fikri Kulakoğlu and Cécile Michel. KIM 1; Subartu 35. Turnhout: Brepols.

———. 2017. "Balance Stone Weights and Scale-Pans from Kültepe-Kanesh: On One of the Basic Elements of the Old Assyrian Trading System." Pages 341–89 in *Overturning Certainties in Near Eastern Archaeology: A Festschrift in Honor of K. Aslıhan Yener*. Edited by Çiğdem Maner, Mara T. Horowitz, and Allan S. Gilbert. CHANE 90. Leiden: Brill.

Kulakoğlu, Fikri, and Gojko Barjamovic, eds. 2017. *Movement, Resources, Interaction: Proceedings of the 2nd Kültepe International Meeting, Kültepe, 26–30 July 2015; Studies Dedicated to Klaas Veenhof*. KIM 2; Subartu 39. Turnhout: Brepols.

Kulakoğlu, Fikri, and Selmin Kangal, eds. 2010. *Anatolia's Prologue: Kültepe, Kanesh, Karum; Assyrians in Istanbul*. KMMCP 78. Istanbul: Kayseri Metropolitan Municipality.

Kulakoğlu, Fikri, and Cécile Michel, eds. 2015. *Proceedings of the 1st Kültepe International Meeting, Kültepe, 19–23 September, 2013: Studies Dedicated to Kutlu Emre*. KIM 1; Subartu 35. Turnhout: Brepols.

Kulakoğlu, Fikri, and Güzel Öztürk. 2015. "New Evidence for International Trade in Bronze Age Central Anatolia: Recently Discovered Bullae at Kültepe-Kanesh." *Antiquity* 89/34, http://journal.antiquity.ac.uk/projgall/kulakoglu343.

Kuzuoğlu, Remzi. 2005. "Eski Anadolu'da İpotek Kavramının İlk İzleri." *Akademi Günlüğü* 1:77–87.

Lafont, Sophie. 1999. *Femmes, droit et justice dans l'antiquité orientale: Contributions à l'étude du droit pénal of Proche-Orient ancien*. OBO 165. Fribourg: Editions universitaires Fribourg Suisse.

Lambert, Wilfred. G., and Alan R. Millard. 1969. *Atra-ḫasīs: The Babylonian Story of the Flood*. Oxford: Clarendon.

Langlois, Anne-Isabelle. 2017. *Les archives de la princesse Iltani découvertes à Tell al-Rimah (XIIIe siècle avant J.-C.) et l'histoire du royaume de Karana/Qaṭṭara*. Archibab 2. Paris: Société pour l'étude du Proche-Orient ancien.

Laroche, Emmanuel. 1966. *Les noms des Hittites*. EL 4. Paris: Klincksieck.

Larsen, Mogens Trolle. 1967. *Old Assyrian Caravan Procedures*. PIHANS 22. Istanbul: Nederlands Historisch-Archaeologisch Instituut in het Nabije Oosten.

———. 1971. "Slander." *Or* 40:317–24.

———. 1976. *The Old Assyrian City-State and Its Colonies*. Mesopotamia 4. Copenhagen: Akademisk Forlag.

———. 1977. "Partnerships in the Old Assyrian Trade." *Iraq* 39:119–49.

———. 1982. "Your Money or Your Life! A Portrait of an Assyrian Businessman." Pages 214–45 in *Societies and Languages of the Ancient Near East: Studies in Honor of I. M. Diakonoff*. Edited by M. A. Dandamayev, J. Nicholas Postgate, and Mogens Tolle Larsen. Warminster: Aris & Phillips.

———. 1999. "*Naruqqu*-Verträge." *RlA* 9:181–84.

———. 2000. "The Old Assyrian City-State." Pages 77–87 in *A Comparative Study of Thirty City-State Cultures: An Investigation*. Edited by Mogens Herman Hansen. Copenhagen: Reitzel.

———. 2001. "Affect and Emotion." Pages 275–86 in *Veenhof Anniversary Volume: Studies Presented to Klaas R. Veenhof on the Occasion of His Sixty-Fifth Birthday*. Edited by Wilfried Hugo van Soldt, Jan Gerrit Dercksen, N. J. C. Kouwenberg, and Theo J. H. Krispijn. PIHANS 89. Leiden: Nederlands Instituut voor het Nabije Oosten.

———. 2002. *The Aššur-nādā Archive*. OAA 1; PIHANS 96. Leiden: Nederlands Instituut voor het Nabije Oosten.

———. 2007. "Individual and Family in Old Assyrian Society." *JCS* 59:93–106.

———. 2008. "Archives and Filing Systems at Kültepe." Pages 77–88 in *Old Assyrian Studies in Memory of Paul Garelli*. Edited by Cécile Michel. OAAS 4; PIHANS 112. Leiden: Nederlands Instituut voor het Nabije Oosten.

———. 2015a. *Ancient Kanesh: A Merchant Colony in Bronze Age Anatolia*. Cambridge: Cambridge University Press.

———. 2015b. "The Relative Chronology of the Old Assyrian Period and Its Consequences." Pages 23–28 in *Proceedings of the 1st Kültepe International Meeting, Kültepe, 19–23 September, 2013: Studies Dedicated to Kutlu Emre*. Edited by Fikri Kulakoğlu and Cécile Michel. KIM 1; Subartu 35. Turnhout: Brepols.

———. 2017. "Between Slavery and Freedom." Pages 289–99 in *At the Dawn of History: Ancient Near Eastern Studies in Honour of J. N. Postgate*. Edited by Yağmur Heffron, Adam Stone, and Martin Worthington. Winona Lake, IN: Eisenbrauns.

Larsen, Mogens Trolle, and Agnete Wisti Lassen. 2014. "Cultural Interaction at Kültepe." Pages 171–88 in *Extraction and Control: Studies in Honor of Matthew W. Stolper*. Edited by Michael Kozuh, Wouter F. M. Henkelman, Charles E. Jones, and Christopher Woods. SAOC 68. Chicago: Oriental Institute of the University of Chicago.

Lassen, Agnete Wisti. 2010a. "Tools, Procedures and Professions: A Review of the Akkadian Textile Terminology." Pages 270–80 in *Textile Terminologies in the Ancient Near East and Mediterranean from the Third to the First Millennnia BC*. Edited by Cécile Michel and Marie-Louise Nosch. ATS 8. Oxford: Oxbow.

———. 2010b. "The Trade in Wool in Old Assyrian Anatolia." *JEOL* 42:159–79.

———. 2012. "Glyptic Encounters: A Stylistic and Prosopographical Study of Seals in the Old Assyrian Period; Chronology, Ownership and Identity." PhD diss., University of Copenhagen.

———. 2013. "Technology and Palace Economy in Middle Bronze Age Anatolia: The Case of the Crescent Shaped Loom Weight." Pages 78–92 in *Textile Production and Consumption in the Ancient Near East*. Edited by Marie-Louise Nosch, Henriette Koefoed, and Eva Andersson Strand. ATS 12. Oxford: Oxbow.

———. 2014. "Wool in Anatolia in the Old Assyrian Period." Pages 255–63 in *Wool Economy in the Ancient Near East and the Aegean: From the Beginnings of Sheep Husbandry to Institutional Textile Industry*. Edited by Catherine Breniquet and Cécile Michel. ATS 17. Oxford: Oxbow.

Lewy, Hildegard. 1965. "Ištar-ṣâd and the Bow Star." Pages 273–81 in *Studies in Honor of Benno Landsberger on His Seventy-Fifth Birthday, April 21, 1965*. Edited by Hans Gustav Güterbock and Thorkild Jacobsen. AS 16. Chicago: University of Chicago Press.

———. 1969–1970. "Old Assyrian Texts in the University Museum." *HUCA* 40–41:46–85.

Lewy, Julius. 1925. "TC 100, LC 242 und das Eherecht des altassyrischen Rechtbuches KAV Nr. 1." *ZA* 26:139–61.

———. 1937. "Old Assyrian Documents from Asia Minor I." *AHDO* 1:91–108.

———. 1938. "Old Assyrian Documents from Asia Minor II." *AHDO* 2:113–42.

———. 1950. "Hatta, Hattu, Hattuša and 'Old Assyrian' Hattum." *ArOr* 18:366–411.

———. 1956. "On Some Institutions of the Old Assyrian Empire." *HUCA* 27:1–80.

———. 1961. "Amurritica." *HUCA* 32:31–73.

Lion, Brigitte. 1993. "L'idée de bonheur dans la littérature suméro-akkadienne." PhD diss., University of Paris.

———. 2003. "Un idéal de Bonheur atypique, celui des guerriers et des nomades." *EO* 8:13–32.

———. 2009a. "Sexe et genre (1). Des filles devenant fils dans les contrats de Nuzi et d'Emar." Pages 9–25 in *Femmes, cultures et sociétés dans les civilisations méditerranéennes et proches-orientales de l'antiquité*. Edited by Françoise Briquel-Chatonnet, Saba Farès-Drappeau, Brigitte Lion, and Cécile Michel. TopoiSup 10. Paris: de Boccard.

———. 2009b. "Les femmes scribes de Sippar." Pages 289–303 in *Femmes, cultures et sociétés dans les civilisations méditerranéennes et proches-orientales de l'antiquité*. Edited by Françoise Briquel-Chatonnet, Saba Farès-Drappeau, Brigitte Lion, and Cécile Michel. TopoiSup 10. Paris: de Boccard.

———. 2011. "Literacy and Gender." Pages 90–112 in *The Oxford Handbook of Cuneiform Culture*. Edited by Karen Radner and Eleanor Robson. Oxford: Oxford University Press.

———. 2018. "Gender and Methodology in the Study of Second Millennium BCE Family Archives." Pages 233–47 in *Studying Gender in the Ancient Near East*. Edited by Saana Svärd and Agnès Garcia-Ventura. University Park, PA: Eisenbrauns.

Lion, Brigitte, and Cécile Michel, eds. 2016. *The Role of Women in Work and Society in the Ancient Near East*. SANER 13. Berlin: de Gruyter.

Lion, Brigitte, Cécile Michel, and P. Villard, eds. 1997. *Enfance et éducation au Proche-Orient ancien, Actes de la table ronde, Nanterre, Décembre 1997*. *Ktèma* 22. Strasbourg: Presses universitaires de Strasbourg.

Lumsden, Stephen. 2008. "Material Culture and the Middle Ground in the Old Assyrian Colony Period." Pages 21–43 in *Old Assyrian Studies in Memory of Paul Garelli*. Edited by Cécile Michel. OAAS 4; PIHANS 112. Leiden: Nederlands Instituut voor het Nabije Oosten.

Łyczkowska, Krystyna. 1978. "Some Data about Šūbultum." Pages 131–37 in *Festchrift Lubor Matouš*. Edited by B. K. Hruška and Géza Komoroczy. Budapest: Eötvös Loránd Tudományegyetem.

———. 1993. "Anatolian *amtum* in the Texts from Kaneš." *Rocznik Orientalistyczny* 48:23–33.

———. 1998. "Familienrechts-Urkunden bei den Anatoliern in Kaniš." *RO* 51:13–23.

Maekawa, K. 1980. "Female Weavers and Their Children in Lagash: Pre-Sargonic and Ur III." *ASJ* 2:81–125.

Malul, Meir. 1987. "Gag-ru: *Sikkatam maḫāṣum/retûm*, 'To Drive in the Nail'; An Act of Posting a Public Notice." *OA* 26:17–35.

Márquez Rowe, Ignacio. 2003. "Alalakh." Pages 693–718 in *A History of Ancient Near Eastern Law*. Edited by Raymond Westbrook. HdO 72. Leiden: Brill.

Matouš, Lubor. 1965. "Anatolische Feste nach kappadokischen Tafeln." Pages 175–82 in *Studies in Honor of Benno Landsberger on His Seventy-Fifth Birthday, April 21, 1965*. Edited by Hans Gustav Güterbock and Thorkild Jacobsen. AS 16. Chicago: University of Chicago Press.

———. 1973. “Beiträge zum Eherecht der anatolischen, Bevölkerung im 2. Jhts. v.u.Z.” *ArOr* 41:309–18.

———. 1974. “Der Aššur-Tempel nach Altassyrischen Urkunden aus Kültepe.” Pages 181–89 in *Travels in the World of the Old Testament: Studies Presented to Professor M. A. Beek*. Edited by N. A. van Uchelen, Philo H. J. Houwink Ten Cate, M. A. Beek, and Matthieu S. H. G. Heerma van Voss. SSN 16. Assen: Van Gorcum.

———. 1982. “Zur Korrespondenz des Imdīlum mit Taram-kubi.” Pages 268–70 in *Zikir Šumim: Assyriological Studies Presented to F. R. Kraus on the Occasion of His Seventieth Birthday*. Edited by Govert van Driel. Leiden: Brill.

McCarthy, Andrew. 2016. “Businesswomen and Their Seals in Early Mesopotamia.” Pages 101–12 in *Women in Antiquity: Real Women across the Ancient World*. Edited by Stephanie Lynn Budin and Jean MacIntosh Turfa. London: Routledge.

Michalowski, Piotr. 2011. *The Correspondence of the Kings of Ur: An Epistolary History of an Ancient Mesopotamian Kingdom*. MC 15. Winona Lake, IN: Eisenbrauns.

Michel, Cécile. 1986. “Réédition des trente tablettes ‘cappadociennes’ de G. Contenau.” *RA* 80:105–40.

———. 1991. *Innāya dans les tablettes paléo-assyriennes*. 2 vols. Paris: Editions recherches sur les civilisations.

———. 1994. “Règlement des comptes du défunt Huraṣānum.” *RA* 88:121–28.

———. 1997a. “Hommes et femmes prêtent serment à l’époque paléo-assyrienne.” Pages 105–23 in *“Jurer et maudire”: Pratiques politiques et usages juridiques du serment dans le Proche-Orient ancien; Actes de la table ronde*. Edited by Francis Joannès and Sophie Lafont. Méd 10–11. Paris: Harmattan.

———. 1997b. “Propriétés immobilières dans les tablettes paléo-assyriennes.” Pages 285–300 in *Houses and Households in Ancient Mesopotamia*. Edited by Klaas R. Veenhof. CRRAI 40; PIHANS 78. Istanbul: Nederlands Historisch-Archaeologisch Instituut te Istanbul.

———. 1997c. “Une incantation paléo-assyrienne contre Lamaštum.” *Or* 66:58–64.

———. 1997d. “Un témoignage paléo-assyrien en faveur du port du voile par la femme mariée.” *NABU*: art. 40.

———. 1997e. “Les malheurs de Kunnanīya, femme de marchand.” *ArAn* 3:239–53.

———. 1997f. "À table avec les marchands paléo-assyriens." Pages 95–113 in *Assyrien im Wandel der Zeiten: XXXIXe Rencontre assyriologique internationale, Heidelberg, 6.–10. Juli 1992*. Edited by Hartmut Waetzoldt and Harald Hauptmann. CRRAI 39; HSAO 6. Heidelberg: Heidelberger Orientverlag.

———. 1997g. "Les enfants des marchands de Kaniš." *Ktèma* 22:91–108.

———. 1998a. "Quelques réflexions sur les archives récentes de Kültepe." Pages 419–33 in *III. Uluslararası Hititoloji Kongresi: Çorum, 16–22 Eylül, 1996 / Acts of the IIIrd International Congress of Hittitology: Çorum, September 16–22, 1996*. Edited by Sedat Alp and Aygül Süel. Ankara: Uyum Ajans.

———. 1998b. "'Les mites d'Assyrie': Moths in the Assyrian Texts of the Second Millenium B.C." *JAOS* 118:325–31.

———. 2000a. "Les litiges commerciaux paléo-assyriens." Pages 113–39 in *Rendre la justice en Mésopotamie: Archives judiciaires du Proche-Orient ancien (IIIe–Ier millénaire avant J.-C.)*. Edited by Francis Joannès. Saint-Denis: Presses Universitaires de Vincennes.

———. 2000b. "À propos d'un testament paléo-assyrien: Une femme 'père et mère' des capitaux." *RA* 94:1–10.

———. 2001a. *Correspondance des marchands de Kaniš au début du IIe millénaire av. J.-C.* LAPO 19. Paris: Éditions du Cerf.

———. 2001b. Review of *Cuneiform Texts in the Sadberk Hanım Museum*, by Veysel Donbaz. *BiOr* 58:176–81.

———. 2003a. *Old Assyrian Bibliography of Cuneiform Texts, Bullae, Seals and the Results of the Excavations at Assur, Kültepe/Kanis, Acemhöyük, Alishar and Bogazköy*. OAAS 1; PIHANS 97. Leiden: Nederlands Instituut voor het Nabije Oosten.

———. 2003b. "Les femmes et les dettes: Problèmes de responsabilité dans la Mésopotamie du IIe millénaire avant J.-C." *Méditerranées* 34–35:13–36.

———. 2004. "Deux incantations paléo-assyriennes. Une nouvelle incantation pour faciliter la naissance." Pages 395–420 in *Assyria and Beyond: Studies Presented to Mogens Trolle Larsen*. Edited by Jan Gerrit Dercksen. PIHANS 100. Leiden: Nederlands Instituut voor het Nabije Oosten.

———. 2006a. "Bigamie chez les Assyriens du début du IIe millénaire." *RHDE* 84:155–76.

———. 2006b. "Femmes et production textile à Aššur au début du IIe millénaire avant J.-C." *T&C* 46:281–97.

———. 2006c. "Old Assyrian Bibliography 1 (February 2003–July 2006)." *AfO* 51:436–49.

———. 2006d. "Les suidés dans la documentation de Kaniš au début du IIe millénaire avant J.-C." Pages 169–80 in *De la domestication au tabou: Le cas des suidés au Proche-Orient ancien*. Edited by in Brigitte Lion and Cécile Michel. TMRG 1. Paris: de Boccard.

———. 2006e. "Calculer chez les marchands assyriens du début du IIe millénaire av. J.-C." CultureMATH: Site de ressources mathématiques pour les enseignants. Département de mathématiques de l'École normale supérieure de Paris. June 2006. https://tinyurl.com/SBL1539a.

———. 2008a. "'Tu aimes trop l'argent et méprises ta vie': Le commerce lucratif des Assyriens en Anatolie centrale." Pages 37–62 in *La richessa nel Vicino Oriente Antico, Atti del Convegno internazionale Milano 20 gennaio 2007*. Centro Studi del Vicino Oriente, Milan. HAL: Archives-ouvertes.fr. https://tinyurl.com/SBL1539b.

———. 2008b. "Écrire et compter chez les marchands assyriens du début du IIe millénaire av. J.-C." Pages 345–64 in *Muhibbe Darga Armağanı*. Edited by Aksel Tibet, Erkan Konyar, and Taner Tarhan. Istanbul: Sadberk Hanim Muzesi Yayini.

———. 2008c. "Les Assyriens et leurs femmes anatoliennes." Pages 209–29 in *Anatolia and the Jazira during the Old Assyrian Period*. Edited by Jan Gerritt Dercksen. OAAS 3; PIHANS 111. Leiden: Nederlands Instituut voor het Nabije Oosten.

———. 2008d. "Femmes au foyer et femmes en voyage: Le cas des épouses des marchands assyriens au début du IIe millénaire av. J.-C." *ClioH* 28:17–38.

———. 2008e. "The Alāhum and Aššur-taklāku Archives Found in 1993 at Kültepe Kaniš." *AoF* 35:53–67, 359.

———. 2008f. "Les Assyriens et les esprits de leurs morts." Pages 181–97 in *Old Assyrian Studies in Memory of Paul Garelli*. Edited by Cécile Michel. OAAS 4; PIHANS 112. Leiden: Nederlands Instituut voor het Nabije Oosten.

———. 2008g. "La correspondance des marchands assyriens du XIXe s. av. J.-C.: De l'archivage des lettres commerciales et privées." Pages 117–40 in *La lettre d'archive: Communication administrative et personnelle dans l'Antiquité proche-orientale et égyptienne; Actes du colloque de l'Université de Lyon 2; 9–10 juillet 2004*. Edited by Laure Pantalacci. TopoiSup 9. Le Caire: Institut français d'archeologie orientale.

———. 2009a. "Femmes et ancêtres: Le cas des femmes des marchands d'Aššur." Pages 27–39 in *Femmes, cultures et sociétés dans les civilisations méditerranéennes et proches-orientales de l'antiquité*. Edited by Françoise Briquel-Chatonnet, Saba Farès-Drappeau, Brigitte Lion, and Cécile Michel. TopoiSup 10. Paris: de Boccard.

———. 2009b. "Les filles de marchands consacrées." Pages 145–63 in *Femmes, cultures et sociétés dans les civilisations méditerranéennes et proches-orientales de l'antiquité*. Edited by Françoise Briquel-Chatonnet, Saba Farès-Drappeau, Brigitte Lion, and Cécile Michel. TopoiSup 10. Paris: de Boccard.

———. 2009c. "Les femmes et l'écrit dans les archives paléo-assyriennes (XIXe s. av. J.-C.)." Pages 253–72 in *Femmes, cultures et sociétés dans les civilisations méditerranéennes et proches-orientales de l'antiquité*. Edited by Françoise Briquel-Chatonnet, Saba Farès-Drappeau, Brigitte Lion, and Cécile Michel. TopoiSup 10. Paris: de Boccard.

———. 2009d. "Dis-moi ce que tu bois…" Boissons et buveurs en haute Mésopotamie et Anatolie au début du IIe millénaire av. J.-C." Pages 197–220 *Et il y eut un esprit dans l'Homme: Jean Bottéro et la Mésopotamie*. Edited by Xavier Faivre, Brigitte Lion, and Cécile Michel. TMRG 6. Paris: de Boccard.

———. 2010a. "Women of Aššur and Kaniš." Pages 124–33 in *Anatolia's Prologue: Kultepe, Kanesh, Karum; Assyrians in Istanbul*. Edited by Fikri Kulakoğlu and Selmin Kangal. KMMCP 78. Istanbul: Kayseri Metropolitan Municipality.

———. 2010b. "Writing, Counting and Scribal Education in Aššur and Kaniš." Pages 82–93 in *Anatolia's Prologue: Kultepe, Kanesh, Karum; Assyrians in Istanbul*. Edited by Fikri Kulakoğlu and Selmin Kangal. KMMCP 78. Istanbul: Kayseri Metropolitan Municipality.

———. 2010c. "Presentation of an Old Assyrian Document." Pages 98–99 in *Anatolia's Prologue: Kultepe, Kanesh, Karum; Assyrians in Istanbul*. Edited by Fikri Kulakoğlu and Selmin Kangal. KMMCP 78. Istanbul: Kayseri Metropolitan Municipality.

———. 2010d. "Le langage figuré dans les lettres paléo-assyriennes: Expressions relatives à l'homme et à la nature." Pages 347–76 in vol. 1 of *Language in the Ancient Near East: Proceedings of the 53e Rencontre Assyriologique Internationale*. Edited by Leonid E. Kogan. BabBib 4. Winona Lake, IN: Eisenbrauns.

———. 2010e. "The Day Unit within the Old Assyrian Calendar." Pages 217–24 in *DUB. SAR É. DUB. BA. A Veysel Donbaz'a sunulan yazılar*

/ *Studies Presented in Honour of Veysel Donbaz*. Edited by Şevket Dönmez. Istanbul: Ege Yayınları.

———. 2010f. "Les comptoirs de commerce assyriens en Anatolie: Emprunts réciproques et acculturation." Pages 1–12 in *Portraits de migrants, portraits de colons II*. Edited by Pierre Rouillard. CMRG 6. Paris: de Boccard.

———. 2011a. "Old Assyrian Bibliography 2 (July 2006–April 2009)." *AfO* 52:416–37.

———. 2011b. "The Kārum Period on the Plateau." Pages 313–36 in *Handbook of Ancient Anatolian (10,000–323 B.C.E.)*. Edited by Sharon R. Steadman and John G. McMahon. Oxford: Oxford University Press.

———. 2011c. "The Private Archives from Kaniš Belonging to Anatolians." *AoF* 38:94–115.

———. 2012. "Talhai/wum, Talhāyum, Talhat." *RlA* 13:420–21.

———. 2014a. "Considerations on the Assyrian Settlement at Kaneš." Pages 69–84 in *Current Research at Kültepe/Kanesh: An Interdisciplinary and Integrative Approach to Trade Networks, Internationalism, and Identity*. Edited by Levent Atici, Fikri Kulakoğlu, Gojko Barjamovic, and Andrew Fairbairn. JCSSup 4. Atlanta: Lockwood.

———. 2014b. "Old Assyrian Kaniš (Akkadian Texts: Women in Letters)." Pages 205–12 in *Women in the Ancient Near East: A Sourcebook*. Edited by Mark W. Chavalas. London: Routledge.

———. 2014c. "The Assyrian Textile Trade in Anatolia (19th century BCE): From Traded Goods to Prestigious Gifts." Pages 111–22 in *Textile Trade and Distribution in Antiquity / Textilhandel und -distribution in der Antike*. Edited by Kerstin Dross-Krüpe. Philippika 73. Wiesbaden: Harrassowitz.

———. 2014d. "Wool Trade in Upper Mesopotamia and Syria According to Old Babylonian and Old Assyrian Texts." Pages 232–54 in *Wool Economy in the Ancient Near East and the Aegean: From the Beginnings of Sheep Husbandry to Institutional Textile Industry*. Edited by Catherine Breniquet and Cécile Michel. ATS 17. Oxford: Oxbow.

———. 2014e. "Central Anatolia in the Nineteenth and Eighteenth Centuries BC." Pages 111–36 in *Constituent, Confederate, and Conquered Space: The Emergence of the Mittani State*. Edited by Nicole Brisch, Eva Cancik-Kirschbaum, and Jesper Eidem. Topoi 17. Berlin: de Gruyter.

———. 2014f. "The Economic Role of Women in the Old Assyrian Sources." Pages 93–101 in *Le rôle économique des femmes en Mésopotamie anci-*

enne (REFEMA) / Women's Role in the Economy of the Ancient Near East: Report December 31, 2011–December 30, 2014. Edited by Francis Joannès and Fumi Karahashi. Nanterre: REFEMA; Tokyo: Japan Society for the Promotion of Science.

———. 2015a. "Quelle place occupent les femmes dans les sources cunéiformes de la pratique?" *NdA* 140:46–50.

———. 2015b. "Women in the Family of Ali-ahum son of Iddin-Suen (1993 Kültepe Archive)." Pages 85–93 in *Proceedings of the 1st Kültepe International Meeting, Kültepe, 19–23 September, 2013: Studies Dedicated to Kutlu Emre*. Edited by Fikri Kulakoğlu and Cécile Michel. KIM 1; Subartu 35. Turnhout: Brepols.

———. 2015c. "Les lettres des rois d'Aššur découvertes à Kaniš (XIXe siècle av. J.-C.)." Pages 43–60 in *Official Epistolography and the Language(s) of Power: Proceedings of the First International Conference of the Research Network Imperium and Officium; Comparative Studies in Ancient Bureaucracy and Officialdom, University of Vienna, 10–12 November 2010*. Edited by in Stephan Procházka, Lucian Reinfandt, and Sven Tost. PapVin 8. Vienna: Verlag der Österreichischen Akademie der Wissenschaften.

———. 2015d. "Were There Only Merchants at Aššur and Kaneš? Overview of Professions Attested in the Old Assyrian Sources." Pages 171–84 in *Cahit Günbattı Armağan: Studies in Honour of Cahit Günbattı*. Edited by İrfan Albayrak, Hakan Erol, and Murat Çayır. Ankara: Ankara Üniversitesi Dil ve Tarih-Coğrafya Fakültesi.

———. 2015e. "Old Assyrian Bibliography 3 (May 2009–June 2015)." *AfO* 53:525–59.

———. 2016a. "Women Work, Men are Professionals in the Old Assyrian Private Archives." Pages 199–214 in *The Role of Women in Work and Society in the Ancient Near East*. Edited by Brigitte Lion and Cécile Michel. SANER 13. Berlin: de Gruyter.

———. 2016b. "Les médaillons solaires dans la documentation paléo-assyrienne: Des bijoux pour les dieux." Pages 319–29 in *Mille et une empreintes: Un Alsacien en Orient; Mélanges en l'honneur du 65e anniversaire de Dominique Beyer*. Edited by Pascal Butterlin, Julie Patrier, and Philippe Quenet. Subartu 36. Turnhout: Brepols.

———. 2016c. "Estimating an Old Assyrian Household Textile Production with the Help of Experimental Archaeology: Feasibility and Limitations." Pages 118–30 in *Traditional Textile Craft: An Intangible Cultural Heritage?* Edited by Camilla Ebert, Mary Harlow, Eva Andersson Strand, and Lena Bjerregaard. Copenhagen: Centre for Textile Research, University of Copenhagen.

———. 2016d. "Women and Real Estate in the Old Assyrian Texts." *Orient* 51:83–94.

———. 2016e. "Quelques remarques sur les bullæ inscrites de la ville basse de Kültepe." Pages 175–84 in *Parcours d'Orient: Recueil de textes offerts à Christine Kepinski*. Edited by Bérengère Perello and Aline Tenu Oxford: Archaeopress.

———. 2017. "Economy, Society, and Daily Life in the Old Assyrian Period." Pages 80–107 in *A Companion to Assyria*. Edited by Eckart Frahm. BCAW 113. Oxford: Wiley & Sons.

———. 2018. "Constitution, Contents, Filing and Use of Private Archives: The Case of the Old Assyrian Archives (Nineteeth Century BC)." Pages 43–70 in *Manuscripts and Archives: Comparative Views on Record-Keeping*. Edited by Alessandro Bausi, Christian Brockmann, Michael Friedrich, and Sabine Kienitz. SMC 11. Berlin: de Gruyter.

———. Forthcoming a. "Belts and Pins as Gendered Elements of Clothing in Third and Second Millennia Mesopotamia." In *Textiles and Gender in Antiquity: From the Orient to the Mediterranean*. Edited by Mary Harlow, Cécile Michel, and Louise Quillien.

———. Forthcoming b. "Calendars in Old Assyrian Sources." In vol. 2 of *Calendars and Festivals, Cultures and Societies in the Middle Euphrates and Habur Areas in the Second Millennium BC*. Edited by Daisuke Shibata and Shigeo Yamada. StCh.

———. Forthcoming c. "Weighing Units and Weights in the Context of Trade from Upper Mesopotamia to Anatolia (Nineteenth and Eighteenth Centuries BCE)." In *Cultures of Quantification and Computation*. Edited by Karine Chemla, Agathe Keller, and Christine Proust. Why the Sciences of the Ancient World Matter.

Michel, Cécile, and Paul Garelli. 1996. "New Old Assyrian Marriage Contracts." *AMMY* 1995:295–302.

Michel, Cécile, and Marie-Louise Nosch, eds. 2010. *Textile Terminologies in the Ancient Near East and Mediterranean from the Third to the First Millennnia BC*. ATS 8. Oxford: Oxbow.

Michel, Cécile, and Klaas R. Veenhof. 2010. "The Textiles Traded by the Assyrians in Anatolia (Nineteenth–Eighteenth Centuries BC)." Pages 209–69 in *Textile Terminologies in the Ancient Near East and Mediterranean from the Third to the First Millennnia BC*. Edited by Cécile Michel and Marie-Louise Nosch. ATS 8. Oxford: Oxbow.

Moren, S. M. 1980. "Four Old Assyrian Tablets in a Private Collection." *Or* 50:98–105.

Nakata, Ichiro. 2016. "Economic Activities of *Nadītum*-Women of Šamaš Reflected in the Field Sale Contracts (MHET II/1–6)." Pages 255–69 in *The Role of Women in Work and Society in the Ancient Near East*. Edited by Brigitte Lion and Cécile Michel. SANER 13. Berlin: de Gruyter.

Owen, David I. 1980. "A Sumerian Letter from an Angry Housewife?" Pages 189–202 in *The Bible World: Studies in Honor of Cyrus H. Gordon*. Edited by Gary Rendsburg, Ruth Adler, Milton Arfa, and Nathan H. Winter. New York: Ktav.

Öz, Esma. 2014. *Kültepe Metinleri Işığında Eski Anadolu'da Tarım ve Hayvancılık*. TTKY 5.6. Ankara: Türk Tarih Kurumu Basımevi.

Özgüç, Nimet. 1996. "Seal Impressions on Kültepe Documents notarized by Native Rules." Pages 267–78 in *Collectanea Orientalia: Histoire, arts de l'espace et industrie de la terre; Mélanges offertes en hommage à Agnès Spycket*. Edited by Hermann Gasche and Barthel Hrouda. CPOA 3. Neuchâtel: Recherches et publications.

———. 2006. *Seal Impressions on the Clay Envelopes from the Archives of the Native Peruwa and Assyrian Trader Uṣur-ša-Ištar, Son of Aššur-imittī*. TTKY 5.50. Ankara: Türk Tarih Kurumu Basımevi.

Özgüç, Tahsin. 1986. *Kültepe-Kaniş II: Eski Yakindoğu'nun ticaret merkezinde yeni araştirmalar / New Researches at the Trading Center of the Ancient Near East*. TTKY 5.41. Ankara: Türk Tarih Kurumu Basımevi.

———. 1994. "A Boat-Shaped Cult-Vessel from the Karum of Kanish." Pages 369–75 in *Cinquante-deux réflexions sur le Proche-Orient ancien: Offertes en homage à Léon de Meyer*. Edited by Hermann Gasche, Michel Tanret, Caroline Janssen, and Ann Degraeve. Leuven: Peeters.

———. 1999. *Kültepe-Kaniš/Neša sarayları ve mabetleri / The Palaces and Temples of Kültepe-Kaniš/Neša*. TTKY 5.46. Ankara: Türk Tarih Kurumu Basımevi.

———. 2001. "Observations on the Architectural Peculiarities of the Archive of an Assyrian Trader of Kārum Kanesh." Pages 367–71 in *Veenhof Anniversary Volume: Studies Presented to Klaas R. Veenhof on the Occasion of His Sixty-Fifth Birthday*. Edited by Wilfried Hugo van Soldt, Jan Gerrit Dercksen, N. J. C. Kouwenberg, and Theo J. H. Krispijn. PIHANS 89. Leiden: Nederlands Instituut voor het Nabije Oosten.

———. 2003. *Kultepe Kaniš/Neša: The Earliest International Trade Center and the Oldest Capital City of the Hittites*. N.p.: Middle Eastern Culture Center in Japan.

———. 2004. "Archives of the Karum at Kaniš, Level Ib." Pages 445–450 in *Assyria and Beyond: Studies Presented to Mogens Trolle Larsen*. Edited by Jan Gerrit Dercksen. PIHANS 100. Leiden: Nederlands Instituut voor het Nabije Oosten.

Parayre, Dominique. 1997. "Les âges de la vie dans le répertoire figuratif oriental." *Ktèma* 22:59–89.

Parpola, Simo, and Robert M. Whiting, eds. 2002. *Sex and Gender in the Ancient Near East: Proceedings of the Forty-Seventh Rencontre Assyriologique Internationale, Helsinki, July 2–6, 2001*. Helsinki: Neo-Assyrian Text Corpus Project.

Pedersén, Olof. 1986. *Archives and Libraries in the City of Assur: A Survey of the Material from the German Excavations*, part 1: *1985*, part 2: *1986*. Acta Universitatis Upsaliensis 6. Uppsala: Uppsala University.

Postgate, J. N. 2014. "Wool, Hair and Textiles in Assyria." Pages 401–27 in *Wool Economy in the Ancient Near East and the Aegean: From the Beginnings of Sheep Husbandry to Institutional Textile Industry*. Edited by Catherine Breniquet and Cécile Michel. ATS 17. Oxford: Oxbow.

Powell, Marvin A. 1990. "Masse und Gewichte." *RlA* 7:457–517.

Reculeau, Hervé. 2018. "On Some Metrological Issues Affecting Yield Estimates in Second-Millennium BCE Upper Mesopotamia." *JCS* 70:87–114.

Rems, R. 1996. "Eine Kleinigkeit zum altassyrischen Eherecht." Pages 355–67 in *Festschrift für Hans Hirsch zum 65. Geburtstag: Gewidmet von seinem Freunden, Kollegen und Schülern*. Edited by Arne A. Ambros, Markus Köhbach, and Claudia Römer. WZKM 86. Vienna: Institut für Orientalistik.

Renger, Johannes. 1967. "Untersuchung zum Priestertum in der altbabylonischen Zeit, 1. Teil." *ZA* 58:110–88.

———. 1969. "Untersuchung zum Priestertum in der altbabylonischen Zeit, 2. Teil." *ZA* 59:104–230.

Ricetti, Melissa. 2017. "Sealing without a Seal: Alternative Sealing Media at Kültepe during the Old Assyrian Period." Pages 131–60 in *Movement, Resources, Interaction: Proceedings of the Second Kültepe International Meeting, Kültepe, 26–30 July 2015; Studies Dedicated to Klaas Veenhof*. Edited by Fikri Kulakoğlu and Gojko Barjamovic. KIM 2; Subartu 39. Turnhout: Brepols.

Ridder, Jacob Jan de. 2015. "On the Etymology of the Old and Middle Assyrian *Nasbītu*-Festival (<*naṣbutu*)." *NABU*: art. 120–21.

———. 2017a. “Testaments and Division of Assyrian Estates in the Second Millennium BC.” *AulaOr* 35:51–84.

———. 2017b. “Slavery in Old Assyrian Documents.” Pages 49–61 in *Movement, Resources, Interaction: Proceedings of the Second Kültepe International Meeting, Kültepe, 26–30 July 2015; Studies Dedicated to Klaas Veenhof*. Edited by Fikri Kulakoğlu and Gojko Barjamovic. KIM 2; Subartu 39. Turnhout: Brepols.

Rosen, B. L. 1977. “Studies in Old Assyrian Loan Contracts.” PhD diss., Brandeis University.

Roth, Martha T. 1987. “Age at Marriage and the Household: A Study of Neo-Babylonian and Neo-Assyrian Forms.” *CSSH* 29:715–47.

———. 1997. *Law Collection from Mesopotamia and Asia Minor*. WAW 6. 2nd ed. Atlanta: Scholars Press.

Scott, Joan W. 2010. “Gender: Still a Useful Category of Analysis?” *Diogenes* 57:7–14.

Scurlock, Joann. 2002. “Soul Emplacements in Ancient Mesopotamian Funerary Rituals.” Pages 1–6 in *Magic and Divination in the Ancient World*. Edited by Leda Ciraolo and Jonathan Seidel. AMD 2. Leiden: Brill.

Sever, Hüseyin. 1992a. “Anadolu'da nişanın bozulması hakkında verilmiş Kaniş karumu kararı.” *Belleten* 56:667–75.

———. 1992b. “Eine neue Ehescheidungsurkunde.” Pages 483–86 in *Hittite and Other Anatolian and Near Eastern Studies in Honour of Sedat Alp*. Edited by Heinrich Otten, Ekrem Akurgal, Hayri Ertem, and Aygül Süel. Ankara: Türk Tarih Kurumu Basımevi.

———. 1995. “Yeni Belgelerin Işığında Koloni Çağında Yerli Halk ıle Asurlu Tüccarlar Arasındaki İlişkiler.” *Belleten* 59:1–16.

———. 1998. “Köleştı Hakkında Yeni Kültepe Metinleri.” Pages 485–94 in *XXXIVème Rencontre Assyriologique Internationale 6–10; VII. 1987 Istanbul / XXXIV. Uluslararasi Assırıyolojı Kongresi 6–10; VII. 1987 Istanbul / XXXIV. International Assyriology Congress 6–10; VII. 1987 Istanbul*. Edited by H. Erkanal, Veysel Donbaz, and Ayşegül Uğuroğlu. CRRAI 34; TTKY 26.3. Ankara: Türk Tarıh Kurumu Basımevi.

Sever, Hüseyin, and Salih Çeçen. 2000. “‘*Naruqqum*’: Ortaklığı Hakkında Yeni Bir Belge.” *ArAn* 4:167–76.

Sharlach, Tonia M. 2017. *An Ox of One's Own: Royal Wives and Religion at the Court of the Third Dynasty of Ur*. Berlin: de Gruyter.

Soden, Wolfram von. 1976. “Ein altassyrisches Testament.” *WO* 8:211–17.

Stein, Gil J. 2008. "A Theoretical Model for Political Economy and Social Identity in the Old Assyrian Colonies of Anatolia." *TÜBA-AR* 11:25–37.

Stol, Marten. 1991. "Eine Prozessurkunde über 'falsches Zeugnis.'" Pages 333–39 in *Marchands, diplomates et empereurs: Études sur la civilisation mésopotamienne offertes à Paul Garelli*. Edited by Dominique Charpin and Francis Joannes. Paris: Éditions Recherche sur les Civilisations.

———. 1995a. "Women in Mesopotamia." *JESHO* 38:123–44.

———. 1995b. "Private Life in Ancient Mesopotamia." Pages 485–501 in vol. 1 of *Civilizations of the Ancient Near East*. Edited by Jack M. Sasson. New York: Scribner's Sons.

———. 2000a. *Birth in Babylonia and the Bible: Its Mediterranean Setting*. Groningen: Styx.

———. 2000b. "Titel altbabylonischer Klosterfrauen." Pages 457–66 in *Assyriologica et semitica: Festschrift für Joachim Oelsner anlässlich seines 65. Geburtstages am 18. Februar 1997*. Edited by Joachim Oelsner, Joachim Marzahn, Hans Neumann, and Andreas Fuchs. AOAT 252. Münster: Ugarit-Verlag.

———. 2016. *Women in the Ancient Near East*. Berlin: de Gruyter.

Stratford, Edward. 2015a. "Eponyms, Debt Notes, Intercalation, and the Old Assyrian Calendar during Kültepe Level II: A Critical Reappraisal." *JNES* 74:301–24.

———. 2015b. "Old Assyrian Literacy: Formulating a Method for Graphic Analysis and Some Initial Results." Pages 117–28 in *Proceedings of the First Kültepe International Meeting, Kültepe, 19–23 September, 2013: Studies Dedicated to Kutlu Emre*. Edited by Fikri Kulakoğlu and Cécile Michel. Subartu 35. Turnhout: Brepols.

———. 2017. *Time, Narrative, and the Old Assyrian Trade*. Vol. 1 of *A Year of Vengeance*. SANER 17. Berlin: de Gruyter.

Sturm, Thomas. 1995. "Qannuttum, eine Dame in Assur zur aA Zeit." *NABU*: art. 37.

———. 1999. "Datteln und Dattelpalmzweige in den altassyrischen (aA) Texten vom Kültepe." *NABU*: art. 31.

———. 2001. "Puzur-Annā: Ein Schmied des Kārum Kaniš." Pages 475–501 in *Veenhof Anniversary Volume: Studies Presented to Klaas R. Veenhof on the Occasion of His Sixty-Fifth Birthday*. Edited by Wilfried Hugo van Soldt, Jan Gerrit Dercksen, N. J. C. Kouwenberg, and Theo J. H. Krispijn. PIHANS 89. Leiden: Nederlands Instituut voor het Nabije Oosten.

———. 2008. "Allanu - Haselnüsse als Delikatesse im karum-zeitlichen Handel von Anatolien nach Nordmesopotamien (ca. 1930-1730 v.Chr). " *AoF* 35:296–311.

Suter, Claudia E. 2008. "Who Are the Women in Mesopotamian Art from ca. 2334–1763 BCE?" *KASKAL* 5:1–55.

Svärd, Saana, and Agnès Garcia-Ventura. 2018. *Studying Gender in the Ancient Near East.* University Park, PA: Eisenbrauns.

Taggar-Cohen, Ada. 2006. "The NIN.DINGIR in the Hittite Kingdom: A Mesopotamian Priestly Office in Hatti?" *AoF* 33:313–27.

Teissier, Beatrice. 1994. *Sealing and Seals on Texts from Kültepe Kārum Level 2.* PIHANS 70. Istanbul: Nederlands Historisch-Archaeologisch Instituut te Istambul.

Thébaud, Françoise. 1998. *Écrire l'histoire des femmes.* Fontenay-aux-Roses: ENS éditions Fontenay Saint-Cloud.

Thomason, Allison Karmel. 2013. "Her Share of the Profits: Women, Agency, and Textile Production at Kültepe/Kanesh in the Early Second Millennium BC." Pages 93–112 in *Textile Production and Consumption in the Ancient Near East: Archaeology, Epigraphy, Iconography.* Edited by Marie-Louise Nosch, Henriette Koefoed, and Eva Andersson Strand. ATS 12. Havertown: Oxbow.

———. 2018. "Her Share of the Profits: Women, Agency, and Textiles Production at Kültepe/Kanesh in the Early Second Millennium BC." Pages 93–112 in *Studying Gender in the Ancient Near East: Rencontre assyriologique internationale / RAI 59 Workshop.* Edited by Saana Svärd and Agnès Garcia-Ventura. Winona Lake, IN: Eisenbrauns.

Toorn, Karel van der. 1996. *Family Religion in Babylonia, Syria and Israel: Continuity and Change in the Forms of Religious Life.* CHANE 7. Leiden: Brill.

Ulshöfer, Andrea Marie. 1995. *Die altassyrischen Privaturkunden.* FAOS 4. Stuttgart: Steiner.

———. 2000. "Sprachbarrieren und ihre Überwindung: Translatorisches Handeln im alten Orient." Pages 163–69 in *Geography and Cultural Landscapes.* Vol. 2 of *Landscapes, Territories, Frontiers and Horizons in the Ancient Near East: Papers Presented to the XLIV Rencontre Assyriologique Internationale, Venezia, 7–11 July 1997.* Edited by Lucio Milano, Stefano de Martino, Frederick M. Fales, and Giovanni B. Lanfranchi. CRRAI 44; HANE 3/2. Padova: Sargon.

Üstündağ, Handan. 2014. "Human Remains from Kültepe-Kanesh: Preliminary Results of the Old Assyrian Burials from the 2005–2008

Excavations." Pages 157–76 in *Current Research at Kültepe/Kanesh: An Interdisciplinary and Integrative Approach to Trade Networks, Internationalism, and Identity*. JCSSup 4. Atlanta: Lockwood.

Uzunalimoğlu, Ayşe. 1992. "1950 Yılında Kültepe Kazısında Bulunan 5 Adet Mahkeme Kararı." *AMMY* 1990:44–53.

Van de Mieroop, Marc. 1999. *Cuneiform Texts and the Writing of History*. London: Routledge.

Van der Stede, Véronique. 2007. *Mourir au pays des deux fleuves. L'au-delà mésopotamien d'après les sources sumériennes et akkadiennes*. LO 12. Leuven: Peeters.

Veenhof, Klaas R. 1972. *Aspects of Old Assyrian Trade and Its Terminology*. SDIO 10. Leiden: Bill.

———. 1978. "An Ancient Anatolian Money-Lender: His Loans, Securities and Debt-Slaves." Pages 279–311 in vol. 2 of *Festchrift Lubor Matouš*. Edited by Blahoslav Hruska and Géza Komoróczy. Budapest: Eötvös Loránd Tudományegyetem, Ókori Történeti Tanszékek.

———. 1982a. "The Old Assyrian Merchants and Their Relations with the Native Population of Anatolia." Pages 147–55 in *Mesopotamien und seine Nachbarn: Politische und kulturelle Wechselbeziehungen im Alten Vorderasien vom 4. bis 1. Jahrtausend v. Chr*. Edited by Hans Jörg Nissen and Johannes Renger. CRRAI 25; BBVO 1. Berlin: Reimer.

———. 1982b. "A Deed of Manumission and Adoption from the Later Old Assyrian Period." Pages 359–81 in *Zikir Šumim: Assyriological Studies Presented to F. R. Kraus on the Occasion of His Seventieth Birthday*. Edited by Govent van Driel. Leiden: Brill.

———. 1991. "Assyrian Commercial Activities in Old Babylonian Sippar: Some New Evidence." Pages 287–303 in *Marchands, diplomates et empereurs: Études sur la civilisation mésopotamienne offertes à Paul Garelli*. Edited by Dominique Charpin and Francis Joannes. Paris: Éditions Recherche sur les Civilisations.

———. 1992. "*Makkārum*, 'Trader'?" *NABU*: art. 5.

———. 1995. "'In Accordance with the Words of the Stele": Evidence for Old Asyrian Legislation." *CKLR* 70:1717–44.

———. 1996. "The Old Assyrian *Hamuštum* Period: A Seven-Day Week." *JEOL* 34:5–26.

———. 1997a. "Two Marriage Documents from Kültepe." *ArAn* 3:357–81.

———. 1997b. "Old Assyrian and Ancient Anatolian Evidence for the Care of the Elderly." Pages 119–60 in *The Care of the Elderly in the Ancient Near East*. Edited by Marten Stol and Sven P. Vleeming. Leiden: Brill.

———. 1998. "The Chronology of *Kārum* Kanish: Some New Observations." Pages 421–50 in *XXXIVème Rencontre Assyriologique Internationale 6–10; VII. 1987 Istanbul / XXXIV. Uluslararasi Assırıyolojı Kongresi 6–10; VII. 1987 Istanbul / XXXIV. International Assyriology Congress 6–10; VII. 1987 Istanbul.* Edited by Hayat Erkanal, Veysel Donbaz, and Ayşegül Uğuroğlu. CRRAI 34; TTKY 26.3. Ankara: Türk Tarıh Kurumu Basımevi.

———. 1999a. "Silver and Credit in Old Assyrian Trade." Pages 55–83 in *Trade and Finance in Ancient Mesopotamia: Proceedings of the First MOS Symposium (Leiden, 1997).* Edited by Jan Gerrit Dercksen. MOS Studies 1. Leiden: Nederlands Institut voor het Nabije Oosten.

———. 1999b. "Redemption of Houses in Assur and Sippar." Pages 599–616 in *Munuscula Mesopotamica: Festschrift für Johannes Renger.* Edited by Barbara Böck, Eva Christiane Cancik-Kirschbaum, and Thomas Richter. AOAT 267. Münster: Ugarit-Verlag.

———. 2000. "Old Assyrian Chronology." *Akkadica* 119–20:137–50.

———. 2001. "The Old Assyrian Period." Pages 93–159 in *Security for Debt in Ancient Near Eastern Law.* Edited by Raymond Westbrook and Richard L. Jasnow. Leiden: Brill.

———. 2003a. "The Old Assyrian Period." Pages 431–84 in *A History of Ancient Near Eastern Law.* Edited by Raymond Westbrook. HdO 72. Leiden: Brill.

———. 2003b. "Three Unusual Old Assyrian Contracts." Pages 693–705 in *Festschrift für Burkhart Kienast zu seinem 70. Geburtstage dargebracht von Freuden, Schülern und Kollegen.* Edited by Gebhard J. Selz. AOAT 274. Münster: Ugarit-Verlag.

———. 2003c. "Trade and Politics in Ancient Assur: Balancing of Public, Colonial and Entrepreneurial Interests." Pages 69–118 in *Mercanti et Politica nel Mondo Antico.* Edited by Carlo Zaccagnini. SSA 21. Rome: L'Erma di Bretschneider.

———. 2003d. *The Old Assyrian List of Year Eponyms from Karum Kanish and Its Chronological Implications.* TTKY 6.64. Ankara: Turkish Historical Society.

———. 2003e. "Archives of Old Assyrian Traders." Pages 78–123 in *Ancient Archives and Archival Traditions: Concepts of Record-Keeping in the Ancient World.* Edited by Maria Brosius. Oxford: Oxford University Press.

———. 2007. "Sisterly Advice on an Endangered Marriage in an Old Assyrian Letter." Pages 285–304 in *Studies Presented to Robert D. Biggs, June*

4, 2004: From the Workshop of the Chicago Assyrian Dictionary. Edited by Walter Farber, Martha T. Roth, Matthew W. Stolper, and P. von Bechtolsheim. Vol. 2. Chicago: University of Chicago Press.
———. 2008a. "The Old Assyrian Period." Pages 13–264 in part 1 of *Mesopotamia: The Old Assyrian Period*. Edited by Markus Wäfler. Annäherungen 5; OBO 160.5. Fribourg: Academic Press.
———. 2008b. "The Death and Burial of Ishtar-Lamassi in Karum Kanish." Pages 97–119 in *Studies in Ancient Near Eastern World View and Society: Presented to Marten Stol on the Occasion of His Sixty-Fifth Birthday, 10 November 2005, and His Retirement from the Vrije Universiteit, Amsterdam*. Edited by Robartus J. van der Spek. Bethesda, MD: CDL.
———. 2008c. "Across the Euphrates." Pages 3–29 in *Anatolia and the Jazira during the Old Assyrian Period*. Edited by Jan Gerrit Dercksen. OAAS 3; PIHANS 111. Leiden: Nederlands Instituut voor het Nabije Oosten.
———. 2008d. "Communication in the Old Assyrian Trading Society by Caravans, Travelers and Messengers." Pages 199–246 in *Old Assyrian Studies in Memory of Paul Garelli*. Edited by Cécile Michel. OAAS 4; PIHANS 112. Leiden: Nederlands Instituut voor het Nabije Oosten.
———. 2011. "Houses in the Ancient City of Assur." Pages 211–31 in *Correlates of Complexity: Essays in Archaeology and Assyriology Dedicated to Diederik J. W. Meijer in Honour of his 65th Birthday*. Edited by Peter M. Akkermans, Arne Wossink, and Bleda S. During. PIHANS 116. Leiden: Nederlands Instituut voor het Nabije Oosten.
———. 2012a. "Last Wills and Inheritance of Old Assyrian Traders with Four Records from the Archive of Elamma." Pages 169–201 in *Family Cohesion in the Bible and the Ancient Near East: Studies in Honour of Aaron Skaist on the Occasion of His Seventy-Sixth Birthday*. Edited by K. Abraham and J. Fleishman. Bethesda, MD: CDL.
———. 2012b. "Old Assyrian and Old Babylonian Law: Some Comparative Observations." *ZAR* 18:141–74.
———. 2013a. "The Archives of Old Assyrian Traders: Their Nature, Functions and Use." Pages 27–71 in *Archives and Archival Documents in Ancient Societies: Legal Documents in Ancient Societies IV; Trieste 30 September–1 October 2011*. Edited by Michele Faraguna. Trieste: Edizioni Università di Trieste.
———. 2013b. "New Mesopotamian Treaties from the Early Second Millennium BC from *Kārum* Kanesh and Tell Leilan (Šehna)." *ZAR* 19:23–57.

———. 2014. "Families of Assyrian Traders." Pages 341–71 in *La famille dans le Proche-Orient ancien: Réalités, symbolismes et images; Proceedings of the Fifty-Fifth Rencontre Assyriologique Internationale at Paris, 6–9 July 2009*. Edited by Lionel Marti. Winona Lake, IN: Eisenbrauns.

———. 2015a. "Some Contributions to the Old Assyrian Lexicon." *Or* 84:217–75.

———. 2015b. "The Archive of Elamma son of Iddin-Suen and His Family." Pages73–83 in *Proceedings of the 1st Kültepe International Meeting, Kültepe, 19–23 September, 2013: Studies Dedicated to Kutlu Emre*. Edited by Fikri Kulakoğlu and Cécile Michel. KIM 1; Subartu 35. Turnhout: Brepols.

———. 2015c. "Nuhšatum, the Wife of an Old Assyrian Trader: Her Status, Responsibilities and Worries (with Two New Letters)." Pages 271–88 in *Cahit Günbattı Armağan: Studies in Honour of Cahit Günbattı*. Edited by İrfan Albayrak, Hakan Erol, and Murat Çayır. Ankara: Ankara Üniversitesi Dil ve Tarih-Coğrafya Fakültesi.

———. 2017a. "The Old Assyrian Period (Twentieth–Eighteenth Century BCE)." Pages 57–79 in *A Companion to Assyria*. Edited by Eckart Frahm. BCAW 113. Oxford: Wiley & Sons.

———. 2017b. "The Old Assyrian Contract H.K. 1005-5534." *NABU*: art. 8.

———. 2018a. "On Old Assyrian Marriage and Marriage Law." *ZAR* 24:7–56.

———. 2018b. "The Family God in Old Babylonian and Especially in Old Assyrian Sources." *RA* 112:49–90.

Veldhuis, Niek. 2018. "Gender Studies and Assyriology: Expectations of an Outsider." Pages 447–59 in *Studying Gender in the Ancient Near East*. Edited by Saana Svärd and Agnès Garcia-Ventura. University Park, PA: Eisenbrauns.

Waetzoldt, Hartmut. 1972. *Untersuchungen zur neusumerischen Textilindustrie*. Rome: Centro per le antichità e la storia dell'arte del Vicino Oriente.

———. 2010. "The Colours and Variety of Fabrics from Mesopotamia during the Ur III Period (2050 BC)." Pages 201–9 in *Textile Terminologies in the Ancient Near East and Mediterranean from the Third to the First Millennnia BC*. Edited by Cécile Michel and Marie-Louise Nosch. ATS 8. Oxford: Oxbow.

Westbrook, Raymond. 1988. *Old Babylonian Marriage Law*. AfOB 23. Horn: Berger.

———. 1995. "Slave and Master in Ancient Near Eastern Law." *CKLR* 70:1631–76.

———. 2001. "Old Babylonian Period." Pages 361–430 in *Security for Debt in Ancient Near Eastern Law*. Edited by Raymond Westbrook and Richard L. Jasnow. Leiden: Brill.

Westenholz, Joan Goodnick. 1990. "Towards a New Conceptualization of the Female Role in Mesopotamian Society." *JAOS* 110:510–21.

Wilcke, Claus. 1976. "Assyrische Testamente." *ZA* 66:196–233.

———. 1983. "Drei altassyrische Kültepe-Texte aus München." *Or* 52:194–200.

———. 2000. *Wer las und schrieb in Babylonien und Assyrien: Überlegungen zur Literalität im Alten Zweistromland*. München: Bayerischen Akademie der Wissenschaften.

Wilhelm, Gernot. 2008. "Hurrians in the Kultepe Texts." Pages 181–94 in *Anatolia and the Jazira during the Old Assyrian Period*. Edited by Jan Gerrit Dercksen. PIHANS 111. Leiden: Nederlands Instituut voor het Nabije Oosten.

Yazıcıoğlu Santamaria, Gökçe Bike. 2017. "Locals, Immigrants, and Marriage Ties at Kültepe: Results of Strontium Isotope Analysis on Human Teeth from Lower Town Graves." Pages 63–84 in *Movement, Resources, Interaction: Proceedings of the Second Kültepe International Meeting, Kültepe, 26–30 July 2015; Studies Dedicated to Klaas Veenhof*. Edited by Fikri Kulakoğlu and Gojko Barjamovic. KIM 2; Subartu 39. Turnhout: Brepols.

Yılmaz, Şerife. 1998. "Köle Satışı Üzerine Yeni Belgeler." *AMMY* (1997): 103–10.

Zaccagnini, Carlo. 2017. "Two Old Assyrian Letters (Tab. X–XI)." *Or* 86:297–303.

Ziegler, Nele. 1997. "Les enfants du palais de Mari." *Ktèma* 22:45–57.

———. 1999. *La population féminine des palais d'après les archives royales de Mari: Le harem de Zimrî-Lim*. FM 4. Paris: Société pour l'étude du Proche-Orient ancien.

Indexes

Abbreviations

†	deceased
br.	brother of
d.	daughter of
f	female name
f.	father of
gf.	grandfather
hu.	husband of
m.	mother of
REL	eponym no.
REL x + 1	eponym following no.
s.	son of
si.	sister of
w.	wife of (by default *aššutum*)

Personal Names

Ašdu **66**:33
Ašhāni **212**:22
Aššur-amārum
s. Ennum-Aššur, hu. ^{f}Zibezibe **36**:3, 12, 15, 17
Aššur-bāni **121**:33 (witness)
s. Ilī-emūqi **106** seal A:1; **106**:1 (seal)
f. Ikuppiya **56e**:3′; **56t**:42
f. Pilah-Ištar **276**:3
Aššur-bāšti **167**:4
Aššur-bēl-awātim **12**:4; **109**:2; **313**:17
Aššur-bēlī **294**:2 (recipient), 10
s. Tabina **20e**:6 (seal); **20t**:13 (witness)
f. ^{f}Zibezibe **36**:6
Aššur-damiq **176**:36 (witness); **296**:11′
Aššur-dān **56t**:43; **121**:31, 32; **250**:19 (dumu A.)
s. Ennum-Aššur **80t**:12 (witness)
s. Ikuppiya **10e**:3 (seal); **10t**:47 (witness)
f. Ennum-Aššur **250**:8
Aššur-emūqi
s. Edinaya **193**:21 (witness)
Aššur-ennam **158**:8; **309**:8 (recipient)
s. Damqum **301**:13
Aššur-e[x-x] **248**:1 (recipient)
Aššur-idī **88t**:3 (creditor); **162**:5, 9
s. Agūa, br. ^{f}Ab-šalim, Šu-Bēlum, Puzur-Ištar, Uṣur-ša-Aššur, and Abi-ilī **54t**:26
s. Amur-Aššur **173**:8
s. Aššur-malik **182e**:1 (seal); **182t**:14 (witness)
s. Kusaya **316**:18
f. Aššur-taklāku **29e**:1
f. Laliya **33t**:1
f. Puzur-Aššur **30**:6; **72**:19
f. Ṭāb-ṣilli-Aššur **257e**:4; **257t**:41
hamuštum + Šu-Ištar **91e**:12; **91t**:6; **188**:6
limum (REL 95) **77**:15; **261**:5
Aššur-imittī **12**:1 (sender); **47t**:27 (witness); **92**:18 (witness); **93t**:17 (witness); **196**:20; **256**:24; **279**:5′; **297**:13; **320**:14
s. Ah-šalim **11**:1 (witness)
s. Ennānum **209**:18
s. Iddin-Wēr **30**:3 (seal); **72**:16 (witness)
s. Kura **128**:39
s. Mannum-balum-Aššur **324**:8 (witness)
s. Šu-Ištar **322**:7
f. Hunniya **257e**:3 ; **257t**:40
f. Iddin-Aššur **263**:7
f. Ilī-bāni **30**:7
f. Kulumaya **257e**:3; **257t**:39
hamuštum + Innaya **83e**:16; **83t**:9
limum A. *malāhum* (REL 106) **191**:7
Aššuriš-takil **322**:12
s. Sukkalliya **169**:6 (*ellat* A.)
Aššuriš-tikal **24**:24 (witness); **78**:12 (witness)
f. Dān-Aššur **65**:92
Aššur-lamassī **62t**:22 (witness); **113**:5 (uncle Enlil-bāni); **156**:1 (sender); **171**:1 (recipient)
f. Iddin-Suen **324**:11
Aššur-malik **21e**:3 (seal); **52e**:3 (seal); **52t**:22 (witness); **88e**:2 (seal); **88t**:13 (witness); **136**:3 (sender); **137**:2 (sender); **147**:35; **148**:21 (witness); **163**:27; **164**:4; **169**:2, 4 (recipient); **212**:1 (recipient); **213**:1 (recipient), 22; **259**:9; **270**:2 (recipient); **312**:26 (sender); **323**:1 (recipient)
s. Ali-ahum **279**:7′
s. Amur-luṣu **32e**:1 (seal); **32t**:16 (witness)
s. Anīnum **4**:11; **10e**:4 (seal); **10t**:47 (witness)
s. Aššur-šamšī **140**:13
s. Elālī **99**:1 (seal)
s. Lipaya **196**:16 (witness)
s. ^{f}Lušitiya, hu. ^{f}Šuppiašu **31**:2
s. Puzur-Aššur **56e**:6′ (seal)
s. Puzur-Ištar **51**:3, 8
s. Sukkalliya *hamuštum* **89**:6
f. Adad-rabi **323**:11
f. Aššur-idī **182e**:2

Aššur-tukultī **139**:3 (recipient)
Aššur-ṭāb **73**:17 (witness); **77**:16 (witness); **148**:2 (é A.), 7, 13, 18; **198**:5, 32; **287**:7; **297**:25; **333**:1 (sender)
s. Aguza, br. Šu-Ištar **62e**:1′
s. Kīki **214**:5 (witness), 13
f. Abu-šalim **143e**:2
f. Aššur-nādā **19e**:2
f. Dudu **30**:4; **72**:17
f. Ē-nibâš **87**:4
f. fIlina **61**:25
Aššur-[x x] **34**:23′ (witness)
fAšua-elka
w. Šarabuna, m. Tilkanu and Peruwa **92**:5, 13
Atali **185**:2 (debtor)
Atata **37**:1, 9; **81**:1 (seal); **193**:4 (debtor); **285**:9 (*šiprum*)
s. Mannum-balum-Aššur **175e**:2 (recipient); **175t**:1 (recipient)
s. Tudhaliya and fAnna-anna, br. Zuru and Inar **53**:8
Atatiya
f. Aššur-rabi **17e**:5
Ataya **17e**:3 (seal); **17t**:12 (witness); **51**:15 (witness); **59**:2 (recipient); **166**:27 (é A.); **218**:23
f. Abu-šalim **10e**:2
f. Ikuppiya **276**:10, 20
fAwiala
w. [X-x]wa **45**:10
Awiliya
limum **36**: 22 (REL 194)
fAya **135**:32 (†)
Azirum
s. Kurara **258t**:56 (witness)
Aziya
br. Dān-Aššur and Ennum-Aššur **63**:3 (sender)
Azu **132**:18; **144e**:3′ (seal); **144t**:18 (witness); **186e**:2 (seal); **186t**:9 (witness)
br. Agia, Ali-ahum, and Šumi-abiya **115**:1, 8, 17, 27
Azūa
s. [X-x-x]-šar **15e**:1 (seal); **15t**:23 (witness)
f. Ikuppiya **301**:4
fAzu-elka **311**:1, 3 (recipient); **312**:1 (recipient), 25 (recipient)
Azutaya
s. Ememe **158**:28 (*kaṣṣar* A.)
A-[x-x-x] **297**:25
fBabbar-Šimala **225**:2 (recipient)
Badidaya **108e**:3 (seal); **108t**:11 (witness)
Bala
f. Ennam-[x-x] **322**:5
f. Nimar-Ištar **49**:1; **158**:26
Balṭua
f. Ilī-rēṣi **190**:18
Ba[r x x x]
s. Wašinuman **53**:3
Barušga
s. Halkiašu **109**:16 (witness)
fBazaya
d. Iddin-Aššur **196**:10
fBazītum **125**:4′ (sender?)
Baziya **280**:18′; **281**:28, 31
f. Agūa **18e**:1
fBedibedi
si. fTitawašhi **93e**:4, 10; **93t**:2, 11
Bēlānum **9**:9; **71t**:11 (*rābiṣum ša* Pūšukēn); **131**:4 (*amtum* B.); **160**:22; **174**: 1″; **276**:13
s. Šu-Aššur **257e**:5 (seal); **257t**:42
s. Šu-Kūbum **87**:3 (seal)
fBēlātum **174**: 8′, 21′; **253**:3 (sender); **254**:3 (sender), 5; **255**:8 (sender), 11; **256**:3 (sender)
Bēlum-bāni **198**:16; **228**:24
Bubuar **212**:21
Budatum **174**:4″ (son of B.)
f. Ennum-Aššur **6**:19
Bududu
f. Nanaya **224**:12
Bukānum
s. Šu-Suen **105**:1 (seal)

Bulina
hu. fWalawala, br. Ganana **91e**:1 (seal), 7 (debtor); **91t**:2 (debtor)
Bunamuwadi **111**:7
Būr-Ištar **228**:19
Būr-Suen **61**:12
s. Dada 7:26 (witness)
s. Irīšum **20e**:2 (seal); **20t**:10 (witness)
Buṣi
s. [X-x]-num **15e**:3 (seal); **15t**:25 (witness)
fBuṣi
d. Iddin-Adad **191**:5, 14
Buṣiya **121**:28; **217**:21
Butaya
s. Iddin-Aššur **138e**:3 (seal); **138t**:23 (witness)
Buzāzu **134**:1 (sender); **141**:2 (recipient); **160**:1 (sender); **161**:1 (sender); **236**:1 (recipient); **260**:20; **277**:2 (recipient); **278**:2 (recipient); **279**:17′; **280**:3 (sender); **281**:1 (recipient); **282**:6; **284**:6, 10; **307t**:12
s. Pūšu-kēn, br. Sue'a, Aššur-mūtappil, Ikuppaša, and fAhaha **257e**:13 (seal), 18; **257t**:9; **276**:7 (seal)
Buza/uzu(m) **91e**:8 (creditor); **91t**:4 (creditor)
f. Maṣi-ilī **138e**:1; **138t**:22
limum (REL 87) **178e**:22; (REL 87); **208**:9
Buzizi
f. Kuṣiya **56e**:5′; **56t**:42 (witness)
Buzutaya **174**:1″
hamuštum + Laqēpum **193**:12
Dada **25**:22 (d. D.)
f. Būr-Suen 7:27
Dadānum **86**:12 (witness)
Dadaya 57:9, 21
f. Šulmu-Aššur **258t**:56
Dadiya **8**:7 (*pāšer awātim*)
s. Šumi-abiya **64**:78 (witness)
Daki-[x-x]
f. Ṭāb-ṣilli-Aššur **74e**:2
Dakū **258t**:59 (witness)
Dakuna **40**:1 (seal)
Dalaš **35**:31 (witness); **188**:21 (witness)
s. Hamaraya **149e**:5 (seal); **149t**:11 (witness)
f. Šadahšu **38**:18
Dalaša **94e**:24 (seal); **94t**:17 (witness)
Damqaya **190**:2 (*aššat* D.), 5 (*aššat* D.)
Damqum
f. Aššur-ennam **301**:14
Dān-Aššur **13**:2 (recipient); **26**:11 (witness); **115**:39 (witness); **166**:5; **213**:2 (recipient), 22; **222**:6; **247**:5, 22, 26, 30; **282**:4 (*naruq* D.); **283**:5, 17 (*naruq* D.)
s. Aššuriš-tikal **65t**:92 (witness)
f. Iddin-Aššur **257e**:7; **257t**:43
f. Puzur-Ištar **112**:15′
br. Ennum-Aššur and Aziya **63**:1, 3 (recipient)
Darakšu **39**:25 (witness)
Darhašiat **40**:4 (seal)
Da[x-x]
f. Puzur-Šamaš **32e**:5
Dikšar
s. Sasum, br. Harnašarna **41e**:2 (seal); **41t**:12 (witness)
Dišti-[x] **46**:23
Dudiki
f. Ali-ahum **178e**:3
Dudu **103e**:5 (seal); **103t**:4, 12; **159e**:4 (seal); **318**: 31
s. Aššur-ṭāb **30**:4 (seal); **72**:17 (witness)
f. Adad-bāni **317**:6
f. Lulu **98**:4
Duduli **132**:18
Duhušili **39**:23 (witness)
Duwazi **111**:4 (seal)
Ea-šar **237**:18
Edinaya
f. Aššur-emūqi **193**:22
Edi[x]aša **68**:23
Ekiya
f. Nūnu **17e**:2
Ela **165**:5; **176**:30; **271**:9

Ennānum (*cont.*)
s. Ali-abum **37**:12 (witness)
f. Abiaya **224**:14
f. Aššur-imittī **209**:19
hamuštum ša qāti E. **87**:15
E/Inna-Suen **35**:29 (witness); **61**:29; **92**:3, 14; **114**:6, 19; **129**:6 (é E.); **171**:4, 8; **326**:28 (in Hurrama); **327**:3, 8, 23, 27; **329**:17
s. Amur-Šamaš **37**:14 (witness)
s. Iddin-Kūbum **201**:7 (witness)
s. Ikua **71t**:1
s. Ilānum **214**:6 (witness), 14
s. Kurara **263**:19
f. fQannuttum **175e**:5
f. Šamaš-bāni **191**:18
hu. fIštar-nādā **27**:1 (recipient)
limum s. Šu-Aššur **58**: 19 (REL 107)
limum ša qāti (REL 107+1) **4**:8; **180**:15
Enna-[x-x] **296**:8′, 11′
Enna/um-[x-x] **327**:37
s. Bala **322**:4
Ennum-Aya **88e**:2 (seal); **88t**:12 (witness)
Ennum-ilī **115**:38 (witness); **221**:36
s. Kuza **299**:5
fEnnum-Ištar
šawītum of Laqēpum **106**:6 (seal), 12, 24; **106** seal C: 1
Epiš-qabi
f. Kumum **56** seal: A2
Epqum
f. Mannum-balum-Aššur **37**:17
Eririya **225**:10
fEtari
w. Šu-Suen, si. Ennum-Aššur **15e**:4; **15t**:1
fEwanika **2**:[1], 8, 18
Ewarimuša **328**:20, 36, 40
fGadada **114**:8 (slave)
fGadagada **96**:8 (seal), 9, 19, 24
Galgalia **307t**:26
Galua
s. Akabši, hu. fTamnanika **17e**:6 (seal), 8, 13; **17t**:1, 4
fGamu-[x-(x)] **52e**:12; **52t**:12
fGanana
si. Bulina **91e**:23 (pledge); **91t**:17 (pledge)
Gazuba **187**:1 (seal)
Habatali
hu. fNiwahšušar (fNahšušara), f. Šeliara (adoptive son) **120**:1, 6, 7, 12, 15, 19, 21
Habi **313**:35
Habiya **151e**:4 (seal)
Hadaikur
alahhinnum **112**:4
Hadaya
f. Šu-Anum **292**:29
Hadua **219**:32
Haduwan
ša ṭābtim **44e**:6 (seal)
fHahalu(w)an
w. Humadašu **43**:2, 6
Hali(t)ka **42**:22 (witness); **76e**:4 (seal); **76t**:17 (witness)
Halkiašu
f. Apiziašu **97**:2
f. Barušga **109**:17
rabi simmiltim **43**:9′ (*iqqātī*)
Halule **132**:17; **313**:38
Halupa **103e**:5 (seal); **103t**:23 (witness)
f. Hazimel **109**:19
Hamala
hu. fHašum-elka **258e**:1 (from Mada), 10, 15, 19, 25; **258t**:1, 12, 13, 16, 19, 28, 50, 54
Hamanani **22**:15 (witness)
fHamananika
d. fŠuppi-elka, w. Aššur-malik **19e**:5; **19t**:2
Hamaraya **95e**:3 (seal); **95t**:11 (witness)
f. Dalaš **149e**:5
Hamuriya
f. Peruwa **94** seal A: 2
f. Šuppiuman **149e**:6
fHana **79e**:9 (debtor); **79t**:2 (debtor); **94e**: 1 (d. H.), 5, 8, 20, 23 (seal); **94t**:1 (d. H.), 6, 10

br. Amur-Šamaš **64**:1, 2, 50; **65t**:1, 2, 38, 39
Ikuppaša **141**:2 (recipient); **277**:2 (recipient); **278**:3 (recipient); **280**:3 (sender); **282**:6; **284**:2 (recipient)
s. Pūšu-kēn, br. Sue'a, Aššur-mūtappil, Buzāzu, and ^{f}Ahaha **257e**:13 (seal), 18; **257t**:9; **276**:8 (seal)
Ikuppiya **12**:17; **52e**:6; **52t**:3, 10; **54e**:9 (seal); **54t**:44 (witness); **71t**:4 (dam I.), 5 (*mēr'at* I.), 6 (*mēr'ē* I.), 8 (debtor); **137**:19; **166**:11, 27; **184**:17 (witness); **206**:2 (sender); **209**:22; **235t**:35; **240**:15; **249**:3 (recipient); **289**: 2 (recipient); **298**:3 (sender)
s. Agia **74e**:3 (seal); **74t**:16 (witness)
s. Aššur-bāni **56e**:3′ (seal); **56t**:41 (witness)
s. Ataya **276**:10, 20
s. Azūa **301**:4
s. Ilī-bāni and ^{f}Lamassī, br. ^{f}Ahattum and Iaya **56t**:24, 38, 39
f. Aššur-dān **10e**:3
f. Puzur-Aššur **250**:1
dub-sar 57:52 (*bēl šīmtum*)
Ikuppī-Aššur **52e**:4 (seal); **52t**:23 (witness)
s. Pilah-Aššur **71e**:4 (seal); **71t**:20 (witness)
Ilabrat-bāni **248**:3 (sender); **255**:3 (recipient), 5
s. Ah-šalim **31**:20 (witness)
s. Kūn-ilum and ^{f}Ištar-Lamassī, br. ^{f}Šīmat-Ištar and Iliya **59**:24
s. ^{f}Puzur, br. Iddin-Ištar **49**:7, 13
hu. ^{f}Musa **51**:2
Ilabrat-dunnī **190**:1, 4
^{f}Ilališkan **79e**:12 (creditor); **79t**:4 (creditor)
w. Histahšu **100**:3 (debtor)
Ilānum
f. Enna-Suen **214**:7
Ilī-ālum **233**:4, 11, 27; **271**:28 (dumu I.)
f. Enlil-bāni **143e**:3
f. Kuziziya 7:25
Ilī-ašranni
h. ^{f}Talhama **37**:2
Ilī-bāni **62t**:20 (witness); **115**:36 (witness); **128**:8; **164**:33; **168**:27; **175t**:5, 20, 22; **195**:4; **296**:16′; **305**:5
s. Amur-Ištar, br. Suen-rē'ī, Aššur-nīšu, Šu-Labān, ^{f}Ab-šalim, and Iddin-Adad **257e**:10 (seal), 14; **257t**:3
s. Aššur-imittī, hu. ^{f}Tataya **30**:7 (seal), 11, 15, 24
s. Iaya, hu. ^{f}Lamassī, f. ^{f}Ahattum, Iaya, and Ikuppia **56e**:2′ (seal); **56t**:1 (*šīmtum* I.)
s. Ištar-bāni **138** seal: 1
s. Maniya **285**:3 (seal), 7
f. Ali-abum **57**:52
hu. ^{f}Tataya **72**:9, 13, 25
Ilī-dān **121**:7, 20; **297**:20; **329**:14
f. Apil-kēn **54e**:8; **54** seal: D2
f. Zuzua **82**:30; **183e**:2
limum (REL 98/123) **74t**:14; **91e**:15; **91t**:8
Ilī-emūqi
f. Aššur-bāni **106**:3; **106** seal A: 2
Ilī-iddinaššu **217**:21 (dumu I.); **293**:31 (dumu I.)
Ilī-imittī
f. Šu-Suen **5e**:4
Ilī-išar **132**:15; **315**:5, 19
Ilī-kurub
f. Amur-Aššur **81** seal: 2
Ilī-malak
s. Suen-rē'ī, hu. ^{f}Wawala **87**:2 (seal), 10 (debtor), 23 (pledge)
Ilī-malik **136**:9; **137**:17 (*ṣuhārum ša* Ikuppiya); **209**:24; **260**:4 (é I.)
^{f}Ilina
d. Aššur-ṭāb **61**:25
Ilī-nādā
f. Puzur-Anna **109**:15
Ilī-rē'ī
s. Salimanum **56t**:5
Ilī-rēṣi
s. Balṭua **190**:18 (witness)
Iliš-takil **232**:28

(sender); **322**:1 (sender); **323**:4 (sender); **328**:1 (recipient); **328**:34; **330**:2 (recipient); **331**:12′
s. Aššur-malik, hu. ^{f}Waliwali **143e**:12; **143t**:8
s. Aššur-rabi **143e**:4 (seal), 10, 20; **143t**:5, 15
s. Šu-Ištar **258t**:58 (witness)
s. Wardum, hu. ^{f}Hatala **324**:3
f. Aššur-rabi **98**:3
f. Aššur-šamšī **209**:13; **295**:4′
f. Šu-Anum **58**:44
hu. ^{f}Hatala **24**:1, 17
hamuštum + Buzutaya **193**:11
Lihšuman **107**:13 (witness)
Lila **273**:3 (é L.)
Limiššar **217**:5 (dumu L.)
Lipaya
f. Aššur-malik **196**:17
f. Uzua **82**:3
Lulu **152**:3; **332**:2 (recipient)
s. Aranapšu **177**:11 (witness)
s. Dudu **98**:4 (seal)
^{f}Lušitiya
m. Aššur-malik **31**:1
Luzina **285**:8
Madada **151e**:18
^{f}Maganika **199**:2 (recipient)
Mahira **103e**:4 (seal); **103t**:22 (witness)
^{f}Maka **219**:3 (recipient), 12, 19
Malaš
f. Perwahšu **101**:15
^{f}Malawašhina
w. Arawurhina **39**:11
Maliahšu
f. ^{f}Šišawada **98**:7, 15
^{f}Mamala **145e**:2 (recipient); **145t**:1 (recipient)
Manamana **186e**:6 (seal), 11 (debtor); **186t**:4 (debtor)
Manniya
f. Ilī-bāni **285**:4
f. Puzur-Suen and Šarra-Suen **70**:22
Mannukkiya (nickname?) **204**:7, 17
Mannum-balum-Anna **221**:12
Mannum-balum-Aššur **10t**:1, 4, 13, 30, 37; **11**:5, 12; **216**:5
s. Aššur-ṣululī **23**:27 (witness)
s. Epqum **37**:16 (witness)
f. Aššur-imittī **324**:9
f. Atata **175e**:3
Mannum-kī-Adad **99**:3, 7
Mannum-kī-Aššur **13**:26; **47t**:28 (witness); **91e**:8 (creditor); **91t**:4 (creditor); **173**:1 (recipient); **205**:3; **331**:1, 13′ (recipient); **334**:8 (witness)
s. Ahu-waqar **191**:19 (judge)
Mannum-kī-ēnia **204**:2 (recipient), 19
Mannum-kī-iliya **78**:11 (witness)
Manuba
gudu$_4$ *ša* Aššur **174**:4′
Manukaya **159e**:4 (seal)
Mara **111**:1 (seal, from Kammalia)
Masaya **24**:23 (witness)
f. ^{f}Lamassī **80t**:11
Massa-Aššur
s. Al-ṭāb **180**:17 (witness)
Ma/eṣi-(i)lī **51**:18 (witness); **61**:29; **76e**:1 (seal); **76t**:15 (witness); **81**:1 (seal); **221**:11 (*kaṣṣar* Mannum-balum-Aššur); **250**:6
s. Buzuzum **138e**:1 (seal); **138t**:22 (witness)
limum **72**:7 (REL 109)
Mašhi-ilī
f. Šalim-ahum **180**:3
^{f}Mawašhi **76e**:6 (seal), 11 (debtor); **76t**:3 (debtor)
Meišmiš **119**:10
Memē **121**:18; **221**:14
Memē-ibri **89**:14 (witness)
Menānum
f. Šu-Ištar **56t**:4
Merali **85e**:15 (creditor); **85t**:4 (creditor)
s. Ennum-Aššur **104**:17 (witness)
f. Šu-(i)lī **121**:33
^{f}Muati
w. Warad-Kūbi **46**:6
^{f}Mula
w. Peruwa **159e**:5, 7, 14, 18

^{f}Muna'iškan **123**:21
^{f}Musa **182e**:10 (creditor); **182t**:3 (creditor); **189e**:3 (seal); **189t**:8 (witness); **223**:1 (recipient); **232**:1 (recipient)
d. Iliš-tikal, w. Ilabrat-bāni **51**:1; **91e**:22 (slave); **91t**:15 (slave)
si. Iddin-Suen **194e**:1″; **194t**:3 (guarantor), 8, 11; **210**:1, 2 (recipient)
Nabi-Enlil **332**:6
Nab-ilī **13**:28
Nab-Suen **26**:10 (witness)
s. Šu-Bēlum **112**:10′ (witness)
^{f}Nahištum **198**:21 (sender)
Nakile'ed **186e**:4 (seal), 10 (debtor); **186t**:3 (debtor)
s. Šuppiahšu **101**:16 (witness)
s. Šuppiuman **96**:6 (seal)
rabi šariqē **40**:5 (seal)
^{f}Nakilwišwe
w. Aššur-mūtappil **144e**:6′, 15′; **144t**:5, 16
Nakišduar **107**:6
^{f}Nanaya **75e**:5 (creditor); **75t**:3 (creditor)
Nanaya
s. Bududu **224**:4, 12
s. Hannānum **190**:19 (*tappā'um*)
Naniya **61**:10
^{f}Naniya **297**:20
Naplis **105**:5 (é N.), 8, 14 (d. *gubabtum* N.)
Naqidu **186e**:2 (seal); **186t**:10 (witness)
Narām-Suen
f. Ennum-Aššur **30**:5; **72**:18
hamuštum **76e**:15; **76t**:7
^{f}Narāmtum **234**:3 (sender); **235e**:2 (seal); **235t**:3 (sender)
Nazi **305**:4; **332**:3 (recipient)
Nikilit
hu. ^{f}Šašalika **44e**:8; **44t**:1, 23
Nimar-Ištar **123**:1 (recipient); **302**:2, 21 (recipient)
s. Bala **49**:1 (seal); **158**:26
^{f}Ninala **292**:22
^{f}Nini **81**:3 (seal), 7 (debtor); **151e**:1 (seal)
Nišašar **307t**:22 (géme)
Niwahšu **153**:20′ (witness)
^{f}Niwahšušar (^{f}Nahšušara) **97**:5 (seal), 7, 19; **108e**:7; **108t**:3
w. Habatali **120**:1, 21
^{f}Niwalka **144e**:4′; **144t**:3
^{f}Nuhšatum **3**:2 (recipient); **16**:2 (recipient); **212**:2 (recipient), 4; **213**:2 (recipient), 3; **214**:2 (recipient)
Nuhušatum **104**:1, 3, 4
Nūnu
s. Ekiya **17e**:2 (seal); **17t**:11 (witness)
s. ^{f}Šāt-Ištar, br. Amur-Aššur and ^{f}Walawala **35**:8
Nūr-Ištar
f. Šu-Kūbum **178e**:4
Nūr-kī-ilī **218**:24; **225**:21
Palanašwa **101**:3 (debtor)
Palui
f. Hašui **31**:23
Panaka **13**:5 (s. P.)
Papantah'e **99**:4, 20
Pappalum
f. Iddin-Aššur **105**:9
Peri/u(w)a **21e**:20; **33t**:17 (witness); **43**:13′ (witness); **69e**:3 (seal); **69t**:13 (witness); **97**:6 (seal), 8, 19; **152**:13; **196**:19; **210**:19
s. Hamuriya **94e**:25 (seal); **94t**:18 (witness); **94** seal A: 1
s. Karunuwa **41e**:4 (seal); **41t**:14 (witness)
s. Kurkuri **45**:1 (seal)
s. Šarabuna and ^{f}Ašua-elka, br. Tilkanu **92**:5, 12
s. Šuppibra **32e**:2 (seal); **32t**:18 (witness)
s. Walahšina **149e**:4 (seal), 10, 18; **149t**:2, 6
hu. ^{f}Mula **159e**:5 (seal), 7, 14, 18
gudu$_4$ *ša* ^{d}im *ša qaqqidim* **44e**:1 (seal)
ša qanu'e **37**:20 (witness)
Perwahšu **144t**:18 (witness)
s. Malaš **101**:14 (witness)
Perwaš-[x-(x)]
gudu$_4$ *ša* Kubabat **46**:2 (seal)

Pe-[x-x] **42**:24 (witness)
Pilah-Aššur
f. Ikuppī-Aššur **71e**:6 **71t**:20
Pilahaya **130**:17; **317**:16
hu. ^{f}Alayaga, f. ^{f}Huna **47t**:2
Pilah-Ištar **7**:1, 3; **10t**:1, 3, 14, 29, 39, 41; **11**:14, 20; **61**:21; **125**:8′, 9′ (é P.); **264t**:37
s. Aššur-bāni **276**:3 (seal)
s. Elamma, br. ^{f}Ummī-Išhara, Ennum-Aššur, and Šu-Bēlum **58**:2, 10, 29, 36
f. Adad-damiq **5e**:5
f. Amur-Ištar **180**:20
hu. ^{f}Tatana, d. Agiya **28**:5, 7, 14
hu. ^{f}Walawala, f. ^{f}Lamassī **35**:1, 6, 14, 21
hamuštum + Imdīlum 77:6
Pithana **100**:15 (witness)
rubā'um **44t**:19 (*iqqātī*)
rabi qaqqidī **45**:5 (seal)
^{f}Pitian-elka **79e**:5 (seal), 11 (debtor); **79t**:3 (debtor)
Puppurānum **294**:7 (witness); **296**:4′; **297**:16 (tur)
Pūšu-kēn **1**:2 (recipient); **71t**:12 (*rābiṣum* P., creditor); **74e**:6 (creditor); **74t**:2 (creditor); **77**:3 (creditor); **124**:2 (recipient); **139**:1 (recipient); **147**:1 (recipient); **163**:1 (recipient); **164**:1 (recipient); **165**:1 (recipient); **166**:1 (recipient); **167**:1 (recipient); **168**:1 (sender); **169**:1, 8 (recipient); **195**:1 (recipient); **208**:1 (recipient); **209**:1 (recipient); **210**:1 (recipient), 14, 22; **211**:1 (recipient); **222**:1 (recipient); **223**:1 (recipient), 23, 31; **232**:8, 29; **239**:1 (recipient); **245**:4, 8, 18; **246**:1 (recipient); **247**:1 (sender); **254**:1 (recipient); **255**:1 (recipient), 16, 30 (é P.); **256**:1 (recipient), 29; **259**:1 (recipient); **260**:1 (recipient); **290**:20–21; **293**:20, 23; **310**:20, 23
f. Aššur-mūtappil **71t**:10, 12
f. Aššur-mūtappil, Buzāzu, and Ikuppaša **257e**:13, 20, 25, 36; **257t**:10, 18, 19, 33, 34
f. Sue'a, Buzāzu, Ikuppaša, Aššur-mūtappil, and ^{f}Ahaha **276**:6, 7, 8, 9, 11, 16, 21, 25, 26
hu. ^{f}[X]-mazi **34**:1′, 7′
^{f}Puzur
m. Iddin-Ištar and Ilabrat-bāni **49**:15, 19
Puzur-Anna **86**:3 (debtor)
s. Enna-Aššur **257e**:7 (seal); **257t**:41
s. Ilī-nādā **109**:15 (witness)
f. Anīna **320**:22
f. Aššur-nādā **54e**:5; **54** seal: E2
Puzur-Aššur **3**:1 (sender); **59**:1 (sender); **63**:2 (recipient); **83e**:13 (creditor); **83t**:6 (creditor); **99**:3, 6; **113**:4, 13; **115**:6, 11, 28; **129**:7, 17, 41; **139**:2 (recipient); **157**:5; **162**:1 (sender); **168**:5, 10; **279**:1 (recipient); **280**:1′ (recipient); **281**:10, 13, 23; **282**:5, 16, 23 (é P.); **283**:22; **284**:5 (*naruq* P.); **290**:7; **294**:4, 8; **297**:4, 26
s. Aššur-idī **30**:6 (seal); **72**:19 (witness)
s. Ikuppiya **250**:1
s. Šu-Labān **263**:21
f. Agiya **191**:16
f. Aššur-malik **56e**:6′
Puzur-Enna **173**:11
s. Eliya **149e**:2 (seal)
Puzur-ilī **204**:4 (sender); **205**:2 (sender); **271**:11
s. Uṣur-ša-Ištar **273**:5, 13
Puzur-Ištar **86**:4 (creditor); **155**:1 (sender); **172**:25; **192**:2 (recipient), 20; **229**:2 (recipient); **231**:2 (recipient); **255**:2 (recipient), 4; **256**:4
s. Agūa, br. ^{f}Ab-šalim, Šu-Bēlum, Aššur-idī, Uṣur-ša-Aššur, and Abi-ilī **54t**:33
s. Ali-abum **71t**:2
s. Dān-Aššur **112**:14′ (witness)
f. Aššur-malik **51**:4

Šalim-Adad
f. Ennum-Aššur **194e**:1′; **194t**:14
Šalim-ahum **147**:30; **213**:4 (sender); **214**:32; **277**:23 (é Š.)
s. Mašhi-ilī **180**:3 (debtor)
s. Ṭāb-ilī **71e**:19 (*tappā'um*); **71t**:23 (*tappā'um*)
f. Ennum-Aššur **1**:18
Šalim-ālum **312**:27 (in Wahšušana)
Šalim-Aššur **193**:3 (debtor); **209**:17; **240**:15
s. Aššur-malik and f. ^{f}Arala **143e**:7; **143t**:2
s. Iphurum **112**:6
f. Išim-Suen **65t**:92
f. Šamaš-bāni, Amur-Ištar, Šuma-Aššur, Aššur-šamšī, and ^{f}Ziki **258e**:4, 7 (é Š.), 9 (é gal *ša* Š.), 13, 21, 29, 1′; **258t**:4, 5, 8 (é Š.), 9 (é gal Š.), 14, 32, 47, 49, 51
hamuštum + Amurru-bāni **184**:7
Šalim-bēlī **329**:7, 10
hu. ^{f}Kititi **73**:1, 3, 10, 15
Šalim-Ištar
f. ^{f}Tataya **30**:9, 25; **72**:3, 24
^{f}Šalimma **148**:5, 10, 19; **244e**:10, 15; **244t**:6, 11; **253**:1 (recipient)
w. Ir'am-Aššur **264e**:5 (recipient); **264t**:1 (recipient)
Šalim-wardī **331**:10′
Šalini
f. ^{f}Abī-dūrī **102**:4
Šalkuata **159e**:1 (seal)
Šaluata **95e**:13; **95t**:1
Šamaš-abī
s. Zuzānum **112**:2
Šamaš-bāni **148**:20 (witness); **319**:9; **319**:9
s. Enna-Suen **191**:17 (judge)
s. Šallim-Aššur, br. Amur-Ištar, Šuma-Aššur, Aššur-šamšī, and ^{f}Ziki **258e**:2, 27; **258t**:2, 30, 45
f. Ikūnum **98**:2; **98 seal A**: 2
Šamaš-rē'ī **214**:21
Šamaš-taklāku **301**:16; **302**:3 (recipient); **303**:27
Šamaš-ublam **215**:16
^{f}Šamnanika **107**:3 (slave), 10
Šanabū **108e**:1 (seal); **108t**:10 (witness)
Šarabunu(w)a **313**:8; **318**:32
s. Šipana **84**:17 (witness)
f. Tilanu and Peruwa, hu. ^{f}Ašua-elka **92**:4, 11
Šarba **111**:6 (seal)
^{f}Šarika / ^{f}Šariša
d. Hapiya and ^{f}Šuppianika **109**:6, 10
Šarmama **76e**:3 (seal); **76t**:16 (witness); **81**:3 (seal)
Šarnikan **79e**:4 (seal); **79t**:15 (witness)
Sarnikum
f. Iddin-Dagan **71e**:17; **71t**:22
Šarra/u-Suen
s. Manniya, br. Puzur-Suen **70**:21
f. Šu-Rama **258t**:57
^{f}Šarrat-Ištar **172**:2 (sender); **320**:4, 15
Šarua
f. Kulakula **41e**:3; **41t**:13
^{f}Šašalika
w. Nikilit **44e**:9, 11; **44t**:2, 5, 14
^{f}Ša-Šamaš **115**:23; **215**:1 (recipient), 22
^{f}Šāt-Adad
si. Adad-bāni, Šu-Anum, and Ennum-Aššur **57**:4
^{f}Šatahšušar **189e**:4 (seal), 6 (debtor); **189t**:3 (debtor)
^{f}Šāt-Anna **102**:17 (witness); **179**:3 (creditor); **180**:3 (creditor); **181e**:4′ (creditor); **181t**:4 (creditor); **332**:1 (recipient), 5, 20
^{f}Šāt-Aššur **124**:1 (sender); **135**:33; **136**:1 (recipient); **137**:1 (recipient); **280**:3′; **303**:17; **307t**:30; **311**:4 (sender), 20
^{f}Šāt-Ea **184**:4 (creditor); **193**:5 (guarantor)
d. Su'etata **74e**:4 (seal), 6 (debtor); **74t**:2 (debtor); **183e**:4 (seal), 7 (debtor); **183t**:2 (debtor)
^{f}Šāt-ilī **233**:3 (sender)
m. ^{f}Kititi **73**:16

^{f}Šāt-Ištar
m. ^{f}Walawala, Nūnu, and Amur-Aššur 35:7
Šazua **102**:15 (witness)
Šeliara
s. Habatali (adoptive son) **120**:2, 3, 16, 19, 22
Šepana **69e**:3 (seal); **69t**:14 (witness)
Šēṣur **150e**:3 (seal); **150t**:20 (witness); **310**:1 (recipient), 17, 27; **312**:16
Šezizi **103e**:2 (seal); **103t**:20 (witness)
^{f}Šiduna
si. ^{f}Zizizi **230**:4 (†)
^{f}Šī-lamassī **121**:23
Šiliara **44e**:7 (seal)
Šiliuman **85e**:6 (seal), 14 (debtor); **85t**:3 (debtor),18 (witness)
^{f}Šīmat-Aššur **170**:3 (sender); **238**:2 (sender); **252**:3 (sender); **290**:3 (recipient); **292**:19; **295**:13′; **296**:13; **297**:9, 12
^{f}Šīmat-Ištar **68**:7; **121**:21
d. ^{f}Ištar-Lamassī, si. Iliya and Ilabrat-bāni **59**:4 (recipient), 5
^{f}Šīmat-Suen **127**:3 (sender); **142**:2 (sender); **173**:2 (sender); **237**:3 (sender); **272**:1 (sender); **273**:1 (sender); **274**:2 (sender)
Šimnuman
s. Tatalī, hu. ^{f}Šuppianika **22**:4, 11
Šipana
f. Šarabunuwa **84**:18
^{f}Šišahšušar **132**:3 (recipient); **157**:2 (recipient); **313**:2 (sender); **314**:2 (recipient); **315**:2 (recipient); **316**:3(recipient); **317**:2 (recipient); **318**:3 (recipient); **319**:2 (recipient); **320**:8; **321**:4
^{f}Šišawada
d. Maliahšu **98**:6 (seal), 14, 29, 30, 32
Šiwašme'i
utû ša abbul addahšū **96**:2 (seal)
Šu-Anum **115**:39 (witness); **212**:2 (recipient), 21
s. Hadaya **292**:28 (witness)
s. Hanu **171**:6
s. Laqēp **58**:43 (witness)
f. Agūa **54e**:15
f. Ah-šalim **297**:6, 28
f. Tutaya **324**:6
br. Adad-bāni, ^{f}Šāt-Adad, and Ennum-Aššur 57:33, 37, 41
Šu-Aššur **115**:36 (witness); **158**:6
s. Kurub-Ištar **201**:5
f. Aššur-Šamšī **91** seal A: 2
f. Belānum **257e**:5; **257t**:43
f. Enna-Suen **58**:19; **180**:16
Šu-Bēlum **47t**:30 (witness); **88e**:4 (debtor); **88t**:2 (debtor); **115**:38 (witness); **121**:5; **129**:6 (é Š.); **240**:6 (é Š); **268**:6
s. Agūa, br. ^{f}Ab-šalim, Aššur-idī, Puzur-Ištar, Uṣur-ša-Aššur, and Abi-ilī **54t**:9, 10, 24
s. Elamma, br. ^{f}Ummī-Išhara, Ennum-Aššur, and Pilah-Ištar **58**:3, 10, 30, 37
s. Zurzur **183e**:3 (seal); **183t**:13 (witness)
f. Nab-Suen **112**:11′
f. ^{f}Tamnanika **17e**:12, 16; **17t**:3
^{f}Šūbultum **168**:20, 23, 24; **174**:7′; **195**:2 (sender); **222**:3 (sender); **247**:6
Šudaya
limum (REL 82) **208**:3, 11
Šu-Enlil **141**:4 (é Š.); **173**:5, 12
Šu-Hubur **1**:1 (sender); **224**:4
limum **184**: 15 (REL 88)
Šuhurpiya **40**:7 (seal); **43**:12′ (witness)
gudu$_{4}$ *ša* ^{d}im **44e**:4 (seal)
Šu-(i)lī
s. Merali **121**:33 (witness)
^{f}Šuiškuna **150e**:4 (seal), 9, 13; **150t**:5, 7, 11
Šu-Išhara
s. Ušher **258t**:58 (witness)
Šu-Ištar **126**:1 (sender); **154**:28; **212**:3 (recipient), 22; **256**:24, 27; **297**:14; **329**:15
s. Aguza, br. Aššur-ṭāb **62t**:3
s. Iliš-tikal **292**:30 (witness)
s. Menānum **56t**:3
f. Ahu-(wa)qar **292**:27

f. Aššur-imittī **322**:8
f. Iddin-Adad **58**:42
f. Laqēp **258t**:58
hamuštum + Aššur-idī **91e**:12; **91t**:6; **188**:7
Šu-Kūbum **12**:10; **177**:2 (debtor); **181t**:12 (witness); **221**:22
s. Nū-Ištar **178e**:3 (seal), 7 (debtor); **178t**:3
f. Bēlānum **87**:3
f. Elālī **129**:28 (dumu Š.), 34, 36; **206**:11
hamuštum + Elamma **181e**:6′; **181t**:8
Šu-Labān **9**:7; **221**:3 (sender); **237**:18
s. Āl-ṭāb **276**:2 (seal)
s. Amur-Ištar, br. Suen-rē'ī, Ilī-bāni, Aššur-nīšu, fAb-šalim, and Iddin-Adad **257e**:11 (seal), 16; **257t**:4
f. Puzur-Aššur **263**:21
Šuliya **111**:2 (seal, the Sasuean)
Šulmu-Aššur
s. Dadaya **258t**:55 (witness)
Šuma-Aššur
s. Šallim-Aššur, br. Šamaš-bāni, Amur-Ištar, Aššur-šamšī, and fZiki **258e**:3, 28; **258t**:3, 31, 46
Šumi-abiya **59**:42; **60**:22; **75e**:1 (seal); **75t**:12 (witness); **123**:1 (recipient), 18, 20; **219**:2 (recipient), 15, 23, 26; **227**:5; **250**:9 (representing the sons of Kūn-ilum), 20; **285**:14 (witness)
f. Dadiya **64**:78
br. Azu, Agia, and Ali-ahum **115**:40
Šumkum **84**:10
Šu-Nunu **263**:16
f. Ṭāb-ṣilli-Aššur **276**:1
Šuppiahšu **84**:21 (witness); **150e**:2 (seal); **150t**:19 (witness)
f. Nakile'ed **101**:17
fŠuppiahšušar **221**:1 (recipient), 5
fŠuppianika **24**:26 (witness); **138e**:10 (female slave); **138t**:2
d. Kurukuru **97**:4 (seal)
d. Tatalī and fTi-[x]-ama, w. Šimnuman **22**:3, 6, 12
m. Zulī **95e**:6 (seal), 9; **95t**:5
w. Hapia, m. fŠariša **109**:4, 8
fŠuppiašu
d. Happuašu and fUniuni, w. Aššur-malik **31**:3 (*amtum*)
fŠuppiašuwa **152**:4, 5, 10
fŠuppiašwe **93t**:18
Šuppibra
f. Perua **32e**:2
fŠuppi-elka
m. fHamananika **19e**:4 (seal), 6; **19t**:3
fŠuppimani **77**:2 (debtor)
Šuppišamnuman
br. Labarša **69e**:4; **69t**:2
Šuppiuman
s. Hamuriya **149e**:6 (seal); **149t**:12 (witness)
f. Nakile'ed **96**:7
Šuppunahšu **69e**:2 (seal); **69t**:12 (witness); **90**:2 (seal)
Šuppunuman **42**:23 (witness); **185**:13 (witness)
Šu-Rama **187**:3 (seal), 4, 7 (debtor)
s. Šarru-Suen **258t**:56 (witness)
Šu-Suen **157**:19; **203**:2 (sender); **215**:3 (sender); **248**:15
s. Ilī-imittī **5e**:4 (seal)
f. Bukānum **105**:1
hu. fEtari **15e**:4, 20; **15t**:1, 17, 20
Šuzuzu **10t**:2, 5, 14, 30, 38; **11**:6, 13
Tabina
f. Aššur-bēlī **20e**:8
Taha
hu. fHutalathe **42**:4, 11, 17
Tahrunu **313**:22, 25
Talhama
s. fWalawala, br. Hištahšu **138e**:6 (seal), 17, 20, 25; **138t**:8, 13, 19
fTalhama
w. Ilī-ašranni **37**:1, 7
Taliya **24**:25 (witness)
hu. fHašušarna **40**:8, 13, 23
Talwana
f. Tarhuala **97**:3

^{f}Tamnanika
wi. Galua, d. Šu-Bēlum **17e**:10; **17t**:2, 7
Tamura **84**:5 (creditor)
Tamuriya **100**:14 (witness); **101**:4 (creditor), 10; **151e**:6 (seal), 12, 15
s. Hapuašu **138e**:4 (seal); **138t**:24 (witness)
^{f}Tarām-Kūbi **128**:2 (sender); **129**:1 (sender); **170**:2 (sender); **206**:3 (sender); **207**:2 (sender); **252**:2 (sender); **286**:3 (sender); **287**:4 (sender); **288**:3; **289**:3 (recipient); **290**:2 (recipient); **295**:15′; **296**:13′; **297**:8, 11
w. Innaya **285**:5
Tarhišan **330**:13
Tarhuala
s. Talwana **97**:3 (seal)
Tarhunu **89**:3 (debtor)
Tarhušet
gudu$_4$ *ša* Ilalianta **46**:4 (seal)
Tarikuda
s. Kimarniman **19e**:1 (seal); **19t**:18 (witness)
^{f}Tariša **288**:2
^{f}Tarīš-mātum **115**:23; **146**:3 (sender); **174**:8′, 21′; **211**:2 (sender); **254**:2 (sender); **255**:7 (sender); **256**:2 (sender)
Tarmana **160**:7
Tatalī
hu. ^{f}Titinatal, f. Šimnuman **22**:1, 5
^{f}Tatana
d. Agiya, w. Pilah-Ištar **28**:4, 15
^{f}Tataya
d. Šalim-Ištar, w. Ilī-bāni **30**:9 (seal), 13, 16, 24, 26; **72**:11
Tatkipu(š) **95e**:5 (seal); **95t**:13 (witness)
Tattašmiš **119**:6, 11
Tilkanu
s. Šarabuna and ^{f}Ašua-elka, br. Peruwa **92**:2 (slave), 8
Tirikuda **39**:22 (witness)
hu. ^{f}Haštahšušar **102**:1, 11
^{f}Titawašhi
si. ^{f}Bedibedi **93t**:1 (slave), 12
Titinatal **288**:12 (witness)
f. Ennanātum **5e**:3
^{f}Ti-[x]-ama
w. Tatalī, m. ^{f}Šuppianika **22**:1
Tubtuku **89**:13 (witness)
Tudhaliya
hu. ^{f}Anna-anna, f. Zuru, Atata, and Inar **53**:6, 20, 22
rabi šaqē **45**:2 (seal)
Tuhunara **151e**:3 (seal)
Tuhuši **120**:25 (witness)
Tuhušipha **102**:6, 9
Tumana **33t**:19 (witness)
kaššum **89**:11 (witness)
Tumliya **328**:11
Tuna
wardum ša Ahu-waqar **225**:18
Turuhna **160**:9
Tutupiala **17e**:4 (seal)
Tutaya **47t**:30 (witness)
s. Šu-Anum **324**:5
Tutupiala **185**:11 (witness)
Ṭāba **312**:22
Ṭāb-ahhē **73**:18 (witness)
Ṭāb-Aššur **130**:17
f. Abaya **18e**:4, 7; **18t**:2
limum **183e**: 17 (REL 91); **183t**:11
Ṭāb-ilī
f. Šalim-ahum **71e**:20; **71t**:24
Ṭāb-ṣilli-Aššur **172**:27
s. Aššur-idī **257e**:4 (seal) **257t**:40
s. Ānah-ilī **20e**:4 (seal); **20t**:11 (witness)
s. Daki-[x-x] **74e**:2 (seal); **74t**:15 (witness)
s. Šu-Nunu **276**:1 (seal)
f. Ānah-ilī **175e**:9
hu. d. Ānah-ilī **26**:5
Udgariya
f. ^{f}Hašušarna **40**:10, 21
Ukida **278**:29 (é U.)
Ummana **251**:4 (dumu-munus U. †)
^{f}Ummī-Išhara **59**:3 (recipient); **264e**:1 (sender); **264t**:2 (sender)

d. Elamma, si. Ennum-Aššur, Pilah-Ištar, and Šu-Bēlum **58**:1, 11, 15, 33, 40
^{f}Umminara **149e**:18; **149t**:7; **221**:7
w. Ennum-Aššur **150e**:10, 12; **150t**:3, 9, 16
^{f}Uniuni
w. Happuašu, m. ^{f}Šuppiašu **31**:4
Urad-Nana **209**:23
Urani **163**:9, 12; **164**:20; **208**:14
Uraya **55**:7′ (witness)
Urnihšu **22**:16 (witness)
Usānum **271**:32
s. Amur-Aššur **257e**:1 (seal); **257t**:38
Uṣur-pāka
s. Puzur-Ištar **196**:18
Uṣur-ša-Aššur **195**:5; **211**:28; **254**:26; **255**:2 (recipient), 5; **256**:5; **263**:4 (d. is *gubabtum*); **289**:2 (recipient)
s. Agūa, br. ^{f}Ab-šalim, Šu-Bēlum, Puzur-Ištar, Aššur-idī, and Abi-ilī **54t**:34
s. Aššur-malik **297**:5, 27 (witness); **313**:4, 6, 30
s. Iliya **209**:16
f. Anīna **276**:4
Uṣur-ša-Ištar **12**:2 (recipient); **176**: 35; **237**:1 (recipient); r **240**:1 (sender); **265**:1 (recipient); **266**:1 (recipient); **267**:1 (recipient); **268**:1 (recipient); **271**:1 (recipient); **272**:2 (recipient); **273**:2 (recipient); **274**:1 (recipient)
f. Puzur-ilī **273**:5
hamuštum **182e**:13; **182t**:5
Uṣur-[x-x]
f. Salia **54e**:11
Ušher
f. Šu-Išhara **258t**:58
Ušinuman
slave of Amur-Ištar **55**:7
Ušmanahšu **38**:20 (witness)
Ušunaman
s. Zi-[x-x] **95e**:1 (seal); **95t**:10 (witness)
Utnihšu **22**:16 (witness)
^{f}Utruwaššu **113**:15 (slave); **114**:8 (slave)
Uzua **25**:25 (witness); **234**:1 (recipient), 9
s. Lipaya, hu. ^{f}Zuška **82**:2, 4, 32
Wadū **258t**:60 (witness)
Wakle
hu. ^{f}Kapzia, f. ^{f}Kukran **90**:3 (seal), 8 (debtor)
Walahšina
f. Peruwa **149e**:4, 12; **149t**:3
Walahšu **144t**:19 (witness)
Walawala **301**:20; **303**:18 (*wardum*)
^{f}Walawala **98**:9, 18, 26, 35 (slave); **245**:2 (sender)
d. ^{f}Šāt-Ištar, si. Nūnu and Amur-Aššur, w. Pilah-Ištar **35**:1 (*amtum*), 6
w. Bulina **91e**:1 (seal), 7 (debtor); **91t**:3 (debtor)
w. Hapuala, m. Talhama and Hištahšu **138e**:10, 19, 22, 28; **138t**:3, 11, 15, 20
w. Ilī-malak **87**:6 (seal), 11 (debtor)
^{f}Walha/išna **152**:1, **152**:3 (é W.); **300**:21; **307e**:3 (recipient); 1 (recipient); **309**:1 (sender)
f. Alulu **38**:17
Wališra **96**:1 (seal)
^{f}Waliwali
w. Laqēp, s. Aššur-malik **143e**:12, 16; **143t**:7, 12
Walkua **111**:9, 21
^{f}Waqqurtum **162**:2 (recipient); **197**:2 (sender); **236**:3 (sender)
Warad-Kūbi
hu. ^{f}Muati **46**: 6
Wardum **221**:14; **298**:11
s. Ikūnum **199**:21
f. Laqēpum **324**:4
Waršuma
rubā'um **43**:8′ (*iqqātī*)
Wašhuba
rabi mahirim **159e**:2 (seal)
Wašinuman **153**:19′ (witness)
f. Ba[r x x x] **53**:4
Wazawa **120**:25 (witness)
Wa-[x x x x]
ša mun **53**:1 (seal)

Geographical Names and Nisbe

é/bēt Ālim (City Hall) **125**:12′; **128**:23; **175t**:19; **207**:9, 16; **235t**:27; **277**:12
dīn Ālim (verdict of the city) **66**:32; **175t**:10
mahar/igi *Ālim* **206**:21
mēr/dumu *Aššur* (male Aššur inhabitant) **15e**:17; **15t**:12
mērat/dumu-munus *Aššur* (female Aššur inhabitant) **2**:13; **7**:17; **25**:14
naṣir Ālim (protector of the city) **53**:33–34
nīš Ālim (oath of the city) **34**:3′; **37**:3; **47t**:5; **62e**:3′; **72**:21; **115**:4; **257e**:22; **257t**:15
ṭuppum ša Ālim (tablet of the city) **139**:8, 19, 24; **175t**:27; **206**:21, 24
Arahtum-canal **117**:2, 13
Burušhattum **19e**:13; **19t**:11; **23**:5; **27**:3, 17; **168**:25; **198**:4; **217**:11
Durhumit **19e**:16; **19t**:12
kārum Durhumit **71e**:10; **71t**:15; **112**:3′
Haburā **300**:8
Hahhum **27**:28, 30; **302**:16
kārum Hahhum **8**:1
Hanaknak
Haqqa **301**:6
Hattum **23**:6; **99**:14
Hurrama **203**:24; **326**:29
Kaneš (Kaniš) **6**:6, 10; **15e**:14; **15t**:8; **19e**:17; **19t**:10; **23**:9; **25**:9; **27**:8, 20, 26; **28**:8; **49**:11, 24; **54t**:10; **55**:2; **56t**:15, 20; **57**:2, 49; **62e**:4′; **62t**:7; **64**:56; **65t**:86; **89**:2; **99**:17; **105**:11; **116**:13; **123**:14; **135**:6; **139**:9; **172**:9; **172**:28; **190**:1; **198**:6; **205**:20; **229**:27; **276**:11; **300**:19; **311**:5, 24
awāt Kaneš **81**:14; **91e**:20; **91t**:13
kārum Kaneš **7**:21; **10e**:6; **10t**:45; **36**:1; **64**:75; **139**:22; **244e**:2 (seal); **244e**:29
dīn k. K. **244e**:1, 3
kārum Kaneš *ṣaher rabi* (tur gal) **48**:1; **65t**:9; **99**:26
māt Kaneš **99**:18
rubā'um Kanišium **258t**:10
Katila **328**:5
Kilarian **154**:22 (géo)
Kunanamit **314**:21
māt Kunanamit **145t**:14
Luhusaddiya **65t**:74
Mada **258e**:1 (nisbe), 10; **258t**:1, 12
Nihriya **15e**:14; **15t**:8; **161**:3
Purattum **99**:21
Qabrā **231**:5
Sasu (nisbe) **111**:2
Šaladi/uwar **205**:5
Šamuha **213**:18
Šanā **132**:14
Šubartum
Subarian female slave: **129**:35
Šurbu (nisbe, wool) **167**:6, 16
Talhad (nisbe, textiles) **97**:30; **98**:22; **247**:16
Tegarama **200**:8, 9
kārum Tegarama **6**:23
Timilkiya **27**:12, 19; **156**:11
Tišmurna **302**:11
Uršu **157**:21
Wahšušana **3**:20; **14**:9; **19e**:15; **19t**:14; **28**:23; **139**:25; **190**:9; **200**:17; **226**:16; **312**:27; **332**:16
dumu-munus Wahšušana **3**:21
kārum Wahšušana *ṣaher rabi* **28**:1 (seal); **190**:14–15
Wašhaniya **316**:30
Zalpa **158**:4; **332**:7
Zizum **160**:25

Gods and Goddesses

Amurrum **129**:28
fAnna **34**:13′ (*nīš* A.) **35**:11
(festival) of Anna **186e**:16
paššurum ša A. **247**:14
Anum **118**:4 (daughter)
(d)Aššur **66**:13; **122**:3; **145t**:26; **235t**:29; **237**:10, 24; **252**:7
bāb Aššur **13**:22
é/bēt Aššur **287**:8; **295**:11′

ēn Aššur **129**:24; **229**:20; **252**:15; **265**:23
igi Aššur *karābum* **238**:14; **239**:18; **240**:13
ikribū ša Aššur **261**:15
kasap Aššur **197**:17
kumrum ša Ašur **174**:4′
nīš ^{d}Aššur **34**:12′; **35**:11
paṭrum/gír *ša* ^{d}Aššur **7**:22; **10e**:7; **10t**:46; **64**:76; **65t**:75, 91; **71e**:12; **71t**:17; **112**:5′; **243**:2–3, 9; **244e**: 7; **244t**:4
šēp Ašur **272**:23
sūn Aššur **147**:10; **163**:23; **166**:39
šugaria'um ša Aššur **190**:16; **318**:17
šugaria'ēn ša ^{d}Aššur **99**:29
^{f}Aššurītum **122**:5
Bēlum **121**:28, 30
(the festival of) Bēlum **185**:4
ikribū ša Bēlum **247**:10
taphirum ša Bēlum **262**:9
Harihari
(the festival of) Harihari **189e**:9; **189t**:5
Ilalianta
gudu$_4$ *ša* Ilalianta **46**:5
^{d}im **44e**:5; **45**:7
gudu$_4$ *ša* ^{d}im **44**:5; **45**:7
^{d}im *ša qaqqidim* **44**:1–2
^{f}Išhara **245**:6, 7
^{f}Ištar **14**:61; **122**:4; **245**:5
huppum ša Ištar **243**:11–12; **244e**:18; **244t**:14
igi Ištar *karābum* **241t**:13
^{f}Ištar-ZA-AT
igi Ištar-ZA-AT *karābum* **241t**:14
^{f}Kubabat
gudu$_4$ *ša* Kubabat **46**:3
^{f}Ninkarrak **118**:20
ikrībū ša Ninkarrak **206**:5
^{f}Ninkilil **117**:21, **118**:18
Nipas
(the festival of) Nipas **85e**:16; **85t**:5
é Nipas **91e**:18; **91t**:10
Parka
(the festival) of Parka **75e**:6; **75t**:4
Su'en **57**:50
Šamaš **121**:31
^{f}Tašmētum **64**:22; **242**:1 (recipient)
ikrībū ša Tašmētum **65t**:16; **246**:16

Eponyms (*limum*)

REL	Name	Qualification	Text reference
82	Šudaya		**208**:3, 11
87	Buzuzu(m)		**178e**:22; **208**:9
88	Šu-Hubur		**184**:15
89	Ilšu-rabi		**193**:20
91	Ṭāb-Aššur		**183e**:17; **183t**:11
92	Elālī		**9**:20
95	Aššur-idī		**77**:15; **261**:5
97	Kubiya		**188**:12
98/123	Ilī-dān		**74t**:14; **91e**:15; **91t**:8
106	Aššur-imittī	*malāhum*	**191**:7
107	Enna-Suen	s. Šu-Aššur	**58**:19
107 + 1	Enna-Suen		**4**:8; **180**:15

REL	Name	Qualification	Text reference
108	Akūtum		**87**:18
109	Ma/eṣi-ilī		**72**:7
110	Iddin-ahum		**182e**:16; **182t**:8
194	Awiliya		**36**:21
227a + 1	Ahiaya	s. Adunaya	**258t**:55

Weeks (*hamuštum*)

Agūa
+ Išme-Adad **88e**:7
Ali-ahum **86**:6
Amua **78**:6
Amurru-bāni
+ Aššur-nādā **183e**:12; **183t**:4 (REL 91)
+ Šalim-Aššur **184**:7 (REL 88)
Aššur-idī
+ Šu-Ištar **91e**:12; **91t**:6 (REL 98/123); **188**:6 (REL 97)
Aššur-imittī
+ Innaya **83e**:16; **83t**:9
Aššur-malik **4**:4 (iii/REL 107 + 1)
s. Sukkalliya **89**:6
Aššur-nādā
+ Amurru-bāni **183e**:13; **183t**:5 (REL 91)
Aššur-ṣululī
+ Imdī-ilum **177**:5
Aššur-taklāku **74e**:10; **74t**:4 (REL 98/123)
Buzutaya
+ Laqēpum **193**:12 (REL 89)
Elamma
+ Šu-Kūbum **181e**:6′; **181t**:7
Ennam-Anum
dumu E. **180**:6 (REL 107 + 1)
Ennānum
ša qāti Ennānum **87**:15
Iliš-tikal
+ Puzur-šadu'e **178e**:12; **178t**:6 (REL 87)
Imdīlum
+ Aššur-ṣululī **177**:5
+ Pilah-Ištar 77:5 (REL 95)
Innaya
+ Aššur-imittī **83e**:15; **83t**:8
Išme-Adad
+ Agūa **88e**:7
Karwaya
+ Kurub-Ištar **179**:5
kaššum
ša qāti Ennānim **87**:13
Kurub-Ištar
+ Karwaya **179**:5
Laqēp(um)
+ Buzutaya **193**:11 (REL 89)
Narām-Suen **76e**:15; **76t**:7
Pilah-Ištar
+ Imdīlum 77:6 (REL 95)
Puzur-šadū'e
+ Iliš-tikal **178e**:13; **178t**:6 (REL 87)
Šalim-Aššur
+ Amurru-bāni **184**:7 (REL 88)
Šu-Ištar
+ Aššur-idī **91e**:12; **91t**:6 (REL 98/123); **188**:7 (REL 97)
Šu-Kūbum
+ Elamma **181e**:6′; **181t**:8
Uṣur-ša-Ištar **182e**:13; **182t**:5 (REL 110)

Months

i Bēlet-ekallim 124:13
ii/iii Narmak-Aššur **124**:33
iii ša Kēnatim **4**:5; **258t**:54 (REL 227a + 1)
iv Mahhur-ilī **91e**:14; **91t**:7 (REL 98/123); **180**:12 (REL 107 + 1); **184**:13 (REL 88)
v Ab-šarrāni **89**:8; **188**:11 (REL 97)
vi Hubur **268**:11

Professions and Titles

alahhinnum **112**:5
ašlākum **167**:12
bārītum **252**:5; **253**:5
ēmiqtum **199**:12; **219**:9; **263**:5
dayyānum **191**:1
gubabtum (nin-dingir) xxviii; **56**:10, 13; **61**:35; **62e**:2′; **62t**:5; **64**:5; **65**:32, 36, 76; **105**:8; **257e**:21, 35, 36; **257t**:12, 32, 35; **258e**:5, 12; **258t**: 6, 16; **262**:3; **263**:4
iššiʾakkum (ensí) **122**:3
kaššum **13**:21; **89**:12
  hamuštum kaššum ša qāti Ennānim **87**:13
kumrum (gudu$_4$) **44**:1, 5; **45**:7; **46**:3, 5; **174**:4′
malāhum (*limum* REL 106) **191**:7
mūṣû-official **147**:19
naggārum **129**:42; **279**:16′
nappāhum **158**:12
naṣir ālim **53**:33–34
qadištum **15e**:12; **15t**:7; **24**:6; **55**:9
rabi haṭṭim **143** seal A: 1 (Zatipra)
rabi mahirim **159e**:2 (seal)
rabi nāgirim **44**:3
rabi qaqqidim **45**:5
rābi sikkatim
  nīš rābi sikkatim **34**:15′
rabi simmiltim **26**:22; **43**:10′; **44**:22; **45**:27; **53**:35
rabi šāriqē **40**:6
rābiṣum **70**:2 (sender), 29; **139**:20; **256**:21; **257e**:8; **257t**:1
rubāʾum **43**:8′ (*iqqātī*); **91e**:17; **100**:16; **174**:15′, 17′; **258t**:10
  nīš rubāʾim **34**:14′; **35**:12; **47t**:5
rubāʾum gal **45**:24 (*iqqātī*); **46**:21 (*iqqātī*); **53**:34 (*iqqātī*)
šaduštum **173**:15
šaʾiltum **226**:20; **252**:4; **256**:7
ša qānuʾē **98**:5
ša ṭābtim (mun) **44**:6; **53**:2
šawītum **15e**:9; **15t**:4; **54**:26; **106** seal C
tamkārum (dam-gàr) **10**:9, 17, 22, 28, 33; **38**:8; **44**: 13; **59**:39; **64**:6, 18; **65**:33; **67**:27; **86**:18; **130**:4; **145**:4; **174**:11′; **193**:2; **200**:21; **202**:12; **203**:4; **209**:8; **215**:7; **234**:14; **235**:29; **277**:7; **278**:6; **280**:11′; **327**:10, 15
utû ša abbul addahšī **96**:3–6 (seal)
wardum ša ekallim **174**:14′

Commented Words and Expressions

ahāzum 46
allānum **202**:3
arhalum **223**:5
arhālum **258**:21, 34
arhatum **117**:2
arhum **117**:1
amtum xxviii, 26, 70
aššutum 26, 69–70
babrum **223**:6
badutum **223**:6
balāṭum **122**:i10
bētum 155, 223, 236; **148**:16; **153**:7′; **244**:11; **249**:12
  bēt abini 256, 272, 358
damamtum **67**:34
dappurtum **67**:23
dittum **171**:17
ebābum **194**:3″
ekallum 237
elītum **46**:36; **57**:51
ēmiqtum 379
ennānum **230**:24
eṭemmū 356–58
ewaztum **319**:12

Cited Texts

Subjects

Lightning Source UK Ltd.
Milton Keynes UK
UKHW010630160622
404522UK00001B/204

9 781628 372823